History
in the Media

History *in the Media*

Film and Television

Robert Niemi

ABC-CLIO

Santa Barbara, California • Denver, Colorado • Oxford, England

Library of Congress Cataloging-in-Publication Data
Niemi, Robert.
    History in the media : film and television history in the media /
Robert Niemi.
        p.   cm.
    Includes bibliographical references and index.
    ISBN 1-57607-952-X (hardback : alk. paper) — ISBN 1-57607-953-8
(ebook)   1. Historical films—History and criticism.   2. Historical
television programs—History and criticism.   3. Biographical
films—History and criticism.   4. Biographical television
programs—History and criticism.   I. Title.

    PN1995.9.H5N54 2006
    791.43'658—dc22

                                                        2006007457

This book is also available on the World Wide Web as an eBook. Visit abc-clio.com for
details.

Acquisitions Editor: Jim Ciment
Production Editor: Laura Esterman
Associate Production Editor: Cisca Schreefel
Media Editor: Giulia Rossi
Production Manager: Don Schmidt
Manufacturing Coordinator: George Smyser

ABC-CLIO, Inc.
130 Cremona Drive, P.O. Box 1911
Santa Barbara, California 93116–1911

This book is printed on acid-free paper.
Manufactured in the United States of America

To the memory of my father
Alfred Antii Niemi
March 7, 1915–April 7, 2005
"Ei ole koiraa karvoihin katsominen"

Contents

4   *Military History on Film and Television: Korean War to Bosnia, 147*

Acknowledgments

First of all, I offer special thanks to my friend, Alan Harris Stein, oral historian and archivist extraordinaire, for facilitating this project. Thanks to my editors, Jim Ciment and Laura Esterman, for their expert advice, good cheer, and patience. Thanks to my colleagues in the English Department and other departments at St. Michael's College: Mike Arena, Jeff Ayres, Nick Clary, Carrie Kaplan, Bill Grover, Nat Lewis, Jack MacDonald, Will Marquis, Susan Ouellette, Christina Root, Kerry Shea, Lorrie Smith, and Erin Stehmeyer. Thanks to Laurence Suid and Jim Leger who read and commented on portions of the manuscript in progress. I owe a heartfelt thanks to Don and Lynn Feeser for all their help and support and also acknowledge Paul Malone, Richard Davis, Mick, Cindy, Alex, Andy, Buzz, Karen, my mom, my brothers Tom and Al, my sister, Karen, my daughter, Elena, foster son, Dima, and my good friends Mark Madigan and Steve Soitos for many years of loyalty. Finally, I owe my continuing spiritual well-being to my wife, best friend, and life partner, Gretchen.

Introduction

From 1981 to 2005, thirteen of the twenty-five Oscar winners for Best Picture have been movies based in history. Over the same period, 32 of the 100 films nominated for Best Picture have had their basis in historical events. Both statistics testify to the continuing power and prestige of history as source material in the film business. Likewise, when members of a viewing audience see the familiar phrase, "based on a true story," flash on the screen during the opening credit sequence, they tend to assume, rightly or wrongly, that the movie they are about to watch will deliver more significance than a pure fiction and will therefore require a heightened level of attentive engagement and respect. The irony is rich: in a constantly accelerating culture of consumption that fosters short attention spans and shorter memories, historical subject matter somehow continues to hold strong sway over filmmakers and moviegoers.

Perhaps much of the appeal of history films has to do with an unsatisfied popular hunger for some sort of grounding in "truth" and "reality." As postmodern business civilization becomes more standardized, authoritarian, and alienating, its culture industries have had to aspire to new depths of insipidity and escapism to mask and compensate for the real, and really depressing, social conditions that prevail. Though never of great quality, a preponderance of contemporary movie and television fare is weird, puerile, banal, and slyly contemptuous of its audience. Sizable fractions of the populace are quite aware that products of corporate media do not emanate from, or reflect, any reality they know. In a world of simulacra and contrivance, people want some recognizable token of life on planet Earth before "Commodity" became a ravenous god.

As a field of study, film and history have undergone a tremendous upsurge in interest in recent years that is commensurate with the growing public appetite for historical representations on film and television. First-rate history-film reference guides, essay anthologies, and critical-theoretical works are now being published on a regular basis (see the Bibliography at the end of this volume). Typically a "history film" is defined, in very broad and loose terms, as either a "true story" or simply a period piece that conjures a bygone era (e.g., *All Quiet on the Western Front* or *The Searchers*). The theory goes that, even if the narrative and characters are largely fictional, the setting is real and evocative enough to qualify the film as "historical." There is nothing wrong with this idea; historical fiction films can be profitably "read" as both reflective and productive of the ideological temperament that informed the time in which they were made, as well as the time they purport to represent. Indeed, virtually any film can be analyzed as a revealing "historical" document.

To stake out new and exclusive ground, the present study applies a somewhat more rigorous litmus test: the film in question needs to be firmly "based on a true story," that is, it has to deal with an actual, documented historical incident. The movie can contain fictional elements—every history film does—but must describe a once real moment in a real place involving real people. Consequently I have sidestepped the enormous repertoire of historical fiction films that most other film-history studies treat as their bread and butter. I have also avoided films dealing with ancient history topics because the existing documentation to support the film's veracity is often weak. Finally I have to confess to being much more interested in films engaging modern history because the political and ideological ramifications hit much closer to home.

As for theoretical presuppositions, while I have narrowed the definition of what I consider to be a true "history" film, I have expanded the notion of what constitutes "history" beyond the conventionally dominant categories of military, social, and political history. Half the book treats these standard categories but the other half examines films dealing with the history of sports, music, art, race relations, and crime—types of human endeavor not necessarily tied up with shaping and reshaping nation-states but important nonetheless as specimens of ideology and psychohistory. Furthermore, I have opted to treat the films under consideration not as discreet artifacts but as *events*—an axiom that precludes an alphabetical, encyclopedic arrangement. Instead the ten chapters herein are generally laid out in uninterrupted chronological sequences to delineate patterns of stylistic and ideological development that may arise from or reflect changes in political temperament over periods of time. Treating a film as an event also means dealing with the aesthetic, personal, and political character of the people who conceived it, the historical moment in which it was spawned, the film's genre kin and immediate antecedents, the resources the filmmaker had at hand, the commercial requisites that shape tone and narrative structure, the concrete circumstances of the film's production, and the sort of critical and popular reception it received. All these factors make up the gestalt of the film as representative of history, as an historical event in its own right, and as part of a larger historical mosaic formed by the entire body of films on the subject.

As for conclusions arrived at after intensively researching, studying, and analyzing some 375 history films, a few things come to the fore. Because it focuses exclusively on the "true story," this book deals with two types of history film: the docudrama and the documentary. Docudramas invariably streamline, distill, and radically simplify historical events. In keeping with the Anglo-American ideology of heroic hyperindividualism, docudrama narratives have room for one or two protagonists but no more than that. Consequently, docudramas routinely create composite characters or erase important participants in the real event altogether because the requisites of economical storytelling dictate as much. Docudramas also tend toward melodrama as they exaggerate internal and interpersonal conflicts and emotional *Sturm und Drang*. In a similarly reductive way, they posit Manichaean moral schemes with clearly recognizable heroes and villains, jump to arbitrary conclusions when the evidence is incongruous, and structure the historical incident into a classic three-act drama that ends with the requisite satisfactory closure. These common narrative tropes militate against the ambiguity and complexity that naturally inheres in any real event. Docudramas also get lots of great and small details wrong, either deliberately—to argue a partisan political point or drum up sympathy or antipathy for a particular person—or inadvertently, due to poor research or fallacious assumptions. Ultimately historical accuracy is a function of the filmmakers' political and intellectual integrity and varies wildly depending on the persons involved and the lasting ideological significance of the historical event being depicted.

The popular perception is that a documentary film is far more objective and reliable a source of historical truth than a docudrama. This is, of course, not true. Documentaries are susceptible to the same sorts of narrative distortions that characterize docudramas and are even more dangerously seductive because they *appear* to adhere to a higher standard of epistemological neutrality by typically showcasing authoritative and explanatory voice-overs; interviews with experts and other real people in the know; and obviously genuine archival footage, maps, still photographs, and other sorts of visually compelling graphic evidence to prove their cases. The source materials are all real enough and the interviewees supposedly sincere. The documentary filmmaker manipulates in a more subtle way, through what he or she inserts or omits and how the film's materials are edited. Finally both docudrama and documentary filmmakers tend to skew history by offering a partisan interpretation, or perhaps two simple, opposing interpretations, of an historical event when the event calls for many more points of view to do justice to its mysterious aspects, insoluble contradictions, and complexities. In sum, a history film of any sort might be emotionally compelling, intellectually persuasive, and an artistic triumph but none of these apparent strengths mean that it is good history—buyer beware.

Military History on Film and Television: Wallace's Rising to the Boer War

A t the outset of this chapter, a crucial distinction needs to be drawn between the vast war film genre and a subset of the war film: the military history film. The Internet Movie Database (http://www.imdb.com) lists over 4,500 war films. Of that number, less than 150 (or about 3 percent) qualify as films that more or less accurately deal with authentic episodes in military history. The remaining 4,350 war movies have to be classified as *war fiction films*—that is, films that superimpose largely or entirely fictional narratives onto war history settings. As is true of all genre classifications, there are a number of gray areas here. For example, films like *Gallipoli* and *Das Boot* involve fictional characters, but the settings and war action depicted are so specific and realistic as to qualify them as military history films. Conversely, even a fastidiously accurate military history film like *Gettysburg* will inevitably fabricate much of its dialogue; historical sources can only supply so much. Genre conventions, narrative requisites, and ideological imperatives also introduce distortions into otherwise credible renditions of military history. Still, all caveats aside, the distinction between the war history and the war (fiction) film is clear enough to allow meaningful classification. Military history on film essentially represents actual incidents involving real persons. A war film may, in many ways, be a fairly accurate pictorial representation of a particular conflict and may allegorize its salient political, psychological, and moral issues brilliantly (for example, *The Deer Hunter*) but it is still a fiction; the events depicted never happened. Quite a number of books have concerned themselves with ideological analyses of war films per se. What is offered in what follows is a focused ideological-historicist reading of military history on film.

Wallace's Rising (1297–1304)

Braveheart (1995)

The moment of inspiration for *Braveheart*, Mel Gibson's 1995 biopic about Scotland's greatest hero, Sir William Wallace (1272?–1305), apparently occurred sometime in 1983 when the film's screenwriter, Randall Wallace, came across a statue of William Wallace outside of Edinburgh Castle while he was researching his family genealogy. (An alternate version of the story is that Randall Wallace happened on a plaque in a wall of St. Bartholomew's Hospital near London's Smithfield Market commemorating the site of William Wallace's execution.) Whatever the exact impetus, an intrigued Randall Wallace began to research and write a screenplay based on the life of his legendary namesake. At least eight biographies of Wallace had been published between 1830 and 1983, but all had their origins in a single, highly speculative, source: *The Actes and Deidis of the Illustre and Vallyeant Campioun Schir William Wallace* (circa 1477), an epic poem by Scottish poet, Henry the Minstrel (aka, "Blind Harry," circa 1440–1493) (Mackay 1995). Written 172 years after Wallace's death, Henry's poem drew on the stories passed down over the generations; it was adulatory and patriotic but of very dubious accuracy. No matter, Randall Wallace was not overly concerned with historical exactitude; as an American of Scottish ancestry, his aim was to write an exciting swashbuckler of epic proportions that would captivate audiences and pay homage to his courageous ancestors.

In broad terms, the story *Braveheart* tells is true enough. William Wallace (Mel Gibson) did, indeed, rebel against King Edward I (1239–1307) "Longshanks" (Patrick McGoohan); he handily defeated the English in battle at Loudon Hill, Ayr, Scone, and, most notably, Stirling Bridge (after which he was knighted and appointed Guardian of Scotland by Robert the Bruce); behind the scenes, the Scottish nobles likely sold out the popular revolt against the English; Wallace's forces lost the Battle of Falkirk (June 1298); stripped of his prestige after Falkirk, Wallace went into hiding but was eventually captured, tried, and executed for treason. It also appears to be true that Edward's son and heir apparent, the Prince of Wales (Peter Hanly), was effeminate, probably homosexual, and neglectful of his wife, Princess Isabelle (Sophie Marceau). The film's falsifications and distortions are equally significant, however. Wallace did not swear eternal enmity against the Crown for the murder of his young wife—the alleged murder never happened. (One source suggests that Wallace became an outlaw in a much more prosaic manner—after a deadly quarrel with British soldiers over some fish he had caught.) In the film, King Edward I is portrayed as a sinister, devious character but was, in fact, a strong and well-respected king; the real Wallace did not

A scene still of actor and director Mel Gibson from Braveheart. *(Icon/Ladd Co/Paramount/The Kobal Collection)*

have an affair with Princess Isabelle; the English did not take heavy losses at Falkirk; the film's depiction of the Scottish warriors in blue face paint and kilts is anachronistic; the historical William Wallace was a giant of a man (6 feet, 7 inches tall) whereas Mel Gibson is of average height (5 feet, 11 inches).

Whatever its failings as history, *Braveheart* certainly has epic grandeur and plenty of bloody, frenetic battle sequences, romance, and high-minded sentiment. Shot in Ireland and Scotland, *Braveheart* used 1,700 Irish army troops as extras for its battle scenes and cost a hefty $70–$80 million to make (http://www.imdb.com). But Gibson's gamble paid off handsomely. A huge international hit, *Braveheart* received rave reviews, generated revenues in excess of $200 million, was nominated for ten Oscars, and won five (including two for Gibson, for Best Director and Best Picture). On a more ominous note, filmmaker (*Hoop Dreams*) Steve James saw *Braveheart*'s celebration of Anglo-Saxon chauvinism as playing to crypto-fascist elements in American society: "It is apparent that sections of the US far right . . . find a mythical version of Scottish history useful for their present political purposes. This fabricated Scotland closely echoes contemporary rhetoric. This nation of 'Bravehearts' has no social classes, only Scots. It devotes itself to defending 'ancient freedoms'—that are thankfully bound up with land, property and religion—against a foreign threat, both external and internal" (James 1999).

The Jacobite Rebellion of 1745

Culloden (1964)

Radical media critic and filmmaker Peter Watkins started out in the mid-1950s, in Britain, making short amateur (8mm) films. Two of his films—*Diary of an Unknown Soldier* (1959) and *The Forgotten Faces* (1960)—won "Ten Best" awards (the equivalent of the Oscar for amateur films in the UK) and were screened at the London National Film Theatre. Impressed by his work, Huw Wheldon, head of BBC-TV's Documentary Film Department, hired Watkins as an assistant film producer in 1962. In 1964 Watkins was granted a small budget to make a film version of John Prebble's *Culloden* (London: Secker & Warburg, 1961), a best-selling historical account of the British army's destruction of Bonnie Prince Charlie's Scots Jacobin forces at Culloden Moor on April 16, 1746, the last battle fought on British soil. Filming at Inverness, Scotland, with an all-amateur cast in August 1964, Peter Watkins eschewed the conventional historical docudrama in favor of a cleverly mounted faux cinema verité approach that employed handheld cameras and direct-to-camera address of battle participants that quite deliberately imitated contemporary television news coverage of the unfolding war in Vietnam. Screened on BBC-TV on December 15, 1964 (exactly four months after the Gulf of Tonkin Resolution), *Culloden* presented "you are there" coverage of a battle that had occurred 218 years before: a surreal Brechtian gambit that proved to be a major success with critics and the viewing public and set the tone and style for much of Watkins' later work.

The Napoleonic Wars (1799–1815)

Kolberg (also known as *Burning Hearts*) (1945)

After the envelopment and destruction of the German 6th Army at Stalingrad in the winter of 1942–1943, it became obvious that Hitler's war with the Soviet Union was going to be a protracted and exceedingly difficult struggle that Germany might well lose. On June 1, 1943, convinced that the German people needed a great inspirational film to galvanize their fighting spirit, Propaganda Minister Josef Goebbels commissioned *Kolberg* [also known as *Burning Hearts*] (1945), a period epic directed by Veit Harlan (*Jud Süss*) about a small Baltic port's stubborn fight against Napoleon's army. Written by Harlan in close collaboration with Goebbels, *Kolberg* actually conflates two distinct events: the resistance of the citizens of Kolberg to French invasion in 1806–1807 and an insurrection against French occupation forces led by Prussian Lt. Ferdinand Baptist von Schill's Freikorps in the Hanseatic city of Stralsund in 1809. The historical reality is as follows. Under the military command of Prussian Field Marshal Neidhardt von Gneisenau (1760–1831), Kolberg became famous for its long and spirited resistance to capture by the French after the larger fortresses in the area had surrendered. The Stralsund story was quite different. After three quick victories against the French and their allies, Schill (Gustav Diessl in the film) led his rebel solders to the seaport of Stralsund to seek support from English warships harbored there. Unfortunately, the English had already departed by the time Schill arrived. Unable to stir a wider rebellion in Pomerania, Schill and his men (about 2,000 Prussians and Swedes) fortified Stralsund against the inevitable counterattack. It came on May 31, 1809, when 5,000 mostly Dutch and Danish troops stormed the town and overwhelmed Schill's men in heavy fighting. In Stralsund's market square Dutch soldiers dragged Lieutenant Schill from his horse, bayoneted him, stripped him of his uniform, and cut off his head, which was preserved and put on display in a Dutch army museum until 1839. The French executed Schill's fellow officers by firing squad and sent his surviving soldiers into forced labor at Brest and Cherbourg.

For Harlan and Goebbels, Kolberg's staunch resistance to Napoleon's armies served as an allegorical example of what could be accomplished by a patriotic people united at home and on the battlefront, despite the defeatism of the generals. But eventually Kolberg did fall to the French, a historical fact omitted from the Harlan-Goebbels version for obvious reasons. Likewise, the real fate of the charismatic Lieutenant Schill—an allegorical stand-in for Hitler—was elided from the movie. Though they played fast and loose with the historical facts, Harlan and Goebbels made sure that *Kolberg* would rival *Gone With the Wind* (1939) for pageantry and epic scope. Shot near Potsdam under constant threat of air raids, *Kolberg* took two years to make, cost 8.5 million Reich marks, and involved elaborate sets, 10,000 specially made uniforms, and trainloads of salt for artificial snow. The film also used thousands of soldiers—Harlan makes the unlikely claim of 185,000 in his memoir (Harlan 1966)—and 4,000 sailors as extras at a time when the Third Reich needed every available combatant at the front.

Kolberg's public premier was one of the strangest in cinematic history. A print of the film was parachuted into the besieged U-boat base garrison at La Rochelle, France, and shown on January 30, 1945, the twelfth anniversary of Hitler's takeover, to exhort the surrounded troops to hold out—which they did until a general surrender on May 9. Still, the overall propaganda effectiveness of *Kolberg* was negligible and the yawning gap between Goebbels' wish-fulfillment fantasy and the war's reality was manifest when the real Kolberg fell to advancing Soviet forces in early February 1945. Heinrich George, the actor who played Joachim Nettelbeck (1738–1834), Kolberg's heroic mayor, died of starvation in a Soviet concentration camp in 1946. Twenty years after its initial release, *Kolberg* was rereleased in West Germany as *30. Januar 1945*, with an accompanying documentary that corrected *Kolberg*'s many misrepresentations.

The reputation of French writer-director Abel Gance (1889–1981) rests primarily on his 1927 silent masterpiece, *Napoléon*, a stirring and technically innovative 4-hour epic that depicts Napoleon's early life up to the beginning of his military career. In 1981 director and film historian Kevin Brownlow released a restored version with a new music score by Carmine Coppola. Gance had intended to cover the remainder of Napoleon's saga with another five films, but when *Napoléon* proved to be a financial disaster, he had to abandon his ambitious plan. Gance's fascination with Napoleon never waned, however. In 1934 Gance released *Napoléon Bonaparte*, a reedited 2-hour, 20-minute version of *Napoléon* with sound effects and dubbed dialogue added. Gance also released a third reedited version, *Bonaparte et la Révolution*, in 1971.

The Battle of Austerlitz (1960)

Toward the end of his career, an aging Abel Gance hoped to revive his standing in world cinema with a rewritten version of what would have been the third part of his Napoleon project: *The Battle of Austerlitz* (1960). Financed by French, Italian, Yugoslavian, and Liechtensteinian interests, *Austerlitz* likewise featured an international cast: Pierre Mondy as Napoleon (1769–1821), Claudia Cardinale as Pauline Bonaparte (1780–1825), Martine Carol as Joséphine de Beauharnais (1763–1814), Leslie Caron as Mlle. de Vaudey, Orson Welles as American inventor Robert Fulton (1765–1815), Jack Palance as Russian General Weirother, and Vittorio De Sica as Pope Pius VII (1740–1823). Fastidious to a fault about historical accuracy, Abel Gance and cowriters Nelly Kaplan and Roger Richebé wrote a screenplay that lays out the complex political situation in 1804, exhaustively examines the strategic decisions made by Napoleon and his Russian and Austrian adversaries as they maneuvered their forces into battle, and presents the battle itself in great tactical detail. Unfortunately, such detailed exposition necessarily involves copious amounts of dialogue, which makes for a very slow film. Combine poor pacing with choppy editing (especially in the first hour), laughably bad dubbing in the English-language version, hammy acting (especially by the bombastic Jack Palance), and Gance's failure to adequately orient the viewer as to the basic geography of the sprawling battlefield, and the final result is a film that falls far short of its epic aspirations.

Waterloo (1970)

The subject of a number of silent films and short documentaries over the years, Napoleon's defeat at Waterloo (June 12–15, 1815) received its definitive filmic treatment with Sergei Bondarchuk's eponymous epic, *Waterloo* (1970). Through most of the 1960s, Bondarchuk (1920–1994) poured his heart and soul into his masterpiece, *Vojna i Mir* (*War and Peace*), a 7-hour adaptation of Leo Tolstoy's great novel that was released in four parts between 1965 and 1967 and in its entirety in 1968. At the height of the Cold War, when American and Soviet military, geopolitical, economic, and cultural competition were at fever pitch, the Soviets spared no resources in assuring that *War and Peace* would be the most lavishly mounted and, consequently, the most expensive film ever made (ultimately costing the equivalent of about US$540 million in 2005). The film deservedly won the 1969 Oscar for Best Foreign Film, advanced Russia's international prestige, and prompted film producer Dino De Laurentiis to throw in his lot with Bondarchuk and the Soviet-state studio, Mosfilm, in the making of

Waterloo, a joint Russo-Italian project that would further mine the grand cinematic potential of the Napoleonic Wars. Shot mostly in Russia using tens of thousands of Soviet troops (as did *War and Peace*), *Waterloo* cast prominent British and American actors to maximize its appeal to Western audiences: recent Oscar winner Rod Stieger as Napoleon; Christopher Plummer as Arthur Wellesley, Duke of Wellington, also known as the "Iron Duke" (1769–1852); Orson Welles in a cameo as King Louis XVIII (1755–1824); Michael Wilding as Sir William Ponsonby (1772–1815); Jack Hawkins as Lt. Gen. Sir Thomas Picton (1758–1815); and Dan O'Herlihy as Marshall Michel Ney (1769–1815). Originally released in a 4.5-hour version (shortened by half for video release), *Waterloo* bifurcates into two parts. The first, much shorter, part chronicles Napoleon's exile on Elba, his escape and march on Paris, Ney's defection to Napoleon, the overthrow of Louis XVIII, and the formation of the "Seventh Coalition" between Britain, Austria, Prussia, and Russia to oppose Napoleon's return to power. The second part of the film accurately chronicles the decisive 9-hour battle: Napoleon's main force of 70,000 conducting a series of furious assaults on Wellington's lines, which nonetheless hold; Blücher's Prussian army evading Grouchy's army and linking up with Wellington in the late afternoon; and the combined British and Prussian armies counterattacking the French on two sides, overpowering and ultimately routing Napoleon's exhausted and outnumbered main force. Authentic looking except for the appearance of bolt-action rifles, which did not yet exist, *Waterloo* combined the lavish use of battlefield extras with brilliant cinematography and the inclusion of much actual dialogue from historical sources to create a scrupulously accurate depiction of the era and the battle. The effectiveness of the film was also aided by the relative tactical simplicity of the battle itself; unlike Austerlitz, the Battle of Waterloo did not involve especially complex deployments and maneuvers. All its considerable strengths notwithstanding, *Waterloo* was a box office flop, returning a small fraction of the $25 million it cost to make and scaring the living daylights out of MGM executives, who backed away from financing a proposed Stanley Kubrick film on Napoleon (which, unfortunately, was never made, despite extensive research and a finished script). The commercial failure of *Waterloo* had nothing to do with its inherent qualities and everything to do with the moment of its release. In 1970 the international counterculture, then at its apogee, valorized personal liberation, contemporary relevance, iconoclasm, and revisionist attitudes toward history. A conventional historical epic centering on an early nineteenth-century battle did not stand a chance in such a cultural climate.

The Texas Revolution (1835–1836)

The thirteen-day defense of the Alamo in February–March 1836 by a small band of Texians (U.S.-born Texans) and Tejanos (Mexican-born Texans) against Santa Ana's Mexican army stands as the central mythic event in the history of Texas. The Alamo is, by extension, a quintessential American myth, putatively illustrating courage, idealism, and steadfastness in the face of overwhelming odds and near-certain doom. In a darker vein, one could argue that sanctifying the slaughter at the Alamo valorizes righteous vengeance against a foreign foe as a prime engine of historical destiny. The Alamo myth also intervenes in the history of the European conquest of the Americas by selectively fixating on one of those rarer instances when the Anglo settler was the one outnumbered, outgunned, and strictly on the defensive—ergo, a perfectly innocent victim.

As film critic J. Hoberman has noted (2004), "Each epoch gets its Alamo"— that is, the evolving Alamo film subgenre has functioned as a kind of mirror reflecting changing cultural attitudes toward patriotism and Manifest Destiny. The first film version, William Haddock's *Immortal Alamo* (also known as *Fall of the Alamo*), now lost, appeared in 1911. A second silent film version, Christy Cabanne's *Martyrs of the Alamo* (1914; rereleased in 1921 as *The Birth of Texas* and released on video in 2000), unself-consciously expressed the jingoistic, white supremacist tenor of its era by positing the racist notion that the Texian revolution was a reaction to Mexicans lusting after American women. A. D. Sears, the

The Texans are overrun by the Mexican army at the Alamo on March 6, 1836, during the Texas Revolution. (Library of Congress)

actor who plays Davy Crockett, had just played a Klansman in D. W. Griffiths' infamous *Birth of a Nation*. A third (mostly lost) silent film version, Robert N. Bradbury's [*With*] *Davy Crockett at the Fall of the Alamo*, appeared in 1926. During the centennial year of the Alamo, Dallas theater owner and film producer Anthony J. Xydias made the first "talkie" Alamo movie: *Heroes of the Alamo* (1937; rereleased by Columbia Pictures in 1938), a patriotic Depression-era morale booster.

Early in his long career John Wayne (real name: Marion Michael Morrison, 1907–1979) became obsessed with the idea of someday making his own movie about the Alamo. An actor since 1926 and a well-known Western star since 1930, Wayne came to epitomize the American masculine ideal, that is, tough, solitary, independent, taciturn, fearless, and combative. (As most things Hollywood, the image was a fanciful one; Wayne, who was dominated by a judgmental mother, avoided service in the military and never worked as a real cowboy.)

From 1949 to 1953, at the height of the Red Scare, Wayne headed the Motion Picture Alliance for the Preservation of American Ideals (MPA), an ultra-Right Hollywood group formed in 1944 that blacklisted suspected Communists and sympathizers, reported their names to the FBI, and pressured Congress to open the infamous House Un-American Activities Committee (HUAC) hearings in 1947. That same year Wayne began producing films and a few years later tried his hand at some uncredited second-unit directing on John Ford's *The Quiet Man* (1952) and William Wellman's *Blood Alley* (1955).

Davy Crockett and *The Last Command* (1955)

Circa 1948 Wayne engaged his favorite screenwriter, James Earl "Jimmy" Grant, to write an Alamo script, and in 1951 Wayne approached Republic Pictures executive Herbert Yates with an ambitious Alamo project proposal. Unwilling to risk a large investment on a movie in which all the heroes are killed, Yates turned Wayne down. Three years later, to promote the Frontierland section of his new Disneyland theme park in Anaheim, California, fellow MPA alumnus Walt Disney aired *Davy Crockett, King of the Wild Frontier*, starring former Texas football star Fess Parker as Crockett. A multipart television series (1954) converted to a theatrical release (1955), *Davy Crockett* was a puerile, highly romanticized rendition of the Crockett-Alamo myth that touched off an astonishing $100 million Crockett outfit and coonskin cap craze among American schoolboys that lasted throughout 1955. Encouraged by Disney's success and bent on punishing Wayne for leaving Republic Pictures after a fifteen-year association, Yates went ahead with his own Alamo movie: Frank Lloyd's *The Last Command* (1955), a modestly budgeted but realistic quickie starring Sterling Hayden as Jim Bowie, Richard

Carlson as Travis, and Arthur Hunnicutt as Davy Crockett that—thanks to the Davy Crockett fad—just broke even at the box office.

The Alamo (1960)

Unfazed by Herbert Yates's attempt to steal his thunder, Wayne went ahead with his own Alamo project and, in 1956, finally secured a deal with United Artists. Wayne put in his own money and acquired additional funding from several right-wing Texas oil millionaires. Though he initially planned to film in Mexico to keep down production costs, Wayne was persuaded that, given its superpatriotic ideological aims, the movie had best be shot in Texas. The Daughters of the Republic of Texas, custodians of the real Alamo in downtown San Antonio, would not allow filming there so Wayne decided to build an Alamo set at James T. "Happy" Shahan's 30-square-mile ranch outside of Brackettville, Texas, 125 miles west of San Antonio. Ironically dozens of Mexican craftsmen labored two years to construct a meticulously authentic adobe facsimile of the Alamo and a twenty-building replica of the adjacent town of San Antonio de Béxar (pronounced Bayhar) on Shahan's ranch. "Alamo Village," as it came to be called, cost $1.5 million to build and is still in use as a movie set and tourist attraction.

The casting of *The Alamo* (1960) proved as problematic as the location of the shooting. Originally John Wayne wanted to cast Richard Widmark as Col. Davy Crockett (1786–1836) and himself in the lesser role of Sam Houston (1793–1863) so that he could concentrate on directing the film. However, United Artists insisted that he maximize his star power by playing Crockett to help ensure the movie's commercial success. Wayne obliged, but his iconic status as the archetypal American cowboy hero had the unintended effect of seriously compromising any suspension of disbelief; the viewing public tended to forget about the character he was playing and simply saw and heard the always imposing John Wayne playing himself in a funny-looking coonskin cap. It hardly mattered that Richard Boone played Sam Houston; Widmark played Col. James Bowie (1796–1836); and British actor Laurence Harvey played Col. William B. Travis (1809–1836). Though all solid actors in their own right, their job was to play second fiddle to John Wayne's frontier superhero. Indeed, the film's elitist "great man" orientation tends to work against its primary ideological aim, which is to affirm American nation-building within widely accepted populist traditions: a fundamental contradiction that has always vexed American conservatism as a political philosophy.

In broad outline James Earl Grant's script was a fairly accurate rendition of the historical facts. As the film depicts, the thirteen-day fight at the Alamo was a holding action by fewer than 200 irregulars against 4,000 Mexican troops under General Antonio López de Santa Ana (1794–1876). The defense of the Alamo was only meant to gain time for Sam Houston to assemble an insurgent army of Texans further to the east. Though the physical structures, uniforms, weapons, and personages involved stay close to reality, *The Alamo* is marred by slow pacing, Western genre clichés, Wayne's clumsy direction of his actors—despite some uncredited and unsolicited help from Wayne's old mentor, John Ford—and a number of fallacious representations that distort history and damage the film's credibility. For example, Wayne locates the Alamo on the Rio Grande when it is 150 miles distant. Wayne's Davy Crockett is always dressed in fabled buckskin and raccoon cap but the real Crockett rarely wore such an outfit. Jim Bowie receives a letter at the Alamo informing him that his wife and children have died of cholera, an event that actually took place four years earlier. Bowie is depicted as bedridden after being wounded in an explosion during the siege but in reality was sick in bed from the outset. Davy Crockett is shown being killed in battle but historical evidence indicates that he surrendered and was subsequently executed. The Mexican army is shown to have something like 100 cannons when, in fact, they only had about 15. Though portrayed as zealous pro-annexation (and proto-American) patriots, many of the 186 defenders of the Alamo were actually hired mercenaries fighting for a promised reward of free land and cash. In point of fact, most Texans did not want independence from Mexico; they merely wanted (1) Texas to be its own state within Mexico and (2) the restoration of the Mexican constitution, which had been abrogated by the dictatorial Santa Ana. Taken together, all of these distortions oversimplify history while emphasizing the righteousness of the cause and the heroism of the defenders.

When *The Alamo* was released on October 24, 1960, two weeks before the presidential election, John Wayne, who had just joined the John Birch Society, hoped that his film's fiery celebration of American patriotism would help elect Republican candidate Richard Nixon. Having put his heart, money, and reputation on the line, Wayne desperately wanted *The Alamo* to be a hit, win the accolades of critics and colleagues, and make him a politically powerful Hollywood producer-director. None of these hopes were realized. Nixon lost a closely contested election to John Kennedy, and film critics politely damned *The Alamo* with faint praise. In deference to Wayne's stature in the industry, the Academy disingenuously nominated the movie for seven Academy Awards, including Best Picture. Despite, or because of, shamelessly hyperbolic patriotic hype by Wayne's publicist, Russell Birdwell, *The Alamo* won only one Oscar for Best Sound and did poorly at the box office, initially recouping only about a tenth of its record-setting cost of $12 million (US$76 million in 2005).

The Alamo's disappointing performance was partly the result of its inherent mediocrity and partly the result of bad timing. Hatched during the height of the Red Scare, *The Alamo* became something of an anachronism in the decade it took John Wayne to bring the movie to fruition. By 1960 the national mood had changed sufficiently for anticommunist hysteria to lose much of its force. Part and parcel of a more politically paranoid and jingoistic time, John Wayne would find himself increasingly out of step with the chaotic and conflicted culture of the 1960s, a state of affairs made embarrassingly evident by Wayne's dim-witted and justly reviled pro-Vietnam War movie, *The Green Berets* (1968).

Viva Max! (1970)

Dallas newspaper journalist (and future PBS *NewsHour* anchorman) Jim Lehrer undoubtedly had John Wayne in mind when he wrote his first novel, *Viva Max!* (New York: Duell, Sloan, and Pearce, 1966), a satire of nationalism and militarism featuring a modern, deranged Mexican general who decides to recapture the Alamo. Ely Landau and Oliver A. Unger (cofounders, with Harold Goldman, of National TelaFilm Associates) bought the film rights to Lehrer's book and hired Elliott Baker to adapt it to the screen, Mark Carliner to produce, and television veteran Jerry Paris to direct. With exteriors shot at the real Alamo and interiors shot on a set in Rome, *Viva Max!* (1970) boasted a stellar cast of politically liberal comedic actors headed by Peter Ustinov as General Maximilian Rodrigues de Santos; Pamela Tiffin as Max's girlfriend; Jonathan Winters as General Billy Joe Hallson of the Texas National Guard; John Astin as Sgt. Valdez; Keenan Wynn as General Lacomber; and Harry Morgan as Chief of Police Sylvester. Coming at the height of the Vietnam War protests and on the heels of John Wayne's aforementioned *Green Berets*, *Viva Max!* was quite clearly meant to serve as a liberal rejoinder to Wayne's reactionary politics. Indeed, the film shows a painting of Wayne as Davy Crockett defending the Alamo and includes the following disclaimer: "All characters depicted in this motion picture except John Wayne are fictitious . . ."

The Alamo: Thirteen Days to Glory (1987)

At the end of the Reagan era and the twilight of the Cold War, John Wayne protégé James Arness of *Gunsmoke* fame brought out a made-for-television movie, *The Alamo: Thirteen Days to Glory* (1987), based on Lon Tinkle's straightforward historical account, *13 Days to Glory* (New York: McGraw-Hill, 1958). In adapting his book to the screen, writers Clyde Ware and Norman Morrill followed Tinkle's lead by eschewing myth and emphasizing the flawed humanity of the main personages. Unfortunately, Arness's version was hamstrung by a very limited budget and generally poor casting choices. Though the then twenty-eight-year-old Alec Baldwin made a fitting William B. Travis (twenty-seven years old at the Alamo), and the prodigiously talented Raul Julia delivered a memorable rendition of General Santa Ana, the rest of Arness's ensemble was embarrassingly miscast. At sixty-four the 6-foot, 7-inch Arness was too old and too big to play Jim Bowie, who was forty years of age and a lanky 6 feet tall; sixty-six-year-old Brian Keith made an absurd Davy Crockett, who was only forty-nine; and Lorne Green, at sixty-eight, was twenty-five years older than his character, Sam Houston. Lacking sufficient funds for the necessary extras to fill out Santa Ana's army, director Burt Kennedy resorted to using battle footage from 1955's *The Last Command*, which was shot at a set built on Hobbs Ranch in Brackettville, not at the nearby Alamo Village, where *13 Days* was mostly shot. The resulting mismatches made the film's shoddy production values look even shoddier. Suffice it to say, *13 Days to Glory* is the weakest of the modern Alamo movies.

The Alamo (2004)

In May 2002 Disney CEO Michael Eisner announced that Disney subsidiary, Touchstone Pictures, would make a new movie about the Alamo that would "capture the post-September 11th surge in patriotism" (Barra 2002). Eisner also noted that the film would not stint on the Mexican side of the story, prompting the press to speculate that a "politically correct" (that is, revisionist) version of events was in the works. Ron Howard was slated to produce and direct the film and Russell Crowe was to star as General Sam Houston, with Ethan Hawke playing the part of William Barrett Travis. Intent on historical accuracy, Howard teamed up with leftist writer/director John Sayles (*Eight Men Out; Matewan*) to write a script that would avoid the pat mythologizing that Disney had been guilty of in the 1950s. But patriotism, political correctness, and money considerations are uneasy bedfellows, and Disney's new Alamo project soon ran into trouble. The epic that Howard, Sayles, and script polisher Stephen Gaghan (*Traffic*) envisaged was dark and bloody and would require an R rating. Furthermore, Howard and his producing partner, Brian Glazer, were asking $10 million and superstar Russell Crowe's fee was $20 million, bringing the total cost of the film to about $125 million. Michael Eisner balked at the downbeat script, the R rating, which would narrow its box office potential, and the enormous budget, prompting Ron Howard to quit as director in July 2002. Crowe and Hawke also dropped out. At this point Disney scaled down the scope of the project to a projected $75 million and brought in Leslie Bohem (*Dante's Peak*) to help make script revisions that would render the desired PG-13 rating. Texas native John Lee Hancock (*The Rookie*) replaced Howard as director (who nonetheless stayed on as coproducer with Mark Johnson); Dennis Quaid replaced Russell Crowe; Patrick Wilson replaced Ethan Hawke; Emilio Echevarría was hired to play General Santa Ana; Jason Patric took on the role of Jim Bowie; and Billy Bob Thornton signed on to play Davy Crockett in what proved to be the film's best casting choice. Opting not to use John Wayne's forty-three-year-old Alamo Village in Brackettville, Disney built an elaborate and incredibly expensive 51-acre set on Reimer's Ranch in Dripping Springs outside of Austin, Texas—the largest movie set ever built in North America.

As Roger Ebert noted in his review, "The arc of the Alamo story is a daunting one for any filmmaker: long days and nights of waiting, followed by a massacre" (Ebert 2004). In the early twenty-first century the filmmakers' task was made even more difficult by a confluence of new factors: (1) the perceived need to meet higher standards of historical accuracy (that is, given enlightened attitudes and more sophisticated research, a new Alamo film had to be more balanced and realistic than previous versions); (2) the need to *not* offend America's substantial Hispanic population; (3) the urgent need, post 9/11, to affirm patriotism; and (4) the usual imperative that the film be entertaining and, therefore, make money. All of these somewhat contradictory requisites would have been difficult enough to negotiate but Disney also wanted to hedge its bets by serving up a happy ending! Struggling mightily to fashion a script that covered all the bases, *The Alamo*'s various screenwriters and script doctors came up with a story line that borrowed the old film noir device of putting the aftermath at the beginning, then flashing back to the events leading up to the final battle, which is then shown in detail. The happy ending requirement is addressed by devoting the last part of the movie to the Battle of San Jacinto (April 21, 1836), when Sam Houston's army utterly routed Santa Ana's forces in a mere 18 minutes and won independence for Texas, thus compensating for the defeat at the Alamo.

Scheduled for release just before Christmas 2003, *The Alamo* was rescheduled for Easter 2004 release after negative test screenings in November prompted massive cuts, rewrites, and reshooting. Particularly irksome to test audiences was the film's depiction of Davy Crockett cravenly begging for his life at the feet of Santa Ana. What was originally a 3-hour film was reduced to a more digestible 2 hours and 15 minutes. However, the four-month delay needed to revamp *The Alamo* ultimately pushed its price tag to $107 million (or $32 million over budget), garnered bad advance publicity, and forfeited untold tens of millions of dollars by missing the peak Christmas season. But Hancock and Disney were between a rock and a hard place. In its original, more politically correct form, the film would have failed. In its revised form, *The Alamo* was perhaps more (white) audience-friendly, but excessive tinkering had compromised any dramatic focus it might have had, and the film's best showcasing opportunity had been irrevocably lost. Most critics found the film visually impressive and historically accurate but dramatically diffuse and rather dull. Soon after *The Alamo* made its April 11, 2004, national premier on some 2,600 screens, it was painfully apparent to Disney executives that they had a major bomb on their hands. The film ultimately earned about $24 million at the box office: less than a fourth of what it cost to make and market. Despite international and future rental business, *The Alamo* is unlikely to ever turn a profit: a sign perhaps that the American culture wars have reached such a state of bitter divisiveness that any ideologically charged historical epic seeking a broad audience is now simply an impossible proposition.

The Crimean War (1854–1856)

The Charge of the Light Brigade (1936)

Following sound marketing practice, Warner Brothers made Michael Curtiz's *The Charge of the Light Brigade* (1936) to capitalize on the box office success of *Lives of a Bengal Lancer* (1935), a Paramount action-adventure film about the British imperialist experience in India. Furthermore, Warner Bros. deemed *The Charge* a perfect vehicle for its new action star, Tasmania-born Errol Flynn, who had just won fame playing the highly idealized, heroic, and impeccably British title character in Michael Curtiz's hit film, *Captain Blood* (1935). As originally conceived, the script called for the events leading up to the famous Charge of the Light Brigade to have their basis in the siege and annihilation of the British garrison at Cawnpore during the Sepoy (sepáhi) Rebellion, a widespread mutiny of Indian soldiers in the British colonial army. When some astute observer pointed out that the Sepoy Rebellion actually took place in 1857, three years *after* Balaclava, Warner Bros. hurriedly changed the fort's name to Chukoti and its attackers became mythical "Suristani" hill tribesmen led by an equally mythical and suitably diabolical potentate named Surat Khan, perhaps a conflation of the Sepoy Mutiny leaders Hajimullah Khan and Nana Sahib.

One might well ask what colonial hostilities in India have to do with the Crimean War. Not a thing, but the film needed to link these two distinct crises of Victorian imperialism for reasons both logistical and ideological. First, screenwriters Michel Jacoby and Roland Leigh had to supply a noble and plausible reason for the suicidal and otherwise inexplicable Charge of the Light Brigade at Balaclava that would also square with Errol Flynn's emerging star persona as a dashing, high-minded figure. In his famous poem, Alfred Lord Tennyson had simply noted, "someone had blundered." The elaborate plot Jacoby and Leigh devised has Surat Khan's minions slaughtering British women and children after the fall of the fort at Chukoti: an atrocity that cries for British vengeance. Transferred to the Crimea after service in India against the Suristanis, the fictional Geoffrey Vickers (Errol Flynn) learns that Surat Khan (stock villain C. Henry Gordon) has allied himself with the Russians. Quite predictably, Vickers forges orders for an attack of the 27th Lancers on the Russian batteries at Balaclava Heights to exact personal revenge on the Khan. The Light Brigade is butchered but British honor is restored when Vickers manages to kill Surat Khan before succumbing to his own wounds. Faring worse in reality were some 200 horses deliberately tripped and killed during the filming of the cavalry charge scene: an atrocity that prompted tighter controls on the use of animals in motion pictures.

The Charge of the Light Brigade (1968)

While Michael Curtiz's *Charge of the Light Brigade* reflected the romantic-escapist tendencies of 1930s Hollywood and its none-too-discriminating audience, Tony Richardson's *The Charge of the Light Brigade* (1968) bespoke a starkly different time, place, and cultural sensibility. One of Britain's "angry young men" and a leading figure in British cinema's iconoclastic New Wave in the late 1950s and early 1960s, Richardson (*Look Back in Anger*; *Tom Jones*) was a major antiestablishment figure, as were Richardson's screenwriters, noted playwright John Osborne (*Look Back in Anger*) and Charles Wood (who cowrote Richard Lester's *Help!* and *How I Won the War* and revised Osborne's screenplay). Like most of their peers in mid-1960s London, Richardson, Osborne, and Wood were staunchly opposed to the ongoing Vietnam War, to war in general, and to the authoritarian, sclerotic bureaucracies that promoted war and all manner of oppression. Knowing something of their own country's history, Richardson and his cohorts were well aware that Michael Curtiz's 1936 version of events was a preposterous fabrication. In point of fact, the Crimean War was a farcical masterpiece of incompetent leadership for which, as usual, the rank and file had to pay dearly.

Working with a substantial budget (the equivalent of US$43.3 million in 2003), Richardson and producer Neil Hartley secured a superb cast: Trevor Howard as Lord Cardigan (1797–1868); John Geilgud as Lord Raglan (1788–1855); Harry Andrews as Lord Lucan (1800–1888); David Hemmings as Captain Louis

Edward Nolan (1818–1854); Richardson's wife, Vanessa Redgrave, as Mrs. Clarissa Morris; and John Osborne's wife, Jill Bennett, as Mrs. Frances "Fanny" Duberly. For their main source, Osborne and Wood relied on Cecil Woodham-Smith's scathing exposé of the Balaclava fiasco, *The Reason Why: The Fatal Charge of the Light Brigade* (New York: McGraw-Hill, 1954). According to Woodham-Smith the slaughter of the Light Brigade chiefly owed to Lord Raglan's tendency to extemporize and issue vague orders. Indeed, an ambiguously worded order caused the Light Brigade to charge into the wrong valley where they encounter the Russian artillery batteries head-on. Another error on Raglan's part was his placing Lord Cardigan under the command of Cardigan's brother-in-law, Lord Lucan. The two men loathed each other and carried on a steadily escalating feud that made their respective commands incapable of working together. In a more general sense, the gross mismanagement of the Crimean War stemmed from the absurdities of the British class system. Though it had its share of able soldiers, a good part of the British army's senior officer corps in the early Victorian era was comprised of aged veterans of Waterloo and wealthy gentry who had simply purchased their commands when the war started: a dubious practice that ensured the placement of inexperienced and inept amateurs leading professional soldiers into battle.

An officer of the latter category, James Thomas Brudenell, the 7th Earl of Cardigan and commander of the Light Brigade, was an insufferably petulant martinet who flew into childish rages at the smallest annoyances. His hated brother-in-law, George Charles Bingham, the 3rd Earl of Lucan and overall commander of the cavalry, was a hot-tempered, pompous peer of the realm promoted over better officers because of his connections and high social standing. Richardson's *Charge* does not need to exaggerate the deficiencies of Cardigan and Lucan; both men were detestable upper-class twits and incompetent commanders. Overall commander of British forces in the Crimea, Fitzroy James Henry Somerset (Lord Raglan), a sixty-five-year-old, one-armed Waterloo veteran, was well intentioned but woefully ineffectual. John Geilgud's amusing rendition of Lord Raglan as nearly senile is exaggerated, but not by much.

In partial contrast to the privileged ninnies who run the show, the film posits Captain Louis Nolan (David Hemmings), a strident but combat-tested officer who quite rightfully despises Cardigan, Lucan, and Raglan—who respond in kind. Indeed, as regards Capt. Nolan, Raglan utters one of the film's more memorable lines: "It will be a sad day for England when her armies are led by men who know too well what they are doing—it smacks of murder." To further emphasize the characteristic 1960s theme of enlightened youth versus benighted, hidebound middle age, Richardson pairs Hemmings with Vanessa Redgrave, the wife of his friend, Capt. Morris (Mark Burns), whose amorous advances he piously spurns. As the two had already starred opposite each other in Michelangelo Antonioni's ultrahip mystery-thriller, *Blowup* (1966), contemporary audiences were meant to see them as iconic representatives of the rebellious youth culture. Finally, in marked contrast to the glorious charge visualized by Michael Curtiz, Richardson shoots his version of the event with a certain gritty realism. The culminating image—a freeze-frame shot of a dead horse—nicely encapsulates the sense of slaughter, waste, and futility as the commanding officers try to lay blame on each other for the fiasco. Though a sometimes effective satire of Victorian hubris, Richardson's *Charge* lacks overall dramatic cohesion, nor does it present a protagonist with whom the audience can identify. Richard Williams' *Monty Python*–like animated linking sequences inspired by Crimean War–era *Punch* magazine cartoons are witty but shatter the carefully cultivated verisimilitude of the film proper and date the movie as quintessentially 1960s in style and temperament.

The American Civil War (1861–1865)

The Andersonville Trial (1970)

Early in 1864 the Confederacy, struggling to cope with a massive influx of Union prisoners of war, built Camp Sumter near Andersonville, Georgia, where some 43,000 POWs were interned in a camp designed for 8,000. Over the next fourteen months, 12,912 of those men (30 percent) died of starvation, disease, and exposure: a humanitarian tragedy of horrifying proportions. After the war, the victorious Federals put the camp commandant, Capt. Henry Wirz (1822–1865), on trial for the hideous conditions at Andersonville, found him guilty of war crimes, and had him hanged. Almost a century later (on December 29, 1959, to be exact) *The Andersonville Trial*, a play by war correspondent, Pulitzer Prize–winning journalist, and ex-Communist Saul Levitt, premiered on Broadway and was a great success. Based on the actual court-martial transcripts, *The Andersonville Trial* starring George C. Scott as Capt. Wirz was a dramatic tour de force that posed troubling questions about authority and moral responsibility. Sounding very much like the Nazis who stood trial at Nuremberg after World War II, the arrogant, unrepentant Wirz protested that he was only following orders. In May 1970 the Public Broadcasting Service (PBS) released a 2-hour, 30-minute telecast of Levitt's play, *The Andersonville Trial*, directed by George C. Scott and starring Richard Basehart as Henry Wirz, Cameron Mitchell as Advocate General Lew Wallace (1827–1905), and William Shatner as Lt. Col. Norton Parker Chipman

(1836–1924), the army's chief prosecutor. True to the facts and brilliantly acted, *The Andersonville Trial* was nominated for five Emmys and won three (for best drama, camera work, and writing). Released just six months after *New York Times* correspondent Seymour Hersh first broke the shocking story of the massacre of over 500 Vietnamese civilians at My Lai on March 16, 1968, the film also carried renewed and enormous political resonance.

Glory (1989)

Edward Zwick's *Glory* (1989) pursues an ideological agenda that differs markedly from that of *The Andersonville Trial*. Basing his screenplay on Peter Burchard's *One Gallant Rush* (New York: St. Martin's, 1965), Lincoln Kirstein's *Lay This Laurel: An Album on the Saint-Gaudens Memorial on Boston Common Honoring Black and White Men Together Who Served the Union Cause with Robert Gould Shaw and Died with Him July 18, 1863* (New York: Eakins Press, 1973), and the letters of Robert Gould Shaw, writer Kevin Jarre (*Rambo: First Blood Part II*) recounts the story of the 54th Massachusetts Regiment, one of the first black units assembled during the Civil War. On July 18, 1863—just two weeks after Gettysburg—the 54th led eleven other Union regiments in an unsuccessful assault on Fort Wagner, near Charlestown, South Carolina, and predictably sustained the heaviest casualties: 256 dead or wounded out of 600 men. Among the dead was Colonel Robert Gould Shaw (1837–1863), the regiment's white commander from a prominent Boston abolitionist family. Though the attack was disastrous, the 54th proved its fighting mettle and paved the way for the eventual recruitment of another 180,000 African Americans into the Union army (10 percent of their total number): a development that helped turn the tide of the Civil War in favor of the North.

The story that *Glory* tells is an exceptionally important one but the film itself is less than great. Among its weaknesses: a tendency toward bombastic dialogue and, especially, the casting of the cherubic-faced Matthew Broderick as Colonel Robert Gould Shaw. Primarily a comic actor, Broderick lacked the gravity needed to deliver a convincing depiction of Col. Shaw. Likewise, the supposed glory of being slaughtered in a suicidal frontal assault on a well-defended enemy fortress is a dubious proposition that unavoidably casts the larger significance of the event into doubt. As Robert Burgoyne (Film Studies, Wayne State University) argues, "In the shots of the mass burial of the soldiers of the 54th that end the film, the national narrative is hauntingly evoked not as a triumphal story of social progress, but as a collective narrative of social loss" (Burgoyne 1997, 37).

The Civil War (1990)

In 1984 fledgling documentarian Ken Burns read Michael Shaara's *The Killer Angels* (New York: McKay, 1974), a Pulitzer Prize–winning novel about the Battle of Gettysburg. Inspired by Shaara's book, Burns undertook a massive documentary about the Civil War. Scouring dozens of libraries and museums, Burns and his team filmed 16,000 photographs, paintings, and newspapers from the period, recruited an impressive contingent of commentators for interviews and actors for dramatic recitations, and proceeded to make *The Civil War*, a nine-part (11-hour) PBS film series narrated by David McCullough. On the PBS website devoted to the film, Burns grandiloquently describes his filmmaking style (which had been evolving since his first film, *Brooklyn Bridge*, in 1981) as "the careful use of archival photographs, live modern cinematography, music, narration, and a chorus of first-person voices that together did more than merely recount a historical story. It was something that also became a kind of 'emotional archaeology,' trying to unearth the very heart of the American experience; listening to the ghosts and echoes of an almost inexpressibly wise past" (http://www.pbs.org).

    Episode One of *The Civil War*, *The Cause (1861)*, introduces the major figures of the era and details the signal events leading up to the firing on Fort Sumter: the publication of Harriet Beecher Stowe's *Uncle Tom's Cabin* in 1850; the pro-slavery Dred Scott Decision of 1857; John Brown's failed raid at Harpers Ferry in 1859; and the controversial election of Abraham Lincoln in 1860. The episode culminates with General McClellan's crushing defeat at Mannasas, Virginia (First Battle of Bull Run). Episode Two, *A Very Bloody Affair (1982)*, recounts the revolutionary use of "ironclad" ships on both sides and contrasts the inaction of McClellan on the Virginia peninsula with the able leadership of Ulysses S. Grant, whose Union forces prevail at the extremely bloody Battle of Shiloh (Tennessee). Episode Three, *Forever Free (1862)*, focuses on Lincoln's firing of McClellan, followed by reinstatement after McClellan's replacement, General John Pope, is defeated at the Second Battle of Bull Run, followed by McClellan's permanent ouster after his indecisive performance against Robert E. Lee's forces at Antietam (Sharpsburg, Maryland), September 16–18, 1862. Episode Three also traces Lincoln's Emancipation Proclamation, from idea to actuality, made politically possible by the Union victory at Antietam. In Episode Four, *Simply Murder (1863)*, Union forces under General Ambrose Burnside suffer another withering defeat at Fredericksburg, Virginia (December 1862); Lincoln replaces Burnside with Joseph Hooker but the Union army sustains another trouncing by Lee's forces at Chancellorsville, Virginia (April–May, 1863); General Grant lays siege to Vicksburg. Episode Five, *The Universe of Battle*

(1863), deals primarily with Robert E. Lee's invasion of Pennsylvania, culminating in General George Meade's decisive victory over Lee's army at Gettysburg (July 1–3, 1863), a battle that resulted in over 50,000 total casualties. Episode Six, *Valley of the Shadow of Death (1864)*, examines the backgrounds of Generals Grant and Lee and then chronicles Grant's Overland Campaign (May–June 1864), an incredibly bloody offensive against Lee's Army of Northern Virginia that resulted in stalemate outside of Petersburg, Virginia. Episode Seven, *Most Hallowed Ground (1864)*, focuses on the presidential election of 1864, when Abraham Lincoln handily defeated the Democratic candidate, his former army commander, George McClellan, after Union victories at Mobile Bay, Atlanta, and the Shenandoah Valley renewed the North's faith in eventual victory. Episode Eight, *War Is All Hell (1865)*, begins with General William T. Sherman's devastating march to the sea, covers Lincoln's second inauguration, recounts the fall of Petersburg and Richmond, and culminates with Lee's surrender to Grant at Appomattox. Episode Nine, *The Better Angels of Our Nature (1865)*, concludes the series with Lincoln's assassination on April 14, 1865, just five days after Lee's surrender, and ruminates on the meaning and consequences of the Civil War.

When it aired in the fall of 1990, after almost six years of painstaking research and production, *The Civil War* won two Emmys, broke all ratings records for public television, and instigated a passionate national dialogue on the Civil War 135 years after the war ended. In part, the astonishing cultural impact of Burns's achievement can be gauged in dollars and cents. A companion book, priced at $50, sold 700,000 copies, and gross revenues associated with the film eventually topped $100 million: an amazing performance for a documentary series. While it is difficult to pinpoint the reasons for *The Civil War's* tremendous success, a number of factors probably came into play: nostalgia for a simpler, more idealistic—and astonishingly more literate—time; the war's enduring fascination for hundreds of thousands of Americans; Burns's considerable narrative gifts and a multifaceted expositional approach that made for compelling viewing; the film's intellectually middlebrow and politically centrist orientation that refused to take sides (except to unequivocally condemn slavery), that is, a stance that guaranteed the widest possible audience. No doubt *The Civil War* was also a triumph of style. Its stately pace, reverential tone, epic scope, and richness of detail practically demanded a respectful, attentive reception.

But was it good history? Historians are divided on the question. In 1996 Oxford University Press published *Ken Burns's 'The Civil War': Historians Respond*, a collection of critical essays edited by film historian Robert Brent Toplin (University of North Carolina at Wilmington) that also featured strident rebuttals by Ken Burns and Geoffrey C. Ward (*Civil War* cowriter with Burns and Burns's brother, Ric). Toplin and C. Vann Woodward (retired Johns Hopkins history professor who served as a consultant to Burns) praise the film; Gabor S. Boritt (director of the Civil War Institute at Gettysburg) and Gary W. Gallagher (professor of the history of the American Civil War at the University of Virginia) give it mixed reviews; Catherine Clinton (expert on nineteenth-century gender issues), Leon F. Litwack (University of California at Berkeley; expert on African American history), and Eric Foner (Columbia University; expert on slavery and the Reconstruction era) find it wanting in its coverage of women, blacks, and the Reconstruction, respectively. Responding to his detractors, Burns has argued that contemporary academic history, with its arcane specializations, abstract discourse, and emphasis on social structure and ideology, make history not only boring but virtually unintelligible to the layperson. For Burns, the historical documentary calls for orderly, audience-friendly storytelling that assiduously avoids current academic debates about competing research methodologies and representational modes and the ideological biases that inform them. Some academics, usually on the radical Left, counter that Burns would do well to present opposing interpretations rather than a homogenized version of American history that tends to repress darker truths (that is, exploitation, inequality, imperialism) by submersing them in a sea of wholesome period detail. In Ken Burns's favor, it must be noted that he has been instrumental in bringing reasonably accurate treatments of historical subjects to millions of Americans who would not otherwise seek such knowledge. An unintended consequence of *The Civil War* series was that it brought the sorry state of contemporary political discourse into sharp relief by reminding Americans they once had a president of very high moral and intellectual stature.

The Battle of Gettysburg (1955)

As the battle that arguably sealed the doom of the Confederacy, Gettysburg is far and away the most famous engagement of the Civil War. At least five films were made about the Battle of Gettysburg (or Lincoln's Gettysburg Address) during the silent film era. In 1955, at the nadir of the Cold War, Dore Schary, the politically liberal CEO of Metro-Goldwyn-Mayer, wrote and produced *The Battle of Gettysburg*, a patriotic 30-minute color documentary shot on location at Gettysburg National Military Park. Voice-over narrator Leslie Nielsen (ironically, a Canadian by birth) recounts the battle, his commentary accompanied by battle sounds, period music, and shots of the numerous memorials and empty fields where the carnage took place ninety years before. There are no reenactments. In 1956 *The Battle of Gettysburg* was nominated for two Oscars (Best Documentary, Short Subject, and Best Short Subject, Two Reel).

Gettysburg (1993)

In 1978, when he was just starting out as a film director, Ronald F. Maxwell read Michael Shaara's *The Killer Angels*. As deeply moved by the book as Ken Burns would be a few years later, Maxwell resolved to make a film version of *The Killer Angels*, but it would take nearly fifteen years before he could obtain sufficient financing. Ironically, the release of Burns's *The Civil War* did the trick. Encouraged by the series' tremendous success, Atlanta media mogul Ted Turner contracted with Maxwell to make *Gettysburg*, a 6-hour Turner Network Television (TNT) miniseries. Once filming began, Ted Turner was so impressed by the quality of the evolving project that he became convinced it could be his entrée into major feature film production. Accordingly, Turner approved a 4-hour version for theatrical release that was budgeted at $25 million: a considerable sum but still modest for a movie of such epic proportions.

A faithful adaptation of Michael Shaara's historically accurate novel, *Gettysburg* (1993) starred Martin Sheen as Robert E. Lee (1807–1872); Tom Berenger as Lt. Gen. James Longstreet (1821–1904); Stephen Lang as Major General George E. Pickett (1825–1875); Richard Jordan as Brigadier General Lewis A. Armistead (1817–1863); Jeff Daniels as Colonel Joshua Lawrence Chamberlain (1828–1914), and, literally, a cast of thousands of unpaid Civil War reenactors who provided their own, scrupulously authentic, uniforms and equipment: a key ingredient that kept the film realistic and the production affordable. With its final cut coming in at some 4 hours and 20 minutes, *Gettysburg* was an exhilarating experience for Civil War fanatics—an overwhelmingly white, male, Southern demographic—but a tad slow and ponderous for most laypersons, who stayed away in droves. The film lost about $14 million. A lugubrious score by Randy Edelman (*Last of the Mohicans*) protested too much the film's mythic pretensions, as did pompously noble speeches by the principal actors, some of whom were accoutred in outsized false beards that bordered on the unintentionally funny. To his credit, Ken Burns tried to be as inclusive as his own biases allowed, examining the Civil War from social, cultural, military, and personal perspectives. Made during and released after the unambiguous triumph of the first Gulf War, Ron Maxwell's *Gettysburg* is a portentous military docudrama that revels in the supposed glory of the clash of arms. As with most conventional war movies, there is a great deal of spectacular simulated killing and dying but the film does not dwell on the general squalor and gore, the pitiful screams of the wounded, the fields strewn with bloated corpses, or the hundreds of grisly amputations that were as integral to the battle as Pickett's Charge.

Pharoah's Army (1995)

Diametrically opposite to *Gettysburg* in scope, tone, and ideological valance is Robby Henson's *Pharoah's Army* (1995), a low-budget independent production that accomplishes much more with much less. In 1941 an elderly mountaineer returned to a remote sinkhole outside the now defunct hamlet of Meschack's Creek, Kentucky, where seventy-nine years earlier he had secretly buried a Union soldier he had killed during the Civil War. Noted Appalachian folklorist-writer-activist Harry M. Caudill (1922–1990) recorded the mountaineer's story and Robby Henson adapted it to the screen with stunning results.

In 1862 a small party of Union cavalry, sent out to forage for provisions in the Cumberland Gap region of south-central Kentucky, is forced to linger at a Confederate partisan's farm after one of their number (Huckleberry Fox) is injured in a fall. The farm's beautiful mistress, Sarah Anders (Patricia Clarkson) and her young son (Will Lucas)—who will become the elderly narrator recalling the events—despise the Federals for trespassing and stealing their food but are forced to tolerate them. What ensues is a battle of nerves and emotions between the soldiers and their reluctant hosts. The leader of the Union detachment, recent widower Captain John Hull Abston (Chris Cooper), is a decent, compassionate man caught between duty, romantic attraction to Sarah Anders (whose husband is off fighting with the Confederate army), and the often deeply personal hatred that prevails between the North and South. A farmer himself, Abston plows the woman's field and chops her wood—signs of kindness one of his embittered soldiers chooses to interpret as weakness. After a tumultuous stay, the men are departing the farm when Sarah's idealistic young son shoots and kills the injured soldier: an act that enrages Captain Abston, who nonetheless chooses not to punish his "enemies." In marked contrast to the epic-heroic pretensions of *Gettysburg*, *Pharoah's Army* presents the Civil War in intimate terms: as a Faulknerian story about individuals struggling to morally navigate the inevitable brutalities, injustices, and conflicted loyalties that marked the war. Despite the superb performance of Chris Cooper and a small but notable part played by Kris Kristoffersen (as a hard-hearted Southern preacher), *Pharoah's Army* received very limited distribution and publicity—a sad irony given the film's clear superiority to most films about the Civil War.

Andersonville (1996)

Not long after *Gettysburg*, Ted Turner bankrolled another Civil War project: John Frankenheimer's *Andersonville* (1996), a two-part miniseries for TNT that sought to capture the horrors of the Civil War's most notorious prison camp. Written by David W. Rintels, *Andersonville* presented two story lines: (1) the prisoners' battle against the "Raiders," that is, renegade Union soldiers who prey on their comrades and (2) an escape attempt by tunnel. An overlong but better-than-average television film, *Andersonville* was nominated for seven Emmys and won one (for Frankenheimer's direction). *Andersonville* should not, however, be confused with *The Andersonville Trial*. Made during the politically charged era of the Vietnam War, *The Andersonville Trial* was implicitly antiwar and specifically aimed at evoking moral questions surrounding the My Lai Massacre. *Andersonville*'s politics are, by contrast, decidedly conservative. Made well after Ronald Reagan orchestrated national amnesia about Vietnam, *Andersonville* and to a lesser extent, its predecessor, *Gettysburg* reflected the manful, right-wing Southern populism of its backer, Ted Turner, and was geared toward military enthusiasts, Civil War buffs, and reenactors, not for those interested in pondering the philosophical and moral vagaries of war.

Gods and Generals (2003)

During his long quest to make *Gettysburg*, Ronald Maxwell became close friends with Michael Shaara and Shaara's son, Jeff. After *Gettysburg* appeared, Maxwell suggested to Jeff that someone should be commissioned to write the prequel and sequel to *The Killer Angels* that his father had planned to write before he died of a heart attack in 1988. Taking up Maxwell's suggestion himself, Jeff Shaara quit the antique business and proceeded to write his first book, *Gods and Generals* (New York: Ballantine, 1996), the *Killer Angels* prequel that focuses on the military career and personality of legendary Confederate General Thomas "Stonewall" Jackson (1824–1863; killed at the Battle of Chancellorsville, two months before Gettysburg). Though primarily a hagiography about Jackson, the novel also deals with Robert E. Lee and Union officers Winfield Scott Hancock (1824–1886) and Joshua Lawrence Chamberlain. Much to Shaara's surprise, *Gods and Generals* garnered strong reviews and resided on the *New York Times* bestseller list for fifteen weeks; the nation's Civil War flame, never dead but fanned into a major conflagration by Ken Burns six years earlier, apparently still burned bright.

As was always his intention, Ron Maxwell bought the rights to *Gods and Generals*, wrote a screen adaptation, and once again received the personal backing of Ted Turner to the tune of $56 million to make the film version (another $24 million would be spent on marketing). Released in February 2003, *Gods and Generals* starred *Gettysburg* veteran Stephen Lang as "Stonewall" Jackson; Jeff

Daniels reprising his *Gettysburg* role as Joshua Chamberlain; Robert Duvall as Robert E. Lee (ironically, the politically archconservative Duvall replaced Martin Sheen, an outspoken liberal activist off-camera), and 7,500 reenactors who gladly filled in as cinematic cannon fodder. Lacking the narrative focus and compressed time frame that held *Gettysburg* together, *Gods and Generals* was nearly as long but far less compelling. Most reviews were derisive and box office proceeds dismal; Turner may have lost as much as $70 million on the project. The film's stunning failure seemed to indicate that American Civil War fever had finally run its course, some twelve years after Burns's miniseries. Perhaps the topic, in true American fashion, had simply been beaten into the ground. Or perhaps *Gods and Generals* too obviously glorified Confederate military prowess, conservative Christianity, insane physical courage, and the chivalric values of a bygone era: all part and parcel of a reactionary romanticism that still exerts influence in parts of the (white) South but is steadily losing ground in the national imagination at the start of a new millennium. A bitter Ron Maxwell admitted that *The Last Full Measure* (the projected third part of his Civil War trilogy) would have to be postponed indefinitely and accused Roger Ebert and other "politically correct" film critics of colluding or even conspiring to suppress *Gods and Generals* because it presented an adulatory view of Stonewall Jackson and the retrograde ideals of the Confederacy (Moore 2003).

Custer and the Indian Wars

They Died with Their Boots On (1942)

Since his demise at the Little Bighorn, General George Armstrong Custer (1839–1876) has remained one of America's most controversial figures, both admired for his heroism in the Civil War and reviled for his reckless ardor as an Indian fighter. Made in the months before Pearl Harbor, Raoul Walsh's *They Died with Their Boots On* (1942) is a fanciful biopic of the colorful, young general appropriately starring Errol Flynn (1909–1959), the swashbuckling actor already notorious for his alcohol-drenched, sybaritic lifestyle away from the set. Flynn's growing mystique, as a devil-may-care maverick, dovetailed nicely with Custer's legend. As America braced itself for inevitable involvement in World War II, Walsh and screenwriters Wally Kline and Æneas MacKenzie were avid to make a thrilling action picture and, in the process, do their patriotic duty by depicting Custer as a true American original and martyr to the nation's swarthy enemies. Consequently, the George Custer they constructed was a bizarre distortion of the real man. In the film, which was shot entirely in California, Custer becomes a mild-mannered, righteous friend of the Indians who seeks to protect them from gold prospectors swarming to their sacred Black Hills. In reality, Custer himself spread the news of the gold discovery. A cruel scourge of the Indians (and his own men), Custer was likely a sociopath; his principal focus was on himself and his chief aim was to recapture the glory and excitement of his Civil War days. The film's whitewashing of Custer was matched by the Hollywood whitewashing of Errol Flynn in the aftermath of the film's release. Acquittal on statutory rape charges in early 1943 cemented Flynn's priapic reputation with American males. During World War II, tales of Flynn's licentiousness functioned as fantasy material for sex-starved U.S. servicemen (hence the popularity of the leering slogan "In like Flynn"). Before the war ended Flynn teamed with director Raoul Walsh to make a half dozen other patriotic films that cast him as a brave and righteous fighter against the tyranny of the Axis powers—perhaps another irony; biographer Charles Higham alleges that Flynn was a secret Nazi sympathizer.

Sitting Bull (1954) and *Custer of the West* (1967)

Twelve years after Walsh's film, B-movie writer-director Sidney Salkow reprised the Battle of the Little Bighorn from the Indians' perspective with *Sitting Bull* (1954), a poorly made, forgettable Western (starring J. Carroll Naish as Sitting Bull) that is every bit as inaccurate as its predecessor. On a more grandiose scale is Robert Siodmak's *Custer of the West* (1967), a would-be epic using 70mm "super-cinerama," a process made specifically for outsized, curved theater screens that would create the illusion, for the viewer, of total immersion in the action. Shot in Spain and starring Robert Shaw as Custer; Lawrence Tierney as Custer's mentor, General Philip Sheridan (1831–1888); Mary Ure as Elizabeth ("Libby") Custer (1842–1933); Ty Hardin as Major Marcus Reno (1834–1889); and young heartthrob Jeffrey Hunter as Captain Frederick Benteen (1834–1906), *Custer of the West* made no pretensions to historical accuracy. Nor did it attempt to present a significantly more critical view of Custer. Its goal, pure and simple, was to be a larger-than-life spectacle designed to wow patrons with exciting action sequences and impressive, grand-scale cinematography. The true historical significance of the film lies behind the scenes. Writer-producer and noted blacklist front man, Philip Yordan financed the movie; two veterans of the Hollywood blacklist—Bernard Gordon and frequent collaborator, Julian Zimet (originally credited under the pseudonym, Julian Halevy)—wrote it; and noir master Robert Siodmak (*The Killers; Criss Cross*) directed it: his first American film in the fifteen years since the second round of HUAC hearings. In sum, *Custer of the West* was one of many manifestations in the mid-1960s of the steadily waning power of the Hollywood blacklist, which had been effectively broken in 1960 when the blacklisted screenwriter Dalton Trumbo received credit under his own name for Stanley Kubrick's *Spartacus.*

Son of the Morning Star (1991)

In 1979 distinguished writer, editor, and essayist Evan S. Connell embarked on an unconventional biography of George Armstrong Custer. Reading dozens of books, journals, and accounts on and by participants in the Battle of the Little Bighorn, Connell also visited the battlefield in Montana on four separate occasions. The resulting work, *Son of the Morning Star* (San Francisco: North Point Press, 1984), was a magisterial biography of Custer that provided what cultural anthropologist Clifford Geertz has termed "thick description" of its subject and his sociohistorical milieu (Geertz 1973). Not concerned with conventional, diachronic narrative structure, Connell proceeded to examine, in exhaustive and often fascinating detail, Custer; his military career; his 7th Calvary officers and soldiers; his Oglala Sioux adversaries (especially Crazy Horse, Sitting Bull, and Gall); and the attitudes and values that animated both sides during the entire history of relations between whites and Indians—all by way of providing an especially vivid context for the final showdown at Little Bighorn. Wary of its hybrid characteristics, major publishing houses refused Connell's manuscript, forcing him to place it with North Point, a small, independent publisher. The book was, however, a major critical and popular success, selling over 80,000 copies in hardcover and winning the *Los Angeles Times* Book Award in history and a National Book Critics Circle nomination.

By its very nature, *Son of the Morning Star* presented a host of problems for screen adaptation. Nonetheless, Connell sold the rights to Republic Television, and respected screenwriter Melissa Mathison produced a suitably linear teleplay for Mike Robe's "*Son of the Morning Star,*" a two-part television miniseries that aired on NBC in February 1991, only nine weeks after the national opening of Kevin Costner's wildly successful and multiple Oscar-winning *Dances with Wolves*, a revisionist Western that played to the "politically correct" zeitgeist of the 1990s by siding with the Native Americans over their white enemies. (Indeed, Kevin Costner was originally slated to play Custer in Robe's miniseries but scheduling problems interfered; Gary Cole replaced him.) Seeking to preserve some of the ideological evenhandedness and perspectival complexity of Connell's book, Melissa Mathison told Custer's saga through two, contrasting points of view: Custer's wife, Libby (Rosanna Arquette) and an Indian girl/woman, Kate Bighead (Demina Becker/Kimberley Norris, voice-over by Native

American singer-songwriter Buffy St. Marie). Faithful to Connell's rigorously accurate account—except for the highly speculative notion that Custer fathered a child with an Indian woman—*Son of the Morning Star* belatedly corrected the lies and distortions of earlier Custer movies and won four Emmys (for costume, makeup, sound editing, and sound mixing) in the process.

Geronimo Fights Back

Geronimo and the Apache Resistance, 1851–1886 (1988)

The Chiricahua Apache warrior-chieftain, Geromino (Goyathlay "one who yawns") (1829–1909) is legendary for the incredible skill and tenacity he displayed in resisting Mexican and American attempts to tame him and his people over a twenty-five-year period. In the decades after his death, Hollywood dramatized Geronimo's story a number of times, with Paul Sloane's *Geronimo* (1939), John Hoffman's *I Killed Geronimo* (1950), Ray Nazarro's *Indian Uprising* (1952), and Arnold Laven's *Geronimo* (1962). With the exception of the surprisingly progressive *Indian Uprising*, the early Geronimo films were stock Westerns told from the Anglo point of view that depicted Geronimo in generally stereotypical terms as the inscrutable embodiment of Indian savagery. In the late 1980s and early 1990s, cultural attitudes toward Native Americans began to change, at least in the realm of popular culture. One barometer of the change was the PBS *American Experience* series program, *Geronimo and the Apache Resistance, 1851–1886* (1988), a revisionist documentary that examined the Apache wars in terms of the clash of civilizations. In 1990 the Arts & Entertainment Network (A&E) *Biography* series followed suit with a well-researched and fair-minded reassessment of Geronimo that helped dispel some of the old stereotypes. Soon thereafter the success of such revisionist films as Kevin Costner's *Dances with Wolves*, Mike Robe's *Son of the Morning Star*, Michael Mann's *Last of the Mohicans* (1992), and Clint Eastwood's quasi-revisionist *Unforgiven* (1992) breathed renewed life, and a more progressive political consciousness, into the Western genre as the United States moved out of the Reagan-Bush era and into the nominally more liberal Clinton years.

Geronimo and *Geronimo: An American Legend* (1993)

It was into this new climate of opinion that the two latest Geronimo films were released within a week of each other in December 1993: *Geronimo*, a TNT movie,

Geronimo was the last major recalcitrant Indian leader to surrender, yielding for the final time to General Nelson A. Miles in 1886. (National Archives)

and *Geronimo: An American Legend,* a big-budget theatrical release. In the first instance, veteran television director Roger Young (*Lou Grant; Murder in Mississippi*) teamed with neophyte screenwriter, J. T. Allen, to make *Geronimo* for TNT. Starring Joseph Runningfox as Geronimo, Young's version was probably the most sympathetic to the Native American side of the story but was instantly overshadowed by the more ambitious *Geronimo: An American Legend,* a $50 million movie cowritten by macho reactionary John Milius (*Conan the Barbarian; Red Dawn*) and action film specialist Larry Gross (*48 Hrs.; Another 48 Hrs.*) and helmed by Gross's compatriot, action director Walter Hill (*48 Hrs.; Another 48 Hrs.*). Given the anti-white-supremacist implications of the subject matter, Milius and his cohorts seemed an unlikely creative team for such a project and the movie they ended up making is predictably incongruous. In an interview with Marianne Cotter (*MovieMaker,* Sept. 1994), Walter Hill spoke of his desire to be evenhanded since the "distinction as to what passes as a good guy and a bad guy is often blurred in life and in history and in the telling of a story." John Milius's position was similarly ambivalent and even more disingenuous. A longtime admirer of Geronimo as the very embodiment of the tough-as-nails American warrior ethos he venerates, Milius nonetheless remains committed to the side that won. Though willing to acknowledge that "White-Eyes" disgracefully mistreated Native Americans, Hill et al. are unwilling to repudiate Manifest Destiny: an ideological and narrative contradiction that results in a meandering story line and weak characterizations. Consequently, the film is "about" Geronimo's heroic struggle to evade capture but unfolds from the *white* point of view, with the action centering on the sympathetic character of Lt. Charles B. Gatewood (Jason Patric) of the U.S. 6th Cavalry and narration supplied by Gatewood's morally scrupulous young subordinate, 2nd Lt. Britton Davis (Matt Damon). Likewise, Gatewood's commanding officer, Brig. Gen. George Crook (1828–1890, played by Gene Hackman) and the cavalry's Chief of Scouts, Al Sieber (Robert Duvall), are depicted in almost wholly sympathetic terms. Inasmuch as Geronimo (Wes Studi) is justified in defending his people and ancestral lands against foreign incursion, there are no villains in the piece, nor much dramatic tension. Despite excellent location cinematography by Lloyd Ahern and an evocative sound track by Ry Cooder, *Geronimo: An American Legend* suffers from the same culture wars muddle that would blight Disney's *Alamo* almost a decade later.

British Colonial Wars in Africa

A relatively small-scale conflict in the overall history of British imperialism, the Anglo-Zulu War of 1879 nonetheless spawned two major films: *Zulu* (1964) and

Zulu Dawn (1979). The first of these projects, *Zulu*, was the result of a three-way collaboration between distinguished Welsh actor, Stanley Baker (1927–1976); American ex-patriot director, Cy Endfield (1914–1995); and Scottish popular historian, John Prebble (1916–2001). All three men hailed from working-class backgrounds and two of them—Prebble and Endfield—had been members of the Communist Party in their respective countries. Indeed, Endfield fled the United States for Britain during the 1951 HUAC hearings, rather than name names or submit to the blacklist. Endfield and Baker first worked together in 1955, became close friends, and teamed up on four other British films in the late 1950s. Endfield and Prebble first collaborated on a 1961 screen adaptation of Jules Verne's *Mysterious Island*. But the main impetus behind the making of *Zulu* was Stanley Baker, who formed a production company, Diamond Films, and supplied, out of his own pocket, much of the £1.2 million (US$2.1 million) needed to make the film. It was Baker who enlisted Endfield and Prebble to collaborate with him in transforming an article Prebble had written on the Battle of Rorke's Drift into an epic war film.

Some background on the origins of the Anglo-Zulu War is in order. In the 1840s a British colony sprang up in Natal, on the southern edge of Zululand (which is located in the northeast corner of present-day South Africa). By the 1870s the British had begun to pursue an imperialistic "forward policy" aimed at the economic and political consolidation of the various British colonies, Boer republics, and autonomous African tribes in the region. Convinced that the fiercely independent Zulu were a threat to British interests and could only be brought into line by force, Sir Henry Bartle Frere (1815–1884), the British High Commissioner in South Africa, fabricated a quarrel with Zulu King Cetshwayo kaMpande (circa 1827–1884). Frere quite reasonably assumed that the Zulu, armed primarily with rawhide shields and assegai (short spears), would quickly fall to the modern technology and superior training of the British military. On January 11, 1879, Frere's military commander, Lt. Gen. Lord Chelmsford (1827–1905), led three columns of British imperial and irregular troops in an invasion of Zululand.

At noon on January 22, after Chelmsford had split his forces to try and find the main Zulu army, 25,000 Zulu warriors staged a surprise attack on the poorly defended British base encampment at Isandhlwana Rock and slaughtered most of the 1,800 British and colonial soldiers left behind there. Just two and a half hours after the battle at Isandhlwana ended, the 4,000 warriors who formed the rear guard of the Zulu army descended on 140 British troops stationed at nearby Rorke's Drift, a Christian missionary compound converted into a supply station and hospital for Chelmsford's forces. Though outnumbered about thirty-to-one, the men of the 2nd Battalion, 24th (2nd Warwickshire) Regiment of Foot had capable leadership, good cover, plenty of ammunition, and advance warning of the impending attack. In a series of desperate battles that started on the afternoon of January 22 and raged into the small hours of the next morning, the defenders of Rorke's Drift fought off every assault and ultimately avoided the ghastly fate that had just befallen their brethren at Isandhlwana. Spotting British reinforcements approaching on horseback at dawn on January 23, the exhausted Zulu warriors finally withdrew, leaving behind some 370 dead and scores of wounded. The British lost only 18 men. Ultimately, eleven Victoria Crosses were awarded to the defenders of Rorke's Drift: a record number for a single engagement. Recipients included the two commanders of the defense: Lt. John R. M. Chard (1847–1897) of the Royal Engineers and Lt. Gonville Bromhead (1845–1892) of the 24th Regiment. An admiring Queen Victoria, who met with Chard twice, termed the defense of Rorke's Drift "immortal."

Zulu (1964)

Stanley Baker's interest in the battle—and his particular identification with Lt. John Chard—had its basis in Baker's intense pride in his Welsh working-class roots. Though B Company of the 24th was actually comprised of English, Irish, Scottish, and Welsh soldiers, the regiment was based in Brecon, South Wales, and thus had a strong Welsh character, which is nonetheless exaggerated in the film. Furthermore, *Zulu* goes out of its way to emphasize Chard's proletarian identity, as opposed to the more refined pedigree of his foppish, haughty fellow officer, Lt. Bromhead (played by Michael Caine, in his first film role). With his hardheaded pragmatism, mordant attitude toward the British caste system, and mental toughness under pressure, Stanley Baker's Lt. Chard exhibits the no-nonsense outlook of the disillusioned subaltern that implicitly condemns the jingoistic, elitist, freebooting tendencies of English imperialism. As written by Endfield and Prebble, the film admirably refuses to engage in triumphalism; in their battle with the Zulu, Chard and his men fight only for their own survival, not for the greater glory of the British Empire. And while the action is presented entirely from the British point of view, the Zulu are depicted as fierce, courageous, unrelenting warriors. Indeed, to heighten the sense of primal combat between worthy foes, *Zulu* fabricates a scene toward the end of the film showing the Zulu warriors chanting homage to the fighting prowess of the British: a respectful concession of defeat that disguises the historical fact that the Zulu actually retreated because they saw Chelmsford's column advancing toward them. In reality, the immediate aftermath of the battle was much more prosaic and brutal, with the British finishing off wounded Zulu warriors left behind on the battlefield. There are other inaccuracies as well. The filmmakers, indulging in anti-clericalism consistent with their own biases, wrongly depict the original custo-dian of the mission, Reverend Otto Witt (Jack Hawkins), as a drunk. They also entirely omit Witt's colleague, Rev. George Smith, who stayed on at Rorke's Drift and played a significant part in the battle. On a more general level—despite intro-ductory and closing voice-over commentary by Stanley Baker's friend, Richard Burton—the film does not adequately acknowledge the justice of the Zulus defending their homeland or explain the battle (and war) in the context of British colonialism in Africa. Though these additions and omissions tend to dehistori-cize the Battle of Rorke's Drift, the film *as a wide screen action epic* is superbly realized and absorbing. Shot (in 70mm "Super Technirama") at Royal Natal National Park in then-apartheid South Africa about 90 miles southwest of the actual battle site, *Zulu* accurately depicts the protracted ferocity of the fighting. And, a menacing score by celebrated film composer John Barry, who scored the James Bond films, greatly contributes to the film's power. A perennial favorite with war film aficionados, *Zulu* often airs on television. A DVD edition appeared in 2003.

Khartoum (1966)

Appearing two years after *Zulu*, Basil Dearden's *Khartoum* (1966) was, at least superficially, in the same vein: a wide-screen epic about an Alamo-like stand of British colonial forces against rampaging African natives during the Victorian era. The events portrayed in *Khartoum* occur a few years after those depicted in *Zulu* and much further north: in the Sudanese city of Khartoum. In the fall of 1881, after a nationalist coup destabilized Egypt, an Islamic fanatic named Mohammed Ahmed, calling himself the Mahdi (Expected Guide), took advantage of the chaos to instigate a jihad against the British and their Egyptian allies in the Sudan. The Mahdi's followers, numbering some 80,000 men, ambushed and destroyed a British-led Egyptian army of 8,000 sent to quell the rebellion and then went on, over the next two years, to trounce the Egyptians in battle after battle and liberate much of the Sudan from Egyptian (and British proxy) control. In February 1884, with the Mahdi's army poised to capture the strategically vital port of Khartoum at the fork of the white and blue branches of the Nile, Her Majesties' government dispatched General Charles George "Chinese" Gordon (1833–1885) to coordinate the evacuation of British and Egyptian citizens from the city. A singularly fervent Christian who took the white man's burden seri-ously, Gordon had no intention of ceding Khartoum to the Madhi without a fight. Gordon fulfilled his mandate by evacuating 2,000 people from Khartoum but also exceeded it by organizing and directing the city's defenses during the ensuing 317-day siege (March 12, 1884–January 26, 1885), all the while holding out hope that British Prime Minister William Ewart Gladstone (1809–1898) would send a relief army. Though firm in his resolve to defend British-controlled Egypt and the newly completed Suez Canal, Gladstone was reluctant to pursue the kind of colonial expansionism that support of Gordon would have entailed. By the time Gladstone finally bowed to mounting popular sentiment it was too late; Khartoum had fallen, and Gordon slain, two days before a British vanguard force arrived.

The most significant thing about *Khartoum*, the film—starring a somewhat miscast Charlton Heston as Gordon; Laurence Olivier, in blackface, as the Mahdi; and Ralph Richardson as Gladstone—was that Robert Ardrey (1908–1980) wrote it. A trained anthropologist (University of Chicago, 1930) turned screenwriter, Ardrey believed that the engine of evolution is aggression. Extrapolating from studies of animals, Ardrey held that animals and human beings always ferociously defend their territory as an exclusive preserve when it is invaded and that the strongest will prevail, thrive, and evolve. In the 1960s, when scientific debates over human nature raged between conservative and liberal points of view, Ardrey propounded his deterministic "might makes right" theories in three books of popular anthropology: *African Genesis: A Personal Investigation into the Animal Origins and Nature of Man* (New York: Simon & Schuster, 1961); *The Territorial Imperative: A Personal Inquiry into the Animal Origins of Property and Nations* (New York: Atheneum, 1966); and *The Social Contract: A Personal Inquiry into the Evolutionary Sources of Order and Disorder* (New York: Atheneum, 1970). Writing *Khartoum* to illustrate the primacy of territoriality and aggression, Ardrey slighted the complex socioeconomic and political forces at play before, during, and after the siege of Khartoum. One might also add that an explication of these complicated background issues would not have readily lent itself to cinematic treatment. Although producer Julian Blaustein was a stickler for historical accuracy, *Khartoum* grossly oversimplifies the war between the Mahdi and the British. It also contains outright falsifications. For example, the film depicts two face-to-face meetings between Gordon and the Mahdi that never happened in order to dramatize the clash of wills between two fanatics—an emphasis that contributes to the now long discredited "Great Man" approach to historiography. Furthermore, Charlton Heston's romanticized portrayal of Gordon as a calm, stalwart English hero renders Gordon bland and minimizes the man's eccentricity, which was well documented in Lytton Strachey's brilliantly sardonic *Eminent Victorians* (1918).

Zulu Dawn (1979)

Released 15 years after *Zulu* and 100 years after the actual event, *Zulu*'s prequel, *Zulu Dawn* (1979), deals with the whys and wherefores of the slaughter at Isandhlwana that immediately preceded the Battle of Rorke's Drift. Judicious use of the Aristotlean unities of time and place and its concentrated dramatic focus on just a few key figures (such as Chard, Bromhead, or Rev. Witt) made *Zulu* a tour de force. By contrast, *Zulu Dawn*'s screenwriters, Anthony Story and Cy Endfield (also *Zulu*'s cowriter and director), opted for a broader narrative approach that better explained the war's geopolitical background and more systematically revealed the dubious British attitudes and tactics that led to disaster at Isandhlwana. The more circumspect tone of *Zulu Dawn* also reflected growing anticolonial and antiapartheid sentiment throughout the world in the late 1970s. In sum, what *Zulu Dawn* lost in dramatic intensity it made up for in historical accuracy and depth. The film's depiction of British arrogance and incompetence is devastatingly accurate. Underestimating the resourcefulness of the enemy, Lord Chelmsford (Peter O'Toole) foolishly splits his forces; the complacent British officers at Isandhlwana refuse to listen to the admonitions of their Boer scout, Colonel Durnford (Burt Lancaster), who advises tight perimeter security; once the fighting starts, priggish quartermaster Edward Bloomfield (Peter Vaughn) is reluctant to distribute ammunition for fear the troops will waste it. While *Zulu* is a tribute to the guts of the ordinary foot soldier, *Zulu Dawn* is its polar opposite: a searing indictment of a sclerotic British imperialism that was coming to the end of its days. The political climate had changed considerably in the intervening years between the two films.

The Spanish-American War and the Philippine Revolution (1898–1901)

Though hundreds of still photographs were taken during the American Civil War, the Spanish-American War was the first for which aspects were captured on motion picture film. William Kennedy Laurie Dickson, the man Thomas Edison appointed to develop the kinetoscope (the first motion picture camera and viewer), successfully completed a prototype in 1891 and the first public demonstration of the kinetoscope was held at the Brooklyn Institute of Arts and Sciences on May 9, 1893. In the early 1890s Dickson and his assistant William Heick made a series of short experimental nonfiction films, called "actualities," of celebrities, performances, and sporting events. In 1895 W. K. L. Dickson left Edison's employ to start his own film company, the American Mutoscope & Biograph

Company. In 1896 the invention of a portable movie camera made it possible to film extensively "on location," prompting the development of travelogues and embryonic newsreels of current events that were shown to eager audiences at vaudeville theaters (the nickelodeon did not arrive on the scene until 1905).

When the Battleship USS *Maine* mysteriously blew up and sank in Havana Harbor on February 15, 1898, the Edison Manufacturing Company and Dickson's rival American Mutoscope & Biograph Company rushed camera operators to Cuba to film the aftermath of the event. Both companies then proceeded to make dozens of short, black-and-white films that recorded the ensuing war between Spain and the United States (April 25–August 14, 1898). The Library of Congress has gathered many of these rare films at the Spanish American War in Motion Pictures home page, at http://lcweb2.loc.gov/ammemsawhtml/sawsp1.html.

Rough Riders (1997)

Having indirectly competed with Ted Turner on respective Geronimo movies in 1993, writer-director John Milius joined forces with Turner to make *Rough Riders*, a TNT 4-hour, two-part miniseries that originally aired on July 20–21, 1997. Passionate about all things martial, Milius suffered the disappointment of a lifetime when he was rejected for military service due to asthma. Not surprisingly, he has always idolized Theodore "Teddy" Roosevelt (1858–1919) who overcame childhood asthma to become an outdoorsman, soldier, politician, and ultimately the twenty-sixth president of the United States (1901–1909). The story of Roosevelt's celebrated exploits with the 1st U.S. Volunteer Cavalry Regiment, popularly known as the "Rough Riders," during the Spanish-American War was tailor-made for Milius (and Turner); it had the ebullient Teddy Roosevelt, proud and ascendant American imperialism, swashbuckling adventure, and military glory.

Nor had the story already been done to death. Other than the actual silent film footage taken at the time of the war, only a couple of films had been made: Victor Fleming's long-forgotten silent, *The Rough Riders*, also known as *The Trumpet Calls* (1927), starring Noah Beery, and a nineteen-minute biopic, Ray Enright's *Teddy the Rough Rider*, which won the 1941 Oscar for Best Short Subject. The relative neglect of the topic is probably due to the fact that the Spanish-American War was a small-scale, short-lived conflict that soon paled in comparison to the wholesale carnage of World War I. By midcentury popular culture treatments of Teddy Roosevelt tended toward caricature. During a Broadway run that lasted throughout much of World War II, Joseph Kesselring's black comedy *Arsenic and Old Lace* (also a 1944 Frank Capra movie) mocked the heroic posturing of the Teddy Roosevelt ethos through the character of the demented Teddy

Brewster. Laboring under the delusion that he *is* Teddy Roosevelt, Brewster dresses in mufti, digs the Panama Canal in his basement, and races up and downstairs yelling "Charge!" Compared to the catastrophe engulfing the world in the early 1940s, the Spanish-American War looked like a Gilbert and Sullivan operetta. After Fidel Castro seized power in Cuba in 1959, Americans were even less likely to dwell on the distant days of the Rough Riders. Yet, almost forty years later, as the centennial of the Spanish-American War approached, John Milius's personal passion coalesced with Ted Turner's interest in dramatizing military history—and a general groundswell of right-wing frustration over President Bill Clinton's perceived misuse of the armed forces, especially after the disastrous Battle of Mogadishu on October 3, 1993, that drove the United States out of Somalia.

Relying especially on Teddy Roosevelt's memoir, *The Rough Riders* (1899), Milius and his co-screenwriter, Hugh Wilson (*Police Academy; Guarding Tess*)

Lieutenant Colonel Theodore Roosevelt with his "Rough Riders" (1st Volunteer Cavalry) in a victory photo after the famed Battle of San Juan Heights. (National Archives)

took Teddy Roosevelt's account at face value and proceeded to make *Rough Riders* a rousing cinematic celebration of masculinity, esprit de corps, militarism, and Manifest Destiny writ large. In 1898 Teddy Roosevelt (Tom Berenger), assistant secretary of the Navy under President William McKinley (Brian Keith, who played Teddy Roosevelt in Milius's 1975 film, *The Wind and the Lion*), is watching growing anti-Spanish unrest in Cuba and is determined to "take this opportunity of driving the Spaniard from the Western World."

Once war is declared Roosevelt eagerly sets out to form his own volunteer regiment. The 23,000 men who heed the call to arms from all over the country are winnowed down to a regiment of about 600 men that then learn to put aside petty differences and cohere as an effective fighting unit. In an astute review of *Rough Riders* ("Film & History," *H-Net Reviews*, June 1998), Ron Briley (Sandia Prep. School, Albuquerque, NM) notes that this first part of the movie has all the elements of a standard World War II film: "First [there] is the forging of a melting pot society (today we call it multiculturalism) in which Native Americans, Afro-Americans, Hispanics, and Anglos (both North and South), from every walk of life, come together to form a cohesive unit based on national pride. The war experience brings mutual respect across class and social barriers. Of course, this mythology does not reflect reality. What about the racist society of 1898? Did it just vanish?" As Briley points out, racism in the United States was at its worst in the 1890s; on average 100 blacks were murdered by lynch mobs every year of that decade. But the film's sunny view of social relations was also Teddy Roosevelt's. In his memoir Roosevelt makes no mention of racial, ethnic, or class tensions among his men; such an admission would have worked against his narrative purpose, which was to allegorize the founding of the nation in the forming of the Rough Riders.

Briley observes that a "second key element of traditional war cinema is established when a group of disorderly recruits is molded into a disciplined fighting unit by a tough but caring noncom. In *Rough Riders*, [Henry] Nash [Brad Johnson], an enlisted man, is an outlaw who despises his superior, [Bucky] O'Neill [Sam Elliot]. However, over time—much like John Agar's character with John Wayne's Sergeant Stryker in the classic *Sands of Iwo Jima* (1949)—the recruit comes to love and respect the soldier. When O'Neill dies, Nash—now a man—prepares to carry on the struggle" (Briley 1998). Obviously, such an emphasis on male bonding creates a world that devalues and excludes women: certainly an accurate reflection of the zeitgeist in 1898 but one that surely requires some ironic distance or implicit critique from a twenty-first-century vantage point.

Briley is also critical of Milius's handling of the film's historical context:

He does present the role played by yellow journalists, such as William Randolph Hearst [George Hamilton], in initiating the war, but fails to note that most historians believe that the *Maine* was destroyed by an ammunition explosion rather than foul play. Milius makes much of Spanish atrocities against the Cuban people, but both groups are kept in the background . . . In his tale of glory and valor, [Milius] omits how the war concluded with the Platt Amendment, making Cuba a virtual protectorate of the United States, and the Peace of Paris, allowing the United States to acquire Guam, Puerto Rico, and the Philippines. American Marines were soon dispatched to the Philippines on a military operation designed to put down the Aguinaldo Revolt opposing American annexation, while Puerto Ricans were inspired by the words of patriot Jose De Diego calling for resistance to the American conquest. The Spanish-American War appeared to many anti-imperialist critics . . . to simply make the United States another . . . imperialist power. This seemed confirmed when President Theodore Roosevelt seized the Panama Canal at the expense of Colombia, establishing a legacy of Latin American suspicion regarding American motives in the region.

Though it seems bizarre, even surreal, that a modern film about the Spanish-American War could uncritically adopt the crude ideological assumptions that prevailed in 1898, that is precisely what *Rough Riders* did.

The Anglo-Boer War (1899–1902)

"Breaker" Morant (1980)

In the 1970s Australia's Labor Party regime headed by Edward Gough Whitlam (succeeded in 1975 by Liberal Prime Minister John Malcolm Fraser) granted massive infusions of funding that not only rescued the Australian film industry from almost certain oblivion but actually spawned a filmmaking renaissance. Between 1970 and 1985 the Australian "New Wave" produced nearly 400 movies: more than had been made in the industry's entire history up to that time. Among these efforts was Bruce Beresford's *"Breaker" Morant* (1980), a film that Beresford, David Stevens, and Jonathan Hardy adapted from the eponymous 1978 stage play by Kenneth Ross, which was in turn based on Kit Denton's novel, *The Breaker* (London: Angus and Robertson, 1973). Inspired by a conversation with a Boer War veteran who actually knew Morant, Denton freely adapted his story from George Witton's *Scapegoats of the Empire: The True Story of Breaker Morant's Bushveldt Carbineers* (Melbourne, Australia: D. W. Patterson, 1907).

Witton's book was a firsthand account of a controversial incident during the Boer War in which Witton and two of his fellow officers—Lt. Harry "Breaker" Morant and Lt. Peter Handcock—were court-martialed for alleged war crimes.

The complex chain of events leading up to the incident began on October 11, 1899, when Sir Alfred Milner (1854–1925), high commissioner of the Cape Colony in South Africa, forced war on the Dutch Boer republics of the Transvaal and the Orange Free State to expand British influence in Africa and gain control of the Boers' gold mines. After a series of humiliating defeats in December 1899, heavily reinforced British imperial forces launched a counteroffensive in the spring of 1900 that resulted in the March 13 capture of Bloemfontein, capital of the Orange Free State, and the June 5 capture of Pretoria, capital of the Transvaal. But instead of surrendering, the Boers turned to guerrilla tactics. Waging the kind of warfare that would characterize anticolonial struggles throughout the twentieth century, small, mobile Boer units conducted devastating hit-and-run raids on British outposts, blew up trains, and sometimes committed atrocities. Field General Horatio Kitchener (1850–1916), the newly appointed chief of staff to Lord Frederick "Bobs" Roberts (1832–1914), commander in chief of the British forces, responded with equal ferocity. To deprive the Boer commandos of their civilian support base, Kitchener ordered the burning of some 30,000 farms, which displaced thousands of African and Boer families, who were then rounded up and interned in concentration camps (an invention of the Spanish in Cuba a couple of years earlier) where over 42,000 died. Kitchener also established several regiments of irregulars to fight the Boers using their own no-holds-barred tactics; among them were the Bushveldt Carbineers (BVC), a unit mostly comprised of Australians.

On the night of August 5, 1901, Capt. Simon Hunt and a small BVC contingent were ambushed by a much larger enemy force as they stormed a Boer farmhouse. Wounded in the fight, Hunt was subsequently captured by the Boers, who tortured him with knives, stomped him to death, and then mutilated his body. When Hunt's close friend and subordinate, Lt. Harry Morant, learned of the atrocity he flew into a fit of grief and rage and vowed vengeance. In the weeks following Hunt's death, Morant had a dozen Boer prisoners of war summarily shot. Rev. Predikant C. H. D. Hesse, a witness to some of the shootings, was also found dead of a bullet wound. In October 1901 Morant, Lt. Handcock, Lt. Witton, and four other BVC members were arrested. Though their British comrades were quietly discharged, Australian Lts. Morant, Handcock, and Witton were charged with the murder of more than twenty people, including women and children. Though hardly baseless, the indictments were a political gesture designed to placate Germany, which was threatening to enter the war on the side of the Boers. After a perfunctory court-martial, all three men were convicted—despite an intelligent and vigorous defense mounted by Major J. F. Thomas, who argued, in part, that his clients were being judged by legal standards that were impossible to live up to under the combat conditions that prevailed. Witton received a life sentence but was freed by the British House of Commons after serving only twenty-eight months. Harry "Breaker" Morant and Peter Handcock were executed by firing squad on the morning of February 27, 1902.

Starring Edward Woodward as "Breaker" Morant, Jack Thompson as Major Thomas, Bryan Brown as Lt. Handcock, and Lewis Fitzgerald as Lt. Witton, *"Breaker" Morant* stays close to the historical facts as they were known in the late 1970s. Morant is portrayed as a hot-blooded romantic—a published poet, horse tamer ("breaker"), soldier, adventurer—but ultimately a fatalistic soul. Handcock is shown to be a lady's man with a sardonic wit, and Witton is depicted as a naïve patriot. Following the dramatic trajectory of Ross's play, the film shows Major Thomas's development as the defense attorney. Inexperienced, nervous, and woefully underprepared at the outset, Thomas steadily gains self-confidence and righteous passion as the court-martial proceeds. Thomas's eloquently articulated defense is persuasive but futile; the empire has already determined that these three Australian colonials will serve as scapegoats for all the atrocities, injustices, and inhumanity caused by Lord Kitchener's realpolitik. Beautifully staged and acted and incredibly moving, *"Breaker" Morant* was the biggest hit in the history of Australian cinema. Nominated for thirteen Australian Film Institute (AFI) Awards, the movie won ten of them. It was also nominated for an Academy Award for Best Writing, Screenplay Based on Material from Another Medium. The huge success of *"Breaker" Morant* owed much to the anti-imperialist temperament of the post-Vietnam era and to Australia's emerging sense of itself as a nation apart from its British roots: nationalistic pride partly fueled by the productions of the Australian Film Board. The film's thesis—that Morant and his comrades were victims of British cynicism and hypocrisy—resonated deeply with Australians tired of deriving their identity from the motherland.

On the centennial of the executions of Morant and Handcock, Nick Bleszynski's *Shoot Straight, You Bastards! The Truth behind the Killing of "Breaker" Morant* (New York: Random House, 2002) presented a somewhat revisionist rejoinder to Beresford's film. Bleszynski amply confirms the obvious fact that the court-martial was rigged and even presents new evidence that the prosecution suppressed a secret field order by Kitchener not to take any Boer commandos alive: a piece of evidence that would have exonerated the accused. However, Bleszynski also argues that Morant and Handcock were indeed guilty of the murder of the Reverend Hesse and should not be thought of as merely victims of imperial injustice. After Bleszynski's book appeared, Kenneth Ross published an article admitting that his own play tended to wrongly romanticize Morant.

2

Military History on Film and Television: World War I

Filming the Front Lines

For the first year of the Great War, Britain's war minister, Lord Kitchener, declared the front lines off-limits to journalists and cameramen, forcing the country's leading commercial newsreel companies—Topical, Pathé, and Gaumont—to film well behind the lines and on the home front. In November 1915 the War Office established the British Topical Committee for War Films and appointed two official frontline cinematographers—Geoffrey Malin (1886–1940) and John Benjamin McDowell—to make propaganda films.

The Battle of the Somme (1916)

Malin and McDowell's most successful effort was *The Battle of the Somme* (1916), a documentary that follows the advance of the British 7th and 29th divisions on the first day of the battle (July 1, 1916). The film begins with shots of the massive artillery bombardment that preceded the infantry attack; shows the troops getting into position for the attack; going over the wire (staged footage actually shot before the attack began); the attack itself; the resulting casualties, prisoners taken, and wounded evacuated and treated; the British consolidating their gains and German prisoners of war being marched to the rear. After a quick job of editing by Charles Urban (1867–1942) of Topical Newsreel, the War Office released *The Battle of the Somme* on August 10, 1916, while the British offensive was still under way. The film proved wildly popular, selling some 20 million tickets, which represents almost half the total population of the British Isles at that time. Though successful as pro-British propaganda, *The Battle of the Somme* could scarcely avoid exceeding its mandate by showing numerous images of the killed and wounded; the first day of the Battle of the Somme yielded an astonishing 60,000 casualties, making it the bloodiest day in British military history.

Though such graphic images aroused controversy, the film became the classic cinematic treatment of the Great War and established the paradigm for war documentaries thereafter. Stock shots from the film, especially of the massive mine explosion that created the Hawthorne Crater, are routinely used in films about World War I. In 1993 London's Imperial War Museum released a restored version of *The Battle of the Somme* (now available in a 60-minute DVD version from Pegasus in the UK).

On October 2, 1918, just five weeks before the Armistice, German forces surrounded overextended elements of the 307th and 308th Infantry Regiments of the 77th (U.S.) "Liberty" Division in an Argonne Forest ravine near Charlevaux, France. Over the next five days what became known as the "Lost Battalion" (which was neither lost nor a single, unified battalion) held out in cold, rainy weather against constant, withering enemy fire with a dwindling supply of ammunition, no food or shelter, and little potable water. When American forces finally broke through the German cordon and began to rescue the Lost Battalion on the night of October 7, only 252 survivors of a force of 679 walked or were carried out of "the pocket," that is, the area held by the Lost Battalion while it was surrounded. The unit's stubborn refusal to surrender instantly became a legendary example of American bravery and resolve under the worst conditions. The Lost Battalion's commanding officer, Major Charles W. Whittlesey, and two key subordinates, Captains George McMurtry and Nelson Holderman, were awarded the Congressional Medal of Honor.

The Lost Battalion (1919)

A few months after the Armistice, film producer Edward A. McManus enlisted Burton King as director, Charles A. Logue as writer, and a dozen repatriated survivors of the pocket (including Whittlesey and McMurtry) to play themselves in a semiofficial silent film version, *The Lost Battalion* (1919), that was sanctioned by the U.S. government and included Signal Corps footage. Deploying the oft-repeated melting pot thesis of the American war film genre, the first half hour of *The Lost Battalion* establishes the ethnic and social class diversity of the men of the 77th Division, who hail from the New York metropolitan area. After receiving training at Camp Upton on Long Island, the Division is shipped to France in March 1918. In late September the 77th is an integral part of the Allied Expeditionary Force (AEF) as it launches the massive Meuse-Argonne Offensive that would win the war. In the early days of the offensive, Major Whittlesey's command, advancing too rapidly on the 77th's left flank, is cut off from reinforcements and surrounded. Over the course of the ensuing 123-hour siege, thirty-four runners attempt to reach American lines for help but almost all are killed. Despite being severely wounded by German gunfire, a carrier pigeon named Cher Ami does reach headquarters, and what is left of the Lost Battalion is saved. The film was well received in its day but did not quell the demons of Charles Whittlesey. Haunted by the deaths of so many of his men, Whittlesey committed suicide in November 1921, shortly after attending the dedication of the Tomb of the Unknown Soldier at Arlington National Cemetery.

Films in the Time between the World Wars

All Quiet on the Western Front (1930)

The interwar period saw a powerful backlash against the naïve patriotism that prevailed before, and during the early days of, World War I. Though it took a few years for a widespread and mature understanding of the full horror and futility of the war to dawn on noncombatants, general disgust with the Great War was evident by the end of the 1920s. The new, more sober consciousness was probably best epitomized by Erich Maria Remarque's compelling antiwar novel, *Im Westen Nichts Neue* (*Nothing New in the West*) (1929). Translated into English as *All Quiet on the Western Front* (1929), Remarque's story of youthful disillusionment with the promise of martial glory transcended nationalist considerations, garnered great critical acclaim, and was a hugely popular international bestseller. Immediately adapted to the screen by Universal Pictures' Carl Laemmle Jr. (producer) and Lewis Milestone (director), and starring Lew Ayres as Remarque's young protagonist, Paul Bäumer, *All Quiet on the Western Front* (1930) unflinchingly followed the novel in presenting World War I—and all war— as a fraudulent, pointless exercise in destruction, suffering, and death. The film won the Best Picture Oscar of 1930 and amply confirmed antiwar, antiwar profiteering, and isolationist sentiments held by millions of Americans in the early days of the Great Depression—when the capitalist world order was at its lowest ebb and militarism seemed the stupidest of human endeavors when mere economic survival was so precarious for so many. However, by the end of the decade, the looming threat of the increasingly aggressive Axis powers presented pacifists and noninterventionists with a moral quandary. From the outbreak of the war in September 1939 to Pearl Harbor in December 1941, American antiwar sentiment still made sense but stopping Hitler, Mussolini, and Imperial Japan was beginning to look like an unavoidable necessity.

A movie poster from All Quiet on the Western Front *from 1930. (Universal/The Kobal Collection)*

The Fighting 69th (1940)

During this transitional period Warner Brothers made *The Fighting 69th* (1940), a curious admixture of fact and fiction about a regiment in the 42nd ("Rainbow") Division that distinguished itself in World War I and included such noted personages as future Office of Strategic Services (OSS) director William J. "Wild Bill" Donovan (1883–1959); the poet [Alfred] Joyce Kilmer (1886–1918); and Father Francis P. Duffy (1871–1932), the Division's legendary chaplain commemorated by a statue in Times Square. Formed during the Civil War as the 69th New York, "the Fighting Irish" was actually redesignated the 165th Infantry in 1917 but remained known as the 69th. Predominantly comprised of street-tough Irish-Catholic New Yorkers, the 69th participated in six major offensives in 1918, including St. Mihiel and the Meuse-Argonne, fought bravely, and sustained 3,500 casualties, including 644 killed in action.

As fashioned by contract screenwriters Norman Reilly Raine, Fred Niblo Jr., and Dean Riesner, William Keighley's film version of the 69th's history in World War I hinges on the entirely fictional character of Private Jerry Plunkett (James Cagney), an impulsive maverick who refuses to submit to military discipline. Plunkett's antisocial antics culminate in acts of cowardice on the battlefield that get a number of his comrades killed or wounded. Court-martialed and awaiting death by firing squad, Private Plunkett is inspired by the calm courage of Father Duffy (Pat O'Brien). Escaping confinement and rejoining his embattled comrades at the front, Plunkett redeems all his past sins by fighting with great courage. In the end, he dies a hero, sacrificing his own life to save the life of his sergeant, "Big Mike" Wynn (Alan Hale). Plunkett's evolution from shiftless hoodlum to war hero dramatizes the need in wartime to subordinate individualism to collectivist imperatives. When Plunkett finally embraces his duty he does so because he has guiltily accepted the Christian ideology of personal sacrifice personified by Father Duffy: a conversion scenario that Cagney and O'Brien had already enacted in *Angels with Dirty Faces* (1938).

As it was originally envisioned, *The Fighting 69th* was supposed to be centered on Father Duffy. Film historian Daniel J. Leab speculates that the Plunkett character was created to accommodate James Cagney's outlaw screen persona and perhaps also to address concerns of some Catholic clergy who felt that, through the lionization of Father Duffy, the Church was being used to validate a pro-war stance (Rollins 1997, 113). One could argue that Plunkett is needed to provide dialectical tension to what would have been a blandly didactic narrative. On the level of political allegory the Plunkett character represents selfish, nihilistic isolationism, whereas the Duffy character represents social responsibility actualized by Christian faith. The conversion and martyrdom of Plunkett thus celebrates the righteousness of abandoning egocentric isolationism for altruistic involvement—even though it ends in one's own death. On the other hand, *The Fighting 69th* does not gloss over the horrors of combat or the scale of the slaughter. In the film, war is not glorified but seen as a tragic necessity: a stance in perfect concert with the ambivalent temper of the times in 1939–1940.

Sergeant York (1941)

Released on the Fourth of July, 1941, five months before the attack on Pearl Harbor, Howard Hawks' *Sergeant York* is more forcefully pro-interventionist than *The Fighting 69th*. But, then again, so is the story of Alvin Cullom York. Hailing from the mountain hamlet of Pall Mall, Tennessee, Alvin C. York (1887–1964) grew up in rural poverty, received almost no formal education, and had never traveled more than 50 miles from home before the war. York did, however, resemble the fictional Jerry Plunkett in his fondness for drinking, fighting, and gambling. In 1914, at the age of twenty-six, a chastened York attended a religious revival after his best friend, Everett Delk, was killed in a barroom brawl. Soon thereafter, York joined the Church of Christ in Christian Union, an obscure southern fundamentalist sect that strictly forbade dancing, drinking, swimming, cursing, and movies and condemned violence and war. Through the Church York also met his future wife, Gracie Williams. When York received a draft notice in June 1917 his pastor, Rosier Pile, encouraged him to apply for Conscientious Objector status on religious grounds, but York's plea was rejected and he was sent to Camp Gordon, Georgia, for basic training. A crack shot since boyhood, York incongruously taught marksmanship to his fellow recruits in the 82nd ("All American") Division but adamantly refused to assume the role of a combatant. Pressured by his company commander, Major George Buxton, to reconsider his position, York finally agreed to fight after much debate and soul-searching. In action in the Argonne on October 8, 1918, Corporal Alvin C. York stormed a German machine-gun nest that had decimated his unit, personally killed nine enemy soldiers, and with the help of seven other surviving comrades knocked out other machine-gun nests and captured 123 Germans. For his extraordinary heroism, York was promoted to sergeant, awarded the Medal of Honor and Croix de Guerre, and became a much-celebrated national hero. Though Alvin York could have easily exploited his celebrity by accepting lucrative movie and endorsement deals, he chose instead to return to a 400-acre farm in Tennessee presented to him—with certain strings attached—by the Nashville Chamber of Commerce.

As war clouds gathered in the late 1930s, Alvin York reemerged into public life and began to speak out against isolationism, especially after the formation of the pro-isolationist America First Committee (AFC) in September 1940. Prominent AFC spokesman Charles A. Lindbergh, an admirer of Nazi Germany, preached an increasingly vociferous nonintervention policy and York countered with equally strident calls for intervention. Having resisted offers from Hollywood for twenty years to bring his story to the screen, York saw that the time was right, politically, for a film that would argue the justice, in extraordinary circumstances, of abandoning an isolationist stance and taking up arms. So when Hollywood producer Jesse L. Lasky approached York with yet another offer, York accepted and Warner Bros. began work on *Sergeant York* in 1940.

Starring Gary Cooper as Alvin York, Walter Brennan as Rosier Pile, and Joan Leslie as Gracie Williams, *Sergeant York* stays fairly close to the facts of York's life; it had to, because Alvin York was given an unusual degree of editorial say-so in exchange for his permission to make the film in the first place. The general contours of York's story are adhered to: his humble origins, his rowdy youth, his religious conversion, his initial pacifism, his combat heroics, his discomfort in the spotlight, and his return to Tennessee. *Sergeant York* becomes ideological in the *way* it dramatizes these events. Gary Cooper's Alvin York is naturally courageous because he is a stolid American Adam—rustic, bashful, modest, hardworking, religious, and, above all, honest and pure of heart. No doubt the real Alvin York exhibited many of these qualities but probably not with the perfect pitch rendered by Cooper, whose portrayal suggests a mythic pioneer hero in the nostalgic tradition of Daniel Boone. Where the film fabricates scenes and events it always does so in ways that underscore York's preternatural purity and innocence. York's Herculean efforts as a hardscrabble farmer remind viewers of the country's early settlers. His moral conversion after being struck by lightning resembles the conversion of Saint Paul. His infallibly perfect marksmanship conjures images of Robin Hood and other legendary heroes. Key, though, is a fanciful and deeply romanticized scene in which York retreats to a mountaintop, like Moses, to ponder the wisdom of pacifism. Tellingly, York is converted to the ways of war not by Bible study but by a reading of American history suggesting that war is sometimes an unavoidable paradox: killing in order to save lives. In sum, all these tropes idealize Alvin York as the living embodiment of American foundational values, thus granting him an unassailable moral authority in his decision to go to war. Furthermore, York performs magnificently in combat, is duly recognized, but ultimately allowed to return to his essentially Jeffersonian life: an outcome sure to put Americans at ease about the consequences of taking up the gun.

World War I Filmed in Hindsight

Paths of Glory (1957)

In geopolitical scope, complexity, and sheer ferocity—over 50 million dead—the Second World War eclipsed the First World War in every way. Not surprisingly, the postwar period spawned very few films about the earlier conflict. Under the shadow of the death camps, the Cold War, and the atomic bomb, the 1914–1918 war seemed but a distant nightmare. There is, however, one notable exception from the 1950s: Stanley Kubrick's *Paths of Glory* (1957), a powerful film adaptation of Humphrey Cobb's novel of the same title (New York: Viking, 1935). Cobb (1899–1943), a World War I veteran who served with a Canadian regiment in 1917–1918, was wounded and gassed and came out of the war bitter until the day he died. His novel concerns three French infantrymen unjustly tried and executed for cowardice after a failed attack on a German fort. The specific incident was fictional but based on numerous actual incidents culled from historical sources that Cobb lists at the end of the book: R. G. Réau's *Les crimes des conseils de guerre* (*The Crimes of the Court-Martials*) (1926); Paul Allard's *Les dessous de la guerre révélés par les comités secrets* (*The Underside of the War Revealed by Secret Committees*) and *Images secrètes de la guerre* (*Secret Images of the War*) (1933); Jean Galtier-Boissiere and Daniel de Ferdon's "Les fusillés pour l'exemple" ("Shoot Them for the Example") and *Le Crapouillot* (July 1934); "French Acquit 5 Shot for Mutiny in 1915; Widows of Two Win Awards of 7 Cents Each," *New York Times* (July 2, 1934); and *Le fusillé* (*The Shooting*) by Blanche Maupas, "one of the widows who obtained exoneration of her husband's memory and who was awarded damages of one franc" (Cobb's note).

It appears that Cobb based his narrative on at least three separate incidents: (1) a stalled attack by the French army's 5th Company, 63rd Infantry Regiment on April 19, 1915 (just before the Second Battle of Ypres), in the St. Mihiel sector. As reported by the *New York Times* article referred to earlier, the 5th Company of the 63rd was pinned down by incessant enemy machine-gun fire and could not attack. In the aftermath, five soldiers were chosen by lot and shot by firing squad; (2) another probable source: costly French efforts to recapture Fort Douamont during the Battle of Verdun (February–July, 1916); and (3) the third likely source: General Robert-Georges Nivelle's catastrophic offensive on the Aisne River (April–May, 1917) that caused wholesale mutiny in the French army, terrifying France's ruling elite. Nivelle was relieved of his command, and his replacement, General Henri-Philippe Pétain (of later Vichy infamy), instituted widespread reforms—regular leave, better food and pay, no more reckless offensives—to calm the troops and restore morale. But the stick also accompanied the carrot.

The High Command court-martialed thousands of soldiers for mutinous conduct, found 3,426 guilty, and sentenced 554 men to death. Of that number only a token 45 were actually shot. The rest of the condemned were sent to Devil's Island. Remarkably the French managed to keep secret a string of mutinies and executions that occurred throughout the war until well after its end.

In his novel Humphrey Cobb combines these events into a single and much smaller-scale incident in which an opportunistic, glory-seeking general fittingly named Assolant orders the exhausted 181st Regiment to attack "The Pimple," an impregnable German stronghold. The assault inevitably fails and a furious Assolant orders the entire regiment arrested for cowardice but eventually settles for the court-martial of just three soldiers who will serve as scapegoats for the whole fiasco. After a show trial, the three—Férol, Didier, and Langlois—are summarily shot. The novel's bitter, brutal ending encapsulates Cobb's salient themes: (1) that war is an obscene waste and (2) that the rank and file pay with their lives for the stupidity and arrogance of the generals: an implicit condemnation of the oppressive social hierarchies that have been the plague of human history.

Having read and been impressed by *Paths of Glory* in his youth, Stanley Kubrick wrote a screenplay based on the book but he and his producing partner, James B. Harris, had trouble selling it to the studios until actor Kirk Douglas became interested. On the strength of Douglas's star power, United Artists agreed to fund the film for a modest $950,000. Though it is set in France, Kubrick chose to shoot *Paths of Glory* near Munich using Bavaria's Geiselgasteig Studios for interior shots, the Schlessheim Palace for exterior shots of French army headquarters, and a rented field, meticulously transformed into a shell-pocked moonscape, for the battle scenes. In adapting Cobb's novel to the screen, Kubrick, with help from pulp novelist Jim Thompson and script doctor Calder Willingham, did the usual streamlining. They eliminated much of the detailed background Cobb supplied for his characters, changed some names and unit numbers (for example, "the pimple" became "the anthill," Assolant became Mireau, and the 181st became the 701st), combined or cut a number of characters, and centered the narrative on Colonel Dax (Kirk Douglas), the regimental commander forced to lead the futile attack. A criminal lawyer in civilian life, Dax also acts as defense attorney at the court-martial of his men but his strenuous efforts are of course in vain. Or at least they are in the final version of the film. Fearing that such a depressing ending would ruin any commercial prospects the film might have had, Kubrick initially wanted to shoot a happy ending in which the three soldiers are granted a last-minute reprieve. Fortunately, Kirk Douglas persuaded Kubrick to change his mind and go with Humphrey Cobb's more realistic and thematically meaningful ending. To hedge his bets, though, Kubrick did include an upbeat coda in which a group of soldiers from the 701st drinking in a tavern are deeply moved by the singing of a German woman played by Christiane Harlan. (A niece of Nazi filmmaker Veit Harlan, Christiane Harlan became Kubrick's third wife.) The film's final scene suggests reconciliation between enemies and a reaffirmation of humanity that runs counter to Cobb's deeply pessimistic outlook.

Though generally lauded by critics for its technical artistry, brilliantly rendered battle sequences, and solid performances—especially George Macready as the loathsome General Mireau and Adolph Menjou as the blithely Machiavellian General Broulard—*Paths of Glory* did not do well at the box office. Leftist and antiestablishment in its orientation, the film was too radical for the Cold War zeitgeist of the 1950s, which affirmed social conformity, military preparedness, and the inherent legitimacy of government and legal apparatuses. Indeed, *Paths of Glory* generated intense controversy throughout Europe. The French were, of course, particularly incensed. They saw the film not as a universal condemnation of military incompetence and political corruption but as a mockery of the French army at a most sensitive time—when France was in the midst of an unpopular colonial war in Algeria. There were no screenings of *Paths of Glory* in Paris until 1978. Though a superb antiwar film, perhaps Stanley Kubrick's unacknowledged masterpiece, *Paths* was utterly and unconscionably ignored at the 1958 Oscars, no doubt due to its international notoriety as a political hot potato. It did, however, enjoy a revival during the Vietnam era and its standing as a classic is secure.

Lawrence of Arabia (1962)

Of a more politically ambiguous character is David Lean's *Lawrence of Arabia* (1962). Eager to repeat the success they had with *The Bridge on the River Kwai* (1957), British director David Lean (1908–1991) and American producer Sam Spiegel (1903–1985) joined forces again three years later to begin work on an epic biopic about Thomas Edward Lawrence (1888–1935), the legendary "Lawrence of Arabia" who led the successful Arab revolt against Ottoman Turkey during World War I. Oscar-winning screenwriter (and ex-Communist) Michael Wilson (1914–1978; *A Place in the Sun; Salt of the Earth*), who had anonymously cowritten *The Bridge* with fellow blacklist victim, Carl Foreman, wrote the first version of a Lawrence script based on Lowell Thomas's book, *With Lawrence in Arabia* (New York: Century, 1924). David Lean then commissioned British playwright Robert Bolt (1924–1995; *A Man for all Seasons*), incidentally also an ex-Communist, to rewrite Wilson's dialogue but Bolt decided to create an entirely new script relying almost exclusively on Lawrence's voluminous memoir, *Seven Pillars of Wisdom* (Lawrence 1926), to which Lean had just secured the rights. Though he shared

Film portrait from Lawrence of Arabia, *starring Peter O'Toole and directed by David Lean. (Columbia/The Kobal Collection)*

Michael Wilson's leftist views and retained his predecessor's overall dramatic structure, Bolt veered away from Wilson's emphasis on the politics of European colonialism versus nascent Arab nationalism in the Middle East. Instead, with David Lean's blessing, Bolt made the film a character study that depicted the complex and enigmatic T. E. Lawrence as a half-mad, homosexual Nietzchean genius with pronounced sadomasochistic tendencies—a decidedly strange and anti-heroic hero.

After an expensive screen test, Lean offered the role of Lawrence to Albert Finney, who had impressed audiences in Tony Richardson's *The Entertainer* (1960) and was about to achieve stardom in Karel Reisz's *Saturday Night, Sunday Morning* (1960). Unwilling to commit to a long-term contract, Finney declined the part, which went to another Irish Shakespearean actor, Peter O'Toole. The great Alec Guinness, who had played Colonel Nicholson in *Bridge on the River Kwai*, was cast as Prince (later King) Feisal (1885–1933); Anthony Quinn as the ferocious Bedouin chieftain Auda abu Tayi; and Jack Hawkins as Lawrence's commanding officer, General Lord Edmund Allenby (1861–1936). The screenplay by Wilson also called for the creation of a number of fictional characters used to embody certain political positions or present various viewpoints on Lawrence. The suave Mr. Dryden (Claude Rains) represents European colonialist machinations; the judicious Colonel Harry Brighton (Anthony Quayle) stands for the conventional British military mind-set that Lawrence bedevils; the dashing Sherif Ali ibn Kharish (Omar Shariff) embodies emergent Arab nationalism; the cynical Jackson Bentley (Arthur Kennedy), based on American journalist and filmmaker Lowell (Jackson) Thomas (1892–1981), epitomizes the press, especially its self-serving tendency to distort and mythologize public figures.

Lawrence's *Seven Pillars of Wisdom* is a long book, richly detailed and peopled with hundreds of places, incidents, and personalities. Robert Bolt later said, "Ten different dramas could be got from it" (Bolt 1995).

 Adapting the book to film involved the usual streamlining and distillation, but taken to a radical degree. Rather than attempt to encompass Lawrence's finely textured narrative, *Lawrence of Arabia* opts to tell its story visually, through the brilliantly evocative 70mm cinematography of Freddie Young, and aurally, through the lush and moving musical score of Maurice Jarre. As for plotting, the film pins its story line on four key events: the crossing of the Nefud Desert and conquest of the strategically vital port of Akaba (July 1917); Lawrence's capture, torture, and rape by the Turks at Deraa (November 1917); Lawrence's vengeful massacre of a Turkish police battalion at Tafas (September 1918); and the culminating capture of Damascus and its disillusioning aftermath (October 1918–April 1919).

In an online review of the film for *T. E. Lawrence Studies*, Jeremy Wilson (www.telstudies.org) observes that Lawrence saw the Arab Revolt as a triumph for the Arabs but a tragedy for himself because he understood his own complicity in "a deceit which others had framed and set afoot," that is, his work to unite the warring Arab factions in common cause against the Ottoman Empire was not for their benefit, as he professed, but to advance British war aims and preserve its colonial interests in the Middle East. In *Seven Pillars of Wisdom*, Lawrence admits that the duplicitous role he played vis-à-vis the Arabs became an almost unbearable psychological and moral burden: "Suffice it that since the march to Akaba I bitterly repented my entanglement in the movement, with a bitterness sufficient to corrode my inactive hours, but insufficient to make me cut myself clear of it. Hence the wobbling of my will, and endless, vapid complainings." Yet the film's interpretation of Lawrence as egomaniacal, sexually ambiguous, and increasingly unhinged by the trauma he suffered at Deraa transforms political guilt into psychosexual angst and pushes the geopolitical legacy of the Arab Revolt—the contrived creation of the state of Iraq by and for the Western powers—in the background. Had the film been more attentive to the political implications of Lawrence's crusade it would have enjoyed greater relevance in later decades, when the always deeply factionalized Iraq repeatedly became a battleground in the conflict between the Islamic world and the West. At any rate, Jeremy Wilson conjectures that the Deraa theme was favored over Lawrence's moral and political dilemma because it was "fundamentally sexual, therefore . . . more commercial."

If that is, indeed, the case, David Lean and his colleagues were quite right in emphasizing the subjective, lurid aspects of Lawrence's saga. Shot on location in England, Spain, Morocco, and Jordan, *Lawrence of Arabia* was, for its day, a costly film to make (US$14 million in 1962; US$85 million, adjusted for inflation, in 2005) but earned substantial profits at the box office, was immediately recognized by critics as a classic, and went on to win seven 1963 Oscars, including Best Picture. In the final analysis, *Lawrence of Arabia* follows T. E. Lawrence's own Orientalist tendencies in romanticizing the primitive nobility of the Bedouins. The film also plays loose with history, inventing people and events at every turn in service to a mythic vision of T. E. Lawrence as neurasthenic desert mystic and warrior demigod. Still, the film's strengths outweigh its weaknesses. Appearing in the early days of American involvement in Vietnam, David Lean's masterpiece presents a prescient view of the ultimate futility of one nation's intervention into the internal affairs of another.

World War One (1964–1965)

The success of *Lawrence of Arabia* revived popular interest in the First World War that carried over into 1964, the year marking the fiftieth anniversary of its start. Over a six-month period—from late September 1964 to March 1965—CBS Television broadcast weekly half-hour episodes of *World War One*, an ambitious twenty-six-part documentary miniseries narrated by Robert Ryan, with music by Morton Gould. Nine and a half hours in total length, *World War One* could afford to be detailed and comprehensive in scope. Using still photographs and a good deal of spectacular and previously unreleased film footage, this superbly researched series covered the war's beginnings, the German army's invasion of neutral Belgium, the sinking of the *Lusitania*, Verdun, Jutland, and Gallipoli, the Russian Revolution, aerial combat, Caporetto, American intervention, the Argonne, and the war's terrible legacy. Overshadowed by the escalating war in Vietnam, *World War One* was largely forgotten until it was rebroadcast on A&E's History Channel in the late 1980s. In 1994, 20th Century Fox released a five-part VHS video version (augmented with new material) entitled *World War One: The Complete Story.*

Johnny Got His Gun (1971)

In the 1930s novelist-screenwriter Dalton Trumbo (1905–1976) happened upon a newspaper report on the Prince of Wales visiting a hospital where he encountered a World War I casualty who had lost his limbs and his ability to speak, hear, smell, and see. Haunted by the ghastly image of a living soul trapped inside the ruined corpse of a body, Trumbo went on to write *Johnny Got His Gun* (Philadelphia: J. B. Lippincott, 1939), an antiwar novel centered on Joe Bonham, an American soldier hideously injured by a shell blast. Like his real-life counterpart Joe has lost his limbs, his face, and all his senses except for the sense of touch through his skin. He does, however, retain his mental faculties and his memory, and the novel oscillates between flashbacks of Joe's halcyon life before the war and his present, solipsistic existence inside the back ward of a veterans hospital. Given his horrible injuries, medical personnel assume that Joe must be a vegetable and treat him as such until a sympathetic day nurse suspects that he may still harbor some vestigial awareness. After establishing rudimentary communication through a system of simple signals—she "writes" on his chest or forehead with her finger and he moves his head in reply—the nurse excitedly alerts colleagues, and a man who knows Morse code is brought in. Finally given back a "voice," Joe expresses his wish to be used as a living exhibit of war's terrible effects. Officials tell him it is against regulations, sedate him, and tuck him away again in the recesses of the hospital: a perfect metaphor for society's willful repression and denial of the true consequences of war. In the end, Joe Bonham has to face the horrifying realization that he has been abandoned to a hellish solitude because he is a political embarrassment.

In a classic example of bad timing, *Johnny Got His Gun* was published two days after the start of the Second World War. The novel garnered excellent reviews and sold well but Trumbo, a confirmed Marxist, allowed the book to go out of print when, with exquisite irony, its antiwar message was embraced by right-wing elements hoping to keep America from going to war against the Axis powers. One of the infamous Hollywood Ten in 1947, Trumbo was blacklisted and did not write for the screen under his own name until 1960 when he was given screen credit for Stanley Kubrick's film, *Spartacus*. At the height of the Vietnam War, Trumbo wrote a screen adaptation of his novel and shopped it around the studios until he netted a production deal with a couple of independent firms: World Entertainment and Cinemation Industries. Coproducing and directing with his son, Christopher, Trumbo cast newcomer Timothy Bottoms (*The Last Picture Show*) as Joe Bonham, Jason Robards as Joe's father, Dianne Varsi as the nurse, and Donald Sutherland as a rather outlandish Christ figure. Shooting Joe's elegiac flashbacks in color and his present situation in black and white, Trumbo adhered to the content of his own book but could not capture its power—probably because he lacked directorial experience but also because Joe's stream-of-consciousness musings did not translate well from the page to cinematic voice-over. Still, Trumbo was able to compensate for the novel's poor timing by perfectly timing the film adaptation to coincide with the rising tide of anti–Vietnam War sentiment in 1971.

Gallipoli (1981)

A decade later Australian director Peter Weir brought out *Gallipoli* (1981), a film that complements *Lawrence of Arabia* by focusing on another aspect of the British campaign against Ottoman Turkey in World War I. Perhaps the most talented of the Australian "New Wave" auteurs, Weir had already made *Picnic at Hanging Rock* (1975) and *The Last Wave* (1977) before writing a story treatment about the disastrous 1915 Australia and New Zealand Army Corps (ANZAC) campaign in the Dardanelles based on Anthony Asquith's 1931 film, *Tell England* (U.S. title: *Battle of Gallipoli*). *Tell England* was, in turn, based on Ernest Raymond's novel, *Tell England: A Study in a Generation* (London: Cassel, 1922). Raymond's novel features Edgar Doe and Rupert Ray: two boyhood friends who enlist in the British army at the start of the war in 1914. At Gallipoli Doe suffers something akin to a nervous breakdown but later recovers his courage and redeems himself by single-handedly neutralizing a Turkish trench mortar that had been wreaking havoc on the ANZAC lines. Unfortunately, Doe is mortally wounded in the process. Weir and Australia's leading playwright, David Williamson, took Ernest Raymond's story and made it into something much darker.

Falling closely on the heels of Bruce Beresford's *"Breaker" Morant* (1980) and developed at the same time as Hugh Hudson's *Chariots of Fire* (1981), *Gallipoli* bears some interesting thematic resemblances to both films. With its tale of Australian soldiers serving the British and then being made scapegoats for Boer War atrocities, *"Breaker"* emphasized Aussie male bonding while it appealed to an aggrieved sense of Australian nationalism: key features of *Gallipoli* as well. *Chariots of Fire* involved runners in fierce competition who likewise bond and become "mates": also a key narrative element of *Gallipoli*.

The first section of the film takes place in the outback of southeastern Australia and contrasts the naïve romanticism of Archie Hamilton (Mark Lee) with the urbane realism of Frank Dunne (Mel Gibson), both purely fictional characters. The two compete against each other running track, become mates, and ponder the wisdom of going off to fight the Turks in the Great War alongside the British and French. A pure-hearted idealist avid to achieve manhood, Archie seeks enlistment in the 8th Light Horse Regiment (and is accepted even though he is too young because he is an excellent horseman). Frank, older and wiser, is initially reluctant to join up but changes his mind once he discovers that nubile young ladies admire men in uniform and that there is a real chance for advancement in the military. In allegorical terms Archie and Frank are clearly meant to serve as opposing aspects of the Australian national psyche: isolated "down under" and uninformed about modern world affairs but savvy, tough-minded survivalists nonetheless. In the second part of the film, the ANZAC troops ship to Cairo, Egypt. Camped in the shadow of the pyramids waiting for marching orders, the men generally enjoy themselves as they casually engage in war games under petulant British commanders, consort with the locals, and are lectured about venereal diseases. In May 1915 Archie, Frank, and their comrades in the 10th Light Horse are ordered to Gallipoli as infantry reinforcements; their horses, which will be of no use, are left behind in Egypt.

The third act begins with the eerie nighttime arrival of the 8th Light Horse at the Gallipoli beachhead, and the formerly sunny look and mood of the film literally and figuratively darkens. Having failed in their initial assaults in late April to dislodge the Turks from the ridges overlooking the beach, ANZAC troops hunker down in a broken line of hillside trenches and foxholes under constant bombardment by enemy artillery. In the trenches, where soldiers die randomly from Turkish shells and snipers, the sense of high adventure quickly disappears and the grim reality of war makes itself felt. Frank experiences real fear and even Archie begins to have some glimmering awareness that warfare is not the glorious enterprise he had imagined it to be. After three months of bloody stalemate on the Gallipoli peninsula, compressed into 10 minutes of screen time in the film, a major ANZAC offensive commences in the early morning hours of August 7, 1915. A small part of that offensive is a diversionary action that came to be known as the Battle of The Nek, in which the 8th and 10th Australian Light Horse regiments were sent, in four waves of 150, against the Turkish trenches just 30 meters away. The film accurately shows that a simple failure to synchronize watches resulted in disaster. The naval bombardment preceding the attack ends 7 minutes too soon, allowing the Turks plenty of time to reoccupy their trenches and mow down the advancing first wave with machine-gun and rifle fire. In the film, Weir and Williamson heighten suspense by having Frank Dunne frantically sprint to Brigade Headquarters to have the attack called off. Tragically he is just a moment too late. But the calamity does not end there. On mistaken information that red signal flags have been spotted indicating that the Turkish trenches have been taken, a second wave is sent out 2 minutes later and is duly slaughtered. When Dunne fails to convince the British commander that the attack is futile, a third wave is likewise sent out and annihilated. Archie Hamilton is among those killed. The film ends with a heart-wrenching freeze-frame of Archie, arms splayed, at the precise moment of death, an image clearly patterned after Robert Capa's famous Spanish civil war photograph, "Falling Soldier" (also known as "Loyalist Militiaman at the Moment of Death, Cerro Muriano, September 5, 1936").

Though indisputably an antiwar film in its depiction of official bungling leading to senseless carnage, *Gallipoli* also reflects the emergent, class-conscious Australian nationalism of the time it was made. Much emphasis is placed on the male bonding that occurs between working-class "mates"—especially Archie and Frank—an important facet of Aussie male culture. Equally typical is the film's emphasis on the rigid, incompetent leadership of the British, who treat the Australians and New Zealanders as second-class citizens of the empire, only worthy as cannon fodder. The death of Archie symbolizes the end of Australian innocence—about the supposed righteousness of the British cause and the putative glories of war. In a larger sense, Archie's death symbolizes the death of all youthful innocence in wartime.

Anzacs (1985)

A few years after the resounding success of *Gallipoli*, *Anzacs* (1985), a five-part miniseries, aired on Australian television to critical acclaim and high viewer ratings and has since been rebroadcast numerous times. Featuring Paul Hogan (of *Crocodile Dundee* fame) and covering not just Gallipoli but the entire ANZAC experience in World War I from 1914 to 1918, *Anzacs* follows the fortunes of a dozen ANZAC soldiers from the war's outbreak through the hells of Gallipoli, the Somme, Ypres, Amiens, Beaumont Hamel, and so on. Interspersed with episodes of combat and life in the trenches are glimpses of the lives of the soldiers' loved ones back home—a narrative strategy that slows down the action but makes for a more fully realized depiction of the manners and mores of early twentieth-century Australia and New Zealand. Predictably, *Anzacs* casts the British military leadership as incompetent, arrogant, and cruel.

The Great War and the Shaping of the 20th Century (1996)

Historical fiction films and films more closely based in real history have naturally tended to focus on the purely military aspects of World War I. Reflecting recent trends in historiography that favor more comprehensive and multifaceted treatments, KCET/Los Angeles teamed with the BBC and London's Imperial War Museum to produce *The Great War and the Shaping of the 20th Century* (1996), a well-researched, ambitious eight-part PBS documentary miniseries that surveys the social, cultural, economic, political, and personal ramifications of the war, then and thereafter. Under the guidance of executive producer Blaine Baggett and chief historian Jay Winter (Cambridge University), directors Lyn Goldfarb, Margaret Koval, Carl Byker, and Isaac Mizrahi patterned *The Great War* on the popular expositional style of Ken Burns' documentaries. The series draws on interviews with, and writings by, leading historians and makes ample use of music, photographs, maps, film footage, period art, poetry, soldiers' and citizens' journals, and letters—recited in voice-over by forty-three well-known actors—to present a rounded view of the war and its cataclysmic impact on modern times.

The first episode, "Explosion," attributes the onset of the Great War to tensions caused by rapid industrial expansion, national rivalries, an international arms race, political and cultural dissonance between old and new forms of government and economy, and the yawning gap between the powerful ruling elites and the masses. The specific event that ignited the conflagration was, of course, the assassination of Archduke Franz Ferdinand of Austria on June 28, 1914. The second episode, "Stalemate," chronicles the early weeks of the war, when the German army swept through Belgium in an attempt to capture Paris and defeat the French. After the Allies stopped the Germans at the Marne, what was supposed to have been a brief and glorious war devolved into a protracted deadlock characterized by the building of thousands of miles of trenches on both sides and a

Archduke Franz Ferdinand and his wife in Sarajevo on June 28, 1914, moments before they were shot to death by an assassin working with the Black Hand terrorist group. (The Illustrated London News Picture Library)

daily round of mud, rats, and death that lasted for years. The third episode, "Total War," examines the spread of the conflict across all borders and into the lives of civilian populations to an unparalleled degree. The new standard of state violence and barbarity is most graphically demonstrated by the Turkish massacre of a million Armenians in 1915. The fourth episode, "Slaughter," deals with the Battle of Verdun in 1916, followed by Ypres (Passchendaele). Together, the two battles result in 1.5 million total casualties, including more than half a million dead, and accomplish little. The fifth episode, "Mutiny," set in 1917, examines the growing sense of despair on all sides after three years of bloodletting on a grand scale. A third of the French army mutinies, which forces the generals to make some concessions to sanity. Demoralization in Russia results in the overthrow of the tsar. The sixth episode, "Collapse," deals with the failed German offensive in the spring of 1918 and the mass arrival of American troops in Europe; the disintegration of the German army, revolt of the German navy, and rioting at home result in the abdication of the kaiser and an armistice on November 11, 1918. The seventh episode, "Hatred and Hunger," concerns the grim aftermath of the war for Germany, when a continuing Allied blockade brings mass starvation and undying bitterness. Woodrow Wilson's diplomatic struggle to secure a reasonably humane settlement at the Paris Peace Conference is betrayed by America's European allies with the harshly punitive Treaty of Versailles (1919), sowing the seeds for World War II twenty years later. The eighth episode, ominously titled, "War without End," surveys the costs of the war (over 9 million dead), its gruesome innovations (poison gas, tanks, aerial bombardment, genocide), and its enduring effects on modern civilization. Highly informative and, at times, deeply moving, *The Great War* was a critical success. The series won two Emmy awards, the Alfred Du Pont Journalism Award, the George Foster Peabody Award, the Producers Guild of American Vision Award, the International Documentary Association (IDA): Best Limited Series Award, and a Director's Guild nomination. An accompanying book and PBS website further augment the value of the series as a teaching tool. *The Great War* was not, however, a great popular success, probably because it was culturally sophisticated, politically progressive, and not *exclusively* concerned with military matters or an American historical topic. Writing in *The New Criterion*, right-wing film critic James Bowman probably expressed widely held views in the United States when he attacked the series for its implicit antiwar agenda and political evenhandedness.

The Lost Battalion (2001)

Eighty-two years after Edward A. McManus's *Lost Battalion*, the Arts & Entertainment (A&E) Television Networks released a made-for-TV remake, *The Lost Battalion* (2001). Helmed by television and film director Russell Mulcahy (*Highlander*) and written by Vietnam War veteran James Carabatsos (*Heartbreak Ridge; Hamburger Hill*), A&E's *Lost Battalion* features Rick Schroeder as Charles Whittlesey leading a cast of unknowns in an appropriately gory docudrama that owes much to Steven Speilberg's *Saving Private Ryan* (1999) in terms of cinematographic and editing styles, that is, lots of handheld camera shots, tight framing, and rapid cutting simulate the terrifying chaos of combat. Made before but released after the September 11 terrorist attacks, Mulcahy's *Lost Battalion* was perfectly timed to tap into the American patriotic upsurge as it showed an earlier generation sorely tested in battle but unbowed and ultimately triumphant.

Shattered City: The Halifax Explosion (2003)

At 8:44 on the morning of December 6, 1917, in a narrow section of Halifax harbor, Nova Scotia, the *Imo*, a Belgian relief vessel, collided with the *Mont-Blanc*, a French munitions ship. The *Mont-Blanc* was fully loaded with 2,300 tons of wet and dry picric acid (a highly explosive derivative of phenol); 200 tons of TNT; 10 tons of guncotton (nitrocellulose); and 35 tons of benzol (a highly flammable liquid hydrocarbon). When sparks from the collision set fire to the benzol, the crew of the *Mont-Blanc* hastily abandoned ship. Now essentially a floating time bomb billowing flame and clouds of thick black smoke, the *Mont-Blanc* drifted into Pier 6 in the Richmond section of Halifax. At 9:04:35 local time, the 5 million pounds of high explosives on board the *Mont-Blanc* blew up, sending a fireball a mile into the sky. In one-fiftieth of a second, a 325-acre swath of downtown Halifax was obliterated, a thousand people were instantly killed, and another 9,000 were injured (of whom another 900 would soon die of their wounds). Flying glass shards permanently blinded 200 people. The explosion set off fires throughout the city and stirred up a tidal wave that wreaked further havoc. The Halifax explosion would come to be known as the greatest nonnuclear explosion in history.

Eighty-six years after the tragic event, Salter Street Films and Tapestry Films with $10 million in funding from Téléfilm Canada and the CBC produced *Shattered City: The Halifax Explosion* (2003), a two-part, 4-hour miniseries that first aired on Canadian television in late October 2003. Directed by Bruce Pittman and written by Keith Ross Leckie, *Shattered City* presents the disaster and its aftermath through the eyes of the fictional Collins family, a narrative device that gives the film dramatic unity but somewhat undermines the film's historicity. A plodding pace, sketchy characterizations, and a number of anachronisms further blunt the effect of the series. Nonetheless, *Shattered City* did at least succeed in bringing an important event in Canadian history back into contemporary consciousness.

3

Military History on Film and Television: World War II

uthentic history films about World War II can be divided into three broad historical phases, each with its own formal and ideological characteristics, with the important caveat that World War II, like every war before or since, has been a hotly contested topic in matters of filmic representation. The phases delineated merely mark dominant trends that are contradicted by particular films. The first of these phases coincides with U.S. involvement in the war, 1941–1945. Fiction war films made during the war are typically jingoistic; the Japanese are always referred to as "Japs" and are depicted as bloodthirsty savages. Feature films based on real incidents are likewise propagandistic but in a more muted way, in keeping with the somewhat more stringent requisites of historical accuracy. Military setbacks and casualties are acknowledged but the true, deep horror of combat is generally glossed over. There was, after all, a war to win, and the rending of human bodies and souls had to be kept in the background for morale purposes. After the war, widespread repression of the war's true costs continued to prevail for three decades—and even morphed into a kind of mythic triumphalism. This second phase of World War II films encompasses the period from war's end to the end of the Vietnam era, 1945–1975. For the most part the films of this period reflect stalwart Cold War ideology by celebrating the courage, ingenuity, and teamwork exhibited by the victorious soldiers of the Western alliance (especially the United States and Great Britain). There was, after all, a war against communism to win; any large-scale coming to terms with the true nature of the second global war would have to wait for some halcyon future moment. However, the reality of history unexpectedly intervened. America's disastrous involvement in Vietnam instigated a sweeping legitimation crisis that made radical skepticism about government war policies and motives an acceptable mode of thought and discourse—applied not only to that present moment but also retrospectively to earlier wars. Thus, a third phase of the World War II history film began after the Vietnam War ended in 1975. This type of film, which continues to be made, is plainly revisionist. Perhaps inevitably, it took decades before some of the darker truths of "The Good War" could be brought to light. The enormity of a global, genocidal war that took more than 50 million lives could not be confronted until sufficient time had passed to blunt the emotional awareness of such a hideous reality.

Contemporaneous World War II History Films

Wake Island (1942)

Following the surprise attack on Pearl Harbor (December 7, 1941), Japanese bombers struck the isolated U.S. outpost on Wake Island, a small and barren V-shaped Pacific atoll 2,300 miles west-southwest of Hawaii. After three days of aerial bombardment, a Japanese naval task force attempted to launch an amphibious assault on Wake Island but was repulsed with heavy losses by U.S. shore batteries and a few remaining F4F Grumman Wildcat fighters—an engagement hailed as America's first victory in the Pacific. On December 16 U.S. Task Force 14, commanded by Admiral Jack Fletcher and consisting of an aircraft carrier, three heavy cruisers, and nine destroyers, left Pearl Harbor to provide relief and reinforcement to the embattled troops at Wake Island. On December 23 with Task Force 14 about 500 miles from Wake Island, Vice Admiral William S. Pye (acting commander in chief of the decimated U.S. Pacific Fleet) decided that a large-scale rescue operation was too risky, given sketchy intelligence on enemy strength, and recalled the task force to Pearl Harbor. On the same day, after thirteen days of air raids, the Japanese launched a second and more powerful amphibious assault on Wake Island. Outnumbered, outgunned, and without air cover, the small American garrison finally surrendered after 12 hours of fierce fighting. Of the 513 Navy and Marine personnel stationed on Wake Island, 49 were killed, 41 wounded, and 423 were taken prisoner. Among the 1,146 American civilian construction contractors on the island, 70 were killed, 12 wounded, and 1,064 taken prisoner. Though the Japanese paid a heavy price for Wake Island—approximately 1,000 killed—the island's fall was another humiliating defeat for America after the catastrophe at Pearl Harbor just sixteen days earlier.

Even before the battle for Wake Island was over, Paramount began making *Wake Island* (1942), a patriotic docudrama cowritten by W. R. Burnett (*Little Caesar; High Sierra*) and Frank Butler (*Road to Zanzibar*), directed by John Farrow, and shot in San Diego and at the Salton Sea, a 375-square-mile lake in southeastern California. Burnett and Butler wrote a screenplay that augments the story of the Marines' heroic but hopeless defense of the island with two sub-

Aerial photograph of Wake Island taken from a U.S. PBY patrol plane on May 25, 1941. (U.S. Navy)

plots, one dealing with the conflict between the Pan Am civilian contractors and the Marines and another that focuses on the friendship between Private Joe Doyle (Robert Preston) and Private Aloysius K. "Smacksie" Randall (William Bendix). The first subplot seems to have been fashioned to contrast the principled discipline of the Marines, as embodied by the upstanding Major Geoffrey Caton (Brian Donlevy) with the cynical individualism of the construction contractors, personified by the surly Shad McCloskey (Albert Dekker). As was the norm for war films of the period (such as *The Fighting 69th*), emphasis was placed on group solidarity, patriotism, and teamwork in marked contrast to the mercenary opportunism that is characteristic of business as usual in capitalist civilization. The other subplot, involving Preston urging working-class New Yorker Bendix to reenlist and Bendix stubbornly determined to return to civilian life and marry his beloved "Moittle" (Myrtle), acts as comic relief and helps to makes the common soldier more sympathetic. The main story line, chronicling the defense of Wake Island, contained well-executed combat footage but too readily succumbed to propaganda requisites by implying that all of the island's defenders died in an Alamo-like last stand. Flawed history but compelling entertainment, *Wake Island* was nominated for four 1943 Oscars (Best Picture, Best

Director: John Farrow, Best Supporting Actor: William Bendix, and Best Original Screenplay: W. R. Burnett and Frank Butler). An A&E History Channel documentary, *Wake Island: Alamo of the Pacific* (2003) presents a scrupulously accurate version of the events, including interviews with surviving defenders of Wake Island who express their disdain for Farrow's film.

In Which We Serve (1942)

Though more restrained when it came to nationalist cheerleading, the British also had their propaganda films. Easily the best and most famous of these was Noël Coward's *In Which We Serve* (1942), a film based on the twenty-one-month career of HMS *Kelly* (FO1), a 1,700-ton Royal Navy K-class destroyer that was commissioned on August 23, 1939, and sunk by a Stuka dive-bomber at the Battle of Crete, May 23, 1941. What made the *Kelly* distinctive was that her commander was Lord Louis Mountbatten (1900–1979), great-grandson of Queen Victoria.

As England's most celebrated writer of drawing room comedies and light operettas, Noël Coward (1899–1973) moved in the most exclusive social circles. Hailing from a petit bourgeois background, Coward embraced Englishness and aristocratic snobbery with a vengeance. A close friend of Winston Churchill, Lord Mountbatten, and other illuminati, Coward was anxious to please his high-placed friends, reinvent himself as a more serious artist, and contribute to the war effort by making a patriotic movie. Accordingly, Coward fashioned a film script based on Mountbatten's stories about his service on the *Kelly*, recruited David Lean to help him direct, and cast himself as Captain Edward V. Kinross, the stolidly heroic Mountbatten figure who commands HMS *Torrin*, the fictional version of the HMS *Kelly*. To structure his film, Coward borrowed the noir flashback device then at the height of its popularity. In the present time frame of the film, the *Torrin* has just been sunk. Clinging to wreckage while awaiting rescue, the *Torrin*'s survivors flashback to their home lives, family, and loved ones, thus providing ample opportunity to dramatize what the men value and why they are fighting. *In Which We Serve* fully acknowledges the elaborate social class system that permeates British society but argues, rather disingenuously, that the war has brought all the classes together in their common fight against the Axis powers.

Just three days after Pearl Harbor, Brigadier General Frederick H. Osborn (chief of the U.S. Army's Morale Branch, newly renamed Special Services) met with Colonel Richard Schlosberg (Army Pictorial Service) to establish a program that would make orientation films for soldiers in basic training to explain and justify America's fight against the Axis powers. There are various accounts as to how Hollywood director Frank Capra became involved with the resulting "Why

We Fight" film series but media scholar Thomas W. Bohn gives best credence to Osborn's official memorandum. Therein, Osborn states that he asked the U.S. Army Signal Corps to induct Capra and assign him to Special Services (Bohn 1977). Capra joined the army in February 1942 and was immediately made chief of the Film Production Section of Special Services and commander of the 834th Signal Service Photographic Detachment, a unit later attached to the Signal Corps. Wasting no time, Capra quickly assembled a staff of topflight Hollywood professionals. Englishman Eric Knight (1897–1943) initially headed Capra's writing team. The author of *Lassie, Come Home,* Knight largely wrote the first film in the series and probably would have written the others had he not been killed in a mysterious plane crash in Dutch Guiana on January 13, 1943. Capra's other screenwriters were Leonard Spigelgass (*All Through the Night*), Edward E. Paramore Jr. (*The Bitter Tea of General Yen*), John Sanford (Julian Shapiro) (*Honky Tonk*), Jerome Chodorov (*My Sister Eileen*), Julius J. and Philip Epstein (*Yankee Doodle Dandy; Casablanca*), S. K. Lauren (*Jennie Gerhardt*), and Anthony Veillor (*Stage Door*). For his film editors, Capra enlisted William Hornbeck (*Jungle Book*), Henry Berman (*Kitty Foyle*), Leon Levy (*Marusia*), and John Hoffman (*Boom Town*). Walter Huston, Anthony Veillor, and Lloyd Nolan served as voice-over narrators; the great Dimitri Tiomkin scored and conducted the music; Sam Briskin, former general manager of Columbia Studios, took on the job of Capra's production manager; film historian Richard Griffith was put in charge of research; and Anatole Litvak (*Confessions of a Nazi Spy*) shared directorial duties with Capra. An extraordinary gathering of world-class talent, these artists would, in the course of their careers, collectively rack up more than two dozen Oscar nominations and win eight Oscars. In sum, the 834th was easily the finest filmmaking outfit the U.S. Army Signal Corps ever had and among the best ever assembled anywhere. Ironically government regulations proscribed screen credit for anyone involved.

"Why We Fight" Film Series

Capra's filmmaking team researched, scripted, assembled, edited, and scored the first film in the "Why We Fight" series, *Prelude to War* (1942), in just seven months. Despite its rapid preparation, *Prelude* is a very carefully wrought propaganda piece. The film surveys the events that precipitated the Second World War: the rise of fascism in Italy, Nazism in Germany, Japanese aggression in Manchuria, and the U.S. lack of military preparedness that led to the disaster at Pearl Harbor. Using animated maps, graphics, newsreel footage, and Japanese, German, and Italian propaganda footage in such a way as to subvert the enemies' message, *Prelude to War* argues a decidedly Manichean—but largely accurate—view of the world in which the Axis powers represent barbarism and slavery and the Allied powers stand for civilization and freedom. As a mandatory part of boot camp, the army started showing *Prelude* to new recruits on October 30, 1942, at the height of the grueling Battle of Guadalcanal (August 1942–February 1943). Seven months later, on orders from President Roosevelt, the U.S. government made *Prelude to War* available for general release. The 54-minute film won the 1943 Oscar for Best Documentary.

Close on the heels of *Prelude to War* the government released *The Nazis Strike* (1943), a 41-minute documentary that examines the implementation of Hitler's plans for world conquest (laid out in *Mein Kampf*) through diplomatic treachery and armed aggression. *Divide and Conquer* (1943), the third episode of "Why We Fight," deals with the early phase of the war in Europe, when German blitzkrieg tactics resulted in the fall of most of central Europe in 1939–1940. The series' fourth episode, *The Battle of Britain* (1943), recounts Britain's successful air war against Nazi Germany in 1940, a victory against formidable odds that prevented a planned invasion. The series' feature-length fifth episode, *The Battle of Russia* (1943), looks at Hitler's massive invasion of the Soviet Union ("Operation Barbarossa") in June 1941 that stalled before the gates of Moscow in the winter of 1941–1942 and sustained a crucial defeat at Stalingrad in the winter of 1942–1943. Inevitably, given the political circumstances that prevailed in 1943, the film portrays the Russians as brave and determined allies while glossing over Soviet communism, a politically expedient stance that would change radically after the end of the war in 1945. *The Battle of China* (1944), the sixth installment in the series, also proved politically sensitive. The film quite deliberately fails to acknowledge that Chinese Communist forces were instrumental in checking Japanese aggression in China. This was a viewpoint that the U.S. government saw as a potential source of political embarrassment after the war—especially if the Communists won their civil war against Chiang Kai-Shek (which they did in 1949). Consequently the government did not release *The Battle of China* to the general public. *War Comes to America* (1945), the seventh and final film in the series, released to theaters after V-E day but before Japan's surrender in August, surveys the events leading up to Pearl Harbor. *War Comes to America* also recapitulates the message presented by the other films: that ethnically diverse, freedom-loving, democratic America is well worth defending. Cumulative attendance by military personnel at the seven films topped 45 million by 1945. Countless millions of civilians in the United States and Allied nations also saw one or more of the films, making "Why We Fight" the most widely viewed documentary series of its time. In 2000 "Why We Fight" was added to the Library of Congress's National Film Registry.

December 7, 1941 (1943)

It was inevitable that Pearl Harbor would become the object of a propaganda film. Some months after the attack the U.S. government tapped superpatriotic, multiple-Oscar-winning director John Ford (*The Informer; Drums along the Mohawk; Grapes of Wrath*) to make *December 7, 1941* (1943). Already in the process of making a series of short documentaries for the Field Photography section of the Office of Strategic Services (OSS)—*Sex Hygiene* (1942); *The Battle of Midway* (1942); *Torpedo Squadron* (1942); *We Sail at Midnight* (1943)—Ford assigned the Pearl Harbor film project to one of his subordinates—would-be director Gregg Toland, the brilliant cinematographer who shot Ford's *The Grapes of Wrath* (1940) and Orson Welles' *Citizen Kane* (1941). Novelist-screenwriter Budd Schulberg (who went on to write *On the Waterfront* and *A Face in the Crowd*) wrote a strange, jingoistic script. Most of the first half of the original 82-minute version of *December 7* featured Walter Huston as an allegorical Uncle Sam (U.S.) on vacation in Hawaii debating the loyalty to America of Japanese Hawaiians with Mr. "C" (for Conscience) (Harry Davenport). The complacent, pacifist Uncle Sam maintains that Hawaiian islanders of Japanese extraction consider themselves Americans while his wary conscience argues that Japanese Americans are more closely identified with Japan by race, religion, and custom and therefore cannot be trusted. The second half of *December 7* recounts the attack on Pearl Harbor by mixing newsreel footage with a realistic reenactment of the attack using model ships, planes, and Douglas SBD Dauntless dive-bombers posing as Japanese aircraft. A coda features Dana Andrews as the ghost of a U.S. sailor killed at Pearl Harbor debating the event with the ghost of a World War I soldier (Paul Hurst). Put off by the contrived and bizarrely xenophobic Uncle Sam prologue, Army Chief of Staff General George C. Marshall ordered that portion of the film excised, whereupon John Ford stepped in and cut Tolland's film by a full 48 minutes. A recognizably conventional documentary, Ford's 34-minute version won the 1944 Oscar for Best Documentary, Short Subjects. In 1991 VCI Home Video released a special fiftieth anniversary VHS edition of the film restored to its original 82-minute length and titled *December 7th: The Pearl Harbor Story* (a DVD edition appeared in 2001).

Bataan (1943)

Hours after bombing Pearl Harbor the Japanese air force struck U.S. Army Air Corps installations in the Philippines and destroyed most of the American aircraft on the ground. A few days later Japanese land forces led by Lt. Gen. Masaharu

Homma invaded the Philippines in Northern Luzon and the Southern Mindanao Islands. After the fall of Manila in early January 1942, outnumbered Filipino American forces led by Gen. Douglas MacArthur retreated south into the mountainous and heavily forested Bataan peninsula on the western side of Luzon. After three months of desperate fighting the United States surrendered Luzon on April 9 and more than 70,000 half-starved, exhausted, and disease-ridden men were force-marched north to the Japanese P.O.W. compound at the former Camp O'Donnell. The so-called "Bataan Death March" resulted in the deaths of thousands of prisoners. On May 6 the United States surrendered its last stronghold in the Philippines: the fortified island of Corregidor.

An ignominious and crushing defeat, Bataan could only be recuperated for propaganda purposes by (1) stressing the savagery of the Japanese military—not hard to do—and (2) emphasizing the heroism of the Filipino American resistance—also not hard to do. In short, a filmic representation of the defense of Bataan called for the familiar Alamo motif, which had to admit defeat but glorified the courage of the besieged, pleaded mitigating circumstances, and promised revenge in the very near future. This was precisely the kind of scenario that screenwriter Robert Hardy Andrews conjured for *Bataan* (1943), borrowing the plot from John Ford's *The Lost Patrol* (1934). A somber, atmospheric, and exceptionally violent MGM production directed by Tay Garnett, *Bataan* stars Robert Taylor as tough-as-nails Sgt. Bill Dane and features the usual roster of character actors—George Murphy, Thomas Mitchell, Lloyd Nolan, Barry Nelson, and newcomer Desi Arnaz—filling out the racially, ethnically, and occupationally diverse squad epitomizing the American melting pot. Shot entirely on a Hollywood soundstage, *Bataan* keeps its focus local and narrow by concentrating on its small band of U.S. soldiers committed to slowing the Japanese advance by destroying a tactically important bridge. Though picked off one by one, the Americans never lose their fighting spirit. Indeed, the film's closing shot shows Robert Taylor's Sgt. Dane, the last survivor, firing his machine gun directly at the camera and declaring he will never relent—a rousing image for stateside audiences in the summer of 1943, still hateful toward the Japanese for Pearl Harbor and all the rest.

In early June 1942 the United States achieved its first victory against the Imperial Japanese Navy at the Battle of Midway. Two months later (August 7, 1942) the U.S. 1st Marine Division launched an amphibious invasion of the jungle island of Guadalcanal (in the southern part of the Solomon Island chain, northeast of Australia). The invasion marked America's first land offensive against the Japanese and was strategically and symbolically of enormous importance. The Marines caught the Japanese by surprise, quickly seized the airfield they were building, completed it, and renamed it Henderson Field. But the Japanese Imperial Army was not about to cede the island without a fight. From a major base at

Rabaul in the northern Solomon Islands, the Japanese rushed in reinforcements and, over the next six months, a series of desperate land, sea, and air battles for control of the island ensued. Both sides faced fetid heat, torrential rains, malaria and dysentery, food and supply shortages, and took heavy losses in the continued fierce fighting. By the time the Japanese were finally driven from the island on February 9, 1943, the United States had sustained more than 6,000 casualties and the Japanese lost four times that number. The hard-won American victory at Guadalcanal marked the real turning point of the war in the Pacific.

Guadalcanal Diary (1943)

Landing with the Marines on August 7 was Richard Tregaskis (1918–1973), a volunteer war correspondent who remained on the island for seven weeks and witnessed the bloody "Battle of Edson's Ridge" (September 11–14). Tregaskis's journal, in which he recorded the day-to-day travails of his comrades, was published as *Guadalcanal Diary* (New York: Random House, 1943). The book, a major publishing sensation, immediately prompted a 20th Century Fox movie version adapted to the screen by Lamar Trotti (*Drums along the Mohawk; The Ox-Bow Incident*) and Jerome Cady, directed by Lewis Seiler (*Divide and Conquer*), and starring Preston Foster, Lloyd Nolan, William Bendix (reprising his *Wake Island* role as squad buffoon), Richard Conte, Anthony Quinn, and Richard Jaeckel as members of the stereotypical group of American soldiers from all walks of life. Though containing some combat sequences based on actual events, most of the action of *Guadalcanal Diary* (1943) is fictitious. Furthermore, in the interests of patriotic propagandizing, the film characterizes the enemy soldiers as bloodthirsty "monkey men" and offers a highly sanitized view of the battle that elides terrifying Japanese night attacks, airplane losses at Henderson Field, and the filth and misery of living conditions on the island.

The Sullivans (1944)

The Guadalcanal campaign also spawned another major 20th Century Fox film: *The Sullivans* (1944). On Friday, September 13, 1942, the USS *Juneau* (CL-52), a newly commissioned 6,700-ton *Atlanta*-class light cruiser, was torpedoed by the Japanese submarine *I-26* off Guadalcanal. Having already been badly damaged by a torpedo the previous day, the *Juneau* exploded, broke in half, and sank in 20 seconds. Of a complement of 623, only 10 sailors survived. Among the lost were Albert, Francis, George, Joseph, and Madison Sullivan—five brothers from

Waterloo, Iowa, who all joined the navy together after Pearl Harbor and insisted that they not be separated. Because the Sullivans were already famous for being the only group of five brothers serving on one vessel ("we stick together" was their motto), their deaths made headlines throughout the United States and were exploited by the War Office for propaganda purposes. Though the navy adopted a new policy that discouraged family members from serving together, it also named a new destroyer (DD-537) in the Sullivans' honor in 1943.

A poignant example of unusually intense family solidarity and courage, the Sullivan saga presented rich opportunities for wartime patriotic propaganda. Recognizing as much, Hollywood agent and producer Sam Jaffe contracted a Sullivans film project. Written by Edward Doherty, Jules Schermer, and Mary C. McCall and directed by Lloyd Bacon (*Knute Rockne All American*), *The Fighting Sullivans* (later retitled *The Sullivans*) (1944) is a war film that contains very little battle footage. Instead, the filmmakers concentrate on presenting a rounded and deeply sentimental (some would say cloying) portrait of the five Sullivan brothers from their shared childhood and adolescence in Depression-era Iowa to their ultimate fate in the South Pacific. From a working-class Irish American midwestern background that affirmed God, country, family, hard work, and basic decency, the Sullivans embodied the wholesome bedrock social values that rationalized the war effort for millions of average Americans. The film reinforces and sentimentalizes this image of innocence by scripting the Sullivan boys' youth as an idyllic Huck Finn odyssey presided over by firm but loving parents (played by Thomas Mitchell and Selena Royale). It was a maudlin cliché that served as a model for the sanitized television families of the 1950s and 1960s (for example, *Ozzie & Harriet; Father Knows Best; Leave It to Beaver*). While the tragic deaths of the Sullivans would seem to weaken their pro-American and pro-war propaganda value—no one wants to die, after all—the film transforms the story's disheartening closure into a virtue by turning the Sullivans into heroic martyrs who provide martial inspiration and, in a muted key, another reason for holy vengeance against the enemy. Likewise, the surviving family's devastating grief is recouped by the heartbreaking dignity and stoicism they display in their suffering: a model for thousands of other American families that had to face the deaths of loved ones in the war. Released in February 1943, during the Battle of Anzio, *The Sullivans* proved to be extremely popular and was, perhaps fancifully, nominated for an Oscar for Best Writing, Original Story.

All of this smacks of bitter irony when one stops to consider that there was a dark and bizarre side to the tragedy of the *Juneau*, long suppressed by the navy. Between 115 and 140 sailors, many grievously injured, survived the explosion and sinking of the *Juneau* but the task force of which she was a part steamed away to avoid more losses. Although the position of the *Juneau*'s sinking was well known, a search for survivors was delayed for more than a week. By the time a search was mounted only 10 sailors were pulled from the water alive. More than 100 others had drowned, died of exposure, exhaustion, trauma, or had been eaten by sharks. Needless to say, *The Sullivans* made no mention of this aspect of the story, which contained little positive propaganda value.

Much easier to exploit for propaganda purposes was the celebrated Doolittle raid on Japan. After four months of humiliating military reverses at the hands of the Japanese, the United States desperately needed some good news. On April 18, 1942, Lt. Col. James H. "Jimmy" Doolittle obliged by leading an all-volunteer squadron of sixteen Mitchell B-25 medium bombers from the U.S. aircraft carrier *Hornet* (CV-8) in a bombing raid on industrial targets in Tokyo, Yokohama, Kobe, Osaka, and Nagoya. Launched sooner than intended after the Japanese apparently spotted the American carrier task force, the raid was more arduous than anyone anticipated. Almost all the B-25s successfully bombed their targets but lack of fuel forced most to ditch or bail out into the China Sea instead of landing, as planned, at bases on the Chinese mainland. Of the eighty Air Corps crewmen involved, eight were captured and four killed. Though the raid inflicted only minor damage, it was an inestimable boost to American morale. Doolittle was awarded the Medal of Honor and promoted to brigadier general and his returning raiders were treated as great heroes. Furthermore, the raid shocked the Japanese and forced them to review their strategic options to keep U.S. warplanes from their homeland: a development that led to the decisive American victory at the Battle of Midway in June 1942.

The Purple Heart and *Thirty Seconds over Tokyo* (1944)

A resounding propaganda coup, the Doolittle raid spawned two Hollywood feature films: 20th Century Fox's *The Purple Heart* (February 1944) and MGM's *Thirty Seconds over Tokyo* (November 1944). Directed by Lewis Milestone (*All Quiet on the Western Front*) and written by studio mogul, Darryl F. Zanuck (as "Melville Crossman") and Jerome Cady, *The Purple Heart* focused its treatment of the raid on the eight flyers captured afterward by the Japanese: Lt. Robert Hite, Lt. William G. Farrow, Lt. George Barr, Sgt. Harold A. Spatz, Cpl. Jacob De Shazer, Lt. Dean G. Hallmark, Lt. Robert Meder, and Lt. Chase J. Nielsen (all names were changed for the film, perhaps to lend the story greater universality but most probably because the exact fate of the men was unknown when the film was being made). At a cursory trial held at Police Headquarters in Shanghai, China, on October 14, 1942, Japanese officials convicted the eight of war crimes and sentenced them to death. At dawn on the next day Farrow, Spatz, and Hallmark were executed by firing squad but the other five men had their death sentences commuted to life imprisonment. Lt. Meder died of dysentery on December 1, 1943. The four remaining survivors were freed when Japan surrendered in August 1945, after forty months of starvation and torture in a Japanese prison in Nanking, China.

The actual trial of the captured Doolittle raiders only lasted 20 minutes and was conducted entirely in Japanese. For dramatic and propaganda purposes *The Purple Heart* exercised gross poetic license by inventing long, passionate speeches by the captives' defiant leader, Capt. Harvey Ross (Dana Andrews), justifying the raid and promising Japan terrible retribution for waging unprovoked war on the United States. The film incorrectly depicts all eight airmen being executed by the Japanese, having adamantly refused to divulge any information about their mission—a refusal that causes their Japanese prosecutor, General Mitsubi (stock Asian villain, Richard Loo), to commit suicide in frustration and disgrace. A small and overly zealous film, *The Purple Heart* quickly sank into oblivion.

Such was not the fate of the second film on the Doolittle raid. After Captain Ted W. Lawson, one of the B-25 pilots on the Doolittle raid, wrote a best-selling eyewitness account called *Thirty Seconds over Tokyo* (edited by Robert Considine; New York: Random House, 1943), Hollywood producer Sam Zimbalist sold Metro-Goldwyn-Mayer on a screen adaptation. MGM assigned experienced contract director Mervyn Leroy (*Madame Curie*) to make the picture, hired screenwriter Dalton Trumbo to write it, and Captain Lawson to serve as a technical advisor: a move that ensured an unusually high level of historical accuracy. Starring Van Johnson as Ted Lawson, Spencer Tracy as Jimmy Doolittle, and Robert Mitchum as Lawson's friend and comrade, Lt. Bob Gray, *Thirty Seconds over Tokyo* (1944) eschewed the agitprop sermonizing of *The Purple Heart* and also avoided the bathos so characteristic of other World War II propaganda films. Instead, *Thirty Seconds* presented a detailed, factual, and straightforward account of the raid. The only major concession to sentiment was a subplot that focused on Lawson's devoted wife, Ellen (Phyllis Thaxter), their romance, married life, and her brave acceptance of her husband's dangerous mission and his later having to have his leg amputated after his B-25 crashes off the China coast. Perhaps owing something to Dalton Trumbo's leftist politics, *Thirty Seconds* refuses to caricature the Japanese and depicts our Chinese allies in a very sympathetic light. On the other hand, the film unconscionably neglects to acknowledge the terrible price paid by the Chinese for aiding the Americans. After the raid, vengeful Japanese troops murdered thousands of Chinese civilians. A box office hit lauded by critics, *Thirty Seconds over Tokyo* won an Oscar for Special Effects.

The Memphis Belle: A Story of a Flying Fortress (1944)

Equally successful was William Wyler's Army Air Corps documentary, *The Memphis Belle: A Story of a Flying Fortress* (short title: *Memphis Belle*) (1944). One of nearly 13,000 four-engine B-17 heavy bombers (aka, flying fortresses) manufactured by Boeing Aircraft during the war, Memphis Belle (named after the pilot's sweetheart, Margaret Polk) became the most famous of its type due to Wyler's film. Piloted by Captains Robert K. Morgan and James A. Verinis, the Memphis Belle flew its requisite twenty-five bombing missions with the 91st Bomber Group, 8th Air Force, over France, Belgium, and Germany between November 7, 1942, and May 17, 1943. Over that seven-month period Morgan's 30-ton airplane was in the air for almost 149 hours (i.e., more than six and a half days), covered some 20,000 combat miles, dropped 60 tons of bombs, shot down eight enemy interceptors, and damaged or destroyed another seventeen. Though frequently riddled with holes from Nazi fighter bullets and antiaircraft flak bursts, Memphis Belle did not lose a single crew member. *Memphis Belle*, the movie, centers on the bomber's twenty-fifth and last mission, to bomb German U-boat pens at Lorient, France. After covering mission preparations at RAF Bassingbourn, Cambridgeshire (north of London), *Memphis Belle* follows the bomber in formation, taking flak, bombing its target, dueling enemy fighters, and returning to base in triumph. The relieved crew is congratulated by no less than England's King George VI (1895–1952) and Queen Elizabeth, aka, the Queen Mother (1900–2002). The overall impression the viewer takes away is of a young crew (average age twenty) that exudes stolid courage, competence, and quiet professionalism; clearly the air war is in good hands. Forty-four years after her last mission, the Memphis Belle was fully restored and placed on permanent display at the Memphis Belle Pavillion on Mud Island in Memphis, Tennessee. Three years after that, William Wyler's daughter, Catherine, took advantage of renewed interest in the famous bomber to make *Memphis Belle* (1990), a docudrama staring Matthew Modine as Capt. Dennis Dearborn, the equivalent of Capt. Robert Morgan.

The True Glory (1945)

Two months after V-J day, the U.S. Office of War Information joined Britain's Ministry of Information in releasing *The True Glory* (1945), an 87-minute documentary personally prefaced by General Dwight D. Eisenhower that traces the final year and a half of the war in Europe, from the massive preparations for D-day to the German surrender in May 1945. Distilled from 10 million feet (i.e., 2,000 miles) of black-and-white film shot by some 1,400 cameramen from a dozen different nations (of whom 10 percent were killed or wounded in action), *The True Glory* uses interviews, combat footage, and animated maps to present a sweeping depiction of the invasion and liberation of Hitler's Europe. The project was an enormous undertaking supervised by two directors—Garson Kanin and Carol Reed—and developed by a stable of writers including Peter Ustinov, Harry Brown (*A Walk in the Sun; Sands of Iwo Jima*), Guy Trosper (*The Stratton Story*), and Saul Levitt (*The Andersonville Trial*). An important source of World War II footage, *The True Glory* remains fascinating in its own right.

The Battle of San Pietro (1944)

In marked contrast to the officially sanctioned and mostly celebratory *True Glory* is John Huston's *The Battle of San Pietro* (aka *San Pietro*) (1944), a controversial documentary that bears stark witness to a minor but exceedingly bloody battle. In mid-December 1943 the U.S. Army's 36th Infantry Division was ordered to take San Pietro Infine, a mountain village in southern Italy overlooking the Liri Valley through which ran Highway 6, the strategically vital road from Naples to Rome. Defending San Pietro and its mountainous environs were three well-dug-in battalions from two *Panzergrenadier* regiments (the 2/15th, 3/15th, and 2/71st). After a series of assaults (December 9–10) failed to dislodge the Germans, a second major effort was launched on December 15 that involved an ill-advised frontal assault from the east by sixteen M4 Sherman tanks and one British Valentine tank; an attack from the south by the 141st Regiment; and an attack from the west on the German right flank at Monte Lungo by the 142nd and 143rd regiments. Proceeding along a narrow mountain road with a steep rock slope to the right and a precipitous drop-off on the left side, the advancing armored column was halted and then demolished by mines and deadly accurate Nazi antitank fire; only four tanks returned. The attacking infantry also took terrible losses—the 143rd sustained 1,100 casualties out of a force of 2,565 men—but was ultimately successful. Wary of being cut off from a means of retreat, the Germans abandoned the ruins of San Pietro on the night of December 16.

Hollywood director turned Signal Corps Captain John Huston (*The Maltese Falcon; High Sierra*) directed five cameramen attached to the 143rd to record the fierce tank and infantry fighting at San Pietro with 35mm hand held Bell & Howell Eyemo newsreel cameras. Before the battle Huston interviewed a few of the American soldiers on camera, who waxed eloquent on their understanding of the war. Afterward the corpses of some of the same men appear on camera with their earlier words as voice-over commentary on their fate. In its original form, *The Battle of San Pietro* was a harrowing and sometimes grotesque 80-minute tour of hell, full of the terrifying immediacy of combat. When Huston first screened his film for high-ranking army officers stateside they all eventually walked out (in order of rank, of course). As he relates in his autobiography, *An Open Book* (New York: Macmillan, 1981), Huston later recalled thinking, "What a bunch of a**holes! There goes *San Pietro*." The army found the film pacifistic and demoralizing. An irate Huston responded that he made *San Pietro* as a tribute to the incredible bravery of the foot soldier but not to glorify war. He told army officials, "Well, sir, whenever I make a picture that's for war—why, I hope you take me out and shoot me" (Huston 1981). The film would have been suppressed altogether were it not for the intervention of the always levelheaded army chief of staff, General George C. Marshall, who felt that *San Pietro* would make an excellent training film by showing new soldiers what the shock of combat was really like. A pariah for months, Huston suddenly found himself rehabilitated and even promoted to major. Reduced from five reels to two—with all its most graphic footage excised—*San Pietro* finally appeared in a 32-minute version that included a new preface, dutifully written by Huston and recited by General Mark Clark, disingenuously insisting that the Battle of San Pietro was important and necessary and casualties were not excessive. Even in this form the film was never screened publicly because it showed dead American soldiers being prepared for burial. Four years after John Huston's death in 1987, the Library of Congress added *San Pietro* to the National Film Registry.

The Story of G.I. Joe (1945)

The Battle of San Pietro also figured in *The Story of G.I. Joe* (1945), a film inspired by the writings of Ernie Pyle (1900–1945), the war correspondent with Scripps Howard Newspapers who won national fame and a 1944 Pulitzer Prize for his coverage of the experience of the ordinary U.S. foot soldier in World War II. Always at or near the front lines, Pyle wrote ground-level accounts of the North Africa landings in late 1942, the Sicily campaign, the fighting in southern Italy, D-day, and the fighting in France. Pyle's earthy and unpretentious vignettes of frontline "dogfaces" (popular slang for WWII-era GIs) coping with homesickness and constant physical misery and danger gained great popularity among the troops and on the home front, prompting the release of two best-selling compilations: *Here Is Your War* (New York: Henry Holt, 1943) and *Brave Men* (New York: Henry Holt, 1944).

In 1944 film producer Lester Cowan approached Pyle with the idea of making a film based on people and incidents recounted in Pyle's syndicated columns. Pyle agreed to such a film on three conditions: (1) that Cowan include other real war correspondents in his movie so they could share the spotlight; (2) that the movie's focus be on the infantrymen; and (3) that it not glorify Pyle himself. Pledging to meet Pyle's criteria, Cowan hired writers Leopold Atlas, Philip Stevenson, and Guy Endore to create a script. Ironically, all three writers were Communists and never would have been allowed to work on a populist-patriotic film save for the fact that Russia was a U.S. ally at the time. Leopold Atlas had established anti-Nazi credentials by writing a 1944 film adaptation of James Gow's play about a psychopathic Hitler Youth member, *Tomorrow the World!* Philip Stevenson (aka Lars Lawrence) translated *Pobyeda*, Mikhail Ruderman's play glorifying Russian resistance to the Nazi invasion. He and John Howard Lawson (of later Hollywood Ten notoriety) then cowrote *Counter-Attack*, a screen adaptation for a 1945 film version by leftist director, Zoltan Korda. Guy Endore, a fervent Stalinist, had written *Babouk* (New York: Vanguard Press, 1934), a Depression-era radical novel about the 1791 Haitian Slave Revolt. He also wrote about the infamous Scottsboro Trial, pre-Hitler-Stalin Pact antiwar tracts, and *Song of Russia* (1943), a propaganda film exhorting Americans to support our Soviet allies against Hitler, a work later condemned by supercapitalist Ayn Rand and the House Un-American Activities Committee (HUAC) for presenting too rosy a picture of life in Russia—without considering the historical context in which it was made.

Ideologically predisposed to identify with ordinary working-class conscripts and enlistees, Atlas, Stevenson, and Endore fashioned a screenplay that eschewed the usual war movie clichés involving raucous battle sequences, combat heroics, and idealistic speechifying. In keeping with the style of Ernie Pyle's episodic dispatches, *The Story of G.I. Joe* also avoided plot. What was offered instead was Pyle's realistic vision of the typical GI: an often grimy, exhausted, fatalistic soul trudging from one bloody skirmish to the next, mainly hoping to survive the war and return home to his family. (Though unacknowledged, some of the dialogue used in the film was gleaned from Bill Mauldin's popular "Willy and Joe" cartoons.) Directed by Hollywood journeyman, William A. Wellman (*The Public Enemy; A Star Is Born*), *The Story of G.I. Joe* featured Burgess Meredith as Ernie Pyle, Robert Mitchum in his breakthrough role as Lt./Capt. Bill Walker, and a large contingent of actual war correspondents and soldiers, many of whom would soon be killed in the Pacific. Mitchum's character, Bill Walker, was loosely based on Captain Henry T. Waskow of Belton, Texas, a much beloved company commander in the 36th Division's 143rd Regiment—the very same outfit filmed by John Huston and his colleagues at the Battle of San Pietro. Sadly, Waskow was killed by a German mortar round at San Pietro on December 15, 1943. Ernie Pyle's January 10, 1944, column on Waskow's death, "Beloved Captain," became his most famous, moving, and oft-reprinted piece. Fittingly, the film ends with a dramatization of the incident. After the battle, Waskow's body is brought down a hill on a mule and laid beside a wall awaiting Graves Registration. There, one by one, Walker's men somberly view the corpse: some curse, some offer their condolences or apologies to the dead man. The film closes quietly, with the soldiers moving on to the next battle. Combat veterans who saw *The Story of G.I. Joe* pronounced the film the most authentic depiction of their experience.

They Were Expendable (1945)

Similarly realistic and elegiac is John Ford's unjustly neglected *They Were Expendable* (1945), a postwar film about Motor Torpedo Boat Squadron 3, aka RON (short for "squadron") MTB 3, a flotilla of six PT boats that participated in a losing battle to defend the Philippines against Japanese invasion (December 1941–May 1942). The source for the film was the reportage of William Lindsay White (son of William Allen White, famous author and longtime editor of the *Emporia* [KS] *Gazette*). After the fall of the Philippines W. L. White wrote *They Were Expendable* (New York: Harcourt Brace, 1942), a rousing though not entirely factual account of the exploits of RON MTB 3, primarily based on interviews with Lt. (later Vice Admiral) John D. Bulkeley, its commanding officer, and his second officer, Lt. Robert B. Kelly. By September 1944 former U.S. Navy aviator turned screenwriter Frank "Spig" Wead had completed a film script based on White's book. John Ford began shooting *They Were Expendable* off the coast of south Florida in February 1945. The film starred Robert Montgomery, a PT boat and destroyer commander in the war, as Lt. John Brickley, the character based on Lt. Bulkeley; John Wayne as Lt. (j.g.) "Rusty" Ryan, the character based on Lt. Kelly; Donna Reed as 2nd Lt. Sandy Davys, nurse and John Wayne's love interest; Jeff York as Ensign Tony Aiken, based on Ensign Anthony Akers; and Cameron Mitchell as Ensign George Cross, based on Ensign George Cox. Further contributing to authenticity was the fact that the U.S. Navy provided real PT boats and other navy veterans were involved with the film: cinematographer Joseph August, a former lt. commander, and Second Unit Director James Havens, a former navy captain. Though largely realistic, *They Were Expendable* did take a few liberties with historical accuracy. Actor Robert Barrat portrays the insufferably vain and incompetent General MacArthur in highly idealized terms consistent with MacArthur's inflated reputation at the time. Conversely, John Wayne's rendition of the Lt. Kelly character as a hotheaded maverick offended the real Lt. Kelly who joined the nurse portrayed by Donna Reed in suing MGM for defamation. The studio subsequently settled out of court for a nominal sum.

Your Job in Germany (1945)

Far different in tone was Frank Capra's *Your Job in Germany* (1945), a one-reel Signal Corps training film made just before V-E day to discourage fraternization between American occupation troops and German civilians. Written by Theodor S. Geisel (aka Dr. Seuss, 1904–1991) and narrated by the ubiquitous Dana Andrews, *Your Job* is a remarkably bitter and angry anti-German propaganda film that uses newsreel footage to characterize the German mind as "diseased" and the German people as "never [to] be trusted." Released commercially by Warner Bros. as *Hitler Lives* on December 29, 1945, the film won the 1946 Academy Award for Best Documentary, Short Subjects—a sad commentary on the political zeitgeist in 1945.

Our Job in Japan (1946)

After V-J day Theodor Geisel wrote *Our Job in Japan* (1946), a one-reel training film for U.S. occupation troops in Japan that does not display the xenophobic bile so evident in *Hitler Lives*. Instead, Geisel argues that the Japanese peoples' guileless respect for authority and tradition allowed them to be duped by a cynical ruling elite bent on aggression and cautioned that such a herd mentality must be altered before Japan can be welcomed back into the world community. Evidently General MacArthur disliked *Our Job in Japan;* it was never shown to troops.

World War II History Films of the Cold War Era

Design for Death (1947)

After his discharge from the Army Signal Corps in 1946 (as a Lt. Col.), Theodor Geisel and his first wife, Helen (Palmer) Geisel, revised *Our Job in Japan* and expanded it into *Design for Death* (1947), a three-reel documentary that uses captured Japanese newsreel, historical, and propaganda films gathered by Isaac Kleinerman (who would later work on Stanley Kubrick's second film, *Flying Padre* (1951), and the NBC-TV *Victory at Sea* series). *Design for Death* traces the history of the Japanese people from thirteenth-century feudalism to the modern era, a national saga rife with brutal repression and exploitation that helps to explain the political pliancy and conformism of the Japanese citizenry. It won its producers Sid Rogell (*Murder, My Sweet; The Devil Thumbs a Ride*), Theron

Warth (Lupe Velez's "Mexican Spitfire" films), and Richard Fleischer (Flicker Flashback comedy shorts) a 1948 Oscar for Best Feature Documentary.

Battleground (1949)

Made just a few years after the war, William A. Wellman's *Battleground* (1949) takes its place beside his *Story of G.I. Joe* as another unusually authentic depiction of the ordinary combat soldier's experience—despite the fact that it was shot entirely on an MGM soundstage in Culver City, California. Modest in scale, *Battleground* focuses on a squad of soldiers with the 101st Airborne Division, surrounded by superior German forces at Bastogne during the Battle of the Bulge and literally fighting for survival. Though the squad, led by Sgt. Kinnie (James Whitmore), is entirely fictional, the incidents depicted actually occurred. Screenwriter Robert Pirosh (creator of *Combat*, the 1960s TV series), a trooper with the 101st at Bastogne, relied on his recent memories to create a convincing scenario that conveys the somber landscape, full of fog and snow; the bitter cold; and the intense psychological stress experienced by the besieged but ultimately successful defenders of Bastogne. Nominated for six Academy Awards in 1950, *Battleground* won Paul Vogel an Oscar for Best Black-and-White Cinematography and Robert Pirosh an Oscar for Best Writing. Pirosh also won Golden Globe and Writers Guild of America awards.

The Wooden Horse (1950)

The first postwar British film on a World War II subject was Jack Lee's *The Wooden Horse* (1950), a film written by former RAF bomber pilot Eric E. Williams (1911–1983), later published in book form as *The Tunnel* (New York: Coward-McCann, 1952). In late 1942 Flight Lieutenant Williams was shot down over Germany, captured, and later imprisoned in the East Compound of Stalag Luft III, a newly established POW camp for Allied aviators near Sagan, Germany (present-day Zagan, Poland), 100 miles southeast of Berlin. Williams contrived to escape from the camp by digging a tunnel but the prisoners' huts were too far from the perimeter fences so he came up with an audacious idea inspired by the Trojan Horse: build an enclosed wooden vaulting horse for daily exercise, place it every morning 30 meters from the wire, hide a man inside it, and proceed to use it as cover to dig an escape tunnel. Starting in early July 1943, Williams and two compatriots—Michael Codner and Oliver Philpot—dug for 114 days until their tunnel reached just beyond the outside fence. They escaped on October 29.

Wearing imitation civilian clothes and carrying false identity papers, the three made their way by train to the North Sea port of Lübeck, where a Danish resistance worker smuggled them to Copenhagen by boat. The trio later reached neutral Sweden by boat and eventually repatriated to Britain. In keeping with characteristic British reticence, Jack Lee and producer Ian Dalrymple shot *The Wooden Horse* in an understated, quasi-documentary style. Likewise, Leo Genn, David Tomlinson, and Anthony Steel play "Peter" (Williams), "Phil" (Philpot), and "John" (Codner) not as archetypal war heroes but as weary and frightened human beings with strengths and failings. Involving very little violent action, *The Wooden Horse* showcases ingenuity, tenacity, and teamwork as the sorts of traits that lead to nearly miraculous results.

The Desert Fox: The Story of Rommel (1951)

Released six years after the rabidly anti-German *Your Job in Germany/Hitler Lives*, Henry Hathaway's *The Desert Fox: The Story of Rommel* (1951) is a highly sympathetic biopic of the exemplary "good German": Field Marshall Erwin Rommel (1891–1944) of Afrika Korps fame. Forced to commit suicide for having joined in the failed plot against Hitler (July 20, 1944), Rommel (James Mason in the film) was a legendary figure to Germans and their Allied adversaries for his brilliance as a military tactician and for his irreproachable reputation as an honorable, even chivalric soldier, good to his own men and humane in his treatment of prisoners of war. At the height of the Cold War in 1950, British Brigadier Desmond Young's biography, *Rommel* (New York: Collins, 1950), both verified and consecrated Rommel's heroic image and prompted Nunnally Johnson (1897–1977; *The Grapes of Wrath; The Moon Is Down*), a powerful screenwriter-producer with 20th Century Fox, to write and produce an adaptation of Young's book. Though the career of a German general may seem a strange topic for Hollywood, *The Desert Fox* concentrated on Rommel's opposition to Hitler in the last two years of his life: a narrative focus that made Erwin Rommel a palatable hero for Anglo-American audiences. The film also met U.S. ideological requirements in the early 1950s by affirming the sanity and competence of the professional soldier in stark contrast to dangerously erratic civilian leadership: an unsurprising attitude when the military was at the height of its prestige as an American institution. Furthermore, *The Desert Fox* bolstered relations with a newly remilitarized West Germany vital to NATO as the first line of defense against Russia and her Eastern European satellites—indeed the same sort of anti-Soviet stance held by Rommel, who saw Communist Russia as a dire threat to civilization. In sum, Hollywood refashioned Rommel into something of a Cold War icon.

General Erwin Rommel in Libya with the 15th Panzer Division between Tobruk and Sidi Omar. Rommel and the 15th Panzer Division were sent to Libya in early 1941 to aid the defeated Italian troops. (National Archives)

Victory at Sea (1952–1953)

Another major product of the emerging American Cold War temperament was Henry Salomon's *Victory at Sea* (1952–1953), of enduring historic significance as the first television documentary series, a media form that would be widely imitated in the years that followed. During the war the U.S. Navy assigned Salomon to work as researcher for Samuel Eliot Morison (1887–1976), the distinguished Harvard history professor appointed by FDR in 1942 to write the official *History of the United States Naval Operations in World War II* (Little, Brown; 15 volumes, 1947–1962). In the course of his work for Morison, Salomon learned that the Allied and Axis navies had accumulated vast amounts of documentary footage and concluded that a complete filmic record of the war at sea was entirely feasible, though a formidable undertaking. When Salomon left the navy in 1948 he discussed the idea with his former Harvard roommate, Robert W. Sarnoff (1918–1997), the son of David Sarnoff, the head of RCA, NBC's parent company. When Robert Sarnoff took over NBC's new film division in 1951, he secured $500,000 in funding from his father for the proposed project and hired Salomon to produce it. Salomon secured the full cooperation of the U.S. Navy and pulled together a staff of veteran newsreel editors who spent much of the next year scouring ten countries for film footage. Salomon's project team eventually collected an astounding 60 million linear feet (i.e., 11,300 miles or 11,700 hours) of film footage, which had to be edited down to a mere 62,000 feet or 728 minutes' worth (i.e., twenty-six 28-minute programs). From raw footage to finished product, this represented an editing ratio of close to 1,000 to 1. Switching between the Atlantic and Pacific theaters of war, *Victory at Sea* dealt with campaigns (e.g., antisubmarine warfare, the liberation of the Philippines) and specific engagements (e.g., Pearl Harbor, Midway, Gaudalcanal). Using only archival footage, somewhat pompous voice-over narration by Leonard Graves, and a suitably bombastic musical score written by Richard Rogers, each *Victory at Sea* episode followed the same pyramidal narrative trajectory: it traced the action leading up to a battle, the battle itself, and the aftermath. Aired in half-hour segments on Sunday afternoons from late October 1952 to early May 1953, *Victory at Sea* proved to be a stunning success. In the midst of the frustrating and unpopular Korean War, the nation was given a chance to relive the supposedly unambiguous glory of World War II.

The Dam Busters (1954)

The typically less demonstrative style of the British in matters of nationalistic self-congratulation is once again manifest in Michael Anderson's *The Dam Busters* (1954). A film based on Wing Commander Guy Gibson's book, *Enemy Coast Ahead* (London: M. Joseph, 1946) and Paul Brickhill's *The Dam Busters* (London: Evans Bros., 1951), *The Dam Busters* recounts the planning and execution of Operation Chastise, a daring and unorthodox bombing raid on three Ruhr Valley dams. On the moonlit night of May 16/17, 1943, nineteen Lancasters of No. 617 Squadron under Gibson's command took off from RAF Scampton (Lincolnshire) to attack the Möhne, Eder, and Sorpe dams in the heart of Germany's industrial region. Each specially modified Lancaster was carrying a 9,000-pound cylindrical "bouncing bomb" (code-named "Upkeep") designed to skip on the surface of the water to avoid antitorpedo netting, then sink against the dam wall, explode, and breach the dam.

The man who conceived the raid and perfected the Upkeep mine was Dr. Barnes Neville Wallis (1887–1979), a brilliant scientist, engineer, and inventor employed by Vickers Aircraft. In 1940 Wallis (Michael Redgrave in the film) had broached the idea that the destruction of the major dams in the Ruhr would bring the vital German steelmaking industry to a standstill and perhaps shorten, even end, the war. Given the sheer massiveness of the targets, conventional high-altitude bombing techniques were simply not accurate enough to work. So Wallis began experimenting with the physics of skipping a sphere-shaped device over water that would detonate up against its target. The amount of high explosive needed, the correct backspin speed of the bomb, the speed and height of the airplane (just 60 feet above the water at 232 mph, as it turned out), the ideal distance from target (i.e., 400 to 450 yards), and so on: all these variables had to be calibrated by a long and painstaking process of experimentation with prototypes, models, and mock-ups. Barnes Wallis also had to convince skeptical officials that his seemingly crazy scheme would work and that precious resources in money, personnel, and materiel be devoted to it. Though fraught by almost insurmountable technical problems and bureaucratic resistance, Wallis and his team eventually prevailed.

The Dam Busters devotes the first third of its running time to telling the absorbing scientific story summarized above. The second third of the film dramatizes Guy Gibson's (Richard Todd) recruitment and training of the elite bomber squadron that would deliver the bombs to their respective targets. After all the deliberate and exhaustive preparation, the film's culminating bombing mission sequence provides the intense action necessary to lift *The Dam Busters* from a procedural narrative to a stirring war film. Flying dangerously low into a barrage of antiaircraft tracer bullets, Gibson's bombers succeed in breaching the Möhne and Eder dams and damaging the Sorpe Dam, causing extensive flooding in the Ruhr Valley, disrupting German industry for months, and scoring a major propaganda coup, much in the manner of the Doolittle raid on Japan. The cost was high, however. Of the nineteen bombers deployed, eight were shot down (a loss rate of 42 percent) and fifty-three of their fifty-six crewmen were killed—deaths that weighed heavily on the conscience of Barnes Wallis and lent the film a poignancy that is often lacking in the war film genre.

Released during the second tenure of Winston Churchill—having been deposed in 1945 by Labour's Clement Atlee, Churchill was restored to power by the 1951 election—*The Dam Busters* reflects the conservative Cold War politics of that time. Though the actual Dam Busters raid involved hundreds of people—technicians, ground crew, ordinary workers, and military personnel—the film keeps its elitist focus mostly on Barnes Wallis and Guy Gibson, as if the mission was their personal accomplishment. Furthermore, *The Dam Busters* offers an idealized characterization of Gibson as a lonely, stern warrior, too serious for normal fraternization with his comrades. In point of fact, Guy Penrose Gibson (1918–1944), though enormously courageous and a great pilot, was arrogantly class conscious: a stance that made him widely reviled by his fellow airmen. The U.S. release of the film also needed to alter an important detail. The real Gibson had a pet black Labrador retriever he called "Nigger" and used the word to radio in code that the raid had been successful. A deeply offensive racial epithet in the United States, the word was changed to "Trigger" to avoid controversy.

To Hell and Back (1955)

Every war needs its archetypal hero. For America, World War I had Alvin York. World War II had Audie Leon Murphy (1924–1971). The orphaned son of poor white Texas sharecroppers—a humble country background not unlike York's— Audie Murphy was America's most decorated soldier in the Second World War. Fighting in nine major campaigns in Europe, Murphy is credited with killing some 240 enemy soldiers and wounding or capturing many others. Wounded three times, Murphy rose from private to 2nd lieutenant and was awarded a total of thirty-three decorations for valor including the Medal of Honor and five military awards from Belgium and France. When Murphy was featured on the cover of *Life* magazine (July 16, 1945), he became an instant national legend. After his discharge from the service in September 1945, Audie Murphy ventured to Hollywood at the invitation of actor James Cagney. Despite his notoriety Murphy initially struggled to find work in the film industry but eventually signed a long-term actor's contract with Universal Pictures in 1949 and went on to make forty-six films, mostly Westerns, until his death in a plane crash in 1971.

Murphy's most famous film was Jesse Hibbs' *To Hell and Back* (1955) in which Murphy, playing himself, reprised his extraordinary combat exploits in the war. Based on his eponymous memoir (New York: Henry Holt, 1949), *To Hell and Back* traced Murphy's dirt-poor youth in northwestern Texas; his struggle to support his eleven siblings after the death of his parents; his enlistment in the army in June 1942 at age seventeen; and his grueling tours of duty in Sicily, Italy, France, and Germany, during which he continually distinguished himself as a combat soldier and became a legend among his comrades in the 3rd Infantry Division. The film culminates with a filmic re-creation of an engagement near Holtzwhir, France, that won Murphy the Medal of Honor. Climbing atop an abandoned and burning U.S. tank destroyer, which threatened to blow up any second, Murphy manned its .50-caliber machine gun, and though wounded, felled dozens of advancing German infantrymen, thus single-handedly foiling an attack that might have engulfed and destroyed his entire company. Supported by sturdy character actors—Marshall Thompson, David Janssen, Denver Pyle— playing cheerful, wisecracking soldiers, the amiable and photogenic Audie Murphy delivered a credible but essentially one-dimensional performance. A movie perfectly attuned to the patriotic Cold War consensus of the 1950s, *To Hell and Back* was a huge box office success for Universal that was not surpassed until the *Jaws* phenomenon twenty years later. The film's semiofficial status as pro-American propaganda is manifest from its introduction, delivered on camera by Undersecretary of State General Walter Bedell Smith (1895–1961), Eisenhower's former chief of staff during the war and a recent director of the CIA (1951–1953).

What the film did *not* show was the grimy, dreary life of the foot soldier (recounted in *The Story of G.I. Joe* and *Battleground*); the gore of combat (as seen in the original version of *San Pietro*); or war's lasting psychological damage, exemplified by Murphy himself. Admiring moviegoers had no idea that the handsome and smiling Audie Murphy privately suffered severe symptoms of what is now known as post-traumatic stress disorder (PTSD). Haunted by his combat experiences, Murphy struggled with chronic insomnia and recurring nightmares and in the immediate postwar years he slept (or tried to sleep) with a loaded .45 under his pillow. Inchoate anxiety destroyed his first marriage to movie actress Wanda Hendrix and manifested in other forms of dysfunction. Murphy remained tense and restless and battled alcoholism, depression, and a gambling addiction the rest of his life. *To Hell and Back* buries these darker truths in order to present a sanitized vision of martial glory without its concomitant costs: ideological myopia very much in keeping with the repressive cultural climate of the 1950s.

The Court-Martial of Billy Mitchell (1955)

Somewhat more subversive is Otto Preminger's *The Court-Martial of Billy Mitchell* (1955), ostensibly an admonitory docudrama about military preparedness that, on closer inspection, looks more like an allegory about the political persecution of visionary nonconformists by hidebound ideologues and bureaucratic timeservers. Brigadier General William "Billy" Mitchell (1879–1936), aviator and commander of the U.S. Army Air Corps in World War I, was a fervent advocate of a vastly expanded, independent, and strategic air arm after the war— a view that contradicted the received wisdom that airpower should serve as mere tactical support for ground troops. In September 1925, after the accidental loss of a navy seaplane and the navy dirigible *Shenandoah,* the always outspoken Mitchell fired off a scathing 6,000-word statement to the press that lambasted the navy and War Department for administrative incompetence and "almost treasonable negligence" in their handling of aeronautical matters. The government countered by arresting Mitchell and charging him with insubordination under the catchall 96th Article of War. His court-martial before a dozen senior officers (none of whom was a flier) began on October 28, 1925, and ended just before Christmas of that year. After a brief period of deliberation, the military court convicted Mitchell of insubordination and sentenced him to a five-year suspension of rank, command, and duty with forfeiture of pay and allowances. Rather than submit to his punishment, Mitchell promptly resigned but continued to agitate for a strong air force until his death in 1936. Among other things, Mitchell predicted that the Japanese would launch a surprise air attack on Pearl Harbor.

The movie version of Billy Mitchell's court-martial had its genesis in an eponymous play by Emmet G. Lavery (1902–1986), a lawyer turned playwright and screenwriter who was especially interested in historical figures subject to public censure for their beliefs (during the Red Scare, studio mogul Louis B. Mayer fired Lavery for alleged Communist sympathies). Crucial to the tone of the film is Preminger's casting of Gary Cooper as General Mitchell. Unlike the tall, laconic Cooper, the real Billy Mitchell was short, brash, and nasty-tempered and his family thought that James Cagney would have been far more appropriate in the role. Yet Preminger wisely chose Cooper for the ideological baggage associated with his well-established star persona. As Sergeant York, Lou Gehrig in *Pride of the Yankees*, Robert Jordan in *For Whom the Bell Tolls*, Howard Roark in *The Fountainhead*, Marshal Will Kane in *High Noon*, and many other roles, Gary Cooper came to embody the stoical integrity of the old-fashioned individualist Western hero, short on words but long on character. In that respect he better fit the film's implicit agenda, which was to indict the mean-spirited conformism that sought out and destroyed the recalcitrant outsider. Released a year and a half after Joe McCarthy's downfall during the nationally televised Army-McCarthy hearings, *The Court-Martial of Billy Mitchell* reminded its audience that adhering to one's beliefs, though not always easy, was an honorable and courageous thing to do.

Nuit et brouillard (Night and Fog) (1955)

While *To Hell and Back* and *The Court-Martial of Billy Mitchell* celebrate the quintessential American virtue of strong individual agency, Alain Resnais' contemporaneous *Nuit et brouillard* (*Night and Fog*) (1955) in more typically French fashion broods over the absolute victimization of the powerless. Asked to make a documentary about the Holocaust, Resnais initially refused until his friend, the writer Jean Cayrol, agreed to compose the voice-over narration. Cayrol and his brother, both members of the Maquis (French Resistance), were arrested by the Gestapo in June 1942 and sent to Mauthausen Concentration Camp, near Linz, Austria (Hitler's birthplace). Cayrol's brother died there. Cayrol survived but was profoundly scarred by what he had endured and witnessed—even to the point of suffering amnesia. After the war, he published two books of poetry that grappled with the netherworld of the camps and the paralyzing sense of life's meaninglessness that he experienced after liberation: *Poemes de la nuit et du brouillard* (*Poems of Night and Fog*) (1946) and *Passe-temps de l'homme et des oiseaux* (*Pastimes of the Man and the Birds*) (1947). Resnais' film obviously takes its title from the first of these volumes. In turn, the phrase "night and fog" ("Nacht und Nebel") refers to a 1941 order by Hitler that called for the secret deportation, imprisonment, and/or extermination of those suspected of anti-German activities. Hence, the title of the film is literal but also richly figurative, referring (1) to the bewilderment of the victims as to their whereabouts and eventual fate and (2) to the collective forgetting that envelops any historical event, even the most cataclysmic. As time passes eyewitnesses die off, and the once-lived reality becomes more and more abstract: "history" in the worst sense. The title also resonates with connotations of nightmare.

Faced with the near-impossible task of making a short documentary that would somehow do justice to the horrifying evils of Hitler's death camps, Resnais and Cayrol managed to fashion a cinematic masterpiece that gradually overwhelms through an accretion of haunting images and plainspoken, almost banal description. The overall structure that Resnais employs is brilliant in its simplicity. He oscillates between eleven segments of recently shot color footage of the long-abandoned sites of Auschwitz and Majdanek and an equal number of black-and-white archival segments that show the camps right after they were liberated. Of much longer duration, the black-and-white archival segments comprise about 80 percent of the film (that is, 25 minutes of its 32-minute running time). Yet the color footage of the deserted camps is equally crucial to the psychological and aesthetic effect of the film. Or better said, the *interaction* between these two kinds of filmic representation and the two kinds of time they embody—the bucolic present, absent of horror, and the hellish past, full of it—make for a dialectical montage of stunning power—a visual style fully exploited by Claude Lanzmann with his 9-and-a-half-hour Holocaust documentary, *Shoah* (1985). The film ends with footage of the camps being liberated and several Germans in court, who declare, "I am not responsible." After a final shot of a mountain of naked, emaciated corpses, the film counters with a hard question: "Then who is responsible?" Over closing shots of the camp ruins, the voice-over narration suggests the most chilling of possibilities: if it could happen once, it could happen again. The precedent has been set. A moral and psychological boundary has been breeched that can never be fully repaired, as the film continues: "And there are those of us who sincerely look upon the ruins today, as if the concentration camp monster were dead and buried beneath them. Those who pretend to take hope as the image fades, as though there were a cure for the plague of the camps. Those of us who pretend to believe that all this happened only once, at a certain time and a certain place, and those who refuse to see, who do not hear the cry to the end of time."

British World War II Exploits in Film

From the mid-1950s to the early 1960s, a spate of film releases appeared that were concerned with British exploits in World War II: *The Colditz Story* (1955), *The Battle of the River Plate* [U.S. title: *Pursuit of the Graf Spee*] (1956), *The Man Who Never Was* (1956), *The Bridge on the River Kwai* (1957), *I Was Monty's Double* and *Dunkirk* (both 1958), and *Sink the Bismark!* (1960). Mostly British but sometimes joint Anglo-American productions, all these war films are in the more genteel British tradition of the war film genre, that is, less overt action, more drama, suspense, and an emphasis on ingenuity, military professionalism, courage, and perseverance much in the manner of *The Wooden Horse* and *The Dam Busters* of a few years earlier. With the British struggling with postwar shortages and the once-vaunted British Empire defunct, these films demure from the triumphalism of their American counterparts and stick to modest celebrations of British character that addressed the difficulties of the 1950s.

The Colditz Story (1955)

Guy Hamilton's *The Colditz Story* (1955), another prime example of the British war drama, was based on Major Patrick "P. R." Reid's popular book of the same title (London: Hodder and Stoughton, 1952). In 1941 the German High Command made Schloss Colditz, an eleventh-century castle on top of a cliff in Saxony, into a *Sonderlager*, that is, a maximum-security prison for Allied POWs who had escaped from other facilities at least once. Though Reichmarschall Hermann Göring declared Colditz Castle (Oflag IVC) *flucht-beweis* (escape proof), its international assemblage of escape-prone prisoners made 300 such attempts during the war that resulted in 120 "gone aways" (escapees who managed to break out of the castle but were recaptured) and 31 "home runs" (escapees who made it all the way home). In his book Reid, himself a Colditz escapee, detailed some of the most remarkable of these attempts while also painting a seriocomic picture of daily life at Colditz, the colorful personalities involved, and the friendly rivalries that developed between POWs of various nationalities. The film, starring John Mills as Reid and Eric Portman as Colonel Richmond, is faithful to its source material and, though low-key in the British style, absorbing. The Colditz saga has continued to fascinate. A dozen other books on Colditz have since supplemented Reid's book and more Colditz media projects have appeared since the mid-1950s. These include *Colditz,* a successful BBC television docudrama series (1972–1974); *Nazi Prison Escape,* a PBS-TV *Nova* documentary program (2001); *Escape From Colditz,* a BBC-TV Channel 4 documentary (2001); and even "Escape From Colditz," a 1970 Parker Bros. board game.

The Battle of the River Plate (1956)

Written, directed, and produced by visionary filmmakers Michael Powell and Emeric Pressburger (*The Red Shoes; Black Narcissus; Peeping Tom*), *The Battle of the River Plate* recounts the saga of the German pocket battleship *Admiral Graf Spee,* a surface raider that sank nine cargo ships before being engaged by Allied cruisers *Ajax, Exeter,* and *Achilles* off the coast of Montevideo, Uruguay, in mid-December 1939. Damaged in the fight (as were her opponents), the *Graf Spee* sailed into neutral Montevideo Harbor to make repairs. When the *Graf Spee*'s Captain Hans Langsdorf (Peter Finch in the film) discovers that repairs will not be completed in the required 72 hours, he has his crew evacuated to Argentina and the ship scuttled before the Uraguayans can seize it or the British finish it off. Then, like Rommel, Langsdorf commits an honorable suicide. In keeping with the respectful, even conciliatory spirit of *The Desert Fox, The Battle of the River Plate* downplays the horrors of combat while foregrounding tactical thinking, waiting, and strategizing. Powell and Pressburger accurately depict Captain Langsdorf as a chivalric officer of the old school who always removes enemy sailors to safety before sinking their ships. Honorable warriors on both sides are shown doing nothing more or less than their duty: a somewhat selective, even sentimental, view of a war that soon became totalistic and genocidal.

The Man Who Never Was (1956)

More narrowly focused on exemplary British resourcefulness is Ronald Neame's *The Man Who Never Was* (1956), a 20th Century Fox adaptation of Ewen Montagu's book of the same title (Philadelphia: J. B. Lippincott, 1954). Prior to the Allied invasion of Sicily in the summer of 1943, Sir Archibald Cholmindley, a senior officer in British Intelligence, hatched a unique plan to fool the Germans into thinking that the northern coast of Sicily was targeted for invasion when, in fact, the invasion site was on the southern coast. Montagu's scheme, dubbed Operation Mincemeat, was slightly macabre but quite brilliant: take the corpse of some anonymous soul, fabricate an identity for him as Major William Martin, a Royal

Marine courier, plant misleading documents on the body, and float it to shore off the Iberian coast where it is sure to be discovered by the Abwehr (German military intelligence). The plan, executed in detail by Lieutenant Commander Ewen Montagu of British Naval Intelligence, did, indeed, work. The Germans found the body, examined the documents, concluded they were genuine, and accordingly stripped forces from southern to northern Sicily, thus making the Allied invasion far less costly.

Neame's film version gets this story fundamentally right but also muddies the waters in several ways. Clifton Webb plays Ewen Montagu: an odd casting choice inasmuch as Webb was a sixty-six-year-old American playing a forty-two-year-old Englishman. The film also adds two fanciful subplots to increase drama and suspense. One subplot involves aging film noir actress Gloria Grahame as Lucy Sherwood, the roommate of Montagu's beautiful assistant, Pam (Josephine Griffin), and the other subplot involves Stephen Boyd as Patrick O'Reilly, an anti-British Irish national doing the Germans' bidding by trying to determine if Major Martin is real or a hoax. The subplots add something to the dramaturgy but detract from the film's historical accuracy. A final note: in 1995 writer Roger Morgan claimed to have discovered the identity of the corpse who unwittingly played Major Martin: a forty-three-year-old alcoholic from Wales named Glyndwr Michael who died of chemical pneumonia after ingesting rat poison.

The Bridge on the River Kwai (1957)

A decidedly more ambiguous take on British grit and ingenuity is presented in David Lean's epic film, *The Bridge on the River Kwai* (1957). Adapted for the screen by Lean and blacklisted writers Carl Foreman and Michael Wilson, Pierre Boulle's novel, *Le Pont de la rivière Kwai* (Paris: Rene Julliard, 1952; English translation, London: Secker & Warburg, 1954), is a mostly fictional story superimposed on a factual setting. A prisoner of war of the Japanese in Indochina from 1942 to 1944, Boulle (who later wrote *Planet of the Apes*) was well acquainted with the hideous cruelties the Japanese military visited on its war captives. Boulle's story takes place in Burma (present-day Myanmar) in 1943. The Japanese are building the Thai-Burma Railway, the so-called Death Railway, a 429-kilometer (267-mile) line of narrow-gauge track through thick jungle from Bangkok to Rangoon to transport supplies and troops. The actual project that forms the backdrop of the novel took eighteen months and relied on the slave labor of a quarter million starving, disease-ridden prisoners of war—mostly Asian but also British, Dutch, Australian, and American—working twelve hours a day, seven days a week in sweltering heat and monsoon rains. Conditions were so atrocious that, by the time the railway was completed on October 16, 1943, 94,000 prisoners had died: a death rate higher than Andersonville.

Boulle's novel focuses on just one aspect of this exceedingly grim endeavor: the building of a 600-foot-long wooden railroad bridge over the River Kwai. His fictional protagonist, Colonel Nicholson, is a spit-and-polish martinet who engages in a war of nerves and wits with the Japanese labor camp commandant, Colonel Saito, a sadist with an inferiority complex. Knowing he must keep his men occupied to preserve their tenuous hold on sanity, Nicholson approaches the design and building of the bridge as a means to ward off despair and demonstrate superior British tenacity, industriousness, and honor. Indeed, Nicholson becomes so fixated on the task that he loses sight of the obvious problem with such a coping strategy: it abets the Japanese war effort by building them an excellent bridge, which the Allies will need to destroy. In short, *Le Pont de la rivière Kwai* allegorizes the self-defeating absurdity of war and satirizes the rigid cultural codes and rituals of East and West that fuel such protracted and grueling exercises in futility. More specifically Boulle's depiction of Nicholson was meant to evoke the actions of Vichy collaborationists after the fall of France in 1940. The fact that Boulle's collaborationist is British helps to mask the political allegory and also suggests that anyone is capable of such behavior. Perhaps having borrowed his central motif of the bridge—a resonant metaphor for Meaning spanning Nothingness—from Ernest Hemingway's *For Whom the Bell Tolls*, Boulle also follows Hemingway by dramatizing the contradictory human impulses expressed in the bridge's construction and attempted destruction (in the novel the British commandos fail to blow up the bridge).

To make it properly cinematic, David Lean and his screenwriters wrote and rewrote the script to tighten the slack pacing of Boulle's novel, flesh out his somewhat thinly drawn characters, and underscore the clash of wills between Nicholson (Alec Guinness) and Saito (Sessue Hayakawa). The film also invents Major Shears (William Holden), an opportunistic and cynical American (not unlike Holden's Joe Gillis in *Sunset Boulevard* or George Segal in *King Rat*) who serves as a dramatic foil to his stiff-necked counterparts and contrasts American pragmatism with the inflexible probity of older, more hierarchical civilizations. Lean and his cohorts also changed Boulle's ending and had the bridge destroyed, which entailed building a full-sized bridge in Ceylon (now Sri Lanka) and blowing it up while a real train was passing over it. Shot while trying to prevent the bridge's detonation, Colonel Nicholson falls on the detonator and inadvertently destroys his beloved bridge: a rather far-fetched outcome designed to achieve maximum irony.

While the film veers away from the book, both works veer away from the history. In point of fact, there were a total of nine bridges built across the Kwai Noi River. The bridge on which Boulle modeled his was probably one of two bridges at Makhan, Thailand (one wooden and one made of steel and concrete), that were completed in May 1943 by British and Dutch POWs under the command of Lt. Col. Philip John Denton Toosey (1904–1975). Nicholson's real-life counterpart, Toosey was no traitor but rather a hero who did everything possible to sabotage the bridges under construction and to protect his men from the Japanese. Indeed, only nine of Toosey's men died, a remarkably low number compared to the slaughter on the railway as a whole. In the film Major Shears leads a British commando team to the site. Having escaped from the camp, Shears could have remained in rear echelon comfort but—perversely inspired by Nicholson's fanaticism—dutifully returns and helps to take out the bridge. In reality, the British bombed both bridges at Makhan from the air in 1945: satisfying closure but not sufficiently dramatic in filmic terms.

I Was Monty's Double (1958)

Myrick E. Clifton-James (1898–1963) was an Australian-born English actor and a lieutenant in the British Pay-Corps who happened to do an uncanny impersonation of Field Marshall Bernard Law "Monty" Montgomery (1887–1976). During the planning of the Allied invasion of Europe in early 1944, a British Intelligence officer caught Clifton-James's "Monty" impression at a London theater and hatched a scheme to fool the Germans into thinking that the imminent invasion would be launched from North Africa instead of Britain. Posing as Monty, Clifton-James did indeed hoodwink the Germans into diverting forces from the Normandy area. Some years after the war he published an account of his adventure entitled *I Was Monty's Double* (London: Rider & Co., 1954) and later starred in *I Was Monty's Double* (aka *Hell, Heaven, or Hoboken*) (1958), a film version directed by John Guillermin that amusingly contrasts Clifton-James's consummate ordinariness with the extraordinary role he is called on to play.

Dunkirk (1958)

Among the last films made at West London's original Ealing Studios (1938–1957) was Leslie Norman's *Dunkirk* (1958), a docudrama about the naval evacuation of 338,000 Allied troops trapped on the French coast after the German army overran France and the Low Countries in May 1940. Adapted to the screen by

David Divine and W. P. Lipscomb from two sources—*Keep the Memory Green*, by British Expeditionary Force (BEF) evacuees Maj. J. Selby Bradford and Lt. Col. Ewan Butler (London: Hutchinson & Co., 1950) and *The Big Pick-Up*, a novel by Elleston Trevor (London: Heinemann, 1955)—*Dunkirk* superimposes Trevor's fictional narrative onto Bradford and Butler's historical account to give the Dunkirk story a human perspective. The foreground story, which comprises the bulk of the film, concerns British corporal "Tubby" Bins (John Mills) who must lead his squad to the coast to be rescued by the *Heron*, a small boat captained by John Holden (Richard Attenborough) that is part of the motley fleet of 700 vessels that rescued the defeated Allied armies. With typical British pluck, *Dunkirk* focuses on the redemptive elements of a great defeat.

Sink the Bismarck! (1960)

Almost nineteen years after the sinking of the German battleship *Bismarck*, 20th Century Fox released Lewis Gilbert's *Sink the Bismarck!* (1960), adapted to the screen by Edmund H. North (*Patton*) from C. S. Forester's *The Last Nine Days of the Bismarck* (Boston: Little, Brown, 1959). Heading an international cast is Kenneth More who plays the fictional Captain Jonathan Shepard, a troubled, emotionally reserved British naval officer brought in to run the Admiralty's Naval War Room at Whitehall just as the *Bismarck* is unleashed on the Atlantic to disrupt vital British shipping. True to the historical facts, salvos from the *Bismarck* destroy the battleship HMS *Hood* and badly damage the HMS *Prince of Wales* in the Battle of Denmark Strait on May 24, 1941. Two days later fifteen obsolete Swordfish biplane bombers from the British aircraft carrier *Ark Royal* attack the *Bismarck* with torpedoes, two or three of which find their mark, jamming both of the ship's rudders at a 12-degree angle to port. (Ironically, the ancient Swordfish were too *slow* for the *Bismarck*'s antiaircraft guns to properly target.) Now only capable of cruising in wide circles, the *Bismarck* is doomed. On May 27, 1941, HMS *King George V* and accompanying warships engage the crippled *Bismarck*. In a battle that lasts two hours they send her to the bottom with the loss of most of her crew. While *Sink the Bismarck!* accurately depicts the salient historical facts, it also engages in some distortions for heightened dramatic effect. For example, besides sinking the *Hood*, the *Bismarck* is shown sinking a British destroyer and downing two British aircraft—events that never occurred. Furthermore, the film portrays German Admiral Gunter Lütjens (Karel Stepanek) as an intemperate, glory-seeking Nazi fanatic and his subordinate, Captain Lindemann (Carl Möhner), as a somewhat passive lackey—exaggerated, stereotyped characterizations meant to stress the all-important distinction between the Nazi ideologue and the honorable military professional (cf. *The Desert Fox*). The film also avoids showing the terrible carnage aboard the disabled *Bismarck* as it is blown to pieces at close range or the Royal Navy's reluctance to save survivors; these painful truths would have dulled the glory of victory.

Films of Wartime Events

Hell to Eternity (1960)

On the American side of the ledger, the story of Guy "Gabby" Gabaldon (1926–) is a remarkable one and should be better known, as should the film based on it: Phil Karlson's *Hell to Eternity* (1960). A Chicano boy from the tough Boyle Heights section of East Los Angeles, Gabaldon was orphaned at an early age and subsequently raised by a Japanese American (Nisei) family. Already fluent in Spanish and English, Gabaldon learned Japanese from his foster family. After Pearl Harbor, Gabaldon's foster parents and sister, like most other West Coast Nisei, spent the war years in internment camps while he and his two Nisei foster brothers were allowed to enlist in the service. In 1943 Gabaldon, age seventeen, joined the Marine Corps and his fluency in Japanese got him attached to an intelligence unit. The following year Gabaldon was part of a three-division amphibious landing force numbering more than 50,000 men that invaded the Japanese-held island of Saipan in the Marianas on June 15, 1944. The Japanese garrison fought with its usual fanatical zeal and the Battle of Saipan raged for more than three weeks before U.S. officials declared the island more or less secured on July 9. American casualties numbered over 16,000 (3,225 killed; 13,061 wounded) while almost 24,000 Japanese soldiers were killed. Despite its high cost, Saipan was a major strategic victory for America, finally providing an air base location within striking distance of mainland Japan 1,200 miles to the northwest.

Because of his fluency in Japanese, PFC Guy Gabaldon was able to play a major, if highly unorthodox, role in the closing stages of the battle. On his own initiative, Gabaldon repeatedly approached the enemy hiding in caves and single-handedly talked more than 1,500 Japanese soldiers and civilians into surrender, saving their lives and the lives of hundreds of American soldiers. On July 8, 1944, he managed to round up an astonishing 800 prisoners and earned the moniker "The Pied Piper of Saipan." Though his superiors recommended him for the Congressional Medal of Honor, the Marine Corps awarded him only a Silver Star— perhaps because his actions were directed at pacifying enemy soldiers rather than killing them. That he was a dark-skinned Mexican American raised by Nisei also factored against him.

Despite Guy Gabaldon's personal involvement with *Hell to Eternity* as a technical advisor, his depiction in the film tended to reiterate the prejudice directed against him by the U.S. military. Bowing to commercial pressures and unspoken cultural dictates, the filmmakers cast Hollywood pretty boy Jeffrey Hunter as Gabaldon. A tall, blond-haired, blue-eyed Adonis, Hunter looked nothing at all like Gabaldon, who was small of stature, dark-haired, and swarthy (Sal Mineo would have been a much better fit). The film also took gross liberties with the historical facts. To provide the movie Gabaldon with suitably heroic motivation to capture hundreds of Japanese, writers Gil Doud (*To Hell and Back*), Ted Sherdeman (*The McConnell Story*), and Walter Roeber Schmidt provided Gabaldon with a beloved sidekick named Bill (David Janssen), whose death at the hands of the enemy sets Gabaldon on a frenzied war path quite unlike the deliberate and calculated one-man campaign waged by the real man. Though it was hardly a faithful representation of Private Gabaldon's actions on Saipan, *Hell to Eternity* did generate enough renewed interest to prompt the Marine Corps to promote Gabaldon's Silver Star to the more prestigious Navy Cross. In 1990 Gabaldon self-published an account of his military adventures—*Saipan: Suicide Island, A True Story*—and since then efforts have been afoot to persuade the U.S. Congress to grant him the Medal of Honor.

The Diary of Anne Frank (1960)

A German Jewish girl named Annalise "Anne" Frank (1929–1945) became the most famous victim of the Holocaust when her diary, *Het Achterhuis* (*The Secret Annex*), was published in Amsterdam in 1947 (first English-language translation, retitled *The Diary of a Young Girl*, 1951; first U.S. edition: New York: Doubleday, 1952). For twenty-five months (July 1942–August 4, 1944) Anne Frank, her family, and four unrelated persons hid from the Nazis in the attic of her father's factory building at 263 Prinzengracht, Amsterdam, until an anonymous tip alerted the *Sicherheitsdienst* (*SD* or Security Police). The eight were arrested and deported to concentration camps. Anne and her older sister, Margot, died of typhus in Bergen-Belsen only a few weeks before British troops liberated the camp in mid-April 1945. Of the eight in hiding only Anne's father, Otto, survived the camps. When he returned home, he discovered her diary: an eloquent, spirited, and perceptive day-to-day record of the two years in the secret annex. Amazed and moved, Otto Frank transcribed the diary, carefully edited out Anne's references to her budding sexuality, and had the work published. It was eventually translated into sixty-five languages and continues to be an international bestseller (30 million copies sold), perhaps the most widely read book of the modern era.

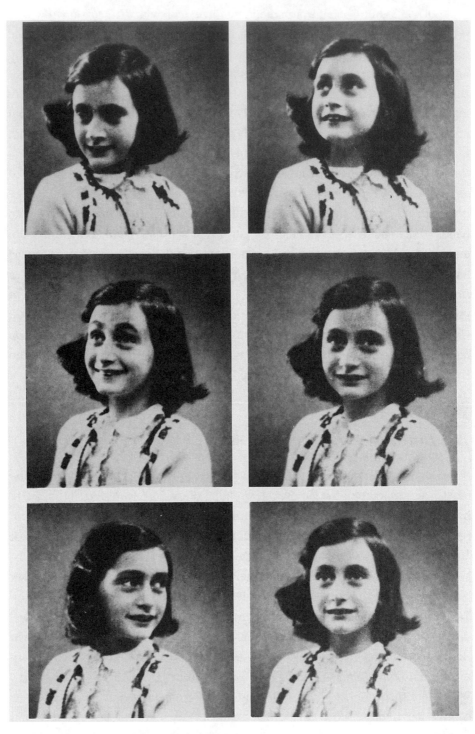

Photographs of Anne Frank taken by her father, Otto Frank, October 1942. (Mirisch/ United Artists/The Kobal Collection)

In 1953 the American husband and wife writing team of Albert Hackett and Frances Goodrich (*The Thin Man; It's a Wonderful Life; Father of the Bride*) began to adapt Anne Frank's diary into a Broadway play. Working with Otto Frank's already sanitized version of the diary, Hackett and Goodrich played up Anne's childish innocence and played down her mordant wit in order to convey maximum saintliness. Directed by Garson Kanin and starring Susan Strasberg as Anne Frank, the play opened on October 5, 1955, and ran for 717 performances (until June 22, 1957). *The Diary of Anne Frank* won five 1956 Tony Awards and the 1956 Pulitzer Prize for Best Drama. During its Broadway run, producer-director George Stevens decided to make a film version. Having filmed Nazi concentration camps as evidence used at the Nuremberg war crimes trials, Stevens considered himself well suited to bring the Anne Frank story to the screen. Though he retained Joseph Schildkraut (as Anne's father, Otto Frank), Gusti Huber (as Anne's mother, Mrs. Edith Frank), and Lou Jacobi (as Mr. Hans Van Daan) from the Broadway cast, Stevens brought in seasoned movie actors— Diane Baker, Shelley Winters, Ed Wynn—for the other major roles. George Stevens initially offered the role of Anne Frank to Audrey Hepburn. When she turned it down, Stevens did scores of screen tests before casting Millie Perkins, a nineteen-year-old model with no prior acting experience.

As has been pointed out by numerous film historians, the work of George Stevens (1908–1975) became increasingly ponderous and self-important after the war. Likewise, his films tended to grow longer and longer. For example, *Giant* (1955) had a running time of 3 hours and 21 minutes; the uncut version of *Anne Frank* ran to 3 hours; the original version of *The Greatest Story Ever Told* (1965) ran an unheard of 4 hours and 20 minutes. Clearly Stevens was captivated by grand themes, treated in suitably grandiose fashion. Though *The Diary of Anne Frank* certainly fulfilled Stevens' demand for epic seriousness, the setting of the film was necessarily small and intimate—eight people living in cramped conditions in an attic hideout—and the action mostly limited to small talk and bickering amost the bored, restless, stress-ridden fugitives. Though the rest of the cast delivered credible performances, Millie Perkins played Anne Frank in a cloying, stagy manner that reduced a complex, evolving personality to a saccharine caricature. An overlong, sometimes tedious viewing experience, *The Diary of Anne Frank* was nonetheless acknowledged for the nobility of its subject matter by eight 1960 Oscar nominations. The movie won three: Best Cinematography, Black-and-White Cinematography; Best Art Direction and Set Decoration; Best Actress in a Supporting Role (Shelley Winters). It was not, however, a box office success.

Judgment at Nuremberg (1962)

On Tuesday evening, April 16, 1959—a month after the movie premier of *The Diary of Anne Frank*—CBS's live television drama anthology series, *Playhouse 90*, aired Abby Mann's *Judgment at Nuremberg*, a 90-minute courtroom melo-drama dealing with "Military Tribunal III," a later phase of the Nuremberg War Crimes trials that weighed the guilt of sixteen Nazi judges who sanctioned Hitler's policies. Taking place in 1947, during the early stages of the Cold War and well after the top echelon of Nazi leadership had been tried and sentenced, the Third Military Tribunal was not exactly front-page news. Indeed it was hardly noticed by a world engulfed in new and more pressing postwar concerns. For television writer Abby Mann (real name: Abraham Goodman), however, these proceedings provided a valuable source of material for a drama that would probe the amoral underpinnings of the Third Reich, especially the collaboration of professional civil servants in the German judiciary who quite willingly did Hitler's bidding. In the interests of dramatic focus, Mann concentrated on the top four Nazi defen-dants: Franz Schlegelberger (Dr. Ernst Janning in the play), Acting Reich Minister of Justice; Herbert Klemm (Werner Lampe), Director of the Legal Education and Training Division in the Ministry of Justice; Oswald Rothaug (Emil Hahn), Senior Public Prosecutor of the Volksgerichtshof (People's Court); Rudolf Oeschey (Friedrich Hofstetter), Judge of the Special Court in Nuremberg and successor to Rothaug as Chief Justice. The charges against these men were complex and lengthy but essentially boiled down to one thing: that Hitler's justices had per-verted law in service to political repression and the persecution of the innocent.

On viewing the *Playhouse 90* broadcast of *Judgment at Nuremberg*, direc-tor Stanley Kramer (1913–2001) decided at once to make a feature-length film version. At the time, the courtroom drama was enjoying a vogue on television and feature films, for example, Sidney Lumet's *Twelve Angry Men* (1957), Robert Wise's *I Want to Live!* (1958), Otto Preminger's *Anatomy of a Murder* (1959), Kramer's own *Inherit the Wind* (1960), Robert Mulligan's *To Kill a Mockingbird* (1962). Furthermore, the fit between Kramer and Mann was an especially good one. Kramer was Mann's senior by thirteen years but both men were Jewish American media artists from northeastern cities (New York and Philadelphia, respectively) who had an intellectual bent, were politically liberal, and were pas-sionately interested in issues of social justice. Indeed, by the late 1950s Kramer had established himself as America's foremost producer-director of the "social problem" film, a genre that explores controversial contemporary social issues like race relations (*The Defiant Ones*), nuclear war (*On the Beach*), or science versus religious ideology (the aforementioned *Inherit the Wind*). *Judgment at Nuremberg* was perfected suited to Stanley Kramer's artistic and political agenda, and Abby Mann was suddenly afforded the opportunity to graduate from television production in New York City to the feature-film business in Hollywood. Mann moved to Hollywood and wrote a screenplay based on the trial transcripts that expanded *Judgment* into a 3-hour movie.

Shot on location at Nuremberg in the spring of 1961—just as the trial of infamous Nazi war criminal Adolf Eichmann was getting under way in Jerusalem—*Judgment at Nuremberg* (1962) starred Maximilian Schell as the fictive Hans Rolfe, lead defense attorney (in point of fact there was no such position at the tribunal); Spencer Tracy as Judge Dan Haywood (a conflation of Judges Carrington T. Marshall and Judge James T. Brand); William Shatner as Capt. Byers, Haywood's aide; Kenneth McKenna as Judge Kenneth Norris (based on Judge Mallory B. Blair); Richard Widmark as Col. Ted Lawson (based on Prosecution Chief of Counsel Telford Taylor); Burt Lancaster as Ernst Janning (Schlegelberger); Werner Klemperer as Emil Hahn (Rothaug); Torben Meyer as Lampe (Klemm); Martin Brandt as Hofstetter (Oeschey); Marlene Dietrich as widow Madame Bertholt; Judy Garland and Montgomery Clift as witnesses for the prosecution. A courtroom drama with a running time of just over 3 hours, *Judgment at Nuremberg* was a challenging experience for viewers. That it was more respected than enjoyed is evident by how seldom it has been broadcast since its initial release and by its weak showing at the 1962 Academy Awards. Though nominated for eleven Oscars, *Judgment* won only two, for Best Actor in a Leading Role (Maximillian Schell) and for Best Writing, Screenplay Based on Material from Another Medium (Abby Mann).

The Longest Day (1962)

Eighteen years after D-day, Darryl F. Zanuck released *The Longest Day* (1962), a long, big-budget Cinemascope epic about the Normandy landings based on Cornelius Ryan's best-selling book, *The Longest Day: June 6, 1944* (New York: Simon & Schuster, 1959). Anxious to make the film as accurate, large-scale, and momentous as possible, Zanuck filmed on location in Normandy and used four directors (Ken Annakin, Andrew Marton, Bernhard Wicki, and himself); five writers (Romain Gary, James Jones, David Pursall, Cornelius Ryan, and Jack Seddon); and forty-eight movie stars in major, minor, or cameo roles (including John Wayne, Henry Fonda, Robert Mitchum, Edmond O'Brien, Eddie Albert, Red Buttons, Roddy McDowell, Richard Burton, Sean Connery, Kenneth More, Rod Steiger, George Segal, Richard Todd, Peter Lawford, and Curt Jürgens). Zanuck even cast teen idols Fabian, Paul Anka, and Sal Mineo to appeal to the burgeoning youth audience. Closely following Ryan's book in viewing D-day from a host of shifting vantage points—Allied and German—*The Longest Day* presents a fairly comprehensive and historically accurate picture of a complex, chaotic event. What is lacking, however, is a realistic sense of the mortal fear experienced by the ordinary soldier or the unspeakable gore of combat: representational weaknesses not remedied by the film's gaudy surplus of Hollywood celebrity. *The Longest Day* also tends to give the false impression that D-day was *the* turning point of the war in Europe. Though the Normandy landings were hugely important, the Russians had already eviscerated the German army at Moscow, Stalingrad, and Kursk, and the Third Reich was well on its way to oblivion when the Western Allies finally made their belated move. Fortuitously released during the Cuban Missile Crisis in October 1962, *The Longest Day* reminded Americans of their recent heroic past and was a huge hit, grossing almost $18 million in the United States and $50 million (US$300 million in 2005) worldwide.

The Great Escape (1963)

Close on the heels of the remarkable success of *The Longest Day*, producer-director John Sturges (*Bad Day at Black Rock; The Magnificent Seven*) brought out another big-name-cast World War II epic: *The Great Escape* (1963). Adapted for the screen from Paul Brickhill's eponymous book (New York: W. W. Norton, 1950) by former POW James Clavell (*King Rat*) and W. R. Burnett (*Wake Island*), *The Great Escape* recounts the process by which seventy-six Allied POWs managed a mass tunnel escape from Stalag Luft III in Sagan, Germany (the same prison camp that is the setting of *The Wooden Horse*), on the night of March 24, 1944. Most were quickly recaptured but three managed to make it back home. A furious Hitler wanted all seventy-three recaptured POWs shot but was persuaded that executing fifty would be sufficient for purposes of vengeance. Of the remaining twenty-three, seventeen were returned to Stalag Luft III, four were sent to Sachsenhausen, and two others were sent to Colditz.

In general terms, Sturges' film version is extraordinarily faithful to history. Though it was shot near Munich, far from the original site of Stalag Luft III, the film achieves exactitude as to the look of the huts, fences, and guard towers; the layout of the compound; the local topography; the cat-and-mouse game between POW "stooges" (lookouts) and "ferrets" (German guards trained to detect escape activity); the construction of the three long, deep tunnels (called "Tom," "Dick," and "Harry") through sandy soil; the forging of identity documents, the fashioning of civilian clothes from military uniforms, and other preparations; the actual escape and its terrible the aftermath. As for the personalities involved, *The Great*

Film still of Steve McQueen in The Great Escape. *(Library of Congress)*

Escape is necessarily distilled and compressed. With some 600 prisoners involved in one way or another with the escape effort, the film concentrates on a small group of key individuals, all of whom are composites of a number of real persons: Capt. Virgil "The Cooler King" Hilts (Steve McQueen); Fl. Lt. Bob "The Scrounger" Hendley (James Garner); Squadron Leader Roger "Big X" Bartlett (James Attenborough); Fl. Lt. Danny "The Tunnel King" Velinski (Charles Bronson); Fl. Lt. Colin "The Forger" Blythe (Donald Pleasance); Flying Officer Louis "The Manufacturer" Sedgwick (James Coburn); Lt. Cmdr. Eric "Dispersal" Ashley-Pitt (David McCallum). Specific tasks—for example, materials acquisition, tunneling, dirt disposal, security, and so on—fall to those with the best aptitude for them but, even with such remorseless division of labor, dedication to the overall goal is always foremost. In sum, *The Great Escape* valorizes the ideology of what William H. Whyte famously termed "Organization Man," that is, the worker who sacrifices his own individuality for the good of the organization. Yet the film has it both ways, countering its conformist-collectivist message through its most charismatic character, Steve McQueen's Virgil Hilts, an inveterate escape artist unfazed by spells in "the cooler" (solitary confinement) for bucking the system. McQueen's already well-defined star persona as the archetypal American rebel enables him to function in the film as the embodiment of a rugged individualist that nonetheless dovetails with the larger aims of the Organization: an implicit assurance to the audience that the new corporate society can accommodate the maverick (and vice versa). Accordingly, Hilts, recaptured after trying to jump the fences at the German-Swiss border on a motorcycle, survives the mass reprisals that claim his comrades. The film closes with sounds of "The Cooler King" bouncing a baseball against his cell walls—the quintessential image of the resilient, irreverent American spirit. In point of fact, though many Americans helped prepare for the Great Escape, none actually participated: they were moved to another compound just before the escape took place.

On November 16, 2004, PBS's *NOVA* science documentary series aired *Great Escape*, a 52-minute documentary by Mark Radice that chronicles a recent archaeological excavation of the tunnel known as "Dick" at the long abandoned site of Stalag Luft III in what is now western Poland. Accompanied by former POWs Davy Jones, Jack Lion, Jimmy James, and Charles Huppert, battlefield archaeologists Peter Doyle and Larry Babits manage to find the remains of the tunnel and various artifacts connected with the escape effort. Concentrating on the daunting technical challenges involved, *Great Escape* vividly evokes the incredible resourcefulness and bravery of the POWs and also constitutes a fitting elegy for the fifty victims of Hitler's Gestapo.

P.T. 109 (1963)

Aging, bald, and comfortably dull, President Dwight D. Eisenhower exemplified the dominant 1950s cultural style that favored the circumspect Organization Man. The political ascendancy of the charismatic, movie star–handsome, media-savvy John F. Kennedy ushered in a new ideal for the American male—sexy, youthful, and adventurous—in keeping with the dawn of a new decade and a "New Frontier." While Steve McQueen was one of many screen surrogates for JFK, Hollywood decided to exploit the star power of the president himself by dramatizing his World War II exploits in Leslie Martinson's docudrama, *P.T. 109* (1963). Based on Robert J. Donovan's adulatory *P.T. 109: John F. Kennedy in WWII* (New York: McGraw-Hill, 1961), *P.T. 109* starred Cliff Robertson as Lt. (j.g.) Kennedy (although JFK would have preferred the sexier Warren Beatty).

Robertson's Lt. Kennedy is, of course, idealized. Though Kennedy was a competent naval officer and responded bravely and resourcefully to the sinking of his P.T. boat by a Japanese destroyer (August 1943), the book and film suppress the reckless playboy side of JFK to present a sanitized image of the future president as an affable, self-effacing war hero in the Audie Murphy tradition. Never before or since has a sitting U.S. president been glamorized by a Hollywood feature film; for whatever reason, the usual taboos that disallow such public fawning were not applied to John Kennedy. Indeed, it would take revisionist historians and biographers many years to uncover the libidinous, arrogant, self-destructive man beneath the romantic myth of Camelot.

Battle of the Bulge (1965)

On December 16, 1965, the twenty-first anniversary of the start of Hitler's Ardennes Offensive or "Battle of the Bulge," producers Phillip Yordan, Milton Sperling, and Dino De Laurentiis released Ken Annakin's *Battle of the Bulge*, a Cinerama blockbuster meant to emulate the epic scope and box office success of *The Longest Day*. Indeed, *Battle of the Bulge* recycles Henry Fonda, Robert Ryan, and Hans Christian Blech in roles similar to the ones they played in *The Longest Day*. *Battle* also features Charles Bronson in order to capture some of the heroic aura of *The Great Escape;* Dana Andrews to lend the film 1940s authenticity; and Robert Shaw as Nazi panzer leader Col. Martin Hessler—a fictional version of SS Lt. Col. Joachim Peiper of Malmedy Massacre infamy—to present the Allies with a worthy adversary. Meant to be both scary and sexy in his cold fanaticism, Shaw's heavily German-accented Aryan Superman is, unfortunately, a rather ridiculous character.

Though the makers of *Battle of the Bulge* managed to assemble the requisite cast of big-name stars, efforts were markedly subpar in terms of the film's production values and script. With his production company based in Spain, where production costs and taxes were low, producer Phillip Yordan had the film shot in the Castille region near Segovia, where topography and weather are nothing at all like that of the Ardennes Forest in the bitterly cold winter of 1944–1945. Spanish soldiers fill the ranks of the German and American forces and various types of U.S. Korean War–era tanks masquerade (poorly) as Tiger and Sherman tanks. The script is, likewise, hokey and simplistic, positing Allied victory by having Hessler's gas-starved panzers stopped just short of a massive Allied fuel dump that never existed as such. So egregious were *Battle*'s inaccuracies that former President (and WWII Supreme Allied Commander in Europe) Dwight D.

Eisenhower came out of retirement for a press conference denouncing the film. Ike was, of course, right but did not understand the economic and cultural forces driving a film like *Battle of the Bulge.* In order to compete with television, 1960s historical movies often resorted to epic pretensions and the spectacle of Cinerama to lure viewers. Catering to the big screen meant prioritizing visual impact over plot or historical verisimilitude. Furthermore, twenty years having elapsed, the cultural immediacy of the Second World War had faded and a new kind of audience has arisen. Mostly young, materially comfortable, weaned on television and pop music, moviegoers in the 1960s wanted exciting spectacle; the facts of a time they had not lived through were largely irrelevant to them.

Anzio (1965)

Later in the decade, as the Vietnam War was reaching its full fury and the draft generated growing domestic unrest, the war film genre began to become problematic for obvious reasons. Into this contested cultural moment, Dino De Laurentiis released *Anzio* (1965), an Edward Dmytryk film about the stalled Allied landings on the western coast of Italy (January 22–May 25, 1944). Loosely based on British war correspondent Wynford Vaughan-Thomas's book, *Anzio: The Massacre at the Beachhead* (New York: Holt, Rinehart & Winston, 1961), *Anzio* was a joint Italian-American production (mostly Italian crew, mostly American cast) filmed near Naples. Plotted something like *Dunkirk,* the film follows the fortunes of six soldiers struggling to return to friendly lines after a failed frontal attack on German machine-gun emplacements. Though such suicidal tactics were seldom if ever practiced by U.S. forces, the battle is based on an actual one that occurred at Cisterna on January 30, 1944, when four attacking Ranger battalions were ambushed, encircled, and destroyed by elements of the Hermann Göring Division. As adapted by H. A. L. Craig (*Waterloo*), Frank de Felitta, Duilio Coletti, and Giuseppe Mangione, *Anzio* has cynical (anti)war correspondent Dick Ennis (Robert Mitchum) perplexed by a fundamental question seldom broached by war films: Why do men make war? In the end war-loving Corporal Jack Rabinoff (Peter Falk) supplies an honest answer that speaks to the existential vacuity of everyday life in the modern world: "Because I like [war]. I want this. A guy sells shoes for forty years and I live more in one day. I see more. I feel more, I think more. I'm more. Do you understand? I'm more." Though episodic and plagued by a trite title song and a sententious script, *Anzio* reflects the rising antiwar sentiment that was rife in Europe and was beginning to animate a sizable part of the American populace in the late 1960s.

Battle of Britain (1969)

Canadian-born film producer Harry Saltzman (1915–1994) began his career in England in the late 1950s, making "Angry Young Men" films with Tony Richardson such as *Look Back in Anger* (1958), *The Entertainer* (1960), and *Saturday Night and Sunday Morning* (1960). Thereafter Saltzman changed his stripes and became a movie mogul specializing in Cold War spy blockbusters. From 1962 to his retirement in 1975 Saltzman produced all the classic James Bond films and other espionage thrillers, for example, *The Ipcress File* (1965), *Funeral in Berlin* (1966), and *Billion Dollar Brain* (1967). In the same ideological vein is Saltzman's *Battle of Britain* (1969), a big-budget, wide-screen, would-be epic in the spirit of *The Longest Day*. Directed by Guy Hamilton (*The Colditz Story; Goldfinger*), *Battle of Britain* featured the cream of Britain's thespian community—Laurence Olivier, Ralph Richardson, Trevor Howard, Michael Caine, Harry Andrews, Kenneth More, Michael Redgrave, Christopher Plummer (actually a Canadian)—and so many WWII airplanes that the assemblage was thought to be the world's eleventh-largest air force at the time. What the film lacked was a compelling script and action sequences commensurate with the historical reality.

For France, May 1968 was a critical month politically, a time when millions of disaffected students and workers engaged in mass demonstrations, strikes, and walkouts that paralyzed the country and threatened to bring about a populist revolution. The Confédération Générale du Travail (CGT, or trade union federation) and the Parti Communiste Français, or PCF (French Communist Party)—ostensibly progressive bureaucracies—feared the unpredictable consequences of a popular uprising. They ended up betraying their constituencies by supporting the conservative Gaullist government as it took all the necessary repressive measures. The rebellion fizzled out as suddenly as it had begun. However, the unrest eventually took its political toll on Charles DeGaulle, who was voted out of power by national referendum in April 1969.

Le Chagrin et la pitié: Chronique d'une ville Française sous l'occupation (The Sorrow and the Pity: Chronicle of a French City under Occupation) (1969)

It was during this turbulent time that Marcel Ophüls made *Le Chagrin et la pitié: Chronique d'une ville Française sous l'occupation (The Sorrow and the Pity: Chronicle of a French City under Occupation)* (1969), a fascinating 4-and-a-half-hour documentary that decisively debunks the myth of widespread French resistance to German occupation during the war. A segment director for *Zoom*, a current-affairs program that aired on state-owned O.R.T.F. (L'Office de Radiod- iffusion-Television Française) [Office of French Television Broadcasting], Ophüls, along with producers André Harris and Alain de Sedouy, made *Munich, ou la paix pour cent ans* (1967) (*Munich, or Peace for One Hundred Years*), an examination of the political intrigues and diplomatic compromises that led to the start of the Second World War. Ophüls and his associates planned *The Sorrow and the Pity* as a sequel to the Munich documentary but all three men quit (or were fired from) O.R.T.F. when DeGaulle called for a media embargo of the May 1968 demonstrations. After securing funding from German and Swiss sources— Norddeutscher Rundfunk (NDR) and Télévision Suisse-Romande (TSR), respectively—Ophüls et al. prepared the groundwork for the new film by study- ing the period and exploring film archives all over Europe for relevant newsreel and propaganda film footage. To anchor the film in a specific locale, Ophüls' team chose the industrial city of Clermont-Ferrand, 400 kilometers south of Paris, capital of the Auvergne region of central France and close to Vichy, seat of Philippe Pétain's puppet government.

Over the course of several months Ophüls, André Harris, and their camera crews conducted on-site interviews with three dozen people, mostly French of course, but also a few Germans and British. Some of Ophüls' interviewees are famous (Pierre Mendès-France; Anthony Eden) but the majority are ordinary folk representing various political persuasions, social strata, and levels of collabora- tion or resistance. Crosscutting between interviews, staking out conflicting posi- tions and stock footage that either enhances or contradicts the preceding inter- view segment, Ophüls creates a dialectical narrative that accrues phenomenal depth and complexity as it goes along. *The Sorrow and the Pity* is divided into two parts. Part I, "L'Effrondrement" (The Collapse), examines how France's rigid class divisions and deep-seated, pervasive anticommunism and anti-Semitism rendered it especially vulnerable to Hitler. Part II, "Le Choix" (The Choice), pro- vides a sobering look at how the French coped with four years of occupation by a foreign power. Contrary to the Gaullist myth of heroic national resistance, most French citizens were apolitical or nominally collaborationist in order to survive. Some elements of the *haute bourgeoisie*, following the logic of their class posi- tion, segued easily from rabid anticommunism to enthusiastic support for Nazism. Interestingly, Ophüls found that genuine members of the Resistance tended to be social misfits willing to risk everything because they had little to lose. Contrary to the conventional wisdom prevailing in the late 1960s, De Gaulle and his rightist "Free French" movement are shown to be a relatively marginal wartime phenomenon. Finally, the disgraceful history of Vichy's willing deporta- tion of 75,000 Jews who ended up in gas chambers is the film's darkest truth. In a coda, *The Sorrow and the Pity* reiterates long-standing charges of collaboration leveled at the famous singer-actor Maurice Chevalier (1888–1972), who lamely tries to rationalize a concert he gave in Nazi Germany.

As a committed leftist, Ophüls' agenda was to weaken the sway of conservative Gaullism, but *The Sorrow and the Pity* achieved much more than ideological demystification. Once it was finally shown in a small Left Bank theater in April 1971, the film proved an immediate sensation. Sparking an impassioned and often bitter national debate about France's troubled past, Ophüls' masterpiece ran in Paris until the end of 1972, was shown at film festivals all over world, and has received universal accolades as one of the greatest films ever made.

Tora! Tora! Tora! (1970)

By the mid-1960s the U.S. former mortal enemy, Japan, had embraced corporate capitalism with characteristic zeal and was well on its way to transforming itself into a Western-style, putatively pro-American bulwark in Asia, countering the regional sway of Soviet Russia, Red China, and Communist North Korea and North Vietnam. One small sign of the economic and political rehabilitation of Japan was the initiation of a joint American-Japanese film project on Pearl Harbor. Hoping to repeat the success of *The Longest Day*, Elmo Williams (among many other credentials, producer of Theodor Geisel's *Your Job in Japan* and

A captured Japanese photograph shows the smoke rising from Hickam Field during the attack on Pearl Harbor on December 7, 1941. (National Archives)

associate producer and second unit director of *The Longest Day*) and 20th Century Fox mogul, Darryl F. Zanuck, joined forces with Masayuki Takagi and Keinosuke Kubo of Japan's Toei film studios to make the Pearl Harbor epic, *Tora! Tora! Tora!* (1970). Based on Ladislas Farrago's *The Broken Seal: The Story of "Operation Magic" and the Pearl Harbor Disaster* (New York: Random House, 1967) and the life's work of preeminent Pearl Harbor expert Gordon W. Prange (1910–1980), *Tora! Tora! Tora!* was conceived and executed as two distinct films woven together, one telling the American side of the story and the other presenting the Japanese perspective.

Richard Fleischer (*The Vikings; Che!*) was hired to direct the American segments, and Japan's greatest filmmaker, Akira Kurosawa (*Rashômon; The Seven Samurai*), agreed to direct the Japanese segments after being told (falsely) that David Lean would be directing the U.S. segments. When Kurosawa learned that Lean was not involved in the film, he got himself fired and was replaced by Kinji Fukasaku and Toshio Masuda. New directors notwithstanding, the guiding credo for the makers of *Tora! Tora! Tora!* (Japanese for "Tiger," the radio code word for a successful attack) remained historical accuracy at all costs—a doctrine that proved to be both the film's greatest strength and its greatest weakness. With much of its dialogue culled from official records, *Tora! Tora! Tora!* provided a faultless representation of the political, bureaucratic, and diplomatic intrigues in the months leading up to December 7, 1941. The problem with such an approach was that it was dramatically monochromatic, too "talky," and rather dull until the spectacular culminating attack. The enormous logistical challenges—shooting in far-flung locations, disguising modern ships as WWII-era vessels, restoring some thirty period aircraft, building and destroying mock-ups and model ships and planes, and so on—pushed up the cost of making *Tora! Tora! Tora!* to a then exorbitant $25 million (US$120 million in 2003). Though, predictably, a huge hit in Japan, the film generated poor box office returns in the United States: a result that nearly bankrupted 20th Century Fox and forced Daryll F. Zanuck into retirement. Indeed, the American public's derisive rejection of an evenhanded treatment of December 7 was probably best expressed by the bitterly sardonic title of Jerry Della Femina's best-selling exposé of the advertising industry that was published four months before the film came out: *From Those Wonderful Folks Who Gave You Pearl Harbor* (New York: Simon & Schuster, 1970).

Patton (1970)

General George Smith Patton Jr. (1885–1945), commander of the U.S. 7th Army in North Africa and Sicily and the U.S. 3rd Army in France and Germany, was one of the most colorful and controversial figures in modern American history. Known as "Old Blood and Guts," George Patton was a strutting, profanity-spouting egomaniac with a penchant for saying and doing scandalous things. Patton was, at the same time, a brilliant strategist and an effective military leader much feared by the Germans—and his own men. Hollywood producer Frank McCarthy (1912–1986), a brigadier general on General George C. Marshall's staff in WWII, struck a Patton film deal with 20th Century Fox in the early 1950s but would have to wait nearly twenty years to make the film a reality. Robert Brent Toplin notes that army officials and members of Patton's family discouraged McCarthy from making a film on Patton, fearing it would caricature him and sully his memory (Toplin, 1996, 158–159). Indeed, McCarthy was not able to move forward until the publication of Ladislas Farago's magisterial *Patton: Ordeal and Triumph* (New York: Ivan Obelensky, 1963), which finally provided a source large and detailed enough on which to base the kind of film McCarthy envisioned. After buying the film rights to Farago's biography and General Omar N. Bradley's *A Soldier's Story* (New York: Henry Holt, 1951), 20th Century Fox hired director Franklin J. Schaffner (*The War Lord; Planet of the Apes*), veteran screenwriters Edmund H. North (*Sink the Bismarck!; Twelve O'Clock High*) and James Webb (*Cape Fear; Cheyenne Autumn*), and a newcomer named Francis Ford Coppola to carve a coherent narrative out of the voluminous material on Patton's life and military career.

Securing an actor to play General Patton proved a bit more problematic. McCarthy and the studio wanted George C. Scott, a superb actor and, ironically, an avowed pacifist perhaps best known for his hilarious rendition of the war-mongering General "Buck" Turgidson—a satirical portrait of SAC's ultrahawkish General Curtis LeMay (1906–1990)—in Stanley Kubrick's *Dr. Strangelove* (1964). Unhappy with an early version of the script that he found too reductive, Scott bowed out. Robert Mitchum, Burt Lancaster, Rod Steiger, and Lee Marvin turned down the role. John Wayne badly wanted to play Patton but his utterly dissimilar physical appearance, laconic manner, and narrow range as an actor made him an inappropriate choice to play the shorter, more volatile, and markedly more educated and intelligent Patton. Thankfully, after considerable revision of the script, George C. Scott agreed to take the part, a fortuitous decision for all involved.

In the broadest terms *Patton* (1970) is an accurate recounting of George Patton's World War II years (1942–1945), and George C. Scott's impersonation of Patton is mesmerizing. Patton's theatrical posturing, his rhetorical and sartorial flamboyance, his zeal for military history and martial glory, his almost mystical sense of destiny, his deep love of war, his competitiveness (especially with British Field Marshall Montgomery), his unpredictable temper—Scott conveys all of these traits with an astonishing range of nuance and skill. While Scott's virtuoso performance rightly came to be seen as one of the great acting achievements of his generation, its singularity may have had the unintended effect of obscuring the ideological nature of the film as a whole.

At first glance, *Patton* seems remarkably evenhanded in its depiction of the man. Patton is shown as an energetic, fearless, inspired, and resourceful leader but also possibly deranged when he spouts hellfire and brimstone to his troops, slaps, kicks, and berates a shell-shocked soldier for cowardice—an outburst that nearly destroyed Patton's career—or displays an exuberant and politically dangerous contempt for America's erstwhile allies, the Russians, after V-E day. In his chapter on *Patton* in *History by Hollywood*, historian Robert Brent Toplin follows the findings of contemporary film critics in judging the film a carefully balanced presentation, a Rorschach test that confirms leftist viewers' antiwar sentiments by showing Patton's fanaticism as more or less insane while serving up an equally plausible vision to rightist viewers of Patton as a warrior whose skills and ambitions rival Alexander the Great. The problem with the Rorschach test interpretation of *Patton* is that it ignores too many of the film's omissions that soften Patton's character and make him a more attractive figure on-screen than the man was in life. The real George S. Patton Jr. was something of a reactionary thug who helped his superior officer, Douglas MacArthur, rout the WWI veteran Bonus Marchers on Washington in 1932; a philanderer who engaged in a well-documented twelve-year affair with his niece; a rabid and vociferous racist and anti-Semite; a Red-baiting cold warrior; a manipulator who affected the persona of a foul-mouthed boor to unsettle his peers and bully his subordinates. The real Patton, who had a high-pitched voice, peppered every sentence with numerous profanities. Given the long-standing taboo against the use of expletives in movies—a taboo that still prevailed in 1970—Scott's rendition of Patton could not be expected to accurately convey Patton's typical speaking style, but the film could have taken on his anti-Semitism and other, equally egregious traits. That it chose not to makes it ideologically suspect. Tellingly, one viewer who identified with Patton and appreciated the film's sly glorification of retrograde attitudes was U.S. President Richard Milhous Nixon (1913–1994). After screening the film at the White House at least twice in April 1970, Nixon, inspired in part by Patton's reckless audacity, ordered the invasion of Cambodia shortly thereafter. Nixon's newfound aggressiveness, which widened the war in Indochina and enflamed the antiwar movement, led to the National Guard killings of four unarmed college students at Kent State University on May 4, 1970.

Sixteen years after *Patton* George C. Scott would reprise his role as the flamboyant general in Delbert Mann's made-for-TV movie, *The Last Days of Patton* (1986), a slow-paced, lugubrious docudrama that centers on Patton as he is slowly dying an excruciatingly painful death in a hospital bed in Germany after an automobile crash (December 9, 1945) leaves him paralyzed. Scott, at fifty-nine, was now closer to George Patton's age when he died (sixty-five) and was well suited to convey Patton's growing sense of exhaustion and uselessness with no wars left to fight. In the years between the two films, the American defeat in Vietnam had cast an entirely different light on Patton's legacy.

The World at War (1973–1974)

As usual it was left to the British to produce a documentary record of World War II that steered a prudent middle course between triumphalism and cynical deconstruction. Between October 31, 1973, and May 8, 1974, Britain's ITV network aired *The World at War*, a twenty-six-part weekly documentary series on World War II produced by Sir Jeremy Isaacs for Thames Television in cooperation with the Imperial War Museum. Superbly written by a dozen distinguished historians led by Neal Acherson and Peter Batty and sonorously narrated by Shakespearean actors Eric Porter and Sir Laurence Olivier, *The World at War* is a series of 52-minute-long compilation-interview documentaries arranged in rough chronological order that cover all the major WWII military campaigns and many other related topics, for example, life during Nazi occupation, life on the home front, the Holocaust, the atomic bomb, and so on. Still shown on television in the United Kingdom and many other countries, *The World at War* was released in VHS and DVD versions in 2001. Widely regarded as the definitive visual history of the Second World War, *The World at War* was named nineteenth among "the 100 greatest British television programmes" by the British Film Institute (BFI) in 2000.

World War II History Films of the Post-Vietnam Era

The Execution of Private Slovik (1974)

The United States was in the process of terminating its disastrous involvement in Vietnam when a made-for-TV docudrama entitled *The Execution of Private Slovik* was broadcast on network television on March 13, 1974. The film, directed by Lamont Johnson, was adapted to the small screen by lifelong writing collaborators Richard Levinson and William Link (the Columbo films) from William

Bradford Huie's controversial book, subtitled *The Hitherto Secret Story of the Only American Soldier since 1864 to Be Shot for Desertion* (New York: Duell, Sloan & Pearce, 1954).

The saga of Private Edward Donald "Eddie" Slovik (1920–1945) is a sad one. A petty criminal and self-described "born loser" from Detroit, Slovik was reclassified from 4-F "unfit for duty" to 1-A and drafted by the U.S. Army in November 1943. Shipped to France in August 1944, Slovik was one of a group of raw replacements assigned to Company G, 109th Infantry Regiment 28th Infantry Division. However, in early October, Slovik refused to join his unit, claiming he was "too scared" (Huie 1954) to serve in a frontline rifle company. Repeatedly given the option of rejoining his company in lieu of legal action, Slovik repeatedly refused, verbally and in writing, and was subsequently court-martialed for desertion under fire. On November 11, 1944, nine senior officers found Slovik guilty and sentenced him to death. Slovik pled for clemency to General Eisenhower but Eisenhower felt he needed to set an example for other would-be deserters; Slovik's plea was denied. On the morning of January 31, 1945, outside the village of Sainte-Marie-aux-Mines, Eddie Slovik was executed by firing squad: the only one of forty-nine condemned U.S. Army deserters actually put to death. Slovik's fate was a closely guarded secret, unknown even to his wife, Antoinette, until the publication of Huie's book in 1954. Originally interred in a secret cemetery in Fere-en-Tardenois, France, Slovik's remains were exhumed and reburied next to his wife's grave in Michigan in 1987.

A politically active liberal Democrat until the early 1960s, singer-actor Frank Sinatra was intrigued by the subversive political implications of Huie's book. He bought the screen rights in 1959 and hired the blacklisted screenwriter Albert Maltz (*This Gun for Hire*) to write an adaptation that would star Steve McQueen as the ill-fated Pvt. Slovik. Denounced by the American Legion and right-wing newspapers for hiring Maltz, Sinatra later fired Maltz at the request of Joseph P. Kennedy (JFK, a friend of Sinatra's, was running for president and the Kennedy family patriarch did not want his son implicated in the controversy). Ultimately Sinatra decided to cancel the project. It lay in limbo for more than a decade before being revived by Levinson and Link, who took Huie's linear narrative and created a more cinematic treatment that relied on a series of flashbacks to show how Slovik came to stand before a firing squad. Well cast in the role of Slovik was Martin Sheen (*The Andersonville Trial; Catch 22*), a progressive activist fully supportive of the film's antiwar message. Similar in spirit to Stanley Kubrick's *Paths of Glory, The Execution of Private Slovik* dramatizes the fact that the ordinary soldier is often the pawn and scapegoat of overlords who cannot be bothered by the human consequences of their grand schemes.

Nominated for eight Emmy Awards in 1974, *The Execution of Private Slovik* won two Emmys for editing.

Midway (1976)

As if to prove that *The Execution of Private Slovik* was, ideologically speaking, an aberration, Walter Mirisch's Universal studios released (*The Battle of*) *Midway* (1976), a big-cast, big-budget spectacle in the tradition of *The Longest Day* and *Tora! Tora! Tora!* just in time for the U.S. bicentennial celebrations. Written from scratch by television screenwriter Donald S. Sanford and directed by B-movie specialist Jack Smight (*Airport 1975*), *Midway* purported to tell the story of the Battle of Midway (June 4–7, 1942), the naval-air engagement in which the U.S. Navy sank four Japanese aircraft carriers, effectively turning the tide of the sea war in the Pacific. Starring Henry Fonda as Admiral Chester W. Nimitz (1885–1966); Glenn Ford as Rear Admiral Raymond A. Spruance (1886–1969); Robert Mitchum as Vice Admiral William F. "Bull" Halsey Jr. (1882–1959); and Toshiro Mifune as Admiral Isoroku Yamamoto (1884–1943), *Midway* also inserts a fictional Captain Matthew Garth (Charlton Heston); a fictional son, Ensign Thomas Garth (Eddie Albert Jr.); and a fictional love interest for the son, Miss Haruko Sakura (Christina Kokubo), in order to give the film a gratuitous dramatic dimension. Clichéd dialogue and the use of too much stock footage gave *Midway* a shopworn quality that signaled the end of the heroic era of American-made World War II epics (1962–1976), a time span that almost exactly coincides with direct U.S. involvement in Vietnam. Coming just after the end of the Vietnam War, *Midway* was a final, anachronistic attempt to recapture World War II glories in a radically altered geopolitical era, when the old good-versus-evil dichotomies no longer made sense.

A Bridge Too Far (1977)

Distinguished WWII correspondent-historian Cornelius Ryan (1920–1974), author of the aforementioned *Longest Day* and *The Last Battle* (New York: Simon & Schuster, 1966), presented a detailed account of the ill-fated Operation Market-Garden in *A Bridge Too Far* (New York: Simon & Schuster, 1974), the third installment in his World War II trilogy and his final book before succumbing to prostate cancer at the age of fifty-four. His dying wish was that the book be made into a film. Producer Joseph E. Levine (*Zulu; Soldier Blue*) obliged, hiring screenwriter William Goldman (*The Stepford Wives; All the President's Men*) to adapt Ryan's book to the screen and Richard Attenborough (*Oh! What a Lovely War; Young Winston*) to direct.

At first glance *A Bridge Too Far* (1977) looks like another installment in the bombastic World War II epic genre. It has all the usual earmarks: focus on a famous battle, epic grandeur—and length, at 3 hours running time—plenty of action, and a large, all-star cast including Laurence Olivier, Robert Redford, Dirk Bogarde, Michael Caine, Sean Connery, Gene Hackman, Anthony Hopkins, and many others of note. There are, however, two essential differences: (1) Attenborough was/is staunchly antiwar and (2) *A Bridge Too Far* deals with a stunning Allied defeat. Cooked up by British Field Marshall Bernard Montgomery as a means to flank the Siegfried Line (aka "West Wall"), cross the Rhine into Germany's Ruhr district at Arhem, Holland, and speed an end to the war in Europe, Market-Garden (September 17–26, 1944) was a large-scale, coordinated airborne ("Market") and armored ("Garden") assault that involved securing key bridges along a 65-mile corridor that led across Nazi-occupied Holland into Germany. Sadly, the operation was probably doomed from the outset because Montgomery refused to credit intelligence reports indicating that the 9th and 10th SS Panzer divisions were refitting in the vicinity of the furthest drop zone, near Arnhem. Shoddy planning, logistical difficulties, poor communications, and bad weather made a bad situation worse. The ensuing Battle of Arnhem, pitting the lightly armed paratroopers of the British 1st Airborne Division against crack panzer forces, quickly devolved into a desperate fight for survival for the Allies. Surrounded and battered for nine days, the 1st Airborne sustained 80 percent casualties before its few remaining survivors were rescued. Likewise, the U.S. 82nd and 101st Airborne divisions took heavy losses in fighting over bridges at Eindhoven and Nijmegen. In the end, Operation Market-Garden accomplished nothing and cost twice the casualties that were incurred at D-day. The vainglorious Montgomery never acknowledged that his grand scheme was an unmitigated disaster, later prompting Dwight Eisenhower to call him a "psychopath" incapable of admitting his mistakes.

As with his other books, Cornelius Ryan was a stickler for historical comprehensiveness and accuracy, assembling his narrative only after doing meticulous research and conducting hundreds of interviews with veterans and other participants. Respectful of Ryan's high standards, Levine, Attenborough, and Goldman went to great lengths to fashion a film that was true to history in almost every way—except for some fabricated dialogue. The result was a well-paced, realistic film. Shot at the actual locations in the Netherlands, *A Bridge Too Far* did justice to the complexities of Market-Garden and effectively conveyed the terrible waste of war. A box office hit and a success with critics, *A Bridge Too*

Far demonstrated that audiences were ready for a new, hybrid war film: a fast-paced, sweeping military epic without the usual flag-waving.

Ike (1979)

The post-Vietnam shift away from the standard battle heroics in World War II history films to the human side of the story was beginning to look like a trend with the May 1979 airing of Melville Shavelson's *Ike*, a 6-hour ABC television miniseries that focused on General Eisenhower's relationship with Kay Summersby (1908–1975), his chauffeur during the war. It was well known at the time that Eisenhower and Miss Summersby were close and rumors persisted that the two were having an affair. At war's end, Eisenhower returned to Mamie, his wife of some thirty years, and Summersby faded out of his life. For her part, Kay Summersby dealt with the end of her relationship with Ike by writing *Eisenhower Was My Boss* (New York: Prentice-Hall, 1948), an adulatory memoir that described an intense but platonic relationship. Five years after Eisenhower's death in 1969 at age seventy-eight, a gossip journalist named Merle Miller published *Plain Speaking, An Oral Biography of Harry S. Truman* (New York: Berkeley Publishing/G.P. Putnam, 1974), which quoted Truman as saying that, during the war, Eisenhower had asked his superior, General George C. Marshall, about the political advisability of divorcing Mamie in order to marry Kay Summersby. Marshall reportedly disabused Eisenhower of the notion in no uncertain terms. Though Miller's book seemed to bear out the old rumors about Ike and Miss Summersby, it could not be corroborated. Marshall died in 1959, Truman died in 1971, and no one else in a position to know could or would confirm the story—except Kay Summersby, who put in her own oar with a second memoir, published twenty-eight years after the first one and plainly titled *Past Forgetting: My Affair with Dwight Eisenhower* (New York: Simon & Schuster, 1976). In her second book, Summersby alleges that she and Eisenhower were, *in terms of emotional intimacy*, lovers—despite the fact that two attempts at consummation failed due to Ike's impotence. That Eisenhower and the rest of his staff always denied any such goings-on took place does not prove anything. Likewise, Summersby's assertions deal with private assignations that cannot be verified. Her motivation for writing *Past Forgetting* is also a bit murky. At the time she was preparing the book, Kay Summersby Morgan was in her late sixties, twice divorced, childless, short of money, and dying of cancer. *Past Forgetting*, which was published posthumously, may have been a final, desperate bid for some lasting recognition. On the other hand, Kay Summersby may have only wished to set the record straight before she died. No one knows for sure. Whatever the truth of *Past Forgetting*, Shavelson's miniseries, *Ike*, takes the book at face value and portrays Eisenhower (Robert Duvall) and Summersby (Lee Remick) as soul mates well aware that their love will not survive the war. Very much a product of changing cultural mores instigated by the sexual revolution of the 1960s and 1970s, the story *Ike* tells could not have been told in the sexually reticent climate of the 1940s.

Playing for Time (1980)

Thirty years after being liberated from Auschwitz, a half-Jewish Parisian cabaret singer turned resistance fighter named Fania Fénelon (real name: Fanny Goldstein, 1918–1983) published *Sursis pour l'orchestre* (*A Break for the Orchestra*) (1976, U.S. title: *Playing for Time* (New York: Atheneum, 1977), her story of surviving Auschwitz-Birkenau by singing, playing in, and arranging music for the women's orchestra there. Celebrated playwright Arthur Miller adapted Fénelon's book into a film script and teamed with producers Linda Yellen, John E. Quill, and Louise Ramsey to make a television movie. Even before filming began, the production was the subject of intense controversy. After Jane Fonda and Barbra Streisand passed up offers to play the lead role, the filmmakers cast the prodigiously talented British actress Vanessa Redgrave as Fania Fénelon. When it was announced in August 1979 that Redgrave—a strident supporter of the Palestine Liberation Organization (PLO)—would play a Jewish victim of the Holocaust, a tremendous uproar ensued. The American Jewish Congress, B'nai B'rith, the Simon Wiesenthal Center of Los Angeles, and a number of Hollywood notables (e.g., Martin Balsam, Larry Gelbart, David L. Wolper, Mel Brooks) protested Redgrave's involvement with the project and pressured CBS to fire her. The most powerful voice raised against Redgrave was that of Fania Fénelon herself, who publicly denounced the actress as an anti-Israel "fanatic" (Lask 1979). Despite the uproar, Vanessa Redgrave refused to step aside and Arthur Miller used his considerable prestige to defend her on the grounds that her removal would constitute a form of political blacklisting. CBS also stood firm and Redgrave ended up playing Fénelon. Broadcast on September 30, 1980, *Playing for Time* drew scattered demonstrations against CBS and some of its affiliate stations but also captured the largest share of the American television audience that evening. Nominated for a Golden Globe, the Peabody Award, and six Emmys, *Playing for Time* won the Peabody and garnered four Emmys. Producers Yellin and Quill won for Best Drama Special, Jane Alexander won for Outstanding Supporting Actress, Arthur Miller won for Outstanding Writing, and—to the chagrin of many Jewish Americans—Vanessa Redgrave won for Outstanding Lead Actress. Perhaps intended as more of a rebuttal than a supplement to *Playing for Time*, the

Simon Wiesenthal Center produced *Genocide* (1981), Arnold Schwartzman's grim documentary of the Holocaust, narrated by Elizabeth Taylor and Orson Welles.

Let There Be Light (1946; 1981)

Thirty-five years after its confiscation by the U.S. War Department, John Huston successfully prevailed on President Jimmy Carter to help liberate his film, *Let There Be Light* (1946; 1981), from government vaults. The third installment in Huston's WWII Signal Corps documentary trilogy—*Report from the Aleutians* (1943) and *San Pietro* (1945) being the first two—*Let There Be Light* was suppressed because it documented the psychiatric treatment of a group of seventy-five U.S. soldiers suffering from "war neurosis" (shell shock) at Mason General Hospital in Brentwood, Long Island. Narrated by the director's father, Walter Huston, *Let There Be Light* featured the evocative music of the prolific Dimitri Tiomkin (who scored the *Why We Fight* series) and the stark cinematographic style of Huston's director of photography, Stanley Cortez (*The Magnificent Ambersons*). When Huston's film was finally exhibited, critics were surprised to discover that it was resolutely conventional, mild-mannered, and unabashedly affirmative of the powers of psychiatry to affect miraculous cures of traumatized combat veterans. Why would the government suppress such an innocuous film? In his autobiography, *An Open Book*, Huston speculates that the War Department "wanted to maintain the 'warrior' myth, which said that our American soldiers went to war and came back all the stronger for the experience, standing tall and proud for having served their country well. Only a few weaklings fell by the wayside. Everyone was a hero, and had medals and ribbons to prove it. They might die, or they might be wounded, but their spirit remained unbroken" (Huston, 125). In the immediate aftermath of the Vietnam debacle, the macho ideology of the fearless warrior was at least temporarily open to examination and critique.

Oppenheimer (1980)

Peter Goodchild's *Oppenheimer*, a television miniseries coproduced by WGBH (Boston) and the British Broadcasting Corporation (BBC), first aired in the United Kingdom in October 1980 and later aired on PBS's *American Playhouse* in May 1982, presents a revisionist view of the advent of the atomic age. The debut of *Oppenheimer* on American public television coincided with a period of intense ferment over the issue of nuclear weapons proliferation. In response to

President Ronald Reagan's extremely aggressive stance toward the Soviet Union, a major antinuclear demonstration was held at the Nevada Test Site on February 24, 1982, the first since 1957. Four months later—between June 7 and July 10— the United Nations convened its Second Special Session on (Nuclear) Disarmament and a few days into the conference an antinuclear demonstration in solidarity drew a million people to New York's Central Park: the largest antiwar demonstration in history.

The ideological thrust of *Oppenheimer* was consonant with the political tenor of these events. Portrayed by Sam Waterston (a well-known liberal activist), J. Robert Oppenheimer (1904–1967), "the father of the atomic bomb," emerges as a complex personality, a scientific genius, and a martyr to McCarthyism. As scientific director of the Manhattan Project, which developed the atomic bomb, Oppenheimer was instrumental in bringing about the atomic age but he soon came to have serious misgivings about "the bomb," especially after Hiroshima and Nagasaki. During his tenure as postwar chair of the General Advisory Committee (GAC) of the Atomic Energy Commission (AEC), Oppenheimer was reluctant to develop the hydrogen bomb, a thermonuclear weapon exponentially more powerful than the atomic bomb. He feared that such a bomb would be, perforce, a genocidal weapon. In 1949, after the Soviets shocked the world by testing their first atom bomb, the U.S. government decided to go ahead with the H-bomb. Oppenheimer's continuing aversion to a superbomb irritated some of his more hawkish colleagues, especially the hydrogen bomb's chief advocate, physicist Edward Teller (1908–2003; the man later caricatured as "Dr. Strangelove" in Stanley Kubrick's 1964 film). As the Cold War intensified and Senator Joe McCarthy brought anticommunist paranoia to a fever pitch in the early 1950s, Oppenheimer came under increasing suspicion. On December 23, 1953, Colonel K. D. Nichols, AEC security chief, acting on behalf of President Eisenhower, sent Oppenheimer a letter detailing charges that he had had Communist ties until 1943 and compromised national security by opposing the H-bomb. Nichols also notified Oppenheimer that his security clearance had been suspended until a final determination could be made of his "veracity, conduct and . . . loyalty." In a long letter published in the *New York Times* (April 13, 1954), Oppenheimer answered Nichols' charges and requested a hearing before the AEC's Personnel Security Board to defend himself against the government's allegations. Over a four-week span in April–May 1954, the hearing board took thousands of transcript pages of testimony from some forty witnesses including Oppenheimer. In the end, the board voted to strip Oppenheimer of his security clearance—an outcome that surprised the public and angered many in the scientific community. Though the U.S. government shamed and politically marginalized Oppenheimer, the American scientific community acknowledged Oppenheimer's stature by appointing him head of Princeton University's Institute for Advanced Study after Albert Einstein's death in 1955. Dr. Oppenheimer held the post until his own death, from throat cancer, in 1967.

Oppenheimer covers much of this ground with a fair degree of accuracy. Nonetheless, screenwriter Peter Prince had to resort to the typical sorts of condensations and fictionalizations necessary to fit a highly complex life into a fluid and sufficiently dramatic seven-episode (350-minute) miniseries. In "Oppenheimer and History according to Television," an article for *Air University Review* (November–December 1982), Lawrence H. Suid criticizes *Oppenheimer* for the dramatic license it takes with the historical record. Suid notes that the series falsely portrays General Leslie Groves (1896–1970, director of the Manhattan Project, played by Manning Redwood) as a boorish, overbearing, and not-very-intelligent figure. Suid also observes that *Oppenheimer* depicts Col. Nichols as a vengeful and mean-spirited Machiavellian bent on destroying Oppenheimer for reasons both political and personal. Suid further notes that *Oppenheimer* condenses weeks of security hearing testimony into a 20-minute segment: an example of extreme distillation that is bound to distort the record. In general, Suid objects to the film's placing most of the blame for Oppenheimer's persecution on the military when, in his view, the impetus fell on McCarthyism's pernicious influence on Congress and the White House. This assertion is somewhat debatable; while the military may not have instigated Oppenheimer's downfall, it was certainly a willing accomplice.

Das Boot (1981)

On an entirely different note, but also strongly revisionist in its own way, is Wolfgang Petersen's superlative antiwar film, *Das Boot* (*The Boat*) (1981), based on Lothar-Günther Buchheim's eponymous novel (Munich: Piper, 1973), his nonfiction book, *U-Boat-Krieg* (*U-Boat War*) (Munich: Piper, 1976), and other writings. An accomplished artist turned war correspondent with the *Kriegsmarine* (German navy) during WWII, Buchheim served on minesweepers and destroyers before going on several patrols in 1941–1942 with *U-96*, a type VII-C U-boat commanded by Kapitänleutnant Heinrich Lehmann-Willenbrock (1911–1986), one of Nazi Germany's top U-boat aces. In the course of the war, U-boats commanded by Lehmann-Willenbrock sank twenty-eight Allied ships, totaling more than 190,000 tons.

Buchheim's stint aboard *U-96* occurred at a time when Germany was winning the battle of the Atlantic. In the first three years of the war—from September 1939 to the end of 1942—U-boats sank some 1,900 Allied ships in the North

Scene still from the movie Das Boot, *directed by Wolfgang Petersen. (Bavaria/Radiant/ The Kobal Collection)*

Atlantic while losing about 150 boats: a kill ratio of almost 13 to 1. Book and film are set in the final weeks of 1941 when the U-boats were beginning to experience difficulties. By this time, with the broken Enigma code (August 1941) and improvements in British antisubmarine technology and tactics, the tide   was beginning to turn in favor of the Allies. (In 1943 U-boats sank 285 enemy ships but lost 237 boats; in 1944 U-boats sank only 31 ships in the North Atlantic while losing 242 boats; results were even more lopsided in the final months of the war.)

Though drawing on events from several patrols, much of Buchheim's narrative is based on the *U-96*'s seventh patrol in the fall of 1941. Four days after departing its base at St. Nazaire, France (October 27, 1941), *U-96* located and attacked Convoy OS-10, a thirty-five-vessel merchant fleet two days out of Liverpool and bound for Freetown, Sierra Leone, on Africa's Atlantic coast. In the ensuing engagement *U-96* torpedoed and sank the SS *Bennekom*, a 6,000-ton Dutch freighter. Of a crew of fifty-four, eight Allied sailors lost their lives. For the remainder of the patrol, *U-96* had no other kills. En route to the Mediterranean in heavy seas, *U-96* had the unlikely experience of encountering another U-boat: *U-572*, commanded by Kapitänleutnant Heinz Hirsacker ("Thomsen" played by Otto Sander in the film). Attempting to enter the Mediterranean Sea through the

Straits of Gibraltar on November 31, 1941, *U-96* was attacked and damaged by a WWI-era RAF Fairey Swordfish biplane (the same type that fatally damaged the *Bismarck* six months earlier). Forced to return to its base for repairs, *U-96* arrived back at St. Nazaire on December 6, 1941, after thirty-nine days at sea.

Novel and movie represent the alternately tedious and terrifying reality of submarine warfare with meticulous accuracy (Heinrich Lehmann-Willenbrock himself served as an advisor to the film). The massive U-boat pens in France; the dank, congested interior of the U-boat; the increasingly ratty look of the crew; the unspeakable terror of depth-charge attacks: all are rendered with an unmatched degree of realism. At the same time, *Das Boot* exaggerates and fictionalizes certain things. While Jürgen Prochnow delivers a dazzling performance as Lehmann-Willenbrock, the real man was huskier, more even-tempered, and in 1943 ten years younger than Prochnow was in 1980, that is, more ordinary than Prochnow's craggy, fiercely intense warrior. Likewise the long and hellish submersion of *U-96* on the ocean floor after being damaged in the Straits of Gibraltar never happened. The film's culminating air raid just as the boat returns to base didn't happen either (though similar air raids on the U-boat pens were common). The former event was added to increase dramatic intensity and the latter event added to drive home, with bitter irony, the heartbreaking futility of war. After having achieved and endured so much, the men of *U-96* find only devastation and grief. Fascinating, harrowing, and elegiac, *Das Boot* ranks as one of the greatest (antiwar) films ever made. By showing German combatants in all their suffering humanity, in a small way *Das Boot* helped to rehabilitate Germany in the Anglo-American imagination.

Empire of the Sun (1987)

After more than twenty years spent writing his inimitable, apocalyptic brand of science fiction–fantasy, J. G. Ballard departed from his usual métier with *Empire of the Sun* (London: Victor Gollancz, 1984), a fictionalized memoir of his coming-of-age in China during World War II. "Jim" (a quasi-fictional version of the author) is the precocious, self-absorbed, persistently cheerful eleven-year-old son of British aristocrats living in conspicuous luxury in Shanghai's International Settlement, a guarded enclave for the city's 30,000 foreigners, mostly British and American. But in December 1941 Jim's halcyon world is irrevocably changed. In conjunction with the attack on Pearl Harbor, the Japanese military, which had already occupied Shanghai proper, take over the hitherto sacrosanct International Settlement. During the ensuing chaos Jim is separated from his parents and forced to fend for himself. For four months he stays alive by foraging for food in his neighbors' abandoned mansions. Thereafter Jim meets up with Frank and Basie, two wily American merchant seamen, who take him in tow and instruct him in the ways of long-term survival. Soon Jim, Frank, and Basie find themselves among 2,000 other foreign nationals incarcerated at the Lunghua Civilian Assembly Center, a Japanese internment camp located near a military airfield at Hungjao, on the outskirts of Shanghai. Over the next four years, while waiting out the war's end at Lunghua, Jim moves from boyhood innocence to a mature understanding of life, death, and his own protean capacities for adaptability and survival when it comes to dealing with his fellow internees and his powerful captors. In the end, Jim survives, is liberated, reunited with his parents, and on his way back to a normal life in a postwar world utterly and ominously transformed by the atomic bomb.

For filmmaker Steven Spielberg, Ballard's novel presented itself as a highly attractive property. It had everything Spielberg looked for at that time: a neatly episodic structure congenial to cinematic treatment, a colorful historical setting, a touch of surrealism, the added narrative prestige of a true story, and the trademark Spielberg element: a youthful protagonist trying to find his way in a suddenly alien world. Once he acquired the rights, Spielberg hired noted playwright-screenwriter Tom Stoppard (*Brazil*) to produce an adaptation and later brought in Menno Meyjes (Speilberg's screenwriter for *The Color Purple*) to revise Stoppard's work. After auditioning thousands of young actors, Spielberg chose a twelve-year-old Welshman named Christian Bale to play the film's protagonist, James Graham. The rest of the cast included the prodigiously talented John Malkovich (*Places in the Heart; The Killing Fields*) as Basie, Joe Pantoliano as Frank, and Miranda Richardson as Mrs. Victor, a woman who takes in James at Lunghua. Shot on location in Shanghai, *Empire of the Sun* (1987) stayed close to Ballard's story but also prettified it in typical Spielberg fashion. For example, in the novel, Jim learns that Basie and Frank routinely extract gold teeth from corpses floating in the Yangtze River—a practice not alluded to in the film. The movie also downplays the stark contrast between Western affluence and the grinding poverty and misery of the Chinese. Likewise, Speilberg's version tends to soft-pedal the harsh living conditions at Lunghua and enhances certain scenes with clichéd ethereal choral music that too insistently evokes a sense of childlike wonder. Despite these flaws the film does stay close to the overall tone and content of Ballard's novel. Anxious to get it right, Spielberg sought Ballard's advice during filming and received his wholehearted endorsement once the film was released. Not a huge success by Spielberg standards, *Empire of the Sun* garnered lukewarm reviews and did only mediocre box office.

Fat Man and Little Boy (1989)

A more extreme example of the bureaucratic routinization of violence is the topic of *Fat Man and Little Boy* (1989), a docudrama about the Manhattan Project at Los Alamos, New Mexico, which developed the atomic bomb during World War II. Roland Joffé and Bruce Robinson, British director and writer, respectively, of the highly regarded Vietnam-era political drama, *The Killing Fields* (1984), joined forces again to produce a cinematic reflection on the dawn of the nuclear age. Starring Paul Newman as Gen. Leslie R. Groves (1986–1970), the military director of the project, and Dwight Schultz as J. Robert Oppenheimer (1904–1967), the scientific director of the project, *Fat Man and Little Boy* explores the uneasy relationship between the nascent military-industrial complex and scientific community that made it all possible. Though it deals with an inherently fascinating and important story, in the hands of Joffé and Robinson, *Fat Man and Little Boy* comes off as rather dull and tepid.

July 20th and *The Plot to Kill Hitler* (1990)

Six weeks after D-day (June 6, 1944) a group of high-ranking German army officers and civilian officials led by Colonel Claus von Stauffenberg (1907–1944) attempted a coup (code-named Operation Walküre) that would bring the war to an end and save what was left of Germany. The plan, directly involving nearly 200 other conspirators, was to assassinate Adolf Hitler at his military headquarters (*Wolfsschanze* or "*Wolf's Lair*") in East Prussia, arrest Hitler's key subordinates, and take over the German government. On July 20 the bomb that Stauffenberg placed under Hitler's conference table did explode, killing four and making a shambles of the room, but Hitler, protected by the thick oak table, was only slightly injured. In the wake of the failed coup Hitler had the conspirators and nearly 4,000 other suspected enemies of the Reich rounded up and executed. Count von Stauffenberg was shot by firing squad. Other key conspirators were hung from piano wire and filmed, for Hitler's sadistic edification, as they were writhing in the agony of their slow strangulation.

Keen to repudiate the horrors of its Hitlerian era, postwar West Germany began "*Vergangenheitsbewaeltigung*" ("coping with the past"), a concerted national effort to confront and atone for the crimes of the Third Reich. Accordingly, the Germans made Stauffenberg an enduring national icon and have, over the years, produced a number of films about the July 20 plot. The first two of these films appeared almost simultaneously in the summer of 1955: Falk

Harnack's *Der 20. Juli* (*July 20th*) and G. W. Pabst's *Es geschah am 20. Juli* (*It Happened on the 20th of July*). In 1971 West German television aired Franz Peter Wirth's *Operation Walküre*, an award-winning miniseries that combined docudrama with interviews of witnesses and survivors. Another version, with additional material, aired on French television in 1973. Thirty years later writer-director Jo Baier presented *Stauffenberg* (2004), another television docudrama for a new generation of Germans born decades after WWII.

The British and Americans have also contributed films about the July 20 plot. In 1964 the BBC aired Rudolf Cartier's docudrama, *The July Plot*, starring veteran mystery–horror film actor John Carson as Stauffenberg. A quarter century later noted American television miniseries producer David L. Wolper (*Roots*) brought out *The Plot to Kill Hitler* (1990), a docudrama directed by investigative journalist Lawrence Schiller (a frequent collaborator of Norman Mailer) and starring Brad Davis (*Roots; Midnight Express*) as Count von Stauffenberg, Madolyn Smith as his wife, Nina, and Ian Richardson as General Ludwig Beck (1880–1944), another leading conspirator. While none of the above-mentioned Stauffenberg films is fully adequate to its subject, all succeed in sustaining the historical memory of the German anti-Nazi resistance.

Tragedy at Sea and *Mission of the Shark: The Saga of the U.S.S. Indianapolis* (1991)

While *The Plot to Kill Hitler* and other films on the July 20 plot have helped to mitigate the sense that Germany's enthrallment to Nazism had been monolithic, American filmmakers dealing with World War II history topics continue to produce work that revises the myth of the Good War in the other direction, toward a more nuanced view that admits the U.S. military made some terrible mistakes during the war and committed worse injustices trying to cover them up. Easily the most notorious among these cases is that of the USS *Indianapolis* (CA-35), a *Portland*-class heavy cruiser that delivered the Hiroshima atomic bomb from San Francisco to the island of Tinian, 5,000 miles distant, on July 26, 1945. After completing her top-secret mission, the unescorted *Indianapolis* was en route to the Leyte Gulf in the Philippines when she was sunk 14 minutes after midnight on Monday morning, July 30, 1945, by Japanese submarine *I-58*. Hit by two torpedoes, the *Indianapolis* heeled over and went under in just 12 minutes, and 300 of its 1,200-man crew went down with it. But far worse was yet to come. Over the next several days some of the ship's surviving crew, possibly numbering almost 900 at the time of the sinking, huddled in the few available life rafts but most treaded water in their life vests, desperately waiting for a rescue that might never come. Wounds, saltwater ulcers, extreme thirst, hunger, exhaustion, exposure, madness, and ravenous sharks steadily thinned their ranks until there were less than 350 left alive when they were accidentally spotted on the morning of the fourth day by a PV-1 Ventura bomber on antisubmarine patrol in the area. The PV-1 radioed its base and a PBY Catalina seaplane was directed to the location, as were the USS *Cecil J. Doyle* (DE-368), a *Butler*-class destroyer escort, and three high-speed transports: the USS *Ringness* (APD-100), the USS *Register* (APD-92), and the USS *Bassett* (APD-73). On Thursday, August 8, the seaplane and naval vessels converged on the site and eventually rescued 316 half-dead survivors who had endured an unimaginably hellish experience.

Horror-struck by the most gruesome catastrophe in the history of the U.S. Navy, navy officials proceeded to sweep the ghastly occurrence under the carpet. First, the navy deliberately downplayed the loss of the *Indianapolis* by delaying a public announcement until August 14, the day Japan surrendered: momentous news sure to push every other news item into relative insignificance. Second, the navy opted to place almost all the blame for the tragedy on the commander of the *Indianapolis*, Captain Charles Butler McVay III, who survived the sinking. At his court-martial, which started on December 3, 1945, in Washington, D.C., McVay was essentially charged with two offenses: (1) failing to issue timely orders to abandon ship and (2) failing to practice evasive maneuvers, that is, zigzagging, which is supposed to lessen the probability of submarine attack. The first charge was dropped when it was established that the enemy torpedoes instantly knocked out the ship's electrics, preventing intercom broadcast of an abandon ship order. McVay was found guilty of the second charge and lived out the rest of his life a disgraced and broken man. He committed suicide on November 11 (Veteran's Day), 1968.

Over the years a series of books have come out dealing with the tragedy: Richard F. Newcomb's *Abandon Ship!* (New York: Henry Holt, 1958); Thomas Helm's *Ordeal by Sea* (New York: Dodd, Mead, 1963); Raymond Lech's *All the Drowned Sailors* (New York: Military Heritage Press, 1982); Dan Kurzman's *Fatal Voyage* (New York: Atheneum, 1990); Doug Stanton's *In Harm's Way* (New York: Henry Holt, 2001); Peter Nelson's *Left for Dead* (New York: Delacorte, 2001). The first cinematic mention of the disaster occurs in Steven Spielberg's 1975 blockbuster, *Jaws*, when the grizzled shark hunter, Quint (Robert Shaw), recounts the story. Many viewers of *Jaws* did not realize that Quint's chilling tale was a true one until the airing of the made-for-television movie, *Mission of the Shark: The Saga of the U.S.S. Indianapolis* (1991). Written by Alan Sharp (*Night Moves; The Osterman Weekend*), *Mission of the Shark* stars Stacey Keach as Capt. McVay and Richard Thomas as the ship's doctor, Scott. Bookended by scenes from a reunion of survivors in the 1960s, *Mission*'s main narrative, told in flashback, accurately recounts the sinking, its horrific aftermath, and the trumped-up navy court-martial of Capt. McVay, which ended in his disgrace and eventual suicide. Thus a cinematic treatment of the true story of the *Indianapolis* had to be deferred for almost half a century for the scandal to lose most of its political relevance and force. Though *Mission of the Shark* was a better-than-average made-for-TV movie, the horrifying saga of the USS *Indianapolis* still deserves feature-film treatment.

Stalingrad (1993)

The Battle of Stalingrad (late August 1942–February 2, 1943) was the fiercest and bloodiest military slaughter in history, producing upward of 1.5 million dead. Stalingrad also proved to be the first major defeat for Nazi Germany, a defeat that sealed the eventual doom of the Third Reich. Encountering fanatical Soviet resistance, Hitler's forces became embroiled in street-to-street fighting in the bombed-out rubble of the city that lasted weeks on end and produced heavy casualties. Obsessed with taking Stalingrad, his nemesis' namesake, Hitler neglected to shore up his flanks along the Volga to the north and south of the city. The Soviets exploited this glaring weakness by unleashing a massive counteroffensive aimed at those areas on November 19–20, 1942. Quickly overrun and/or surrounded, the Axis (German, Italian, and Romanian) armies that had been besieging the city were themselves besieged and destroyed. By the time the German 6th Army surrendered, there were fewer than 90,000 left of a force of a quarter million men. Only a few thousand made it back from Soviet captivity years after the war ended.

As the single most important battle of World War II, Stalingrad has been the subject of a number of films over the years, mostly by Russian and German filmmakers aimed at and limited to their respective audiences. The first feature film on the topic afforded international distribution was Joseph Vilsmaier's *Stalingrad* (1993), a German-made docudrama that follows the fortunes of Hans Witzland (Thomas Kretschmann), an inexperienced lieutenant who leads a *Wehrmacht* unit sent from Italy to the East Front in the fall of 1942. Produced by a group headed by Günter Rohrbach, the producer of *Das Boot*, *Stalingrad* bears some marked similarities to the earlier film. Resolutely antiwar, both films present remorselessly realistic depictions of the psychological terrors of war, but *Stalingrad* exceeds *Das Boot* in its graphic depiction of the dehumanizing and demoralizing effects of all-out combat: horrible wounds, atrocities, insane levels of destruction. The devastating air raid on La Rochelle that comes at the end of *Das Boot* is small potatoes compared to the apocalypse that engulfs the German soldiers at Stalingrad. Yet, as *Washington Post* critic Desson Howe points out in a March 29, 1996, review, *Stalingrad* "feels dutifully exhaustive rather than emotionally insightful: it doesn't shed more than conventional light on war and suffering."

Schindler's List (1993)

On a very hot day in October 1980, Australian novelist Thomas Keneally paid a visit to a Beverly Hills leather goods store to buy a new briefcase. The proprietor, Leopold Page (real name: Poldek Pfefferberg, 1913–2001), a Holocaust survivor, told Keneally the story of Oskar Schindler (1908–1974), a Sudeten German factory owner in Krakow during the war who risked his own life to save the lives of 1,098 Polish Jews (801 men and 297 women). Intrigued by Schindler's saga, Keneally went on to research and write *Schindler's Ark* (London: Hodder & Stoughton, 1982), a partially fictionalized but largely historical account that won the 1982 Booker Prize (for best novel by a citizen of the United Kingdom). Film producer Sid Sheinberg immediately purchased the rights and, a decade later, Steven Spielberg made a film version written by Steve Zaillian (*Awakenings; Searching for Bobby Fischer*) titled *Schindler's List* (1993).

Oskar Schindler's factory, Czech Republic, 2004. (Miaow Miaow)

Herr Oskar Schindler (Liam Neeson) is in many ways an unlikely humanitarian hero. A charming, gregarious bon vivant, a greedy businessman with more than a touch of the con artist in him, a heavy drinker, inveterate womanizer, and a Nazi Party member, Schindler comes to Krakow from his hometown of Zwittau-Brinnlitz in the wake of Hitler's panzers in 1939 to profit from the war. Secretly securing financing from a Jew named Itzhak Stern (Ben Kingsley), Schindler takes over an idle enamel-wear factory and compels hundreds of Jews to work for him. NSDAP membership notwithstanding, Schindler tends to be both amoral and apolitical—until he witnesses the brutal liquidation of the Krakow Ghetto by SS troops on March 13, 1943. (To mark the moment as Schindler's moral epiphany, the camera follows the fortunes of a young Jewish girl in a red coat who is soon murdered. The image of the red coat is especially conspicuous and haunting as the film is shot in black and white.) From that moment until the end of the war, Schindler uses bribery, deception, and personal influence to rescue Jews from the gas chambers: an increasingly risky endeavor after the tide of war turns against Germany.

Ironically, Schindler sometimes enlists the unwitting aid of his evil counterpart, SS Hauptsturmführer Amon Göth (Ralph Fiennes), the sadistic Nazi who carried out the razing of the Krakow Ghetto and commands the Plaszow forced labor camp nearby. In the autumn of 1944, as the Soviet army closes in, the Germans attempt to conceal their crimes by unearthing the bodies of thousands of murdered Jews and burning them. Schindler's factory is closed, as is the Plaszow labor camp. In a bid to save his thousand Schindlerjuden (Schindler's Jews), Schindler pays Göth a hefty bribe to authorize their transport to his hometown of Zwittau-Brinnlitz, Czechoslovakia, 370 miles to the west, where he sets up a munitions factory that turns out (defective) artillery shells. Schindler and Stern draw up a list, that is, "Schindler's List." Those whose names appear on it are sent to relative safety in Zwittau instead of the death camps. The film ends with a present-day coda shot at Schindler's grave in the Catholic churchyard on Mount Zion in Jerusalem, with cast members and actual Schindlerjuden following ancient tradition by placing commemorative stones on the grave marker.

A grim 3-and-a-quarter-hour tour de force well scripted, strongly acted, and beautifully shot by Janusz Kaminski, *Schindler's List* won almost universal praise from critics and audiences. It also won a host of industry accolades, including seven Academy Awards. The film ultimately made almost $300 million worldwide but to his lasting credit, Steven Spielberg refused to take profits for himself. When NBC televised *Schindler's List* in late February 1997, 34 percent of all households watching television (65 million Americans) tuned in, despite the fact that Christian fundamentalist and evangelical groups denounced the broadcast—ostensibly because the film contained graphic violence, nudity, and profanity but more likely due to underlying ideological issues. A few years later the film's considerable prestige was somewhat diminished when historian David M. Crowe (Elon University) published what is considered the definitive Schindler biography: *Oskar Schindler: The Untold Account of His Life, Wartime Activities, and the True Story behind the List* (Boulder, CO: Westview Press, 2004). In his researches Crowe discovered that Oskar Schindler and Itzhak Stern did not prepare the famous list; Schindler could not have because he was in jail at the time for bribing Amon Göth, and Stern was no longer in Schindler's employ. The transport list was actually drawn up by a clerk named Marcel Goldberg, who allegedly accepted bribes by wealthier Jews to include their names. Furthermore, Crowe challenged the film's depiction of Schindler's sudden and decisive moral epiphany as fanciful and simplistic. In fact, Schindler's decision to save "his" Jews evolved over a long period of time as he witnessed Nazi acts of barbarism. In a *Salon* interview with Richard Covington (October 24, 1997), Jewish playwright and screenwriter David Mamet publicly criticized the film as "exploitative," even though Spielberg obviously did not intend it to be.

Tuskegee Airmen (1995)

Though the relatively little-known story of the Tuskegee Airmen, an all-black fighter unit in the U.S. Army Air Corps during World War II, had been told a number of times in the postwar period, it was not until the 1990s that the history of the 99th Air Squadron (332nd Fighter Group) achieved a kind of critical mass with the publication of a half-dozen books on the subject between 1992 and 1997. The historical recuperation of the 99th was reflective of a larger effort to rehabilitate and finally acknowledge key black contributions to twentieth-century American life and culture, for example, in the areas of sports and music, revisionist efforts that reached full flowering in the waning years of the century. Robert Markowitz's made-for-HBO (Home Box Office) movie, *The Tuskegee Airmen* (1995), starring Laurence Fishburne, Malcolm-Jamal Warner, Andre Braugher, and Cuba Gooding Jr. presents a credibly authentic representation of the racism that black airmen faced in Army Air Corps (which was not integrated until after World War II).

Paradise Road (1997)

Bruce Beresford, the Australian director behind *"Breaker" Morant* (1980), took on a very different sort of war history topic with *Paradise Road* (1997). Based on two books—Betty Jeffrey's *White Coolies* (Sydney, Australia: Angus and Robertson, 1954) and Helen Colijn's *Song of Survival: Women Interned* (Ashland, OR: White Cloud Press, 1995)—*Paradise Road* recounts the true story of an international group of women held in a Japanese prison camp in southern Sumatra during World War II who formed a vocal orchestra to pass the time and sustain morale. Heading a large ensemble female cast are Glenn Close as Adrienne Pargiter and Pauline Collins as Daisy "Margaret" Drummond, characters based on real people: Norah Chambers, the conductor of the vocal orchestra, and Miss Margaret Dryburgh (1890–1945), a Presbyterian missionary and nurse who transcribed and arranged the music. A story of courage, imagination, and distaff solidarity in brutal conditions, *Paradise Road* both evokes and transcends the clichés connected with human uplift stories.

Saving Private Ryan (1998)

In 1992 Stephen Ambrose (1936–2002), historian and biographer of Eisenhower and Nixon, published *Band of Brothers: E Company, 506th Regiment, 101st Airborne from Normandy to Hitler's Eagle's Nest* (New York: Simon & Schuster, 1992), a chronicle of the combat experiences of a group of U.S. paratroopers in the last eleven months of World War II. Included in *Band of Brothers* is an account of the four Niland brothers from Tonawanda, New York: Edward (Eddie), Robert (Bob), Preston, and Frederick (Fritz). The oldest brother, Eddie, was shot down over Burma on May 20, 1944, and a telegram reporting him MIA arrived at his parents' home on D-day, June 6. (A year later Eddie turned up alive, having escaped from a Japanese prison camp.) The other brothers—Bob, Preston, and Fritz—all participated in the Normandy landings. Bob, a sergeant with the 82nd Airborne, was killed in action on June 6 and Preston, a 2nd lieutenant with the 4th Infantry Division, was killed a day later. Fritz, a sergeant with the 101st Airborne, was inadvertently dropped too far behind enemy lines. Reported missing in action, he eventually made his way back to friendly lines nine days later. Nonetheless, in the course of a week, four telegrams arrived at the Niland home, reporting two sons killed and two missing in action. In his book Ambrose erroneously reports that *three* Niland brothers were killed and that their mother, Augusta ("Gussie"), received all three telegrams *the same day*, prompting Fritz's immediate removal from the front lines to spare the family further grief. Though factually inaccurate, Ambrose's account of the Niland saga made for great melodrama, on a par with the story of the fighting Sullivans.

Stephen Ambrose's next book, *D-Day (June 6, 1944): The Climactic Battle of World War II* (New York: Simon & Schuster, 1994), timed to coincide with the fiftieth anniversary of D-day, was a runaway bestseller that catapulted Ambrose from academic obscurity to national prominence. It was also a major factor in touching off a national wave of nostalgia for the World War II generation, a wave that crested with two high-profile media products four years later. On the publishing front, NBC network news anchorman Tom Brokaw brought out *The Greatest Generation* (New York: Random House, 1998), a celebrity-laden rip-off of Studs Terkel's *The Good War: An Oral History of World War II* (New York: Pantheon, 1984). While Terkel's massive compilation of interviews added up to a complex, morally ambiguous picture of the supposedly "good war," Brokaw went out of his way to deify the WWII generation.

On the cinematic front, Steven Spielberg's superpatriotic blockbuster, *Saving Private Ryan* (1998), outdid *The Greatest Generation* in its dogged focus on heart-tugging affirmation and praise. Spielberg's screenwriter, Robert Rodat (*Fly Away Home; The Patriot*), based his script on the Niland brothers' story, or at least Stephen Ambrose's distorted version of that story. Indeed, Rodat, script doctor Frank Darabont, Spielberg, and other writers took Ambrose's exaggerated account and further mythologized events by positing an unlikely mission, led by Tom Hanks, to rescue the Fritz Niland figure, Private James Francis Ryan (Matt Damon), from the front lines and spirit him to safety after his brothers are killed in combat. An odd mixture of meticulous realism and sheer balderdash, *Saving Private Ryan* opens with an incredibly graphic, ferocious, and jarring 23-minute combat sequence depicting the storming of Omaha Beach that far outstrips similar but more tepid scenes in *The Longest Day*; graphic screen violence has increased exponentially since the 1960s. Other compelling combat action follows but the overall tenor of the film is unabashedly propagandistic as regards the near-saintly dedication and manly heroism of the American GI. To further highlight the righteous fortitude of the ordinary soldier, Rodat invents a foil: Corporal Upham (Jeremy Davies), an educated GI who speaks fluent German and is too refined to kill when it is necessary to do so. Upham functions as a none-too-subtle slam at leftist intellectuals who display an internationalist outlook and too many scruples when it comes to war's dirty business. The emotionally and ideologically manipulative nature of *Saving Private Ryan* is especially evident with the culminating death of Hanks' virtuous Captain John Miller, a death not in the original version of the script. Miller, while breathing his last, admonishes Ryan to "Earn this," that is, lead a life worthy of the ultimate sacrifice of America's fallen heroes. Also added, to further hammer home the point, are opening and final framing scenes that feature a now elderly Ryan (Harrison Young) visiting the

Normandy American Cemetery, Colleville-sur Mer, a half century later. Coming upon the grave marker of Captain Miller, presumably for the first time, Ryan collapses to his knees in grief and survivor's guilt, wondering aloud to his wife if he has led a good life. She assures him he has and the image fades into a huge, fluttering American flag filling the screen. With so much carefully cultivated righteousness on its side, the film brooks no ambiguity; it demands that viewers accept its premises at the risk of being deemed unpatriotic or worse—morally and emotionally perverse. In an article in *Progressive* magazine (October 2001), radical historian and WWII air combat veteran Howard Zinn offered a dissenting view on the Greatest Generation phenomenon and films like *Saving Private Ryan:*

> I refuse to celebrate [WWII veterans] as "the greatest generation" because in doing so we are celebrating courage and sacrifice in the cause of war. And we are miseducating the young to believe that military heroism is the noblest form of heroism, when it should be remembered only as the tragic accompaniment of horrendous policies driven by power and profit. Indeed, the current infatuation with World War II prepares us—innocently on the part of some, deliberately on the part of others—for more war, more military adventures, more attempts to emulate the military heroes of the past.

The Good War and Those Who Refused to Fight It (2000)

In agreement with Howard Zinn's sentiments regarding naïve patriotism and warmongering, filmmakers Rick Tejada-Flores (*The Fight in the Fields*) and Judith Ehrlich made *The Good War and Those Who Refused to Fight It* (2000), a 57-minute documentary, narrated by Ed Asner, on the 43,000 Americans who refused to fight in World War II for reasons of conscience. Of that number, 25,000 served in the military as noncombatants, 12,000 lived in Civilian Public Service (CPS) camps and worked on public projects (e.g., forestry and firefighting), and the remaining 6,000 went to prison. Though there have been draft resisters to every U.S. war since the American Revolution, Tejada-Flores and Ehrlich chose to focus on COs in World War II because that war seemed morally unassailable and had overwhelming national support. Those who refused to fight were subjected to intense public disdain, ridicule, social ostracism, and worse—yet very few abandoned their stance on nonviolence. *The Good War* pays tribute to the extraordinary courage and idealism of the WWII CO and recuperates a part of the history of the war that has been long suppressed.

Nuremburg (2000)

Besides coauthoring Colin Powell's autobiography, *My American Journey* (New York: Random House, 1995), former Nelson Rockefeller speechwriter Joseph E. Persico has published a number of popular military and political histories. Among these is *Nuremberg: Infamy on Trial* (New York: Viking, 1994), a novelistic re-creation of the Nuremberg trials of 1945–1946 that *New York Times* reviewer James E. Young somewhat unflatteringly termed "literary nonfiction or 'faction'" (Young 1994). Pitched toward a general audience, Persico's *Nuremberg* generally follows the court transcripts but also frequently departs or extrapolates from strict historical facts by imagining the inner thoughts and feelings of defendants, attorneys, prosecutors, and judges—a technique popularized by biographical novelist Irving Stone.

Though slightly dubious as history, *Nuremberg* made for compelling drama. A few years after the book's publication, a group of Canadian filmmakers teamed with American actor Alec Baldwin to produce *Nuremberg* (2000), a 4-hour television miniseries adapted from Persico's book by David W. Rintels. Shot at St. Vincent-de-Paul Prison in Laval, Québec, and locations in Montreal in the summer of 1999, *Nuremberg* stars Baldwin as Supreme Court Justice Robert H. Jackson (1892–1954), the man President Truman appointed U.S. chief of counsel for the International Military Tribunal prosecuting the top Nazis for war crimes. Other name actors in the cast include Jill Hennessy (*Law and Order*) as Mrs. Elsie Douglas, Jackson's secretary (with whom he is having an affair); Christopher Plummer as Sir David Maxwell-Fyfe (1900–1967), British prosecutor at Nuremberg; Brian Cox as Reichsmarschall Hermann Wilhelm Göring (1893–1946); and Max von Sydow as prosecution witness Samuel Rosenman. Though not deficient in production values, *Nuremberg* shows signs of being a vanity project for Alec Baldwin. To a greater extent than is typical for cinematic dramatizations, the film glorifies individual heroism by giving the impression that Justice Jackson engineered the tribunal and carried out the prosecution almost single-handedly. In reality, scores of lawyers, researchers, clerks, translators, and other officials were involved with the elaborate process of negotiating the ground rules for a then-unprecedented international war crimes trial, amassing huge amounts of prosecutorial evidence, and conducting the complex court proceedings. Furthermore, the love affair between Justice Jackson and Mrs. Douglas never happened; it was written into the script to give the film more human interest. Finally, Brian Cox's rendition of Hermann Göring as a charming bon vivant obscures Göring's psychopathic tendencies and skews the tone of the film in ways the filmmakers could not have intended.

To End All Wars (2001)

On February 15, 1942, the British army surrendered Singapore to the Japanese. Members of the 69th Scottish Regiment (the Argyle and Sutherland Highlanders), trying to evade capture, fled the Malay Peninsula by boat but soon surrendered to a Japanese warship and were subsequently sent to the Chungkai POW Camp in Thailand, in an area where tens of thousands of Allied prisoners were being used as slave labor to build the infamous Thai-Burma "Death Railway" (as recounted in *The Bridge on the River Kwai*). Among the officers of the 69th was Capt. Ernest Gordon, an agnostic who experienced a profound religious conversion during his hellish captivity, as did a number of his fellow captives. After the war Gordon attended Hartford Theological Seminary, was ordained a minister, and went on to serve as Presbyterian chaplain at Princeton University from 1955 until his retirement in 1981. Twenty-eight years after the war ended, Gordon published *Through the Valley of the Kwai* (New York: Harper, 1962), published in Britain as *The Miracle on the River Kwai* (London: Collins, 1963), his sermonizing account of spiritual transformation occurring in the midst of horror, brutality, and degradation.

Nearly forty years after the book's initial publication, writer-producer-director David L. Cunningham made *To End All Wars* (2001), an amateurish movie version starring Ciarán McMenamin as Capt. Gordon; Robert Carlyle as Major Ian Campbell; Mark Strong as British POW "Dusty" Miller; and Kiefer Sutherland as Lt. Jim Reardon, an American. Adapted by right-wing Christian zealot Brian Godawa, *To End All Wars* is an extremely heavy-handed piece of propaganda for fundamentalist Protestantism. The figurative crucifixion of the saintly Dusty Miller inspires Gordon and other POWs to embrace the Christian faith as the best, perhaps only, means of enduring a profane world. In sum, *To End All Wars* is partisan religious ideology masquerading as a World War II epic.

Pearl Harbor (2001)

Reprehensible in a different way is the cynically vapid Michael Bay-Jerry Bruckheimer blockbuster, *Pearl Harbor* (2001). Written by Mel Gibson with collaborator Randall Wallace (*Braveheart; We Were Soldiers*), *Pearl Harbor* features young Hollywood idols Ben Afleck (as Capt. Rafe McCawley), Josh Hartnett (as Capt. Danny Walker), and Kate Beckinsale (as Nurse Lt. Evelyn Johnson) in a cliché-ridden ménage à trois plot that dominates what is ostensibly a war movie. Expensive to make at an estimated $135 million, *Pearl Harbor* had to be geared to the widest possible youth demographic in order to recoup its costs and turn a profit; hence the inane love story at its core. The film's elaborate, CGI-aided rendition of the Japanese attack on Pearl Harbor is suitably realistic, spectacular, and ferocious but historical inaccuracies are too numerous to mention. No matter, as any discussion of *Pearl Harbor*'s alleged historicity would grant the film too much credit, it was conceived and made solely to generate maximum profits for the filmmakers. Overlong, dull, and poorly acted and directed, *Pearl Harbor* has achieved the dubious distinction of being judged one of the worst films ever made. Nonetheless, the film took in an astonishing $200 million.

Enemy at the Gates (2001)

Eight years after Joseph Vilsmaier's *Stalingrad*, director Jean-Jacques Annaud (*The Name of the Rose; Seven Years in Tibet*) revisited the epic battle with *Enemy at the Gates* (2001), a film loosely based on the military exploits of Chief Petty Officer Vasily Gregorievich Zaitsev, a Russian navy payroll clerk who volunteered for frontline duty at Stalingrad with the 284th Siberian Rifles Division. A crack shot, Zaitsev became an expert sniper who racked up 149 confirmed kills over a four-month period (October 1942 to January 1943) and ended up with almost 400 kills. Though Zaitsev told his own story in *Notes of a Sniper* (1956), Zaitsev's book was not translated into English until 2003. The film script, by Annaud and frequent collaborator Alain Godard, is actually based on overlapping portions of three books: Alan Clark's *Barbarossa* (New York: Signet, 1966); William Craig's *Enemy at the Gate: The Battle for Stalingrad* (New York: Reader's Digest/E. P. Dutton, 1973); and David L. Robbins' novel, *War of the Rats* (New York: Bantam, 1999). The movie recounts a cat-and-mouse duel between Zaitsev (Jude Law) and Major König (Ed Harris), a highly skilled German sniper flown in from Berlin to kill Zaitsev, who is rapidly becoming a legend to both sides for his prowess with a sniper rifle equipped with telescopic site.

The problem with the story is that it is most likely apocryphal. While Zaitsev's achievements are amply documented and the Soviets did indeed develop a cadre of devastatingly effective snipers at Stalingrad who shot and killed 1,200 German officers, NCOs, and other key personnel, there is no hard evidence that a Nazi sharpshooter (variously referred to as König or Thorwald) ever existed. Soviet propaganda officials probably fabricated the duel between Zaitsev and his deadly nemesis to reduce the immense struggle at Stalingrad to identifiably human terms and bolster the morale of sorely tested troops. Though of dubious historicity, the legend of Zaitsev's duel makes for suitably compelling cinema. With a production budget of $70 million, Jean-Jacques Annaud is able to create a highly realistic vision of the ruins of Stalingrad. (Particularly brilliant is an opening sequence that shows Soviet vessels being strafed by Luftwaffe aircraft as they attempt to ferry reinforcements across the mile-wide Volga.) On balance, though, *Enemy at the Gates* suffers from the kind of operatic grandiosity that Vilsmaier's more somber *Stalingrad* wisely avoids.

Band of Brothers (2001)

Inasmuch as Stephen Ambrose's book, *Band of Brothers: E Company, 506th Regiment, 101st Airborne from Normandy to Hitler's Eagle's Nest* (New York: Simon & Schuster, 1992) spawned *Saving Private Ryan* (1998), it is not surprising that Ambrose, Steven Spielberg, and Tom Hanks teamed up again after *Ryan*'s tremendous success to make *Band of Brothers* into a ten-part HBO television miniseries. Funded by Spielberg's studio, Dream Works SKG, in conjunction with HBO and BBC to the tune of an estimated $125 million, *Band of Brothers* (2001) was a massive undertaking. Shot mostly in huge hangars at the Hatfield Aerodrome in Hertfordshire, England, *Band of Brothers* called for some 500 speaking parts, hundreds of extras, $17 million worth of set construction, and tens of millions more expended on authentic-looking uniforms, equipment,

Steven Spielberg (left) and Tom Hanks in the press room with their awards for Band of Brothers *at the 54th Annual Prime Time Emmy Awards in Los Angeles, September 22, 2002. (Mark Avery/Orange County Register/Corbis)*

and vehicles. The ever-fastidious Spielberg went to great pains to ensure authenticity in the look, sound, and feel of the production. Indeed, Spielberg, Hanks, and Ambrose had their series scripts vetted by veterans of the 101st Airborne to ensure impeccable realism in terms of action and dialogue. Commanding vast sums and the best technical expertise in the film business, Steven Spielberg could afford a degree of perfectionism only dreamt of by ordinary mortals.

Almost predictably, *Band of Brothers* proved to be a superb production in every way—sharply scripted, beautifully mounted, well acted, and consistently authentic in its depiction of Easy Company's hard progress through Hitler's Europe, from Normandy to Obersalzberg, including the Battle of the Bulge and the liberation of one of Hitler's concentration camps. Nominated for Emmys in nineteen different categories, *Band of Brothers* won six, including an Emmy for Outstanding Miniseries. A reiteration of the Greatest Generation ideology that had already proved so successful in the mid-1990s, *Band of Brothers* first aired in the fall of 2001. After the devastating September 11 terrorist attacks on the Pentagon and World Trade Center, the series took on a different cultural function than what might have been anticipated. Rather than merely serve a comfortable nostalgia, *Band of Brothers* proved to be something of a morale stiffener for a shaken and demoralized nation.

The Pianist (2002)

Right after World War II Polish Jewish classical pianist and composer Wladyslaw Szpilman (1911–2000) published *Smierc Miasta* (*Death of a City*) in his native Poland, a harrowing memoir of surviving alone in the Warsaw Ghetto during the Nazi occupation. Suppressed by Communist authorities, the book sank into oblivion—until fifty years later, when Szpilman's book, retitled *The Pianist*, was finally republished first in Germany then in a host of other countries. Belatedly hailed as a masterpiece of Holocaust literature, *The Pianist: The Extraordinary True Story of One Man's Survival in Warsaw 1939–1945* (New York: Picador, 1999) garnered adulatory reviews and caught the attention of director Roman Polanski, himself a survivor of the Warsaw Ghetto. (Polanski's mother, Bula Polanska née Katz, died in a Nazi concentration camp.)

Embracing a work uncannily close to his own traumatic experience under the iron heel of Hitler's Reich, Polanski undertook a film adaptation of Szpilman's book with almost preternatural dedication, understanding, and a mastery of technique developed over a forty-five-year career in cinema. Accurately adapted to the screen by Ronald Harwood (*Cry, the Beloved Country*) and starring Adrien

Brody (*Bread and Roses*)—who lost 30 pounds for the role—as Wladyslaw Szpilman and Thomas Kretcshmann as *Wehrmacht* Captain Wilm Hosenfeld (who risks his life to help Szpilman survive), *The Pianist* unforgettably evokes the cruelties and horrors of the Warsaw Ghetto but also shows—contra moralistic clichés—that humanity and compassion can come from the most unexpected sources. Masterfully filmed by Pawel Edelman (who shot Andre Wajda's *Pan Tadeusz*), edited by longtime Polanski collaborator Hervé de Luze (*Bitter Moon; Death and the Maiden*), and designed by Allan Starski (*Schindler's List*), *The Pianist* was rightly hailed as a superlative achievement. It went on to win a slew of international film awards including Oscars for Best Actor (Brody), Best Director (Polanski), and Best Writer (Harwood).

Blind Spot (2002) and *The Downfall* (2004)

In 2001, after almost sixty years of silence, Traudl Junge (née Gertrude Humps, 1920–2002), Adolf Hitler's personal secretary from December 1942 to April 1945, published her memoirs (edited by Melissa Müller): *Bis zur letzten Stunde. Hitlers Sekretärin erzählt ihr Leben* (*Until the Final Hour: Hitler's Secretary Recounts Her Life*). Shortly thereafter filmmakers André Heller and Othmar Schmiderer filmed ten hour's worth of interview sessions with Junge that were edited down to an 82-minute film, *Im toten Winkel: Hitlers Sekretärin* (*Blind Spot: Hitler's Secretary*, 2002). In memoir and film, Traudl Junge recalls Hitler as soft-spoken, fatherly to her, a sharp dresser, and kind to his dog, Blondi. At the same time Junge expresses profound guilt for being so fond of a man now recognized as one of history's worst monsters. Some critics complained that Traudl Junge's recollections humanized Adolf Hitler, while others noted that was precisely the point: in his private life Hitler was able to project the persona of a rational, civilized gentleman far removed from his familiar—and reductive— image as a hate-filled, raving madman.

On the heels of Traudl Junge's belated remembrances, Nazi expert Joachim Fest published *Der Untergang Hitler und das Ende des Dritten Reiches. Eine historische Skizze* (*The Downfall of Hitler and the End of the Third Reich: An Historical Sketch*, 2002), a gripping depiction of the last surreal days spent by Hitler and his entourage in the Führerbunker as the Red Army closed in on Berlin. Soon thereafter Bernd Eichinger wrote a screenplay based on both books. The resulting film, *Der Untergang* (*The Downfall*, 2004), directed by Oliver Hirschbiegel and starring Bruno Ganz (*Wings of Desire*) as Hitler and Alexandra Maria Lara as Traudl Junge, succeeds brilliantly in conveying the bizarre atmosphere in the bunker—full of dread and evasion—and showing

Hitler as a sick, desperate, deluded man in marked contrast to the mythic Antichrist figure that has haunted the popular imagination since the end of World War II. The net effect is not to render Hitler more sympathetic but to remind later generations that almost unfathomable evil can be perpetrated by relatively ordinary human beings.

4

Military History on Film and Television: Korean War to Bosnia

Since the unambiguous patriotism of World War II–era war films, the war film genre has undergone considerable evolution. In an increasingly more sophisticated ideological climate, war history and fiction films risk absurdity when they trumpet the old, gung-ho verities. Emerging from a century that saw the violent deaths of more than 100 million people, even the most politically oblivious viewers sense that they are being sold a bill of goods when they watch a film that revels in the supposed glories of war—which is not to say that war cannot be sold to a modern populace; it is just a harder sell, involving more oblique, veiled, and complicated representations.

The Korean War

An unpopular, unwinnable conflict poorly understood by the American public, the Korean War (1950–1953) has never received its fair share of media representation. Only a handful of feature films and television series have been devoted to the "forgotten war," most of them made decades after it occurred. Only two feature films based on actual incidents of the Korean War appeared during the 1950s: *The McConnell Story* (1955) and *Pork Chop Hill* (1959).

The McConnell Story (1955)

Captain Joseph C. "Mac" McConnell Jr., a B-24 navigator in World War II, went on to become America's leading jet fighter ace in the Korean War. In a four-month period (January 14–May 18, 1953) McConnell, flying an F-86, became a "triple ace" by downing sixteen North Korean MiG-15s. Not wanting their leading ace shot down again—McConnell had already been shot down once and rescued—

Credited with downing sixteen MIGs, Captain Joseph McConnell Jr. was the U.S. Air Force's top jet ace during the Korean War. (Bettmann/Corbis)

air force officials grounded McConnell and sent him home immediately after his sixteenth kill. Taking on the role of test pilot at Edwards Air Force Base Flight Test Center on the edge of California's Mojave Desert, McConnell was killed on August 25, 1954, when the F-86-H "Sabre" he was test-flying experienced total hydraulic failure. Attempting to land with only throttle and rudder, McConnell crashed.

In 1954 veteran Hollywood producer Henry Blanke (*The Treasure of the Sierra Madre; The Fountainhead*) took on the task of making a patriotic biopic about McConnell for Warner Bros. Directed by Gordon Douglas (*I Was a Communist for the FBI*) and cowritten by Ted Sherdeman (*Hell to Eternity*) and Sam Rolfe, *The McConnell Story* starred Alan Ladd as McConnell and June Allyson as his wife, Pearl "Butch" Brown. It also featured James Whitmore as McConnell's mentor and an uncredited cameo by General O. P. "Opie" Weyland, commander of Far East Air Forces (FEAF) during the Korean War. Captain Manuel J. "Pete" Fernandez Jr., the third-leading Korean War ace, served as the movie's technical advisor. Captain McConnell's death occurred during principal photography and necessitated a rewrite of the film that reflected McConnell's tragic fate.

Pork Chop Hill (1959)

On the night of April 16, 1953, elements of the Chinese Communist 141st Division attacked Hill 255 (more famously known as Pork Chop Hill due to its shape as seen from the air). Defending the hill were two platoons of Easy Company, 31st Infantry Regiment, 7th Infantry Division: a force of less than seventy men. After two hours of fighting, the Chinese Communist Forces (CCF) managed to capture most of the American positions on Pork Chop Hill. Ceding what was a relatively unimportant position to the enemy would have been the prudent move, but with peace talks under way at Panmunjam the U.S. command opted to retake and hold Pork Chop Hill to show the enemy its resolve. In a series of fierce firefights, hand-to-hand encounters, and artillery duels that raged over a 48-hour period, a few companies of the 7th Infantry wrested control of the hill from numerically superior Chinese forces and hung on until the enemy finally withdrew on April 18.

Three and a half years after the battle, war historian Samuel Lyman Atwood "Slam" Marshall (1900–1977) published *Pork Chop Hill: The American Fighting Man in Action—Korea Spring 1953* (New York: William Morrow, 1956). Committed to presenting war from the perspective of the ordinary combatant, S. L. A. Marshall had, in World War II, perfected the practice of interviewing large numbers of infantrymen right after a battle so as to reconstruct the engagement in all its minutiae. He did the same with U.S. survivors of Pork Chop Hill and his book was widely praised for providing an unusually vivid evocation of close combat. Among Marshall's fans was the movie actor Gregory Peck (*Twelve O'Clock High; Moby Dick*), who was so taken with the book that he bought the rights to make a film version for his new film production company, Melville Pictures.

Peck subsequently hired screenwriter James R. Webb (*Cape Fear; Cheyenne Autumn*) to adapt Marshall's book to the screen and veteran war movie director Lewis Milestone (*All Quiet on the Western Front; A Walk in the Sun*) to direct *Pork Chop Hill* (1959). At forty-two, Gregory Peck was really too old to play the lead role of Lt. Joe Clemons of Company K who would have been in his twenties during the Korean War but Peck's performance was convincing enough. Cast in supporting roles were a group of unknowns who would all make their mark later on: Norman Fell, Harry Guardino, Martin Landau, Gavin McLeod, George Peppard, Harry Dean Stanton, and Rip Torn. A faithful rendition of S. L. A. Marshall's putatively authentic account of what was a very chaotic mêlée, *Pork Chop Hill* managed to convey the brutality and horror of the battle without being unduly graphic—thanks to the stark black-and-white cinematography of Sam Leavitt (*The Court-Martial of Billy Mitchell*).

MacArthur (1977)

Eighteen years after *Pork Chop Hill*, Gregory Peck revisited the Korean War with *MacArthur* (1977), a biopic on General Douglas MacArthur (1880–1964) that appeared a year before William Manchester's biography, *American Caesar: Douglas MacArthur 1880–1964* (Boston: Little, Brown, 1978). Produced by Frank McCarthy (*Patton*) and written by the screenwriting team of Hal Barwood and Matthew Robbins (*The Sugarland Express*), *MacArthur* concentrates on the period from 1942 to 1952 that encompasses MacArthur's World War II leadership in the Pacific, his role as military governor of Japan after its surrender, and his Korean War command up to his firing by President Truman for insubordination (April 11, 1951). As was the case with *Patton*, *MacArthur* appears to offer a balanced, "warts-and-all" account of the general that dramatizes his brilliance as a military tactician (and orator) but also admits to the man's colossal egotism, arrogance, and a dangerous tendency toward brinkmanship with America's Cold War enemies.

Still, a host of darker truths are left out of the film. For example, the publicly pious MacArthur kept a mistress named Isabel Rosario Cooper in the early 1930s (MacArthur was in his fifties and Cooper was a teenager). Also not mentioned is MacArthur's excessive brutality in breaking up the so-called WWI veteran "Bonus Marchers" encampment in Washington, D.C., in the summer of 1932. Nor does the film touch on MacArthur's disastrous mismanagement of the defense of the Philippines or the fact that "Dugout Doug"—as his men derisively called him—ensconced himself on the well-supplied and fortified island of Corregidor while his beleaguered troops starved on Bataan. Incredibly, MacArthur enriched himself and some of his lackeys by pressuring Philippines President Manuel L. Quezon (1878–1944) to bestow large monetary "rewards." After order-ing his forces on Bataan to fight to the last man, MacArthur escaped to safety in Australia via PT-boat—and was awarded the Medal of Honor by FDR for publicity purposes! Later, during the Korean War, MacArthur's deluded confidence that the Chinese would not intervene in the conflict caused thousands of American casualties. Even more ominously MacArthur vigorously advocated an all-out war with China that would include the use of nuclear weapons. Though criticized at the time, President Truman was well advised to relieve MacArthur of his command. In the final analysis, *MacArthur* distorts history by presenting the five-star general as a charmingly flawed great man when in fact he was a vain, opportunistic hypocrite; a patrician reactionary who despised democratic institutions; a grossly incompetent field commander who always managed to avail himself of the lion's share of the glory.

Inchon (1981)

In 1973 ultra-right-wing religious cult leader Rev. Sun Myung Moon moved his Unification Church headquarters from South Korea to the United States. Over most of the next decade Moon aggressively sought to attain greater social and political influence in America. His Church wrapped itself in the American flag, supported Richard Nixon during the Watergate scandal, and held mass rallies in New York and Washington during the bicentennial year. Toward the end of the decade Moon decided to produce a movie epic that would further heighten the profile of the Unification Church. Not wanting the public to know that he was the producer, Moon laundered $46 million through one of his disciples, Japanese newspaper publisher Mitsuharu Ishii, to finance the project. Avid to advance Moon's peculiar version of anticommunist Christianity (starring himself as the modern Messiah), Moon and Ishii pondered film biographies of Jesus Christ and Elvis Presley (comparable figures?) before finally settling on a film about General Douglas MacArthur's landing on the Inchon peninsula during the Korean War as the ultimate vehicle for Moonie propaganda. To confirm their choice, Moon and Ishii supposedly channeled the late General MacArthur through tabloid psychic Jeanne Dixon (1918–1997) and were relieved to hear that MacArthur's spirit approved the project wholeheartedly! (Using her preternatural intuition Dixon also appointed the film's director, Terence Young, director of a number of James Bond movies in the 1960s.) To attain proper credibility and star power, Moon's organization paid Sir Laurence Olivier $1 million to portray MacArthur, a role that was a low point in an otherwise distinguished film career. Plagued with a terrible script, horrendous production problems, and shoddy performances all around, the resulting film, *Inchon* (1981), was bad beyond belief.

After a disastrous box office performance, *Inchon* was quickly withdrawn from theaters and all involved tried their best to live down their participation. Reverend Moon never made another film.

The Korean War on Television

Almost half a century after the Korean War ended with a cease-fire but no peace treaty, three television projects recapitulated the military and political history: *The Korean War: Fire and Ice* (1999), a four-part miniseries for the History Channel; *Battle for Korea* (2001), a PBS documentary; and *Korea: The Unfinished War* (2003), a Canadian documentary written, directed, and narrated by Brian McKenna.

The Vietnam War

The most controversial conflict in the history of the United States, the Vietnam War nearly tore the country apart in the 1960s and early 1970s and continues to cast a long shadow over the national psyche. During the war and in the decades since, fiction and nonfiction films about Vietnam have engaged in an elaborate and always emotionally charged dialogue about the war's meaning and consequences. From rancorously partisan defenses and denouncements of American involvement, Vietnam War cinema has generally evolved into something more ideologically nuanced and elegiac.

The Mills of the Gods: Viet Nam (1965)

Ironically, it took a Canadian filmmaker to broach the subject of the Vietnam War on film. Filmed in 1964, Beryl Fox's 56-minute black-and-white documentary, *The Mills of the Gods: Viet Nam* (1965), was made for broadcast on CBC's *This Hour Has Seven Days* (1964–1966), a slyly subversive 1-hour newsmagazine-variety show that attained phenomenal popularity in Canada before being canceled for its controversial content. Working without a script, Fox went to Vietnam with portable equipment and shot two kinds of cinema verité footage: placid images of the ordinary life of the Vietnamese peasantry and shocking images of the war's carnage and destruction as wrought by sometimes disturbingly cheerful American pilots and soldiers. Edited together, the contrasting images brought home the horrible brutality and injustice of the war without the use of voice-over narration or an emotionally manipulative musical score. The film's debut on Canadian television generated intense excitement and controversy. Shown in Britain on the BBC, *The Mills of the Gods* also made the rounds of American college campuses but was shunned by mainstream American television and condemned by the U.S. government for presenting a highly unflattering view of its involvement in Vietnam. Indeed, the film is said to have resulted in chilled diplomatic relations between the United States and Canada and was partially responsible for the premature cancellation of *This Hour Has Seven Days.* Nonetheless, *Mills of the Gods* won the 1966 Film of the Year Award in Canada and a Polk Award in the United States for excellence in journalism. Beryl Fox went on to make two more Vietnam documentaries in the direct cinema style: *Saigon* (1967) and *Last Reflections on a War* (1968).

Loin du Vietnam (Far from Vietnam) (1967)

To protest the war in Vietnam, French filmmaker Chris Marker (real name: Christian François Bouche-Villeneuve) prevailed on a half dozen of his illustrious colleagues in the European cinema to participate in the making of an omnibus documentary entitled *Loin du Vietnam (Far from Vietnam)* (1967). Marker, Joris Ivens (*The Spanish Earth*), William Klein, Claude Lelouch (*A Man and a Woman*), Alain Resnais (*Night and Fog*), Agnès Varda, and Jean-Luc Godard (*Alphaville*) each contributed segments to the film. Among the scenes: footage of aircraft carrier ordnance crews loading bombs onto U.S. warplanes; antiwar demonstrations in New York City and Paris; clips from Godard's *La Chinoise* (*The Chinese*) (1967); interviews with Ho Chi Minh and Fidel Castro; combat footage from Vietnam culled from newsreels and supplied by Joris Ivens and Marceline Loridan who were in Vietnam filming *The 17th Parallel: Vietnam at War* (1968). Marred by pretentious narration, disjunctive styles, and an overly partisan approach to its subject matter, *Loin du Vietnam* provides a revealing glimpse into the aesthetic and political mentality of France's 1960s avant-garde, especially its instinctive anti-Americanism.

The Anderson Platoon (1967)

In the fall of 1966 filmmaker Pierre Schoendoerffer (former *Life* correspondent and a French army veteran of Dien Bien Phu) and cinematographer Dominique Merlin spent six weeks with the 1st Platoon, B Company, 12th Regiment, 1st Cavalry Division as it roamed the central highlands of South Vietnam. Led by Lt.

Joseph B. Anderson, a twenty-four-year-old African American West Point graduate, the racially integrated thirty-three-man platoon is shown in *La Section
Anderson* (*The Anderson Platoon*) (1967) on search-and-destroy patrol in the
jungle, interrogating prisoners, securing the site of a helicopter crash, on leave in
the forbidden red-light district of Saigon. While not filled with close combat sequences of the kind seen in war fiction films, *The Anderson Platoon* does convey
the constant tension experienced by troops in a hostile country. After it was initially broadcast without commercial interruption on French television in January
1967, an edited and translated version of *The Anderson Platoon* (narrated by
actor Stuart Whitman) aired with commercials on CBS July 4, 1967, was rebroadcast on July 25, and began a limited run in theaters five months later. Praised as
remarkably evenhanded in its depiction of American soldiers, *The Anderson Platoon* went on to win the 1968 Oscar for Best Documentary, Feature.

In the Year of the Pig (1968)

Not evenhanded at all is *In the Year of the Pig* (1968), a brilliantly conceived and
executed compilation and interview montage documentary by Scranton-born
Marxist filmmaker Emile de Antonio (1919–1989). Highly resourceful when it
came to locating obscure archival footage, conducting trenchant interviews, and
fashioning didactic juxtapositions of images, de Antonio surveys the modern history of Vietnam from Ho Chi Minh's fight against Japanese occupation in World
War II through the French defeat at Dien Bien Phu in the spring of 1954 to direct
American involvement from 1961 up to the Tet Offensive in early 1968. Featured
are numerous clips of pro-interventionist pronouncements by presidents Eisenhower, Kennedy, Johnson, and Nixon; State Department officials John Foster
Dulles, Henry Cabot Lodge, and Dean Rusk; and generals Curtis LeMay, William
Westmoreland, and George S. Patton IV (who proudly proclaims his men a
"bloody good bunch of killers"). In rebuttal, de Antonio interviews a number of
antiwar figures, among them Fr. Daniel Berrigan, historians Harrison Salisbury
and Arthur Schesinger Jr., journalist David Halberstam, and professors Paul Mus
(author of *Viêt-Nam: Sociology of a War* [1952]) and David Wurfel, a Southeast
Asia expert. Archival material also includes extensive combat footage and such
haunting images as the self-immolation of Buddhist monk Thich Quang Duc on
June 11, 1963, in the middle of a busy Saigon intersection (to protest President
Diem's persecution of Buddhists) and ARVN General Nguyen Ngoc Loan's sum-
mary execution of a Viet Cong prisoner with a .38 bullet to the man's head at
close range (February 1, 1968). A haunting postmodern score by John Cage protégé, Steve Addiss, is supplemented by versions of "La Marseillaise" and "The

Battle Hymn of the Republic" disconcertingly played on Asian folk instruments. Released in the fall of 1968, at the height of the antiwar movement, *In the Year of the Pig* earned de Antonio a 1969 Academy Award nomination and a spot on Richard Nixon's infamous enemies list.

The Selling of the Pentagon (1971) and *Hearts and Minds* (1974)

While he was a writer-producer for the current affairs show, *CBS Reports*, Peter Davis made *The Selling of the Pentagon* (1971), a daring and highly persuasive hour-long exposé revealing that the Pentagon spent anywhere from $30 to $160 million annually on the manufacture and dissemination of pro-U.S. military propaganda. Aired on February 23, 1971, *The Selling of the Pentagon* ignited the proverbial firestorm of controversy but also won Peabody, Emmy, Polk, Saturday Review, and Writers Guild awards. A few years later, Peter Davis made *Hearts and Minds* (1974), a compilation-interview documentary that owes a good deal to de Antonio's *In the Year of the Pig* in terms of structure, content, and montage technique, that is, the skillful juxtaposition of bits of archival footage and interview clips to create implicit assertions about the tragic absurdity of the Vietnam War. Like de Antonio before him, Davis reviews the history of the Vietnam conflict using newsreel clips of combat and interviews with various government officials and then goes on to sketch both sides of the ideological divide. For example, the petulance of State Department war planner Walt Rostow (1916–2003) provides sharp contrast to a sad and repentant Daniel Ellsberg. To cite another example, George Coker, a blandly xenophobic ex-POW, is contrasted to ex-pilot Randy Floyd, who expresses deep remorse for bombing and napalming Vietnamese peasants. A third example: a clip of General William Westmoreland asserting that "life is cheap in the Orient" is crosscut with a scene showing a Vietnamese family in almost hysterical grief by a loved one's grave. In sum, Davis's thesis is that America's military-industrial complex was so vested in the global Cold War against communism, so myopically convinced of its invincibility, righteousness, and cultural and technological superiority, that it utterly misapprehended the nature of the Vietnam conflict—with resoundingly tragic results for both countries.

    Hearts and Minds proved to be highly controversial even before its release. In April 1974 Columbia Pictures backed out of its distribution agreement with the film's producer, Bert Schneider (*Easy Rider; The Last Picture Show*), after nervous studio executives concluded that the film was too radical in its critique of American involvement in Vietnam. After the film was a hit at the Cannes

Film Festival (April 1974), Warner Bros. took over distribution but later withdrew its name from promotion advertising. Disgruntled interviewee Walt Rostow twice petitioned California courts to issue temporary restraining orders barring the release of the film if it contained his interview segment. Following a successful run in Los Angeles in late December 1974, *Hearts and Minds* opened nationally early the next near and was still playing in some theaters when Saigon fell to Viet Cong–NVA forces on April 30, 1975. Almost universally praised by critics, *Hearts and Minds* won the 1975 Academy Award for Best Documentary, Feature—which turned out to be an occasion for further controversy. During his acceptance remarks on Oscar night, producer Bert Schneider read a telegram from Madame Nguyen Thi Binh, head of the Provisional Revolutionary Government (PRG) of Vietnam's delegation to the Paris Peace Talks, that read, in part, "Please transmit to all our friends in America our recognition of all they have done on behalf of peace." Hundreds of irate viewers called to complain to NBC during the telecast and an enraged Bob Hope persuaded master of ceremonies, Frank Sinatra, to deliver a disclaimer and apology, which read: "We are not responsible for any political references made on this program tonight and we are sorry that they are [*sic*] made."

Vietnam: A Television History (1983)

Not long after the fall of Saigon, Stanley Karnow, a foreign correspondent, and L. Richard Ellison, a freelance television writer-producer, began to plan a multipart documentary history of the Vietnam conflict. As arrangements began to crystallize, Dr. Lawrence Lichty (a journalism professor at the University of Wisconsin at that time) signed on as director of media research for the project. In the summer of 1977 Ellison's production company, LRE, acquired $1.2 million in funding from the National Endowment for the Humanities (NEH), $350,000 from the Chubb Group of Insurance Companies, $285,000 from eight other foundations, and $50,000 in funding from both ABC-TV and WGBH-TV (Boston). Due to the controversial nature of the program, longtime PBS sponsors such as Exxon, Mobil, and the Corporation for Public Broadcasting (CPB) refused to lend their support. To make up the shortfall Ellison signed production deals with Antenne–2 (France) and Associated (later Central Independent) Television (UK). Professor Lichty and his team located, selected, and edited a half million feet of archival film footage from governments and news agencies of six countries. In 1981 and 1982 some 300 new interviews were conducted to supplement the compilation material, many of them taking place in Vietnam. After more than six years of research and production work costing $4.5 million (US$8.6 million in 2005), *Vietnam: A Television History* (1983) premiered in the United Kingdom to strong reviews and was then aired on PBS in the fall of 1983. At the same time Viking Press published Stanley Karnow's *Vietnam: A History, The First Complete Account of Vietnam at War*, a hefty companion volume to the series that went into much more detail.

From the outset Stanley Karnow and Richard Ellison were determined to make a fair-minded documentary series that would present many points of view and encompass the entire modern history of the Vietnam War, not just U.S. involvement. Consequently, the thirteen 1-hour episodes of *Vietnam: A Television History* range over more than three decades, from World War II to the fall of Saigon in 1975 and its aftermath. *Episode 1: Roots of a War* shows that Ho Chi Minh was initially in favor of a pro-American, democratic Vietnam but French (and British) colonial interests pushed him toward communism. *Episode 2: The First Vietnam War (1946–1954)* recounts the eight-year French colonial war against Ho Chi Minh's Vietminh guerrillas—a war heavily subsidized by the United States—that ended in defeat for France at Dien Bien Phu. *Episode 3: America's Mandarin (1954–1963)* deals with the U.S. takeover from the French and its support for the decade-long presidency of Ngô Đình Diệm (1901–1963), a regime that ended with Diệm's murder by rebellious generals on November 2, 1963—just twenty days before the assassination of John F. Kennedy. *Episode 4: LBJ Goes to War (1964–1965)* covers the political chaos after the coup, resulting in an escalating civil war in South Vietnam and America's deepening involvement after the Gulf of Tonkin incident. In *Episode 5: America Takes Charge (1965–1967)* the U.S. military takes over the prosecution of the war from crumbling South Vietnamese forces (ARVN). *Episode 6: America's Enemy (1954–1967)* offers a rare glimpse inside the sociopolitical culture of the North Vietnamese and Viet Cong—in contrast to the perspective of American prisoners of war in Hanoi. *Episode 7: Tet, 1968* focuses on the massive NVA (North Vietnamese Army)-NLF (Viet Cong) offensive against a host of major South Vietnamese strongholds, so named because it began on Tết Nguyên Đán, the Vietnamese Lunar New Year (January 29, 1968). Though a costly military defeat for the North Vietnamese, the Tet Offensive was a public relations disaster for the United States inasmuch as it proved that the enemy was still very much in the war. At the end of the LBJ administration and the beginning of Richard Nixon's, the United States began handing the war back to the South Vietnamese, a process detailed in *Episode 8: Vietnamizing the War (1968–1973)*. *Episode 9: Cambodia and Laos* deals with the spread of the war into neighboring Laos and Cambodia, with genocidal results. *Episode 10: Peace at Hand (1968–1973)* examines the course of the Paris Peace Talks amid continued U.S. troop with-drawal and heavy bombing. *Episode 11: Homefront USA* follows the evolution of American public opinion about the Vietnam War, which went from initial wide-spread support to mass protest in the space of three or four years. *Episode 12: The End of the Tunnel (1973–1975)* traces the final collapse of ARVN forces and the fall of Saigon on April 30, 1975. The series closes with *Episode 13: Legacies*, which examines the political consequences for a chastened United States and for a reunited but still poor and war-torn Vietnam.

Watched by a surprisingly large television audience, praised by most crit-ics for its impressive depth and balance, and winning the 1984 Erik Barnouw Award by the Organization of American Historians (OAH), *Vietnam: A Televi-sion History* also generated considerable controversy. Reed Irvine (1920–2004), founder of Accuracy in Media (AIM), a right-wing media watchdog organization, took umbrage at the allegedly leftist orientation of the series. Awarded a $30,000 grant by then NEH Chairman William Bennett, AIM made *Television's Vietnam: The Real Story*, a 56-minute documentary narrated by right-wing movie star Charlton Heston that chastises *Vietnam: A Television History* for suggesting, among other things, that Ho Chi Minh was more of a Vietnamese nationalist than a Communist; that Ngô Đình Diệm was an American puppet, not a demo-cratically elected leader; that the Viet Cong were semiautonomous politically; that the role of the media was *not* decisive in America's defeat. Pressured by the Reagan White House to show *Television's Vietnam*, PBS did indeed air the pro-gram on June 27, 1985. Coming a year and a half after the screening of *Vietnam: A Television History*, Irvine's polemic had little discernible effect on public opinion.

The Killing Fields (1984)

Though not about Vietnam per se, Roland Joffé's *The Killing Fields* (1984) deals with the closely related topic of the holocaust inflicted on Cambodia (Kam-puchea) by the Khmer Rouge. In power from April 1975 to January 1979, the fanatically doctrinaire Khmer Rouge killed anywhere from 1.7 to 3.3 million of their countrymen through forced labor, mass starvation, and executions. In his controversial book, *Sideshow: Kissinger, Nixon, and the Destruction of Cam-bodia* (New York: Simon & Schuster, 1979), British journalist William T. Shaw-cross argued that heavy, continual U.S. B-52 bombing raids on Cambodia (begun in March 1969 to disrupt the Ho Chi Minh Trail) so damaged the social fabric of that country that the Maoist Khmer Rouge were able to win their five-year civil war against pro-U.S. Cambodian President Lon Nol (1913–1985). The issue of

American complicity in Cambodia's destruction is still hotly debated; what is not debated is the fact that the Khmer Rouge committed genocide.

Pulitzer Prize–winning *New York Times* journalist Sydney Schanberg witnessed and reported on the Cambodian civil war and the fall of Phnom Penh on April 17, 1975 (two weeks before the fall of Saigon). Three days later Schanberg's interpreter, guide, and close friend, Dith Pran, was, as a native Cambodian, forced to leave the safety of the French Consulate and fend for himself as hardened Khmer Rouge guerrillas began the ominous process of herding people into internment camps deep in the interior. Under diplomatic protection, Schanberg and his colleagues Jon Swain (a British journalist) and Al Rockoff (an American photographer) escaped Cambodia and returned home. An anxious and guilt-ridden Schanberg spent the next several years trying to find out what happened to his friend. Amazingly, almost four and a half years after his disappearance, Dith Pran emerged alive in Thailand on October 3, 1979, having survived an ordeal of forced labor, near-starvation, scenes of horror in the killing fields, and a grueling escape trek that would have destroyed lesser men. He and Sydney Schanberg were reunited six days later. Three months after that Schanberg published a long and deeply moving account of Dith Pran's extraordinary odyssey entitled "The Death and Life of Dith Pran," *New York Times Magazine* (January 20, 1980).

Much taken with Dith Pran's story, British producer David Putnam and director Roland Joffé (*The Mission; City of Joy*) set out to make a film version adapted for the screen by actor-writer Bruce Robinson and starring Sam Waterston as Sydney Schanberg, Haing S. Nigor (himself a survivor of the killing fields) as Dith Pran, John Malcovich as Al Rockoff, and Spalding Gray as a U.S. consul. Shot in fits and starts in Thailand, Toronto, and New York City from March 1983 to August 1984, *The Killing Fields* opened in early November 1984 to strong reviews and excellent box office returns. Ironically, Haing S. Nigor, the Cambodian nonprofessional actor who won an Oscar for his brilliant portrayal of Dith Pran, survived the killing fields only to be murdered by Los Angeles streets thugs in the garage of his apartment building on February 26, 1996.

Hamburger Hill (1987)

Situated on the Laotian border in western Thua Thien Province, northern South Vietnam, the 25-mile-long A Shau Valley served as a strategically vital spur of the Ho Chi Minh Trail that channeled NVA troops and supplies toward Danang and Hué. In May 1969, in response to increased enemy activity in the area, seven U.S. and three ARVN battalions were sent in to make a sweep (code-named Operation Apache Snow) of the valley. The objective assigned to the 506th Regiment of the

101st Airborne Division and the 3rd Battalion of the 187th Airborne Division (nicknamed the Rakkasans) was to capture Dong Ap Bia (Hill 937), a steep, rugged, and heavily foliated 970-meter (3,182-ft.) mountain held by the 29th NVA Regiment, which was well dug in, amply supplied, and grimly determined to hold their ground. Fought during the monsoon season, the fight for Hill 937 became known as the Battle of Hamburger Hill for its savage intensity and heavy casualties. On May 20, after nine days of bloody struggle, U.S. paratroopers finally took the summit of Dong Ap Bia. Total American casualties were heavy—70 dead and 372 wounded—but the 29th NVA Regiment was virtually wiped out. Not long after their hard-won victory, U.S. forces simply abandoned the area, causing many to wonder if all the carnage and sacrifice had been worth it.

Scene of unremitting gore and extraordinary heroism, but ultimately a meaningless objective, Hamburger Hill served as a perfect metaphor for the entire American experience in Vietnam—a fact recognized by James Carabatsos (*Heartbreak Ridge; No Mercy*), a screenwriter who had served in Vietnam with the 1st Air Cavalry Division in 1968–1969. After conducting years of painstaking research and interviewing dozens of veterans of Hamburger Hill, Carabatsos fashioned a meticulously accurate script that was subsequently made into *Hamburger Hill* (1987) under the capable if conventional direction of John Irvin (*Turtle Diary*), a British television director who made the transition to Hollywood

A wounded U.S. paratrooper is rushed to an evacuation helicopter amid fierce fighting against the North Vietnamese during the Battle of Ap Bia Mountain ("Hamburger Hill") on May 18, 1969. (UPI-Bettmann/Corbis)

feature films in the early 1980s. In marked contrast to better-known fiction films about Vietnam—*The Deer Hunter* (1978), *Apocalypse Now* (1979), *Platoon* (1986), *Full Metal Jacket* (1987)—*Hamburger Hill* eschews hyperbole, surrealism, and lofty allegory to present close combat in all its straightforward horror. Though almost clinically naturalistic in tone and neutral as to the larger merits of the Vietnam War, *Hamburger Hill* is unabashedly reverent in its depiction of the American infantryman as stalwart, brave, competent, and long-suffering: a point of view that anticipates the center-right ideology of later American war films like *Band of Brothers* (2001), *Black Hawk Down* (2001), and *We Were Soldiers* (2002).

Good Morning, Vietnam (1987)

In 1979 Vietnam War veteran Adrian Cronauer finished a screenplay for a proposed television sitcom that was based on his experiences as a disc jockey on the Armed Forces Radio Service (AFRS) in Saigon in 1965–1966. In the early 1980s Cronauer's agent, Larry Brezner, optioned the script but could not sell it until comedian Robin Williams (*Mork & Mindy; Popeye*) read it and recognized it as the perfect format for his own brand of rapid-fire improvisatory humor. Thanks to Williams' rising star power, Brezner was able to sell Cronauer's script to Touchstone Pictures, a recently formed film division of the Walt Disney Company. Mitch Markowitz, a writer for *M*A*S*H*, the hit television series, worked with Cronauer on five full revisions of his original script. The resulting film, *Good Morning, Vietnam* (1987), was a smash hit that earned back its $13 million budget tenfold and elevated Williams to major stardom.

The film was not, however, an accurate rendition of Cronauer or his stint on Armed Forces Radio. In marked contrast to Williams' frenetic brand of comedy, Cronauer's on-air persona was droll, his specialty the kind of gentle but zany situational humor associated with Bob & Ray or Rege Cordic (1926–1999), a legendary disc jockey on Pittsburgh's KDKA in the 1950s and 1960s who was a direct influence on Cronauer. While Williams' Cronauer is manic, superficially cynical, and rebelliously antiestablishment, the real Adrian Cronauer was never antiwar or antimilitary. (A lifelong conservative Republican, Cronauer now works in the Pentagon as senior vice chairman of the Vietnam Veteran's Institute.) Yet, in a convoluted way, *Good Morning, Vietnam* is every bit as ideologically conservative as the real Adrian Cronauer. In keeping with the patriotic zeitgeist of the late Reagan era, Williams' character learns, through bitter experience, that his comedic compulsion affords him an unhealthy detachment from his environment and, more important, from his brave and sincere comrades-in-arms. Dismissed for his antics, he leaves Vietnam a more sober and mature individual. Thus *Good Morning, Vietnam* gets to have its cake and eat it too: it showcases the improvisatory brilliance of Robin Williams but ultimately repudiates the wise guy oppositional mentality that sometimes makes wars so hard to prosecute.

Dear America: Letters Home from Vietnam (1988)

If *Good Morning, Vietnam* is largely fanciful, Bill Couturié's *Dear America: Letters Home from Vietnam* (1988) is very much the real thing. Based on a best-selling book of the same title authorized by the New York Vietnam Veteran's Memorial Commission and compiled and edited by Vietnam veteran Bernard Edelman (New York: W. W. Norton, 1985), *Dear America* is an HBO documentary that presents authentic letters from young soldiers in Vietnam read in voice-over by thirty-six leading actors (among them Tom Berenger, Ellen Burstyn, Willem Dafoe, Robert DeNiro, John Heard, Harvey Keitel, Sean Penn, John Savage, Martin Sheen, and Kathleen Turner). Arranged in chronological order, the visual part of the film is comprised of sometimes shockingly graphic footage from Defense Department and NBC-TV news archives and contemporaneous 8mm home movies made by American soldiers at camp, on leave, or in combat. To further conjure the aura of the times Couturié laces the film with 1960s rock music (except for an orchestral rendition of "Silent Night" and Bruce Springsteen's "Born in the USA," which concludes the film). Because it presents the actual words of the soldiers themselves, *Dear America* avoids the pitfalls of other Vietnam films, real or fictive, that lean too much to the Left or Right. A poignant and profound viewing experience, *Dear America* won two Emmys and the Special Jury Prize at the Sundance Film Festival.

Born on the Fourth of July (1989)

On January 20, 1968, at the start of the Tet Offensive, U.S. Marine Corps Sgt. Ron Kovic took a bullet in the spine that rendered him a paraplegic for life. After an agonizing seventeen-month recovery in and out of a rat-infested Bronx VA hospital, Kovic returned home, in the summer of 1969, to live with his parents in Massapequa, Long Island, but rage, depression, and incipient alcoholism made him impossible to live with. After a period of aimless wandering, Kovic ended up in California where he formed friendships with fellow veterans opposed to the war. Kovic also discovered Dalton Trumbo's antiwar novel, *Johnny Got His Gun* (1939). Deeply affected by the book, Kovic attended the premier of the film in

1971, met Trumbo, and was inspired by the once-blacklisted writer's personal courage and political integrity. Becoming increasingly radicalized, Ron Kovic joined other disabled Vietnam vets and attended the Republican National Convention in Miami in late August 1972—and was forcibly ejected from the convention hall for trying to shout down Richard Nixon during Nixon's acceptance speech. Four years later, at the invitation of candidate Jimmy Carter, Kovic addressed the Democratic National Convention in New York City and a month after that, Kovic's autobiography, *Born on the Fourth of July*, was published by McGraw-Hill to critical acclaim. Therein Kovic described his odyssey, from naïve patriotism—fueled by jingoistic war films that glorified combat—to profound remorse (for accidentally killing Vietnamese civilians and another American soldier) and bitter disillusionment with his government after his horrific treatment in VA hospitals. A Barry Goldwater–style anticommunist when he enlisted in the Marines in 1964, Kovic ultimately became an unyielding disabled veteran's advocate and antiwar activist.

Around 1977 Ron Kovic met and befriended fellow Vietnam veteran and kindred spirit, Oliver Stone. The two collaborated on a film treatment of *Born on the Fourth of July*, engaged Brian De Palma to direct and Al Pacino to play Ron Kovic, but financing fell apart at the last minute. Stone promised a crestfallen Kovic that, if he made it big in Hollywood, he would see to it that their script was made into a film. Stone did indeed make it big when his Vietnam film, *Platoon* (1986), grossed $138 million and won a raft of film awards including eight Oscar nominations and four Oscars, including Best Picture and Best Director. Starring Tom Cruise as Ron Kovic, *Born on the Fourth of July* (1989), though a long and complex film, proved to be everything that Stone and Kovic hoped it would be. Cruise was mesmerizing as an all-American working-class romantic shattered by the ugly truth of Vietnam but later reborn into a sadder and deeper idealism dedicated to peace. A box office success widely lauded by critics, *Born on the Fourth of July* won eight Oscar nominations and two Oscars. More importantly Stone's film furthered the recuperation of the Vietnam veteran in the popular imagination.

Heaven and Earth (1993)

Having made films that dealt with the American soldier in combat in Vietnam (*Platoon*) and with the war's aftereffects on veterans stateside (*Born on the Fourth of July*), Oliver Stone turned his attention to the Vietnamese side of the story with *Heaven and Earth* (1993), the third film in his Vietnam trilogy. In the summer of 1989, while *Born on the Fourth* was in postproduction, Stone read Le Ly Hayslip's autobiography, *When Heaven and Earth Changed Places* (with Jay

Wurts, New York: Doubleday, 1989), and, to his lasting credit, grasped the ideological and ethical importance of embracing the Vietnamese perspective the book offered.

Born Phung Thi Le Ly in 1949 in the hamlet of Ky La near Da Nang in South Vietnam's central highlands, Le Ly Hayslip joined the Viet Cong at age thirteen in 1962. Though she was repeatedly interrogated and tortured by Republican troops, she refused to give up her comrades. Ironically, the Viet Cong suspected that she had betrayed them. Sentenced to death, she was raped instead. A disgraced Le Ly then ventured with her mother to Saigon to work as housekeepers for a wealthy Vietnamese couple. The man impregnated Le Ly, and his jealous wife threw her out of the house. Exiled to the streets of Da Nang with a son and mother to support, Le Ly resorted to black market dealing and occasional prostitution to survive. In 1970 a fifty-five-year-old American civilian named Ed Munro married Le Ly and took her back to live with him in the United States. (She left Munro for a time and returned to Vietnam with an American military advisor named Dan De Parma.) Two years after Munro's death in 1973, Le Ly married Dennis Hayslip, a thirty-eight-year-old Vietnam veteran who had rescued her sister, Chi Lan, from South Vietnam just before its surrender to the Communists. Le Ly's second marriage soon deteriorated as Hayslip, suffering from post-traumatic stress, became increasingly violent, alcoholic, and gun-obsessed. After Hayslip committed suicide in March 1982, Le Ly borrowed money to start a delicatessen and soon became a successful businesswoman. In 1988 she established the East Meets West Foundation to help repair the damage decades of war inflicted on her native country and to foster better relations between Vietnam and the United States.

Though Stone's *Heaven and Earth* condenses Ed Munro, Dan De Parma, and Dennis Hayslip into a single, tormented character named Major Steve Butler (Tommy Lee Jones), the film remains scrupulously faithful to the saga of Le Ly (Hiep Thi Le), as recounted in *When Heaven and Earth Changed Places* and its sequel, *Child of War, Woman of Peace* (New York: Doubleday, 1993). Unfortunately, in his characteristic zeal to cover every aspect of the history, Stone made an overly long and diffuse film that lacked the dramatic unity and visceral impact of his earlier Vietnam pictures. Met with lukewarm reviews, *Heaven and Earth* earned back only a fraction of the estimated $33 million it cost to make.

Maya Lin: A Strong Clear Vision (1994)

On May 7, 1981, Vietnam Veteran's Memorial Fund officials announced that they had chosen a design for a national Vietnam War memorial from 1,421 contest entries: two intersecting walls of black granite embedded in a knoll at one corner of the Washington mall and etched with the names of the 57,692 Americans killed in the war. The author of the design was Maya Ying Lin, a twenty-one-year-old Yale University senior majoring in architecture. Lin's stark design immediately came under fire by the usual right-wing demagogues—Pat Buchanan, H. Ross Perot, Henry Hyde, among others—all of whom strenuously objected to the monument's obvious lack of conventional monumentality. The design's supporters suspected that the controversy had more to do with the fact that Maya Lin was young, female, and Asian American than with the memorial's intrinsic merit. At any rate, Lin and the Memorial Fund held firm and what came to be known as "The Wall" was built as planned (though the VVMF compromised by also erecting a more traditional sculpture nearby). The Vietnam Veteran's Memorial has since become the most visited and beloved war monument in the United States.

More than twenty years after Maya Lin's spectacular debut as an artist-architect, the husband and wife filmmaking team of Frieda Lee Mock and Terry Sanders brought out *Maya Lin: A Strong Clear Vision* (1994), a biographical documentary on Maya Lin that covers the tumultuous story of the Vietnam Veteran's Memorial and, anticlimactically, Lin's career since then. Though highly informative, *Maya Lin* is not particularly well structured or illuminating. Indeed, there was much grumbling when *Maya Lin* won the 1995 Academy Award for best feature-length documentary over such obviously better films as *Hoop Dreams* and *Crumb*.

Return with Honor (1998)

After the release of *Maya Lin*, Frieda Lee Mock and Terry Sanders were approached by ex-POWs who suggested they make a film about the 591 American aviators shot down over North Vietnam and held at Hoa Lo Prison, aka the "Hanoi Hilton," between August 5, 1964, and March 29, 1973. Mock and Sanders obliged by making *Return with Honor* (1998), a patriotic documentary that juxtaposes rare North Vietnamese archival footage of pilots being captured with recent interviews involving some two dozen former POWs (and their wives in some instances). Tellingly avoiding larger political questions regarding the war's propriety, the film concentrates instead on the very human story of the POWs, especially their ingenuity and resilience in staying alive and sane in the face of horrendous living conditions that included near starvation, constant beatings, and torture. *Return with Honor* ends on an upbeat note by recounting the repatriation of the POWs in 1973 and their joyous family reunions. The viewer feels a warm identification with these brave and long-suffering men but their job—to bomb mostly civilian targets in a Third World country—is carefully kept outside the bounds of ethical interrogation. After screenings on the film festivals circuit, *Return with Honor* aired on PBS's *American Experience* series in November 2000.

Regret to Inform (1998)

On February 29, 1968, an enemy mortar round killed twenty-four-year-old army Lt. Jeffery Gurvitz of Chicago in Quang Nam (near Khe Sanh), South Vietnam, while Gurvitz was trying to rescue his radio operator. Gurvitz's wife, Barbara Sonneborn, later remarried and pursued a successful career as a visual artist and photographer but remained haunted by her first husband's death and by the Vietnam War in general. On New Year's Day, 1988, with the twentieth anniversary of Jeff Gurvitz's death approaching, Sonneborn vowed to go to Vietnam—and make a film about the experience—to come to terms with the past. Over the next decade Sonneborn wrote, produced, and directed *Regret to Inform* (1998), a 72-minute compilation-interview documentary loosely structured around her visit to Vietnam that more centrally focuses on the story of her translator, Xuan Ngoc Nguyen, an Americanized Vietnamese woman and other war widows on both sides of the conflict. While *Return with Honor* was obviously pro-American, *Regret to Inform* transcends partisanship by emphasizing the universal nature of the tragedy that is war. A prizewinner at a number of film festivals, *Regret to Inform* won a Peabody Award and was nominated for a 1999 Oscar for Best Documentary, Feature.

A Bright Shining Lie (1998)

On the night of June 9, 1972, a helicopter crash near Kontum, South Vietnam, took the life of U.S. Army Lt. Col. John Paul Vann (1924–1972), a very high-level advisor and war strategist. When Vann was buried with full military honors at Arlington National Cemetery a week later, UPI and *New York Times* war correspondent Neil Sheehan was in attendance and noticed that the other mourners—Daniel Ellsberg, CIA chief William Colby, Sen. Edward Kennedy, and Gen. William Westmoreland—represented wildly divergent views on the Vietnam War. To Sheehan, Vann epitomized the ambiguous, conflicted American experience in Vietnam; more than metaphorically Vann *was* America in Vietnam. Sixteen years later, after almost 400 interviews, two trips to Vietnam, and a preliminary draft nearly half a million words in length, Sheehan finally finished *A Bright Shining Lie: John Paul*

Vann and America in Vietnam (New York: Random House, 1988), a massive biography of Vann that also plots the course of the war, from early confidence, to official denial (despite Vann's vociferous calls for policy changes), to the final, bitter disillusionment. On the *New York Times* bestseller list for months, *A Bright Shining Lie* went on to win the 1989 Pulitzer Prize for General Nonfiction.

Almost a decade later Irish writer-director Terry George (*In the Name of the Father*) adapted Sheehan's book into the made-for-HBO film, *A Bright Shining Lie* (1998). Starring Bill Paxton as John Vann and Amy Madigan as Vann's wife, Mary Jane, *A Bright Shining Lie* had to take a densely detailed and vastly complicated 860-page book covering a fifty-year period and turn it into an exciting 2-hour television movie (when a miniseries would have better suited the scope of the material). In his efforts to make *A Bright Shining Lie* compelling drama, Terry George resorted to fabricating too many incidents while sacrificing too much of the real John Vann's complex character. The final result was so sketchy and misleading that Daniel Ellsberg, David Halberstam, John Paul Vann's son, and Neil Sheehan all distanced themselves from the project.

We Were Soldiers (2002)

On November 14, 1965, sixteen Bell HU-1 Iroquois "Huey" helicopters shuttled 450 soldiers of the 1st Battalion, 7th Regiment, 1st Cavalry "Airmobile" Division ("1/7 CAV") into a landing zone code-named X-Ray in the Ia Drang Valley of the central highlands, near Pleiku, South Vietnam. The battalion's mission was to search for and destroy Viet Cong elements in the area. Led by Lt. Col. Harold G. "Hal" Moore, the 1/7 CAV soon found itself in the thick of battle with some 2,000 to 3,000 People's Army of North Vietnam (NVA) regulars grimly determined to destroy the entire American force. In what proved to be the first major engagement between U.S. and NVA forces in the Vietnam War, Moore's surrounded and beleaguered 1/7 CAV held off numerous assaults for three days, took heavy casualties, but survived as a fighting force and inflicted much heavier losses on the enemy—thanks in large part to massive, effective tactical air support. When the NVA finally withdrew on the morning of November 16 helicopters airlifted the battered remnants of the 1/7th out of LZ X-Ray. Casualties numbered 79 men dead and 121 wounded, a 44 percent casualty rate. In a second, disastrous battle at nearby LZ Albany (November 17–20), an NVA battalion ambushed and annihilated the 1/7 CAV's sister battalion, the 2/7th Cavalry. Both engagements came to be known under one rubric: the Battle of the Ia Drang Valley.

More than two decades after the carnage at Ia Drang, 1/7's former commander (retired Lt. Gen.) Hal Moore collaborated on a book with the only journalist present at the battle for LZ X-Ray, UPI photographer-journalist Joseph L. Galloway. The book, elaborately entitled *We Were Soldiers Once . . . And Young: Ia Drang—The Battle That Changed the War in Vietnam* (New York: Random House, 1992), collected first-person accounts by many of the soldiers involved and their wives back home. Appearing on the market a scant year after the stunning success of Operation Desert Storm, *We Were Soldiers Once* was perfectly timed to take advantage of a renewed pride and confidence in American military prowess to rectify the tarnished image of the Vietnam-era American soldier—an ideological rehabilitation project begun in earnest by Ronald Reagan twelve years earlier. The book garnered strong reviews, was seventeen weeks on the *New York Times* Bestseller list, and was the Marine Corps Commandant's Choice for 1993's Book of the Year.

We Were Soldiers Once also caught the enthusiastic attention of war film specialist Randall Wallace (*Braveheart; Pearl Harbor*) who wrote a screen adaptation and then approached General Moore and Joe Galloway for the film rights, which they sold to him in 1996. Having already had a highly successful collaboration with Mel Gibson on *Braveheart* (1995), Wallace joined forces again with Gibson for his new Vietnam project. Gibson signed on to play Hal Moore and his production company, Icon Entertainment, joined with Wallace's production outfit, Wheelhouse Entertainment, to finance the project. Other cast members included Madeleine Stowe as Hal Moore's devoted wife, Julie; Greg Kinnear as stalwart Huey pilot, Major Bruce "Snake" Crandall; Sam Elliott as Moore's tough-as-nails right-hand man, Sgt. Major Basil Plumley; Chris Klein as the doomed 2nd Lt. Jack Geoghegan; and Barry Pepper as the inquisitive Joe Galloway, a role oddly reminiscent of David Janssen's George Beckwith, the repentant war correspondent in John Wayne's 1968 pro-war propaganda film, *The Green Berets*.

Although Hal Moore's book covered the action at landing zones X-Ray and Albany, Randall Wallace chose to focus only on the more cinematically and ideologically palatable story of the successful defense of X-Ray. Interestingly, *We Were Soldiers* (2002) opens with a sequence showing an oblivious French army detachment being ambushed and massacred by stealthy Viet Minh guerrillas in the early 1950s. No doubt designed to serve as a chilling demonstration of Vietnamese fighting proficiency, the segment also implicitly suggests the military inferiority of the French compared to their American successors. The film then moves ahead a decade to Fort Benning, Georgia, home of the 1st Cavalry Division, and introduces Mel Gibson's highly idealized Hal Moore, a man of impeccable character: tough but deeply religious and family oriented, a scholar of military history, and a caring and capable commanding officer. (Perhaps Moore was all of those things but it is likely that, as a real human being, he had certain failings.) In a similar manner, Lt. Col. Moore's battalion is idealized, in familiar war film genre terms, as an ethnically and racially diverse microcosm of America where esprit de corps cancels out the racism and ethnic bigotry found in the larger society: a characterization at odds with the racially tense conditions that actually prevailed in the U.S. military during the Johnson era. Likewise, the wives of the soldiers—all young, pretty, earnest, and kind—seem to have stepped out of a Norman Rockwell painting. The film refrains from demonizing the enemy but does not afford the NVA troops a commensurate humanity. In marked contrast to its idealized characterizations, most of *We Were Soldiers* is taken up with a hyperrealistic depiction of the ferocious firefight that raged for three days at LZ X-Ray. Elaborate stunt work, exploding blood squibs, CGI, massive pyrotechnics, fastidiously simulated wounds, and thunderous sound effects all combine to produce a suitably intense filmic experience of close combat. Furthermore, the 1/7th's desperate stand against superior enemy forces at Ia Drang conjures images of all other Fort Apache–type defensive battles: the Alamo, Custer's last stand (indeed Hal Moore's unit, the 7th Cavalry, is the same as Custer's), Rorke's Drift, Khartoum, the Lost Battalion, Wake Island, and the 1993 Battle of Mogadishu recounted in the film, *Black Hawk Down* (2001). All of the movies based on such scenarios share the common premise that—whether or not the battle ends in the massacre of the righteous—the valor, discipline, and solidarity shown by the outnumbered, surrounded defenders is something to celebrate and honor. No doubt true, but the emphasis placed on hard-won martial glory eclipses any analysis as to why the besieged troopers were there in the first place. In a telling scene in *We Were Soldiers* Lt. Col. Moore tries to explain America's intervention in Vietnam to his cherubic young daughter, Cecile (Sloane Momsen), when she asks, "Daddy, what's a war?" Moore's answer—"Well a war is when people hurt other people, and people like daddy try to stop them"—is an explanation suitable for a child but wholly inadequate as geopolitical analysis. Book and film take pains to argue that they are not glorifying war but only warriors. As in *Zulu*, *Band of Brothers*, and *Black Hawk Down*, the soldiers do not fight for a larger political cause but only for each other: a politically safe but logically (and ideologically) disingenuous premise. While they fail to explain the need for war, such films nonetheless end up apotheosizing the *culture* of the military, a culture dedicated to making war.

The true ideological function of *We Were Soldiers*, to legitimize American militarism by further recuperating the reputation of the Vietnam veteran, was amply demonstrated when Gibson, Wallace, Hal Moore, and Joe Galloway held a private screening of their film at the White House for President George W. Bush, Vice President Dick Cheney, Secretary of State Colin Powell, National Security Advisor Condoleeza Rice, and Secretary of Defense Donald Rumsfeld on February 26, 2002. In all the patriotic hoopla, no one seemed to notice the exquisite irony of the occasion. While Moore, Galloway, and Powell were genuine Vietnam War heroes, hawkish ideologues Gibson, Wallace, Bush, Cheney, and Rumsfeld carefully avoided Vietnam, though all could have fought—even Gibson who was a U.S. national living in Australia at the time.

United States's Somalia Engagement

In December 1992, President George H. W. Bush sent U.S. military detachments to Somalia to help UN peacekeeping forces intervene in a civil war that was driving that East African country toward anarchy and mass starvation. Ten months later, the American mission in Somalia, now under the Clinton administration, encountered its moment of reckoning. On Sunday afternoon, October 3, 1993, 123 soldiers of the elite Delta Force and U.S. Army Rangers ventured into Mogadishu, the capital city of Somalia, to arrest two lieutenants of the ruling warlord, Mohamed Farrah Aidid. What was supposed to be an hour-long extraction quickly deteriorated into a chaotic and bloody 17-hour firefight when thousands of heavily armed "skinnies," that is, Somali militiamen and civilians including women and children, ambushed the American soldiers and kept them pinned down in the center of the city. By the time the fighting was over on the morning of October 4, two $6 million Black Hawk helicopters had been destroyed, three more were badly damaged, eighteen U.S. soldiers were dead, and seventy-three were wounded. The Somalis sustained between 300 and 500 dead and hundreds more wounded.

In the wake of the Battle of Mogadishu, widely circulated news video footage showed the nearly naked body of a dead U.S. soldier being dragged through the streets of Mogadishu by a jubilant Somali mob: an image that sent shock waves of anger and disgust throughout the United States. As is typical with any military fiasco, heads rolled. The man in charge of the operation, Major General William F. Garrison, demoted to a desk job, soon retired, and Les Aspin, President Bill Clinton's secretary of defense, was forced to resign. President Clinton, having been recently rebuffed and humiliated in his efforts to lift a long-standing ban against homosexuals in the military, feared another disastrous incident that would further erode his already shaky prestige. Consequently the United States pulled out of Somalia and thereafter the Clinton administration showed extreme reluctance to intervene on the ground in other conflicts around the world.

Casting a pall over Clinton's foreign policy decisions, Mogadishu also came to haunt the public imagination during and after the Clinton years. Four years after the battle, *Philadelphia Enquirer* staff writer Mark Bowden produced a gripping account of the battle that appeared in twenty-nine daily installments of the *Enquirer* from November 16 to December 14, 1997. On September 29, 1998, PBS's *Frontline* series broadcast *Ambush in Mogadishu*, a balanced and informative documentary that uses candid interviews with officials, soldiers, and Somalis to trace the developments leading up to the battle—the civil war, the famine, Aidid's escalating attacks on UN and U.S. forces—and to explore the firefight in depth. In March 1999, Bowden brought out a book version of his acclaimed article series entitled *Black Hawk Down: A Story of Modern War* (New York: Atlantic Monthly Press, 1999) that became a national bestseller and soon spawned "a major motion picture" based on the incident.

Black Hawk Down (2001)

Aware that the Mogadishu tragedy was still in the air in the late 1990s, the powerful action-spectacle producer Jerry Bruckheimer (*Beverly Hills Cop I & II; Days of Thunder; Top Gun; Con Air; Armageddon; Enemy of the State; Pearl Harbor*) and like-minded director Ridley Scott (*Alien; Blade Runner; G. I. Jane; Gladiator*) decided to exploit the high-octane kinetic potential of the incident. Predictably the film they made, *Black Hawk Down* (2001), was nothing more or less than a nonstop 144-minute cinematic firefight that, despite an explanatory prologue, had little to say about the geopolitical situation that put American soldiers in Somalia. In part, the political sanitization of the battle was shaped by purely commercial imperatives: flying bullets, swooping helicopters, rappelling Rangers, and rocket-propelled grenade explosions are infinitely more exciting than footage establishing historical context. The Pentagon constituted another vital factor in the shaping of *Black Hawk Down*. Unhappy with the unflattering picture of the first Iraq war presented by David O. Russell's Left-leaning *Three Kings* (1999), the U.S. military establishment was determined to guide a more military-friendly film to the screen. In exchange for the filmmaker's use of advisors, eight Black Hawk helicopters, and 100 soldiers from the Ranger unit that actually fought at Mogadishu, the Pentagon insisted on the right to vet the script and to veto anything that took a dim view of the military. As it turned out, except for correcting some technical inaccuracies, the Pentagon had few objections. Book adapter Ken Nolan and screenwriters Eric Roth (*Forrest Gump*), Steve Zaillian (*Clear and Present Danger; Mission: Impossible*), and Stephen Gaghan (*Rules of Engagement*) crafted a pristine war film that was all furious action and action-driven dialogue and—unlike Bowden's book—contained virtually no background information on those involved in the fight, American or Somali. In sum the film's terrific bloodletting took place in a sociopolitical vacuum: an ideological foreshortening of perspective suggesting that U.S. soldiers were, once

U.S. soldier mans an MK-19 grenade launcher during a weapons sweep in Mogadishu, Somalia. (Defense Visual Information Center)

again, simply the good guys defending themselves against inexplicably hateful, dark-complexioned, anti-American bad guys. Made and marketed for a hefty $90 million, *Black Hawk Down* earned back all its costs and showed a modest profit four months after its Christmas, 2001, release. Pentagon officials were so pleased with *Black Hawk Down* that they contracted with Jerry Bruckheimer and Bertram van Munster (*Cops*) to produce *Profiles from the Front Line*, an unscripted reality television program focusing on U.S. troops battling terrorism in Afghanistan. ABC-TV aired *Profiles* in February 2003 but quickly pulled the show, supposedly due to low ratings.

The Intervention of the United States in Bosnia

On Sunday, June 2, 1995, a surface-to-air (SAM) missile fired by Serb forces hit a USAF F-16 fighter jet piloted by Capt. Scott F. "Zulu" O'Grady while enforcing the NATO no-fly zone over Bosnia. O'Grady survived the downing largely unhurt and then spent the next six days in the countryside evading capture by Bosnian Serb troops before being rescued on June 8 by a Marine Corps Search and Rescue team. Four days after his rescue, Capt. O'Grady was at the Pentagon being feted as a genuine American hero by President Bill Clinton, Defense Secretary William Perry, Gen. John M. Shalikahvili, chairman of the Joint Chiefs of Staff, and a crowd of 500 well wishers. Not unexpectedly, the U.S. press devoured the O'Grady story as an exemplary saga of American ingenuity, true grit, and military competence under pressure.

Behind Enemy Lines (2001)

A few years after the O'Grady incident, producer John Davis (*Predator; Water-world*) teamed with Irish director John Moore to make *Behind Enemy Lines* (2001). A wholly predictable action film written by screenwriting brothers Jim and John Thomas (*Predator; Wild, Wild West*), *Behind Enemy Lines* exploits and embellishes O'Grady's adventure for maximum suspense, thrills, and patriotic feeling—and also adds further gravitas with a subplot that involves the O'Grady figure, Lt. Chris Burnett (Owen Wilson), taking valuable reconnaissance photos of a Serbian massacre and illegal troop movements, photos that need to get back to friendly lines. Though pursued by hundreds of frantic Serbian troops, Burnett and his vital photographs are ultimately and predictably rescued by U.S. forces, thanks to the risk-taking bravado of Admiral Leslie McMahon Reigart (Gene Hackman), a volatile, fly-by-the-seat-of-the-pants officer who subscribes to the American cowboy ethos as opposed to the excessive political scrupulosity of the United Nations. A shameless ploy to enlist simpleminded patriotic fervor in service to a conventional macho-thriller plot, *Behind Enemy Lines* did well at the box office, easily recouping its estimated $40 million budget and showing a healthy profit. Ironically, the real Scott O'Grady, since retired from the military, sued 20th Century Fox for its quasi-fictional depiction of him in the film. Owen Wilson's Lt. Burnett is a "hot dog" pilot who uses foul language and disobeys orders—characteristics that most assuredly do not apply to the devout and politically conservative O'Grady.

5

Sports History on Film and Television

Fiction films on sports topics abound. Films that deal with sports *history* comprise a relatively small but significant subset of the sports film genre. Such films were initially confined to baseball and boxing: two of the three iconic spectator sports that dominated American popular culture in the first half of the twentieth century (the other sport being horse racing). In the decades that followed, baseball and boxing were joined by basketball and football as major spectator sports, the Olympics gained global prominence, and numerous participatory sports enjoyed burgeoning popularity (e.g., surfing, skiing, running, mountaineering, skateboarding, to name a few). Quite naturally sports cinema has reflected the increasing popularity of the major spectator sports and the proliferation of a host of other athletic activities. Commercial sports events are everywhere in the media and popular culture, proof that vicarious experiences of physical grace, achievement, and victory serve an important compensatory function in the era of postmodern capitalism, when large segments of the populace are relegated to underpaid, stultifying work and experience a depressing lack of meaningful community and political power. Nonetheless, more recent sports history films have reflected a growing public cynicism about sports heroism and official sports history. It would have been unthinkable for a film, in the early decades of the twentieth century, to deliberately tarnish the luster of a sports icon. Now such films are commonplace. In keeping with recent revisionist tendencies, there has been a major recuperation of hitherto repressed black sports history in film: a belated offshoot of the Civil Rights movement that has corrected an otherwise woefully skewed image of sports history.

Baseball

The Pride of the Yankees (1942)

Sam Wood's *The Pride of the Yankees* (1942) was the first baseball biopic and still the most famous and best loved. Written by Paul Gallico, Herman J. Mankiewicz (*Citizen Kane*), Casey Robinson, and Joe Sterling, *Pride* recounts the life of Henry Louis "Lou" Gehrig (1903–1941), New York Yankees first baseman from 1923 to 1939, an excellent hitter (.340 lifetime batting average), twice voted the American League MVP (1927 and 1936), and known as "The Iron Horse" for most consecutive games played (2,130), a record that stood for fifty-six years until it was broken by Cal Ripken Jr. in 1995. By all accounts a modest and decent man, Gehrig was much admired by sports fans for his formidable skills, fierce work ethic, and unassuming ways. His forced retirement, after becoming afflicted with the always-fatal motor neuron disease, amyotrophic lateral sclerosis (ALS, later known as Lou Gehrig's disease), was a tragedy mitigated by Gehrig's graceful acceptance of his fate. His dignity and courage were amply manifest when Gehrig made his famous farewell speech at Yankee Stadium (July 4, 1939). He declared himself "the luckiest man on the face of the earth" for having had the opportunity to play ball as long as he did. So revered a figure was Gehrig that he was voted into the newly established Baseball Hall of Fame by special election immediately after his retirement, and his team number (4) was the first to be retired in any professional sport.

Made right after Gehrig's death and released shortly after America's entry into the Second World War, *The Pride of the Yankees* was a tribute to Gehrig's tragic stature. The film also had the obvious ideological purpose of reminding its audience of the ideal American virtues: personal modesty, fair play, team spirit, self-discipline, and psychological resilience, especially in times of crisis and adversity. Baseball was at the height of its cultural prestige as America's pastime, so lionizing a baseball hero was tantamount to saluting America itself. In the film, Gary Cooper plays Lou Gehrig: good casting, in a way, because Cooper bore an uncanny resemblance to Gehrig and Cooper's established star persona, as the archetypal American hero—taciturn but strong and brave—dovetailed nicely with Gehrig's heroic legend. Less than ideal was Gary Cooper's age (forty-one at the time of filming), rank ineptitude as a ballplayer, and the fact that he was right-handed, whereas Gehrig was left-handed, a quandary circumvented by reversing the lettering on Cooper's uniform and flipping the film when Cooper was shown batting. In the final analysis, *The Pride of the Yankees* erred on the side of sentimentality but still managed to retain a level of dignity in keeping with its subject.

The Babe Ruth Story (1948)

Far less successful as sports hagiography was Roy Del Ruth's *The Babe Ruth Story* (1948), a biopic rushed to the screen while its ailing subject, George Herman "Babe" Ruth—who had appeared playing himself in *The Pride of the Yankees*—was still alive to appreciate the tribute. Freely adapted by George Callahan from Ruth's eponymous 1948 memoir ("as told to" Bob Considine), *The Babe Ruth Story* suffered from every sentimental and melodramatic cliché in the book. As played by the oafish character actor, William Bendix, Babe Ruth comes off as something of a buffoon. Though its makers undoubtedly meant well, *The Babe Ruth Story* probably damaged Ruth's legend rather than enhanced it.

The Stratton Story (1949)

As the director of *The Pride of the Yankees*, Sam Wood was uniquely qualified to make *The Stratton Story* (1949), a biopic about Chicago White Sox pitcher, Monty "Gander" Stratton (1912–1982). After five seasons with the White Sox, Stratton was showing great promise when his career in the majors was tragically cut short by the loss of a leg in an off-season hunting accident in Greenville, Texas, on November 28, 1938. Bitterly demoralized by his misfortune, Stratton— with the cheerful encouragement of his wife, Ethel—soon regained his fighting spirit and returned to baseball as a pitching coach for the White Sox from 1939 to 1941. Thereafter he mastered the tricky art of balancing and pivoting on an artificial leg and subsequently had a successful career as a minor league pitcher in his home state of Texas. In 1948 MGM producer Jack Cummings approached the Strattons with a movie deal. Cummings was likely motivated by the success of William Wyler's *The Best Years of Our Lives* (1946), a highly patriotic Samuel Goldwyn production that featured nonactor Harold Russell essentially playing himself as a double amputee adapting to postwar civilian life. Not to be outdone by Goldwyn as a postwar booster of pure Americanism, MGM (which had ousted Goldwyn at its merger) felt that Stratton's courageous recovery from the loss of a limb made for good, morally unassailable drama and could approximate the kind of inspiration for the disabled delivered by *The Best Years*. Furthermore, Stratton's story was an entirely safe property politically at a time when Hollywood was nervous about the ideological content of its films. Joshing, folksy American icon and war hero, James Stewart, was predictably cast as Monty Stratton (and at 6 feet, 3 inches Stewart nearly matched the real Stratton's 6-foot, 5-inch stature). The strenuously perky June Allyson was cast as Stratton's wife,

Ethel. In sum, *The Stratton Story* easily combined two venerable Hollywood feel-good plots, the rags-to-riches saga and the overcoming adversity story, and won its screenwriter, Douglas Morrow, an Oscar.

The Jackie Robinson Story (1950)

On April 15, 1947, Jackie Robinson (1919–1972) made history by breaking major league baseball's long-standing color barrier when he started with Branch Rickey's Brooklyn Dodgers. Three years after Robinson's historic debut, Eagle-Lion Films released *The Jackie Robinson Story* (1950), an inspirational biopic directed by Alfred E. Green that acknowledged Robinson's signal contribution to the Civil Rights movement and the end of American apartheid. Highly unusual was the fact that the film starred Jackie Robinson playing himself. Though a superb athlete (the first UCLA athlete to win varsity letters in four different sports), Robinson's talents did not extend to acting. His self-conscious delivery and wooden mannerisms in front of the camera are slightly painful to watch. The film also suffers from ragged production values and the adverse political climate in which it was made. Tellingly, no mention is made of Robinson's prior struggles with segregation while he was in the military during the war years. The film also

Lobby card promoting The Jackie Robinson Story *showing Minor Watson (as Dodgers president Branch Rickey) and Jackie Robinson as himself. (Library of Congress)*

obviates Robinson's brief stint with the Kansas City Monarchs of the Negro leagues. Such a mention would have acknowledged the *institutionalized* nature of American racism. Both of these omissions indicate a desire to avoid embarrassing truths about the persistence of racism in a nation allegedly standing for freedom and justice.

The Pride of St. Louis (1952)

On a much lighter note is Harmon Jones's *The Pride of St. Louis* (1952), a biopic about Jay Hanna (aka Jerome Herman) "Dizzy" Dean (1910–1974), star pitcher for the St. Louis Cardinals in the 1930s who was one of baseball's most colorful characters. Son of a poor itinerant Arkansas cotton farmer, the uneducated Dean was famous for loud boasting of his prowess on the mound in drawling, mangled English that distressed educators but was popular with the public at large. Dean had six successful seasons with the Cardinals until he suffered a broken toe in the 1937 All-Star game. Returning before his injury had healed properly, Dean pitched when his timing was off, injured his arm, struggled on the mound, was traded, and eventually retired after soldiering through several lackluster seasons with the Chicago White Sox. Cowritten by Guy Trosper and Herman J. Mankiewicz (*The Pride of the Yankees*), *The Pride of St. Louis* portrays Dean (Dan Dailey) as a great athlete and amiable clown. Film historian John Nesbit astutely notes that Mankiewicz copied the rags-to-riches and career-cut-short plot formula he had employed on his earlier *Pride* film point by point: "1. The scout spots the prospect; 2. Early days in the big leagues—a breakthrough success; 3. Get a girl and marry her; 4. Baseball successes, told through stock footage and newspaper headlines; 5. Career ending disaster strikes; 6. Poignant speech required for ending" (Nesbit 2002). Nesbit further conjectures that the film was likely prompted by Dizzy Dean's popularity as a radio and TV baseball announcer in the early 1950s.

Fear Strikes Out (1957)

During his rookie days with the Boston Red Sox, Jim Piersall quickly developed a reputation as a difficult player. Disputatious, emotionally erratic, given to bizarre, clownish antics on the field, Piersall was a more frightening version of Dizzy Dean at his dizziest. Piersall's unruly ways were the unheeded warning signs of a worsening mental illness that culminated in a devastating nervous breakdown in 1952. After seven months of hospitalization, extensive psychotherapy, and numerous shock treatments, Piersall was well enough to return to baseball for the 1953 season (and would play for the Red Sox and other major league clubs for a total of seventeen seasons). Two years after his psychotic break Piersall bravely submitted to a candid interview with *Chicago Sun-Times* columnist, Irv "Kup" Kupcinet. Overwhelmingly positive response to Piersall's painful disclosures about his battle with mental illness prompted him to coauthor a "tell-all" book with sportswriter Al Hirschberg, entitled *Fear Strikes Out: The Jim Piersall Story* (Boston: Little, Brown, 1955). In 1957 movie producer (later director) Alan J. Pakula teamed with director Robert Mulligan and screenwriters Raphael Blau and Ted Berkman to bring *Fear Strikes Out* to the screen. In his first leading role in a motion picture, actor Anthony Perkins delivered a sensitive portrayal of Piersall as an emotionally frail young man hounded to distraction by his overbearing father (competently played by Karl Malden). Though it made for stirring melodrama, the problem with the pathogenic father-son conflict posited by writers Blau and Berkman was the fact that it was simplistic, reductive, and simply not true. The real Jim Piersall scoffed at the notion that his father was the sole cause of his mental problems and also thought Tony Perkins' rendition of a pro baseball player bespoke a questionable masculinity. Whatever its shortcomings, *Fear Strikes Out* did break new ground by dealing with the largely taboo topic of mental illness. At the nadir of the Cold War, a time when conformist pressure to affirm heroic individualism was at its height, the film acknowledged that there was plenty of mental and emotional suffering underneath the Ayn Rand competitive success ethos that has dominated American life.

With the phenomenal rise in the popularity of football and basketball in the 1960s and 1970s—faster-paced sports for a quickening society—baseball, a product of the nineteenth century, began to lose its primacy as *the* American sport. Free agency, burgeoning salaries, and a decades-long series of strikes and lockouts starting in 1972 also had a deleterious effect on baseball's prestige as the national sport. Reflecting baseball's diminishing aura and a more wary and critical post-Vietnam cultural sensibility, more recent feature and television films about baseball have tended to deal with heretofore unexamined issues (particularly race) and have offered revisionist interpretations of baseball history and its icons.

It's Good to Be Alive: The Roy Campanella Story (1974)

Roy "Campy" Campanella (1921–1993) followed Jackie Robinson as one of the first black players admitted to major league baseball. After nine stellar seasons as a catcher in the Mexican and Negro leagues, Campanella signed with Branch Rickey's Brooklyn Dodgers in 1948. Over the next decade, the amiable and popular Campanella capably anchored the Dodgers' defense, played in five World Series, and was selected the National League's Most Valuable Player three times (in 1951, 1953, and 1955). Tragically, on January 28, 1958, the car Roy Campanella was driving near his home on Long Island skidded on icy roads and hit a telephone pole. The accident fractured his fifth cervical vertebra, rendering him quadriplegic. In 1959 he published *It's Good to Be Alive*, an autobiography in which he reminisced about his baseball career and movingly described his physical therapy and emotional recovery after the accident that left him paralyzed and deeply depressed. Campanella was elected to the Baseball Hall of Fame in 1969. In 1974 television writer Steve Gethers adapted Campanella's book into *It's Good to Be Alive: The Roy Campanella Story* (1974), a made-for-TV movie helmed by neophyte director, Michael Landon, and starring Paul Winfield as Campanella and Lou Gossett Jr. as Sam Brockington, his dedicated physical therapist. A sort of hybrid of *The Jackie Robinson Story* and *The Stratton Story*, *It's Good to Be Alive* combined several narratives: the dramatic saga of the struggle to integrate baseball intermeshed with Campanella's rise to prominence and, finally, his struggle to come to terms with his devastating injury. In a finale borrowed from *The Pride of the Yankees*, Campanella tells a reverential audience at the Los Angeles Coliseum, "It's good to be alive."

One in a Million: The Ron LeFlore Story (1978)

Inspiring in a different way is Ron LeFlore's story. Hailing from Detroit's brutal black ghetto, LeFlore turned to crime at an early age, committing burglaries and robberies and selling drugs on the street. Convicted of armed robbery in the spring of 1970, LeFlore, twenty-two years of age, drew a five- to fifteen-year sentence at Jackson State Prison in southwest Michigan. While incarcerated he joined a prison baseball team and showed amazing talent. As luck would have it, a fellow inmate knew someone on the outside who knew Tigers manager, Billy Martin. After paying a visit to Jackson to see LeFlore play ball, Martin arranged to have LeFlore try out for the Tigers in the summer of 1973. Proving himself a solid hitter, fielder, and an unusually fast base runner, LeFlore won a contract with the Tigers. Released from prison in July 1973, LeFlore joined the team for its 1974 season, played extremely well, and became a favorite among Tigers fans (until he was traded to Montreal in 1982). During his fourth season in the majors LeFlore brought out his autobiography, *Breakout: From Prison to the Big Leagues* (New York: Harper & Row, 1978), a book that immediately prompted *One in a Million: The Ron LeFlore Story* (1978), a rags-to-riches made-for-TV movie starring the impressively talented LeVar Burton (*Roots*) as LeFlore. Shot by veteran cinematographer Jordan Cronenweth (*Cutter's Way; Blade Runner*) and edited by Aaron Stell (who also edited *Fear Strikes Out*), *One in a Million* was terse, unsentimental, and documentary-like in style: a better-than-average television movie that also featured a number of LeFlore's Detroit Tiger colleagues: Billy Martin, Norm Cash, Bill Freeman, Jim Northrup, and Al Kaline. Sad to say, LeFlore's life after his active player days gives the lie to the Hollywood happy ending. The beneficiary of a very modest annual baseball pension, LeFlore has survived by taking a series of coaching and managerial jobs with obscure minor league teams in the United States and Canada. The ironic distance between movies and real life was amply demonstrated on September 27, 1999, when LeFlore was feted by thousands of fans at a Tigers Stadium pregame ceremony and then promptly arrested on a standing warrant for nonpayment of $57,000 in child support.

Don't Look Back: The Story of Leroy "Satchel" Paige (1981)

Leroy Robert "Satchel" Paige (1906–1982) may well have been the finest baseball pitcher of all time. Longtime star of the Negro leagues, Paige won nearly 2,000 of the 2,500 games he pitched and was credited with more than *fifty* no-hitters between 1926 and 1948. No less an authority than Joe DiMaggio declared Paige the "best and fastest pitcher" (Ribowsky 2000) he ever faced. Unfortunately, because he was black, Paige was barred from the major leagues until July 1948, when he started for Bill Veeck's Cleveland Indians as the world's oldest rookie (at least forty-two at the time). Though well past his prime, Paige made a respectable showing in his six seasons in the majors, posting a 28–31 win-loss record and a 3.29 earned run average. A pitcher of enormous skill and stamina, Paige was equally famous for his sardonic wit, his powers as a raconteur, and his knack for droll witticisms (e.g., "Don't look back. Something might be gaining on you"). In short, Paige was the black Dizzy Dean—though smarter, funnier, and undoubtedly a better pitcher. Shortly before his death, Paige finally got a modicum of the recognition he deserved, with a modest made-for-TV movie entitled *Don't Look Back: The Story of Leroy "Satchel" Paige* (1981) starring Lou Gossett Jr. as Paige. For a true American folk hero and legend, it was hardly enough.

New York Yankees (The Movie) (1987)

Since their founding in 1903, the New York Yankees (called the Highlanders until 1913) have consistently been baseball's richest, most famous, and most successful franchise. Boasting the likes of Babe Ruth, Lou Gehrig, Joe DiMaggio, Casey Stengle, Phil Rizzuto, Mickey Mantle, Roger Maris, Reggie Jackson, and a host of other baseball luminaries, the Yankees have won forty-one American League pennants and twenty-six World Series: far more than any other major league team. In 1987 Gary A. Blase and Lawrence Miller produced *New York Yankees (The Movie)*, a well-made documentary history of the team that uses newsreels, game footage, and interviews with Yankee greats. Wholly adulatory and nostalgic, the film is essentially a shameless souvenir for Yankees fans.

Still We Believe: The Boston Red Sox Movie (2004)

Not to be outdone by the Yankees, their archrivals, the Boston Red Sox, got their own commemorative documentary in 2004: Paul Doyle Jr.'s *Still We Believe: The Boston Red Sox Movie*. The film chronicles the 2003 season and examines enduring fan loyalty despite the team's failure to win a world championship since 1915. Ironically, the Red Sox did win their long-sought championship the very next year.

Eight Men Out (1988)

Of an entirely different political character is John Sayles' *Eight Men Out* (1988), a revisionist docudrama about the infamous 1919 "Black Sox" scandal. Based on Eliot Asinof's meticulously researched exposé, *Eight Men Out: The Black Sox and the 1919 World Series* (New York: Holt, 1963), Sayles' film manages to stay close to its source material and do justice to a highly complex story—no mean feat when one considers that Sayles was contractually bound to bring the film in at under 2 hours running time. The received wisdom about the "Black Sox" was that the eight players who colluded with gamblers to throw the 1919 World Series to the Cincinnati Reds were inexcusably greedy and corrupt. Asinof's thesis, ably dramatized by Sayles, is that the eight disgraced Chicago White Sox players were certainly culpable but the real villains of the piece were the gamblers and the notoriously stingy, dishonest, and dictatorial White Sox owner, Charles Comiskey (1859–1931), who grossly underpaid his players and treated them like slaves, thus setting the stage for their mutiny. A lover of baseball, John Sayles is also something of a Marxist. His agenda in making *Eight Men Out* was to show how greed and the kind of desperation that comes out of radically skewed power relationships can destroy otherwise good men and poison American institutions.

The Babe (1992)

In the same revisionist vein is Arthur Hiller's *The Babe* (1992), a somewhat bombastic and unflattering biopic of Babe Ruth written by John Fusco (*Thunderheart*) that is almost as nasty as Roy Del Ruth's *The Babe Ruth Story* was sugarcoated. As portrayed by the corpulent John Goodman, Babe Ruth comes off as hedonistic, puerile, and self-absorbed, that is, an immature and oversexed boozehound, glutton, and full-time carouser who happened to have extraordinary baseball talent. Babe Ruth was all of these things but perhaps not to the extent

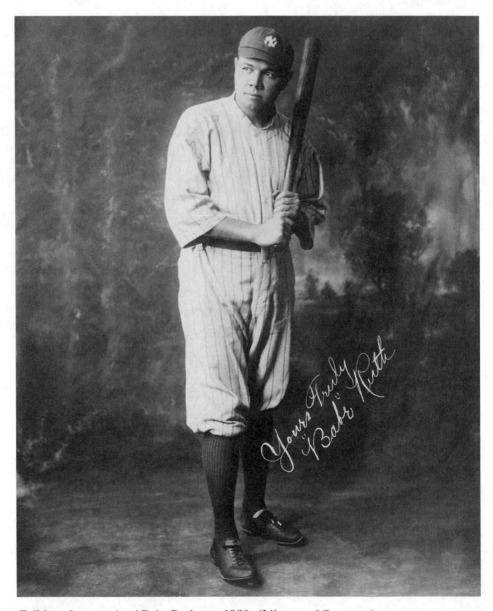

Full-length portrait of Babe Ruth, ca. 1920. (Library of Congress)

depicted or implied in *The Babe*. The film's psychological thesis—that Ruth's excesses compensated for a lonely childhood—is probably accurate but also smacks of a kind of perverse sentimentality.

Baseball (1994)

In a major counterattack against the gradual slide of baseball's stature, documentary filmmaker Ken Burns brought out *Baseball* (1994), an ambitious, learned, and adulatory 18-and-a-half-hour (1,140 minutes) PBS miniseries that surveys the entire history of the sport, from its gradual origins in the early 1800s to the present day. Burns' characteristic method is to explore great swaths of American history through signal events (e.g., the Civil War), long-standing cultural traditions (e.g., baseball, jazz music), or key personages (e.g., Huey Long, Mark Twain). Baseball's near-mythic cultural centrality and its obsession with its own history and traditions made it a perfect vehicle for a Burns epic. The film is divided into nine consecutive 2-hour "innings," each episode dealing with a particular period (usually a decade) in baseball history. Using the tried-and-true Burns documentary formula (reverent voice-over narration, copious stills, clips, and interviews, carefully chosen musical accompaniment, dramatic recitations, and so forth), *Baseball* engages in a protracted saturation bombing of its target. Few, if any, key figures, events (e.g., the Black Sox scandal), or issues (Jim Crow) are left unexamined. Commenting on his subject, Burns rather pompously noted, "You have everything [in baseball]—the immigrants and the rise of the cities, the racial tension, then the decline of cities and the rise of suburbs, the Sun Belt, conflicts between management and labor, the birth of popular culture and the media, the cult of heroes and celebrity, the nature of democracy itself. To a large extent, to a really astonishing extent, the story of baseball is the story of this country." Overlong but still extraordinarily informative and (mostly) well made, Burns' *Baseball* functions as a kind of semiofficial record. Ironically, when it first aired in September 1994, the documentary became a substitute for baseball itself. At that time a particularly unpopular players' strike obliterated half the season and forced the cancellation of the 1994 World Series. Deprived of the real thing, fans could at least revel in baseball's glorious past.

Cobb (1994)

While Ken Burns worshipped at baseball's shrine, producer-director team David V. Lester and Ron Shelton (*Bull Durham*) brought out *Cobb* (1994), a revisionist biopic on Tyrus Raymond Cobb (1886–1961), aka "The Georgia Peach," Detroit Tigers outfielder considered one of baseball's greatest all-around talents. An excellent fielder (.944 lifetime fielding average), aggressive base runner, and superb hitter (.367 lifetime batting average—the highest ever), Ty Cobb set numerous records during his twenty-four years in the majors. These include most career hits (4,191), most career runs (2,245), and most stolen bases in a single season (96), all records that stood up for many decades. Though a truly gifted athlete, Cobb was probably the most reviled baseball player who ever lived. Tense, proud, humorless, misanthropic, ruthlessly competitive, and a die-hard racist, Cobb got into countless arguments and fistfights with teammates, opponents, fans, and any ordinary citizens who happened to rub him the wrong way.

Near the end of his life, Cobb recruited sports writer Al Stump ("Stumpy" to Cobb) to help him write his autobiography, *My Life in Baseball: The True Record* (1961). Despite the misleading subtitle, *My Life* was a thoroughly self-serving and sanitized version of Cobb's career. Observing him up close for months on end, Stump (played by Robert Wuhl in the film) kept secret notes on the real Ty Cobb with an eye toward writing a more truthful biography later on. The human being behind the legend was a lonely, embittered, alcoholic old man dying of cancer who frantically shuttled between his palatial home at Lake Tahoe and a Georgia hospital. Packing a pistol and a paper bag full of negotiable securities, Cobb struggled with his impending mortality and battled his demons to the very end. Stump's conflicted relationship with Cobb becomes the film's framing device, interspersed with flashbacks that fill in Cobb's background and further delineate his complex psyche. While not stinting on Ty Cobb's atrocious personal traits, the movie does offer a plausible causative thesis for the man's fierce and violent nature. Just before Cobb entered the majors in 1905, his mother, Amanda, killed Cobb's father, William, with a shotgun blast, supposedly mistaking him for an intruder when he was, in fact, surreptitiously checking up on her marital fidelity. Admonished by his beloved father not "to come home a failure," Cobb compensated for his father's gruesome death by playing his heart out.

In the movie the very capable Tommy Lee Jones plays the elderly Ty Cobb with great brio but his casting in the role remains somewhat problematic. While his depiction of Cobb is powerful, Jones was only forty-six at the time of filming: too young, healthy, and handsome to convincingly impersonate a wizened, dying seventy-five-year-old alcoholic. Nor does Jones even vaguely resemble the pinched-faced Cobb. Those quibbles aside, *Cobb* remains an absorbing exercise in psychological portraiture and ideological demystification: a film that never would have been made in a more innocent time.

Hank Aaron: Chasing the Dream (1995)

A wholesome chaser to the bitter tonic of *Cobb* was writer-director Michael Tollin's *Hank Aaron: Chasing the Dream* (1995), an inspirational documentary on Henry Louis Aaron, the man who, on April 8, 1974, broke Babe Ruth's hallowed record of 714 career home runs. Produced by a team that included Tollin, Brian Robbins, and actor Denzel Washington, *Hank Aaron* is as much about race as it is about baseball. Aaron entered the major leagues during their integration phase and suffered racist taunts and threats from players and fans alike. Overt racism broke out again for Aaron when he neared Babe Ruth's record in the waning days of his career in the early 1970s. Some bigoted white baseball fans felt that Ruth's record was somehow sacred and the idea of its being surpassed by a nonwhite player was anathema. Undaunted, Aaron did break Ruth's record, demonstrating in a most dramatic way that black athletes were, at the very least, on a par with their white counterparts.

Soul of the Game (1996)

In keeping with the revisionist, race-conscious temper of the times, Home Box Office brought out *Soul of the Game* (1996), a made-for-TV docudrama about the end of the Negro leagues and the postwar racial integration of major-league baseball. Written by Gary Hoffman and David Himmelstein and directed by African American director, Kevin Rodney Sullivan, *Soul* focuses on Satchel Paige (Delroy Lindo), Josh Gibson, "the Babe Ruth of the Negro leagues" (Mykelti Williamson), and Jackie Robinson (Blair Underwood): the three Negro league players being considered by Brooklyn Dodgers General Manager, Branch Rickey (Edward Hermann), for the historic role of integrating the majors. Though viewers know that young Robinson got the nod over established stars Gibson and Paige, the film manages to be suspenseful all the same. As baseball history, though, *Soul of the Game* is less than accurate. In keeping with an understandable tendency to romanticize, the film deceptively portrays Satchel Paige as a devoted husband and attributes Josh Gibson's mental problems to the brain tumor that killed him in 1947, failing to mention that Gibson's sometimes erratic behavior was just as likely triggered by alcohol and heroin use.

The Life and Times of Hank Greenberg (1998)

While racism plagued baseball for much of its history, anti-Semitism has been an equally deplorable but somewhat less obvious blight on the sport and on American cultural life. A documentary biopic, *The Life and Times of Hank Greenberg* (1998), by Aviva Kempner (*Partisans of Vilna*), addresses anti-Semitism while it celebrates the illustrious career of Henry Benjamin "Hammerin' Hank" Greenberg (1911–1986), Detroit Tigers slugger who was the first Jewish baseball star. At the height of his powers in the late 1930s, Greenberg fell just 1 RBI short of Lou Gehrig's single-season record of 184 and only 2 home runs short of Babe Ruth's record of 60 home runs. A quietly devout man who agonized over playing ball on Jewish holy days, Greenberg was also a genuine patriot. As the first baseball player to enlist after Pearl Harbor, Greenberg sacrificed his best potential years in the majors to serve in the U.S. Navy during the Second World War. After eleven (nonconsecutive) seasons with the Tigers and a year with Pittsburgh, Greenberg retired in 1947 with an impressive .313 lifetime batting average and two American League Most Valuable Player awards (1935 and 1940). Greenberg was elected to the Baseball Hall of Fame in 1956. More than just a great hitter, Hank Greenberg was an icon to Jewish Americans in the 1930s and 1940s, a living symbol of Jewish hope and pride at a time of virulent international anti-Semitism and its attendant horrors.

Preparing to write an autobiography in the last months of his life, Greenberg tape-recorded many hours of what Kempner calls "oral testimony." Excerpts from these tapes form the running voice-over narrative of the film, which is comprised of archival footage, audio, and still photographs and interviews with baseball colleagues and celebrity admirers. Interviewees include fellow ballplayers Bob Feller, Hal Newhouser, and Charlie Gehringer, Greenberg's book editor Ira Berkow, Michigan Senator Carl Levin, celebrity lawyer Alan Dershowitz, and sportswriters Shirley Povich and Dick Schaap.

Babe Ruth (1998)

Six years after Arthur Hiller's extremely unflattering biopic, *The Babe* (1992), veteran sports producer Ross Greenburg (*Legendary Champions* and twenty-seven other features) joined forces with frequent television sports films collaborators—producer Rick Bernstein, writer Stephen Hilliard Stern, and producer-editor George Roy—to create *Babe Ruth* (1998), an hour-long documentary for HBO that displays a degree of technical competence and editorial evenhandedness conspicuously lacking in the smarmy *Babe Ruth Story* or the excessively harsh *Babe*. Rather than focus on Ruth's well-known baseball exploits, the film-makers examine the figure of Babe Ruth as an American popular culture icon to distinguish between the man and the prodigious myth that grew around him.

*61** (2001)

Distinguished comic actor and die-hard Yankees fan, Billy Crystal, teamed with longtime HBO Sports producer Ross Greenburg to present *61** (2001), an HBO made-for-TV docudrama about the famous 1961 battle between Mickey Mantle (Thomas Jane) and Roger Maris (Barry Pepper) to break Babe Ruth's single-season record of sixty home runs. Filmed by Oscar-winning cinematographer, Haskell Wexler (*Eight Men Out*), *61** faithfully recounts the highly dramatic rivalry that cast the popular Mantle against his upstart (and decidedly less charismatic) Yankee teammate. Hank Steinberg's well-crafted script and Billy Crystal's sure direction make for a surprisingly effective and suspenseful drama, even though it is well known that Maris won the "race."

Boxing

The Leonard-Cushing Fight (1894)

The first motion picture footage of boxers in action is also among the first motion picture footage of any kind. It was produced by Thomas Edison's protégé W. K. L. (William Kennedy Laurie) Dickson and shot by cameraman William Heise at Thomas Edison's legendary "Black Maria" studio at Menlo Park in West Orange, New Jersey, in May or June 1891. The flickering film, which lasts only a few seconds but is looped to make it appear longer, shows two men warming up but not throwing any punches. The first actual bout committed to film was *The Leonard-Cushing Fight* (1894), a well-fought six-round contest between Mike Leonard and Jack Cushing filmed by William Heise at Edison's Black Maria studio on June 14, 1894. The complete film was 730 feet long and lasted 6 minutes, a minute per round (at about thirty frames per second).

The Corbett-Courtney Fight (1894)

On September 8, 1894—the second anniversary of his victory over John L. Sullivan—James J. "Gentleman Jim" Corbett ventured to West Orange to fight

Peter Courtney in front of Thomas Edison's kinetograph. Edison had wanted to secure John L. Sullivan against Corbett in a filmed rematch of their 1892 World Championship bout but Sullivan's asking price of $25,000 was prohibitive. Peter Courtney, a young prizefighter living in nearby Trenton, replaced Sullivan. Game but badly overmatched against Corbett, Courtney was battered bloody and finally knocked out in the sixth round. He received a paltry $150 for his pains while Corbett took home $5,000. *The Corbett-Courtney Fight* (1894) was the first fight film ever shown commercially.

The Corbett-Fitzsimmons Fight (1897)

One of the most heralded sporting events of the late nineteenth century was the Jim Corbett–Bob Fitzsimmons Heavyweight World Championship fight held at an outdoor arena in Carson City, Nevada (where boxing had been recently legalized), on St. Patrick's Day, 1897. Heavyweight champion since his famous knockout of John L. Sullivan on September 7, 1892, "Gentleman Jim" Corbett successfully defended his title against Charlie Mitchell with a third-round knockout on January 25, 1894. A title fight with British-born New Zealander, Robert Fitzsimmons, was originally scheduled for October 31, 1895, in Dallas, Texas, but was canceled. More interested in his burgeoning acting career than in boxing, Corbett retired in November 1895 at the age of twenty-nine but soon returned to the ring, after a fashion. Fighting only three exhibitions and one real bout (with "Sailor" Tom Sharkey) in 1896, the somewhat rusty Corbett finally met an inferior but determined "Ruby Robert" Fitzsimmons on March 17, 1897. At ringside with three "Veriscope" 63mm movie cameras of his own invention, former Edison associate Enoch J. Rector filmed the fight from beginning to end. Corbett, the sentimental favorite, consistently outfought his rival but was felled a minute into the fourteenth round by a punch to the solar plexus that knocked the wind out of him and gave Fitzsimmons the championship.

Assembled from some 11,000 feet (2 miles) of film, *The Corbett-Fitzsimmons Fight* (1897) was the world's first feature-length film with a running time of 90 minutes. After his movie premiered at the Academy of Music on 14th Street in New York City, Rector built another twenty Veriscope machines and held screenings all over the country and abroad. Rector's film proved so popular and lucrative that Sigmund "Pop" Lubin, a Philadelphia-based film entrepreneur, staged a reenactment of the Corbett-Fitzsimmons fight using two burly Pennsylvania railroad workers as stand-ins. Lubin's version was nearly as popular as Rector's, even though it was a fake. Another interesting aspect of *The Corbett-*

Fitzsimmons Fight was the nature of its audience. Reviewers at Chicago screenings of Rector's movie reported the surprising fact that 60 percent of the audience was comprised of women. Film historian Miriam Hansen (University of Chicago) argues that the "cinematic mediation of the [Corbett-Fitzsimmons fight] gave women access to a spectacle from which they were traditionally excluded . . . At one remove, however, it afforded women the forbidden sight of male bodies in semi-nudity, engaged in intimate and intense physical action" (Hansen 1991). Indeed, an advertisement for a screening of the movie appearing in the *Indianapolis News* (March 19, 1898) touted it as "especially attractive to the ladies"—quite a risqué claim for late Victorian America.

Jeffries-Sharkey Contest (1899)

The huge popularity of the Corbett-Fitzsimmons fight movies spawned a slew of silent-era boxing films, some shot at the actual event, some reenactments or "reproductions." Perhaps the most remarkable of the real films was the *Jeffries-Sharkey Contest* (1899). Having won the world heavyweight championship with an eleventh-round knockout of Bob Fitzsimmons (Coney Island, Brooklyn, June 9, 1899), Jim "The Boilermaker" Jeffries defended his title, for the first time, against Sailor Sharkey in a *twenty-five*-round night bout at Coney Island on November 3, 1899. Jeffries' manager, William A. Brady, and a promoter named O'Rourke sponsored the fight and contracted with the American Mutoscope and Biograph Company to film it. No less than 500 arc lamps were rigged above the ring to light it bright enough for night filming: an arrangement that resulted in temperatures in excess of 115 degrees for the fighters! Cameramen Frederick S. Armitage, Georg William "Billy" Bitzer, and Arthur Marvin each operated a Mutoscope camera. To ensure continuous coverage, one cameraman shot footage while another focused and the third reloaded film. Though the scorching heat of the overhead lamps turned the ring into an oven, the fighters managed to go the distance. Jeffries was declared the winner in a brutal and close contest that could just as easily have gone to Sharkey. In order to cover all twenty-five rounds, 35,000 feet (7 miles) of 68mm film was exposed. Rented to commercial exhibitors in any number of 200-foot rounds they requested, the *Jeffries-Sharkey Contest* was a popular favorite and was shown (in various forms) in hundreds of nickelodeons that sprang up after 1904.

The Johnson-Jeffries Fight (1910)

When Arthur John "Jack" Johnson of Galveston, Texas, won the world heavy-weight title by knocking out Canadian boxer Tommy Burns in Sydney, Australia (December 26, 1908), he returned home expecting a hero's welcome for recapturing the championship for the United States. He was sadly mistaken. Though an American, Johnson was black. As such, he was despised, ridiculed, and slandered by thousands of white boxing fans who could not abide the notion that blacks were superior to whites in any field of endeavor, especially boxing, which was considered the ultimate test of virile manhood—and racial mastery. Johnson further inflamed white racist ire by refusing to be modest and self-effacing. He openly reveled in the high life and, most scandalous of all, bedded and even married dance hall girls and prostitutes, all of them white women. Because no white boxer could beat Johnson, writer Jack London led the hue and cry to coax former champion Jim Jeffries out of rustication to humble the upstart black man. Having retired undefeated six years earlier, Jeffries had become an alfalfa farmer in southern California and had ballooned to nearly 300 pounds. A long and rigorous training regimen got Jim Jeffries (dubbed "The Great White Hope") down to 227 pounds by the time he met Johnson at a specially built outdoor stadium in Reno, Nevada, on July 4, 1910. Nonetheless, Jeffries, thirty-five, was past his prime and it was soon evident that he was badly overmatched. His right eye swollen shut by the seventh round, Jeffries endured a brutal battering and was knocked down three times in the fourteenth round. His seconds finally threw in the towel in the fifteenth round. Their dream of white racial supremacy shattered, the crowd of some 20,000 white spectators dispersed in stunned silence. As word of Jeffries' ignominious defeat spread nationwide, rioting broke out in numerous American cities as blacks celebrated and whites retaliated, resulting in scores of injuries and at least eight reported deaths. In sum, "The Fight of the Century" was, from race-baiting advance publicity to violent aftermath, an exceedingly ugly episode in the appalling annals of American racial bigotry. On a more positive note, Johnson's win over Jeffries was a genuine early victory for black pride and presaged the fight for racial equality that would begin in earnest some forty-five years later.

Naturally, given the extraordinary level of public interest, the Johnson-Jeffries fight was filmed for commercial exhibition. The fight's promoter, George "Tex" Rickard, sold exclusive film rights to a syndicate representing the Essanay, Selig Polyscope, and Vitagraph film companies for the then huge sum of $200,000. Nine cameramen recorded the action and the resulting 2-hour film was released as a reserved-seat attraction in northern states and abroad (an early forerunner of the pay-per-view sports event). Unfortunately for the film syndicate, *The Johnson-Jeffries Fight* (1910) did not do nearly as well as was hoped.

Antiboxing crusaders forced the cancellation of dozens of screenings on the grounds that the film would only incite more interracial violence. Sour grapes about Johnson's victory over Jeffries robbed the film of a white audience in the South and dampened (white) enthusiasm everywhere else. African Americans were, of course, eager to see *The Johnson-Jeffries Fight*; clandestine showings of the film took place in urban black neighborhoods all over the country years after the fight. The film's ideological significance was not lost on white southern politicos. In the spring of 1912, on the eve of Jack Johnson's first title defense after the Jeffries bout, Georgia Representative Seaborn A. Roddenberry and North Carolina Senator Furnifold McLendel Simmons cosponsored a bill before Congress that would prohibit the interstate transportation of fight films. The ostensible reason for the proposed law was to shield American youth from the brutal spectacle of boxing. In reality both Roddenberry and Simmons were hidebound adherents of Jim Crow and sworn personal enemies of Jack Johnson. The bill passed into law and was not repealed until 1929.

Gentleman Jim (1942)

When Hollywood finally turned its attention to boxing history, it chose to sidestep the bitter racial politics of the Jack Johnson era by making *Gentleman Jim* (1942), an innocuous and largely fanciful biopic about James J. Corbett (aka "Handsome Jim" or "Pompadour Jim"), the first great fighter of the gloved era. Adapted for the screen by Vincent Lawrence and Horace McCoy from Corbett's autobiography, *The Roar of the Crowd* (New York: Grosset & Dunlap, 1925), *Gentleman Jim* is less a boxing movie than a rags-to-riches film about social class mobility. The son of an Irish liveryman from San Francisco, Jim Corbett (1866–1933) always aspired to rise above his proletarian background. He went to college and worked as a bank clerk before becoming a professional fighter and eventual world champion after his 1892 knockout of John L. Sullivan (played memorably by Ward Bond in the film). In the film Jim Corbett (played by Errol Flynn) personifies the quintessential American desire to achieve wealth, fame, and social position: American dream values in need of ideological justification during the Second World War.

The Great John L. (1945)

Probably inspired by the commercial success of *Gentleman Jim*, popular crooner Bing Crosby joined Milt Carter, James Earl Grant, and Frank Mastroly to produce *The Great John L.* (1945), a mediocre biopic of legendary bare-knuckle prizefighter, John Lawrence Sullivan, aka "the Boston Strong Boy" (1858–1918), world heavyweight champion from 1882 to 1892—until he was defeated by Gentleman Jim Corbett. Starring Greg McClure as Sullivan, *The Great John L.* uses both the rags-to-riches and comeback plot trajectories as it follows Sullivan's rise from working-class obscurity to greatness, his descent into alcoholism and poverty after his loss of the championship, and his eventual attainment of sobriety and self-respect. Lacking the narrative verve of *Gentleman Jim* or the star power of an Errol Flynn, *The Great John L.* was a less-than-great boxing picture that was quickly forgotten.

Day of the Fight (1951)

The nature of the fight film (and world cinema, for that matter) was changed forever when an obscure young New York City photographer named Stanley Kubrick did a photo shoot for "Prizefighter," a pictorial profile of Irish middleweight boxer Walter Cartier (1922–1995) that appeared in the January 18, 1949, issue of *Look* magazine. Fascinated by the gritty noir culture of boxing, Kubrick decided to parlay his work for *Look* into *Day of the Fight* (1951), a 16-minute documentary about Walter Cartier that became the first film of Kubrick's illustrious forty-eight-year career. Narrated in somber tones by television journalist Douglas Edwards, *Day of the Fight* is divided into three parts, each one about 5 minutes in duration. In the first part of the film, boxing historian Nate Fleischer provides some background that serves to contextualize the second and third parts, which take place on the eponymous day of the fight: April 17, 1950, when Cartier fought Bobby James at Laurel Gardens in Newark, New Jersey. The second part of the film follows Cartier from the start of his day at the West 12th Street apartment he shares with his twin brother, Vincent (also a boxer at the time), to Cartier's arrival at the arena 14 hours later. The third part of the film shows glimpses of the tense 2-hour wait until the bout's scheduled 10:00 P.M. start time and depicts Cartier's physical and mental preparations for the fight. The film climaxes with the brutal fight, which resulted in Cartier's quick victory over James by knockout in the first round (shot live at ringside by Kubrick and his Taft High School buddy, Alexander Singer). Of enduring significance as Kubrick's first effort as a filmmaker, *Day of the Fight* also has considerable value as a historical and anthropological document of professional boxing in midcentury America.

The Joe Louis Story (1953)

Joseph Louis Barrow (1914–1981), better known as Joe "The Brown Bomber" Louis, held the world heavyweight title from June 22, 1937, to June 25, 1948. Many boxing historians rank Joe Louis as the greatest heavyweight champion of all time. After dominating his sport for more than a decade, Louis announced his retirement at the age of thirty-four on March 1, 1949. Not quite done with boxing, Louis returned to the ring for a final, unsuccessful, title bid against Ezzard Charles on September 7, 1950. In the twilight of his career, Louis fought and won another eight bouts against some middling (for example, Omelio Agramonte and Andy Walker) to very good opponents (such as Freddie Beshore, Lee Savold, and Jimmy Bivins). On October 26, 1951, a tired and badly outgunned Louis was knocked out in the eighth round by Rocky Marciano at Madison Square Garden, bringing down the final curtain on a legendary career. A genuine folk hero for blacks and whites, especially for his celebrated 1938 rematch victory over the German boxer, Max Schmeling, Louis was not about to be forgotten. Two years after the Louis-Marciano fight, prolific writer-producer Stirling Silliphant teamed

Joe Louis (right) takes on Max Schmeling in a heavyweight championship rematch on June 22, 1938. (Library of Congress)

with writer Robert Sylvester and director Robert Gordon to make *The Joe Louis Story* (1953), a biopic starring Golden Gloves boxer Coley Wallace (1927–2005) as Louis and integrating actual footage from many of Louis's greatest fights. Avid to uphold Louis's carefully cultivated public image, as a wholesome, likeable, and nonthreatening black champion, the film assiduously avoided any mention of his marital indiscretions or tax problems.

The Harder They Fall (1956)

Afflicted with an overactive pituitary gland as a child, Primo Carnera, aka "The Ambling Alp" (1906–1967), grew into a near giant who stood 6 feet, 6 inches tall and weighed over 270 pounds. An Italian "strongman" and wrestler, Carnera was discovered by French boxing promoter, Leon See, who turned him into something resembling a professional fighter. After two years on the European boxing circuit and seventeen wins in eighteen bouts, twelve by knockout, Carnera came to the United States in January 1930—where he immediately came under the control of organized crime. Carnera continued to win, usually by knockout, but many of his fights were fixed by the mob, which took most of his winnings. Fighting a grueling schedule of two or three times a month over the next three and a half years, Carnera "won" fifty-seven of sixty-one bouts, forty-six allegedly by knockout, before earning a heavyweight title fight against Jack Sharkey in New York on June 29, 1933. Carnera knocked out Sharkey in the sixth round and officially became heavyweight champion. After only two successful title defenses, Carnera lost the championship to challenger Max Baer in Long Island City on June 14, 1934. Knocked down by Baer a dozen times before throwing in the towel in the fourteenth round, Carnera looked so awful that the syndicate dropped him.

Thirteen years after Primo Carnera's downfall, former and future Hollywood screenwriter, Budd Schulberg, published his second novel, *The Harder They Fall*, a gripping exposé of corruption in professional boxing that was loosely but obviously based on Carnera's career. The ironies surrounding the making of *The Harder They Fall* into a 1956 film are many. A fledgling screenwriter and member of the Communist Party in the late 1930s, Budd Schulberg lost his job at Paramount in 1939 after the film version of his second screenplay, *Winter Carnival*, flopped. In the years that followed, Schulberg garnered occasional script work, wrote novels, and served in the U.S. Navy in World War II. Fingered as a former Communist in the first set of House Committee on Un-American Activities hearings in October 1947, Schulberg happily volunteered, in April 1951, to appear before the second round of HUAC hearings to name names of old Communist comrades. Whether it was an act of conscience or career opportunism is debatable but Schulberg's testimony did get him back into Hollywood's good graces. He was invited to write the story and screenplay of *On the Waterfront* for fellow HUAC "friendly witness," Elia Kazan, a hit film that made informing on former comrades tantamount to a saintly act. In the wake of the ideological and commercial success of *On the Waterfront*, writer-producer Philip Yordan brought *The Harder They Fall* to the screen. Yordan's story is also an interesting one. Having moved from Hollywood to Paris in 1955, Yordan fronted for a stable of blacklisted writers in exile, not out of a sense of idealism but because "he got the better people cheaper" as no one else would hire them. In sum, Yordan's collaboration with Schulberg on *The Harder They Fall* was a classic case of psychological and political displacement in which two Hollywood blacklist survivors condemned organized crime as a means to distance themselves from the stain of radical politics, much in the way Kazan and Schulberg had done with *On the Waterfront*. A further irony is that Humphrey Bogart starred in *The Harder They Fall* as Eddie Willis, a has-been sportswriter hired by promoter Nick Benko (Rod Steiger) to tout the Carnera figure (Mike Lane), called Toro Moreno in book and film versions. In 1947 Bogart had initially come out in support of the Hollywood Ten but distanced himself from them after their rancorous testimony at the initial HUAC hearings made them look almost as bad as their inquisitors.

Somebody Up There Likes Me (1956)

After his retirement from boxing in September 1952, the charismatic and popular former middleweight champion Rocky Graziano went on to enjoy a brief period of television stardom, cohosting both *The Martha Raye Show* and *The Henny* [Youngman] *and Rocky Show*. The same year he became a media celebrity, Graziano published his autobiography, *Somebody Up There Likes Me: My Life So Far* (New York: Simon & Schuster, 1955). Taking advantage of Graziano's national profile, Hollywood writer-producers Charles Schnee and James E. Newcom secured the movie rights to *Somebody Up There* and brought Graziano's story to the screen the following year. Starring Paul Newman (in his first major film role) as Graziano, *Somebody Up There Likes Me* (1956) constitutes a classic rags-to-riches saga as it chronicles the fighter's grim youth in the slums of Manhattan's Lower East Side, frequent brushes with the law, his discovery of boxing, the courting of future wife, Norma (Pier Angeli), his rise to the championship, and his fabled rivalry with fellow middleweight, Tony Zale. Directed by the great Robert Wise, and boasting the likes of Newman, Angeli, Everett Sloan, Sal Mineo, and Robert Loggia, *Somebody Up There* coalesced into a remarkable, if slightly romanticized, tour de force. Though he delivered a brilliant performance, Paul Newman was inexplicably passed over for an Oscar nomination. The film did win Oscars for Best Art and Set Direction and for Best Cinematography.

Legendary Champions (1968)

Before Harry Chapin (1942–1981) became a popular folksinger-songwriter and antihunger activist, he tried his hand at filmmaking. After a stint in Los Angeles making airline commercials, Chapin went to work for William Cayton, a New York City filmmaker. Written and directed by Chapin, *Legendary Champions* (1968) focused on some of the great boxers of the early decades of the twentieth century. The fighters featured in archival footage with voice-over narration by Norman Rose were: James J. Jeffries (1897–1953), champion from 1899 to 1905; Jess Willard (1881–1968), champion from 1915 to 1919; Georges Carpentier (1894–1975), champion from 1920 to 1922; Jack Dempsey (1895–1983), champion from 1922 to 1926; and Jack Sharkey (1902–1994), champion in 1932–1933. Chapin's prodigious research and flair for storytelling resulted in an excellent film. *Legendary Champions* won top honors at the New York and Atlanta film festivals as best documentary and was nominated for a 1969 Academy Award as Best Feature-Length Documentary.

The Great White Hope (1970)

At the end of the 1960s Hollywood finally turned its attention to the long shunned Jack Johnson story; the political temper of the times had finally caught up with Johnson's controversial story. Martin Ritt's *The Great White Hope* (1970) started out as a free-verse play by former Stanley Kubrick collaborator, Howard Sackler. Debuting in 1967 at Zelda and Tom Fichandler's Arena Stage, a regional resident theater in Washington, D.C., *The Great White Hope* garnered lukewarm reviews but generated tremendous controversy and ticket sales because it dealt so graphically with racism, black sexuality, and miscegenation: extremely heady topics at a time when the Black Power movement was at its height. In a precedent-setting move, producer Howard Levin brought the production to Broadway, where it ran for 500 performances and swept American theater's highest honors, winning three 1969 Tony Awards (for Best Actor, Best Actress, and Best Drama), the 1968–1969 New York Drama Critics' Award for Best Play, and the 1969 Pulitzer Prize for Best Drama. With its huge success onstage it was perhaps inevitable that *The Great White Hope* would be adapted into a movie. Likewise, Martin Ritt's involvement with the project seemed almost foreordained, given Ritt's progressive political leanings and his abiding interest in American history, ethnography, and the so-called "social problem" film.

Anxious to preserve the integrity of a proven winner as it shifted from stage to screen, Ritt hired Howard Sackler to adapt his own play and cast stage leads James Earl Jones and Jane Alexander to reprise their roles for the film. Sackler's play and script follow Jack Johnson's life story in broad outline: his rise to the world heavyweight championship (to the anguish of white boxing fans); his relationships with white women (distilled into a single interracial relationship); his trumped-up imprisonment for violation of the Mann Act; his exile from America and his wandering in foreign countries up to his final defeat in Cuba. Though the film has lost much of its power to shock in the decades since its release, *The Great White Hope* remains an extremely powerful and historically instructive viewing experience.

Mohammed Ali Films

Three-time heavyweight champion of the world, Mohammed Ali (born Cassius Marcellus Clay Jr. in Louisville, Kentucky, in 1942), dominated boxing in the 1960s and 1970s and is universally acknowledged as one of the greatest sports figures of the twentieth century. His life and boxing career also function as a remarkably vivid barometer of the zeitgeist of his times.

A.k.a. Cassius Clay (1970)

Not surprisingly, a number of films on Ali have appeared over the years. The first of these was the documentary, *A.k.a. Cassius Clay* (1970). Produced by William Cayton (*Legendary Champions*, 1968), directed by Jim Jacobs, and narrated by actor Richard Kiley, *A.k.a. Cassius Clay* was made while Ali's life and boxing career were in limbo. Having joined the Nation of Islam in 1964, Ali sought conscientious objector status as a Black Muslim when the government attempted to induct him for military service in 1967. Convicted of draft evasion, stripped of his heavyweight title, and banned from boxing in the United States, Ali spent what probably would have been his best years as an athlete (March 1967 to October 1970) fighting in court instead of the ring. *A.k.a. Cassius Clay* traces Ali's boyhood in Louisville, his teenage years as an amateur boxer, his gold medal at the 1960 Olympics, his turning professional, his attainment of the world heavyweight title by beating Sonny Liston in 1964, and his highly controversial stand against the Vietnam War. Completed before Ali's successful return to the ring against Jerry Quarry, *A.k.a. Cassius Clay* posits the then-reasonable possibility that Ali might be forced to forsake boxing altogether and become some sort of black revolutionary.

Ali, the Fighter (1971)

Ali, the Fighter (1971), a little-known but excellent cinema verité documentary directed by William Greaves and Rick Baxter and produced by Greaves and Shintarô Katsu, takes up where *A.k.a. Cassius Clay* leaves off. Having beaten Jerry Quarry and Oscar Bonavena, Ali won the right to challenge "Smokin' Joe" Frazier, the reigning heavyweight champion, in a contest touted "The Fight of the Century" at Madison Square Garden on March 8, 1971. *Ali, the Fighter* prefaces the bout with candid footage of (and interviews with) the fighters, their promoters, managers, and rabid fans. In doing so, *Ali* provides a revealing glimpse of the general politico-cultural milieu at a particularly volatile moment in recent American history. Those siding with the controversial Ali were obviously of a more radical temperament. Expertly shot by a dozen ringside cameras, the fifteen-round bout is presented in its entirety and without any blow-by-blow commentary—an inspired directorial trope that enormously enhances the dramatic impact of the bout (which Frazier won by decision).

Mohammed Ali, The Greatest (1974)

Bereft of the world championship for seven years, Ali was back on top when master photographer and filmmaker William Klein made *Mohammed Ali, The Greatest* (1974). Really more of a cultural observer than a boxing fan, Klein sought to explore the facets of Ali's enormous charisma and pay tribute to his stature as a pop culture icon, not just for African Americans but for people of all races, colors, and creeds. Accordingly, Klein concentrates on Ali's phenomenal ability to promote himself at every bout, interview, and press conference, as "the Greatest"—braggadocio that is entertaining at first but wears somewhat thin over the long haul. The same could be said about Klein's documentary, which neatly bifurcates into two films. The first half, shot in starkly beautiful black and white, revolves around Ali's (then Cassius Clay) underdog victory over Sonny Liston for the world title in 1964. The second half, shot in color, chronicles Ali's stunning title win over George Foreman a decade later in Kinshasa, Zaire (the so-called "Rumble in the Jungle"). Critics faulted *Ali, The Greatest* for failing to deliver Ali, the boxer. No film footage is offered of Ali's fights, only a series of still photographs that reduce the fast and brutal action to mythic images.

The Greatest (1977)

After the "Rumble in the Jungle," when Ali's international fame was at its zenith, he brought out a somewhat sanitized autobiography (coauthored with Richard Durham), *The Greatest: My Own Story* (New York: Random House, 1975). Shortly thereafter directors Tom Gries (*Will Penny*) and Monte Hellman (*Two-Lane Blacktop*) turned Ali's memoir into a biopic entitled *The Greatest* (1977), starring Ali himself. Despite the contributions of some seasoned supporting players (Ernest Borgnine as Ali's trainer, Angelo Dundee; James Earl Jones as Malcolm X; Roger E. Mosley as Sonny Liston; Robert Duvall as an early backer), *The Greatest* proved to be far less than great. The film's most glaring drawback was Ali, who could not act or even approximate a credible performance and looked especially awkward at age thirty-five trying to play himself as a much younger man. Likewise, the script was mediocre and the direction tepid, making *The Greatest* little more than an odd historical curiosity.

When We Were Kings (1996)

As one of the high points of Ali's career, the fabled "Rumble in the Jungle" deservedly received its due with Leon Gast's long-awaited and Oscar-winning documentary, *When We Were Kings* (1996). The man who arranged the October 30, 1974, bout was notorious boxing promoter, Don King, who persuaded Zaire's ruthless dictator, Mobutu Sese Seko (1930–1997), to put up $10 million to lure Ali and George Foreman to Kinshasa for an international media event that was guaranteed to put Zaire on the map. Reigning heavyweight champion with thirty-nine wins (thirty-six by knockout) and no losses, the heavily muscled, brooding Foreman was twenty-five years old, in peak physical condition, and an absolutely menacing presence. Having demolished Joe Frazier (who had beaten Ali) in less than two rounds, Foreman was expected to handle Ali with ease. Some even feared that Ali could be badly injured or even killed. Incredibly, things did not turn out that way. Employing his celebrated "rope-a-dope" strategy, Ali absorbed inhuman levels of punishment for seven rounds and managed to stay on his feet and keep moving. Once Foreman had exhausted himself Ali finally went on the offensive and felled his opponent in the eighth round with a series of stunning rights. Ali's dramatic victory, against all odds, was hailed as one of the most courageous, gritty, and dexterous feats in sports history and marks the moment when Mohammed Ali was transformed from controversial celebrity to boxing legend. Skillfully shot and edited, Leon Gast's film not only documents the fight but also provides vivid behind-the-scenes glimpses of Don King's machinations, Mobutu's Zaire, the boxers in training and at press conferences, Ali's charisma and popularity in Africa, and the carnival-like atmosphere that surrounded the proceedings (which included a prefight concert featuring B. B. King, James Brown, and Miriam Makeba). Complicated and protracted legal wrangling between Gast and his Liberian financial backers deferred the film's release for twenty-two years. Finally debuting in 1996, *When We Were Kings* played like a time capsule of a bygone era, when the now always lovable George Foreman was a mean and sullen young man and when the now Parkinson's-afflicted Ali was still his arrogant, ebullient, magnificent self.

Ali (2001)

With a production budget exceeding $100 million and featuring an enormous cast headed by such stars as Will Smith (as Ali), Jon Voigt (as Howard Cosell), and Mario Van Peebles (as Malcolm X), Michael Mann's biopic *Ali* (2001) obviously aspired to be *the* definitive filmic statement on Mohammed Ali. While vastly superior to its hapless predecessor, *The Greatest*, *Ali* was not the great film it might have been. Although Will Smith delivered an astonishingly convincing depiction of Ali and Jon Voigt was eerily brilliant as Cosell, the film as a whole proved to be curiously lifeless and uninspiring, perhaps defeated by the sheer magnitude of the Ali myth. It did not come anywhere near making its huge production and marketing costs.

Post-Vietnam-Era Boxing Films

Raging Bull (1980)

Though primarily psychological portraiture, Martin Scorsese's *Raging Bull* (1980) nonetheless ranks as one of the greatest boxing movies ever made. Frequent Scorsese collaborators Paul Schrader (*Taxi Driver*) and Mardik Martin (*Mean Streets*) took *Raging Bull: My Story*, the autobiography of former middleweight champion Giacobe "Jake" LaMotta ("The Bronx Bull"), and turned it into a searing indictment of paranoid machismo run amok. Raised in the Bronx slums, Jake LaMotta was a street fighter and petty criminal turned pugilist best known for his hard-fought rivalry with the great Sugar Ray Robinson (real name: Walker Smith Jr., 1921–1989). As a human being, LaMotta was, for half his life, a nasty piece of work. Poorly educated and emotionally stunted, Jake LaMotta seethed with rage and insecurity. Whenever he was frustrated, sexually jealous, or vexed—which was often—LaMotta lashed out verbally and physically. After his retirement from boxing in 1954, LaMotta's life spun out of control. Increasingly erratic behavior, marital difficulties, business reverses, and alcoholism ultimately landed him in a Dade County jail, broke, friendless, and literally banging

Movie poster for Raging Bull. *(MGM/Corbis)*

his head against his cell wall. On the verge of suicidal despair, LaMotta experienced something akin to a spiritual conversion experience and began to turn his life around in the years that followed. By the time he wrote his autobiography in 1970, LaMotta had become a successful businessman, entertainer, and all-around raconteur and sports legend.

A lower-middle-class Italian American Catholic from New York City, Martin Scorsese could relate to LaMotta's background and was instinctually drawn to his harrowing life story. It had sex, violence, melodrama, the primal blood sport of boxing, and the tough urban noir atmospherics of the 1950s and 1960s (which Scorsese underscored by filming in black and white). Most important of all, LaMotta's saga could serve as a modern allegory of spiritual ruin and redemption: perennial themes in Scorsese's work. Along with writers Schrader and Martin, actor Robert De Niro also shared Scorsese's identification with LaMotta and his tormented struggle to find inner peace. A staunch practitioner of "The [Stanislavski] Method," De Niro delved into LaMotta's life and psyche with an intensity that bordered on the fanatical. (Michael Mills defines "The Method" by saying that "actors [are] not to emote in the traditional manner of stage conventions, but to speak and gesture in a manner one would use in private life." Moderntimes Classic Film Pages, http://www.moderntimes.com.) To play LaMotta in his boxing prime, De Niro trained diligently and became, for all intents and purposes, a highly competent professional fighter. To play LaMotta in his later years, De Niro eschewed a "fat suit" and actually gained some sixty pounds (which he promptly shed after the film was completed). Beyond the torturous physical transformations, De Niro turned in the performance of a lifetime; his rendition of LaMotta as a moody, menacing sociopath was convincing in the extreme. Scorsese's incredibly fastidious direction—he spent six weeks shooting just *10 minutes* of boxing footage—resulted in a movie that was technically flawless. Brilliant editing by Scorsese stalwart Thelma Schoonmaker and excellent supporting performances by Joe Pesci (who played LaMotta's long-suffering brother and manager, Joey) and Cathy Moriarty (who played LaMotta's long-suffering wife, Vickie) rounded out Scorsese's masterpiece. Nominated for eight Academy Awards, *Raging Bull* won Oscars for De Niro and Schoonmaker and put Scorsese's career back on track. Whether or not the story of Jake LaMotta was worthy of such impassioned and expert cinematic treatment is another matter entirely.

Broken Noses (1987)

Charles Saumarez Smith, the director of London's National Portrait Gallery, has observed that, "in the public mind [internationally famous fashion photographer], Bruce Weber (*Let's Get Lost*) is most obviously associated with a photographic version of the American dream of innocence" (www.bruceweber. com). It is therefore fitting that Weber segued into films with *Broken Noses* (1987), a documentary about twenty-five-year-old Andy Minsker, Oregon Golden Gloves champion turned professional boxer, featherweight class, who retired in 1991 with a record of 12–1–1. Presumably Weber was attracted to Minsker for the man's athletic physique, tough good looks, and his courage and perseverance in the pursuit of boxing success: a pure, proletarian, and romantic version of the American dream. Mixing color and black-and-white cinematography with a jazz music soundtrack, *Broken Noses* manages to be amusing, chic, and mildly homoerotic—unusual traits for a boxing movie. In cinema verité style Minsker is shown mentoring a dozen aspiring young boxers at his Mt. Scott Boxing Club in Portland, Oregon; goofing around; reminiscing about his glory days; and candidly revealing the residual pain of a poverty-ridden, abusive upbringing. The film won a 1988 International Documentary Association (IDA) Award and a Grand Jury Prize nomination at the 1988 Sundance Film Festival.

Champions Forever (1989)

A modern update of Harry Chapin's *Legendary Champions* (1968), Dimitri Logothetis's *Champions Forever* (1989) is an unnarrated anthology documentary about the five great heavyweight boxing champions of the 1960s and 1970s: Muhammad Ali (1964–1967, 1974–1978); Joe Frazier (1970–1973); George Foreman (1973–1974); Larry Holmes (1978); and Ken Norton (1978–1979). Inevitably concentrating on Ali, indisputably first among equals, *Champions Forever* presents highlight clips from the key fights, contemporary interviews by baseball great Reggie Jackson with the former champions, and a markedly uncomfortable "Dinner with the Champs," awkwardly hosted by Jackson. Though somewhat compromised by a saccharine musical score, too many short clips, and erratic editing, *Champions Forever* does succeed in conveying the personalities of the five fighters and functions as a basic cinematic history of the golden era of heavyweight boxing.

Sonny Liston: The Mysterious Life and Death of a Champion (1995)

A memorable part of that era was Charles "Sonny" Liston (1932–1970), one of the most controversial, mysterious, and tragic figures in modern boxing. Over a professional career that lasted almost seventeen years (1953–1970), Sonny Liston won fifty of fifty-four bouts, thirty-nine by knockout. After knocking out Floyd Patterson for the title (September 25, 1962), Liston was world champion for the next seventeen months until he lost the crown to the upstart Cassius Clay on February 25, 1964, in Miami. Liston also lost a rematch to Clay in Lewiston, Maine, on May 25, 1965, after refusing to reenter the ring after being knocked down. Speculation continues to this day as to whether or not one or both of the Clay-Liston fights were fixed by the mob. Liston continued to box until his death, under mysterious circumstances, on December 30, 1970. Outside the ring, Sonny Liston's life was hellish. Jeff Lieberman's made-for-HBO documentary, *Sonny Liston: The Mysterious Life and Death of a Champion* (1995), explores Liston's brutal, illiterate upbringing in abject poverty in rural Arkansas; his two prison stints (for armed robbery and beating a policeman); his career-long manipulation by mobsters; and his mysterious death by drug overdose (which may have been murder).

Don King: Only in America (1997)

The infamous, wild-haired fight promoter, Don King, has had a checkered past to say the least. King's criminal background was never a secret but was not known in its nauseating entirety until longtime *New York Post* sports columnist Jack Newfield's damning exposé: *Only in America: The Life and Crimes of Don King* (New York: William Morrow, 1995). Newfield reveals that, before King broke into the fight promotion business in 1974 by staging the "Rumble in the Jungle," he had been a Cleveland pimp, numbers runner, street thug, and a (twice) convicted killer. Since he has become rich and famous King has continued to break the law but now his crimes are of the white-collar variety—fraud, extortion, bribery, income tax evasion, felony theft of clients' earnings, and so on. Ironically, Don King has often cited his lowly origins and checkered past to tout himself as a living example of the viability of the American dream! Considered with the appropriate level of irony, King's favorite axiom, "Only in America," is grimly amusing. Shortly after Newfield's book appeared, HBO bought the television rights and hired actor-writer Kario Salem to turn King's lurid saga into a made-for-TV movie, *Don King: Only in America* (1997). Starring the talented Ving Rhames in an utterly convincing impersonation of Don King, Salem's adaptation was fast-paced, funny, well acted, and did not stint on the ugly aspects of King's American dream odyssey. Among a host of other accolades, *Don King: Only in America* was nominated for eight Emmys and won for Outstanding Made for Television Movie and Outstanding Writing for a Miniseries or a Movie.

On the Ropes (1999)

Critically acclaimed but still little known and underappreciated is *On the Ropes* (1999), a gut-wrenching documentary by NYU film school graduates Nanette Burstein and Brett Morgen that does considerably more for boxing than the somewhat overrated *Hoop Dreams* did for basketball. Burstein and Morgen took their movie camera into the poverty-ridden, crack-infested Bedford-Stuyvesant (Brooklyn) ghetto and spent a year following the careers of Noel Santiago, George Walton, and Tyrene Manson, three amateur black boxers hoping to qualify for the 1997 Golden Gloves Tournament at Madison Square Garden. All three fighters are coached by forty-one-year-old trainer Harry Keitt, an ex-boxer (and onetime sparring partner of Mohammed Ali) who has overcome drugs, jail, and homelessness and hopes to be catapulted into major success as a trainer through the fortunes of one (or more) of his charges. Noel Santiago, an academically dysfunctional seventeen-year-old high school student, is the son of a mostly absent, formerly crack-addicted mother and a father dead from AIDS. Deficient in self-esteem and the requisite boxing talent, Santiago soon falls by the wayside; he hopes, instead, to get his GED and enter the military. Mickey Marcello, a professional manager of dubious reputation, lures the gifted George Walton away from Harry Keitt and introduces Walton to Eddie Mustafa Muhammad, a former trainer of Mohammed Ali. Increasingly unhappy under new management, Walton eventually returns to the unassuming but honest Keitt. The most compelling of the three stories is that of Tyrene Manson, a talented Golden Gloves aspirant who inadvertently falls afoul of the law. After the police arrest her AIDS-infected uncle for selling crack on the street, they search his house and find a packet of crack cocaine in a bedroom Tyrene Manson shares with four other persons. A reformed drug user with no criminal history, Tyrene is the one who is charged with possession with intent to sell even though it is plainly evident that her uncle is the real culprit. Facing a four-and-a-half- to twenty-five-year prison sentence, Tyrene Manson is convicted and sentenced to the minimum penalty at a trial that coincides with the Golden Gloves Tournament: a grotesque, heartbreaking miscarriage of justice that vividly demonstrates how class and race oppression work in contemporary America.

Southpaw: The Francis Barrett Story (1999)

Liam McGrath's modest documentary, *Southpaw: The Francis Barrett Story* (1999), presents a two-year segment in the ongoing saga of Francis Barrett, a light welterweight Irish boxer. Though he hails from a community of Travelers (Irish gypsies) who live in squalor on the outskirts of Galway, young "Francie"

Barrett is cheerful, earnest, and a fighter of some promise. Chick Gillen, an ex-boxer turned Galway barber, assumes the role of Barrett's trainer and mentor and their relationship becomes a central element in McGrath's film. After qualifying for the 1996 Olympics in Atlanta, nineteen-year-old Barrett is chosen to carry the Irish tricolor flag at the opening ceremonies: an unprecedented honor for a man from a despised minority. Though he does not win an Olympic medal, Francis Barrett returns to Ireland something of a national hero, gets married, moves to London, fathers a child, and continues to pursue his career as an amateur boxer. As the film closes, Barrett is torn between turning professional or attempting to qualify for the 2000 Sydney Olympics. Funded on a shoestring budget, *Southpaw* is somewhat ineptly shot and edited; consequently it lacks narrative focus. Nonetheless, McGrath's documentary manages to pay sincere tribute to an underdog's courage and persistence. After premiering in Ireland, *Southpaw* was shown at the 1999 Sundance Film Festival and later saw limited release in the United States and the United Kingdom.

Joe and Max (2002)

In 2001 German and American film production companies joined forces to create *Joe and Max* (2002), a made-for-TV docudrama about the highly politicized Joe Louis–Max Schmeling rivalry of the late 1930s. When Louis (played by Leonard Roberts) and Schmeling (played by Til Schweiger) first met in the ring (at Yankee Stadium on June 19, 1936), Schmeling knocked out an overconfident and underprepared Louis in the twelfth round: a stunning upset that was touted by Hitler's propaganda minister, Josef Goebbels, as proof of Aryan superiority. Chastened by his loss to Schmeling, Louis took his training seriously, won the heavyweight championship by knocking out James J. Braddock (June 22, 1937), and was in peak condition when he met Schmeling for a rematch at Yankee Stadium on June 22, 1938. Somewhat disingenuously—for Jim Crow still prevailed in America—the media portrayed the second Louis-Schmeling fight as a mythic battle between righteous American democracy and racist Nazi totalitarianism. To the joy of most Americans, Louis felled Schmeling in the first round and went on to retain his heavyweight title until 1947.

As *Joe and Max* dramatizes, both men struggled after their boxing careers ended but Schmeling ultimately did much better. Plagued by horrendous tax problems, Louis ended up broke and publicly humiliated; he eventually took a job as an official greeter at a Las Vegas casino. Though destitute after the war, Schmeling went on to become a spokesperson for Coca-Cola in Germany and prospered accordingly. When Joe Louis died in 1981, Max Schmeling paid for his funeral. In the years since their epic bouts the two men had become friends.

Their friendship is rightly depicted in the film as a triumph of mutual respect and sympathetic humanity over cynically manipulated issues of race, nationalism, and ideology.

Cinderella Man (2005)

Joe Louis's predecessor as heavyweight champion, James J. Braddock (1905–1974), is the subject of Ron Howard's *Cinderella Man* (2005), a film about boxing but even more about attaining—and affirming—the American dream through sheer grit, decency, and wholesome family values. Over a professional boxing career that spanned almost twelve years (1926–1938), Jimmy Braddock (Russell Crowe in the film) fought eighty-four bouts, posting fifty-two wins, twenty-one losses, three draws, two no-contests, and six no-decisions. What Braddock lacked in technical proficiency he made up for with hard hitting, toughness, and resilience. In his first year as a pro fighter, Braddock won thirteen of his first fifteen bouts. After that Braddock's fortunes in the ring fluctuated wildly. Knocked out twice in the spring of 1927, he went winless for seven bouts over a three-month period, did better for a time, but then suffered another slump in the spring of 1928. Fighting well again in the latter part of 1928 and the first half of 1929, Braddock earned a light heavyweight title shot against Tommy Loughran (July 18, 1929) but narrowly lost that fifteen-round bout and then went into a protracted decline. Over a year (September 1931 to October 1932) Braddock won only two of eleven bouts. In a fight with Abe Feldman (September 25, 1933) Braddock broke his right hand, which caused his boxing license to be revoked. Having lost all his investments in the 1929 stock market crash, James Braddock found himself injured, in debt, and with a wife and three young children to feed. Once his hand healed sufficiently, Braddock took work as a stevedore on the New Jersey docks but, with the Great Depression in full swing, such work was erratic—two or three days a week at best. Unable to feed his family, Braddock was forced to go on public relief in September 1934. He and his family received $24 over the next ten months: not enough to live on but enough to keep starvation at bay. But Braddock's luck had already started to change. After a nine-month layoff from boxing, Braddock was pressed into last-minute service as an opponent for a heavyweight contender named John "Corn" Griffin. On June 14, 1934, Braddock a 2 to 1 underdog, knocked out Griffin in the third round. Five months later Braddock defeated a heavily favored John Henry Lewis and then went on to beat Art Lasky on March 22, 1935—a victory that earned him the right to challenge Max Baer for the heavyweight championship. On June 13, 1935, James Braddock, a 6 to 1 underdog, defeated Max Baer on points to become heavyweight champion of the world: a title he held until June 22, 1937. Dubbed the "Cinderella Man" by sportswriter Damon Runyan, Braddock epitomized the triumph of the underdog when the American masses were desperate for just that kind of vicarious experience.

Football

Knute Rockne All American (1940)

Knute Kenneth "Rock" Rockne (1888–1931), the legendary head coach of Notre Dame from 1918 to 1931, was indisputably America's greatest college football coach. With a career record of 105 victories versus 12 losses and 5 ties in thirteen seasons, Knute Rockne still holds the greatest all-time winning percentage (.881) in college and professional football. He led the "Fighting Irish" to several national championships in the 1920s. Moreover, it was Rockne who initiated intersectional rivalries, invented the two-platoon system, and popularized the forward pass and the backfield shift (i.e., starting all four running backs in motion before the snap). Rockne even revolutionized the design of equipment and uniforms. Sadly, after winning another national championship in 1930, Rockne was killed in a plane crash on March 31, 1931, en route to Los Angeles from Kansas to make a football training film. He was only forty-three years old. At the time of his death Rockne was a towering national hero, in demand for product endorsements, book deals, and inspirational speeches. Most of the nation's 1,700 newspapers carried Rockne editorials the week of his death. His funeral was broadcast live on the radio throughout the United States and in parts of South America, Europe, and Asia. A crowd of over 100,000 mourners lined his funeral procession at South Bend, Indiana.

Toward the end of the Great Depression, B-movie actor Ronald Reagan talked of making a film about Rockne's life that would dramatize American dream ideology by stressing Rockne's immigrant journey from Norway to the pinnacle of American sports success. Hal B. Wallis and Robert Fellows at Warner Brothers adopted Reagan's idea as their own and initiated a Rockne biopic project. Ironically, Reagan was very nearly passed over for the role of George "The Gipper" Gipp (1895–1920), Rockne's gridiron protégé, who died of pneumonia in 1920 and became the object of Rockne's famous inspirational halftime speech to his team ("Win one for the Gipper!") in a celebrated game against Army on November 10, 1928. (After a scoreless first half, Notre Dame went on to win 12–6.) Veteran character actor Pat O'Brien was cast as Rockne and Gale Page as Rockne's wife, Bonnie Skiles Rockne. Written by Robert Buckner (*Dodge City*) and directed by Lloyd Bacon, *Knute Rockne All American* (1940) is an exercise in maudlin sentimentality and wooden acting that is often unintentionally funny. Though a bad movie, *Knute Rockne All American* remains an important example of American mythmaking: a fact acknowledged in 1997 when it was included in the National Film Registry.

Jim Thorpe—All-American (1951)

Wa-tho-huck (that is, "Bright Path"), better known as James Francis "Jim" Thorpe (1887–1953), of the Sac and Fox Indian tribe in Oklahoma, was one of the twentieth century's greatest athletes. An all-American halfback (under the tutelage of legendary coach Glenn S. "Pop" Warner) at Carlisle [Pa.] Indian Institute in 1911 and 1912, Jim Thorpe also excelled at baseball and track and field. Indeed, Thorpe won two gold medals at the 1912 Stockholm Olympics for the pentathlon and decathlon—only to have them confiscated when it was discovered he had once played baseball for a small sum of money, thus negating his amateur status. From 1913 to 1919 Thorpe played major-league baseball, as an outfielder with the New York Giants, Cincinnati Reds, and Boston Braves. During many of those same years Thorpe also played semiprofessional football, with the Canton (Ohio) Bulldogs. In September 1920 Thorpe, Ralph Hay (owner of the Bulldogs), and business associates founded the American Professional Football Association (APFA), now known as the National Football League (NFL). Thorpe was elected the first president of the APFA and played professional football until 1928. Sadly, after the death of his son in the 1918 flu pandemic, Thorpe sank into alcoholism. Retiring from football at age forty, Thorpe, twice divorced, spent his last twenty-two years playing stereotypical Indians in B westerns and at public events. Near the end of his life, Thorpe was afforded one final burst of (dubious) recognition when producer Everett Freeman brought out *Jim Thorpe—All-American* (1951), a lifeless and cliché-ridden biopic directed by Warner Brothers stalwart, Michael Curtiz (*Casablanca*) and starring non-Indian Burt Lancaster as Thorpe. Very much a product of benighted midcentury American cultural attitudes, *Jim Thorpe—All-American* engages in the shameless stereotyping of Native Americans, even down to the familiar broken speech patterns ("Ugh!") and buckskin dress. Also, in typical Hollywood fashion, the film acknowledges Thorpe's descent into alcoholic ignominy but fabricates a happy ending by which Thorpe regains his dignity and sense of purpose by coaching youth football. An honest assessment of Thorpe's life would have had to acknowledge his victimization at the hands of racist whites as a factor in his downfall. In 1952, at the height of the Red Scare, Hollywood was not predisposed to make such acknowledgments.

Hailed as the greatest athlete of the first half of the twentieth century, Jim Thorpe excelled in football, baseball, and track. (National Archives)

Crazylegs (1953)

In his nine seasons as a halfback with the Los Angeles Rams (1949–1957), NFL Hall of Famer Elroy Leon "Crazylegs" Hirsch (1923–2004) racked up over 7,000 yards, scored sixty touchdowns, and was instrumental in the Rams winning an NFL championship in 1951. At the height of his fame, Crazylegs Hirsch was approached by writer-producer-director Hall Bartlett (*Changes*) with a biopic offer that involved Hirsch portraying himself, a publicity gambit first used with Jackie Robinson three years earlier and soon used again with war hero, Audie Murphy. *Crazylegs* (1953), the low-budget Republic Pictures movie that resulted, was long on good-natured corn but short on meaningful narrative; apart from his gridiron prowess, Hirsch's life was not particularly eventful. The film's editor, Cotton Warburton, was nominated for an Oscar for his facility in weaving documentary footage of Hirsch on the playing field into the film proper.

Brian's Song (1971)

Often cited as the finest television movie ever made, Buzz Kulik's *Brian's Song* (1971) tells the tragic but ultimately uplifting story of Louis Brian Piccolo (1943–1970), a running back for the Chicago Bears who succumbed to a rare form of cancer after just four seasons in the NFL. Under the tutelage of head coach George Hallas (Jack Warden in the film), Piccolo (James Caan) and Gale Sayers (Billy Dee Williams) compete for the same running back slot on the team. What begins as a fierce rivalry soon develops into a close and loving friendship, socially significant because Piccolo was white and Sears black and race relations in America in the early 1970s were at low ebb. When Piccolo falls ill, he deals with his impending fate with unfailing humor and courage and is staunchly supported until the end by his wife, Joy (Shelley Fabares), Sayers and his wife, Linda (Judy Pace), and of course the rest of the Bears team. The movie works because mortality so obviously transcends social issues.

Friday Night Lights (2004)

In 1988 H. G. "Buzz" Bissinger, a *Philadelphia Enquirer* journalist, took a year-long leave of absence from the paper to follow the fortunes of the Permian Panthers (nicknamed "MO-JO"), a celebrated high school football team from the economically depressed West Texas city of Odessa (population: 90,000). Allowed total access to head coach Gary Gaines and the entire Panthers team, Bissinger also immersed himself in the social milieu of Permian High School and Odessa. What he found was not pretty: drugging, racism, shoddy academics, and a community-wide football fixation that borders on the maniacal. Permian's warped priorities are perhaps best illustrated by its budget. Having already spent millions of dollars on a state-of-the-art 20,000-person capacity football stadium, Permian spent $70,000 in 1988 on chartered jets to transport the Panthers to away games while allocating only $5,000 for teaching materials for its English department. Painstakingly researched and wellwritten, Bissinger's book—*Friday Night Lights: A Town, a Team, and a Dream* (Reading, MA: Addison-Wesley, 1990)—won critical acclaim, resided on the *New York Times* nonfiction bestseller list from October 1990 to January 1991, and was optioned by film director Alan J. Pakula (*All the President's Men*) for $50,000. Not unexpectedly Odessa residents found *Friday Night Lights* a bitter pill to swallow. The once amicable Coach Gaines never spoke to Bissinger again after the book came out and numerous death threats forced Bissinger to cancel a book promotion visit to Odessa in the fall of 1990.

Ultimately producer Brian Grazer (*Apollo 13; 8 Mile*) acquired the film rights formerly owned by Alan Pakula and hired David Aaron Cohen (*V. I. Warshawsky*) to write a screen adaptation. The original director, Richard Linklater (*Dazed and Confused; SubUrbia*), was replaced by Buzz Bissinger's cousin, Peter Berg, a neophyte director who helped Cohen polish the screenplay. Starring Billy Bob Thornton as Coach Gaines, *Friday Night Lights* (2004) alters much of the factual details to distill and heighten drama. Some of these changes are relatively insignificant (e.g., season schedule order, final scores); some are major. For example, the injured Boobie Miles (Derek Luke) did not make the heartwarming gesture of unselfish solidarity by rejoining the team during the play-offs, nor did Permian lose to Dallas Carter in a Division 5A championship game at the Houston Astrodome. (It lost to Dallas Carter in a less dramatic semifinal game at Darrell K. Royal-Texas Memorial Stadium at the University of Texas, Austin.) While *Friday Night Lights* clearly depicts Odessa as football-crazed, it downplays the racism and anti-intellectualism that mark the city's cultural climate: serious changes in emphasis that minimize the human costs of sports fanaticism and emasculate Bissinger's critique.

Basketball

Hoosiers (1986)

Basketball is to the American Midwest what football is to Texas: a way of life. In 1954 the Milan (Indiana) Indians capped a stellar 28–2 season by beating the Muncie Central Bearcats 32–30 to win the state high school basketball championship: a remarkable achievement for a school with an enrollment of 161 students, only 75 of whom were boys. Some thirty years later Indiana natives Angelo Pizzo (writer-producer) and David Anspaugh (director) brought out *Hoosiers* (1986), a loose adaptation of the so-called "Milan Miracle" that invokes a number of tried-and-true sports saga clichés.

Scene from Hoosiers, *starring Gene Hackman and Dennis Hopper. (MGM/Corbis)*

Gene Hackman plays Head Coach Norman Dale, a heavily fictionalized version of Marvin Wood (1928–1999), Milan's legendary coach. Perhaps based on the volatile Bobby Knight, Hackman's Norman Dale is a hot-tempered former collegiate coach banned from college basketball for striking one of his players, now forced to take a high school coaching job at tiny, obscure Hickory High School. He alienates the townsfolk by promptly firing the interim coach, closing practices to the public, and racking up an early losing streak. Soon, however, Dale's stress on mastering the basics and building team cohesion begins to produce victories. In addition to revitalizing Hickory High's basketball program, Dale undertakes to rehabilitate the town drunk, Shooter (Dennis Hopper), by appointing him assistant coach and engages in self-rehabilitation by falling in love with teacher Myra Fleener (Barbara Hershey). Also transformed is Jimmy Chitwood (Maris Valainis), Hickory's star player who sits out half the season in mourning for the deceased coach that Dale replaced. Indeed, it is Jimmy who scores the winning field goal at the buzzer to win the state championship at Butler University's Hinkle Fieldhouse.

To achieve maximum melodrama, *Hoosiers* departs from the historical facts in almost every way. Milan's championship year was 1954; Hickory's is 1952. Milan's previous basketball coach—the popular Herman "Snort" Grinstead (1908–1979)—did not die in his prime; he was fired in 1953 for buying new team uniforms without permission. At the time of the championship Milan's Marvin

Wood was not a rookie but in his second, successful year as coach. Furthermore, Wood was a mild-mannered twenty-six-year-old, married and with two children—nothing at all like the abrasive and lonely Norman Dale, played by fifty-five-year-old Gene Hackman. Neither of Wood's assistant coaches were drunks. Nor was Milan's star player, Bobby Plump, at all like the moody, troubled Jimmy Chitwood. All of these distortions are designed to maximize the emotional thrill of Hickory's against-all-odds victory; in keeping with the spirit of the age of Reagan, winning becomes the wellspring for all forms of redemption.

Hoop Dreams (1994)

A bracing antidote to the underdog triumphant sports movie is Steve James's *Hoop Dreams* (1994), an epic documentary that follows the fortunes of two working-class black Chicago teenagers—William Gates and Arthur Agee—as they strive to become professional basketball players. Shooting on a budget of $700,000, Steve James and his cohorts, Frederick Marx and Peter Gilbert, spent nearly *five years* filming Gates and Agee throughout their high school careers and into college. The 250 hours of raw footage accumulated was laboriously hand-edited down to a 170-minute film that reveals sober truths about inner-city ghetto life, the basketball industry, and American capitalist society in general.

Displaying impressive basketball talent at an early age, both Gates and Agee are recruited by Gene Pingatore, longtime coach at Saint Joseph's, a suburban Catholic prep school with a strong basketball program (Detroit Pistons star, Isiah Thomas, is a St. Joseph's alum). William Gates, the more promising athlete of the two, wins a full scholarship. Arthur Agee is granted a scholarship that covers only half his tuition costs; his financially strapped family must come up with the rest of the money. Essentially fired after a disappointing first year on the court and in the classroom, Agee is forced to transfer to Marshall, an inner-city public high school, where he eventually blossoms into a star player. Gates's fortunes are, likewise, rocky; a knee injury sidelines him for an extended period and casts his whole future in doubt. But, as film reviewer David Walsh points out, "the ups and downs of the two adolescents' careers, the outcomes of even the most decisive games, are less compelling than the traumas one observes taking place at the margin, so to speak, of the film" (Walsh 1994). Particularly emblematic is the story of the Agee family, which must cope with grinding poverty, unemployment, utility shutoffs, and the desertion of Arthur's father, Bo, who is subsequently arrested on drug charges. The picture of the black urban underclass that emerges from *Hoop Dreams* is of generally law-abiding but demoralized working people struggling to survive under the worst conditions: a far cry from stereotypical corporate media depictions that emphasize lazy welfare chiselers, street thugs, and pregnant teenagers. Likewise, *Hoop Dreams* exposes the cynical venality of high school, college, and professional basketball programs that exploit ghetto youth for athletic glory while paying scant attention to their educational needs. Ostensibly about basketball, *Hoop Dreams* ultimately constitutes a searing indictment of the race and class discrimination that permeates American society. Universally praised by critics, the film won a number of awards, including the Audience Award at the 1994 Sundance Film Festival and an Oscar nomination. The film's only weakness is its excessive length; judicious editing could have cut 30–40 minutes of footage without doing any appreciable thematic damage.

Olympics Films

The modern Olympics date from 1896 and have been filmed for commemorative and historical purposes on a fairly consistent basis since the 1930s. Unfortunately, most of these films are relatively unimaginative *Wide World of Sports* highlight compilations that are apt to bore all but the most die-hard sports fans. Only two Olympics films—Leni Riefenstahl's *Olympiad* (1938) and Kon Ichikawa's *Tokyo Olympiad* (1965)—deserve to be called great and just few others have proven worthy of note.

Olympia (Olympiad) (1938)

In 1931, two years before the election of Adolf Hitler as German chancellor, Berlin was chosen as the site of the 1936 summer Olympics. Anxious to tout the virtues of national socialism and present Nazi Germany as an orderly and peaceful Aryan paradise on earth, Hitler and his lieutenants saw to it that the Berlin Olympics were expertly promoted, superbly organized, and carefully sanitized of all evidence of the virulent anti-Semitism and brutal police repression that marked everyday life in the Third Reich. An important aspect of the massive propaganda project that was the 1936 Olympics was a commemorative documentary that would showcase Nordic athletic prowess and racial superiority. Hitler commissioned his favorite filmmaker, Leni Riefenstahl, to make the movie but the resulting film, *Olympia (Olympiad)* (1938), was not quite the propaganda screed that Hitler and Goebbels envisioned. To be sure, Nazi pageantry, beautiful Aryan physiques, and a preponderance of German athletic victories are on display, but *Olympiad* transcends mere propaganda by presenting all of the major athletic achievements (German or not), focusing on the beauty of the human body and presenting a timeless ideal of athletic accomplishment. Indeed, Riefenstahl is manifestly more interested in paying homage to the ancient Olympic tradition than in glorifying Nazism. The film's true ideological orientation is still a matter of debate.

The Bob Mathias Story (1954)

After the Second World War, the United States was unequivocally the preeminent military and economic power on the planet. What should have been the halcyon days of Pax Americana was, instead, a period marked by Cold War paranoia engendered by labor unrest, daunting news of the Russian A-bomb, the frustrating stalemate in Korea, the controversial Rosenberg executions, among other causes. So when Bob Mathias, a clean-cut, genial all-American boy from Tulare, California, won the gold medal in the decathlon at the 1948 summer Olympics in London, Americans had cause for unalloyed national pride. Part of what made Bob Mathias special was his age; at seventeen he was the youngest athlete ever to win a gold medal in any Olympic event. The Amateur Athletic Union (AAU) honored Mathias with the Sullivan Award for the year's best amateur athlete in 1948. Four years later Mathias won another gold medal at the 1952 Olympics in Helsinki, Finland, confirming his stature as the world's best all-around athlete of his day. Quite naturally Hollywood quickly stepped in to exploit Mathias's fame. Shot in a terse documentary style, Francis D. Lyon's *The Bob Mathias Story* (1954) featured Mathias himself reprising his sports victories. (Mathias's wife, Melba, played herself and professional actors played Mathias's parents and sister.) Mathias would later parlay his fame as an American sports hero into a political career; he served four terms (1967–1974) as a Republican congressman representing California.

Tokyo orimpikku (*Tokyo Olympiad*) (1965)

The 1964 summer Olympics, held in Tokyo, are significant as the first games to take place in Asia. Through them, postwar Japan served notice to the world that it had risen from the ashes to become a prosperous and civilized member of the international community. (It was indeed highly symbolic that Yoshinori Sakai, the final torchbearer of the Olympic flame, was born in Hiroshima on the day that city was destroyed by an atomic bomb.) To commemorate the Tokyo games, the government of Japan commissioned filmmaker Kon Ichikawa to make a documentary film. With *Tokyo orimpikku* (*Tokyo Olympiad*) (1965), Ichikawa went well beyond his mandate and created an enduring work of cinematic art that is an absorbing testament to the courage, will, and stamina of all world-class athletes and a visually stunning paean to an ideal of international peace and harmony that the modern Olympic games was supposed to foster (before they were hopelessly tainted by rampant commercialism, doping, jingoistic nationalism, terrorist threats, and cynical professionalism masquerading as amateur competition). Despite a formidable running time of nearly 3 hours, *Tokyo orimpikku* remains a compelling viewing experience because (1) it is brilliantly shot and edited and (2) it eschews the smarmy capsule biographies and contrived human interest segments that have made contemporary Olympic television coverage tiresome. Using the services of nearly 150 camera operators, Ichikawa shot every event with great technical skill, care, and forethought: elements amply manifest in the finished product. Particularly memorable is the closing sequence that records Abebe Bikila's second consecutive victory in the marathon, run just a few weeks after the Ethiopian runner had undergone an appendectomy.

The next two summer Olympics, in Mexico City in 1968 and in Munich, West Germany, in 1972, would prove to be highly politicized, the latter games very tragically so when Palestinian terrorists broke into the Olympic Village, murdered two members of the Israeli team, and held hostage the remaining nine. In a disastrous counterterrorist action by German paramilitary forces, all nine Israelis were killed, as were five Palestinians and one policeman (a tragedy dissected by Kevin Macdonald's controversial, Oscar-winning documentary, *One Day in September* [2000]). The 1976 Olympics in Montreal and the 1980 Olympics in Moscow were also marked by politics. The African nations boycotted Montreal to protest New Zealand's rugby team having played in apartheid South Africa, and the United States led a multination boycott of the Moscow games to protest the 1979 Soviet invasion of Afghanistan.

Chariots of Fire (1981)

Such was the anguished state of the modern Olympic movement when Hugh Hudson brought out *Chariots of Fire* (1981), a nostalgic perspective on Olympic competition that implicitly rebukes the ugly trends of more recent times. Told in flashback, *Chariots of Fire* recounts the dramatic story of Eric Liddell (1902–1945) and Harold M. Abrahams (1899–1978), Cambridge University sprinters who both won gold medals at the 1924 Paris Olympics. The two men were a classic study in contrasts. Liddell (Ian Charleson) was a serenely devout Scottish missionary, born in China to missionary parents, who ran to give glory to God,

Scene still from Chariots of Fire, *starring Ian Charleson (left) and Ben Cross as Cambridge University sprinters who both won gold medals at the 1924 Paris Olympics. (20th Century Fox/Allied Stars/Enigma/The Kobal Collection)*

while the Jewish Abrahams (Ben Cross) was a prickly outsider who ran to gain respect and acceptance. After a failed attempt to qualify for the 1920 British Olympic team, Abrahams hired professional trainer Sam Mussabini (Ian Holm in the film) to help him improve his performance: a gambit frowned upon by the University and British athletic authorities keen on preserving the amateur status of track and field. The move paid off, however, as Abrahams qualified for the 1924 games. By contrast, the moral dilemma at the heart of the film occurs when the scrupulously religious Eric Liddell learns that his 100-meter heat is to be held on a Sunday. Refusing to run on the Sabbath, Liddell runs in the 400-meter race scheduled on another day—and wins the gold medal. To heighten drama, the movie has Liddell learn of the scheduling problem the last minute; in reality, Liddell knew months in advance and adjusted accordingly. Another example of the film's generous use of poetic license: American sprinter, Jackson Scholz, hands Liddell a piece of paper on which is written "he who honors Me, I will honor . . ." (1 Samuel 2:30). In reality an American track coach gave Liddell the note. Stylistic blunders also accompany historical inaccuracies in an otherwise visually beautiful and impeccably textured film. Climactic competitive moments are shot in clichéd slow motion to a throbbing electronic score by Vangelis: a slick and peculiar affectation that tends to date the film. Made for $5 million, *Chariots of Fire* eventually earned ten times that sum, won numerous festival prizes, and was nominated for seven Academy Awards (it won four, for Best Picture; Best Writing, Screenplay Written Directly for the Screen; Best Costume Design; and Best Musical Score). In 1999 the British Film Institute (BFI) listed *Chariots of Fire* among the top twenty British films ever made. The film has not, however, stood the test of time; it is now seldom shown and is virtually unknown to a new generation of viewers.

The Jesse Owens Story (1984)

The post-Vietnam-era recovery of suppressed black sports history already noted in baseball and boxing also extended to Olympic track and field. Six weeks after Max Schmeling knocked out Joe Louis at Madison Square Garden (June 19, 1936), James Cleveland "Jesse" Owens (1913–1980) avenged Louis's defeat and punctured the myth of Aryan superiority by capturing four gold medals at the 1936 Berlin Olympics. (He won the 100-meter dash, the 200-meter dash, the long jump, and was a key member of the U.S. winning 400-meter relay team.) Almost a half century after the Berlin games and four years after Owens succumbed to cancer at the age of sixty-six, he was finally honored with a serviceable but mediocre television biopic, *The Jesse Owens Story* (1984), another example of too little, too late in recognizing one of the great American sports figures of the twentieth century.

Fists of Freedom: The Story of the '68 Summer Games (1999)

Of a very different ideological orientation is Ross Greenburg's *Fists of Freedom: The Story of the '68 Summer Games* (1999), a painstaking and thorough documentary written by Steven Hilliard Stern (*Babe*) that recounts the political controversy that marked the 1968 summer Olympic Games in Mexico City. Mixing archival footage with recent interviews, *Fists of Freedom* focuses on John Carlos and Tommie Smith, African American bronze and gold medal winners in the 200-meter dash who raised black-gloved fists at their medal ceremony to signify their solidarity with the Black Power movement, a ritual moment that shocked the world. Unfortunately, an embittered John Carlos refused to be interviewed for the film—an omission that seriously compromises its value.

Prefontaine (1997) and Without Limits (1998)

Steve Prefontaine (1951–1975) was an all-America long-distance runner from Coos Bay, Oregon, who gained national fame by winning the 5,000-meter race at the U.S. National Collegiate Athletic Association (NCAA) championships four years in a row (1970–1973) while a student at the University of Oregon. A fierce competitor with an unusually high pain threshold, "Pre" (as he was called) held all seven U.S. distance records, from 2,000 to 10,000 meters. He was expected to win a medal in his specialty, the 5,000-meter race, at the 1972 Munich Olympics but came in a disappointing fourth. Off the track "Pre" was a brash and outspoken critic of the Amateur Athletic Union (AAU) and a strident advocate for athlete's rights. Tragically, at the height of his powers, Steve Prefontaine was killed in an alcohol-related one-car accident near his home in Eugene, Oregon, on the night of May 30, 1975—a year before he was due to compete in the Montreal Olympics. Prefontaine's talent and personal charisma, coupled with his death at age twenty-four, made him a legendary figure, something like the James Dean of track.

In the years following Prefontaine's death, jogging and long-distance running steadily gained popularity in the United States. By the late 1990s the time seemed right for a reassessment of Prefontaine's life, and two biopics appeared in quick succession: Steve James's *Prefontaine* (1997) and Robert Towne's *With-*

out Limits (1998). Inevitably film critics were apt to compare the two films though unfairly as they are quite different in tone, approach, and scale (James's film was made for $8 million whereas Towne's film, produced by Tom Cruise and Paula Wagner, had a budget in excess of $25 million). Consonant with his documentary background (*Hoop Dreams*), James made a hybrid film, part pseudo-documentary that features staged interviews with actors playing family members, friends, and associates and part narrative feature film that melds actual race footage with staged sequences. Jared Leto as Prefontaine and R. Lee Ermey (*Full Metal Jacket*) as his college track coach, Bill Bowerman, excel in their respective roles. Nonetheless, *Prefontaine* did poorly at the box office. Released a year after *Prefontaine*, *Without Limits* (originally titled *Pre*) proved to be the better movie. As film reviewer James Berardinelli points out, there are at least two reasons for this. Robert Towne eschewed the interview-flashback structure employed by Steve James in favor of a linearly structured docudrama format, a narrative strategy that made for a more coherent viewing experience. Second, Towne chose to play up conflict between Prefontaine (Billy Crudup in his version) and Coach Bowerman (Donald Sutherland), a slant that produced considerable dramatic tension. Furthermore, Towne cowrote the screenplay with Kenny Moore, a close friend of Prefontaine with inside knowledge of the man's life and personality. Towne also had the advantage of Bill Bowerman's full cooperation. Unfortunately, *Without Limits* was also a box office flop.

Do You Believe in Miracles? The Story of the 1980 U.S. Hockey Team (2001) and *Miracle* (2004)

For citizens of the United States, the most dramatic story of the 1980 winter Olympics at Lake Placid, New York, was the 4–3 upset triumph of the U.S. men's ice hockey team over the heavily favored and seemingly invincible Russian team (a victory paving the way for a 4–2 win over Finland in the final round that earned the United States its first gold medal in hockey since 1960). Any major American sports victory over archrival, Russia, is noteworthy but the 1980 hockey coup carried special ideological significance, given heightened Cold War tensions due to the Soviet invasion of Afghanistan. The underdog factor also helped ramp up the emotional valance of the event, as aptly demonstrated by sportscaster Al Michaels' famous exclamation at the final buzzer: "Do you believe in miracles? Yes!" Patriotic Americans were apt to attach strong mythic values to their team's win, as a victory for the innovative, plucky American entrepreneurial spirit over the grim authoritarianism of the Soviets.

Two films appearing some twenty years after the 1980 miracle on ice victory attest to its enduring value as patriotic propaganda: Bernard Goldberg's hour-long HBO documentary, *Do You Believe in Miracles? The Story of the 1980 U.S. Hockey Team* (2001) and the Disney docudrama, *Miracle* (2004). *Do You Believe* is a well-crafted, if unremarkable, compilation documentary. *Miracle*, made two years after the September 11, 2001, terrorist attacks, could have milked the jingoistic potential of its topic. Thankfully, Eric Guggenheim, *Miracle*'s screenwriter, wisely chose to let the political significance of the American victory over the Soviet team speak for itself. The film's focus is on the American coach, Herb Brooks (Kurt Russell), a stern taskmaster who rightly insists that the key to success is relentless physical conditioning and team solidarity. The film's appearance, nearly a quarter century after the events it depicts, bespoke a perennial need in the United States to reaffirm American dream ideology by glorifying long-shot underdog victories, especially against competing ideologies.

Mountaineering Films

The popularity of modern mountaineering and other extreme sports has grown in proportion to the increasing dominance of technocratic civilization. Understandably, there has been a countervailing impetus to get away from commercial-industrial society with its enervating social pressures, ecological degradation, and stultifying overreliance on technology. Mountaineering began to achieve real prominence as a world sport in the boom years immediately following the First World War. Perhaps inevitably, the earliest mountaineering films focus on Mt. Everest. At 29,035 feet (8,850 meters), Everest is the highest peak on earth and therefore the holy grail for world-class mountaineers. The First British Everest Reconnaissance Expedition led by Lt. Col. Charles Howard-Bury explored the northern and eastern reaches of the mountain in 1921.

Climbing Mount Everest (1922) and *Epic of Everest* (1924)

On the second British expedition in the summer of 1922, George Leigh Mallory made the first (unsuccessful) attempt to climb to the summit of Everest. As the expedition's official photographer and cinematographer, Captain John Noel made *Climbing Mount Everest* (1922), a now extremely rare silent, black-and-white documentary of the attempt that focuses more on the British encounter with Tibetan culture than the actual climbing. Nonetheless, *Climbing Mount Everest* still qualifies as probably the first mountaineering documentary ever made. Noel was also along for Mallory's second attempt to reach the summit of Mt. Everest in 1924, of which the rare *Epic of Everest* (1924) is the filmic record. Sadly, Mallory and his climbing partner, Andrew "Sandy" Irvine, disappeared high on the mountain (their exact fate unknown until Mallory's mummified body was discovered seventy-five years later). In the thirty years after Mallory's death, ten more expeditions were mounted, mostly by the British; all failed and thirteen climbers died (most of the deaths occurring in 1922 and 1924).

The Conquest of Everest (1953)

As fate would have it, Mallory cohort John Noel was part of Edmund Hillary's expedition to Everest in the spring of 1953. Using then state-of-the-art equipment and high-altitude breathing apparatuses, Hillary and his experienced Sherpa, Tenzing Norgay, reached the summit of Mt. Everest on May 29, 1953, a victory of courage, skill, and stamina that was hailed around the world. Noel and fellow cinematographers George Lowe and Thomas Stobart shot the raw footage of the incredibly arduous ascent that became *The Conquest of Everest* (1953), a documentary sonorously narrated by Irish poet Louis MacNeice that is unpretentious, informative, and graciously gives ample credit to the Sherpas whose herculean portage efforts made Hillary's success possible. Winner of the 1954 BAFTA film award for Best Documentary (and Oscar nominee), *The Conquest of Everest* remains an important and enjoyable documentary, despite some editing flaws, its staid, conventional style, and a melodramatic musical score by Arthur Benjamin that adds little to the inherently dramatic subject matter.

Americans on Everest (1963)

After another successful ascent (by a Swiss team in 1956), the (U.S.) National Geographic Society sponsored the first American expedition to Everest in the spring of 1963 that culminated with James "Big Jim" Whittaker becoming the first American to reach the summit. Society cinematographers recorded the feat and *Americans on Everest* (1963), the resulting 60-minute documentary narrated by Orson Welles, was aired on American television that fall (the very first of dozens of National Geographic specials since then). If Edmund Hillary's historic ascent in 1953 marked a final moment of glory for the fading British Commonwealth, Whittaker's successful ascent seemed to confirm the heroic aspirations of John F. Kennedy's "New Frontier"—until Kennedy was assassinated in Dallas shortly after *Americans on Everest* was screened on CBS.

Everest Unmasked (1978)

Though George Mallory used bottled oxygen in his attempts on Everest in the 1920s, he did so grudgingly, believing that the most sportsmanlike method would eschew what the Sherpas sardonically dubbed "English air." In 1933 the British mounted a fourth Everest expedition and four mountaineers—Win Harris, L. R. Wager, Eric Shipton, and Frank Smythe—attempted to climb the mountain without oxygen but ultimately failed. Fifty-five years later, after an initial failure, famed Alpine mountaineers Reinhold Messner and Peter Habeler scaled Mt. Everest without oxygen masks and survived to tell the tale: a seemingly impossible achievement captured on film by adventure filmmaker Leo Dickinson in the aptly titled documentary, *Everest Unmasked* (1978). Never in wide release, *Everest Unmasked* is geared toward hard-core extreme sports enthusiasts rather than the general public.

Into Thin Air: Death on Everest (1997)

Since 1969 Mt. Everest expeditions have been undertaken on an annual basis and climbers have reached the summit *every* year since 1975. Growing steadily over the 1970s and 1980s, the number of people on the mountain in any climbing season began to increase almost exponentially in the 1990s, as professional mountaineers set up commercial enterprises to guide wealthy amateur climbers to the summit for fees in excess of $65,000 per person, not including round-trip airfare to Asia. What had been one of the most forbidding places on earth suddenly began to take on the vestiges of a crowded tourist trap. Statistics bring the commercialization of Mt. Everest into focus. In the decade of the 1990s no less than 882 climbers reached the summit, almost three times as many as had accomplished the feat in the preceding forty years. (Fifty-nine persons died trying, a figure that represents 36 percent of all fatalities on Everest since 1922 but still disproportionately small compared to the decade's total number of climbers.) It was beginning to appear that seasoned guides, advances in scientific knowledge about altitude sickness, and improved equipment and clothing had made the climbing of Mt. Everest almost routine or at least quite feasible for any fit person who could afford the enormous expenses involved. But success can lead to hubris, and hubris to disaster.

Such was the case on the afternoon of May 10, 1996, when nearly thirty climbers were caught in a sudden blizzard near the summit. Eight people died, including world-class mountaineers Rob Hall (New Zealand) and Scott Fischer (United States). Some of the survivors sustained terrible physical damage. All

Photo of the hiking group who climbed Mount Everest with Jon Krakauer (front row, third from left), author of the book Into Thin Air. *(Caroline Mackenzie/Woodfin Camp/ Time Life Pictures/Getty Images)*

were emotionally scarred. One in the latter category was noted journalist Jon Krakauer (*Into the Wild*), who reached the summit earlier that day and was safely on his way back down when the storm enveloped the climbers above him. Deeply shaken by the scale of the tragedy and his own role in it, Krakauer wrote a riveting postmortem of the expedition entitled *Into Thin Air: A Personal Account of the Mt. Everest Disaster* (New York: Villard, 1997). The book was a bestseller, prompting the making of *Into Thin Air: Death on Everest*, a hastily prepared made-for-TV docudrama that aired less than seven months after the book was published. Directed by Robert Markowitz and starring Peter Horton as Scott Fischer, Nathaniel Parker as Rob Hall, and Christopher McDonald as Jon Krakauer, *Into Thin Air* could not cover the catastrophe with the same thoroughness and depth of detail that Krakauer brought to his written account. Still, the film version manages to convey the senselessness of the enterprise and the terrible price nature sometimes exacts for human hubris and stupidity.

Touching the Void (2003)

In a similar vein is *Touching the Void* (2003), Kevin Macdonald's grueling saga of survival that surpasses the most bizarre fiction. In June 1985 British mountaineers

Joe Simpson, twenty-one, and Simon Yates, twenty-four, made the first successful ascent of Siula Grande, a remote and jagged 6,344-meter (20,815-ft.) peak in the Cordillera Huayhuash range of the Peruvian Andes. On the way down, disaster struck when Simpson shattered his leg in a fall: an accident normally tantamount to a death sentence under such circumstances. Not willing to give up on his injured partner, Yates slowly and laboriously began to lower Simpson down the steep, icy mountain with a 300-foot rope, climb down to Simpson's position, and then repeat the procedure. Unfortunately, the attempted rescue soon went awry when Yates inadvertently lowered Simpson over the edge of a deep crevasse. Hanging in space, Simpson could not go up or down or signal his dilemma to Yates. Uncertain as to Simpson's fate and slowly slipping off the mountain himself, Yates was forced to cut the rope—breaking the ultimate mountaineer's taboo— and Simpson was hurled into the deep crevasse. Unhurt by the fall but unable to climb out, Simpson had no choice but to descend further into the crevasse on the remote chance that it would lead to daylight. Miraculously it did and, over the next few days, Simpson hopped, limped, and crawled down the boulder-strewn lower sections of Siula Grande in a delirium of physical and mental agony. Somehow, on the edge of death, he made it back to base camp and was finally rescued by a horrified and guilt-stricken Yates and the astonished base camp keeper, Richard Hawking. Alternating between interview footage with Simpson fifteen years after his ordeal and brilliantly conceived and executed reenactments of the catastrophe, *Touching the Void* is a grim and gripping cinematic experience that wisely avoids the temptation to philosophize (although Simpson refreshingly discloses that his close encounter with death did not dissuade him from an essentially atheistic outlook). The film's net effect is to prompt decidedly mixed emotions: awe at Simpson's incredible will to live but also a deep suspicion that such extreme sports are inherently decadent, insanely egotistical dances with death that ultimately advance human society not a whit.

Contemporary Sports History on Film

After the Second World War a number of major demographic and public policy trends transformed the American landscape. Population density and economic clout began to shift from the Northeast megalopolis to the West Coast and Sunbelt states. In the postwar boom, the United States fully embraced anticommunism, the automobile, and the suburbs and built a vast interstate highway network, dismantled much of its public transportation system, co-opted the union movement, and pursued a conformist and consumerist American dream lifestyle that followed the ideological imperatives of its corporate ruling class, as promulgated by Hollywood and Madison Avenue. The turn toward an affluent, suburban ethos eventually ushered in such sports as surfing, bodybuilding, and skateboarding: all activities that stressed physique, style, showmanship, and individual achievement as opposed to the group effort of team sports.

Surfing

Writer-adventurer Jack London observed natives surfing in Hawaii and introduced the sport to California prior to World War I but surfing needed abundant leisure and the advent of a new pleasure ethic before it would enjoy widespread popularity. In 1958, as surfing began to hit its stride as a major American sport on the West Coast, a twenty-year-old San Clemente lifeguard and surfing enthusiast named Bruce Brown began filming fellow surfers in action with an 8mm movie camera. Surf shop owner and surfing promoter Dale "The Hawk" Velzy (1927–2005) provided Brown with $5,000 to buy 16mm camera equipment, film stock, and six round-trip plane tickets to transport him and five other California surfers (Del Cannon, Henry Ford, Freddy Pfhaler, Kemp Aaberg, and Dick Thomas) to Oahu, Hawaii, to surf Sunset Beach and Makaha. The resulting film, *Slippery When Wet* (1958), though technically crude, was an instant cult hit with surfers and the first of a number of feature-length surfing documentaries Brown would make over the next four decades. For his second feature, *Surf Crazy* (1959), Brown started filming on California beaches and then moved south along the Pacific coast of Mexico, all the way to Acapulco, for prime and previously unexploited surfing locations. The Mexico footage was supplemented by sequences shot at Waimea Bay and Sunset Beach in Hawaii during the winter of 1959–1960. *Surfing Shorts* (1960), *Barefoot Adventure* (1960), and *Surfing Hollow Days* (1961) was followed by *Waterlogged* (1962), a compilation of some of the best surfing footage from the preceding films. All of these films were prologue to Brown's best and most famous film, *The Endless Summer* (1966).

The Endless Summer (1966)

Shooting without sound—Brown's voice-over narration and accompanying music by a group called The Sandals were added in postproduction—Brown follows young surfers Mike Hynson and Robert August as they travel the world, supposedly searching for the perfect wave and a never-ending summer by following the season around the planet. After filming surfing sequences in Malibu, Santa Cruz, and Newport Beach, California, Hynson, August, Brown, and film crew travel to Africa to surf locations that have never been surfed before. The

Africans, who have never seen blond haired white men carrying 10-foot surf-boards, are fascinated. Despite the language barrier, Hynson and August teach the natives to surf: a touching cross-cultural encounter that would be highly unlikely in future decades. After Africa, Brown and the others travel to Australia, where the surfing proves to be disappointing. Better surfing is had in New Zealand, Tahiti, and Hawaii. Though somewhat dated by Bruce Brown's corny narration, *The Endless Summer* is visually stunning and remains the definitive surfing film. In 2002 the Library of Congress selected the film for inclusion in the National Film Registry. In 1994, twenty-eight years after *The Endless Summer*, Brown brought out *The Endless Summer 2*, a more technically adept sequel that retraces the locales explored in the earlier film. (Having worked as an associate producer, writer, editor, and cameraman on *The Endless Summer 2*, Bruce Brown's son, Dana, went on to make his own surfing movie, *Step into Liquid* [2003].)

Bodybuilding

Pumping Iron (1977)

Before George Butler and Robert Fiore released their documentary *Pumping Iron* (1977), the public tended to regard bodybuilding as a fringe sport, the freak-ish pastime of frustrated bullies and well-oiled exhibitionists. For better or worse, *Pumping Iron* not only legitimized the sport and made it hugely popular but also launched the celebrity career of Arnold Schwarzenegger, future action movie star, reactionary politico, and—to the amazement of many—governor of California. Butler and Fiore divide their film into two sections. The first part counterpoises bodybuilders Mike Katz and Ken Waller as they compete for the 1975 amateur title of Mr. Universe (Waller won). The second part crosscuts between the self-assured and charismatic Schwarzenegger, training in sunny Los Angeles, and the shy, hearing-impaired Lou Ferrigno, training in more modest circumstances in Brooklyn. Later, these parallel lines converge at the 1975 Mr. Olympia competition in South Africa, where the perfectly sculpted Schwarzeneg-ger defeats Ferrigno to win his seventh consecutive Mr. Olympia title before retiring from professional bodybuilding to start his movie career. A twenty-five-year anniversary edition of *Pumping Iron* was released in 2002 as Schwarzeneg-ger embarked on a post-Hollywood career in politics. The film offers an unflat-tering depiction of the famed Austrian muscleman, who is shown smoking marijuana, ogling scantily clad women, and generally comporting himself with the sly arrogance of a cynical opportunist. Not surprisingly Schwarzenegger has claimed he merely assumed a loutish persona in *Pumping Iron* in order to help make the film more interesting.

Professional Wrestling

While Greco-Roman wrestling has been part of American physical culture since the post–Civil War period, the birth of *professional* wrestling is reputed to have occurred on April 3, 1908, when Frank Gotch defeated George "The Russian Lion" Hackenschmidt at Chicago's Dexter Park Pavilion for the title of the nation's best wrestler. Some twenty years later pro wrestling abrogated Greco-Roman rules and became a clownish pseudosport when the Great Depression forced promoters to shorten the duration of matches and resort to novelties and gimmicks to attract patrons including manufactured heroes and villains, scripted outcomes, midget wrestling, women's wrestling, tag team matches—even mud wrestling. Always geared toward a none-too-discriminating proletarian audience, pro wrestling eked out a twilight popular culture existence until it enjoyed a surge in popularity with the advent of television in the 1950s. Part theater, part circus since the 1930s, pro wrestling became more garishly absurd and histrionic in the television era. It also became a hugely popular and lucrative business in the 1980s when promoter Vince McMahon purchased Capitol Wrestling Corporation from his father, also a wrestling promoter, won a fiercely contested ratings war with rival Ted Turner's World Championship Wrestling (WCW), and in the process became a billionaire by turning what had been a regional concern into an international conglomerate now known as the World Wrestling Federation (WWF). Two documentaries released in the late 1990s afford a revealing glimpse of the strange world of pro wrestling: Paul Jay's *Hitman Hart, Wrestling with Shadows* (1998) and Barry W. Blaustein's *Beyond the Mat* (1999).

Hitman Hart, Wrestling with Shadows (1998)

For many years Calgary native Bret "Hitman" Hart was a major star of the WWF, playing the role of a righteous good guy routinely vanquishing wrestling villains—until the mid-1990s, when WWF impresario Vince McMahon sensed a change in the zeitgeist. Influenced by the unrestrained vulgarity of heavy metal, shock jock antics, wildly proliferating pornography, no-holds-barred "extreme sports" events, and the like, the pro wrestling demographic began to favor foul-mouthed outlaw types and wrestling bimbos. To shore up ratings, McMahon transformed Hitman Hart into a hectoring cartoon villain who, as a native of

Canada, began trash-talking all things American. Hart chafed under his ugly, new persona but nonetheless signed a $20 million, long-term contract with McMahon. Only eight months into the new arrangement, McMahon concluded that he could not afford the contract and encouraged Hart to seek a deal with Ted Turner's WCW. Hart obliged, but McMahon, afraid that Hart would take his WWF championship belt with him to the WCW, surreptitiously arranged for Hart to lose his final WWF pay-per-view match on November 9, 1997, in Montreal: a betrayal that still angers Hart. Filmmaker Paul Jay also fell afoul of McMahon's machinations. Having contracted to supply stock footage of Hart (and signed public performance privacy release forms) for a percentage of the film's profits, McMahon withheld the materials until Jay signed away distribution support from rival Ted Turner: a concession that probably cost Jay millions of dollars. The alternative was a costly lawsuit that would have delayed release of the film indefinitely.

Beyond the Mat (1999)

Barry Blaustein's *Beyond the Mat* is more broadly focused and more poignant than Paul Jay's film. Interviews with a number of pro wrestling legends, aspirants, and has-beens form the backdrop for in-depth, behind-the-scenes portraits of three pro wrestlers: Terry Funk (also known as "Chainsaw Charlie"), Mick "Mankind" Foley, and Jake "The Snake" Roberts. Fifty-three years old at the time of filming, Terry Funk is a physical wreck after thirty-two punishing years as a professional wrestler but he refuses to retire. Likewise addicted to the limelight, Mick Foley wrestles despite the fact that his violent, bloody profession deeply troubles his wife, Colette, and their four young children. Yet the worst-case scenario for a career in pro wrestling is Jake Roberts. In his late forties at the time of filming, Roberts has gone from a once-charismatic WWF star in his prime to a bloated, depressed, crack-addicted husk of a man who now haunts the regional wrestling circuits. The fakery of pro wrestling is a given; these documentaries by Paul Jay and Barry Blaustein drive home the increasing degradation of popular culture, the venality and ruthlessness of promoters like Vince McMahon, and the very real pain pro wrestlers inflict on themselves and each other.

Skateboarding

Dogtown and Z-Boys (2001)

Though it may seem a trivial pastime, skateboarding has become an international youth culture phenomenon, a multibillion-dollar industry with its own stars, fashions, tours, merchandising tie-ins, and slick publications. A creature of warm and sunny climes, skateboarding started out as a spin-off of the California surf-ing scene, a way to simulate surfing on dry land when the waves were uncoop-erative. The rising popularity of surfing in the late 1950s and early 1960s drove a short-lived national skateboarding craze, circa 1963–1965. During that brief period some 50 million skateboards were sold in the United States. After a decadelong lull, skateboarding enjoyed another great surge in popularity in the mid-1970s. Inspired by G. Beato's article "The Lords of Dogtown" (1999), Stacy Peralta's documentary, *Dogtown and Z-Boys* (2001) chronicles the 1970s skate-board revival at its epicenter in Dogtown, a decrepit Los Angeles suburb between Venice and Santa Monica, where a group of bored lower-middle-class teenagers who were avid surfers began to apply aggressive, acrobatic moves to skateboarding with spectacular results. Three Dogtown skateboarders—Skip Engblom, Jeff Ho, and Craig Stecyk (the film's cowriter, with Peralta)—founded the Zephyr skate team, a loose band of a dozen or so skaters collectively named after a Dogtown surf shop. Narrated by former Dogtown resident Sean Penn, *Dogtown and Z-Boys* intersperses rare archival footage, accentuated by a rau-cous punk and heavy metal soundtrack, with contemporary interviews of former Zephyr team members as it chronicles the sport's spectacular evolution from ille-gal forays into drained swimming pools to corporate-sponsored, media-saturated exhibitions. An absorbing glimpse into a stylish but ultimately vapid subculture, *Dogtown* also serves as an exposé of alienated Southern California street culture in the 1970s.

Stoked: The Rise and Fall of Gator (2002)

Helen Stickler's *Stoked: The Rise and Fall of Gator* (2002) picks up where *Dog-town and Z-Boys* leaves off: in the early 1980s, when "vert" (vertical) skate-boarding, Zephyr team style, was all the rage. Surveying the entire scene but focusing on the disastrous career of Mark "Gator" Rogowski (aka Mark Anthony), Stickler's film is both darker and more penetrating than Peralta's. Agile, fearless, and exceptionally athletic, Gator Rogowski was a spectacularly good skateboarder, so good that he was able to turn professional at the age of fourteen in 1981. Through most of the 1980s Rogowski lived the life of a pop superstar, enjoying continuous media coverage, constant travel, an ample salary, and easy access to all manner of decadence. His young ego ballooned in propor-tion to his fame. Then, in the late 1980s, street-style skateboarding began to sup-plant the vertical style and Rogowski suddenly found himself a has-been. Unable to cope with his straightened circumstances, Rogowski, product of a broken home and probably afflicted with bipolar disorder, began to disintegrate psy-chologically. In October 1989 he was badly injured in a drunken fall from a hotel balcony in Germany. Supposedly chastened by his accident, Rogowski became an ardent "born-again" Christian, which alienated Brandi McClain, his girlfriend of four years, who left him for a blond surfer. Enraged at McClain's rejection of him, Rogowski sought revenge by beating, raping, and murdering Jessica Bergsten, McClain's best friend. Rogowski buried Bergsten's body in the desert but two months later he confessed to the crime and was subsequently sentenced to a thirty-one-year to life prison term. *Stoked* presents Ragowski's lurid saga without editorial comment, but the vapidity of the skateboard scene and, by extension, of suburban life in contemporary America is chillingly dramatized.

A Return to Period Topics

Seabiscuit (2003)

As the sports film genre amply demonstrates, Americans have always loved stories of triumph by underdogs, a cultural tendency reconfirmed by the tremendous success of Laura Hillenbrand's book, *Seabiscuit: An American Legend* (New York: Random House, 2001). Hollywood was quick to sense the potential of the Seabiscuit saga; rights were sold and a movie was under way even before the book was published. Written and directed by Gary Ross (*Dave, Pleasantville*), *Seabiscuit* (2003) tells the story of the famed racehorse that dominated the sport in the 1930s. Undersized and lazy, Seabiscuit (1934–1947; retired 1940) did not display much promise as a racehorse; indeed, he lost his first seventeen races in 1935. It was only after new owner Charles Howard (Jeff Bridges), trainer Tom Smith (Chris Cooper), and jockey Red Pollard (Tobey Maguire) teamed up to manage Seabiscuit that the horse reached his full potential and began to win races and set track records. Much like their equine charge, the men were also underdogs in need of reconstruction: Howard had been demoralized by the loss of his young son in a car accident; other horse trainers regarded Smith as a half-baked eccentric; abandoned by his parents, Pollard was a failed boxer turned unsuccessful jockey. In sum, Seabiscuit's evolution, from rank loser to spectacular winner, reflected the evolution of his handlers (and vice versa). On a larger symbolic level, Seabiscuit's unlikely success captured the imagination of a Depression-weary American public, eager as it was for vicarious experiences of success. Ross's film, an unabashedly sentimental and nostalgic period piece in the Frank Capra vein, served the same function for its contemporary audiences and made a strong showing at the box office and in the video rental market. Furthermore, either Hillebrand's book or Ross's docudrama spawned a number of other Seabiscuit projects: *Seabiscuit* (2002), a documentary directed by Stephen

Jockey Red Pollard rides Seabiscuit to victory in the twenty-eighth Yonkers Handicap in 1937. (Library of Congress)

Ives for PBS's *American Experience* television series; Craig Haffner's *The True Story of Seabiscuit* (2003), a 45-minute Arts and Entertainment (A&E) Network documentary; Laurent Bouzereau's *Seabiscuit: Racing through History* (2003) and *The Making of "Seabiscuit"* (2003), short promotional documentaries for Ross's film; *Seabiscuit: The Making of a Legend* (2003), another short documentary by Adam Hauck and Daniel Soiseth, made for the collector's DVD version of *Seabiscuit.* The revival of the Seabiscuit legend also resulted in the dusting off and re-release of *Seabiscuit: The Lost Documentary* (1939), a 50-minute film by Manny Nathan Hahn commissioned by Seabiscuit's owner, Charles Howard, in honor of Seabiscuit winning the coveted Horse of the Year in 1939.

Bobby Jones: Stroke of Genius (2004)

Robert Tyre "Bobby" Jones Jr. (1902–1971) is one of the undisputed giants in the history of golf. During a strictly amateur career that lasted only fourteen years (1916–1930), Jones won the British Open three times, the U.S. Open four times, thirteen national championships, and the Grand Slam of golf, that is, all four top titles (U.S. and British Opens, U.S. and British amateur championships) in one year (1930), a feat never duplicated. Seventy-four years after Jones's retirement and thirty-three years after his death, Jones's heirs created Bobby Jones Films, LLC, for the sole purpose of making *Bobby Jones: Stroke of Genius* (2004), an unabashedly adulatory biopic directed by Rowdy Herrington (*Road House*) and starring Jim Caviezel (*Passion of the Christ*) as Bobby Jones. A family-sponsored, family-oriented hagiography, Herrington's film suffers from terminal blandness, if not actually a crypto-reactionary agenda (Jones founded the Masters Tournament in Atlanta in 1934, which barred blacks and women). Opening nationally on May 2, 2004, on 1,332 screens, *Bobby Jones* made an abysmal $1.2 million—less than $1,000 per theater—proof positive that, though the Right continues to control America's political economy, it is not always savvy about popular culture.

6

Music History on Film and Television

B ecause of the cultural centrality of music, music history films constitute something of an informal chronicle of American popular culture, from vaudeville to hip-hop. Considered in their historical context, these films also disclose remarkable changes in cultural taste and temperament over the last sixty years. Nonetheless, the abiding issue has always been race. Most forms of American music of any real significance have their roots in the music of West Africa. Gospel, blues, jazz, and rock all derive from African American folk music, which in turn comes out of the long and melancholy history of slavery and Jim Crow, from the first transports to Jamestown in 1619 to the Emancipation Proclamation in 1863, through Reconstruction, into the Civil Rights era. Films devoted to music history topics tend to bifurcate into the few that repress or ignore the African sources of American music and the many that recover and celebrate those sources. Not coincidentally, the first music biopic ever made—*The Jolson Story* (1946)—feted a white Jewish singer famous for his performances in blackface. Likewise, several postwar music biopics focused on *white* swing-era bandleaders and musicians (Glenn Miller, Benny Goodman, Gene Krupa). It took the 1947 desegregation of baseball, the 1948 desegregation of the U.S. military, and the full flowering of the Civil Rights movement in the mid-1950s to establish a legitimizing context for a racially conscious reassessment of the history of American music on film. Allen Reisner's W. C. Handy biopic, *St. Louis Blues* (1958), signaled the modest beginnings of a revisionist history that finally came to fruition in the last decades of the twentieth century with a series of first-rate movies on key black artists working in gospel, folk, jazz, and the blues. Similarly, rock's usurpation of black folk music (especially the blues) has gone largely unacknowledged, at least on film, until quite recently. The sections that follow are divided into music subgenres and each section is then arranged chronologically. Concert documentaries, of which there are hundreds, have been excluded except in the case of hybrid documentaries that include concert footage, interviews, and other material.

Jazz, Blues, Gospel, Motown, and the Swing Era

Young Man with a Horn (1950)

Nostalgia for the music and culture of the 1920s found expression in Michael Curtiz's *Young Man with a Horn* (1950), a cinematic adaptation of Dorothy Baker's fictionalized biography of legendary jazz cornetist Leon Bismarck "Bix" Beiderbecke (1903–1931). In novel and film, the Bix Beiderbecke figure is named Rick Martin, a supremely gifted but tragically self-destructive artist whose Faustian musical ambitions and acute susceptibility to dangerous women and hard booze bring about his demise at an early age. This is a generally faithful depiction of Beiderbecke (played by Kirk Douglas in the film, with his trumpet playing dubbed by Harry James) but also another rendition of the familiar artist-as-doomed-genius cliché that has enjoyed wide currency since the days of Poe, Rimbaud, Van Gogh, and others.

The Glenn Miller Story (1953)

Valentine Davies' *The Glenn Miller Story* (1953) is a nostalgia vehicle of a somewhat different sort. Legendary swing-era bandleader and trombonist, Alton Glenn Miller (1904–1944) achieved great popularity in the last four years of his life with such hits as "Tuxedo Junction," "Pennsylvania 6–5000," "Chattanooga Choo Choo," "Moonlight Serenade," and many other tunes. The patriotic Miller sought and won a captain's commission in the Army Air Corps in 1942 and he and his army band spent the next two years entertaining thousands of Allied troops with hundreds of broadcasts and personal appearances. Sadly, Miller died when his plane strayed off course in heavy fog and went down over the English Channel on December 15, 1944. Made some eight years after Miller's death—and seven years after bebop had decisively displaced swing as the dominant jazz form—*The Glenn Miller Story* sought to recapture the faded glory of the big band era. On a subliminal level, the film was a nostalgic paean to the remarkable national solidarity and sense of purpose that marked America's effort in the Second World War. Appropriately, Miller was played in the film by look-alike James Stewart, himself a bomber pilot in the war and later a brigadier general in the postwar Air

Actor Jimmy Stewart (right), portraying Glenn Miller in The Glenn Miller Story *(1953). (Bettmann/Corbis)*

Force Reserve. The always-smarmy June Allyson played Miller's wife, Helen, as a starry-eyed helpmate. Bland and romanticized, *The Glenn Miller Story* engaged in very little actual biography; its aim was to present an entertaining and patriotic hagiography appropriate to the Cold War temper of its day.

In the years that followed, Hollywood attempted to repeat the success of *The Glenn Miller Story* with three more 1950s tributes to earlier pop music icons: Valentine Davies' *The Benny Goodman Story* (1955), starring Steve Allen as the "King of Swing" (and Donna Reed as the love interest); George Sidney's *The Eddy Duchin Story* (1956), starring Tyrone Power as Duchin (and Kim Novak as his wife, Marjorie); and Don Weis's *The Gene Krupa Story* (1959), starring Sal Mineo as Krupa, with the real Gene Krupa playing drums off camera as Mineo pantomimed his performances. None of these films were accurate depictions of their subjects' lives, nor particularly successful. Newer trends in popular music—bop, "cool" jazz, rock and roll—had long since rendered the big band sound moribund: a reality evidently lost on 1950s studio executives.

St. Louis Blues (1958)

As already noted, Allen Reisner's *St. Louis Blues* (1958) was the first film to present the black side of the story with its somewhat fanciful recounting of the early life of William Christopher (W. C.) Handy (1873–1958). Handy, a classically trained composer and entrepreneur, was the self-proclaimed "Father of the Blues" for having discovered and legitimated the blues: African American folk music indigenous to the Mississippi Delta. Heading an extraordinarily talented all-black cast was Nat King Cole as W. C. Handy. The list of supporting players reads like a roster of the premier black singers and actors of the second half of the twentieth century: Eartha Kitt, Ella Fitzgerald, Mahalia Jackson, Ruby Dee, Pearl Bailey, Cab Calloway, and even future rock star, Billy Preston, playing Handy as a boy. Though weak on biographical particulars, *St. Louis Blues* manages to convey the important fact that gospel music was the progenitor of the jazz and blues traditions. Its relative obscurity undoubtedly has more to do with race than its inherent value.

Wattstax (1973)

The same could be said for *Wattstax* (1973), a long-lost documentary by Mel Stuart (*Willy Wonka & the Chocolate Factory*) that chronicles the "Black Woodstock," a benefit concert by Stax label recording artists at the Los Angeles Coliseum on Sunday, August 20, 1972. Seven years earlier (August 11–17, 1965) Watts, the black ghetto in south-central Los Angeles, erupted into six days of rioting after a routine traffic stop caused seething community tensions to explode. Before state and city police, supplemented by thousands of National Guard troops, were able to quell the uprising, 34 (mostly black) people had been killed, 1,000 injured, almost 4,000 arrested, and hundreds of buildings were burned and looted, resulting in over $200 million in property damage. The Watts Riot of 1965 signaled the eclipse of the nonviolent Civil Rights movement by "Black Power," a term coined by Stokely Carmichael, aka Kwame Ture (1941–1998), to describe a new, militant black consciousness best exemplified by the Black Panther Party founded in Oakland a year after the riot.

By the early 1970s, after years of urban unrest, the assassination of Martin Luther King, white backlash, and the systematic destruction of the Black Panthers by the FBI's Counter-Intelligence Program (CounterIntelPro), Black Power, largely spent as a *political* force, inevitably transmogrified into a powerful *cultural* ethos manifested in "blaxploitation" films, soul music, and distinctively African clothing and "afro" hairstyles. In tune with the new emphasis on gesture and symbolism, the idea behind Wattstax, organized by Stax Records boss, Al Bell, and cosponsored by Stax and the white-owned Joseph Schlitz Brewing Co., was to celebrate and affirm black pride through music, not through revolutionary struggle. Likely Bell's chief motivation was to garner publicity for Stax, which was then relocating from Memphis to Los Angeles.

The capstone event of the Watts Summer Festival, "Wattstax '72," lasted 6 hours, drew a mostly African American audience of some 90,000, and featured almost the entire roster of Stax artists (introduced by Jesse Jackson and other black celebrities): Issac Hayes, Rufus and Carla Thomas, the Staples Singers, the Bar-Kays, Albert King, and many lesser-known acts. To elevate his film above the level of the standard pop concert documentary, Mel Stuart augmented main stage footage with performances at other venues by The Emotions, Johnnie Taylor, and Little Milton; archival newsreel clips of the 1965 riot; contemporary interviews with Watts residents on all sorts of social topics; and hilarious banter by the then up-and-coming black comedian, Richard Pryor. Largely unseen at the time of its initial release in February 1973, *Wattstax* was rereleased in a remastered and reedited thirtieth anniversary edition that premiered at the Sundance Film Festival in January 2003 and first aired on public television in September 2004—another in a series of resurrected 1970s documentaries (e.g., *When We Were Kings; Festival Express*) that help to articulate the temper of that time.

Bix: Ain't None of Them Play Like Him Yet (1981)

Thirty years after Michael Curtiz's *Young Man with a Horn*, Toronto filmmaker Brigitte Berman made a documentary on Bix Beiderbecke entitled *Bix: Ain't None of Them Play Like Him Yet* (1981). Narrated by actor Richard Basehart, *Bix* combines archival footage and new interviews with a number of Beiderbecke's jazz contemporaries (filmed in his hometown of Davenport, Iowa), including singer-songwriters Hoagy Carmichael (1899–1981), Jack Fulton

(1903–1993), and Al Rinker (1907–1982); trumpeter Doc Cheatham (1905–1997); and clarinetist-bandleader Artie Shaw (1910–2004). The subtitle of the film derives from an oft-cited statement by Louis Armstrong: "Lots of cats tried to play like Bix; ain't none of them play like him yet."

Say Amen, Somebody (1982)

George T. Nierenberg's *Say Amen, Somebody* (1982) explores both the history and contemporary state of black gospel music by interspersing rousing performance clips of gospel groups with extensive interviews of three elderly gospel pioneers: "Professor" Thomas A. Dorsey, "The Father of Gospel Music" (1899–1993); Sallie Martin (1895–1988), Dorsey's longtime business manager; and "Mother" Willie Mae Ford Smith (1904–1994), one of gospel's earliest soloists. In its first incarnation in America, gospel was the sacred music of lamentation and prayer for deliverance sung on Southern plantations by black slaves. In the modern era Thomas Dorsey was an instrumental figure in reviving and popularizing gospel. An accomplished blues arranger, composer, and accompanist for the likes of Bessie Smith and Ma Rainey, Dorsey heard some of the religious music of Charles A. Tindley at a Baptist convention in 1930. Having undergone a religious conversion, Dorsey was inspired to write gospel music thereafter. Dorsey's lyrics were suitably pious, but the spirited music he composed owed much to the rhythms of jazz and, especially, the blues—"devil's music" according to devout Baptists. Initially confined to tent revivals, gospel eventually managed to permeate established Baptist churches in the South and later spilled over into the commercial mainstream. An invaluable historical document, *Say Amen, Somebody* also succeeds in conveying the infectious joy of the music.

Artie Shaw: Time Is All You've Got (1985)

Clarinetist Artie Shaw (real name: Arthur Jacob Arshawsky, 1910–2004) is primarily known as one of the most popular big band leaders of the swing era. He is also famous for his eight marriages—all of them to great beauties and movie stars, including Lana Turner and Ava Gardner. Always torn between music and writing, Artie Shaw finally retired from the jazz scene in the summer of 1954 to pursue his other passion: writing quasi-autobiographical fiction. Over the years Shaw wrote three books—*The Trouble with Cinderella: An Outline of Identity* (New York: Farrar, Straus & Giroux, 1952); *I Love You, I Hate You, Drop Dead! Variations on a Theme* (New York: Fleet Publishing, 1965); *The Best of Inten-*

tions and Other Stories (Santa Barbara, CA: John Daniel & Co., 1989)—and an unpublished trilogy entitled *The Education of Albie Snow*. Having interviewed Artie Shaw for *Bix*, her 1981 documentary on Bix Beiderbecke, Brigitte Berman asked Shaw for authorization and cooperation to make a documentary about him (Shaw). Shaw agreed and Berman commenced to make *Artie Shaw: Time Is All You've Got* (1985), a thoroughgoing filmic portrait of Shaw, directed, edited, narrated, and coproduced by Berman on a shoestring budget that includes concert and film footage and interviews with Shaw and some of his swing colleagues—singers Helen Forrest and Mel Tormé, drummer Buddy Rich, and a number of lesser-known artists. Shown at various film festivals around the world in 1984–1985, *Artie Shaw* won the 1986 Oscar for Best Documentary Feature. Unfortunately, Brigitte Berman's Artie Shaw odyssey ended on a sour note when Shaw demanded a 35 percent interest in the film's profits. Berman refused so Shaw sued her in an Ontario court but eventually lost his case due to lack of a written contract. The issue was moot anyway; the film did not make a profit.

Louie Bluie (1986) and *Sweet Old Song* (2002)

On an entirely different note is Terry Zwigoff's low-budget documentary, *Louie Bluie* (1986). Zwigoff (best known for *Crumb*) tracked down Howard Armstrong (1910–2003), aka "Louie Bluie," a black string band violinist, mandolinist, guitarist, and master of nineteen other string instruments who made a few recordings with Sleepy John Estes, Yank Ranchell, Ted Bogan, and Carl Martin in the 1920s and 1930s, dropped out of sight for thirty years—while he worked at a Chrysler auto factory assembly line in Detroit—and then reemerged on the folk festival circuit in the 1970s. Seventy-five at the time of filming, Armstrong dazzles, in interviews and performance, as a string virtuoso, a fascinating raconteur, multilinguist, accomplished painter, and all-around bon vivant. Though he comes off as an amazing character, Armstrong was not happy with Terry Zwigoff's film. He felt that *Louie Bluie* manipulated his image in ways that suggest a wild, sybaritic African American street hustler of loose morals while it downplays his genius as a Renaissance man and artist.

In 1997 filmmaker Leah Mahan (a former intern for Henry Hampton's Blackside Films) began work on another Howard Armstrong documentary, eventually entitled *Sweet Old Song*, which had its debut on July 30, 2002, as part of PBS's television documentary film series, *P.O.V.* Mahan's focus was wider and deeper than Zwigoff: she concentrated on the relationship between Armstrong and the sculptor, Barbara Ward Armstrong. Though Howard Armstrong was thirty years older than his wife, the marriage worked magnificently well. Both nurtured each other emotionally and creatively and Barbara's sympathetic influence probably lengthened Howard's life.

Let's Get Lost (1988)

Another ambiguous example of music history excavation is Bruce Weber's *Let's Get Lost* (1988), a brooding black-and-white documentary on the life of "cool jazz" trumpeter, vocalist (and longtime heroin addict) Chet Baker (1929–1988). In marked contrast to the strained melodrama of a jazz biopic like *Lady Sings the Blues*, *Let's Get Lost* has an ethereal, slightly surrealist aura in keeping with Weber's own mythic vision of Baker as a 1950s-era jazz Adonis who once had the looks and charisma of a James Dean or Neal Cassady. Combining still photographs, performance and studio footage, and interviews with Chet Baker, his family, and associates, *Let's Get Lost* contrasts the movie-star handsome young Baker, possessed of enormous talent and potential, with Baker at fifty-seven years of age—and nearly thirty years of addiction—toothless, haggard, and monstrously jaded. Though lyrical and strangely fascinating at times, *Let's Get Lost* contributes rather predictably to the artist-as-doomed-genius cliché. Thus, with ideological appropriateness, the movie informs viewers in its closing credits that Baker died shortly after filming in a mysterious fall from a hotel window in Amsterdam.

Bird (1988)

If Bruce Weber's *Let's Get Lost* both enhanced and deflated the romantic myth of Chet Baker, Clint Eastwood's biopic, *Bird* (1988), more straightforwardly sought to affirm the mythic stature of Kansas City's Charlie "Yardbird" Parker (1920–1955), widely thought to be the finest improvisational jazz saxophonist who ever lived. A man of huge appetites and passions, Parker was an alcoholic and a heroin addict. After he died at the age of thirty-four, the coroner who examined his body said it looked to be that of a sixty-five-year-old man. Eastwood's film is sprawling (2 hours and 41 minutes long) but richly detailed and factually accurate. The sheer length of the film allows for ample showcasing of Parker's music. Forest Whitaker delivers a moving depiction of Parker and Diane Venora is equally impressive as Parker's devoted and long-suffering wife, Chan. More problematic is the fact that Eastwood and his writer, Joel Oliansky, strive for an impressionistic jazz effect by emphasizing dark, color-saturated visual tones and a complex flashback-within-flashback structure that renders chronology virtually meaningless. The result is a film that lovingly conveys the look, feel, and sound of Parker's life, times, and music but remains strangely obtuse as to the man's true character and deepest motivations.

Thelonious Monk: Straight, No Chaser (1989)

Eastwood, a longtime jazz aficionado, followed up *Bird* by bankrolling Charlotte Zwerin and Bruce Ricker's excellent documentary, *Thelonious Monk: Straight, No Chaser* (1989). An innovative pianist and brilliant composer, Thelonious

Thelonious Monk performing in the early 1950s. (Mosaic Images/Corbis)

Sphere Monk (1917–1982) penned numerous jazz classics (including "Round Midnight") until his career was cut short by mental illness that had its onset in 1973. After documentary filmmaker Christian Blackwood informed Bruce Ricker that he had shot extensive footage of Monk on tour for German television in 1967–1968, Ricker and Zwerin excitedly embarked on a new Monk documentary project. Using Blackwood's film as their basis, Ricker and Zwerin tracked down and filmed interviews with Monk's son; his tenor sax player, Charles Rouse; Monk's road manager, Bob Jones; his personal manager, Harry Colomby, and the Baroness Nica de Koenigswarter, a close friend and caretaker of Monk in his later years. Historically valuable as an intimate and revealing portrait of the life of one of the great bebop jazz musicians, *Straight, No Chaser* remains intriguing for the mysterious tragedy at its core: Monk's inexorable descent into solipsistic madness.

A Great Day in Harlem (1994)

Jean Bach's Oscar-nominated documentary, *A Great Day in Harlem* (1994), is built around an interesting and unusual premise: it celebrates Art Kane's legendary photograph of fifty-seven jazz greats assembled on the stoop of a brownstone at 17 East 126th Street (corner of Lenox Avenue) for a 1958 special jazz issue of *Esquire* magazine. On his very first assignment as a professional photographer, Kane managed to gather three generations of jazz luminaries. Among those included in the photograph were Art Blakey, Jay C. Higginbotham, Charles Mingus, Gene Krupa, George Wettling, Jimmy Rushing, Coleman Hawkins, Oscar Pettiford, Marian McPartland, Sonny Rollins, Thelonius Monk, Lester Young, Gerry Mulligan, Roy Eldgridge, Dizzy Gillespie, and Count Basie—a veritable who's who of midcentury American music. Novice filmmaker Jean Bach, a longtime jazz fan, personally knew many of the people featured in Kane's photograph and was able to secure interviews with most of the twenty-three surviving musicians, who warmly reminisce about the day and about each other. Other photos taken the day of the Kane shoot are supplanted by 8mm color footage taken by Milt Hinton's wife. Quincy Jones' narration and copious samplings of the music round out the texture of the film. Unabashedly sentimental but never cloying, *A Great Day in Harlem* is short (only 60 minutes), unpretentious, and an important jazz history film. Jean Bach followed up *A Great Day in Harlem* with *The Spitball Story* (1998), a 21-minute documentary that focuses on Dizzie Gillespie, Milt Hinton, and Jonah Jones during their tenure with Cab Calloway's touring band.

The Genius of Lenny Breau (1995)

Relatively unknown in the United States is Emily Hughes' documentary, *The Genius of Lenny Breau* (1995). Born in Maine, into a French Canadian musical family, Leonard Breau (1941–1984) was a guitar prodigy at the age of three. Obsessed with achieving total mastery of his instrument, Breau played, practiced, and experimented with remorseless dedication and became a topflight improvisational jazz guitarist. Adept with acoustic and electric guitars, Breau blended fingerpicking techniques from classical, flamenco, and country to develop an intricate style of playing that ultimately defied genre classification and won the admiration and envy of some of the world's best guitarists. He recorded eight albums between 1968 and 1979. Outside of his musical world Breau struggled with alcohol, drugs, and despair. He was found dead in the swimming pool of his Los Angeles apartment complex on August 12, 1984. What looked like an accidental drowning turned out to be murder; an autopsy revealed that Breau had been strangled, not drowned. The case remains unsolved.

The daughter of Breau and jazz singer, Judi Singh, Emily Hughes had barely known her father. Originally intending to write a book, Hughes made a film instead. Concert footage and interviews with illustrious colleagues Chet Atkins, Randy Bachman, Liona Boyd, Pat Metheny, and Steve Vai reveal Breau's enormous talent and complexity. Commenting on the meaning of the film, Hughes told interviewer Craig Elliot "I think he was somebody who experienced great highs and great lows, and you experience that when you watch the film. The music was something that brought him so much joy . . . There are the darker issues but, in the end, it seems to balance out. He had a lot of people around him that love him and he was so passionate about his music, and he really knew 'up' and he really knew 'down.' And the film gives you a sense of both" (Elliot 1999).

Wild Man Blues (1996)

Internationally famous as a filmmaker and equally notorious for his scandalous private life, Woody Allen is less well known as a moderately talented jazz clarinetist. In 1996 distinguished documentarian Barbara Kopple (*Harlan County, U.S.A.; American Dream; Beyond JFK*) brought out *Wild Man Blues*, a cinema verité record of Allen and his seven-piece New Orleans jazz band on a hectic eighteen-city, twenty-three-day tour of Europe in 1996. Allen's distinctive brand of neurotic humor is in evidence but mostly he is shown to be a rather morose little man and a very serious, if unspectacular, musician. Though it includes many concert snippets, *Wild Man Blues* divides its time between onstage and behind-the-scenes segments, the latter essentially prosaic interactions between Allen; his bandleader, Eddy Davis; Allen's sister, Letty Aronson; and most frequently his then-girlfriend (now wife), Soon-Yi Previn. Though Allen kept his promise to Kopple, to allow complete access to him and his entourage, nothing particularly revealing is brought to light—except perhaps the surprising maturity of Ms. Previn and Allen's essentially demoralizing relationship with his very elderly and still judgmental parents, Martin and Nettie Konigsberg.

Charles Mingus: Triumph of the Underdog (1997)

In marked contrast to the musical dilettantism of Woody Allen is the fateful career of Charles Mingus (1922–1979), a mercurial, brooding musical genius. Mingus was not only a superb double bassist but is now widely regarded as one of America's greatest jazz composers. Nine years in the making, Don McGlynn's *Charles Mingus: Triumph of the Underdog* (1997) presents a complex montage of rare audio segments, film clips, and still photographs of Mingus performances enhanced by revealing interviews with many musical cohorts, Charles Mingus's two wives (Celia Mingus Zaentz and Sue Mingus), and his son, Dorian. The portrait that emerges is of a light-skinned black man of mixed-race parentage who endured wrenching artistic frustrations and ill treatment by blacks and whites alike for his uncertain racial identity. A consummate intellectual and visionary musician and composer, Mingus was probably afflicted with bipolar disorder. McGlynn's elegiac documentary biopic presents a convincing case for Mingus's enduring status as one of jazz's key figures.

Buena Vista Social Club (1999)

Easily the most famous feature-length film on a jazz history topic is Wim Wenders' documentary, *Buena Vista Social Club* (1999). The catalyst for the film (and CD) was the versatile American guitarist and musicologist, Ry Cooder, who initially traveled to Havana, Cuba, in the 1970s to explore the music scene there. In 1996 Cooder had the opportunity to return to Havana when British record producer Nick Gold proposed a project that would use West African and Cuban musicians. The West Africans were not able to participate but the project went forward anyway with an assemblage of veteran Cuban musicians who once played at the members-only Buena Vista Social Club in Havana before Castro came to power in 1959. The resulting CD was a smash hit, selling over a million and a half copies and winning a Grammy award. Celebrated German filmmaker Wim Wenders, a longtime collaborator with Ry Cooder, accompanied Cooder on a return trip to Havana in 1998 to produce an album featuring Ibrahim Ferrer, one of the lead singers on the *Social Club* album. Using digital cameras, Wenders and crew shot interviews with the musicians, recorded their rehearsals, and captured daily life in decaying, poverty-stricken Havana, still stuck in a time warp by the long-standing American embargo. The film culminates with triumphal footage of hugely successful concerts in Amsterdam and at New York's Carnegie Hall. The music—Cuban folklore and love songs combining African, American (jazz, blues, gospel), and European forms and set to various Latin rhythms—is emotionally evocative and hauntingly beautiful. Unfortunately, the film *as a cinematic experience* is rather dull. As film critic Roger Ebert rightly notes, the film-makers are overly smitten with a few filmic clichés, for example, the camera slowing and repeatedly circling its subject, and Wender's friend, Ry Cooder, receives an inordinate amount of screen time at the expense of the Cubans. Its politically charged subject and setting notwithstanding, *Buena Vista Social Club* assiduously avoids any overt political commentary. Fidel Castro is not mentioned and the lionization of elderly, pre-Castro-era musicians suggests a vaguely anti-Castro stance. Yet the film implicitly advocates cultural exchange as a

Scene from the movie Buena Vista Social Club, *directed by Wim Wenders. (Corbis Sygma)*

means of further détente between the United States and Cuba: a cautious nod back toward liberalism in keeping with the slightly improving state of relations between the two countries in the late 1990s.

"Jazz" (2001)

Six years in the making, Ken Burns' massive, 19-hour, ten-episode PBS mini-series, *"Jazz"* (2001), is a hugely ambitious attempt to survey the entire history of jazz music in America, from its origins in late nineteenth-century New Orleans to its contemporary manifestations. Almost entirely ignorant about jazz when they undertook the project, Burns and coproducer, Lynn Novick, relied on celebrated jazz trumpeter and impresario, Wynton Marsalis, and a host of other experts for guidance. Creative consensus dictated that great emphasis be placed on the seminal influences of Louis Armstrong (1901–1971) and Duke Ellington (1899–1974). In-depth coverage is also afforded to the other acknowledged giants in the field: Sidney Bechet, Bessie Smith, Bix Biederbecke, Art Tatum, Benny Goodman, Artie Shaw, Count Basie, Ella Fitzgerald, Lester Young, Charlie Parker, John Birks "Dizzy" Gillspie, Thelonious Monk, Dave Brubeck, Gil Evans, Miles Davis, Sonny Rollins, and John Coltrane. At every turn, pains are taken to show the relationship between developments in jazz and trends in American social and cultural history. Burns employs his signature documentary style: a conventionally linear chronological structure that showcases thousands of pans and zooms of still photographs; over 2,000 archival film footage bits; and seventy-five interviews with jazz greats and historians. The entire series is laced with 497 separate samples of jazz music. Professional actor Keith David delivers extensive explanatory voice-over narration (with appropriate solemnity), supplemented by a cadre of other actors reciting illustrative quotations along the way.

The result of such prodigious research and meticulous filmmaking is pure Ken Burns: a work that is beautifully scripted, impressively thoroughgoing, highly informative, occasionally fascinating—but utterly conventional in style and structure and predictably skewed toward reverential Americana, as were Burns' marathon PBS series on the Civil War and on baseball. This is not to say that Burns is naïve or Pollyannish; *"Jazz"* deals honestly with the attendant history of Jim Crow and the terrible hardships and injustices suffered by African Americans. But the underlying ideological intent of a Ken Burns documentary is to encourage its audience to *feel good* about America and Americans, a valid enterprise, to be sure, but one that can too easily lead to smarmy self-congratulation.

Strange Fruit (2002)

An effective answer to the decorous liberalism of *"Jazz"* is Joel Katz's 57-minute documentary, *Strange Fruit* (2002). Katz's film centers on "Strange Fruit," the famous protest song about lynching first performed by Billie Holiday in 1939 at Café Society (then New York City's only integrated nightclub) and recorded by her in 1940 on the leftist Commodore record label after Columbia Records deemed the song too controversial for release. Holiday variously claimed that the song was written for her or that she actually wrote the song herself. Both claims were patently false. After seeing a magazine photograph of a lynching in 1937, a Bronx high school English teacher and "closet Communist" named Abel Meeropol (1903–1986), using the pseudonym Lewis Allan, wrote an antilynching poem called "Bitter Fruit." Meeropol's wife, Ann, set the poem to music and changed the title to "Strange Fruit." Starkly powerful, "Strange Fruit" gained added sociopolitical significance by virtue of having been written by a white, Jewish man in a city often marked by Jewish and African American tensions. Enormously moved by the song, Billie Holiday added it to her repertoire and is forever identified with it. Employing artfully complex documentary exposition, Katz offers concise overviews of Billie Holiday's career, Abel Meeropol's career, and the grotesque practice of lynching in America—an effective blending of social, cultural, and political history that makes for a powerful viewing experience. Viewers will also be surprised to learn that Abel and Ann Meeropol had a second claim to fame: they adopted the sons of Ethel and Julius Rosenberg after the Rosenbergs were executed for espionage in 1953.

Standing in the Shadows of Motown (2002)

Bringing belated credit to unsung heroes is the purpose of Paul Justman's *Standing in the Shadows of Motown* (2002), a documentary based on the book (and accompanying CD set), *Standing in the Shadows of Motown: The Life and Music of Legendary Bassist James Jamerson* (Milwaukee, WI: Hal Leonard Publishing, 1989) by Alan Slutsky, aka "Dr. Licks." The book and film focus on the Funk Brothers, the collective name for a dozen or so hitherto anonymous session musicians behind all of Motown's greatest hits. Mostly black jazz musicians, some classically trained, the Funk Brothers consisted of a core group— Eddie Willis and Joe Messina on guitar, James Jamerson on bass, Joe Hunter on piano, and Benny "Papa Zita" Benjamin on drums—supplemented or replaced by Eddie "Bongo" Brown on congas, Bob Babbitt on bass, Earl Van Dyke and

Johnny Griffith on keyboards, Robert White on guitar, Richard "Pistol" Allen and Uriel Jones on drums, and Jack Ashford on percussion and vibraphone. In various combinations these superb musicians supplied the trademark Motown sound on dozens of hit songs by Marvin Gaye, Stevie Wonder, Smokey Robinson and the Miracles, Martha and the Vandellas, the Supremes, Mary Wells, Junior Walker and the All-Stars, the Temptations, and the Four Tops. Indeed, the film asserts that the Funk Brothers played on more number one records than Elvis Presley, the Beatles, the Beach Boys, and the Rolling Stones *combined*. Not officially credited on most of the records on which they appeared, the Funk Brothers were, for many years, paid scale, a measly $10 per song, while Motown Records founder, Berry Gordy Jr., and his big name stars made millions. To add insult to injury, after fourteen years on Detroit's West Grand Boulevard ("Hitsville, U.S.A."), Berry Gordy moved his operations to Los Angeles in 1972 without prior notice.

Standing in the Shadows combines candid interviews with the eight surviving Funk Brothers, voice-over narration by Walter Dallas and poet Ntozake Shange, reenactments of sessions, and renditions of Motown classics featuring contemporary artists such as Chaka Khan, Joan Osborne, Bootsy Collins, and Me'Shell NdegéOcello fronting the Funk Brothers. As the latter feature achieves decidedly mixed results, the film would have been better served by more Motown archival footage, a probing examination of the business practices of Berry Gordy, and a thorough overview of the sociohistorical background that preceded Motown—the mass African American migration to northern industrial cities like Detroit, Chicago, and New York City after World War I that gave rise to the African American urban experience and the music that expressed it. Nonetheless, *Standing in the Shadows* constitutes an important recuperation of the history of Motown music.

Martin Scorsese Presents the Blues— A Musical Journey (2003)

In 1903, while waiting for a train on a station platform in Tutwiler, Mississippi, W. C. Handy happened to encounter a ragged man playing slide guitar and singing a mournful tune. Haunted by the extraordinary music he heard, Handy went on to compose extensively in the same idiom, which became known as "the blues." On September 5, 2002, the U.S. Senate adopted Resolution 316, designating 2003 "The [Centennial] Year of the Blues."

Most prominent among a host of commemorative events offered in 2003 was a seven-part PBS miniseries entitled *Martin Scorsese Presents the Blues—*

A Musical Journey. Scorsese, a longtime rock and blues devotee, was executive director and producer of the series while a different director made the 90-minute film that comprised each "episode" of the series. The first film, *Feel like Going Home*, directed by Scorsese, written by rock journalist Peter Guralnick, and hosted by Corey Harris, traces the roots and evolution of the Delta blues from West Africa to Mississippi. Supplementing rare archival footage of Son House (Eddie James House, 1902–1988), Muddy Waters (McKinley Morganfield, 1915–1983), and John Lee Hooker (1917–2001) are new performances by (and interviews with) Willie King, Taj Mahal, Otha Turner, Ali Farka Toure, and many other contemporary blues artists. The second film, *The Soul of a Man*, written and directed by Wim Wenders and narrated by Laurence Fishburne, explores the lives of Wenders' favorite blues artists: bottleneck slide guitarist, Blind Willie Johnson (1902–1947); Betonia blues player, Nehemiah "Skip" James (1902–1969); and boogie blues guitarist, J. B. Lenoir (1929–1967). On his own website, Wenders describes his film as "part history, part personal pilgrimage . . . that tells the story of these lives in music through an extended fictional film sequence (recreations of '20s and '30s events—shot in silent-film, hand-crank style), rare archival footage, present-day documentary scenes and covers of their songs by contemporary musicians such as Shemekia Copeland, Alvin Youngblood Hart, Garland Jeffreys, Chris Thomas King, Cassandra Wilson, Nick Cave, Los Lobos, Eagle Eye Cherry, Vernon Reid, James 'Blood' Ulmer, Lou Reed, Bonnie Raitt, Marc Ribot, The Jon Spencer Blues Explosion, Lucinda Williams and T-Bone Burnett" (www.wim-wenders.com). The third film, *The Road to Memphis*, directed by Richard Pearce and written by Muddy Waters biographer Robert Gordon, focuses on the Memphis-centered work of the legendary B. B. King, "folk-funk" avatar Bobby Rush (Emmit Ellis Jr.), blues pianist Rosco Gordon (1934–2002), the infamous Ike Turner, rock-blues vocalist Rufus Thomas (1917–2001), and the great Howlin' Wolf (Chester Burnett, 1910–1976). The fourth film, *Warming by the Devil's Fire*, directed by Charles Burnett (*Killer of Shee; My Brother's Wedding; To Sleep in Anger*), is described on the series official website as "a fictional narrative about a young boy's encounter with his family in Mississippi in the 1950s, and the intergenerational tensions between the heavenly strains of gospel and the devilish moans of the blues" (www.scorsesefilms.com/blues.htm). The fifth film, *Godfathers & Sons*, directed by Marc Levin (*Slam*), follows Marshall Chess (son of Leonard Chess, founder of the premier blues label, Chess Records) and hip-hop star, Chuck D (of Public Enemy), touring Chicago and reflecting on its rich blues history as they produce an album that showcases blues and hip-hop musicians. The film features rare archival footage of Howlin' Wolf, Muddy Waters, and the Paul Butterfield Blues Band and performances by Koko Taylor, Otis Rush, Magic Slim, Ike Turner, and Sam Lay. The sixth film, *Red, White and*

Blues, directed by Mike Figgis (*The Browning Version, Leaving Las Vegas*), focuses on the so-called "British invasion." In the mid-1960s England's top club musicians—Jeff Beck, Eric Clapton, John Mayall, Albert Lee, Peter Green, Mick Fleetwood, Van Morrison, the Rolling Stones, and many others—reintroduced the blues to America with rock songs firmly based in the blues idiom. Interspersing archival footage of 1960s rockers and their blues progenitors with contemporary interviews and performances, Figgis explores the ironic and sometimes controversial process by which Europeans revitalized a black American music tradition. Clint Eastwood's *Piano Blues*, the seventh and final film of the series, features Eastwood himself playing renditions of piano blues classics and showcases interviews with, and performances by, such piano blues masters as Marcia Ball, Dave Brubeck, Ray Charles, Jay McShann, Dr. John (Mac Rebennack), and Pinetop Perkins.

You're the Top: The Cole Porter Story (1990)

Writing both lyrics and music, Cole Porter (1891–1964) was one of America's foremost composers of popular songs. His 800-song repertoire includes such classics as "Anything Goes," "Begin the Beguine," "Don't Fence Me In," "I Get a Kick Out of You," "It's De-Lovely," "Just One of Those Things," "Let's Do It, Let's Fall in Love," "Let's Misbehave," "Miss Otis Regrets," "Red, Hot and Blue," "So in Love," "Too Darn Hot," "You're the Top," and many other tunes instantly recognizable to people of a certain age. With his witty tunes, full of double entendre and sly irony, Porter—a closeted gay man from a wealthy background—came to epitomize high society elegance and urban sophistication with a whiff of blissful decadence, yet tempered by a tragic dimension that was also part of Cole Porter's legend. On October 24, 1937, Porter's legs were crushed in a riding accident and he spent the remaining twenty-seven years of his life a semi-invalid. In constant pain, Porter underwent a seemingly endless series of operations but continued to write music and remained the bon vivant in keeping with his Epicurean philosophy of life—at least until the last part of his life. Porter's wife, Linda, died of emphysema in May 1954. Four years later Porter had to have his right leg amputated. Thereafter he sank into a deep and lasting depression that he medicated with drugs and alcohol. He died on October 15, 1964.

A quarter century after his death at the age of seventy-three, Cole Porter's reputation as a twentieth-century musical giant was resurrected with the television broadcast of *You're the Top: The Cole Porter Story* (1990), an hour-long documentary biopic hosted and narrated by famed New York cabaret singer Bobby Short. Comprised of interviews, photographs, archival footage, and clips of famous artists—Bing Crosby, Judy Garland, Frank Sinatra—performing Porter's songs, *You're the Top* presents a truthful and fairly comprehensive overview of Porter's life and career in music.

Night and Day (1946)

Revived on television, Cole Porter was also given renewed exposure at record stores when the Red Hot Organization, a self-described "leading international organization dedicated to fighting AIDS through pop culture" (www.redhot.org) released *Red Hot + Blue* (titled after a 1936 Cole Porter musical comedy), a 1990 album that featured some twenty contemporary pop singers reinterpreting Porter's songs. Though somewhat uneven in quality, the record was a hit, selling more than a million copies, winning *Stereo Review*'s Album-of-the-Year award, and inaugurating a new and still burgeoning music genre: the tribute album. Thus, through the efforts of AIDS activists and sympathetic artists, Cole Porter's stature as a major figure in twentieth-century popular music, though never in doubt, was revitalized for a new generation. It was, perhaps, only a matter of time before the requisite docudrama appeared. Indeed, one already had, while Porter was just past the height of his fame in the 1940s: Michael Curtiz's *Night and Day* (1946), a typically formulaic and phony musical biopic starring Cary Grant as Cole Porter and Alexis Smith as Linda Lee Porter. Though packed with Porter's music, *Night and Day* bore almost no resemblance to the facts of his actual life. As was de rigeur at that time, the Porters' marriage, which was really one of convenience only, is wildly romanticized. Likewise, Cole Porter's homosexuality is completely suppressed and, among other apocrypha, the film had Porter fighting and getting wounded in World War I: an outrageous tall tale that originated with Porter himself.

De-Lovely (2004)

Fourteen years after *You're the Top* and fifty-eight years after *Night and Day*, producer-director and Cole Porter fanatic Irwin Winkler (*Night and the City; Life as a House*) brought out *De-Lovely* (2004), another Porter biopic utterly unlike its predecessors—except for showcasing the music. Written by Martin Scorsese collaborator Jay Cocks (*Age of Innocence; Gangs of New York*), filmed in London and Venice, and starring Kevin Kline as Porter and Ashley Judd as his wife, Linda, *De-Lovely* reflects its own cultural moment by facing the issue of Porter's homosexuality head-on—though not graphically, in keeping with its PG-13 rating. In terms of structure, *De-Lovely* employs a kind of *This Is Your Life* expositional method that shows Porter, close to death, having the highlights of his life paraded before him in carnivalesque fashion by a fictive producer and symbolic angel named Gabe (Jonathan Pryce). To give the film a more contemporary feel and increase its marketability with a younger audience, Winkler enlisted pop stars—Robbie Williams, Elvis Costello, Alanis Morisette, Sheryl Crow, and Natalie Cole—to perform renditions of Porter's songs. The ambiguous result of all this is a film that plays like a bad Fellini movie—at once colorful, vapid, and strangely uninvolving.

Rock

Don't Look Back (1967)

By the 1960s Hollywood and the emerging youth culture were leagues apart in outlook: a situation starkly manifested, for example, by a long and dismal series of corny Elvis Presley exploitation films. The task fell to independent filmmakers to record the unfolding story of the 1960s counterculture as it grew out of the Beat apostasy, Civil Rights, antiwar ferment, drug experimentation, and the explosive emergence of rock as the dominant pop music form. Poet-avatar of the new counterculture sensibility was Bob Dylan (Robert Allen Zimmerman of Hibbing, Minnesota), a Greenwich Village folksinger-songwriter turned rock star credited with almost single-handedly revolutionizing pop music in the 1960s. Dylan wrote angry, intelligent songs critical of bourgeois-consumerist-conformist values that were light-years beyond the Tin Pan Alley hackwork of the day. In 1965, at the height of Dylan's international fame and mystique, his manager, Albert Grossman, contacted documentary filmmaker, Richard Leacock, and asked if he would be interested in making a film about his famous client. Leacock passed the project on to his associate, D. A. (Donn Alan) Pennebaker, a fellow practitioner of cinema verité who had risen to prominence for his involvement in *Primary* (1960), a groundbreaking 60-minute documentary on the Wisconsin presidential primary contest between Hubert Humphrey and John F. Kennedy. Pennebaker enhanced his reputation as a gifted documentarian with *Jane (Fonda)* (1962), a behind-the-scenes look at Fonda's work on her Broadway debut in *There Was a Little Girl* (1960). Armed with a handheld movie camera, Pennebaker accompanied Dylan and his entourage on a seven-city, eight-show tour of Great Britain in April–May 1965 and shot the young pop star performing onstage, meeting fans, relaxing in hotel rooms with friends and hangers-on, getting into arguments, riding in cars, and sparring with inquisitive, befuddled journalists at press conferences. Some 20 hours of black-and-white footage were eventually edited down to a 96-minute opus entitled *Don't Look Back* (perhaps inspired by the Satchel Paige axiom, "Don't look back. Something might be gaining on you"). Initially released in San Francisco on May 17, 1967, *Don't Look Back* brilliantly captured the mercurial, moody Dylan, age twenty-four, at the height of his creative powers, but the unblinking camera eye also revealed a man obviously troubled and frequently obnoxious to those he considered his intellectual inferiors. A fascinating portrait of the artist as an alienated young lout, *Don't Look Back* disclosed a revealing glimpse of 1960s youth culture: brash, irreverent, and unwilling to live by the received, conservative wisdom of the Cold War consensus. Pennebaker's film broke ground on several fronts. It was the first rock documentary; the first music biopic to be shot in contemporaneous, direct cinema fashion, sans nondiegetic commentary; and the first music biopic that dared to show its subject's dark side: an idea utterly inconceivable to the Hollywood moguls of past decades. In all three respects, *Don't Look Back* was a perfect reflection of its revolutionary historical moment.

Monterey Pop (1969)

A month after the release of *Don't Look Back*, D. A. Pennebaker and cohorts James Desmond, Barry Feinstein, Richard Leacock, Nicholas Profreres, and Albert Maysles were in California to film the Monterey International Pop Festival for an ABC-TV special (that was never aired). In the two-year span between Pennebaker's shooting of his Dylan documentary and this new project, Dylan's fearless and passionate iconoclasm had permeated the psyche of America's youth; psychedelics and hard rock music were de rigeur and the baby boom generation saw itself, however briefly, as uniquely liberated, questing, and rebellious. Occurring during the fabled "summer of love," the three-day pop festival held at the Monterey County Fair Grounds on June 16–18, 1967, before a crowd of some 200,000 concertgoers, was an uncannily synchronistic event, a perfectly timed debutante ball for the 1960s counterculture that celebrated the new, expansive social ethos of the "hippies" as it showcased rock's premier talent. The performers' roster of thirty-two acts included pop's crème de la crème: Otis Redding, the Mamas and the Papas, the Byrds, the Grateful Dead, Simon and Garfunkle, Ravi Shakar, the Animals, the Jefferson Airplane, and many others. Pennebaker's film version of the festival, entitled *Monterey Pop* (1969), covered about a third of the artists who appeared that weekend and featured incendiary debut appearances by The Who, Janis Joplin, and Jimi Hendrix. The film's relatively brief running time of 78 minutes and Pennebaker's adherence to cinema verité precepts dictated a spare, direct, and somewhat clinical approach to cinematography and editing. *Monterey Pop* concentrates almost exclusively on the performances themselves. Interspersed are the obligatory crowd reaction shots but mostly absent are the backstage interviews, behind-the-scenes glimpses, and local color footage that would become an integral part of later rock concert documentaries.

Woodstock (1970)

In marked contrast to the stylistic economy of *Monterey Pop* was Michael Wadleigh's mammoth *Woodstock* (1970), a decidedly expressionistic 3-hour documentary of the legendary four-day rock festival on 600 acres of pastureland at Max Yasgur's dairy farm in Bethel (Sullivan County), New York, on August 15–17, 1969. Woodstock boasted most of rock's top name acts: Blood, Sweat and Tears; the Band; Creedence Clearwater Revival; Crosby, Stills, Nash and Young; Joe Cocker; Arlo Guthrie; the Grateful Dead; Tim Hardin; Jimi Hendrix; Richie Havens; Janis Joplin; the Jefferson Airplane; Ravi Shankar; Sly and the Family Stone; Santana; Ten Years After; Johnny Winter; The Who. Much more than a concert film, *Woodstock* supplemented ample coverage of the music performances— often rendered in split screen or tight close-up—with much direct cinema footage of the massive crowd en route, tearing down fences, listening and dancing to the music, smoking pot, frolicking naked, wallowing in mud after a rainstorm, using filthy portable toilets, and milling about the trash-strewn site and its environs. Also included were interviews with promoters, performers, event staff, concertgoers, and locals who had to bear the brunt of an influx of some 450,000 people to an event set up to accommodate a fraction of that number.

The huge quantity of footage shot by Wadleigh and four other cinematographers was edited by a six-person team that included Martin Scorsese and Thelma Schoonmaker, who edited Scorsese's first film, *Who's That Knocking at My Door?* (1968), and would edit many of his later films. Much like the event itself, *Woodstock* was a sprawling, overlong mess, exciting and boring by turns. Even for its time the music was decidedly uneven. Some of it was exhilarating (e.g., Joe Cocker; Sly and the Family Stone), much of it mediocre (e.g., the Jefferson Airplane), and some of it downright awful (e.g., Joan Baez). But the point of the festival and its filmic record was not to just showcase late 1960s pop music but to celebrate the hippie/antiwar counterculture in all its supposed peace-loving, sensuous, gaudy vibrancy—despite (or perhaps because of) the mud, chaos, and woefully inadequate amenities. Indeed, the film became virtually synonymous with the event itself and cemented the self-congratulatory legend of a generation

Poster promoting the Woodstock Music and Arts Fair in Bethel, New York, August 15–17, 1969. (Library of Congress)

dedicated to peace and harmony while their elders prosecuted a war in Vietnam. The implicit argument was that half a million people sharing a makeshift city for several days without violent incident bespoke a new, enlightening sensibility. The film's tagline said it all: "Three [*sic*] days of peace, music . . . and love." Ironically, by the time *Woodstock* was released in late March 1970, the hippie ethos had already died, defamed by the notorious Manson murders that occurred in Los Angeles just a few days *before* the Woodstock Festival and ultimately done in by the fiasco that was the free Rolling Stones concert at Altamont Speedway near Livermore, California, on December 6, 1969.

Gimme Shelter (1970)

Gimme Shelter (1970), Albert and David Maysles' masterful and still harrowing documentary about Altamont, remains an indispensable corrective to the bloated pro-hippie propaganda of *Woodstock*. During their 1969 U.S. tour, the Rolling Stones met with criticism for charging too much for concert tickets. To assuage their fans and counter negative publicity, Mick Jagger and company decided to stage a free concert at Golden Gate Park in San Francisco at the close of their tour. Unfortunately, the San Francisco City Council denied a concert permit a few days before the scheduled event, forcing the Stones' organization to scramble to find an alternate venue. After a deal to hold the show at nearby Sears Point Speedway fell through, the Stones secured the Altamont site just 48 hours before the announced concert date: too late to make adequate preparations for the expected hordes. Worst yet, the Stones hired members of the notorious Hell's Angels biker gang to provide security and crowd control in exchange for free beer: a practice not unheard of on the West Coast but one that would prove disastrous on this occasion. Heavy drinking and drug taking by the bikers and many of the 300,000 concertgoers started early on the day of the concert and sporadic fighting began to break out in the crowd and between unruly fans and drunken, drug-addled bikers armed with weighted pool cues. By the time the Rolling Stones took the stage that evening, the enormous crowd—cold, intoxicated, sick of being harassed by leather-clad thugs and of waiting all day for the headliners—was close to rioting. After a very brief set that was constantly interrupted by erupting scuffles and beatings, the Stones fled the chaos by helicopter, unaware that a black teenager named Meredith Hunter had been beaten, stabbed, and stomped to death a short distance from the stage by Hell's Angels after pulling out a gun, perhaps in self-defense.

The original mandate for the Maysles brothers and coproducer Charlotte Zwerin was to make a concert documentary that would chronicle the Stones'

1969 American tour. The unexpected reality of Altamont changed all that. Indeed, *Gimme Shelter* neatly bifurcates into two films: a typically adulatory rock concert film and a gripping cinema verité documentary. The first half of the film, mostly shot at three Madison Square Garden shows, depicts the band at its exuberant, swaggering best. The camera inevitably pays rapt attention to the writhing, gesticulating, highly androgynous spectacle of lead singer Mick Jagger who "interprets" the Stones' material with the hyperkinetic energy of a spastic on amphetamines. In this part of the film, concert footage is interspersed with shots of the band in a film editing suite, watching themselves perform; telephone negotiations with their San Francisco celebrity attorney, the notorious "King of Torts," Melvin Belli (1908–1996), to set up the Altamont concert; and the Stones, in a recording studio, listening to radio announcements of the upcoming free concert.

The mood darkens noticeably once the focus shifts to Altamont. Ominously, scuffles keep on breaking out during preliminary acts. While trying to intervene in a fight, Marty Balin of the Jefferson Airplane is knocked unconscious by a Hell's Angel. Mick Jagger is punched in the face as soon as he emerges from his trailer. Once night falls and the Stones finally take the stage, pandemonium erupts and never subsides. Jagger, the strutting rock demigod normally able to bend audiences to his will, is pathetically impotent in his attempts to soothe the mob and tame the rampaging bikers. A particularly telling racking focus shot shifts from the caped and prancing Mick Jagger in the foreground to a well-muscled, menacing biker on the side of the stage, looking Jagger up and down with the icy contempt of an exterminator examining a particularly loathsome insect. The film continually cuts away to the band members in an editing room at a later date, impassively watching the bedlam unfold on film—including inadvertent footage of the actual murder of Meredith Hunter that is rewound, repeated, and reexamined not unlike the Zapruder film of JFK's assassination. The final, brilliant shot of *Gimme Shelter* is a freeze-frame of Jagger emerging from the editing room, his ashen face and haunted eyes providing all the editorial commentary necessary. Thanks, in part, to the powerful impact of *Gimme Shelter*, Altamont came to be seen as the Waterloo of hippiedom and the official end of the 1960s.

Cocksucker Blues (1972)

Their already sketchy public status damaged by the Altamont fiasco, the Rolling Stones soon made matters worse by hiring noted Beat photographer-filmmaker Robert Frank (*The Americans; Pull My Daisy*) to film their 1972 *Exile on Main*

Street tour. The resulting cinema verité documentary, scandalously titled *Cock-sucker Blues* (1972), featured a few stage performances but was mostly comprised of behind-the-scenes footage of hotel living and constant travel from one venue to the next. In the process, amid the tedium of the tour grind, Frank's camera captured all manner of decadent sex and illicit (including intravenous) drug use by the band's motley entourage. Not really an exposé as the Stones were already notoriously debauched, *Cocksucker Blues* tends to turn its rock star subjects into pitiable, pedestrian characters. Fearing that the movie's revelations would cause the Stones to be banned in America thereafter (with financially catastrophic results), Mick Jagger's lawyers went to court to prevent the release of the film. Now it can only be shown theatrically when filmmaker Robert Frank is present but a bootleg VHS tape has circulated extensively.

Jimi Hendrix (1973) and *Janis* (1974)

Declared dead by *Gimme Shelter*, the 1960s were eulogized by back-to-back documentaries in the early 1970s: *Jimi Hendrix* (1973) and *Janis* (1974). The son of a Seattle landscaper, James Marshall Hendrix (1942–1970) began playing guitar at an early age and honed his skills in the military and as an itinerant sideman for the likes of Little Richard and Curtis Knight. Hendrix's big break came in 1966 when Animals bassist Chas Chandler discovered him heading a band called Jimmy James and the Blues Flames at the Café Wha? in New York City's Greenwich Village. Chandler brought Hendrix over to London in the fall of 1966 and built a mixed-race trio around him called the Jimi Hendrix Experience, with Englishmen Mitch Mitchell on drums and Noel Redding on bass. Though his career as an international superstar lasted little more than four years (1966–1970) and he released only three studio albums, Hendrix practically reinvented rock with his virtuoso guitar playing, flamboyant stage presence, a well-deserved reputation for sexual conquests and heavy drug use, and a musical lyricism and intensity that could be both exquisite and frightening. By 1968 Hendrix was the world's top rock performer. Sadly, his moment in the sun would be a brief one; he died of an alcohol and barbiturate overdose in London on September 18, 1970, nine months after Altamont and just four and a half months after the Ohio National Guard shot and killed four student antiwar protesters at Kent State University—yet another death blow to the counterculture already staggering under drug paranoia, political despair, and ideological factionalism.

Financed by Warner Brothers and directed and produced by Joe Boyd, John Head, and Gary Weis, the documentary film *Jimi Hendrix* combined archived interview clips of Hendrix, numerous photographic stills, ample con-

Rock guitarist Jimi Hendrix in an undated publicity photograph. (Reuters/Corbis)

cert footage (e.g., Monterey, Woodstock, Berkeley, Isle of Wight), and candid interviews with some two dozen friends, associates, and contemporaries. Among those interviewed were Hendrix's father, Al Hendrix; road manager, Eric Barrett; girlfriends Fayne "Faye" Pridgeon and Monika Dannemann; sidemen Mitch Mitchell, Noel Redding, Billy Cox, Juma Sutan; and other rocks stars, such as Lou Reed, Mick Jagger, Pete Townsend, and Eric Clapton. Made less than three years after Hendrix's death, *Jimi Hendrix* benefited from the availability and fresh memories of most of the key players in Hendrix's life (with the notable exceptions of his longtime girlfriend, "super groupie" Devon Wilson, who died of a heroin overdose in 1971, and his manager, Mike Jeffrey, who was killed in a plane crash in 1973). The result was a poignant portrait of an essentially shy and conflicted musical genius, a fascinating glimpse into the hedonistic excesses of rock superstardom, and a belated requiem for the psychedelic era. On the downside, the film's proximity to its subject's life deprived it of the considerable benefits of historical perspective and further research that has since revealed much more about the complexities of Hendrix's life.

Produced by Howard Alk, F. R. "Budge" Crawley, and Seaton Findlay, *Janis* documents Janis Joplin's tumultuous life, from her childhood in Port Arthur, Texas, to her ascendancy to rock superstardom, to her early death by heroin overdose on October 4, 1970, less than three weeks after the death of Jimi Hendrix. Intelligent, anguished, passionate, and lonely, Joplin, aka "Pearl," became the most uninhibited and expressive white blues-rock singer of her generation. The documentary, replete with performance clips, captures Joplin's raw intensity onstage, her peculiar mixture of feminism and wounded romanticism, and her all-too-obvious self-destructiveness. Much like *Jimi Hendrix*, *Janis* constitutes an elegy to a unique, unrepeatable cultural moment, when a small but significant sector of America's youth briefly turned away from materialistic status seeking and sought a more direct and honest experience of life. One could even argue, more portentously, that they were seeking some ill-defined spiritual transcendence.

Always highly commercial and populist, rock music was big business by the mid-1970s. Widespread fan adulation, massive concert and album revenues, star hubris, and extreme decadence combined to strip rock music of its freshness and any pretensions it might have had toward the subversive. Firmly established as a mainstream institution, rock became just another branch of the entertainment industry that it had sometimes tried to mutiny against in the 1950s and 1960s. The intuition that the rebelliousness and inventive magic were gone was amply manifest in the rock films that would follow.

Renaldo and Clara (1978)

At the end of the 1970s, what came to be known as classic rock music enjoyed a final, elegiac burst of cinematic attention. In his first bid as a filmmaker, Bob Dylan directed, cowrote (with Sam Shepard), and starred in *Renaldo and Clara* (1978), a 4-hour-long concert documentary-symbolist film that revolves around Dylan's Rolling Thunder Revue Tour of the Northeast in 1975. (A subtopic is Dylan's advocacy on behalf of the supposedly wrongly convicted boxer, Rubin "Hurricane" Carter.) Though it included a good deal of exciting concert footage,

Dylan's film was painfully overlong and suffered from formlessness, erratic editing, and many awkwardly improvised scenes that were largely unintelligible,
even to Dylan cognoscenti. Savaged by critics, *Renaldo and Clara* quickly sank
into oblivion. Never officially released in VHS or DVD format, it leads a spectral
existence as a rare bootleg. Severely damaged by the *Renaldo and Clara* debacle and a subsequent string of mediocre records, Dylan's artistic prestige did not
fully recover until the mid-1990s.

The Last Waltz (1978)

Bob Dylan appeared on film again in 1978, as part of an all-star lineup in Martin
Scorsese's *The Last Waltz* (1978), a reverential documentary record of the Band's
farewell concert at San Francisco's Winterland Arena on Thanksgiving Day, 1976.
Also appearing that night were Paul Butterfield, Eric Clapton, Ronnie Hawkins,
Dr. John (Mac Rebennack), Neil Diamond, Joni Mitchell, Van Morrison, Ron
Wood, Neil Young, the Staples Singers, and Muddy Waters. Interspersed between
performances are rather banal backstage interviews with Band members Robbie
Robertson, Rick Danko, Levon Helm, Richard Manuel, and Garth Hudson reminiscing about their sixteen hectic, arduous years on the road. Expertly directed
by Scorsese and shot by world-class cinematographers Vilmos Zsigmond and
Michael Chapman, assisted by Michael Watkins, *The Last Waltz* is undoubtedly
the best-looking rock concert documentary ever made. As for the performances
themselves, many viewers and critics have noted that the Band and their illustrious colleagues seem rather tired and jaded and that the whole proceeding has a
somewhat perfunctory, long-in-the-tooth aura to it, despite its elegant production
values and celebratory pretensions.

The Kids Are Alright (1979)

In terms of music history on film, the classic rock era came to final closure with
the appropriately nostalgic *The Kids Are Alright* (1979), a documentary by television writer-producer Jeff Stein on the wildly successful British rock group, The
Who. A year before the film was released, the Who's notoriously dissolute drummer, Keith Moon, died of a drug overdose. Although former Small Faces drummer, Kenney Jones, replaced Moon and the Who continued to record and tour for
many years after, the magic died with Moon's demise. Essentially a compilation
of archived concert clips (e.g., *Smother Brothers Show, Shindig, Rock and Roll
Circus*, and *Woodstock*), interspersed with interviews, *The Kids Are Alright*

traces the history of the band from 1964 up to Keith Moon's death thirteen years later. Fascinating, funny, and appalling by turns, the film showcases the band's evolution from "Mod" club band to international sensation and documents the extremely diverse personalities of the band members. Its creative force, Pete Townsend, comes off as neurotic but brilliant; Roger Daltry seems a somewhat dim-witted narcissist; John Entwhistle, quiet and unassuming; Keith Moon, a colorful and unpredictable maniac. In sum, the film effectively showcases the band's reckless exuberance and humor: traits more in keeping with the rebellious 1960s than the decadent 1970s or the generally moribund period that would follow.

History of Rock 'N' Roll (1995)

There is no surer indicator of a cultural trend's demise than the appearance of a comprehensive history of that trend. Accordingly, in 1995, coproducers Andrew Solt, Quincy Jones, Bob Meyerowitz, and Jeffrey Peisch brought out *History of Rock 'N' Roll*, an informative ten-part series of 1-hour made-for-television documentaries that mix contemporary interviews with archival footage and voiceover narration (by actor Gary Busey) to survey the history of rock from its rockabilly roots in the 1950s to the era of MTV and hip-hop. Volume 1, *Rock 'N' Roll Explodes*, recounts the genesis of rock 'n' roll in the mid-1950s with reference to such legendary figures as Elvis Presley, Carl Perkins, Chuck Berry, Little Richard, and Fats Domino. Volume 2, *Good Rockin' Tonight*, covers the second wave of early rock 'n' roll innovators, including Buddy Holly, Bo Diddley, Roy Orbison, Ben E. King ("Stand by Me"), and Jerry Lee Lewis. Volume 3, *Britain Invades, America Fights Back*, deals with the benign "British invasion" of the United States by mid-1960s English rock groups—the Beatles, the Rolling Stones, Herman's Hermits, the Animals, the Who—who often derived their inspiration (and some of their material) from classic American blues singer-guitarists. America fought back with Motown and the Beach Boys. Volume 4, *Plugging In*, examines rock's psychedelic period (ca. 1966–1968), which was marked by surreal lyrics and more elaborate (electric) instrumentation. Volume 5, *The Sounds of Soul*, focuses on the development of soul within the rock genre and features interviews and concert footage with James Brown, Ray Charles, Sam Cooke, Aretha Franklin, Marvin Gaye, Gladys Knight, Wilson Pickett, Otis Redding, Smokey Robinson, Bobby Womack, and many others. Volume 6, *My Generation*, revolves around the apotheosis of the hippie counterculture that was the 1969 Woodstock festival. Volume 7, *Guitar Heroes*, showcases the electric guitar as rock's quintessential instrument and surveys many of its greatest proponents: Les Paul (the inventor of the electric guitar), Chuck Berry, Eric

Clapton, Jimmy Page, Keith Richards, Duane Allman, Carlos Santana, Stevie Ray Vaughan, Mark Knopfler, and others. Volume 8, *The 70s: Have a Nice Decade*, covers the tumultuous 1970s, when rock morphed into a number of distinct subgenres: glam, gay-inflected rock theater, as practiced by David Bowie, the New York Dolls, Lou Reed, and so forth; reggae, the Afro-Caribbean pop music of Jamaica brought to the world by the great Bob Marley; heavy metal, a flamboyant amalgam of guitar histrionics and costume spectacle epitomized by Kiss; the mellifluous California pop sound of Fleetwood Mac; the soul-jazz fusion of Stevie Wonder; and so on. Volume 9, *Punk*, surveys the anarchistic punk phenomenon of the late 1970s through the raucous music of Iggy Pop, the Ramones, Patti Smith, the Sex Pistols, the Clash, and many others. Volume 10, *Up from the Underground*, deals with the birth of the Music Television (MTV) cable channel in August 1981, an event that irrevocably changed the face of rock 'n' roll. MTV videos emphasized the *spectacle* of the performance; the quality of the music (always a bit dubious) inevitably suffered. *Up from the Underground* also points out that, in its early stages, MTV ignored black music: a racist oversight soon corrected when MTV was forced to catch up with the immensely popular hip-hop phenomenon.

Festival Express (2003)

In 1970 two enterprising young concert promoters named Ken Walker and Thor Eaton arranged Festival Express, a five-day rock tour of Canada that began with shows in Toronto on June 27 and 28, proceeded to Winnipeg for a show on July 1, and ended in Calgary with shows on July 4th and 5th (a planned show in Montreal was canceled). Walker and Eaton assembled an impressive, eclectic array of talent—Janis Joplin, the Grateful Dead, the Band, Delaney & Bonnie & Friends, the Buddy Guy Blues Band, Ian and Sylvia, Eric Andersen, Tom Rush, the Flying Burrito Brothers, Mountain—and came up with the novel idea of chartering a private train to transport the performers from one venue to the next. Cinematographers Peter Biziou and Bob Fiore headed camera and sound crews that filmed the concerts and dozens of hours of behind-the-scenes footage of the musicians partying and jamming on the train as it wended its way west over 2,150 miles of Canadian countryside. Unfortunately, the concerts and the film did not materialize as planned. Eaton and Walker charged $14 for tickets to the various shows: exorbitant prices in 1970 that sparked angry protests and left venues half filled. With the tour a financial debacle Eaton Walker Associates, business partners Maclean Hunter Ltd., and film producers Gavin and Willem Poolman were forced to consign the movie to oblivion—until British filmmaker Bob Smeaton (*The*

Beatles Anthology) began, in the early 1990s, to locate the surviving 46 hours of raw footage in archives and garages. After almost a decade of painstaking restoration work, editing in the 1960s style (including split screen), and the filming of contemporary interviews with some of the surviving members of the tour, Smeaton unveiled *Festival Express* at the 2003 Toronto Film Festival, thirty-three years after the events depicted. A fascinating time capsule of a bygone era, *Festival Express* is particularly valuable for offering previous unseen glimpses of the great Janis Joplin, who died two months after the tour ended.

Punk (and Grunge) Rock

A brace of films appeared in the 1970s, 1980s, and 1990s that document and commemorate punk: the loud, raw, and angry rock style that countered mainstream rock's increasingly baroque and overproduced excesses. Punk was more than a reaction to rock's decline into bland, commercial decadence; it was, at base, a barbaric yawp against Western liberal capitalist society, a bitter denunciation of contemporary corporate hegemony and its attendant evils: rampant, soulless commercialism, economic stagnation, massive inequalities of power and wealth, cultural vapidity, and a general sociopolitical climate of disenfranchisement, alienation, and despair. Most of punk's adherents wielded no sophisticated political analysis; they only knew from lived experience that contemporary society was, in all ways, bankrupt.

Despite its relatively short life span and outré characteristics, punk is, cinematically, the most thoroughly documented pop music phenomenon. As film critic Alex Patterson notes, "The persistence of punk has been one of the remarkable art stories of the past quarter-century. Punk may be chaotic, it may be juvenile, but it must have something 'cause it just won't go away" (Patterson 2000). Three major documentaries on the punk music scene were released during its short tenure and immediate aftermath: Don Letts' *The Punk Rock Movie* (1978), Lech Kowalski's *D.O.A.* (1980), and Julien Temple's *The Great Rock 'n' Roll Swindle* (1980). Don Letts, Brixton-born son of black émigrés from Jamaica, began working as the disc jockey at London's Roxy in 1977: the venue where English punk was born the year before.

The Punk Rock Movie (1978)

Armed with an 8mm movie camera, Letts did extensive filming of punk acts on and behind stage at the Roxy (and would play reggae records between live sets).

Though not a technically polished film, *The Punk Rock Movie* is an indispensable historical record that showcases the Sex Pistols, Siouxie and the Banshees, Wayne County, Eater, Joe Strummer, Billy Idol, and others in the fleeting moment of their apotheosis. Martin Scorsese surprised and awed Letts by requesting a private screening.

D.O.A. (1980) and *The Great Rock 'n' Roll Swindle* (1980)

Kowalski's *D.O.A.* and Temple's *The Great Rock 'n' Roll Swindle* both center on England's most notorious punk band, the Sex Pistols. Kowalski's film focuses on the Sex Pistols' weird and disastrous U.S. tour (January 5–14, 1978) but also includes performance clips of X-Ray Spexs, Dead Boys, Generation X (with Billy Idol), Rich Kids (with former Sex Pistols' bassist, Glen Matlock), Sham 69, and Joe Strummer of the Clash. The film's high point may be a famous in-bed interview between Kowalski and Sex Pistols' bassist, Sid Vicious, and his repugnant girlfriend, Nancy Spungen (that satirically references the famous "bed-in" for peace of John Lennon and Yoko Ono at Amsterdam's Hilton Hotel in the spring of 1969). Though Temple's chaotic *The Great Rock 'n' Roll Swindle* shows little evidence of plot, it is built around the half-serious, half-mocking premise espoused by Sex Pistols manager, Malcolm McClaren (proprietor with Vivienne Westwood of *Sex*, a London fetish boutique), who steadfastly maintains that punk rock was a fraud he dreamed up to make "a million pounds." Appropriately anarchic filmmaking that is a jumbled mix of silly posturing, (simulated) sex and violence, remarkable concert footage, and strange animation, *Swindle*'s highlight is Sid Vicious' infamous rendition of the Frank Sinatra standard, "My Way," a brilliantly snide tour de force that makes a mockery of Sinatra's maudlin world weariness.

The Decline of Western Civilization (1981)

Penelope Spheeris's *The Decline of Western Civilization* (1981) documents seven punk bands—Alice Bag Band, Black Flag (featuring Henry Rollins), Catholic Discipline (including future lesbian folk-novelty singer, Phranc), the Circle Jerks, Fear, the Germs, and X—who played the Los Angeles nightclub circuit in late 1979, early 1980. Performance footage and interviews with band members and fans show that punk nihilism, Los Angeles style, is every bit as angry as the punk philosophy espoused on the East Coast or in the United Kingdom. What ultimately makes the L.A. punk scene especially unsettling is the absence of economic crisis and squalor that spawned punk in the first place; children of perennial sunshine, unheard-of affluence, and vapid Hollywood celebrity culture, most southern California punks owe their raison d'être not to the failures of Western business civilization but to its resounding, Orwellian success.

Another State of Mind (1983)

A more obscure and decidedly underrated punk documentary is Adam Small and Peter Stuart's *Another State of Mind* (1983). The cinematic record of a makeshift DIY (do it yourself) bus tour by two fledgling Los Angeles bands—Youth Brigade and Social Distortion—that covered some thirty North American cities in five weeks, *Another State of Mind* mixes raw performance footage with extensive interviews with punks and band members, especially Shawn Stern of Youth Brigade and Mike Ness of Social Distortion. Because the bands are obscure and the venues they play barely qualify as venues at all, *Another State* presents a truly ground-level perspective on the punk phenomenon in North America.

Sid and Nancy (1986)

Though grim, gripping, and sometimes hilarious, Alex Cox's docudrama *Sid and Nancy* (1986) is nonetheless a largely fanciful account of the doomed love affair between Sid Vicious (real name: John Simon Ritchie) of the Sex Pistols and an American groupie named Nancy Spungen. Possessed of no musical ability whatsoever, Sid Vicious was famous for being the archetypal punk—deeply cynical, casually violent, hedonistic in the extreme, and generally out of control. After the demise of the Sex Pistols in January 1978, Vicious and Spungen sank ever deeper into heroin addiction while sequestered at New York City's seedy Chelsea Hotel. On Thursday morning, October 12, 1978, Nancy Spungen was found dead, the victim of a stabbing very likely perpetrated by Sid Vicious. Rather than face the rigors of a trial for Nancy Spungen's murder, Sid (out on bail) committed suicide by heroin overdose on February 1, 1979.

In their screen acting debuts, Gary Oldman plays Sid and Chloe Webb plays Nancy with astonishing assurance and skill; even their physical resemblance to Sid and Nancy is nothing short of eerie. Unfortunately, the film as a whole does not quite match the excellence of its leads. While *Sid and Nancy* more or less accurately depicts the couple's self-destructiveness, the anarchic squalor and cheerful nihilism of the late-1970s London punk scene, and the stark horrors of heroin addiction, it constantly tends toward caricature and cartoon. For example,

Scene still from the movie Sid and Nancy, *a docudrama about the band the Sex Pistols. (Zenith-Initial/Goldwyn/The Kobal Collection)*

Johnny Rotten (real name: John Lydon), the founder of the Sex Pistols, is portrayed by Andrew Schofield as nothing more than a misanthropic dolt: a characterization highly resented by the real Lydon. Though his performance is undeniably superb, Gary Oldman's interpretation of Sid tends to both sensationalize and romanticize the late punk rocker. In the film Sid is almost always a violence-prone, posturing hooligan but contrary to fact he is never shown being violent toward Nancy. (In reality Sid beat her on a regular basis.) Chloe Webb's interpretation of Nancy Spungen as petulant, whining, and generally obnoxious is, by all accounts, accurate. Those who knew the real Nancy Spungen universally proclaim her as being the most troubled and reviled figure in the punk music scene on both sides of the Atlantic.

Sid and Nancy contains the usual number of factual errors, misrepresentations, and anachronisms. For example, Poly Styrene (lead singer of X-Ray Spex) is depicted as an emaciated white woman when she was, in fact, a light-skinned black woman of normal body type. Brightly dyed Mohawks abound in the film but the fashion only emerged after the Sex Pistols broke up. In one scene Sid watches Tom Snyder interview Johnny Rotten on TV: an event that did not occur until a year after Sid's death. These are small things. More egregious is the fact that *Sid and Nancy* seeks to have it both ways. In terms of content, it can pass as a film that grittily depicts the low-life decadence of the punk scene and the terrible consequences of drug abuse. At the same time, its tone is so jaunty, one cannot help but gather that this lifestyle must be great, good fun. Furthermore, *Sid and Nancy* does not give much credence to the *political* dimensions of the so-called "punk" movement in England: its class consciousness, its disgust with the decaying welfare state, its instinctive opposition to the Conservative backlash that would bring Margaret Thatcher to power in 1979. In sum, the sociopolitical context is reduced to mere ambience while Sid and Nancy are slyly glorified as cultural rebels when, in fact, they were pathetic, suicidal sociopaths.

Kurt and Courtney (1998)

A decade after their sordid deaths, the doomed love story of Sid and Nancy was at least partially reprised by West Coast grunge superstars Kurt Cobain and Courtney Love. But unlike Sid and Nancy, Kurt and Courtney were not comparably dysfunctional. Haunted by deep-seated emotional trauma that he self-medicated with heroin, Kurt Cobain steadily disintegrated while his feisty, competitive wife, Courtney Love, grew stronger and more assured. Cobain almost killed himself several times by overdose before he finally succeeded with a self-inflicted shotgun blast on April 5, 1994. After Cobain's suicide, many of his fans blamed Love for hastening, perhaps even *causing* his destruction. Always on the lookout for lurid subject matter, British documentary filmmaker Nick Broom-field put in his oar with *Kurt and Courtney* (1998), a history that advances the improbable notion that Courtney Love had her famous husband murdered. Though the film is not able to prove its conspiracy case against Love, it does suc-ceed in casting her in the worst possible light. Quite understandably, Courtney Love did everything in her power to have the film suppressed.

Born to Lose: The Last Rock and Roll Movie (1999)

Longtime punk aficionado Lech Kowalski finally followed up his 1980 documen-tary, *D.O.A.* with *Born to Lose: The Last Rock and Roll Movie* (1999), a docu-mentary biopic on the life and death of Johnny Thunders (real name: John Anthony Genzale Jr., 1952–1991). As a guitarist for the early 1970s glam group, the New York Dolls, Thunders emulated his hero, Keith Richards, and quickly became a protopunk legend for his remorselessly profane, nihilistic outlook and incessant use of alcohol, cocaine, and heroine. Indeed, Thunders is the direct link between glam and punk; Malcolm McClaren briefly managed the New York Dolls before formulating the Sex Pistols and obviously based his notion of what the Sex Pistols should be on Johnny Thunders' heedlessly self-destructive lifestyle. Another version of the artist-as-doomed-rebel narrative, *Born to Lose* is a deftly edited survey of Thunders' music career, his considerable influence on the punk movement, and an investigation into the circumstances of his ignomin-ious death—apparently due to methadone and alcohol poisoning—in a New Orleans hotel room on April 23, 1991.

The Filth and the Fury (2000)

Twenty years after Julien Temple made *The Great Rock 'n' Roll Swindle*, he reprised much of the same territory with *The Filth and the Fury* (2000), another documentary on the Sex Pistols using archival footage and interviews. The essen-tial difference between the two films is point of view. Made shortly after the Sex Pistols' dissolution as a group, *Swindle* was meant as a myth-deflating parody of a conventional rock hagiography. Malcolm McClaren's supposedly tongue-in-cheek version of events cast himself as puppet master and the Sex Pistols as his willing marionettes in an effort to throw fans off-balance and thus avoid the embarrassing adulation that had befallen other rock bands after breaking up.

Two decades having intervened, *Filth* is free to present a revisionist history of the group that contextualizes the rise of punk in England's moribund welfare state and lends much more agency to Johnny Rotten and his cohorts. The surviving members of the band, interviewed (somewhat pretentiously) in silhouette, reminisce about their brief moment in the limelight as genuine subversives who mocked the moribund English caste system and rocked its household gods.

Hype! (1996)

Practically dead by the beginning of the 1980s, punk rock in America was dramatically revitalized in Seattle, Washington, with the advent, circa 1986, of grunge music—an alternative rock subgenre that melded the music of punk and heavy metal and recombined their characteristic attitudes and styles: social anarchism, alienation, chronic drug use, tattered clothing, tattoos, dyed hair, and so on. In 1996, after grunge had been largely absorbed and tamed by the corporate media and music industry, first-time filmmakers Doug Pray (director) and Steve Helvey (producer) released *Hype!*, a documentary on the Seattle music scene that surveyed its rise, commercial and media co-optation, and fall, marked by the suicide of Nirvana's Kurt Cobain in 1994. *Hype!* is nothing if not thoroughgoing; it seems to cover *every* Seattle grunge band of any note. Performance clips, stills, and interviews showcase the usual suspects—Pearl Jam, Soundgarden, and Mudhoney—but also feature more obscure and frequently awful grunge bands with such colorful names as the Gits, Flop, Love Battery, 7 Year Bitch, Skin Yard, Green River, the Thrown Ups, Gas Huffer, Coffin Break, the Fastbucks, Screaming Trees, Tad, the Melvins, the Walkabouts, the Supersuckers, the Young Fresh Fellows, the Monomen, Seaweed, Zipgun, Crackerbash, Some Velvet Sidewalk, the Posies, Dead Moon, Hammerbox, and others. Though the interview patter is often vapid and pretentious and much of the music unintelligible noise, *Hype!* conveys the grassroots excitement of the Seattle scene before the corporate music machine took over.

Songs for Cassavetes (2001)

Shot in a sketchy, minimalist style using 16mm black-and-white film, Justin Mitchell's underground documentary, *Songs for Cassavetes* (2001), complements *Hype!* by presenting live performance clips of, and interviews with, ten West Coast "indie" punk bands: the Peechees, Henry's Dress, Sleater-Kinney, Further,

Tullycraft, Some Velvet Sidewalk, Dub Narcotic Sound System, the Hi-Fives, the Make-Up, and Unwound. The title is in homage to experimental filmmaker John Cassavetes (1929–1989), not because he had anything to do with punk music but because his work valorized spontaneity and emotional truth over commercial artifice.

Between Resistance and Community: The Long Island Do It Yourself Punk Scene (2002)

In stark contrast to the grungy West Coast punk scene explored by *Songs for Cassavetes, Between Resistance and Community: The Long Island Do It Yourself Punk Scene* (2002), a 44-minute documentary by Joe Carroll and Ben Holtzman, presents an East Coast punk subculture that is overwhelmingly white, male, upper middle class, and politically correct in all the requisite tenets of bourgeois liberalism (e.g., enlightened gender and racial attitudes, anticapitalist economics, and social responsibility). Indeed, despite their affinity for loud, formless music, the basement rockers in *Between Resistance* promulgate a progressive punk ethos that seems to owe more to the legacy of Robert Kennedy than Sid Vicious—a politico-cultural stance that is both refreshing in its guilelessness and problematic in its flirtation with hypocrisy.

End of the Century—The Story of the Ramones (2003)

Unbeknownst to most of the world, punk music was born on Saturday night March 30, 1974, when a leather-jacketed, mop-haired band from Forest Hills, Queens, called the Ramones played its first live show at the Performance Studio in New York City. That evening and from then on, the Ramones played extremely loud, fast, and crude three-chord rock 'n' roll—in marked contrast to the prevailing pop style, which was then becoming increasingly pretentious, over-orchestrated, and synthetic. The audience that first night was sparse but the Ramones soon garnered a cult following. Active from 1974 to 1996, the hardworking Ramones played 2,263 shows (100 shows a year), put out fourteen studio and five live albums, and inaugurated a new rock genre. Lack of radio airplay or a hit single kept them from achieving any significant degree of success. Lead vocalist Joey Ramone (real name: Jeffrey Hyman) died of lymphatic cancer less than a year before the Ramones were inducted into the Rock and Roll Hall of

Fame on March 18, 2002. Ramones bassist Dee Dee Ramone (real name: Douglas Colvin) died of a heroin overdose on June 5, 2002, and Johnny Ramone (real name: John Cummings) died of prostate cancer in 2004.

In the years following the Ramones' breakup, longtime punk rock enthusiasts (and first-time filmmakers) Jim Fields and Michael Gramaglia spared no effort in making *End of the Century—The Story of the Ramones* (2003), an intriguing and exhaustively detailed documentary that features the requisite rare photos, concert footage, and extensive interviews with the band members and their friends, family, fans, and rock music colleagues, most notably the late Joe Strummer (real name: John Graham Mellor) of The Clash, Debbie Harry of Blondie, Glen Matlock of the Sex Pistols, and Roderick "Legs" McNeil, coiner of the term "punk," cofounder of *Punk* magazine, and coeditor with Gillian McCain of *Please Kill Me: The Uncensored Oral History of Punk* (New York: Grove Press, 1996). *End of the Century* (titled after the Ramones' sixth studio album, released in 1980) bifurcates into two movements: the explosive emergence of the band in the 1970s and its long decline, marked by commercial failure, drug abuse, and a general falling out between band members heartily sick of the road and of each other. Though not a big commercial success, *End of the Century* garnered rave reviews from film critics.

Pop Singer Biopics

The Jolson Story (1946)

The first music biopic of the sound era was *The Jolson Story* (1946), a film about the first real pop star of the twentieth century, Al Jolson. Directed by Alfred E. Green and starring Larry Parks (later notorious as an HUAC informer) as young Jolson and Evelyn Keyes as Jolson's wife, film star Ruby Keeler, the decidedly upbeat *Jolson Story* features some sixteen of Jolson's greatest hits, dubbed by Jolson himself. Quite naturally for its time, the film glossed over Jolson's ethnicity (Lithuanian Jew), his egomania, and the political dubiousness of his choice of blackface persona. By the time this highly sanitized film biography came out, Jolson (real name: Asa Yoelson, 1886–1950) was in the twilight of his show business career. Though *The Jolson Story* briefly revived the singer's name and reputation and spawned a sequel, it was primarily a nostalgia piece for Jolson's heyday, the 1920s, a supposedly more celebratory and innocent time subsequently obliterated by the angry years of the Great Depression and apocalyptic events of World War II. Released just after the war, *The Jolson Story* can be seen as a quasi-ironic bid to forget recent horrors and pick up where the Jazz Age left off.

The Helen Morgan Story (1957)

Helen Morgan (real name: Helen Riggins, 1900–1941) emerged from a rural Illinois working-class background to become a Chicago cabaret singer, Ziegfeld Follies chorus girl, Broadway and Hollywood musical star, and a famous night club "torch singer" of romantic ballads (e.g., "Bill," "Can't Help Lovin' Dat Man," "The Man I Love") before alcoholism derailed her career and destroyed her health. She died of cirrhosis of the liver at the age of forty-one. Sixteen years after Morgan's death, Warner Bros. brought out *The Helen Morgan Story* (1957), a typically maudlin biopic of the era starring Ann Blyth (Veda in *Mildred Pierce;* vocals by Gogi Grant) as Helen Morgan and Paul Newman as Larry Maddux, a gunrunner and con man who was the love—and the torment—of Helen Morgan's life.

Lady Sings the Blues (1972)

The precipitous collapse of the 1960s counterculture marked a tailing off of independently produced direct cinema concert documentaries that briefly reigned as the predominant music film form. The return to pop culture business as usual was evident by 1972 when, for the first time since the late 1950s, Hollywood brought out a new music biopic: Sidney J. Furey's *Lady Sings the Blues*, an over-produced Diana Ross star vehicle loosely based on Billie Holiday's eponymous 1956 autobiography, written with professional ghostwriter, William F. Dufty (a book music critic John Bush describes as "notoriously apocryphal" [www. allmusic.com]). Diana Ross delivers a suitably gut-wrenching portrayal of Billie Holiday (real name: Eleanora Fagan Gough, 1915–1959) as a doomed drug addict and the film does manage to depict some of the salient events in the legendary jazz singer's tragic life: her rape at age ten, her life as a prostitute, her discovery as a singer, her bouts with racial bigotry, her chronic drug addiction, and her tragic death at the age of forty-four on July 17, 1959. As entertaining mythmaking, *Lady Sings the Blues* is a powerful albeit melodramatic experience. As music history and biography the film is very seriously flawed. Most of what is wrong with *Lady* can be attributed to screenwriters Chris Clark, Suzanne De Passe, and Terence McCloy, who rely too heavily on Holiday's often fanciful account of her own life. They make matters worse by casting her as a perpetual victim: a perspective that undercuts Holiday's existential responsibility for the life she lived. Equally problematic is the film's failure to keep the music central or to adequately contextualize Billie Holiday's life. Meaningful chronology is all but nonexistent and the larger history of midcentury jazz and the many great artists that Holiday worked with and was influenced by are simply absent from the story. That the film was initially overrated was soon made manifest by its failure to win any of the five Oscars for which it was nominated.

The Buddy Holly Story (1978)

In keeping with the retrospective temper of the times is *The Buddy Holly Story* (1978), a somewhat superficial but well-made biopic of early rock 'n' roll star, Charles Hardin "Buddy" Holly (1936–1959) of Lubbock, Texas. Holly died tragically in a plane crash in Iowa that also took the lives of pop stars Ritchie Valens and the Big Bopper (real name: Jiles Perry Richardson Jr.). Gary Busey plays Buddy Holly (and Busey commendably does his own singing) as the film traces Holly's meteoric rise to rock stardom in the late 1950s. Though *The Buddy Holly Story* follows the general contours of Holly's short life, it tends to unduly romanticize Holly while it depicts his sidemen—Jesse Charles and Ray Bob Simmons ("The Crickets")—as malicious, reactionary yahoos. Indeed, the entire thrust of the film seems to suggest that Holly was a visionary youth culture avatar who epitomized creativity, honesty, and cheerfulness at war with a racist, repressed, puritanical 1950s America. There is some truth to this characterization but not as much as the film would have its viewers believe.

La Bamba (1987)

The logical successor to *The Buddy Holly Story* was Luis Valdez's *La Bamba* (1987), a reverential biopic of late 1950s rock star, Ritchie Valens (real name: Ricardo Valenzuela, 1941–1959), who died in the plane crash in Iowa on February 3, 1959, that also took the lives of Buddy Holly and J. P. "Big Bopper" Richardson. A Mexican American from the Los Angeles suburb of Pacoima, Valens took up guitar at an early age and began to write songs and perform while still in high school. In 1957 Valens' first single, "Come on, Let's Go," proved to be a hit. In 1958 Valens released his second single, which contained "Donna"—a paean to his girlfriend Donna Ludwig—and "La Bamba," a traditional Latin tune sung entirely in Spanish to a more hard-edged rockabilly accompaniment. Both songs were huge hits and Valens was on his way to becoming a rock superstar when he died at the tender age of seventeen. Because Valens died so young, his career as a pop star spanned less than a year. Left with a paucity of narrative material, writer-director Luis Valdez was compelled to fill out his story by delineating, and inevitably exaggerating, the conflicted relationship between Valens (Lou Diamond-Philips) and his jealous and volatile stepbrother, Bob Morales (Esai Morales). Anxious to lionize Valens as the first Hispanic pop music idol, Valdez also exaggerates the extent of the poverty of the Valenzuela family. In reality, Valens' parents held factory jobs and did not work as migrant farm labor: a factual distortion obviously meant to underscore the miraculously steep trajectory of Valens' career and enhance the tragedy of his early death. Rags-to-riches clichés and inaccuracies notwithstanding, *La Bamba* was celebratory, tuneful (music by Los Lobos), and a palpable hit that reflected the emerging pride and cultural self-awareness of America's bourgeoning Hispanic population in the 1980s.

Great Balls of Fire! (1989)

The pop culture mythology of the 1950s as a halcyon time of innocent enthusiasms and cheerfully tuneful music also informed Jim McBride's tame, sanitized, and largely false *Great Balls of Fire!* (1989). A Hollywood docudrama about the notoriously debauched and sinister rocker, Jerry Lee Lewis, aka "The Killer," *Great Balls of Fire* is putatively based on an exposé of the same title by one of Lewis's wives. Lewis (played by Dennis Quaid) is suitably manic at the piano but the film slights his dark and dangerous side: another example of pat mythologizing in the service of nostalgia.

Madonna: Truth or Dare (1991)

Just after the end of the Reagan dispensation, pop diva Madonna launched her four-month Blond Ambition tour of Japan, Europe, and North America. Neophyte music video director Alex Keshihian joined her entourage and shot some 250 hours of color and black-and-white footage that was edited down to a 114-minute pseudodocumentary entitled *Madonna: Truth or Dare* (1991). In terms of cinematic style and approach, *Truth or Dare* is clearly modeled on D. A. Pennebaker's *Don't Look Back;* it purports to be a revealing, even unflattering, glimpse of a pop superstar at career apogee that mixes performance clips with behind-the-scenes cinema verité footage.

A comparison of the two films is, therefore, instructive. Though the presence of movie cameras in everyday situations undoubtedly prompted self-conscious performances on the part of Bob Dylan and his cohorts, Pennebaker's film had freshness and immediacy and really did seem to reveal more than Dylan wanted his public to know about him. Fortuitously timed, *Don't Look Back* also managed to capture an electrifying moment in American popular culture: when, for better or worse, the existentialist-outlaw sensibility of the Beats—drug-inspired, sexually liberated, outspoken, and intellectually iconoclastic—broke into mainstream youth consciousness via Dylan's charismatic influence. Keshihian's *Truth or Dare* attempts to *simulate* the same level of cinematic candor and cultural momentousness but smacks of sly contrivance. There are several reasons for this, not least of which is the fact that Madonna is no Bob Dylan. In his witty, allusive, lyrically complex songs, Dylan mounted a thoroughgoing critique of the repressive, hypocritical, and racist nature of corporate-capitalist America, a critique that was very much in tune with the restive spirit of the 1960s. Emerging in the smug, quiescent age of Reagan, when capitalist greed was fully, finally, and irrevocably emancipated, Madonna was and is essentially an updated edition of an old-fashioned showgirl relying on salaciousness, spectacle, and fancy choreography to dazzle impressionable preteens: a purveyor of show-biz glitter masquerading as a cultural rebel. *Truth or Dare* reveals Madonna Ciccone's insanely fierce ambition, ruthless careerism, and unquenchable thirst for public exposure: sociopathic traits very much in keeping with the corporatist agenda of personal success at all costs. Unfortunately, the film misses the opportunity to interrogate the sources of these dubious compulsions in Madonna's Detroit Italian American working-class roots.

The Doors (1991)

An odd complement to Madonna's vanity film is Oliver Stone's *The Doors* (1991), the third installment in his series of quasi-revisionist films on the history of the 1960s. The title of the film is misleading; it is not really about the notorious Los Angeles rock group but is actually a biopic that more narrowly focuses on the Doors' charismatic lead singer and creative force, James Douglas Morrison (1943–1971). In the space of six frenetic years, Jim Morrison morphed from a UCLA film school dropout to an internationally famous rock demigod to an alcohol-drug casualty to an enduring counterculture legend. As the film abundantly demonstrates, Stone's interest in Morrison is as an iconic rebel-artist and existential trickster figure who came to personify the apocalyptic adventurism of the late 1960s psychedelic era. Rendered with uncanny precision by look-alike Val Kilmer, Morrison comes off as a moody, willful, nihilistic loose canon—charming, menacing, and mystifying by turns. Reenactments of the Doors' concerts brilliantly capture an exciting aura of taboos being broken and are the film's strongest moments. The essential problem with Stone's film is that it concentrates almost exclusively on Morrison's holy fool stage persona, a point of view that merely reiterates the Morrison myth instead of dissecting it.

What's Love Got to Do with It (1993)

While Oliver Stone's *The Doors* sought to recapitulate the somewhat inflated myth of the 1960s as a time of visionary counterculture rebellion and demonic transcendence, Brian Gibson's powerful biopic, *What's Love Got to Do with It* (1993), reminded its audience that the 1960s was also an era of rampant male chauvinism. Based on Tina Turner's autobiography, *I, Tina* (with Kurt Loder, New York: William Morrow, 1986), *What's Love* follows Anna Mae Bullock's (Angela Bassett) arduous and sometimes harrowing evolution from dirt-poor sharecropper origins in Nutbush, Tennessee, to her eventual rise to international pop superstardom. Inevitably, the film's central focus is on Tina Turner's horrendously traumatic sixteen-year marriage to Ike Turner (Laurence Fishburne), the talented rhythm and blues musician who discovered her and made her famous but also turned out to be a violent, paranoid cocaine addict, shameless philanderer, and a cruelly abusive husband. As the film shows, Tina finally left Ike in 1974 and divorced him two years later. Turner struggled as a solo artist until her career began to turn around in 1980 when she acquired Roger Davies (one of the film's coproducers) as her manager. At the age of forty-five, Tina Turner made the most celebrated comeback in pop music history with her best-selling and multiple Grammy-winning album, *Private Dancer* (1984).

Ike and Tina Turner performing at the Olympia Theater in Paris, November 30, 1975. (Richard Melloul/Sygma/Corbis)

Turner's inspiring story of suffering, survival, and ultimate triumph was already well known when she wrote her memoir; given her enormous popularity, the book's adaptation to film was almost inevitable. What was not a foregone conclusion was the quality of the movie, which boasted fine acting, great music, hyperkinetic stage performances, and a gripping narrative. In the final analysis, *What's Love Got to Do with It* makes an especially telling comparison to *Lady Sings the Blues*. A product of the early 1970s, *Lady* seems to accept woman's victimization as a tragic fact of life, only redeemed by the dubious consolation of posthumous secular sainthood. *What's Love* revels in woman's resilience, strength, and independence: a clear barometer of the positive cultural effects of the feminist movement in the years intervening between the two films.

Selena (1997)

Of a similarly affirmative character, despite the tragic fate of its subject, is Gregory Nava's biopic, *Selena* (1997). When she was shot to death by hanger-on Yolanda Salvidar on March 31, 1995, twenty-three-year-old Tejano singer, Selena Quintanilla-Perez, was on the verge of crossing over into mainstream pop superstardom. Ironically, Selena's murder brought her the widespread notoriety that she had not yet achieved in life. For Latinos throughout the Americas, Selena's death was a cataclysmic event, comparable to the 1980 death of John Lennon for Anglo-American rock fans. Distinguished writer-director Nava (*El Norte* [1983] and *My Family/Mi Familia* [1995]) could have made a woman's version of *La Bamba*, emphasizing the seemingly foreordained but still terribly tragic loss of a young, promising talent. Instead, he chose to make a Latin rags-to-riches American dream saga. Consequently, *Selena* (with a decidedly mediocre Jennifer Lopez in the title role) is a cheerfully sanitized hagiography that fails to avoid ethnic stereotypes and show business clichés while it pays scant attention to Selena's grittier side, practically ignores Yolanda Salvidar, and only notes the singer's death symbolically. The film's somewhat smarmy tone comes from its quasi-official status (its executive producer was Selena's father, Abraham Quintanilla) and its ideological function as a point of pride for Latinos struggling to achieve their own American dream.

The Cream Will Rise (1998)

Darker and ultimately more disturbing than Selena's poignant saga is Gigi Gaston's *The Cream Will Rise* (1998), a documentary biopic about controversial pop percussionist and singer-songwriter Sophie B. Hawkins. Starting out as a filmic record of Hawkins' 1996 "Moxie Tour," *Cream* soon becomes an intensive and sometimes uncomfortably revealing character study that showcases Hawkins' troubled psyche, her dysfunctional family rife with rumors of abuse, her inchoate sexuality, and her free-spirited but ultimately simpleminded bohemian ideology. Having intended to capture on film a wild, wise, New Age artiste-savant, Gigi Gaston (Hawkins' manager) inadvertently reveals a rather loosely strung, shallow, and self-involved prima donna who exhibits a flamboyant narcissism that puts Madonna to shame. On a technical level, Gaston's film suffers from formlessness and a sense of arbitrariness that soon becomes tiresome.

Beyond the Sea (2004)

In the works since the mid-1980s, a biopic about pop singer Bobby Darin (real name: Walden Robert Cassotto, 1936–1973) finally began to come to fruition once the Oscar-winning actor Kevin Spacey acquired the film rights to the Darin saga in the year 2000. An extremely self-assured, ambitious, and versatile artist in his own right, Spacey evidently identified with Darin's legendary ambition, versatility, and self-assurance. Some of his contemporaries considered Bobby Darin arrogant but one could argue that his alleged egotism was the very force that enabled Darin to overcome childhood illness and poverty. Whatever the darker truths of Darin's rise to pop stardom, Kevin Spacey chose to focus on Darin's indomitable will and show business resiliency. Throwing himself into every aspect of his vanity project's production, Spacey cowrote the movie, called *Beyond the Sea* (with Lewis Colick), directed it, and starred in it.

Beyond the Sea (2004) concentrates on Darin's fifteen-year career as a popular singer and film star (1958–1973). Born to a recently widowed mother living in poverty in Brooklyn during the Great Depression, Robert Cassotto was eight years old in 1944 when he contracted rheumatic fever, an autoimmune disease brought on by strep throat that damages the heart valves. Well aware that he was likely to die young, Cassotto developed a passion for music and a powerful determination to achieve a kind of immortality through fame. After changing his name to Bobby Darin in 1956, Darin had a number of hit records in the late 1950s and early 1960s (e.g., "Splish Splash," "Dream Lover," "Mack the Knife" from Kurt Weill's *Threepenny Opera*, "Beyond the Sea"). In 1960 Darin embarked on a successful film career and also married the Hollywood starlet, Sandra Dee. The marriage lasted until 1967 and produced a son, Dodd. In the late 1960s Darin groped toward a new professional and personal identity. He continued to make mainstream commercial films and records and played Las

Vegas lounges but also composed and recorded folk music and became avowedly more political after the assassination of Robert Kennedy in the summer of 1968. Unfortunately, Darin's quest for a more resolved identity was cut short by his death on December 20, 1973, immediately following heart valve replacement surgery in Los Angeles.

In the film Kevin Spacey does all his own singing and dancing, is gracefully adept at both, and his impersonation of Bobby Darin is frequently uncanny. Despite Spacey's considerable strengths as a performer, *Beyond the Sea* is marred by an episodic structure, a somewhat hackneyed script, and stagy musical extravaganzas that border on a kind of sophisticated self-parody. As numerous film critics were avid to point out, Spacey was simply too old—forty-four at the time of shooting in the winter of 2003–2004—to convincingly play Darin from the ages of twenty-two to thirty-seven. Costing some $24 million to make, *Beyond the Sea* only managed to generate one-fourth that amount in box office receipts. Reviews were likewise halfhearted.

Ray (2004)

Ray Charles (real name: Charles Ray Robinson, 1930–2004) overcame blindness, abject poverty, childhood trauma, racism, and drug addiction to assume the mantel of one of the leading lights in American popular music in the second half of the twentieth century. Nicknamed "the genius" by Frank Sinatra, the innovative singer-composer-pianist blended gospel, blues, jazz, big band, even country and western into a distinctive personal style that sold millions of records and earned him numerous chart hits and a dozen Grammy Awards. Though he was once a drug addict and philanderer, Ray Charles was ultimately held in high public esteem by virtue of his disability, extraordinary talent, and a genuinely ebullient personality.

In 1987 producer-director Taylor Hackford (*An Officer and a Gentleman; Dolores Claiborne*) secured the film rights to Ray Charles' story (*Brother Ray: Ray Charles' Own Story*, co-written by Ray Charles and David Ritz, New York: Dial Press, 1978) but was not able to interest a major studio in making the film. In the late 1990s Hackford obtained financial backing from Ray Charles Jr. and two high-powered Hollywood producer couples—Howard and Karen Baldwin and Stuart and Elise Benjamin—and was finally able to go ahead with production. With financial support coming from the Charles family and Ray Charles actively involved in the project as a consultant, *Ray* (2004) needs to be considered a quasi-official biography. Indeed, Hackford's screenwriter, James L. White

(*The Better Half; The Bo Jackson Story*), fashioned a politically correct script that acknowledges Charles' well-known shortcomings but is so adulatory and upbeat overall that audiences were more than happy to accept the film's version of Ray Charles' life at face value. Another major factor in the critical and popular success of *Ray* was the luminous, Oscar-winning performance of Jamie Foxx (*Ali; Collateral*) as Ray Charles. Though he did screen a final edit of the film, Ray Charles did not live to see his apotheosis in public release; he died of liver failure at the age of seventy-three on June 10, 2004, during the postproduction phase of the film, which had its premier at the Toronto Film Festival three months later.

Folk Music

Bound for Glory (1976)

Celebrating the nation's bicentennial from a grassroots, populist viewpoint was Hal Ashby's film version of folk legend Woody Guthrie's 1943 autobiography, *Bound for Glory* (1976). The most significant folksinger-songwriter of his era, Guthrie (1912–1967) was young Bob Dylan's main role model for the archetypal American rebel-artist. A rambling folk minstrel, leftist radical, and chronicler of the Great Depression, Guthrie wandered the Texas-Oklahoma dust bowl and wrote about the terrible injustices done to displaced farmers reduced to penury and homelessness, hardships they managed to survive through an instinctive class solidarity and enormous resilience that was cultivated over generations of struggle. Though they tone down Guthrie's politics, Hal Ashby, his screenwriter, Robert Getchell, and his lead actor, David Carradine, manage to capture a good deal of Guthrie's humanity, passion, complexity, and musical genius. Likewise, Ashby's cinematographer, the great Haskell Wexler, brilliantly evoked the desolate beauty of 1930s America and was rewarded with his second career Oscar. Dealing with only the last half of the 1930s, neither book nor film conveyed much about Woody Guthrie's life as a whole but biography was not the principal aim of either work.

Leadbelly (1976)

Covering much the same locale and time period from a black perspective is Gordon Parks' little-known biopic, *Leadbelly* (1976), starring Roger E. Mosley in the title role. Huddie Ledbetter, aka "Leadbelly" (1889–1949), was a hugely talented

African American folk-blues artist (author of "Goodnight, Irene," "Bourgeois Blues," and other classics) whose chaotic life included an apprenticeship with Blind Lemon Jefferson and assault and murder convictions for which he served a total of twelve years in Texas and Louisiana chain gangs in the 1920s and 1930s. Once pardoned on the strength of his musical abilities, Leadbelly was discovered in Louisiana's notorious Angola Penitentiary by John A. Lomax (1867–1948), the celebrated ethnomusicologist who spent his life collecting and preserving folk music for the Library of Congress. A psychologically astute and well-made film on an American icon, *Leadbelly* never found much of an audience—most probably due to the prevailing racial politics.

The Weavers: Wasn't That a Time (1982)

Michael Apted's excellent Loretta Lynn biopic, *Coal Miner's Daughter* (1980), unwittingly helped, in its own small way, to usher in the right-wing hyper-Americanism of the Reagan dispensation by contributing to the valorization of southern white "redneck" culture. Conversely, Jim Brown's concert documentary, *The Weavers: Wasn't That a Time* (1982), flew in the face of Reaganism by celebrating a folk group that had fallen victim to anticommunist blacklisting in the early 1950s: a witchhunt that then Screen Actor's Guild (SAG) president Ronald Reagan enthusiastically supported. The Weavers (Ronnie Gilbert, Lee Hays, Fred Hellerman, and Pete Seeger) were at the height of their popularity in the summer of 1950 when they were denounced by the anticommunist journal, *Red Channels*. Subsequently put under surveillance by the FBI, the group began to lose radio airplay, record distribution, and concert bookings. At the end of 1952 they were forced to disband. Despite successful Carnegie Hall reunion concerts in 1955, 1960, and 1963, the Weavers sank into obscurity and would have remained all but unknown to a new generation of folk music enthusiasts but for Brown's adulatory documentary. Narrated by Lee Hays (who died soon thereafter), the film intersperses clips from two Carnegie Hall farewell concerts in November 1980 with interviews that establish the Weavers' history and political identity, the implications of which could hardly be lost on a Reagan-era audience.

The Ballad of Ramblin' Jack (2000)

Aiyana Elliott's absorbing documentary, *The Ballad of Ramblin' Jack* (2000), sketches out the life of her father, Ramblin' Jack Elliott, an underappreciated but pivotal figure in modern American folk music. Elliott Charles Adnopoz was born in Brooklyn on August 1, 1931, the eldest son of Flossie and Dr. Abraham Adnopoz, both of whom wanted their son to follow in his father's respectable footsteps and become a physician. After attending a rodeo featuring Gene Autry at Madison Square Garden in 1940, Elliott began a lifelong love affair with the romantic image of the footloose cowboy. At the age of fourteen Elliott ran away from home and joined the Colonel Jim Eskew Ranch Rodeo, working as a horse groomer for $2 a day. During his three-month stint with the rodeo, Elliott began to learn guitar. His western idyll terminated by his anxious parents, Elliott returned to Linden Boulevard in Brooklyn where he continued to practice guitar and learn cowboy folk songs. Hearing Woody Guthrie sing on the radio in 1950, Elliott immediately recognized Guthrie as the very embodiment of the wandering cowboy–folk hero that he aspired to be. His own rambling cut short by the onset of Huntington's chorea, a degenerative nerve disorder, Guthrie had settled with his family in nearby Coney Island. Elliott visited his new idol, even lived with him for a time, and the two developed a very close mentor-acolyte relationship with Elliott imitating Guthrie's every twang and mannerism. By the mid-1950s Elliott had become a wandering folk minstrel and raconteur, making a subsistence living with an endless succession of one-night appearances in towns all over North America and Europe. Living in New York's Greenwich Village in the early 1960s, Elliott acquired a young protégé named Bob Dylan who imitated him the way he had imitated Woody Guthrie a decade before. Dylan went on to international superstardom, leaving Jack Elliott in obscurity. Never particularly focused or ambitious, Elliott remained an unsung hero of folk music—at least until the 1990s, when he finally won a Grammy (for Best Traditional Folk Album in 1995) and a National Medal of the Arts, bestowed by President Clinton in 1998.

Daughter of Elliott by his fourth wife, Martha, Aiyana Elliott saw little of her elusive father when she was growing up. A graduate student at New York University's prestigious film school, Aiyana Elliott made a half-hour biopic about her father that she expanded into a feature-length film that was two years in the making. Switching between archived concert footage; present-day interviews with her father, the family, and friends (including Dave Van Ronk and Arlo Guthrie); and cinema verité footage of Ramblin' Jack on the road in his RV, Elliott's *Ballad* combines a conventional compilation-interview documentary with a quest film about her (ultimately futile) attempts to actually sit down and have a real conversation with her father. The net result is a highly informative film about Ramblin' Jack Elliott's place in folk music history and a poignant assessment of his pathological inability to get or stay close to his loved ones. Premiering at the Sundance Film Festival on January 26, 2000, *The Ballad of Ramblin' Jack* won the Special Jury Prize for Artistic Achievement.

Country and Western

Coal Miner's Daughter (1980)

Shot in 1979 and released in February 1980, Michael Apted's *Coal Miner's Daughter* is on the cusp of two decades and two divergent sensibilities. It is most assuredly a product of the 1970s, when hardscrabble working-class authenticity enjoyed a brief vogue in Hollywood (e.g., *Bound for Glory; Norma Rae*). At the same time *Coal Miner's Daughter* is essentially a rags-to-riches saga that presaged the emerging Reagan era's strenuous revival of the American dream ideology of upward mobility supposedly based on hard work, persistence, and true grit. Adapting Loretta Lynn's best-selling autobiography, *Coal Miner's Daughter* (1976, cowritten with George Vecsey), Michael Apted and screenwriter Thomas Rickman opted to stay close to their source material and make a generally accurate film about Lynn's hard life, rather than focus more centrally on the music, as many biopics of musicians tend to do. Starring Sissy Spacek as Loretta (Webb) Lynn and Tommy Lee Jones as her husband, Doolittle "Doo" Lynn, the film chronicles Lynn's dirt-poor origins in Butcher Holler, Kentucky, marriage at age thirteen, teenage motherhood, her early career singing in honky-tonk bars, her rise to stardom in the 1960s, her close friendship with Patsy Cline (played by Beverly D'Angelo in the film), her problems with fame and drug abuse, and her eventual

Sissy Spacek plays country singer Loretta Lynn in Coal Miner's Daughter, *1980. (Bettmann/Corbis)*

nervous breakdown onstage (an incident ridiculed in Robert Altman's film, *Nashville*). One of the better biopics, *Coal Miner's Daughter* was nominated for seven Academy Awards and won an Oscar for Sissy Spacek as Best Actress in a Leading Role.

Sweet Dreams (1985)

The logical, though not entirely necessary, complement to *Coal Miner's Daughter* appeared five years later: Karel Reisz's *Sweet Dreams* (1985), a solid if somewhat tepid biopic about Loretta Lynn's chief rival and close friend, country and western diva, Patsy Cline (1932–1963). Written by *Bound for Glory* screenwriter, Robert Getchell, *Sweet Dreams* is less ambitious in scope than its counterpart, chronicling only the last seven or eight years of Cline's life: a narrative approach that necessarily eschews the rags-to-riches trajectory of *Coal Miner's Daughter*. Instead, *Sweet Dreams* chooses to foreground Patsy Cline's (Jessica Lange) turbulent relationship with her husband, Charlie Dick (Ed Harris) and includes an apocryphal affair with her manager, Randy Hughes (David Clennon). Inexplicably, Getchell's script entirely omits Cline's friendship with Loretta Lynn.

Classical Music

Lisztomania (1975)

Ken Russell's *Lisztomania* (1975) was an attempt to transform or at least camouflage the garish banality of 1970s pop music by opting for an historical subject through which to express that sensibility. An obscenely phantasmagoric rock-opera parody of the life of the Hungarian Romantic composer-pianist Franz Liszt (1811–1886), *Lisztomania* was Russell's hurried attempt to reiterate the huge commercial success he had with *Tommy* (1975), a somewhat insipid but lively film version of The Who's rock opera. Unfortunately for Russell and his cohorts, lightning did not strike twice; *Lisztomania*, starring The Who's lead singer, Roger Daltry (who had also starred in *Tommy*), proved to be an artistic atrocity, box office flop, and perhaps the most wildly and egregiously inaccurate music biopic ever made. The only remotely true information conveyed about Liszt was his enormous popularity as a young pianist and his later friendship with Richard Wagner. In sum, *Lisztomania* said much more about Ken Russell's bombastic tendencies and the weirdly decadent zeitgeist of the 1970s than it said about nineteenth-century European Romanticism.

Amadeus (1984)

In America, where classical music has a small audience, Milos Forman achieved a near-impossible feat with his film, *Amadeus* (1984). Forman managed to make a biopic about the great German composer, Wolfgang Amadeus Mozart (1756–1791) that was hugely popular. Adapted from the Peter Shaffer play of the same name, *Amadeus* approaches the life of Mozart through the viewpoint of a Mozart contemporary, the Vienna court composer, Antonio Salieri (1750–1825). The historical record indicates that Salieri (F. Murray Abraham in the film) and Mozart (played by Tom Hulce) were friendly rivals but legend has it that Salieri, jealous of Mozart's musical genius, murdered him. Nikolay Rimsky-Korsakov's 1897 opera, *Mozart and Salieri* (libretto by the poet Aleksandr Pushkin), institutionalized the entirely speculative murder theory. Peter Shaffer's 1979 Royal National Theatre production, *Amadeus*, further ratified the myth, and Forman's film version of the hit play turned the myth into incontrovertible fact for millions of viewers who came to the film with no prior knowledge of Mozart or Salieri. The truth of the matter is that Mozart probably died of renal failure. Likewise, Salieri's depiction in opera, play, and film versions as a frustrated mediocrity is fatuous; he was, in fact, highly respected in his day and numbered among his pupils Beethoven, Schubert, Czerny, and even one of Mozart's sons.

Thirty Two Short Films about Glenn Gould (1993)

Legendary classical pianist Glenn Gould (1932–1982) was a musical genius and something of an odd duck who, for example, wore a scarf, gloves, and overcoat in the summer. Not one to indulge in the trappings of jet-set celebrity, Gould lived a quiet, semireclusive life in his native Toronto. He never married. After nine highly successful years (1955–1964) on the international concert circuit, Gould unceremoniously retired from live performance to concentrate on studio recording and pursue other interests including writing, composing, and conducting. Over the course of a twenty-seven-year recording career, Gould made some seventy classical recordings. Bach and Beethoven were his favorite composers but he also recorded works by Brahms, Chopin, Debussy, Haydn, Liszt, Mozart, Prokofiev, Schoenberg, Schumann, Sibelius, Wagner, and many others. His most famous and popular recordings were Bach's *Goldberg Variations* (1955 and 1981 versions), now widely regarded as definitive.

A decade after Gould's death from a stroke in October 1982, Barbara Willis Sweete and Larry Weinstein—Canadian film producers who specialize in music topics—presented François Girard's *Thirty Two Short Films about Glenn Gould*

(1993), a series of brief (1- to 6-minute) vignettes in imitation of the structure of the thirty-two *Goldberg Variations*. Written by François Girard and actor-writer Don McKellar and starring Colm Feore as Glenn Gould, *Thirty Two Short Films* sketches aspects of Gould's personality through abstract, symbolic representations and docudrama-like re-creations of Gould at the recording studio or just going about his daily life. As quirky and accomplished as its subject, *Thirty Two Short Films* is a fitting commemoration to the greatest classical pianist of the twentieth century.

Immortal Beloved (1994)

Perhaps inspired by Milos Forman's tour de force on Mozart, young English writer-director Bernard Rose made *Immortal Beloved* (1994), an ambitious biopic about the world's greatest composer, Ludwig van Beethoven (1770–1827). Having assayed the most ridiculous figure in music history (Sid Vicious), Gary Oldman also opted to play the most sublime. Oldman's moving interpretation of Beethoven as an arrogant, irascible, half-mad, lonely genius with an eye for the ladies may be historically accurate but the film's rendition of his life is highly speculative and sometimes hard to follow, given a flashback-within-flashback structure. Adopting the investigative device used by Orson Welles for *Citizen Kane*, *Immortal Beloved* sets Beethoven's secretary, Anton Schindler (Jeroen Krabbe), the task of solving the mystery of the person addressed as "immortal beloved" by Beethoven in a letter that Schindler discovered after his master's death: a narrative trope that allows Rose to explore Beethoven, the man, versus Beethoven, the world historical figure.

Shine (1996)

Less ambitious in scope but more successful dramatically—and vastly more popular—was Scott Hicks's *Shine* (1996), a heavily fictionalized biopic about David Helfgott (Geoffrey Rush), a once-gifted classical pianist from Australia whose budding concert career was derailed by schizophrenia. Intentionally or not, the narrative model for Jan Sardi's screenplay seems to have been Robert Mulligan's *Fear Strikes Out* (1957), a biopic about baseball star Jimmy Piersall, who suffered a nervous breakdown after having allegedly been pushed too hard to succeed by his father. *Shine* disingenuously posits the same etiology for David Helfgott's psychotic break but, according to Helgott's sister, Margaret (*Out of Tune: David Helfgott and the Myth of "Shine"* with Tom Gross, New York: Warner

Books, 1998), David's father, Peter Helfgott (Armin Mueller-Stahl in the film), did not beat, terrorize, or otherwise exert undue pressure on his son. Nor was the elder Helfgott a concentration camp survivor. According to family members, David Helfgott was an introverted and somewhat spoiled child who became arrogant and egotistical in his teens. The mental illness that had its onset in 1970 when Helfgott was twenty-three years old was hereditary schizophrenia and had nothing at all to do with pathological family interactions. In the same vein, the film grossly exaggerates David Helfgott's subsequent isolation and creative impoverishment. During the decade Helfgott was in and out of institutions and halfway houses, he had access to a piano and continued to play and even perform locally. Furthermore, Helfgott's family was actually supportive and caring, as were a host of mental health professionals. The film cleverly distorts the biographical reality in all these ways in order to enlist maximum audience identification and sympathy. Helfgott's victimhood is underscored and idealized, as is the redemptive love of his second wife, Gillian (Lynn Redgrave), a professional astrologer. Indeed, Helfgott's first wife is expunged from the movie.

Unaware of these serious falsifications at its core, critics and audiences embraced the film as a life-affirming, inspirational example of the triumph of the human spirit over adversity, especially the pernicious influence of bad patriar-

British actress Lynn Redgrave (left) is seen with Australian actor Geoffrey Rush (center) and director Scott Hicks (right) at a party after the annual Golden Globe Awards in Beverly Hills, January 20, 1997. (Reuters/Corbis)

chal parenting, a staple target of the 1990s pop psychology zeitgeist. An unalloyed critical success, *Shine* was also a major international hit, returning its makers their $5.5 million production investment at least tenfold. Following suit, Hollywood gave the film its imprimatur by awarding Geoffrey Rush the 1997 Oscar for Best Actor in a Leading Role (although, ironically, he was only on-screen for 30 of the film's 105 minutes). In the wake of *Shine*'s success, the film's soundtrack became a top ten *Billboard* hit, prompting David Helfgott to release CDs and go on a highly lucrative worldwide Shine Tour primarily patronized by first-time classical music concertgoers who were captivated by the movie. Helfgott's wife Gillian also got in on the act with a movie tie-in memoir, *Love You to Bits and Pieces* (New York: Penguin Books, 1997). But the power of cinema to mythologize quickly boomeranged on Helfgott. His concert appearances made it painfully obvious that the film had softened the symptoms of his madness—he sang, grunted, and loudly talked to himself onstage—while wildly exaggerating his musical skills. Mortified by the crass spectacle of a mentally ill person playing classical piano badly to sellout audiences who knew little or nothing about good piano technique, music critics universally panned Helfgott's performances and some journalists called into question the ethics of his handlers for staging a kind of upscale freak show.

Hilary and Jackie (1998)

No doubt the success of *Shine* set the stage for Anand Tucker's *Hilary and Jackie* (1998), a film that traces the complex and emotionally fraught relationship between world-class cellist, Jacqueline Du Pré (1945–1987, played by Emily Watson), and her sister, Hilary (Rachel Griffiths), a somewhat mediocre flautist. The psychological premise of the film is undoubtedly true but also very much in keeping with popular preconceptions of the artist: that genius is a sublime gift but also a kind of madness in that it demands so much that the happiness experienced by ordinary people must be forsaken. Ironically, Hilary is jealous of her sister's extraordinary talent but Jackie is envious of her sister's contented personal life, so much so that she eventually abandons the international recital circuit and leaves her famous composer-pianist husband, Daniel Barenboim (James Frain), to live with Hilary and her husband, Kiffer Finzi (David Morrisey), whom both sisters share—a controversial disclosure in book and film that cast doubt on the intentions of Hilary and Piers Du Pré. Fortunately, the superb acting of Emily Watson and Rachel Griffiths redeem the film's tabloid elements. *Hilary and Jackie* remains a moving tribute to a troubled and tragic artist.

7

Art History on Film and Television

F ilms dealing with famous or merely notorious artists almost invariably reproduce the long-standing cultural cliché of the artist as tormented genius/madman: an image perhaps best epitomized by Vincent van Gogh. The popular viewpoint romanticizes the artist as an exceptional human being but also reinforces the alienation, even revulsion, the public feels toward such odd, cryptic personalities who sin against bourgeois proprieties with their bohemian ways and frequently unconventional sex lives. In sum, the filmic artist biography almost always has an element of titillation and spectacle.

A major progenitor of the tortured artist ideology was Irving Stone (1903–1989), the inventor and acknowledged master of the biographical novel and one of the original creators and chief popularizers of the now-fashionable "art novel." Over a writing career that spanned more than half a century, Stone wrote long, exhaustively researched, richly detailed, sometimes melodramatic biographical novels that attempted to blend fact and speculation about such diverse figures as Vincent van Gogh, Jack London, Michelangelo, Eugene V. Debs, Charles Darwin, Sigmund Freud, and Camille Pissarro. Two of his most famous and popular biographical novels—*Lust for Life* (London: Longman's, Green & Co., 1934) and *The Agony and the Ecstasy* (New York: Doubleday, 1961)—on van Gogh and Michelangelo, respectively, were made into successful feature films.

Lust for Life (1956)

In the mid-1950s venerated stage and film actor-producer John Houseman sold M-G-M on a film version of Stone's twenty-year-old van Gogh book. Adapted for the screen by Norman Corwin and directed by Vincente Minelli (*An American in Paris*) with uncredited help by George Cukor (*The Philadelphia Story*), *Lust for Life* (1956) starred Kirk Douglas (*Ace in the Hole*) as Vincent van Gogh (1853–1890), the manic-depressive genius who produced some of the greatest paintings and drawings of the modern era before dying of a self-inflicted gunshot wound at the age of thirty-seven. Irving Stone based his mostly accurate book on van Gogh's letters to his beloved brother, Theo (James Donald in the film). To ensure authenticity, Stone visited all the places where van Gogh lived and worked. Likewise, Vincente Minelli shot *Lust for Life* at all the actual locations in southern France, Belgium, and the Netherlands and even featured many of van Gogh's actual paintings. Book and film faithfully present the salient features of Vincent van Gogh's life, but while Kirk Douglas, with beard and red dyed hair, bears a remarkable resemblance to van Gogh, Douglas's emphatic acting style, strapping physique, and hypermasculine action star screen persona were somewhat at odds with van Gogh's more fragile and troubled nature. Nonetheless, Douglas was nominated for an Academy Award and his costar, Anthony Quinn, won the Best Supporting Actor Oscar for his rendition of van Gogh's friend, Paul Gauguin (1848–1903). As only Hollywood cinema could, *Lust for Life* brought van Gogh to the masses.

The Agony and the Ecstasy (1965)

Not long after the publication of Irving Stone's best-selling *The Agony and the Ecstasy*, British producer-director Sir Carol Reed (*The Third Man*) mounted a lavish epic film version written by Philip Dunne (*How Green Was My Valley*) and starring Charlton Heston as Michelangelo Buonarroti (1475–1564); Rex Harrison as Pope Julius II, the "Warrior Pope" (1443–1513); and Diane Cilento as the Contessina de Medici (?–1515). While Stone's book dealt with Michelangelo's entire life, the film mostly focuses on his famous commission to paint religious frescoes on the ceiling of the Vatican's Sistine Chapel, which took nearly five years (1508–1512), sorely trying the patience of Pope Julius, but resulted in one of the world's great works of art.

The problem facing Philip Dunne and Carol Reed was how to make an exciting film about a man painting a ceiling. The solution they came up with had a number of components. First, *The Agony and the Ecstasy* (1965) plays up what was a very real clash of wills between Michelangelo, who was reluctant to take on the project, and Pope Julius, who insisted he do it. Second, to minimize the inevitably static nature of the Sistine Chapel scenes, the filmmakers crosscut between them and furious battle scenes of the pope's wars to repel foreign invaders and unite Italy's disparate city-states under the papacy. A third and obvious element was to dazzle viewers with the pomp and splendor of Renaissance

Creation of the Sun, Moon, and Planets *by Renaissance artist Michelangelo. In a detail from the Sistine Chapel, Michelangelo depicts God as the sole creator of the universe. (Web Gallery of Art)*

Italy. Filmgoers who had just seen Rex Harrison play Professor Henry Higgins in George Cukor's *My Fair Lady* (1964) might have noticed that his role as Pope Julius II was analogous—that of the haughty patron struggling to impose his will on a recalcitrant protégé. (In his mid-fifties Harrison was considerably younger than Pope Julius during Michelangelo's Sistine Chapel project and bore no resemblance to him whatsoever; a 1512 portrait of the pope by Raphael shows a gaunt, careworn pontiff with a white beard who looks even older than his sixty-nine years.) Along with making the pope a more virile figure, *The Agony and the Ecstasy* did much the same for Michelangelo. Or at least it sidestepped the issue of Michelangelo's sexuality by suggesting that his disinterest in the smitten Contessina de Medici could be attributed to his obsession with his art. Simply put, the resolutely heterosexual popular culture of the mid-1960s precluded any mention of the polymorphous sexual practices of Renaissance Italy's elite.

Civilisation (1969)

In the late 1960s, when revolution was in the air and French intellectuals (e.g., Michel Foucault and Jacques Derrida) were ushering in postmodernism by assailing Western humanistic and totalistic habits of thought, the British Broadcasting Corporation (BBC) made a bid to shore up the old verities by creating a television documentary series extolling the cultural glories of Western civilization. BBC-TV producers Michael Gill and Peter Montagnon enlisted Sir Kenneth Clark

(1903–1983), long Britain's leading art impresario, to write and host *Civilisation* (1969), a series of thirteen 52-minute programs shot at dozens of galleries, cathedrals, and other locations in Europe and America and covering Western art, architecture, and music from the Dark Ages to the early twentieth century—but stopping short of modernist art, for which Clark had no use. A former director of London's National Gallery, the prolific Clark had already written or edited some two dozen books on art and art history that were geared to a mainstream audience. Likewise pitched at a middlebrow level, *Civilisation* proved to be enormously popular in Britain and the United States. An accompanying coffee-table book was also issued. At a time when the West was in sociopolitical turmoil, it was comforting to reflect on Europe's dazzling cultural achievements.

Ciao! Manhattan (1972)

Nothing could be further removed from the tone, spirit, and ideological bearing of Clark's *Civilisation* than *Ciao! Manhattan* (1972), a film about former Andy Warhol protégé Edie Sedgwick (1943–1971) by David Weisman (*Kiss of the Spider Woman*) and John Palmer. The rich, beautiful debutante daughter of artist Francis Minton Sedgwick (1904–1967), Edie Sedgwick was raised on her parents' ranch near Santa Barbara, California, and privately schooled. She moved to New York in 1964, where she did modeling, socialized, dated Bob Dylan, and did copious amounts of drugs with Manhattan's beautiful people. In early 1965 either television producer Lester Persky or playwright Tennessee Williams (accounts vary) introduced Sedgwick to artist Andy Warhol. Instantly intuiting that he could exploit her charm, beauty, and elegance, Warhol cast Edie Sedgwick in a string of his improvised underground films shot in 1965–1966 at his famous studio, The Factory, then located at 231 East 47th Street, New York City.

In October 1967, in the middle of shooting *Ciao! Manhattan* (aka *Stripped and Strapped*), a disjointed potboiler by former Warhol associates Chuck Wein (*Rainbow Bridge*) and Genevieve Charbin, Segwick abruptly decamped for Los Angeles, leaving the film unfinished. By the end of the 1960s Edie Sedgwick had paid the price of a recklessly wild life by having devolved into a gibbering drug casualty/mental patient. In 1971 neophyte director David Weisman and cameraman John Palmer tracked down Sedgwick in California and persuaded her to finish *Ciao! Manhattan*, revamped with a new script (of sorts) and incorporating, as flashbacks, much of the black-and-white footage shot in New York City four years earlier. In the film Sedgwick plays "Susan Superstar," a thinly disguised version of herself. Once a famous jet-set ingenue, the now seriously addled Susan is reduced to living in an empty swimming pool on her mother's property and rem-iniscing about her glory days as a counterculture icon. A voyeuristic and grotesquely exploitative movie, *Ciao! Manhattan* nonetheless retains a certain macabre fascination, as an intimate look at a woman clearly on the verge of death (Sedgwick died of a barbiturate overdose on November 16, 1971, while the film was in postproduction) and a time capsule glimpse of the New York 1960s art underground.

Caravaggio (1986)

Caravaggio (1986), a highly stylized biopic about Italian Baroque painter Michelangelo Merisi da Caravaggio (1571–1610) by British underground author-painter-filmmaker Derek Jarman (1942–1994), says much more about Jarman's sensibilities than it does about Caravaggio's life. In point of fact, not much is known about Caravaggio other than that he was a passionate, volatile man who rose from poverty to become the great painter who originated chiaroscuro tech-nique and introduced a more naturalistic style to Renaissance depictions of the human body. It is also known that, on a street in Rome in May 1606, Caravaggio killed a man named Ranuccio Tomasoni in a sword fight over a disputed debt and was forced to stay on the run from authorities until his own death four years later. Jarman, a militant gay activist who later died of AIDS, depicts Caravaggio (Nigel Terry in the film) as a bisexual more inclined to the homosexual persua-sion. In Jarman's fanciful biopic, Caravaggio is involved in an ultimately fatal ménage à trios with his gay model-lover Ranuccio (Sean Bean) and his mistress, Lena (Tilda Swinton). Employing a postmodern noir structure and techniques, for example, extravagantly worded voice-over, appropriately chiaroscuro light-ing, disjointed flashbacks, and depictions of lust and murder, *Caravaggio* aims for a phantasmagorical aestheticism but delivers an often confusing and preten-tious gay art film that did not find a wider audience.

Vincent: The Life and Death of Vincent van Gogh (1987)

Some thirty years after Vincente Minelli's *Lust for Life*, Dutch-born Australian director Paul Cox wrote and directed *Vincent: The Life and Death of Vincent van Gogh* (1987), a spare documentary consisting of only a few visual elements—brooding landscape shots, stills of van Gogh's paintings, some period reenact-ments—and a single element on the soundtrack: excerpts from van Gogh's letters to his brother, Theo, recited in voice-over by British actor John Hurt. The gestalt that results from visuals and sound is richly evocative but, at the same time, abstract enough to allow the viewer considerable freedom of interpretation.

Camille Claudel (1988)

When she died at the Montdevergues Asylum near Avignon on October 19, 1943, Camille Claudel (1864–1943) was known, if at all, as the older sister of Paul Claudel (1868–1955), the noted poet, playwright, diplomat, and Catholic apologist. No one would have guessed that the dowdy, elderly, senile Mme. Claudel was once a prodigiously talented and fiercely dedicated sculptor. For a fifteen-year period at the end of the nineteenth century, Claudel was also the model, muse, mistress, and collaborator of the great August Rodin (1840–1917). In 1898 Camille Claudel made a final break with Rodin because he refused to leave his longtime mistress (later wife), Rose Beuret (1844–1917). For the next fifteen years Camille Claudel lived and worked alone and grew increasingly eccentric and paranoid. Just days after the death of her father, Louis Prosper-Claudel, in March 1913, Camille Claudel's family had her forcibly committed and she spent most of the remaining thirty years of her life incarcerated at Montdevergues.

Camille Claudel may have remained an obscure footnote to art history had her name not been recuperated by Anne Delbée, a French feminist actor, director, and writer whose fictionalized biography, *Une Femme* (*A Woman*) (Paris: Presses de la Renaissance), brought Claudel into public awareness in 1982. In 1984 the Musée Rodin in Paris and Musée Ste.-Croix in Poitiers staged major exhibits of Camille Claudel's work, and Editions Gallimard published *Camille Claudel: 1864–1963*, a biography by Claudel's grandniece, Reine-Marie Paris, that became a bestseller. (Over the next several years there would be major Claudel exhibits in Germany, Greece, Japan, and the United States.) Amid the excitement over Camille Claudel in 1984, actor Isabelle Adjani (*L'Histoire d'Adèle H.*; *Le Locataire*) joined cinematographer turned writer-director Bruno Nuytten (*Jean de Florette*) in undertaking a film version of Paris's biography. Co-producer of the film with Christian Fechner, Adjani stars as Camille Claudel opposite Gérard Depardieu as Rodin. The script, by Nuytten and Marilyn Goldin, stays close to the known facts of Claudel's life but resists the urge to provide pat answers. Thus *Camille Claudel* (1988) wisely avoids depicting Claudel as merely the tragic victim of Rodin's mistreatment or the misogyny that permeated the era. Neither influence, pernicious as they were, fully explains Camille Claudel's descent into madness.

Superstar: The Life and Times of Andy Warhol (1990)

By the time he died, after a botched gallbladder operation on February 24, 1987, Andy Warhol (1928–1987) had been the world's most famous and controversial artist for more than two decades. With his distinctive look—acne scarred face, tortoise-shell glasses, and disheveled silver wig—Warhol assumed the deadpan persona of an emotionally detached cynic suffering from terminal boredom, but all the while the real Warhol sought publicity with maniacal determination. Andy Warhol also produced quite a bit of pop art of debatable quality. His many absurdist films, outsized Brillo boxes, brightly colored, repetitive silkscreen paintings of celebrities, Campbell soup cans, bananas, and the like seemed to both mock and elevate the banal mass-produced products and images of modern business civilization. Whether an artistic genius or a colossal fraud (or perhaps both), Warhol was spectacularly successful in attaining his greatest ambitions: to be very hip, rich, and famous—and well connected with other hip, rich celebrities.

Not long after Warhol's death, filmmaker Chuck Workman (*Precious Images*) began work on *Superstar: The Life and Times of Andy Warhol* (1990), a documentary that uses a host of archival clips and interviews with Warhol's family, friends, and entourage to examine Warhol's art and present a portrait of the artist as a shy, sickly working-class boy from Pittsburgh who refashions himself into a showman, art entrepreneur, and avatar of the New York avant-garde. Not much is revealed about Warhol's real personality or motivations but Warhol never disclosed much about himself, perhaps because there was less there than met the eye.

Vincent & Theo (1990)

On the centenary of van Gogh's death, director Robert Altman (*McCabe & Mrs. Miller; Nashville*) supplemented Paul Cox's recent documentary with *Vincent & Theo* (1990), a docudrama beautifully written by Julian Mitchell (*Arabesque; Inspector Morse*) and luminously shot by frequent Altman collaborator, Jean Lépine (*Tanner, '88*). In the thirty-four years since the appearance of the adulatory *Lust for Life*, cultural tastes had changed dramatically. It was now possible to depict an iconic figure like van Gogh in a more realistic and three-dimensional way. As written by Mitchell and interpreted by Tim Roth, Vincent van Gogh is not just an obsessively dedicated artistic genius but also a desperately moody, puerile, grossly ill-kempt albatross around the neck of his long-suffering (and syphilitic) brother Theo, played by Paul Rhys as a quivering nervous wreck.

Vincent & Theo opens with the auction at Christie's in London (March 1987), when van Gogh's *Sunflowers* sold for an astonishing $39.9 million. The film then cuts to Vincent and Theo in van Gogh's chaotic hovel of a studio a century earlier. By contrasting van Gogh's fantastic posthumous success with his miserable commercial failure in life (he sold only one painting), *Vincent & Theo* (1) satirizes the whimsies of the art world; (2) pays homage to the heroic integrity of the visionary artist spurned by his contemporaries; and (3) foregrounds the economic realities that always bedevil the production (and reception) of art. All of these themes are of great relevance to Robert Altman, a filmmaker who has always defied social conventions and commercial imperatives to pursue his unique cinematic vision. Fittingly, *Vincent & Theo* was no great commercial success but has come to be regarded as one of Altman's best films.

Crumb (1994)

In the late 1980s filmmaker Terry Zwigoff (*Louie Bluie*) began filming a documentary on his longtime friend and fellow blues enthusiast, the famous underground comic book artist R. Crumb (creator of Mr. Natural, the Keep on Truckin' logo, and *Fritz the Cat*, among others). Unfortunately, Zwigoff soon found his path was filled with stones. Plagued by lack of money, chronic and severe back pain, depression, and Robert Crumb's ambivalence toward the project, Zwigoff finally completed *Crumb* (1994) after a six-year struggle. *Crumb* premiered at the Toronto Film Festival, September 10, 1994, and was subsequently shown at the Sundance Film Festival (late January 1995), where it won the Grand Jury Prize for Best Documentary. Over the next year *Crumb* won a host of other festival, film industry, and critics' awards, garnered adulatory reviews, earned a distribution deal with Sony Pictures, and achieved cult status.

Much more than just a film biography of Robert Crumb, *Crumb* is a haunting portrait of the incredibly dysfunctional Crumb family; the story of Robert Crumb's personal redemption through artistic self-expression; and an exemplary tale of intergenerational conflict and counterculture rebellion. Robert's father, Charles V. Crumb (1914–1982), was a Marine Corps officer turned businessman and by all accounts a sadistic tyrant who visited countless acts of mental and physical cruelty on his wife, Beatrice, and their five children. (Ironically, the elder Crumb had the temerity to publish a book entitled *Training People . . . Effectively!*) Robert Crumb's two sisters declined to be interviewed for Zwigoff's film but *Crumb* does contain footage of his amphetamine-addicted mother and features extensive interviews with Robert's older brother, Charles, and his younger brother, Maxon. It turns out that Charles was a gifted cartoonist in his

Cartoonist Robert Crumb, photographed in California, 1985. (George Steinmetz/ Corbis)

youth and the one most responsible for Robert's taking an interest in art. Stricken with mental illness in late adolescence, Charles stopped drawing—or doing much of anything else. In his early fifties in the film, Charles is shown still living at home in suburban Philadelphia with his mother. Under heavy antipsychotic medication, Charles seldom leaves his bedroom; his chief amusements are smoking and reading cerebral literary classics. Though obviously disturbed, Charles also comes off as sensitive, eloquent, and sardonically self-aware about the massive psychic damage inflicted by the Crumb family patriarch. (Sadly, we learn at the end of the film that Charles has since committed suicide.) Almost as pathetic as Charles is Robert's other brother, Max, who lives alone in a San Francisco flophouse, paints strange symbolic paintings, sleeps on a bed of nails, and cleanses himself by swallowing a long tape that runs through his intestines.

Deeply alienated, misanthropic, and afflicted with certain weird sexual fetishes, Robert is by no means an exemplar of good mental hygiene. Yet as a devoted husband and father and a highly successful and famous artist, Robert is the only Crumb in the film who could be credibly deemed sane. He owes his sanity to his ability to access and purge his inner demons through his (sometimes distressingly graphic and misogynistic) artwork. If there is a hero in *Crumb* it is art: the only thing that has stood between Robert Crumb and madness. Finally, a probably unintended effect of *Crumb* is to exemplify the breakdown of American dream ideology, the nuclear family, and traditional codes of American masculinity held dear by the World War II generation but not successfully transmitted to or taken up by the baby boomers that followed.

I Shot Andy Warhol (1996)

By the mid-1960s Andy Warhol had achieved the kind of fame and counterculture mystique that sometimes attracts mentally unbalanced hangers-on. One such person was Valerie Jean Solanas (1936–1988), a panhandler, prostitute, radical lesbian, and aspiring polemicist who showed up at Warhol's Factory in early 1967 with a play entitled "Up Your *ss." Warhol neglected to produce Solanas's play but, to mollify her, did put her in a couple of his underground films: *I, a Man* and *Bikeboy* (both 1967) and paid her a small fee. That same year Solanas self-published the *SCUM* (*Society for Cutting up Men*) *Manifesto*, a now legendary diatribe in which she exhorted "civic-minded, responsible, thrill-seeking females" to "overthrow the government, eliminate the money system, institute complete automation and destroy the male sex" (Solanas 2004). *SCUM Manifesto* in hand, Solanas approached Maurice Girodias (1919–1990), founder of Olympia Press (which published Henry Miller's *Tropic* novels, Vladimir Nabokov's *Lolita*, J. P. Donleavy's

The Ginger Man, Pauline Reage's *Story of O*, William S. Burroughs' *Naked Lunch*, Terry Southern's *Candy*, and other underground classics). Intrigued, Girodias had Solanas sign a contract and gave her a $600 cash advance to write a novel based on her manifesto. In the meantime, put off by her pushy personality and fiery political ideas, Warhol and his ultracool entourage soon gave Valerie Solanas the cold shoulder. Over the next year an increasingly paranoid Solanas became convinced that both Andy Warhol and Maurice Girodias were taking advantage of her in some way. She bought a .32 automatic and, on June 3, 1968, sought out Girodias at the Chelsea Hotel where he was a resident. Girodias was out of town that day, so Solanas decided to go to the newly relocated factory and shoot Andy Warhol instead. Hit by bullets on both sides of his abdomen that damaged vital organs, Warhol nearly died from shock and loss of blood before being revived by open-chest heart massage. Patched up by extensive surgery, Warhol spent two months in the hospital recovering. A year after the shooting, Solanas was sentenced to up to three years at the New York State Prison for Women at Bedford Hills. Released from prison in September 1971, Solanas eventually ended up in San Francisco's Tenderloin District, addicted to drugs and continuing to work as a prostitute. She died in a transient hotel of respiratory disease in April 1988 at the age of fifty-two.

Not long after the deaths of both Warhol and Solanas, Canadian filmmaker and Warhol enthusiast Mary Harron began making what she originally conceived of as a documentary about the Solanas saga. Harron's producers—principally Christine Vachon and Tom Kalin—soon persuaded her that a docudrama would better suit the subject matter. Starring Lili Taylor (*Short Cuts*) as Valerie Solanas and Richard Harris's son, Jared Harris (*Dead Man*), as Andy Warhol, *I Shot Andy Warhol* (1996) stays close to the historical facts. Harris as the mincing, passive-aggressive, scheming Warhol is suitably repulsive while Taylor delivers a spellbinding rendition of Solanas as a smart, funny, tough-as-nails protofeminist firebrand deeply scarred by her father's sexual abuse and years of hustling on the streets. After seven years in production, *I Shot Andy Warhol* was screened at the Sundance, Cannes, and a number of other film festivals, where it was always well received, before going into limited theatrical release.

Basquiat (1996)

A few months after the release of *I Shot Andy Warhol*, pop artist turned filmmaker Julian Schnabel added another facet to the Warhol vogue with *Basquiat* (1996), a biopic about Jean Michel Basquiat (1960–1988), an African American painter and Warhol protégé who enjoyed great success and international fame in the last years of his short life. Son of a Brooklyn accountant, Basquiat started out as a New York City graffiti artist but soon graduated to serious painting. His fashionably charismatic persona—young, black, handsome, chic, and with the requisite dreadlocks—and his bold, crudely vibrant canvases quickly made him wealthy and famous in New York's trendy art world but success was fatal to Basquiat: an unbridled heroin addiction led to his death by overdose on August 12, 1988. Written by Julian Schnabel and Michael Thomas Holman—both friends of the late artist—*Basquiat* covers the familiar, clichéd territory but so did Basquiat's life. Perhaps gifted, but certainly naïve and insecure, Jean Michel Basquiat soon fell afoul of the usual traps lying in wait for the overnight sensation. Too much fame, money, and art world intrigue cause the volatile Basquiat (Jeffrey Wright in the film) to lose his bearings and founder. Contrary to the negative depictions of Andy Warhol in other films, rock star David Bowie plays Warhol as emotionally fragile and genuinely solicitous and caring toward his young friend, Jean Michel. This is probably an accurate portrait as Warhol associates note that he mellowed in the last years of his life. Whatever the truth about Warhol, *Basquiat* fails to make a convincing case for the greatness of its protagonist.

The Line King: The Al Hirschfeld Story (1996)

Diametrically opposed to the cometlike transit of Jean Michel Basquiat is the very long and distinguished career of *New York Times* caricaturist Al Hirschfeld (1903–2003). When Hirshfeld was in his early nineties, friend and admirer Susan Warms Dryfoos (great-granddaughter of Adolf Ochs, founding publisher of the *New York Times*) made *The Line King: The Al Hirschfeld Story* (1996), an unabashedly adulatory documentary that traces Hirschfeld's seventy-five-year career doing his elegant line drawings of Broadway and Hollywood stars. Featuring interviews with Hirschfeld, his wife, Dolly Haas, their daughter Nina, and a number of celebrities—Barbara Walters, Lauren Bacall, Carol Channing, Joseph Papp, Joan Collins—*The Line King* is a biography of the famous artist but also equally a survey of American show business through most of the twentieth century, much of which Hirschfeld personally witnessed and commemorated.

Surviving Picasso (1996)

Providing contrast to *The Line King*'s lighthearted, benevolent approach to its subject is James Ivory's *Surviving Picasso* (1996), a docudrama portrait of the artist as a churlish, self-involved, sometimes destructive personality. The film, in turn, had its genesis in Arianna Stassinopoulos Huffington's *Picasso: Creator and Destroyer* (New York: Simon & Schuster, 1988), a biography that concentrated on revealing the private man behind the mythic artist. A caustic, quasi-feminist deconstruction of Pablo Picasso (1881–1973) as a raving sociopath and hateful misogynist, Huffington's controversial book garnered mixed reviews, sent shock waves through the art world, and became an international bestseller (by the 1980s there existed a well-established market for damning biographies of twentieth-century icons). Having purchased the television rights before Huffington even wrote the book, producer David L. Wolper acquired the film rights after reading the manuscript. A number of years later Wolper formed an alliance with Merchant-Ivory Productions to make a film version. As adapted by Merchant-Ivory's screenwriting partner, Ruth Prawer Jhabvala, Huffington's portrait of Picasso (Anthony Hopkins in the film) is considerably softened and made more vulnerable: a function both of the distinctively charitable—some might say smarmy—Merchant-Ivory sensibility and the differing requisites of cinematic representation. Natascha McElhone plays the artist Françoise Gilot, Picasso's mistress from 1946 to 1953 and evidently the only woman formidable enough to leave Picasso and thrive thereafter.

Love Is the Devil: Study for a Portrait of Francis Bacon (1998)

Francis Bacon (1909–1992) was arguably Britain's foremost twentieth-century artist, an iconoclastic painter of eerily distorted human faces and forms that look as though the artist painted under the influence of powerful hallucinogens. Considered works of unmitigated horror by philistines, Bacon's nihilistic figurative paintings are revered by art critics for their technical mastery and as haunting evocations of modern alienation and anxiety. Soon after Bacon's death his long-time friend, Daniel Farson, released *The Gilded Gutter Life of Francis Bacon* (New York: Pantheon, 1993), an intimate biography cowritten by Farson and Bacon that contained such graphic accounts of Bacon's homosexual liaisons that it had to wait until his death to be published. A couple of years later John Maybury, a gay British director of short films and music videos (most famously Sinead O'Connor's "Nothing Compares 2U"), decided to make *The Gilded Gutter Life* into his first feature film.

Starring Sir Derek Jacobi (*I, Claudius; Cadfael*) as Francis Bacon and Daniel Craig (*Elizabeth; The Ice House*) as George Dyer, *Love Is the Devil: Study for a Portrait of Francis Bacon* (1998) focuses on Bacon's love affair with Dyer, a former borstal boy and petty criminal from London's East End. The affair began in 1964, when the two met at a bar, and ended with Dyer's suicide by barbiturate overdose on October 27, 1971—just two days before the opening of a major Bacon exhibit at the Grand Palais in Paris. The relationship between Bacon and Dyer was complex and contradictory. In the bedroom Bacon insisted that Dyer play sadist while he assumed the role of masochist, but in public the monstrously narcissistic Bacon took sadistic pleasure in belittling and humiliating Dyer for his low pedigree and lack of a real vocation. Over the years Dyer, troubled and insecure, eventually succumbed to alcoholism and barbiturate addiction.

Denied use of Bacon's paintings by the estate for his film, John Maybury simulated their grotesque aura through cinematographic techniques—disjunctive editing, oblique compositions, canted camera angles, distorted lenses, and so on—all to the appropriately discordant electronic music of Ryuichi Sakamoto (*The Last Emperor; Sheltering Sky*). Made by BBC for the modest sum of £900,000 (US$1.5 million), *Love Is the Devil* was a hit in Britain and won a number of film festival awards but its resoundingly negative depiction of a homosexual love affair made it controversial in gay circles on both sides of the Atlantic.

Pollock (2000)

Thirty years after his death there was a strong revival of interest in the life and work of Jackson Pollock (1912–1956), the enfant terrible of the New York School (i.e., abstract expressionism). *Jackson Pollock: Portrait*, an hour-long documentary by Amanda C. Pope and Karen Lindsay, aired on New York City's Channel 13 in the spring of 1984 and was soon followed by Jeffrey Potter's *To a Violent Grave: An Oral Biography of Jackson Pollock* (New York: Putnam, 1985); Deborah Solomon's *Jackson Pollock: A Biography* (New York: Simon & Schuster, 1987); and Steven Naifeh and Gregory White Smith's magisterial *Jackson Pollock: An American Saga* (New York: Clarkson N. Potter, 1989). In late November 1986 Ed Harris's father sent him a copy of Jeffrey Potter's book as a birthday present with the suggestion that the material might be suitable for a film. Some months later the elder Harris sent his son Deborah Solomon's book. Soon Ed Harris became fixated on Jackson Pollock and began the decadelong process of developing a feature-length biopic that he would direct (his directorial debut), help produce, and star in as Pollock—to whom he bears a fairly strong physical resemblance.

Working primarily with Naifeh and Smith's biography, screenwriters Barbara Turner (*Georgia*) and Susan Emshwiller fashioned a script for *Pollock* (2000) that skips over the artist's troubled youth in the West to concentrate on the last fifteen years of his life in New York City and environs (1941–1956). After being rejected for military service for psychological reasons, Pollock meets Lee Krasner (1909–1984), another struggling artist, and the two begin a personal and professional relationship that is almost all to Pollock's advantage. An anguished, angry bisexual, probably bipolar, Pollock medicated himself with copious amounts of alcohol. The far more stable Krasner (Marcia Gay Hardin in an Oscar-winning performance) loyally weathered Pollock's alcoholism, rages, infidelities, and depressions and was a tireless advocate for his work. Without her it is highly doubtful that Pollock would have attained the acclaim that he did. Admirably, *Pollock* does not subscribe to the tortured, misunderstood artist cliché to mitigate the man's excesses; innovative genius or not, Ed Harris's Pollock is a reprehensible human being who repays Krasner's devotion by having an affair with Ruth Kligman (Jennifer Connelly), a young devotee, and getting himself killed in a drunken auto accident near his home on Long Island.

Frida (2002)

When Hayden Herrera's meticulously researched *Frida: A Biography of Frida Kahlo* (New York: Harper & Row) was published in 1983, Nancy Hardin, a former book editor and literary agent who had become one of Hollywood's first female studio moguls, seized on Kahlo's story as the perfect vehicle to effect her crossover to independent producing. Hardin marketed her project relentlessly but no studio was interested at the time. By 1990, though, Frida Kahlo (1907–1954) had become an international cult figure. As a bisexual, a Communist, a constantly suffering invalid (badly injured in a Mexico City streetcar accident in 1925), and a heretofore underrated Third World woman artist in the shadow of her famous, philandering husband, muralist Diego Rivera (1886–1957), Kahlo combined all the necessary elements to make her a late twentieth-century feminist heroine.

In 1997 Nancy Hardin signed a production deal with Trimark Pictures and Trimark signed Julie Taymor (*Titus*) to direct, Salma Hayek (*From Dusk Till Dawn*) to play Frida, and Alfred Molina (*Boogie Nights; Magnolia*) to play Diego Rivera (a role that required Molina to gain fifty pounds). To be suitably marketable and to mesh with contemporary sensibilities the screenplay of *Frida* (2002), adapted from Herrera's book by Gregory Nava and Anna Thomas (*El Norte; Mi Familia*), emphasizes the passionate, stormy relationship between Kahlo and Rivera. Consequently, their political radicalism as expressed through their art, though by no means ignored, is given short shrift. Largely dehistoricized and depoliticized, *Frida* functions beautifully as a lush period romance. A success at the box office, *Frida* won numerous film festival and industry awards, including two Oscars (for Best Makeup and Best Music, Original Score).

Salma Hayek on the set of the film Frida *in Puebla, Mexico, 2001. (Servin Humberto/ Corbis Sygma)*

American Splendor (2003)

In marked contrast to the exotic bohemian lives of most of the artists depicted on film is the conspicuously ordinary saga of Harvey Pekar. In 1976 Pekar began writing the ironically titled *American Splendor*, an irregularly published underground comic book series (variously illustrated by G. Budgett, R. Crumb, Gary Dumm, Joe Zabel, and others) that dramatizes small incidents in Pekar's working-class life in Cleveland, where he toiled for many years as a file clerk at a local Veteran's Administration hospital. Pekar's motto—"Ordinary life is pretty complex stuff"— nicely sums up the populist-existentialist rationale for *American Splendor*. Already something of a cult figure by the late 1980s, Pekar gained a national audience when late-night talk-show host David Letterman invited Pekar to make a number of guest appearances on his show. In his television persona, as hypercool postmodern ironist, Letterman sought to use the socially awkward, balding, chubby Harvey Pekar as a whipping boy who exemplified a supposedly passé 1960s-style counterculture sensibility. On a show that aired the night of August 31, 1988, Pekar deftly turned the tables on Letterman by accusing him of being a highly paid shill for General Electric, the parent company of NBC and a key player in America's military-industrial complex. The usually unflappable Letterman exploded into a shouting match with Pekar: a very rare moment of unscripted reality on national television that earned Pekar permanent exile from Letterman's show but also cemented his cult reputation as a genuine, incorruptible social critic and underground hero.

Almost a decade and a half later independent producer Ted Hope (*The Ice Storm*) joined Shari Springer Berman and Robert Pulcini, a husband and wife team of documentary filmmakers (*Off the Menu; The Young and the Dead*), and signed a deal with Home Box Office (HBO) to make *American Splendor* (2003). An innovative biopic, *American Splendor* combines docudrama (with Paul Giamatti as Pekar and Hope Davis as Pekar's wife, Joyce Brabner) with animated and still cartoon sequences and appearances by the real Pekar, Brabner, and friend and coworker, Toby Radloff. Just as Pekar, a nonartist, relied on a number of artists to illustrate his autobiographical tales, the film uses different versions of Harvey Pekar to delineate the complex facets of individual identity as they relate to differing modes of representation—a risky postmodern trope that works surprisingly well. After a triumphant premier at the Sundance Film Festival (January 20, 2003), HBO opted for a theatrical release of *American Beauty* in the fall of 2003. For a small-scale film, it did well at the box office, won a host of film festival and industry nominations and awards, and earned dozens of rave reviews.

8

Labor, Business, and Political History on Film and Television

The Forties

Citizen Kane (1941)

The first great political history film of the sound era is of course Orson Welles' *Citizen Kane* (1941). Based primarily on the life of publishing mogul William Randolph Hearst (1863–1951), *Citizen Kane* also contains allusions to Chicago utilities magnate Samuel Insull (1859–1938) and other major capitalists of the same ilk. Long considered one of the greatest films ever made, *Citizen Kane* has been widely praised for broaching a raft of innovative and influential cinematic techniques introduced by Welles and his cinematographer, Gregg Toland. These include a complex, nonlinear flashback narrative structure, overlapping dialogue, low-angle and deep focus shots, expressive use of low-key lighting, long takes, subjective camera, and convoluted camera movements. At least two of these elements—the flashback expositional structure and use of atmospheric low-key lighting—became staples of the Hollywood style known as film noir (ca. 1941–1958).

The most visually exciting film of its time, *Citizen Kane* also proved to be the most controversial. On January 9, 1941—almost four months before its official premier—right-wing movie gossip columnist Louella Parsons (1881–1972) and two Hearst attorneys screened the film to verify rumors that it was a thinly veiled attack on William Randolph Hearst. Their suspicions were confirmed. The life of the film's protagonist, Charles Foster Kane (Orson Welles), bore a number of pointed parallels to Hearst's life. Both men were sons of mining millionaires who started as newspaper owners in their early twenties and went on to build media empires; both perfected yellow journalism and engineered a war to increase newspaper circulation; both unsuccessfully aspired to high political office; both lost vast sums of money in the Great Depression; both built palatial homes (Hearst's San Simeon near San Luis Opisbo, California, and Kane's

Orson Welles in Citizen Kane, *written, produced, directed, and starring Welles. (Underwood & Underwood/Corbis)*

Xanadu in Florida) filled with precious objets d'art from all over the world; both used their influence to advance the show business careers of their mistresses.

There were also fairly significant differences. Hearst ran for mayor of New York City in 1905 and lost to George B. McClellan Jr. (1865–1940, son of the famous Civil War general) by 3,000 votes out of the almost 220,000 cast. Hearst ran for governor of New York in 1906 and was soundly beaten by Charles Evans Hughes (1862–1948). Welles and his co-screenwriter, Herman J. Mankiewicz, conflated the two campaigns into a single gubernatorial race and invented the scandal of an extramarital affair as the event that derailed Kane's political career. In point of fact, Hearst suffered no such scandal, although a short poem published in a Hearst newspaper by Ambrose Bierce (1842–1914?) on the assassination of Governor-elect William Goebel of Kentucky (February 2, 1900) was wrongly thought to call for the assassination of President William McKinley (1843–1901), who was indeed also assassinated twenty months later. The resulting brouhaha badly damaged Hearst's public image, which was ambiguous at best, and his political career withered.

In the film Kane marries Emily Monroe Norton (Ruth Warrick) for politically opportunistic reasons; she is the daughter of a senator and the niece of the president of the United States. A largely loveless marriage devolves into total estrangement and Kane takes up with Susan Alexander (Dorothy Comingore), young and pretty but dim-witted and an untalented singer. In the midst of scandal, Kane sacrifices his marriage and political aspirations to hold on to Susan, whom Kane tries to groom into an opera star to fulfill his own colossal vanity.

Hearst's love life differed rather markedly from Kane's. In 1903 Hearst, age forty, married Millicent Veronica Willson (1882–1974), a beautiful twenty-two-year-old chorus girl. The couple had five sons between 1904 and 1915. In 1916 Hearst saw a nineteen-year-old beauty named Marion Davies (real name: Marion Cecelia Douras, 1897–1961) perform in a Zeigfeld Follies chorus line and, despite the thirty-four-year age difference, became smitten and made her his mistress. The affair caused Hearst and his wife to permanently separate in 1926 but she refused to grant him a divorce so he was never able to marry Davies. A Hollywood actress from 1917 until she retired in 1937, Marion Davies appeared in thirty-three silent films and fifteen talkies—all of them exclusively financed by Hearst and praised to high heavens in Hearst-owned newspapers. In *Citizen Kane* Emily Norton Kane is the Millicent Willson Hearst figure after her marriage has collapsed. Susan Alexander is something of an amalgam of both Millicent Willson Hearst and Marion Davies (who were both young chorus girls when they met Hearst) but more Davies in the sense that Charles Foster Kane, like Hearst, goes to unreasonable lengths to foster her career. Still, Welles and Mankiewicz engage in egregious distortion when they characterize Susan Alexander as a stupid, crass, mean-spirited alcoholic who came to hate her lover and ultimately leave him. Her real-life counterpart, Marion Davies, was quite talented and much beloved for her emotional generosity and sweet temperament, and her relationship with Hearst endured until his death in 1951. Indeed, William Randolph Hearst's concerted and largely effective campaign to have *Citizen Kane* suppressed in 1941 seems to have had more to do with its defamatory portrayal of his beloved Marion than of himself. Orson Welles later expressed regret that the film had represented such a nice lady in such a vicious way. Nonetheless, *Citizen Kane* was generally on firm ground when it characterized its Hearst figure as arrogant, autocratic, elitist, and reactionary and implicitly called into question the propriety of one private citizen having so much power.

Give Us This Day (1949)

Ironically, the genesis of a cinema of American labor history coincides with the beginnings of the decline of the American labor movement after World War II. A massive wave of commerce-debilitating strikes right after the war and burgeoning paranoia about communists in the labor movement (and just about everywhere else) prompted a Republican Congress to pass, over President Truman's veto, the Taft-Hartley Act of 1947—sweeping and resolutely antilabor legislation that gutted the pro-union provisions of the Wagner Act passed during the depths of the Great Depression in 1935. Management and its minions in government had served notice to labor that much of the progress made in the democratization of the American workplace over the previous two decades would heretofore be discontinued and rolled back wherever possible.

On the Hollywood front, the House Committee on Un-American Activities (HUAC) held hearings in October 1947 that were supposedly intended to ferret out communist influence in Hollywood labor unions. One of the notorious Hollywood Ten who refused to cooperate with HUAC was Hungarian-Canadian movie director Edward Dmytryk (1908–1999). Fired from his job by RKO and then blacklisted in November 1947, Dmytryk sued over his banishment from Hollywood but when nothing came of his efforts at legal redress, Dmytryk left the United States for Britain in the fall of 1948 with blacklisted colleagues screenwriter Ben Barzman (*Back to Bataan*) and actor Sam Wanamaker (1919–1993). Residing in London for a year, Dmytryk made two movies in England: *Obsession* (1949), a film noir written by Alec Coppel, and *Give Us This Day* (1949), an adaptation by Ben Barzman of Pietro di Donato's great proletarian novel, *Christ in Concrete* (Indianapolis, IN: Bobbs-Merrill, 1939), starring Sam Wanamaker. Edward Dmytryk returned to America in September 1949 and later named names at the 1951 HUAC hearings to salvage his own film career: a political apostasy that earned him the undying contempt of his Hollywood associates who held fast under tremendous pressure from the Right.

Nonetheless, Dmytryk's bona fides as a progressive filmmaker were still in tact when he made *Give Us This Day* (later retitled *Salt to the Devil*). The autobiographical novel the film is based on begins with the death of the protagonist's father, Geremio, in a New York City building collapse on Good Friday just as

Pietro di Donato's father was killed on Good Friday, March 30, 1923. Forced to take over as head of the family and chief breadwinner, young Paul (i.e., di Donato) must learn his father's trade as a bricklayer while disabusing himself of the Roman Catholicism that teaches Italian American immigrants pious passivity in the face of intense bigotry, oppression, and exploitation. While most of *Christ in Concrete* concerns young Paul's coming-of-age after his father's death, Dmytryk's screenwriter, Ben Barzman (*The Boy with the Green Hair*), decided to shift the focus of the film to Geremio and deal with his travails in adjusting to America as a first-generation immigrant. In the film Geremio (Sam Wanamaker) and his wife Annuziata (Lea Padovani) move into a dilapidated apartment in a Brooklyn tenement after their honeymoon and begin to save for the day they will own a house. All they want is a modest version of the American dream but their destination seems to keep receding into the distance as they trudge toward it. Children arrive and fluctuations in the building trade make employment sporadic. After the stock market crash of 1929, life is reduced to a daily struggle for survival. Forced to take unsafe building demolition work because he desperately needs the money, Geremio is killed when the building collapses—putting the lie to the promise of upward mobility for poor folk who work hard and abide by the law.

Although *Give Us This Day* won film festival awards in France, Czechoslovakia, and Italy, the Legion of Decency, an organization formed in 1934 by American Catholic bishops to identify and proscribe "immoral" movies, condemned the film. The irony of *Give Us This Day* being blacklisted by the Catholic Church in the United States was that the film refrained from engaging in the scathing critique of Catholicism found in its source, *Christ in Concrete*. Presumably what the Legion of Decency found objectionable was the film's realistic depiction of the plight of the immigrant working classes, which amounted to a powerful demystification of American dream ideology. Virtually unseen in America, *Give Us This Day* was as good as lost for more than a half century until All Day Entertainment, a company specializing in rereleasing obscure films on DVD, brought out a version misleadingly titled *Christ in Concrete* (2003) carefully restored from the 35mm nitrate originals held in the archives of the British Film Institute (BFI).

The Fifties

Salt of the Earth (1954)

In October 1950 in Bayard (Grant County), New Mexico, Local 890 of the International Union of Mine, Mill, and Smelter Workers (Mine-Mill, a radical union founded in 1893 and ejected from the CIO in 1950 for its Communist leanings) went on strike against Empire Zinc Corporation, a subsidiary of the New Jersey Zinc Corporation. The impetus behind the action was Empire Zinc's systematic discrimination against its mostly Mexican American workforce. All facilities were segregated, with Anglo workers receiving safer job assignments, better company housing (with indoor plumbing), more pay, and promotion opportunities not afforded to non-Anglos. Eight months into the strike Empire Zinc used the new Taft-Hartley laws to enjoin the workers from picketing the road that led to the mine. If they continued to picket they would be arrested and jailed and if they stopped picketing the strike would be lost—either way it appeared the company had won. To the consternation of company officials and striking workers alike, the wives and mothers of the strikers took over the picket line inasmuch as the court order only prevented *employees* from picketing. Almost immediately Grant County sheriff deputies swooped down on the picket line and arrested forty-five women and seventeen children and jailed them in the local lockup. However, the incessant, boisterous protest chanting of the detainees so unnerved their jailers that they released them all that evening. In the months that followed the company stepped up efforts to break the strike. At one point four carloads of scabs attempted to barge through the picket line and a riot resulted but the line held. An interesting sidelight: with the women on the picket line, the men had to tend to domestic chores: a gender role reversal that proved highly illuminating to Latino working-class males accustomed to thinking of women and women's work as inferior. After fifteen grueling months, Local 890 won its strike against Empire Zinc on January 21, 1952—a triumph of grit, perseverance, and sheer physical and moral courage in the face of overwhelming repression.

Hollywood screenwriter Paul Jarrico (real name: Israel Shapiro, 1915–1997; *Song of Russia*) happened to be vacationing in New Mexico with his family and learned of the strike while it was still in progress. Having formed Independent Productions Corporation (IPC) with theater owner Simon Lazarus, producer Adrian Scott (*Murder, My Sweet; Crossfire*), writer-director Herbert Biberman (one of the Hollywood Ten), and screenwriter Michael Wilson (who would later write *The Bridge on the River Kwai* and *Lawrence of Arabia*) after all but Lazarus were blacklisted for their Communist affiliations, Jarrico suggested to his colleagues that the Empire Zinc strike would be the perfect subject for IPC's first and, as it turned out, last film project. Biberman and Wilson cowrote a script and then IPC enlisted the support and cooperation of Local 890 and Mine-Mill, which put up a good part of the film's $300,000 production budget. Local 890 vetted and approved the screenplay and supplied most of the film's nonprofessional cast, essentially playing themselves, including 890's union organizer Clinton Jincks and his wife, Virginia, and Local 890 president Juan Chacón who co-starred as Ramon Quintero, the staunch but chauvinist husband of Esperanza Quintero (played by Mexican actress Rosaura Revueltas), the woman who leads the strike after the men are prevented from picketing. Filling out the cast were blacklisted professional actors Will Geer (later famous for his role as Grandpa on *The Waltons*), David Wolfe (*Where the Sidewalk Ends*), and Mervin Williams (*Force of Evil*).

Denounced by right-wing politicos including tycoon Howard Hughes, denied a union film crew by the International Alliance of Theatrical Stage Employees, and its two-month shoot in New Mexico harassed and threatened every step of the way by local vigilantes, it is a minor miracle that *Salt of the Earth* (1954) was made at all. The U.S. Immigration and Naturalization Service deported Rosaura Revueltas back to Mexico on a visa technicality before principal photography was finished, necessitating shooting Revueltas's few remaining scenes in Mexico and using a double, shot from behind, for Revueltas in other scenes. The

Scene still from Salt of the Earth. *(International Union of Mine, Mill, and Smelter Workers/The Kobal Collection)*

Hollywood unions also barred IPC from using industry postproduction facilities; processing and editing the film had to be done at a number of secret locations. In the end, despite all the concerted opposition, Biberman and Jarrico managed to make a good neorealist film that combines the veracity of documentary with the emotional impact of well-scripted drama. Widely and hysterically condemned as a Kremlin-mandated piece of Communist propaganda, *Salt of the Earth* merely dramatizes the need for working men and women to come together in solidarity to fight discrimination and social injustice. Having failed to prevent the making of *Salt of the Earth*, the powers that be were, however, largely successful in blocking the film's exhibition in the United States. After premiering at the Grande Theater on East 86th Street in New York City on March 14, 1954, *Salt of the Earth* had a solid nine-week run there and at about a dozen other urban cinemas but, for the most part, the film was boycotted in America and lost about $250,000. Well received outside of the United States, *Salt of the Earth* won awards at several international film festivals and the 1955 Grand Prize of the Academie du Cinema de Paris. Though largely suppressed and forgotten, *Salt of the Earth* never sank into complete oblivion. The film enjoyed a limited theatrical rerelease in 1965 and was finally aired on public television in 1980. In 1992 the Library of Congress selected *Salt of the Earth* for the National Film Registry.

On the Waterfront (1954)

An especially revealing contrast to *Salt of the Earth* is Elia Kazan's *On the Waterfront* (1954), released four months later on July 28, 1954. The story of Kazan's political apostasy is well known. The most successful and powerful producer-director of his time, Kazan (1909–2003; *A Streetcar Named Desire; Viva Zapata!*) initially chose to defy HUAC's bullying and may have had the personal clout to delegitimize the blacklist had he had the courage to do so, but Kazan soon capitulated and named names rather than forfeit his lucrative Hollywood career, even though he had a highly profitable Broadway career to fall back on. Kazan justified informing on colleagues as a necessary repudiation of communism but his many detractors saw the issue as moral, not political. In their view, a principled refusal to betray friends and associates was not tantamount to an endorsement of Russian totalitarianism; it was simply the right thing to do. At any rate, Kazan found a kindred spirit in screenwriter Budd Schulberg, another HUAC informer anxious to rectify his sullied reputation. In 1950 Joe Curtis (nephew of Columbia Pictures mogul Harry Cohn) and director Robert Siodmak (*The Killers; Criss Cross*) hired Schulberg to write a screenplay based on "Crime on the Water Front," a Pulitzer Prize–winning series of muckraking articles on corruption in the International Longshoremen's Association's (ILA) New York and New Jersey locals that journalist Malcolm Johnson published in the *New York Sun* between November 8 to December 10, 1948, and subsequently expanded into the book, *Crime on the Labor Front: The Inside Story of Murder, Violence, and Organized Gangsterism in Labor Unions* (New York: McGraw-Hill, 1950). At the outset of the project Schulberg met with Johnson, who referred him to Father John M. "Pete" Corridan, SJ (1911–1984), the waterfront priest who ministered to and advocated for dockworkers from his parish at the St. Francis Xavier Church at 30 W. 16th Street in Manhattan's Chelsea neighborhood. Schulberg spent a good deal of time with Father Corridan and came to venerate the priest for his sincere New Testament beliefs, courage, and toughness in the face of considerable danger. Indeed, as it was originally conceived, Schulberg's script made a crusading priest based on Father Corridan the hero of the story. All of Schulberg's research and hard work came to grief—at least initially—when Harry Cohn rejected his script as "communistic" (Talmer 2004).

In 1947, three years before Schulberg began his waterfront script, playwright Arthur Miller (*Death of a Salesman*) was walking in the Red Hook district of Brooklyn when he noticed fading graffiti on building walls: "Dove è Pete Panto?" ("Where is Pete Panto?"). Intrigued, Miller began talking to longshoremen who had known Pietro Panto (1911–1939), a dockworker turned union activist who led a rank-and-file revolt against Joseph P. "King Joe" Ryan, the unutterably corrupt "life president" of the International Longshoremen's Association (ILA) who, with Anthony "Tough Tony" Anastasia and Tony's gangster brother, Albert (1902–1957; head of Murder Incorporated), ruled the Port of New York's 25,000 longshoremen through intimidation and violence. On the night of July 14, 1939, thugs working for Albert Anastasia kidnapped, brutally battered, and then strangled Pete Panto after Panto refused to take a bribe to desist from his dissident activities. His body was found in a shallow grave at a known mafia dumping ground in Lindenhurst, New Jersey, eighteen months later. Taken with Panto's tragic heroism, Miller visited Italy to get a better feeling for the Italian immigrant experience in America before writing a play based on Panto's life entitled "The Bottom of the River" (1949). The next year Miller collaborated with his then-close friend, Elia Kazan, to transform his play into "The Hook," a screenplay they hoped to turn into a film. The project died, though, in 1951 when Columbia Pictures' CEO Harry Cohn submitted "The Hook" to the FBI for analysis as to its subversive qualities. On the advice of the Bureau, Cohn suggested that Miller change the script's corrupt union bosses into Communists to make the work more politically correct! Miller declined.

Refusing to knuckle under to Harry Cohn, Arthur Miller dropped out and the project lay fallow until Elia Kazan allied himself with Budd Schulberg to bring a decidedly different version of the waterfront story to fruition. From late 1951 to the summer of 1953, Kazan and Schulberg produced eight rewrites of a screenplay that blended Schulberg's Father Corridan story with Arthur Miller's saga of Pete Panto. During the long and arduous process of developing their script, both Kazan and Schulberg fell afoul of HUAC and sold out their friends in order to survive in the business—the third and most crucial formative element affecting the ultimate shape of *On the Waterfront*. In its final form, *On the Waterfront* was a thinly veiled and deeply disingenuous political allegory that rationalized its authors' cowardice and opportunism. By having the story's protagonist, Terry Malloy, a failed boxer turned longshoreman, ultimately decide to testify before an anticrime commission against his crooked union bosses, Schulberg and Kazan glorified the informer as a heroic man of conscience. But neither Schulberg nor Kazan faced the situation of their fictional counterpart who was threatened with death whether he testified or not. Nor was the Communist Party both men belonged to in the 1930s at all like the ILA under Joseph Ryan. While most certainly doctrinaire, dictatorial, and controlled by Moscow, the Communist Party was not devoted to racketeering and did not murder its recalcitrant members. Nor was Spruille Braden's Crime Committee of Greater New York that investigated waterfront corruption in any way comparable to HUAC. The Crime Committee (which was active from 1951 to 1956) was formed to combat the very real and pervasive infiltration of the longshoremen's union by organized crime, whereas HUAC's chimerical quest to rid the nation of Communists was largely the fetid product of paranoia and political opportunism. In sum, Schulberg and Kazan had it all backward. While Terry Malloy was most assuredly on the side of the angels, his creators could make no analogous claim to righteousness.

After peddling their script all over Hollywood without luck, Schulberg and Kazan finally signed a contract with Horizon Pictures, an independent production company formed in 1950 by producer Sam Spiegel and director John Huston. Ironically, Spiegel secured $900,000 in financing from the previously disinclined Harry Cohn at Columbia Pictures. Shot in Hoboken, New Jersey, in the final months of 1953, *On the Waterfront* starred Marlon Brando (chosen over Frank Sinatra) as Terry Malloy (a conflation of Peter Panto and Tony Mike De Vincenzo, a dock boss who defected from the mob to Corridan's side); Karl Malden as Father Pete Barry (the Pete Corridan figure); Lee J. Cobb as Johnny Friendly (probably an amalgam of several crime figures including Albert Anastasia, Joe Ryan, and Big Bill McCormack, the "Mr. Big" of the entire New York waterfront); and Rod Steiger as Charley "The Gent" Malloy, Terry's older brother and a mobster associated with Johnny Friendly. Eve Marie Saint rounds out the cast as Terry Malloy's demure love interest. Though reprehensible politically—not only for its fallacious HUAC "friendly witness" allegory but also for stereotyping unionism as gangsterism—*On the Waterfront* is, from an artistic point of view, a great film. Graced with a pitch-perfect script, superb performances, the evocative black-and-white cinematography of Boris Kaufman (*L'Atalante*), and a stirring score by Leonard Bernstein, *On the Waterfront* was a box office smash that earned back its production costs tenfold. The film also garnered a dozen Oscar nominations and won statuettes for Brando, Eve Marie Saint, Elia Kazan, Budd Schulberg, Sam Spiegel, Boris Kaufman, editor Gene Milford, and set designer Richard Day. Critics who joined in the chorus of praise for the film were apt not to notice that New York's ultraconservative Cardinal Francis Joseph Spellman (1889–1967) staunchly opposed Father Corridan's efforts to democratize the waterfront or that closely contested union elections held in December 1952 and March 1953 failed to oust Joe Ryan's ILA as the authorized bargaining agent for New York's longshoremen.

The Sixties

Harvest of Shame (1960)

On Friday night, November 25, 1960, millions of Americans recovering from their Thanksgiving feast of the previous day were subjected to a sobering television viewing experience. That night *CBS Reports* aired *Harvest of Shame* (1960), a 1-hour documentary on the plight of migrant farmworkers created by CBS documentary producer David Lowe at the behest of executive producer Fred W. Friendly and narrated by legendary radio and television journalist Edward R. Murrow (1908–1965). *Harvest of Shame* follows farmworkers from their squalid winter quarters in Florida and Mexico to orchards and fields in the Northeast and Northwest. Working from dawn to dusk four-and-a-half months a year at harvest-time, Hispanic, black, and white migrant workers earned an average annual salary of $900—less than one-fifth of the 1960 U.S. average annual salary of $4,743. Their living conditions were appalling: crowded, filthy shacks without running water, a meager diet, no health care, no educational opportunities for migrant children, transportation to work sites standing packed like sardines in flatbed trucks. One southern grower who hired migrant labor sardonically remarks, "We used to own our slaves, now we just rent them."

Pioneering a new and revolutionary kind of advocacy documentary, David Lowe juxtaposed stark footage of the migrants' living and working conditions with pronouncements by wealthy growers, lobbyists, and government officials that attempted to explain away or minimize the all-too-obvious exploitation. Lowe's construction of an argument by inference using images to ironically refute (or sometimes illustrate) assertions by commentators would have a tremendous and enduring influence on political documentarians from Emile de Antonio to Michael Moore. Furthermore, with its bold and unashamed affirmation of workers' rights, *Harvest of Shame* helped to weaken the muzzling influence of HUAC on the America media just as the decadelong blacklist was being broken on the Hollywood front. The film also set the tone for a host of *CBS Reports* investigative documentaries aired throughout the 1960s and established CBS as the most courageous and innovative of network news organizations.

Ironically, Edward R. Murrow sought to prevent the airing of *Harvest of Shame* on Britain's BBC-TV in March 1961. As JFK's newly appointed director of the United States Information Agency (USIA), essentially a pro-America propaganda arm of the government, Murrow was afraid that foreign broadcast of a film that revealed glaring injustices in American society would only help to strengthen the hand of America's Communist adversaries. The program aired anyway and Murrow was mortified when his attempted intervention was made public. As for David Lowe, the unsung inventor of the muckraking documentary, he made a number of other *CBS Reports* films on current events before dying of a heart attack at the age of fifty-one on September 24, 1965.

The Seventies

The Molly Maguires (1970)

From 1863 to 1877 there existed, in the eastern Pennsylvania anthracite coal mining counties of Carbon, Columbia, Luzerne, Northumberland, and Schuykill, a mysterious organization known as the Molly Maguires (the name derived from a seventeenth-century Irish peasant woman who fought tenant evictions). A shadowy contingent of the Ancient Order of Hibernians (AOH), an Irish benevolent society, the Molly Maguires was formed during the Civil War to resist the draft on the grounds that it discriminated against the white working class by allowing any man with $300—half a year's wage for the average nonskilled worker—to buy his way out of military service. Having immigrated to America en masse during and after the Potato Famine (1846–1850), impoverished Irish Catholics entered American society at the lowest levels and were treated accordingly by a virulently prejudiced Protestant majority. Compelled by law to fight for the liberation of African slaves by a Republican administration perceived as antiproletarian, Irish Americans reacted with bitter class resentment animated by intense racism. In mid-July 1863, when New York City erupted into three days of sustained rioting against the draft (as dramatized in Martin Scorsese's operatic film, *The Gangs of New York*), Irish antidraft riots also occurred in eastern Pennsylvania mining towns. Thus the Mollies, as they were called, embodied a morally and politically ambiguous blend of justified anger at rank injustice with intolerance and mindless, sometimes homicidal, violence.

After the Civil War, the Molly Maguires, perhaps some 3,000–4,000 strong, turned their wrath on mine owners, pit bosses, and other rivals by issuing death warrants that were duly carried out if the intended victim refused to leave the area. In 1873 Franklin B. Gowen (1835–1889), president of the Philadelphia and Reading Railroad—which owned huge parcels of land in the mining counties— hired the Pinkerton Detective Agency to break up the Molly Maguires. The agency's founder, Allan Pinkerton (1819–1884), assigned detective James McParland to infiltrate the Mollies and gather evidence against them. Under the alias Jamie McKenna, McParland became a full-fledged Molly Maguire in December 1873 and over the next two years gathered massive amounts of incriminating information against the group. Suspected of being a spy by Mollie leader John "Black Jack" Kehoe (1837–1878), McParland fled Pennsylvania in late 1875. On May 6, 1876, the authorities arrested twenty Molly Maguires and subsequently tried them for a number of murders. With the trials paid for by the Reading Railroad and prosecuted by Franklin Gowen and associates, featuring McParland as the key witness and juries from which Irish Catholics were barred, the accused never had a chance. All were convicted and eventually hanged. Because of the rigged nature of the trials, suspicion persists than many were convicted on testimony McParland simply fabricated and were martyred so that Gowen could gain economic and political control over the anthracite counties.

The truth of the matter is hard to determine inasmuch as the early historical accounts only support the victorious Gowen point of view, for example, Alan Pinkerton's oft-reprinted book, *The Molly Maguires and the Detectives* (New York: G. W. Carleton, 1877), and Cleveland Moffett's article, "The Overthrow of the Molly Maguires," *McClure's* (1894). In keeping with changes in the zeitgeist, revisionist histories sympathetic to the Mollies appeared during the Great Depression: Anthony Bimba's *The Molly Maguires* (New York: International Publishers, 1932) and James W. Coleman's *The Molly Maguire Riots: Industrial Conflict in the Pennsylvania Coal Region* (Richmond, VA: Garrett and Massie, 1936). A third phase of interest in the Molly Maguires occurred in the early 1960s with Wayne Broehl's scholarly study, *The Molly Maguires* (Cambridge, MA: Harvard University Press, 1964) and Arthur H. Lewis's popular history, *Lament for the Molly Maguires* (New York: Harcourt, Brace & World, 1964).

Not long after Lewis's book appeared, director Martin Ritt (*Hud*) and screenwriter Walter Bernstein (*Fail Safe*)—both blacklisted in the 1950s and previous collaborators on *Paris Blues* (1961)—decided to make a movie based on the books by Coleman and Lewis. A deal was secured with Paramount Pictures in 1967 and, in the tumultuous spring of 1968, the film was shot in Eckley, Pennsylvania, a company mining town in Luzerne County saved from planned demolition and turned into a movie set. Afforded a hefty budget of $11 million (US$60.9 million in 2005), Ritt and Bernstein were able to hire Sean Connery (at the height of his fame as James Bond) to play Jack Kehoe and Richard Harris (*Major Dundee; Camelot*) to play James McParland/McKenna (though, unlike Harris, the real McParland was a big, bearish man). As per Hollywood requisites, Samantha Eggar (*Doctor Dolittle*) was contracted to play Miss Mary Raines, McKenna's landlady and love interest. Shot in color—black and white would have been a better choice—by the great cinematographer, James Wong Howe (*Hud; Seconds*), edited by Frank Bracht (*Hud; Nevada Smith*), and scored by Henry Mancini, *The Molly Maguires* (1970) promised to be a major film. Unfortunately, it turned out to be a major box office flop because Ritt and Bernstein could never quite decide where to put their allegiances. Inclined by political persuasion to side with the Molly Maguires, the filmmakers wanted to stay close to their source material and maintain the sort of moral ambiguity that makes for good storytelling. Though a commercial and critical failure, the film did succeed in reviving sustained interest in the Molly Maguires. The refurbished pseudo-town of Eckley has, for better or worse, become a living history museum run by the Pennsylvania Historical and Museum Commission, and a raft of new books on the Mollies have appeared since the movie.

Joe Hill (1971)

Another instance of labor history almost inextricably tangled in myth is the story of Joe Hill (aka Joseph Hillstrom; real name: Joel Emmanuel Haaglund, 1882–1915). A Swedish immigrant to the United States around 1901, Hill was a talented piano player, songwriter, and poet who in 1910 at the age of twenty-eight joined the International Workers of the World (IWW), the radical anarcho-syndicalist labor union founded in 1905 and popularly known as the Wobblies. The charismatic Hill became a dynamic IWW organizer and composer of a number of popular union ballads including "The Preacher and the Slave" (1911), "Casey Jones—the Union Scab" (1912), and "The Rebel Girl" (ca. 1914). Hill's career as a revolutionary was cut short, however, when he was arrested for the murder of grocer J. B. Morrison and his son in Salt Lake City, Utah, on Saturday, January 10, 1914. At the time of the killings the Morrison family exchanged gunfire with two masked assailants and one of the attackers was heard to exclaim that he had been wounded. The night of the attack Joe Hill was treated by a doctor for a through-and-through gunshot wound to the chest that he refused to explain except to say that it had to do with a romantic imbroglio. Though it had the strong but hardly conclusive circumstantial evidence of Joe Hill's wound, the prosecution could not produce the murder weapon, the bullet that passed through Hill, any of Hill's blood at the scene of the crime, or a positive identification by eyewitnesses. Nonetheless, Joe Hill was convicted of first-degree murder and, despite impassioned pleas from all over the world to Utah Governor William Spry, Hill was executed by firing squad at the Utah State Penitentiary on November 19, 1915. Shortly before he died he sent a final telegram to his friend and Wobbly colleague, William "Big Bill" Haywood (1869–1928), which read, in part, "Don't waste time in mourning. Organize!" (Stegner 1950). Joe Hill's body was shipped to Chicago for a funeral attended by 30,000 people. On May Day, 1916, Hill's ashes were scattered to the winds in the United States (except Utah) and several foreign countries. Larger in death than in life, Joe Hill became an iconic martyr of the radical labor movement. In 1936 activist-composer Earl Hawley Robinson (1910–1991) wrote "Joe Hill," a tribute that became a union anthem. The legend of Joe Hill remained sacrosanct until Wallace Stegner's fictionalized biography, *The Preacher and the Slave* (Boston: Houghton Mifflin, 1950; reprinted as *Joe Hill*, New York: Doubleday, 1969), advanced the troubling view that Joe Hill was probably guilty of the crime for which he was convicted.

As was consistent with his own, dreamy sensibilities, Swedish writer-director Bo Widerberg (*Elvira Madigan*) reverted to the romantic myth when he made *Joe Hill* (1971). A joint Swedish-American production starring Thommy Berggren, *Joe Hill* more or less accurately represents Hill's radicalization but then shades off into unsubstantiated territory when it foregrounds and embellishes Hill's possibly fictitious story that he was shot by a jealous rival in a love triangle. In the end, Widerberg is more interested in Joe Hill as a young, tragic lover of the Tristan variety than he is in Hill as a radical Wobbly: a sentimentalist perspective that serves history poorly.

Harlan County, U.S.A. (1976)

Markedly more tough-minded, informative, and moving is Barbara Kopple's Oscar-winning documentary, *Harlan County, U.S.A.* (1976). Located in southeastern Kentucky, "Bloody Harlan" has a history of labor strife stretching back to the early 1930s, when the United Mine Workers of America (UMWA) encountered fierce opposition from owners as it began to organize coal miners in the region. In 1970 the Eastover Mining Company, a subsidiary of Duke Power, purchased the Brookside Mine from Harlan Collieries and subsequently signed a three-year contract with the Southern Labor Union (SLU), an independent union considered pro-company by the workers. When the SLU contract expired, Brookside's miners opted to affiliate with the UMWA but Eastover's president, Norman Yarborough, refused to negotiate a new contract. On July 29, 1973, Brookside went on a strike that would last for the next thirteen months.

There the whole time to film and record the events was Barbara Kopple, a young leftist cinema verité filmmaker who had gone to college in the mining country of rural West Virginia and was attracted to Harlan County by the rise of Miners for Democracy, a dissident faction of the UMWA led by Joseph A. "Jock" Yablonski (1910–1969), who challenged the corrupt, dictatorial W. A. "Tony" Boyle (1902–1985) for the union presidency in December 1969. Boyle won the election but had Yablonski, his wife, and his daughter murdered in their beds by contract killers on New Year's Eve, 1969, as Yablonski still represented a threat to Boyle's power. Arnold Miller, the new Miners for Democracy candidate, later defeated Boyle, who was subsequently convicted and sentenced to life in prison for masterminding the Yablonski murders.

Unapologetically on the side of the miners, who were fighting for a decent wage and minimally safe working conditions, *Harlan County, U.S.A.* chronicles every aspect of the strike: the hard life at home for striking miners and their families, contentious strategy meetings, the daily grind—punctuated by violent confrontations—on the picket line, negotiations with company officials, the triumphant end of the strike on August 29, 1974 (three weeks after Richard Nixon's resignation). Using union songs throughout as accompaniment, Kopple and her crew contrast the rugged, natural beauty of the southeastern Kentucky countryside with the poverty and squalor of Brookside while also contrasting the bravery of the miners and their wives to the callousness and venality of the owners, cops, paid stooges, and scabs who tried to keep them down. In a society where power and social class relations are often obscured by a compliant corporate media, *Harlan County, U.S.A.* makes for an especially powerful viewing experience because the lines between the haves and have-nots are so clearly drawn. In 1990 the Library of Congress added *Harlan County, U.S.A.* to the National Film Registry.

All the President's Men (1976)

In keeping with the progressive political temperament that prevailed in the mid-1970s but approaching American politics from the opposite end of the power-privilege spectrum is *All the President's Men* (1976). Directed by Alan J. Pakula

Reporters Bob Woodward (right) and Carl Bernstein, whose reporting of the Watergate case won a Pulitzer Prize, sit in the newsroom of the Washington Post *on May 7, 1973. (AP/Wide World Photos)*

(*Klute; The Parallax View*) and adapted by William Goldman (*The Stepford Wives*) from the book of the same title by Bob Woodward and Carl Bernstein (New York: Simon & Schuster, 1974), *All the President's Men* recounts the Watergate affair from the night the watchman Frank Wills discovered a break-in at the Democratic National Committee (DNC) headquarters at the Watergate Office Building (June 17, 1972) to the day more than two years later when Richard Nixon resigned the presidency (August 9, 1974).

The driving force behind the film was actor Robert Redford, a liberal Democrat who was no fan of Richard Nixon. Redford noticed early on that Woodward and Bernstein, two young reporters for the *Washington Post*, were instrumental in exposing the Watergate burglary and subsequent cover-up. He met with them while the scandal was still unfolding and enlisted their cooperation in developing a movie that would dramatize the procedural intricacies of the Watergate investigation and celebrate competent, aggressive, principled journalism as an important force for keeping American democracy on the up and up.

Bringing the story of Watergate to the screen proved to be no easy matter, however. For obvious reasons the filmmakers were not allowed to film in the newsroom of the *Washington Post* so a full-scale mock-up had to built on a Hollywood soundstage at a cost of nearly a half million dollars. The script was even more problematic. Screenwriter William Goldman soon discovered that a docudrama based on the Watergate saga was hard to write; depicting two reporters making phone calls, researching records, interviewing people, and typing at their desks did not exactly make for a scintillating cinematic experience. The solution arrived at involved several components: radical streamlining to simplify a very complex story; documentary-style realism; fast pacing; a strong (and exaggerated) hint of danger and mystery for toying with powerful forces in government; dramatic foregrounding of the working relationship between Woodward and Bernstein and their skeptical, truculent boss, *Washington Post* editor, Ben Bradlee (Jason Robards). Fortunately, Bob Woodward and Carl Bernstein provided an interesting study in contrasts. Woodward was a well-scrubbed Ivy League golden boy being groomed for rapid advancement, while Bernstein was a working-class Jew who had worked his way up from copy boy and was still rough around the edges. The two quite nicely staked out the mythic roles of official hero and outlaw hero and suggested a potent joining of forces across social class lines. Woodward supplied the social graces and sophistication while Bernstein supplied the tenacity and street smarts. Though not promising on paper, *All the President's Men* turned out to be a surprisingly coherent, powerful, and entertaining viewing experience. A major box office hit, the film was nominated for eight 1977 Academy Awards and won Oscars for Best Sound, Best Art Direction, Best Supporting Actor (Jason Robards), and Best Writing (William Goldman). Though it was not apparent at the time, *All the President's Men* (book and film) would turn out to be American journalism's finest moment. In subsequent decades the public's high esteem for the press would evaporate as hardheaded investigative journalism gave over to tabloid-style celebrity gossip, crass sensationalism, and a morbid preoccupation with crime and cultural decadence.

Union Maids (1976)

Throughout the 1960s noted activists Staughton and Alice Lynd conducted tape-recorded oral history interviews with scores of workers regarding their experiences in the American labor movement during the 1930s and 1940s. The product of these interviews was *Rank and File: Personal Histories of Working-Class Organizers* (Boston: Beacon Press, 1973). Not long after the publication of *Rank and File* a trio of young leftist filmmakers—Julia Reichert, Jim Klein, and Miles Mogulescu—made *Union Maids* (1976), a 55-minute black-and-white documentary based on the Lynds' work but narrowing the focus to just three of the Lynds' interviewees, all Chicago-based CIO organizers: Sylvia Woods (1909–1987), a black woman from New Orleans who was the daughter of an ardent union man and an adherent of Marcus Garvey's separatist movement; Kate Hyndman (aka Christine Ellis, 1907–1978), born in Iowa to Croatian émigrés; and Stella Nowicki (aka Vicky Starr, 1916–) who grew up on a farm in the Midwest then moved to Chicago in 1933. At the time of the filming all three women—who come across as funny and vibrant—were still active in labor organizing. The interviews, supplemented by still photographs, newsreel footage, and pro-union songs, nostalgically recall a glorious and exciting time in the union movement, when the ranks were swelling with new members and important victories were being won. But as Linda Gordon points out in "*Union Maids:* Working Class Heroines," *Jump Cut*, no. 14 (1977), the film is misleading in implicitly suggesting that women were welcome in industrial work and in union organizing; for the most part they were not. Nor does *Union Maids* acknowledge that, by 1976, the U.S. labor movement was in serious trouble with the gathering momentum of deindustrialization, manufacturing jobs moving overseas, and a tough new corporatist hegemony being put into place that would deal unionism a crushing blow when Ronald Reagan destroyed the Professional Air Traffic Controllers Organization (PATCO) in 1981.

Norma Rae (1979)

Already something of a local hero in Roanoke Rapids, North Carolina, a cotton mill worker named Crystal Lee (Pulley) Jordan received national attention when freelance journalist Henry P. Leifermann made her the focus of "The Unions Are Coming," *New York Times Magazine* (August 5, 1973), an article on efforts by the Textile Workers Union of America (TWUA) to organize textile giant, J. P. Stevens. When Leifermann turned his article into a book—*Crystal Lee: A Woman of Inheritance* (New York: Macmillan, 1975)—producers Tamara Asseyou and Alexandra "Alex" Rose bought the rights and hired Martin Ritt (*Hud; The Molly Maguires*) to direct, who in turn hired the screenwriting team of Harriet Frank Jr. and Irving Ravetch (*Hud*) to write a script based on Leifermann's book. Never enthusiastic about pro-union movies, Hollywood studios shied away from backing a film about Crystal Lee. Eventually Asseyou and Rose were able to convince 20th Century Fox that their film could be marketed as a triumph-of-the-underdog story, a perennially popular trope in American popular culture.

Mostly shot at a working textile mill in Opelika, Alabama—600 miles from Roanoke Rapids—*Norma Rae* (1979) stars Sally Field as Norma Rae Webster, the Crystal Lee figure. Known to the public from 1960s television sitcoms *Gidget* and *The Flying Nun* and as Burt Reynolds' ditzy sidekick in *Smokey and the Bandit* (1977), the perky, diminutive, Pasadena-born Field seemed a strange casting choice for a tough, southern union maid. As it turned out, Sally Field could act and her surprisingly convincing performance as Norma Rae won her the first of two Academy Awards. Starring opposite Field was Ron Liebman (the memorably psychotic Paul Lazzaro in George Roy Hill's *Slaughterhouse-Five*) as New York–based labor organizer Reuben Warshawsky, a heavily fictionalized version of Eli Zivkovich (1921–1989), a former coal miner from West Virginia who was the TWUA organizer at Roanoke Rapids. No doubt, Harriet Frank and Irving Ravetch made their Zivkovich figure into a handsome, charismatic young New Yorker to create some sexual tension and cultural dissonance between their lead characters—and to generate the jealousy of Norma Rae's husband, Sonny (Beau Bridges), the fictional counterpart to Crystal Lee's second husband, "Cookie" Jordan. Despite these examples of poetic license, *Norma Rae* stays close to Crystal Lee's story. As suggested in the film, Crystal Lee was a sexually vibrant woman who had children with several men: a form of rebelliousness that she later sublimated into union work, a vocation that increased her self-confidence and supplied a sense of purpose previously lacking in her life. As depicted in the film Crystal Lee was indeed fired and arrested for copying an antiunion notice from a company bulletin board and did stand up on her workbench and display an improvised "Union" sign to her coworkers before being hauled out of the mill by police. As also depicted in the film, the workers at all six J. P. Stevens plants in Roanoke Rapids subsequently voted in the union—but fourteen months after Crystal Lee's dismissal, not immediately thereafter as was shown in the movie for maximum dramatic impact. A bona fide hit with box office returns exceeding $22.2 million (US$62.3 million in 2005), *Norma Rae* garnered a number of prestigious nominations and awards. Released during the pro–human rights administration of Democratic President Jimmy Carter, *Norma Rae* proved to be well attuned to the quasi-populist temper of the times.

The Eighties

Reds (1981)

Though tragically short at thirty-three years, the life of John Silas "Jack" Reed (1887–1920) was packed with adventure, drama, and momentous historical significance. Born into a wealthy family in Portland, Oregon, John Reed attended Harvard University (1906–1910), spent some time traveling, immersed himself in New York City's burgeoning arts scene, and then took up a highly successful career as a radical journalist-activist with his wife, Louise Bryant (1885–1936), also a radical. Reed covered the Mexican Revolution, the Ludlow (Colorado) Massacre, World War I, and the Russian Revolution and was a close friend of V. I. Lenin. Reed's eyewitness account of the Bolshevik Revolution, *Ten Days That Shook the World* (New York: Boni & Liveright, 1919), is still considered definitive.

Some time in the late 1960s actor Warren Beatty became fascinated with John Reed and began doing extensive research for a film about him. In 1976 Beatty hired British playwright Trevor Griffiths to write a screenplay and used Griffiths' script (initially titled "Comrades") to sign a production deal with Paramount Pictures. Between August 1979 and July 1980 Beatty (the film's producer, director, and star) and his Oscar-winning cinematographer Vittorio Storaro (*Apocalypse Now*) shot about 130 hours (i.e., nearly a million feet) of film at locations in England, the United States, Spain, and Finland. For added verisimilitude, *Reds* (1981) also includes clips from filmed interviews with thirty-two witnesses to the actual events (e.g., Henry Miller, Scott Nearing, Rebecca West, George Seldes, Roger Baldwin). In a scant five months editors Dede Allen (*Serpico; Dog Day Afternoon*) and Craig McKay (*Melvin and Howard*) distilled the mountain of footage to one-fortieth of its size: a still overlong 3 and a quarter hours.

Released in December 1981 *Reds* stars Beatty as John Reed; Diane Keaton (Beatty's girlfriend at the time) as Louise Bryant; Jack Nicholson as Bryant's lover, playwright Eugene O'Neill (1888–1953); and Polish novelist Jerzy Kosinski (*The Painted Bird*) as Russian revolutionary, Grigory Zinoviev (1883–1936). Concentrating on the last few years of Reed's life, *Reds* tries mightily to capture the moral and political seriousness of the man and his times but—in service to Beatty's vanity and the prerogatives of commercial filmmaking—cannot avoid foregrounding a melodramatic rendition of the often contentious love affair between Reed and Bryant. Rich, pampered, and glamorous Hollywood beautiful people, neither Beatty nor Keaton could project the mental toughness needed to make them believable Communists committed to world revolution. The times also worked against the film's impact. Conceived in a period of leftist ferment, *Reds* was released in the early Reagan era, when such views were once again being consigned to history's dustbin. A film that probably cost upward of $40 million (US$113 million in 2005) to make, *Reds* was not a box office hit—though over the long run, with video rentals and foreign distribution, it did make a profit.

Missing (1982)

On September 11, 1973, Chile's democratically elected Marxist President Salvador Allende Gossens (1908–1973) was deposed from power and murdered (or committed suicide; accounts vary) in a violent coup led by General Augusto Pinochet Ugarte. In the ensuing chaos Pinochet's junta dissolved Chile's congress and began arresting thousands of Allende supporters and incarcerating them temporarily at Santiago's National Stadium (now known as Victor Jara Stadium, after a famous victim of the coup). About 2,000 people, mostly Chileans, were summarily executed. Hundreds of others mysteriously disappeared. Initially in the latter category were two Americans: Charles E. Horman, thirty-one, a freelance journalist, and Frank R. Teruggi Jr., twenty-four, a graduate student. On September 21, four days after Charles Horman went missing, his father, Edmund C. Horman, first learned of his son's disappearance. After spending two weeks making frantic but futile inquiries, Edmund Horman flew to Santiago, Chile, on October 5, 1973. Two anxiety-filled weeks later Ed Horman learned that his son had been murdered by the Chilean military on September 18 and had been secretly buried in a wall at the National Cemetery two days before Ed Horman arrived in Chile. (Frank Teruggi was murdered on September 20.) When he discovered that the U.S. Consulate knew of Charles Horman's arrest but did nothing to intervene, an embittered Ed Horman filed a lawsuit against a number of officials in the U.S. State Department (including Henry Kissinger) but the suit was eventually dismissed because the U.S. government refused to release classified documents relating to the coup and Charles Horman's death. Ed Horman ultimately cast his lot with attorney Thomas Hauser, who felt the best way to publicize the Charles Horman case was to write about it. Hauser could produce no smoking gun but his book, *The Execution of Charles Horman: An American Sacrifice* (New York: Harcourt Brace Jovanovich, 1978), marshaled circumstantial evidence to argue that the Chileans assassinated Horman, with the U.S. government's knowledge and blessing, probably because Horman had been in Vina del Mar on September 11 and had learned too much about American involvement from U.S. military officials stationed in nearby Valparaiso where the coup originated.

Intrigued by the moral and political implications of the Horman family tragedy, Greek-born, Paris-based political filmmaker Constantin Costa-Gavras (*Z; State of Siege*) bought the rights to Hauser's book, secured funding from Universal Pictures, and proceeded to make *Missing* (1982), a powerful docudrama shot in Mexico and starring Jack Lemmon as Ed Horman and Sissy Spacek as Charles Horman's wife, Joyce (called Beth in the film). At the center of the film is Ed Horman's political conversion, from a conservative, patriotic Christian Scientist who firmly believes in the probity of his government to an angry, grief-stricken father who becomes convinced that his government was complicit in his son's killing and tried to cover it up. Coming a few years after the end of the Vietnam War, *Missing* reiterates the same sort of disillusionment that affected much of American society at that time; what was advertised as a benign undertaking was eventually revealed to be a corrupt, wrongheaded, atrociously destructive adventure that cast grave doubt on the nation's fundamental goodness. While

Sissy Spacek's rendition of Joyce Horman as petulant and abrasive is sometimes too shrill, Jack Lemmon's enactment of Ed Horman's transformation, from true believer to grim skeptic, is brilliantly realized and wholly convincing.

Missing, which never specifically refers to Chile, proved controversial from the outset. Two days *before* the film officially opened on February 12, 1982, the U.S. State Department took the highly unusual step of issuing a three-page communiqué taking issue with the film's allegations that its consulate in Chile did nothing to try to locate Charles Horman and that the United States somehow conspired in, or at the very least condoned, Horman's death. Interestingly the State Department did not challenge a third point implicit in the film: that the United States played a major role in the coup. More controversy followed on January 10, 1983, when Nathaniel Davis, former ambassador to Chile, Frederick D. Purdy (Consul Phil Putnam played by David Clennon in the film), former consul to Chile; and Capt. Ray E. Davis (Capt. Ray Tower played by Charles Cioffi in the film), an American military official in Chile at the time of the coup, joined together to file a $60 million libel suit against Costa-Gavras; Universal City Studios, the film's distributor; MCA, the distributor's parent company; and author Thomas Hauser and his publisher, Harcourt Brace Jovanovich. The lawsuit prompted Hauser's publishers to take his book out of print—and keep it out of print—even after a federal judge dismissed libel charges in February 1984. In 1985 Thomas Hauser sued his publishers for $6.5 million and reached a favorable out-of-court settlement in 1988. Hauser and Costa-Gavras were further vindicated in 1999 when President Bill Clinton directed the National Security Council (NSC) to release some 7,000 previously classified documents on Chile. The declassified files show that the U.S. government was indeed complicit in Allende's overthrow and that the State Department gave tacit permission to Pinochet's security forces to arrest Horman and Terruggi though American officials knew full well that the Chileans would deal with them brutally.

Silkwood (1983)

Shortly after 7:00 P.M. on the night of November 13, 1974, a 1973 Honda Civic driven by Karen Gay Silkwood veered off State Route 74, 7 miles south of Crescent, Oklahoma, and struck a concrete culvert. Silkwood, a twenty-eight-year-old lab technician at Kerr-McGee's Cimarron plutonium fuel plant in Crescent, died in the crash. The Oklahoma State Highway Patrol ruled the incident a classic case of a tired driver who had fallen asleep at the wheel. When an autopsy disclosed high levels of the sedative methaqualone (quaaludes) and alcohol in Silkwood's blood, the police theory gained added credibility. Others were not so sure. On the night she died Karen Silkwood was on her way to an Oklahoma City Holiday Inn to meet with David Burnham, a *New York Times* reporter, and Steve Wodka, a health and safety official for the Oil, Chemical, and Atomic Workers International (OCAW), the union to which Silkwood belonged. It was thought that Silkwood was carrying a sheaf of documents proving Kerr-McGee was in flagrant violation of safety regulations: not a small matter when the product being handled was highly radioactive plutonium. Silkwood's associates found no such documents among the items removed from her demolished Honda but the car had already been gone over by the state police and Kerr-McGee officials. Made suspicious by the murky circumstances surrounding Silkwood's death, OCAW hired private investigators to study the car and the accident scene. Their conclusion: a fresh dent in the rear bumper suggested that Silkwood's car was forced off the road by another vehicle. The allegation prompted the FBI to mount its own probe, which eventually upheld the state police finding that Silkwood had fallen asleep at the wheel. But the controversy would not go away. Howard Kohn, a reporter for *Rolling Stone* magazine, published a series of articles on Silkwood that he later fashioned into a partially fictionalized biography, sans footnotes, *Who Killed Karen Silkwood?* (New York: Summit Books, 1981). Investigative journalist Richard Rashke covered the story in far greater precision and depth with his book, *The Killing of Karen Silkwood: The Story behind the Kerr-McGee Plutonium Case* (Boston: Houghton Mifflin, 1981). Based on more than 20,000 pages of pretrial depositions, trial transcripts, FBI reports, and congressional transcripts, Rashke's book provided overwhelming evidence that Kerr-McGee, the Atomic Energy Commission (AEC) (reorganized as the Nuclear Regulatory Commission in 1975), and other government agencies colluded to conceal gross health and safety violations in the plutonium processing industry. Though Rashke could not prove that Karen Silkwood had been murdered, his book thoroughly discredited Kerr-McGee as a law-abiding, safety-conscious energy conglomerate.

Soon after these books appeared—and populist antinuclear fervor had reached its peak—producer-director Mike Nichols (*The Graduate; Catch–22*) took on the task of making Karen Silkwood's story into a Hollywood docudrama. Written by Nora Ephron (former wife of Carl Bernstein of Watergate fame) and Alice Arlen, *Silkwood* (1983) stars Meryl Streep as Karen Silkwood; Kurt Russell as Silkwood's boyfriend, Drew Stephens; and Cher as Silkwood's lesbian housemate, Sherri Ellis (named Dolly Pelliker in the film). Based largely on Howard Kohn's work, the Ephron-Arlen script takes numerous liberties with history. For example, *Silkwood* places inordinate emphasis on the interpersonal relationships among the three protagonists at the expense of dramatizing Silkwood's strident union activism and likewise makes Silkwood politically somewhat naïve, which she was not. The film also depicts the decontamination of Karen Silkwood's mysteriously radioactive house (in reality, an apartment) as having occurred in just one day when, in fact, the process took nearly three weeks and strongly suggests that Silkwood was deliberately run off the road on the night of her death: a plausible scenario but never proved. All of these changes serve to render Karen Silkwood a more sympathetic martyr-victim of despotic corporate power but also tend to diminish the extent of her autonomous political radicalism.

Matewan (1987)

On May 19, 1920, Mayor Cabell Testerman and Police Chief Sid Hatfield of Matewan, West Virginia, supported by a group of armed UMWA members, confronted employees of the Baldwin-Felts Detective Agency who had just illegally evicted striking coal miners and their families from Stone Mountain Mining Company housing. No one knows who fired the first shot but in the ensuing gun battle—which came to be known as the Matewan Massacre—Mayor Testerman, two miners, and seven Badwin-Felts detectives were killed and many more wounded: a rare instance of open, violent class war in a culture dedicated to denying that such conflict exists. The firefight at Matewan turned out to be the prelude to a long and bloody war that the UMWA ultimately won.

In the late 1970s leftist novelist-filmmaker John Sayles was doing research for his second novel, *Union Dues* (Boston: Little, Brown, 1977), which is partially set in West Virginia, when he came across a glancing reference to Sid Hatfield and the Matewan shoot-out in a book about the infamous Hatfield-McCoy feud (1863–1891). Intrigued, Sayles did further research on the labor wars in Mingo County right after World War I, when the UMWA (founded in 1890) was struggling to unionize portions of West Virginia and Kentucky. The nonunion coal producers in these areas still operated on a semifeudal basis. Workers dug coal in mines without any safety provisions, lived in wretched company housing, and were paid ridiculously low wages in company scrip, which could only be used to buy overpriced necessities at company stores. In sum, these Appalachian miners and their families lived the lives of de facto slaves. Because they paid their employees so little, nonunion companies could undersell unionized concerns and therefore continued to jeopardize the movement to unionize the industry. Consequently the battles between the coal companies and the UMWA were particularly fierce.

A nondoctrinaire Marxist, John Sayles has long been interested in stories of class struggle, grassroots community action, solidarity achieved among disparate minorities, and the (preferably nonviolent) ways in which working people gain some say over their economic and political lives. The Matewan saga provided all these elements except a nonviolent resolution. In writing a screenplay based on the "Mingo County Wars," Sayles therefore opted to create a fictional protagonist named Joe Kenehan (Chris Cooper in the film), a Wobbly organizer who tries but ultimately fails to find a nonviolent solution to the owner-miner conflict—but inspires a young acolyte named Danny Radnor (Will Oldham) to carry on the work for peaceful solutions to capital-labor conflicts. Integral to Sayles' artistic and political vision is the conviction that his films not reinforce the hyperindividualist American dream ethos by pinning the narrative on a single hero. Accordingly, *Matewan* (1987) also features David Strathairn as the indomitable Sid Hatfield and James Earl Jones as "Few Clothes" Johnson, the leader of black workers brought in as scab labor who ultimately opt to side with the UMWA against the mining company. Likewise, Fausto (Joe Grifasi) leads a contingent of Italian immigrants also recruited as scabs in switching over to the union side. Shot in somber tones by Oscar-winning cinematographer Haskell Wexler (*Medium Cool; Bound for Glory*) in Thurmond, West Virginia (100 miles from Matewan), *Matewan* faithfully re-creates the grim look and feel of Appalachian coal country in the 1920s.

Tucker: The Man and His Dream (1988)

In July 1946 a former Pierce-Arrow sales manager named Preston Tucker (1903–1956) founded the Tucker Corporation of Chicago for the purpose of mass-producing the Tucker Torpedo, an innovative four-door sedan that would boast a mostly aluminum, long-slung body with fastback styling, push-button controls, a 166-horsepower rear-mounted engine, air-cooled disk brakes, hydraulic torque converter, built-in air conditioning, special safety glass, individual wheel suspension, twin mufflers (and six tailpipes), and a center headlight that turned with the steering wheel. Tucker leased a 475-acre Chrysler-Dodge plant on Chicago's South Side that had been used to make B-29 engines during the war and began to raise capital by selling distributor and dealer franchises. In May 1947 Tucker filed a registration prospectus with the Securities and Exchange Commission (SEC) to offer public shares in his corporation. The following month Tucker whetted the public's appetite for his new car by unveiling a hastily fabricated prototype (actually a mock-up made from a 1942 Oldsmobile) amid much fanfare. By September 1947 Tucker had raised $15 million from stock sales and another $7.7 million from franchises (almost US$215 million in 2005). But the Tucker Corporation was already in deep trouble. Numerous technical problems with the car, a tool and die strike, internecine squabbling, administrative shake-ups, lawsuits, and tax problems led to investor panic and a collapsing stock price. In July 1948 the SEC delivered the coup de grâce by order-ing a massive investigation into the company's finances that forced Tucker to suspend operations. In June 1949 a grand jury indicted Preston Tucker and seven of his associates for SEC violations. On January 11, 1950, after a four-month trial, Tucker and his business partners were acquitted of stock fraud but the Tucker Corporation was in ruins, having made only fifty Tucker 1948 cars (the last thir-teen without engines or transmissions). Preston Tucker died from lung cancer on December 16, 1956, having failed to realize his dream.

Thirteen years after Preston Tucker's death, producer-directors Francis Ford Coppola and George Lucas founded a San Francisco–based independent film studio named American Zoetrope in order to make artistically innovative movies outside the Hollywood system. To his chagrin Coppola had to sell his share of Zoetrope in 1983 after losing more than $25 million on his offbeat musi-cal *One from the Heart* (1982). After two more box office fiascos—*Rumble Fish* (1983) and *The Cotton Club* (1984)—it appeared that Francis Coppola was fin-ished as a filmmaker, but when *Peggy Sue Got Married* (1986) proved a major hit, Coppola's career in movies gained a new lease on life. Having been nearly destroyed for pursuing his own vision somewhat heedless of commercial conse-quences, Detroit-born Francis Coppola saw the saga of Preston Tucker as deeply analogous to his own experience (Coppola's father, Carmine, had indeed pur-chased a Tucker Torpedo in 1948). After making the Vietnam War movie, *Gardens of Stone* (1987), Coppola joined forces with his old partner, George Lucas, to bring Tucker's story to the screen. Not surprisingly, screenwriters Arnold Schulman (*A Chorus Line*) and John Seidler created in *Tucker: The Man and His Dream* (1988) a deeply romanticized film that portrays Preston Thomas Tucker (Jeff Bridges in the film) as a cheerfully naïve idealist and visionary and attributes his downfall to persecution by the established Detroit automakers in collusion with big government: entrenched bureaucracies inimical to the entrepreneurial spirit that built America. Needless to say, such a view is self-serving to Coppola (and Lucas) and downplays Tucker's tendency to generate hoopla for his product with-out devoting the requisite time, money, and attention to research, development, and testing. While it is true that Preston Tucker was subject to unfair harassment by the SEC and other agencies, he also made a series of colossal mistakes that would ultimately render the Tucker a mere automotive curiosity.

Roger & Me (1989)

A very different but strangely complementary take on the American auto indus-try is offered by Michael Moore's *Roger & Me* (1989), a satiric documentary about the economic annihilation of Flint, Michigan, by its chief employer, General Motors Corporation. In the mid-1980s GM Chairman Roger B. Smith ordered the closing of most of GM's facilities in Flint, throwing some 30,000 people out of work and wreaking havoc on the city (population 150,000) and environs. Moore, a Flint native, decided to make a film that would not only document the ruin caused by the plant closings but would also expose laughably inept attempts by municipal government to effect economic recovery. Tying the film together is a third element: Moore's quixotic quest to meet with Roger Smith and convince him to tour Flint to see for himself what his cost-cutting measures have wrought. Moore never expects to actually meet and converse with Smith; the whole point of his pursuit of Smith at GM headquarters in Detroit and at Smith's homes and haunts is to dramatize the man's utter inaccessibility—and by extension, the Olympian distance of the corporate ruling class from ordinary Americans.

A corpulent, baby-faced man with longish hair, eyeglasses, ever-present baseball cap, and casual attire, Michael Moore slyly establishes an on-screen persona as a disarmingly unkempt working-class Everyman (when in reality Moore is a smart, angry, tough-minded critic of American business civilization). Moore's awkward and sometimes hilarious encounters with Roger Smith's guards, flunkies, apologists, and other cheerleaders of corporate capitalism are best

Michael Moore with a television set showing General Motors CEO Roger Smith, who was the subject of Moore's documentary Roger & Me. *(Jacques M. Chenet/Corbis)*

understood as 1960s-style guerrilla theater—the work of a counterculture skeptic baiting dim-witted servants of power and privilege to illustrate some of the patent absurdities of a social system that sanctifies profit accumulation for its ruling elite at the expense of most everyone else. Moore's genial but pointed interviewing methods cause many of his interviewees to hang themselves with their own ropes. GM spokesman Tom Kay sounds heartless when expounding on the corporation's right to fire as many workers as it deems necessary. Conservative Christian crooner and former GM pitchman Pat Boone comes off as vapid, smug, and out-of-touch, as do the equally repugnant Anita Bryant (who offers an unconvincing pep talk to the unemployed), Bob Eubanks (who tells an anti-Semitic joke), and Kaye Lani Rae Rafko (Miss America 1988, whose quest for personal glory contrasts sharply with Flint's wholesale devastation). Moore also highlights Flint's pitiful, idiotic efforts to transform itself into a tourist destination by spending precious millions on a new downtown Hyatt Hotel and Auto World, an amusement park that soon goes out of business. Meanwhile crime, poverty, home abandonment, and rat infestation in Flint soar to unprecedented levels and a deputy sheriff named Fred Ross is depicted, in several scenes, evicting tenants behind in their rent. In sum, *Roger & Me* shows, in a truly visceral way, what happens when a community organized around profit extraction is allowed to go belly up. Critics have pointed out that Michael Moore is not always precise about chronology. Nor does he offer a sophisticated analysis of the macroeconomic factors behind General Motors' huge downsizing in the 1980s (steady loss of market share to Japanese imports that led to ill-advised attempts at business diversification, automation, streamlining, and so forth). Nonetheless, Moore's salient point—that GM built and exploited communities like Flint to serve its business purposes and then deserted them when it proved expedient—remains an irrefutable truth mostly suppressed or ignored by the mainstream media.

A rank amateur with no prior filmmaking experience or training, Michael Moore made *Roger & Me* on a shoestring budget of about $160,000, some of which he raised through a legal settlement, by selling his house, and by holding yard sales and bingo fund-raisers. A surprise hit with critics—except for Pauline Kael, who panned it—and audiences, *Roger & Me* won a million-dollar distribution deal with Warner Brothers and launched Michael Moore as a major and often controversial American polemicist of the Left, whose sometimes bombastic books, television shows, and later films would bedevil corporatist ideologues for years to come. Ironically, *Roger & Me* could not be shown within the city limits of Flint, Michigan—not because it was banned but because all of Flint's movie theaters had gone out of business.

The Nineties

American Dream (1991)

In October 1984, two years before General Motors began to pull the plug on Flint, George A. Hormel & Company unilaterally tightened work rules, reduced benefits, and cut the base pay of line employees at its flagship meatpacking plant in Austin, Minnesota, from $10.69 to $8.25 an hour—even though the company had posted a $26 million profit for 1983. These developments prompted James Guyette, president of Local P-9 of the United Food and Commercial Workers Union (UFCW), to organize protests and to hire Ray Rogers' Corporate Campaign, an aggressive labor-consulting firm that had been instrumental in the unionization of J. P. Stevens. Jim Guyette also sought the help of the 1.3-million member UFCW but Lewie Anderson, head negotiator for the union's packinghouse division, refused to support P-9. Anderson argued several points: that with the virulently antiunion Ronald Reagan in the White House, it was not a propitious time to engage in labor militancy; that Hormel was well positioned to hold out indefinitely; that Hormel's rival, Armour, paid its nonunion workers only $6.00 an hour and that a boycott against Armour had to be given priority over the situation in Austin to stabilize pay scales throughout the meatpacking industry; that Ray Rogers' plan to launch a boycott of Hormel would hurt workers at other Hormel plants.

Though not backed by its parent union, P-9 voted 1,261 to 96 to reject Hormel's new contract on August 14, 1985, and three days later began the first strike against Hormel in fifty-two years—which soon devolved into a grueling stalemate that dragged on into the winter of 1985-1986. By January 1986 P-9 was in dire straits. The bitter cold and snow made picketing an onerous chore and the strikers and their families were living on subsistence terms, many of them facing foreclosure on their homes. To make matters worse, on January 13, 1986, five months into the strike, Hormel reopened the Austin plant and, over the next three weeks, hired more than 700 new replacement workers and rehired 400 strikers who had given up the fight and returned to work. When P-9 picketers tried to block the passage of former comrades and other scabs into the plant, so much violence ensued that Governor Rudy Perpich ordered out the Minnesota National Guard to maintain order. Ray Rogers and many strikers were arrested but nothing was accomplished; by mid-February the Austin plant was back in full operation and the strike was, for all intents and purposes, broken. Still, the remaining members of P-9 soldiered on. There were more picket line clashes, more rallies, more arrests, but all to no avail. In mid-March P-9 voted to reconcile with its parent union but then, a few days later, defied the UFCW and voted to continue the strike. On June 2, 1986, a federal judge granted the UFCW an injunction allowing it to take over P-9 and conduct negotiations with Hormel through an appointed trustee. The union settled with Hormel on September 12, almost thirteen months after the strike started. All told, the Austin strike cost hundreds of workers their jobs, caused bitter and lasting community divisions, and proved a devastating defeat to an American labor movement already reeling from PATCO and other Reagan-inspired debacles.

In Austin for the duration, Barbara Kopple (*Harlan County, U.S.A.*) filmed the strike from its optimistic beginnings to its bitter, disillusioning end. As she had done in Harlan County a decade earlier, Kopple established close relationships with the strikers and was on hand with her film crew to record the often tense negotiations between P-9 and the international union and between the union and Hormel management. Kopple also interviewed strikers on the picket line and in their homes and filled out the story with television news archival footage. The resulting film, *American Dream* (1991), was a depressing and wrenchingly ambiguous saga of organized labor's self-division and defeat that differed markedly from *Harlan County, U.S.A.* The earlier film had easily identifiable heroes, villains, and an upbeat ending. *American Dream* reflected a much more complicated and troubled time that presented not two but *three* antagonists: P-9, the UFCW, and Hormel. The crucial fact of the Austin strike of 1985–1986 is that the local did not have the support of its parent union. Without such support the strike was probably doomed from its inception. Yet Kopple does not fault the UFCW for its seemingly timid recalcitrance or P-9 for its seemingly heedless militancy; both points of view are shown to be valid from their own perspectives. Hormel, a large and profitable concern, had already wrested givebacks from its workers to build its $100 million, 23-acre Austin facility. The work regimen at the new plant (opened in 1982) was brutal, and Hormel's decision to cut wages and benefits in the fall of 1984 caused deep resentment. P-9 had legitimate complaints but UFCW was right, in its own way, to stress industry-wide considerations and an adverse political climate. If anyone comes off badly, it is probably Ray Rogers. Rogers' Corporate Campaign had been highly successful against J. P. Stevens a decade earlier but its aggressive confrontational tactics proved ill suited to the Reagan era. A somber but powerful viewing experience, *American Dream* earned Barbara Kopple a number of awards including a second Oscar.

JFK (1991)

The assassination of President John F. Kennedy in Dallas, Texas, on November 22, 1963, was unquestionably one of the most traumatic events in modern American history. Despite the findings of the Warren Commission—that Lee Harvey

Oswald was the killer and acted alone—Kennedy's gruesome and very public murder, preserved for all time by the Zapruder film, haunts the American cultural psyche like no other event. Conspiracy theories sprung up immediately and have continued to proliferate, and theorists have produced myriad books, articles, films, and websites rehashing every facet of the assassination, its geopolitical background, and its supposed implications. Many unanswered questions do indeed remain but the abiding impetus behind the endless controversy can probably be attributed to human incredulity. It is difficult to believe that such an inconsequential little man as Lee Harvey Oswald could destroy the most powerful man on earth in the span of a few seconds with a cheap, mail-order vintage rifle.

Having already made a number of major films covering salient aspects of American history in the 1960s (*Platoon; Born on the 4th of July; The Doors*), polemical filmmaker Oliver Stone turned his attention to the Kennedy assassination with *JFK* (1991). Stone and his co-screenwriter, Zachary Sklar, based their script on two conspiracy books: Jim Garrison's *On the Trail of the Assassins* (New York: Sheridan Square Press, 1988) and Jim Marrs' *Crossfire: The Plot That Killed Kennedy* (New York: Carroll & Graf, 1989). They also supplemented these works with extensive further research. What Stone and Sklar came up with was truly mind-boggling. *JFK* puts forth the theory that Oswald was, as he himself said, merely a patsy and that the actual killing was carried out by a shadowy team of professional hit men employed by a conspiracy of hawkish U.S. generals, rogue elements inside the intelligence community, organized crime confederates—and Vice President Lyndon B. Johnson! The putative motive: to exact vengeance on Kennedy for his failure to support the invasion of Cuba at the Bay of Pigs (April 17, 1961) and to stop him from pulling out of Vietnam: a move that would supposedly degrade America's world stature, weaken the fight against the global spread of communism, and deprive the military-industrial complex of rich sources of revenue.

Lending some circumstantial plausibility to these notions is the fact that Oswald, as a U.S. Marine, had been stationed at a secret radar facility in Japan, had defected to the Soviet Union and married a Russian woman, had just as suddenly and mysteriously returned to the United States, had become involved with a pro-Castro organization in New Orleans whose offices were adjacent to former CIA and FBI agents involved in *anti*-Castro activities, and so on. In the hands of Oliver Stone and his cohorts, these odd and puzzling tidbits are arranged in powerfully portentous ways to suggest that Lee Harvey Oswald was set up as the designated fall guy for the assassination and that his own assassination by Dallas nightclub owner Jack Ruby (November 24, 1963) had been carefully planned to bring closure to what was in effect a secret coup that overthrew the U.S. government.

Adding prestige to Stone's film is a large ensemble cast made up of some of the finest (or most popular) actors in Hollywood: Kevin Costner as New Orleans D.A. Jim Garrison; Sissy Spacek as Garrison's wife, Liz; Walter Matthau as Senator Russell Long; Edward Asner as former FBI agent Guy Bannister; Jack Lemmon as Bannister's sidekick; Tommy Lee Jones as New Orleans businessman Clay Shaw (aka Clay Bertrand); John Candy as New Orleans lawyer Dean Andrews; Gary Oldman as Lee Harvey Oswald; Joe Pesci as David Ferrie, a paranoid informant; Donald Sutherland as a mysterious government man; and Kevin Bacon as a fictional character named Willie O'Keefe. While Kevin Costner delivers one of the most wooden and insipid performances captured on film, his fellow actors are almost uniformly impressive—even in thankless roles, such as Sissy Spacek's superfluous turn as Garrison's wife who is always unhappy that he is so obsessed with the assassination. Garrison's prime suspect, David Ferrie, dies before he can be brought to trial but Garrison does prosecute Clay Shaw for JFK's murder. In the end Garrison fails to convict Shaw but the film uses the trial to play and replay the Zapruder film, to discredit the Warren Commission's single bullet theory (derisively called the "magic bullet" theory in the film), and to afford Garrison the platform to make a pompous closing statement about the mythic significance of Kennedy's allegedly unsolved murder. Beautifully shot and brilliantly edited, *JFK* creates and sustains an aura of momentous intrigue that is utterly absorbing, despite the film's considerable length.

Before, during, and after its national release on December 20, 1991, *JFK* generated a firestorm of controversy and Oliver Stone was denounced from Left, Right, and Center for playing fast and loose with history. Sadly, viewers of *JFK* who come to the film with no prior knowledge of the assassination will be impressed by its seductive pretensions toward authenticity and will believe that they are seeing a true rendition of history instead of an almost impenetrable admixture of fact, unsubstantiated myth, and ill-founded conjecture. The fallacies and half-truths advanced in *JFK* are too numerous and complex to elucidate here. Readers should refer to an exhaustively researched and authoritative website by Dave Reitzes called "The *JFK* 100—One Hundred Errors of Fact and Judgment in Oliver Stone's *JFK.*"

F.I.S.T. (1978) and *Hoffa* (1992)

President of the two-million-member International Brotherhood of Teamsters (IBT) from 1957 to 1971, James Riddle "Jimmy" Hoffa (1911–1975) forged the Master Freight Agreement of 1964 that regularized labor terms for truckers throughout the country and solidified the Teamsters as America's richest and

most powerful labor union. Though admired by his constituents for his toughness, resolve, and tactical brilliance, Hoffa was hounded by government authorities and widely reviled by the public at large for his underworld connections.
Sentenced to prison in March 1967 for jury tampering and fraud, Hoffa was pardoned four and a half years later by President Nixon—with the proviso, secretly
brokered with a $300,000 bribe by his handpicked surrogate, Frank E. "Fitz"
Fitzsimmons (1907–1981), that he (Hoffa) refrain from union activities until
1980. Enraged by Fitzsimmons' betrayal, Hoffa mounted a determined campaign
to regain the Teamster presidency after his release from federal prison on
December 24, 1971.

Jimmy Hoffa's three-and-a-half-year quest to win back power abruptly
ended on Wednesday afternoon July 30, 1975. On that day Hoffa drove his 1974
Pontiac Grand Ville the 21 miles south from his home in Lake Orion, Michigan,
to the Machus Red Fox Restaurant on Telegraph Road in Bloomfield Hills (a
northwest Detroit suburb) for a 2:00 P.M. meeting to mend fences with mobster
associates Anthony "Tony Pro" Provenzano and Anthony "Tony Jack" Giacalone.
At 2:15 Hoffa called his wife, Josephine, to complain that he had been stood up.
Twelve minutes later Hoffa phoned the office of his friend, Louis Linteau, to
voice the same complaint. Jimmy Hoffa was never seen or heard from again. It
is presumed that Hoffa was abducted and murdered by mafia thugs in cahoots
with Frank Fitzsimmons.

Autocratic, cynical, volatile, foul-mouthed but also fearless, abstemious,
scrupulously self-disciplined, and a devoted family man, Jimmy Hoffa was a
complex individual who lived a fascinating life and met a mysterious fate.
Decades after his disappearance, Hoffa remains America's most notorious and
legendary labor leader. Inevitably Hoffa's story has been dramatized on film and
television a number of times. Director Norman Jewison's *F.I.S.T.* (1978), written
by Joe Eszterhas (*Basic Instinct*) and starring Sylvester Stallone of *Rocky* fame
as Johnny D. Kovack (Hoffa), is a mostly fictionalized biopic that portrays its
protagonist as a principled unionist who has to make alliances with the mob to
defend his truckers' union from company thugs but later comes to realize that
casting his lot with organized crime was a terrible mistake. A lethargic actor of
limited talent, Stallone was not capable of evoking Hoffa's intensity—or even
delivering a very credible performance. *F.I.S.T.* did reasonably well at the box
office but was soon forgotten.

Markedly better but far from perfect is *Hoffa* (1992), an epic biopic written
by acclaimed playwright-screenwriter David Mamet (*House of Games; Glengarry
Glen Ross*), produced and directed by Danny DeVito, and starring Jack Nicholson
as Jimmy Hoffa and DeVito as Bobby Ciaro, a fictionalized Hoffa sidekick who is
an amalgam of several Hoffa lieutenants. Armand Assante plays a fictional

Jimmy Hoffa, 1959, president of the Teamsters Union. (Associated Press)

character named Carol D'Allesandro, a composite of all the influential mobsters who were part of Hoffa's world. Mamet employs a noir structure, telling Hoffa's story through a series of flashbacks as Hoffa and Bobby Ciaro await their rendezvous with mobsters at a roadside café on that fateful midsummer afternoon in 1975. (In reality Hoffa was alone, the restaurant was upscale, and he waited only half an hour, not the several hours depicted in the film.) Though some 4 inches taller than Hoffa (who stood 5 feet 5 and a half), Nicholson in makeup and with a prosthetic nose bears a credible resemblance to his subject and plays the role with great conviction and seriousness. The film's thesis is both straightforward and startling. David Mamet argues that Hoffa formed alliances with the mob only because it had the requisite muscle to help him win labor concessions from a rapacious, brutal capitalist system that routinely crushes worker opposition by political chicanery, intimidation, force, and violence. If Hoffa was mean-spirited, ruthless, and corrupt—which he most certainly was—he was nothing more than a pure product of American class warfare in all its unmitigated, Darwinian savagery. Also revisionist is the film's portrayal of Robert F. Kennedy (1925–1968). In the popular imagination, Bobby Kennedy is remembered as an idealistic politician who might have effected much positive social change had he not been assassinated. In *Hoffa*, Bobby Kennedy (Kevin Anderson) comes across as a peevish, vindictive, opportunistic scion of privilege lacking any real awareness of the plight of working-class people: a refreshingly iconoclastic perspective after all the Kennedy worship perpetrated by the mainstream media.

Cradle Will Rock (1999)

Staking out an entirely different sensibility is Tim Robbins' *Cradle Will Rock* (1999). Both hailing from working-class backgrounds, David Mamet and Danny DeVito were avid to rehabilitate Jimmy Hoffa as an admittedly flawed working-class hero and perhaps slightly alter popular preconceptions about social class. From haute bourgeois stock—his father being folksinger Gil Robbins (real name: Gilbert Rubin) of the Highwaymen and his mother a musician and publishing executive—Tim Robbins espouses a more rarified but also more strident and polemical progressivism. Not surprisingly, *Cradle Will Rock* deals with social class only insofar as it impacts on questions of artistic freedom and censorship. The title of the film refers to *The Cradle Will Rock*, a 1936 pro-union operetta by radical composer-playwright Marc Blitzstein (1905–1964). Produced by John Houseman (1902–1988) and directed by Orson Welles (1915–1985) for Works Progress Administration (WPA) Federal Theatre Project (FTP) 891, *The Cradle Will Rock* was scheduled to open with a preview performance on Wednesday,

June 16, 1937, at the Maxine Elliott Theatre on West 39th Street and 6th Avenue in New York City. When hundreds of people showed up that night, they were informed that the show would not go on—at least not at that venue. The previous day WPA Federal Theatre Director Hallie Flanagan (1890–1969), on orders from Congress, had suspended all WPA theater productions until July 1, ostensibly to allow the agency to implement a 25 percent personnel cut. More likely the FTP pulled the plug because of mounting nervousness in government circles that Mrs. Flanagan's agency was producing ever more overtly Marxist theatrical works at taxpayer expense. Pennsylvania Senator James J. Davis leveled charges of communism at the Federal Theatre Project in April 1936. Thereafter congressional conservatives suspected that the FTP was a subversive organization. Named as a Communist sympathizer by a disgruntled employee named Hazel Huffman (Joan Cusack in the film), Hallie Flanagan (Cherry Jones in the film) was compelled to testify before Texas Representative Martin Dies' Special [House] Committee on Un-American Activities in December 1938—an event Tim Robbins conflates with the debut of *Cradle* in June 1937 to heighten dramatic intensity.

As members of the cast regale the milling crowd with songs from the opera, John Houseman (Cary Elwes) and Orson Welles (Angus Macfadyen) finalize arrangements for another, hastily acquired venue: the Venice Theatre at 59th Street and 7th Avenue. Cast members and audience walk or ride the twenty blocks north and one block west and *The Cradle Will Rock* goes ahead at 9:00 P.M. Marc Blitzstein (Hank Azaria) substituting for a twenty-three-piece orchestra, provides musical accompaniment at a rented piano on a bare stage lit by a single spotlight. Following the spontaneous example of Olive Stanton (Emily Watson), members of the cast sing their parts from the audience so as not violate an order from Actor's Equity against participating in an unauthorized WPA production. At the end of the 2-hour performance (20 minutes in the film), the audience stands and cheers as it did in actuality; everyone knew that theater history had been made that night.

The Cradle Will Rock had a history beyond June 16, 1937. The WPA distanced itself from Blitzstein's operetta but Orson Welles and John Houseman later took it on the road and, in early 1938, Welles's Mercury Theatre staged a 108-performance run at the Windsor Theatre in the Bronx. In the spring of 1983, forty-six years after its first performance, John Houseman mounted a revival of *Cradle* at the American Place, a small off-Broadway theater on West 46th Street. At the time of his death, Orson Welles planned to make a behind-the-scenes docudrama about the operetta called "Rocking the Cradle."

While Tim Robbins makes the legendary debut of *The Cradle Will Rock* the centerpiece of his film, he adds fictional characters (e.g., an alcoholic ventriloquist played by Bill Murray) and rearranges historical chronology to form a cluster of incidents that celebrate Depression-era artistic idealism or disparage censorship and political reaction. One such famous episode—also covered in Julie Taymor's *Frida* (2002)—involves Mexican muralist Diego Rivera (1886–1957) who was commissioned to paint a 17' x 6' fresco for the Great Hall of the new RCA Building in Rockefeller Center. On May 10, 1933, five and a half weeks after Rivera (Rubén Blades in the film) started his mural called "Man at the Crossroads," the Rockefeller Foundation paid him the $14,000 it owed him and ejected him from the work site. Rivera, a Communist, was cashiered because he had audaciously insisted on including an image of Nicolai Lenin (Vladimir Ilich Ulyanov, 1870–1924), the architect of the Russian Revolution, in a work of art installed at one of the shrines of American corporate capitalism! Not amused, Nelson Rockefeller (John Cusack in the film) had the mural destroyed in February 1934.

Though too frenetic, broadly focused, and occasionally heavy-handed in its depiction of political heroes and villains, *Cradle Will Rock* is unusual in its focus on an important and hitherto neglected moment in American cultural history, when politics and art were considered compatible enterprises. Though treated respectfully by critics, *Cradle Will Rock* was too complex and sophisticated for the average moviegoer and proved to be a box office disaster for Touchstone Pictures, earning only $3 million—less than 10 percent of what it cost to make.

The New Millenium

Erin Brockovich (2000)

While Tim Robbins' valiant attempt to interest the moviegoing public in the politico-cultural debates of the 1930s proved to be an exercise in commercial futility, producer-director Stephen Soderbergh (*Gray's Anatomy; The Limey*) hit it big with *Erin Brockovich* (2000), a straightforward, contemporary triumph-of-the-underdog story. As sometimes happens, *Erin Brockovich* had its genesis in a chance encounter. Carla Santos Shamberg, the wife of film producer Michael Shamberg (a partner in Jersey Films with Danny DeVito and Stacey Sher), heard the saga of Erin Brockovich from her chiropractor. In 1991 a twice-divorced single mother of three with no money and no prospects, Erin Brockovich pleaded for work at the law offices of Masry and Vititoe in Westlake Village, a community north of Malibu, California. Lawyer Ed Masry took pity on Brockovich and gave her a job as a file clerk. Assigned to do some case research, Brockovich wondered why medical records were included in real estate files. Further digging revealed that Pacific Gas and Electric (the world's largest utility) was buying up and condemning scores of properties in Hinkley, California, a small town in the Mojave Desert near Barstow. The reason soon became clear. In 1952 PG & E built a compressor station in Hinkley, on a pipeline delivering natural gas from Texas to California. The utility used highly toxic hexavalent chromium (aka Chromium 6) to inhibit corrosion and scaling in the compressor plant's cooling towers and then dumped the contaminated wastewater in unlined ponds nearby. As early as the autumn of 1965, PG & E was aware that Chromium 6 was leaching into the groundwater but did not line its take-up ponds with clay until 1972—after millions of gallons of polluted water had been discharged. In 1988 PG & E officials met with Hinkley residents and reassured them that their drinking water was safe even though the utility was well aware from its own tests that Chromium 6 levels were *thousands of times* higher than EPA recommendations. Once it had compiled exhaustive evidence of numerous illnesses among Hinkley residents, Masry and Vititoe joined forces with Girardi & Keese and Engstrom, Lipscomb & Lack: powerful Los Angeles law firms that specialize in toxic pollution lawsuits. The three firms then organized a direct action lawsuit against PG & E that eventually included some 650 plaintiffs. After losing its case against the first 39 plaintiffs in arbitration, PG & E decided to cut its potential losses and agreed to pay $333 million to settle all claims against it on July 1, 1996. The law firms involved took about a third of the enormous settlement in fees and Brockovich earned a $2 million bonus.

In every conceivable way, the Erin Brockovich story was ideal for cinematic exploitation. Though not highly educated, Brockovich presents as outspoken and supremely self-assured. Her looks also play to her advantage. Young (twenty-eight when she was hired by Masry), shapely, and attractive, Erin Brockovich was/is fond of wearing provocative outfits that accentuate her feminine assets. In sum, Erin Brockovich embodies the kind of uninhibited sexiness, quasi-feminist spunk, and working-class authenticity that make her success story a particularly compelling version of the American dream. Better yet, the Brockovich saga also seemed to pit the proverbial David against a corporate Goliath: a perennial crowd-pleaser in a society rife with inchoate anticorporate sentiment. Written by Susannah Grant (*Pocahontas*) and starring an irrepressible Julia Roberts as Erin Brockovich, the redoubtable Albert Finney (*Tom Jones; Under the Volcano*) as Ed Masry, and the likable Aaron Eckhart as George, Erin's next-door neighbor and love interest, *Erin Brockovich* concentrates on telling an engaging human interest story. Accordingly, the film avoids courtroom scenes to focus on the investigative process, streamlines (and oversimplifies) the complex medical and legal issues, and plays up Erin's eye-popping sartorial excesses and her difficulties in juggling family, love life, and the all-consuming mission to bring an errant corporation to justice—dramatic themes also explored in *Norma Rae* and *Silkwood*. A rather expensive film to make—with $20 million of its $50 million budget going to Julia Roberts' record-setting salary—*Erin Brockovich* proved to be a major international hit that earned back its cost fivefold, garnered five Academy Award nominations (including Best Picture), and won Julia Roberts her first Oscar.

The Weather Underground (2002)

In marked contrast to the wholesome rebelliousness of Erin Brockovich, in *The Weather Underground* (2002), Sam Green (*The Rainbow Man/John 3:16*) and Bill Siegel (*Hoop Dreams*) present a documentary about sedition against the status quo *not* tempered by American dream ideology and $2 million bonuses. In June 1969 about 1,600 delegates of the Students for a Democratic Society (SDS), the largest New Left college campus organization in the 1960s, held their annual convention at the Chicago Coliseum, a grimy 1912 brick building at 15th Street and Wabash Avenue that had been used to mount protests against the 1968 Democratic Convention. On Saturday June 22, after four days of bitter infighting, the SDS expelled Progressive Labor (PL), a well-organized, doctrinaire Maoist faction whose 600 delegates had been making a strong bid to take over. After it expelled the PL, the Action Faction or Weathermen (its name was derived from the 1965 Bob Dylan song, "Subterranean Homesick Blues"), an alliance of white radicals, Black Panther party (BPP) members, and radical feminists took control of the SDS national offices. Six months later the Weathermen convened a war council in Flint, Michigan, and decided to morph into the Weather Underground, a secret revolutionary organization dedicated to strategic acts of sabotage against the U.S. government (the SDS ceased to exist). Between October 7, 1969, and September 5, 1975, members of the Weather Underground carried out some two dozen (mostly nonlethal) bombings of corporate, police, state, and federal offices in California, Connecticut, Illinois, Massachusetts, New York, and Washington, D.C., including the Capitol and State Department buildings. Among other acts the Weathermen/Weather Underground also carried out: the Days of Rage (organized insurgence in Chicago, October 8–11, 1969); LSD guru Timothy Leary's escape from the California Men's Colony Prison, San Luis Obispo, on September 12, 1970; a botched Brink's armored car holdup near Nyack, New York, on October 20, 1981, that resulted in the killing of a Brink's guard and two New York State troopers and the almost immediate capture of the four perpetrators. On March 6, 1970, the Weather Underground blew up three of their own when a bomb factory located in a town house at 18 West 11th Street just off 5th Avenue in New York's Greenwich Village was gutted by a massive explosion and fire when a bomb under construction went off by accident. In the final analysis, the Weather Underground did not shorten the Vietnam War, overthrow capitalist America, or appreciably advance the cause of Third World revolution. If anything, the sect's sporadic acts of violence engendered negative publicity for the radical Left and played into the hands of its rightist enemies by dramatically demonstrating the need for increased law and order.

After the obligatory collage of archival footage that conjures the sociopolitical aura of the 1960s and 1970s, narrated by Pamela Z and Lili Taylor, *The Weather Underground* presents a series of recent interviews with former SDS president Todd Gitlin and former Weather Underground members and associates Bill Ayers, Kathleen Cleaver (former BPP communications director), Bernardine Dohrn, Brian Flanagan, David Gilbert, Naomi Jaffe, Mark Rudd, and Laura Whitehorn. Gitlin, now a Columbia University professor of journalism and sociology, pointedly condemns the Weather Underground as a group of self-indulgent naïfs engaging in radical chic. Brian Flanagan, now a New York City bar owner, regrets his radical days and blames the group's extremist rhetoric and actions on a kind of collective insanity induced by the immorality of the Vietnam War. Mark Rudd, now a math professor at Albuquerque Technical Vocational Institute, defends the group's aim to end the Vietnam War but deplores its terrorist methods as a terrible mistake. The rest of the interviewees—Ayers and Dohrn (long married and both professors at Northwestern University), Gilbert (still serving a life sentence at Attica for his part in the 1981 Brink's robbery), Jaffe (now director of a feminist grant organization), and Whitehorn (in prison between 1984 and 1999 on conspiracy charges)—voice regrets over ways and means but all stand by the philosophical and moral justice of their past actions. Filmmakers Green and Siegel avoid editorializing but the overall tenor of the film seems to indicate that they share a similar mixture of pride and sadness. *The Weather Underground* won several film festival awards and was nominated for a 2004 Oscar. Part of a nostalgic wave of books, films, and memoirs that revisit and reassess 1960s-style radicalism in an era of archconservatism, *The Weather Underground* also speaks to new millennium concerns regarding American military adventures and domestic dissent.

Howard Hughes

Notorious aviator, movie mogul, playboy, political power broker, billionaire industrialist, and ultimately a paranoid, germ-phobic recluse, Howard Robard Hughes Jr. (1905–1976) led a strange and extraordinary life ripe for cinematic treatment—especially after stories of Hughes' bizarre final years emerged following his death on April 5, 1976. In April 1977 CBS aired *The Amazing Howard Hughes*, a 3-hour miniseries starring Tommy Lee Jones as Hughes and based on *The Amazing Mr. Hughes* (New York: Fawcett, 1972) by Noah Dietrich (1889–1982), Hughes' factotum from 1925 to 1957. Three years later Jonathan Demme's comedy, *Melvin and Howard* (1980), evoked the Hughes legend without delving into Hughes' biography. The film mostly concerns the chaotic life of a blue-collar Mormon named Melvin Dummar (Paul LeMat in the film) who claimed to have been bequeathed $156 million by Howard Hughes (Jason Robards) for having picked up Hughes in the Nevada desert near Tonopah in December 1968 and given him a ride back to the Sands Hotel in Las Vegas 150 miles to the south. On June 10, 1978, a Las Vegas jury ruled a handwritten will leaving Dummar part of his estate a forgery. Though Dummar was not prosecuted, he did not receive a penny from Hughes' vast estate.

Over the next twenty-five years a number of Hughes film projects were attempted and abandoned. In early 1982 Warren Beatty acquired the rights to Hughes' life story. Beatty had already written the first draft of a script that would cover Hughes' early life but other interests intervened. In 1993 actor-producer John Malkovich and director Russell Smith attempted to launch a Howard Hughes film project but failed to secure the necessary financing. Young filmmakers Alan and Albert Hughes (*From Hell*) planned a Hughes film starring Johnny Depp that never materialized. Director Brian De Palma nearly secured a Hughes movie deal with Touchstone but the studio balked at the proposed $80 million price tag. In 2002 actor Jim Carey's attempts to go forward with a Hughes film with Castle Rock Entertainment were dropped after it became clear that Martin Scorsese had a viable Hughes film project in the works.

The Aviator (2004)

Produced by Michael Mann (*Heat; Ali*) and written by John Logan (*Gladiator; The Last Samurai*), Scorsese's *The Aviator* (2004) stars Leonardo DiCaprio as a young and already very rich Howard Hughes in the prime of his life. Covering a twenty-year period (1927 to 1947), *The Aviator* depicts Hughes' early career as a maverick Hollywood film producer, focusing on the making of *Hell's Angels* (1930), a movie about brothers Monte and Roy Rutledge (played by Ben Lyon and James Hall): dashing fighter pilots in World War I who both vie for the attentions of Jean Harlow. Originally making *Hell's Angels* as a silent film, Hughes had most of the movie reshot when sound technology became available and also assembled a large private air force of vintage biplanes for the film's aerial combat sequences. Mostly due to Hughes' fanatical perfectionism (and a 250 to 1 shooting ratio), the film cost three stunt pilots their lives and $3.8 million (US$41

Film still from The Aviator, *directed by Martin Scorsese and starring Leonardo DiCaprio. (Andrew Cooper/Miramax Films/Bureau L.A. Collections/Corbis)*

million in 2005), making it the most expensive film of its time—also a major hit, although it did not quite recuperate its huge cost.

As *The Aviator* makes abundantly clear, the younger Howard Hughes had two other passions besides movies: women and airplanes. He is shown dating a bevy of Hollywood stars and starlets in the 1920s and 1030s and having significant relationships with actresses Katherine Hepburn (Cate Blanchett) and Ava Gardner (Kate Beckinsale). Unable to cope with his strange behavior—Hughes suffered from an ever-worsening and undiagnosed case of the anxiety affliction now known as obsessive-compulsive disorder (OCD)—both women ultimately left him, though they remained sympathetic friends. Likewise, Hughes' love of aviation offered both compensations and hazards. Hughes earned his pilot's license during the making of *Hell's Angels*. In 1932 he formed the Hughes Aircraft Company, built and test-piloted an experimental racing airplane called the H-1, and set a world's speed record in 1935 (at 352 miles per hour). Hughes also set coast-to-coast and transcontinental flight speed records in 1937–1938. In 1939 Hughes crowned his aviation triumphs by acquiring Transcontinental and Western Air, a commercial airline he would expand and transform into an international carrier, renamed Trans World Airlines (TWA) in 1950. With the advent of World War II, Howard Hughes was well positioned to turn Hughes Aircraft into a major force in the industry when he obtained government contracts for a twin-engine reconnaissance plane (the XF-11) and a huge, eight-engine "flying boat" transport (the HK-1). (Popularly known as the Spruce Goose though it was made mostly of birch, the HK-1 had a wingspan slightly longer than a football field and was six times larger than any other plane then in existence.) Unfortunately, technical and managerial problems and his own quirks prevented Hughes from delivering a single finished aircraft to the Army Air Corps during the war. Worse, Hughes was very nearly killed when the XF-11 he was test-piloting crashed and burned while he was attempting an emergency landing on a golf course in Los Angeles on July 7, 1946. To add to his woes Hughes was called before the Senate War Investigating Committee chaired by Maine Senator Owen Brewster (Alan Alda in the film) in the summer of 1947 and subjected to a grilling as to why the government's $40 million investment in Hughes' wartime aircraft projects yielded no results. Not one to be intimidated, Hughes fought back by publicly revealing that Senator Brewster was in league with Pan American Airways mogul Juan Trippe (Alec Baldwin) and had tried to blackmail Hughes into merging Transcontinental and Western Air with Pan Am at a time when the two competing airlines were the only ones making flights to and from the United States and Europe. *The Aviator* ends with Hughes winning his fight against Pan Am and Owen Brewster and then making a successful test flight of the Spruce Goose in Long Beach Harbor on November 2, 1947 (though the oft-ridiculed plane was never flown again and no others were built). Ominously, Hughes is shown in the film's final scene compulsively repeating the phrase, "The way of the future"—obviously full-blown madness awaits him.

While remaining generally faithful to the salient facts of the first half of Howard Hughes' life, *The Aviator* suffers from a number of related deficiencies and distortions, some of which have to do with the people involved in the project, some with the requisites of big time filmmaking and some with the cultural moment in which the film was made. Initiated by Leonardo DiCaprio (who hired Scorsese with whom he had worked on *The Gangs of New York*), *The Aviator* is not well served by DiCaprio casting himself as the young Howard Hughes. Though a competent actor, DiCaprio is too boyishly handsome, high-voiced, and naturally cheerful to convincingly evoke the lonely, dour, and deeply neurotic Howard Hughes. The problem is not a lack of physical similarity but is in DiCaprio's temperament, which renders Hughes a much softer, gentler, and simpler man than he was.

The involvement of producer Michael Mann and director Martin Scorsese are likewise problematic. Starting out as a writer for television cop and crime shows in the 1970s, Mann has tended to make loud, bombastic, action-driven pictures not conducive to psychologically subtle characterizations. And while Scorsese has had a long and highly distinguished career as a filmmaker, his more recent films have tended toward melodrama and Hollywood-style visual extravagance (e.g., *Gangs of New York*) that seem to balloon in proportion to his looming stature as one of the world's great directors. Once an edgy independent at the margins of the business, Scorsese has become too successful and respectable to make films that are even mildly subversive. The very scale of *The Aviator*—which involved a dozen far-flung shooting locations, a cast of eighty-five actors, a crew of nearly 500, and cost $116 million to make—dictates that it conform to accepted narrative and ideological patterns to have a reasonable expectation of recouping its enormous cost for its backers. The film's inherent timidity regarding the real Howard Hughes is also a function of the political climate in which it was made. At a moment when American-style corporate capitalism is globally triumphant and its traditional adversaries—labor unions and socialist political formations—are at their lowest ebb in a century, lionizing the business tycoon as glamorous visionary rebel (cf. *Tucker: The Man and His Dream*) is easy, logical, and expedient.

As a number of biographies have established, the real Howard Hughes was a bisexual rake, an anti-Semite, a reactionary, and a racist yahoo whose surface charm and diffidence concealed a steely compulsion to dominate people and control situations. Very little of this comes through in *The Aviator*. Instead, the film posits the more palatable notion that Hughes' problems all spring from his OCD (which the film never names as such because the term did not become official nomenclature until *DSM-III* in 1980, four years after Hughes' death). Using simplistic cinematic shorthand, *The Aviator* includes a single scene showing Hughes as a nine-year-old boy (Jacob Davich) being vigorously bathed by his germphobic mother, Allene (Amy Sloan), who obviously instills her contamination paranoia into her overprotected son. Prima facie, Hughes' character and psychological disorders must have had a far more complex course of development.

An equally serious problem concerns the scope of the film. The fact that *The Aviator* ends in November 1947 has to be considered a deeply ideological choice on the part of its makers. The last twenty-eight years of Howard Hughes' life were marked not only by his inexorable descent into codeine dependency, isolation, and autism but also by his deepening involvement with the mobsters, spies, shady government officials, and businessmen who formed the dark underside of an emerging military-industrial complex. Though Scorsese, Mann, and Logan are well within their artistic rights to focus on a kinder, gentler Howard Hughes, such a focus creates a highly misleading portrait of the man and of the society from which he emerged. Though inferior history, *The Aviator* proved good business; it grossed $213.6 million worldwide—a net profit of $97.6 million. The film also garnered eleven 2005 Academy Award nominations and won five Oscars (for Best Art Direction, Best Cinematography, Best Costume Design, Best Editing (Thelma Schoonmaker's second Oscar), and Best Actress in a Supporting Role (Cate Blanchett). Unfortunately, though nominated for a fourth time, Martin Scorsese did not win the Best Achievement in Directing Oscar that he covets.

Good Night, And Good Luck (2005)

Edward R. Murrow (1908–1965) was America's first television broadcast journalist and remains legendary for his personal courage and professional integrity. One of the events that solidified Murrow's stellar reputation was the March 9, 1954, episode of his show *See It Now*, which devoted its half hour to exposing the true character of Joseph R. McCarthy (1908–1957), the infamous demagogue and anticommunist witch-hunter who had held the country in his thrall for more than four years. Although Murrow did not bring down McCarthy single-handedly, his *See It Now* exposé went a long way toward discrediting the junior senator from Wisconsin and helped set the stage for McCarthy's political ruin on national television during the Army-McCarthy Hearings (June 6, 1954).

The son of a television newscaster, actor-director-writer George Clooney first visited a TV studio in 1966 at the age of five. Since that time he has maintained a deep reverence for the kind of no-nonsense broadcast journalism once practiced by Edward R. Murrow and his protégés. Dismayed by the mostly quietist, compliant, and degraded character of the contemporary corporate media, Clooney cowrote (with Grant Heslov) and directed *Good Night, And Good Luck*, a docudrama that deals with Murrow's heroic stand against McCarthy. (In the film Clooney also portrays Murrow's intrepid producer, Fred W. Friendly.)

Shot in stark black and white and starring David Strathairn as Murrow, *Good Night, And Good Luck* is meticulously researched, superbly acted, and richly evocative of a time when paranoia permeated the national consciousness. Though at least one critic—Jack Shafer for *Slate*—found the film's depiction of Murrow too adulatory, the man did exemplify the highest ideals of journalism in defending democracy against authoritarian bullies. To drive home the implicit message that broadcast journalism needs to return to the high standards set by Edward R. Murrow, Clooney and Heslov frame their film with excerpts from a keynote speech Murrow gave at the Radio-Television News Directors Association convention in Chicago (October 15, 1958). In that speech, Murrow said, in part: "We are currently wealthy, fat, comfortable and complacent. We have currently a built-in allergy to unpleasant or disturbing information. Our mass media reflect this. But unless we get up off our fat surpluses and recognize that television in the main is being used to distract, delude, amuse and insulate us, then television and those who finance it, those who look at it and those who work at it, may see a totally different picture too late."

9

History of U.S. Race Relations on Film and Television

Though often mean-spirited and reductive, the neoconservative critique of political correctness is not without some validity. Especially since the end of the Reagan era, "true story" films dealing with racial matters in American history have become increasingly constrained by the dictates of a Manichaean morality that idealizes victims of oppression while demonizing its perpetrators. These characterizations are not wrong; they are merely too predictably one-sided to do justice to the complexities of real individuals caught in the contradictions and ambiguities of modern capitalist society. Curiously, as social class divisions have deepened, the very concept of class has been exiled from the nation's cultural discourse—only to be replaced by a somewhat self-righteous identity politics that puts excessive, and often excessively rigid, emphasis on race (and gender) as the prime arbiters of individual fate. On the one hand, it is an extraordinarily positive development that films on race history topics have proliferated. On the other hand, most recent race history films stress victimization in ways that do not begin to address fundamental inequalities that have also oppressed a large segment of the white majority. In sum, the unintended result of fetishizing race is to foster a superficial but highly persuasive climate of opinion that ultimately serves status quo interests by obscuring oppressive economic and class structures affecting working-class people of *all* colors. The following chronological survey of race history films from the Civil Rights era to the present brings this ambiguous but perhaps unavoidable trend into sharp relief.

Films Made before the Civil Rights Act of 1964

Crisis: Behind a Presidential Commitment (1963)

On Tuesday morning, June 11, 1963, two young African Americans—James Hood and Vivian Malone—tried to enroll at the hitherto all-white University of

Alabama in Tuscaloosa, which had just been desegregated by court order. Literally blocking the door was Alabama's segregationist governor, George Corley Wallace (1919–1998). Defeated in the 1958 Alabama gubernatorial race for holding liberal-progressive views on racial matters, Wallace thereafter embraced segregation to please his constituents. The confrontation between Wallace, the students, and their legal representatives was filmed and broadcast on national television, making Wallace a household name overnight. Initially deterred, Hood and Malone were enrolled later that same day after President Kennedy federalized the Alabama National Guard.

By prior arrangement documentary filmmaker Robert Drew (*Primary*) had four film crews film the principal players as the crisis unfolded. One team covered George Wallace in Alabama; another filmed JFK at the White House; a third filmed JFK's brother, Attorney General Robert Kennedy, at his office in the Justice Department and at his home in McLean, Virginia; a fourth filmed Nicholas Katzenbach, deputy attorney general and the Kennedys' point man in Alabama. The resulting 52-minute black-and-white documentary, *Crisis: Behind a Presidential Commitment* (1963), is a work of considerable historical importance—not only for representing the issue at hand but also for its revealing glimpses of the inner workings of the Kennedy administration, especially the relationship between JFK and RFK. Ironically, though the Kennedy brothers cut George Wallace down to size, he outlived them both and became a major transitional figure into the transformation of the South into a conservative, even crypto-racist, bulwark against progressive, democratic values in the decades that followed.

Black Like Me (1964)

In 1955, the year of the Birmingham bus boycott, a successful white writer from Mansfield, Texas, named John Howard Griffin (1920–1980) conceived of a daring and risky experiment. He wondered what would happen to him—and how he would react—if he darkened his skin and passed himself off as a black man in the still-segregated Deep South. Some four years later, on November 1, 1959, to be exact, Griffin began the experiment he had long contemplated. Shaving his head and using skin-darkening medication and ultraviolet light, Griffin temporarily "became" a black man. In November and December 1959, Griffin traveled through Louisiana, Mississippi, Alabama, and Georgia with the same name and same credentials but could obtain only menial work. Eliciting anger and incredulity from blacks when he revealed his hidden agenda, Griffin faced discrimination, insult, humiliation, and intense hatred from white southerners on a daily basis. Though increasingly demoralized, Griffin duly recorded his travails

Author John Howard Griffin, known for his controversial and best-selling book, Black Like Me. *(Bettmann/Corbis)*

in journal entries that would form the basis of a series of articles published in 1960 in *Sepia*, an African American magazine published in Fort Worth, Texas. The following year Griffin expanded his articles into *Black Like Me* (Boston: Houghton Mifflin, 1961), a book that caused a firestorm of controversy but also went on to sell 10 million copies. (Translated into thirteen languages, *Black Like Me* has remained in print since its initial publication.) In the wake of the book's appearance Griffin was subject to vituperative attacks and death threats but also internationally recognized as a champion of human rights.

Too controversial for Hollywood, *Black Like Me* was purchased by independent film producer Julius Tannenbaum (*Indian Summer*). South Carolina writer-composer Paul Green (1894–1981, *State Fair*) and the husband and wife team of Carl and Gerda Lerner (both ex-Communists) collaborated on a screen adaptation of Griffin's book. Starring James Whitmore as "John Finley Horton" (John Howard Griffin), *Black Like Me* (1964) faithfully followed the content of Griffin's book but skewed its tone by having Whitmore—who did not look black at all—become increasingly bellicose at his treatment by whites while Griffin actually tended toward despair. The film premiered two months before President Lyndon Johnson signed the Civil Rights Act of 1964 into law, striking down Jim Crow in the South once and for all but also permanently alienating hundreds of thousands of white southerners from the Democratic Party and instigating a white backlash that would contribute to the chaotic temper of the 1960s.

Films Made after the Civil Rights Act

King: A Filmed Record . . .
Montgomery to Memphis (1970)

Shortly after the assassination of Dr. Martin Luther King Jr. in Memphis on April 4, 1968, film producers Ely A. Landau and Richard Kaplan commissioned *King: A Filmed Record . . . Montgomery to Memphis* (1970). Put together by distinguished filmmakers Joseph L. Mankiewicz (*All about Eve; Guys and Dolls*) and Sidney Lumet (*Fail Safe; The Pawn Broker*), *King: A Filmed Record* is a 3-hour compilation documentary that traces King's pivotal role in the Civil Rights movement between 1955 and 1968 through newsreel footage of speeches and marches. To enliven the proceedings the film uses a bevy of Hollywood films stars—Paul Newman, Joanne Woodward, Ruby Dee, James Earl Jones, Ben Gazzara, Charlton Heston, Harry Belafonte, Sidney Poitier—as narrators and commentators. Dr. King's personal courage, charisma, and eloquence as an orator are amply evident, and the film, despite its considerable length, is a powerful viewing experience. It was nominated for Best Feature Documentary in 1971 and added to the National Film Registry in 1999. A shorter version (103 minutes) also exists.

Judge Horton and the Scottsboro Boys (1976)

In 1969 University of Maryland history professor Dan T. Carter published *Scottsboro: A Tragedy of the American South* (Baton Rouge: Louisiana State University Press), a magisterial account of the infamous Scottsboro case that went on to win the Lillian Smith Book Award (for outstanding writing about the American South) and the Bancroft Prize (for distinguished work in American history). Seven years later NBC-TV aired *Judge Horton and the Scottsboro Boys* (1976), an Emmy-nominated docudrama produced by Paul Leaf, adapted from Carter's book by John McGreevey, and starring Arthur Hill as Judge James Edwin Horton (1878–1973). On June 22, 1933, Horton, an 8th Circuit Court judge, set aside the conviction of Haywood Patterson, one of eight black boys sentenced to death for allegedly raping two white women on a freight train in Scottsboro, Alabama, on March 25, 1931. Horton's decision, which paved the way for the overturning of other Scottsboro case convictions, was widely reviled by white Alabamans, who defeated him in his bid for reelection in 1934. Ostracized by his white peers and his career as a jurist ruined, Horton spent the remainder of his long life farming. As the docudrama shows, Judge Horton resisted intense social pressure and rendered a fair verdict: an act of professional integrity and personal heroism hardly recognized in his own time.

King (1978)

On three nights in mid-February 1978, ten years after MLK's murder and a year after the huge success of David L. Wolper's ABC-TV miniseries *Roots*, rival network NBC aired *King* (1978), a miniseries written and directed by Abby Mann (*Judgment at Nuremberg*) on the life of Dr. Martin Luther King Jr. (Paul Winfield in the film). Eschewing idolatry, Mann's script depicts Dr. King in all his complex humanity and foibles, including his tendency to engage in extramarital affairs. Using a flashback structure, the film follows King from his courtship of his wife, Coretta Scott King (Cicely Tyson); his leadership of the Montgomery bus boycott in 1955; his "I Have a Dream" speech in Washington in 1963; and his assassination in Memphis on April 4, 1968. Because its focus is on characterization and melodrama, *King* is somewhat weak on precise chronology. A viewing of *King* is therefore best supplemented by *King: A Filmed Record* and/or a good biography.

Despite its refusal to engage in hagiography, *King* had the full support of the King family, and several of King's children appear in the film, as do friends and supporters Tony Bennett, Julian Bond, and Ramsey Clark.

Who Killed Vincent Chin? (1987)

On Saturday night, June 19, 1982, four friends of Vincent Chin, a twenty-seven-year-old Chinese American automotive engineer, took him to Fancy Pants, a now-defunct strip club in the Highland Park area of Detroit, to celebrate Chin's upcoming wedding. Ronald Ebens, a Chrysler foreman (and an alcoholic), mistakenly assuming that Chin was Japanese, began to taunt him as one of "the little motherf***ers" responsible for the decline of the American auto industry. A fight involving Chin, Ebens, and Ebens' stepson, Michael Nitz, ensued and everyone involved was ejected from the club. Half an hour later Ebens and Nitz spotted Chin outside a nearby MacDonald's restaurant. While Nitz restrained Chin, Ronald Ebens smashed him four times in the head with a baseball bat. Vincent Chin went into a coma and died at the hospital four days later.

In 1983 Wayne County Judge Charles Kaufman found Ebens and Nitz guilty of manslaughter and sentenced both men to three years probation and a $3,000 fine plus court costs—an absurdly lenient verdict for premeditated murder that outraged the Asian Pacific–American community, which strenuously lobbied the U.S. Department of Justice to file civil rights charges against Ebens and Nitz. In June 1984 Ebens was convicted of violating Vincent Chin's civil rights and sentenced to twenty-five years (Nitz was acquitted) but the conviction was overturned on a legal technicality and a new trial ordered. In April 1987 the Justice Department moved the venue to Cincinnati, Ohio, in an effort to get a fair trial but the strategy backfired. The Cincinnati jury had no idea how strong anti-Asian sentiment was in economically depressed Detroit and so could not be persuaded that Ebens' attack on Chin had been racially motivated; Ebens was once again acquitted. Later that year Ebens lost a civil suit for $1.5 million but evaded paying any portion of the penalty by simply disappearing. Aghast at the injustice of it all, Vincent's mother, Mrs. Lily Chin, returned to her native village in Guangzhou Province, China, in 1987. While a judicial travesty, the Vincent Chin case did have the effect of galvanizing the Asian American community to organize and fight discrimination.

Even before verdicts were rendered in the third trial, independent New York filmmakers Christine Choy and Renee Tajima-Pima finished *Who Killed Vincent Chin?* (1987), an 83-minute documentary that explores the case through news footage and interviews with most of the relevant parties including Judge

Kaufman, Ronald Ebens, Vincent Chin's friends, Lily Chin, dancers at Fancy Pants, and many others. Admirably and somewhat surprisingly, Choy and Tajima-Pima go out of their way to achieve a balanced point of view. Their aim was to explore cultural differences between whites and Asian Americans and to puncture stereotypes. *Who Killed Vincent Chin?* won a 1989 Oscar nomination.

Eyes on the Prize: America's Civil Rights Years (1954–1965) (1987)

In 1983 the U.S. Congress passed a bill making Martin Luther King's birthday a national holiday. Four years later King's legacy was explored in great depth in Henry Hampton's incomparable *Eyes on the Prize: America's Civil Rights Years (1954–1965)*, a six-part documentary series on the Civil Rights movement that aired on PBS in late January 1987. The beginnings of the project go back to 1968, when Henry Hampton (1940–1998) founded Blackside, a Boston-based African American film production company specializing in documentaries that became the largest of its kind. One of 25,000 participants in Dr. King's Selma-to-Montgomery March for voting rights in the spring of 1965, Hampton initiated his *Eyes on the Prize* project in the 1970s but a chronic lack of funding and Hampton's thoroughgoing and meticulous production methods tended to impede progress. Hampton and his Blackside team persevered, however, and the finished product exceeded all expectations.

Narrated by Julian Bond, *Eyes on the Prize* is divided into six 1-hour episodes that use extensive archival footage and interviews with participants in the events. *Episode 1: Awakenings (1954–1956)* concentrates on two signal events in the genesis of the Civil Rights movement: Mose Wright's brave court testimony against the white murderers of his nephew, Emmett Till (lynched August 24, 1955, in Money, Mississippi), and Rosa Parks' refusal (on December 1, 1955) to surrender her seat on a Montgomery, Alabama, city bus to a white man, which touched off a yearlong bus boycott. *Episode 2: Fighting Back 1957–1962)* focuses on the landmark 1954 Supreme Court decision, *Brown v. Board of Education* and its practical consequences: the integration of Central High School in Little Rock, Arkansas (September 25, 1957), and the admission of James Meredith to the University of Mississippi on October 1, 1962—both achieved after extensive litigation, protest, and white racist violence. *Episode 3: Ain't Scared of Your Jails (1960–1961)* chronicles civil disobedience actions (e.g., lunch counter sit-ins) in the Deep South led by the Student Nonviolent Coordinating Committee (SNCC). Also highlighted is the Congress for Racial Equality (CORE) and its racially integrated Freedom Rides designed to desegregate interstate bus travel below the Mason-Dixon Line. *Episode 4: No Easy Walk (1961–1963)* documents the Civil Rights movement's adoption of the mass demonstration as a key tactic, a development that culminates in the 200,000-person March on Washington (August 28, 1963) and Dr. King's transcendent "I Have a Dream" speech. *Episode 5: Mississippi: Is This America? (1963–1964)* recounts "Freedom Summer" (1964), a massive voter registration campaign organized by the Southern Christian Leadership Conference (SCLC), the SNCC, and the NAACP and targeted at the state of Mississippi, where only 6.7 percent of African Americans were registered to vote in 1962. White supremacists resisted violently, going so far as to murder three young Civil Rights campaigners: James Chaney, Andrew Goodman, and Michael Schwerner: an atrocity that shocked the nation. The series culminates with *Episode 6: Bridge to Freedom (1965)*, a documentary record of the Selma-to-Montgomery March and the passage of the Voting Rights Act. Seen by a national viewing audience of some 20 million people, *Eyes on the Prize* garnered critical acclaim and a number of awards, including a John Foster Peabody Award (for outstanding achievement in television broadcasting) and an Oscar nomination for Best Feature Documentary. In a deplorable turn of events, *Eyes on the Prize* has not been available since 1995: the year copyright licenses for various content elements expired and were not renewed because Blackside could not afford the exorbitant fees involved.

Mississippi Burning (1988)

Almost two years after PBS broadcast *Eyes on the Prize* British director Alan Parker revisited the Civil Rights struggle with his controversial film, *Mississippi Burning* (1988), a docudrama about the FBI's investigation of the infamous Chaney-Goodman-Schwerner murders by southern reactionaries during Freedom Summer, 1964. Financed by white producers Robert Colesberry and Frederick Zollo; written by Chris Gerolmo, a white, neophyte screenwriter; and directed by Parker (*Midnight Express; Angel Heart*), a white Englishman not deeply conversant with Civil Rights history or America's racial politics, *Mississippi Burning* makes basic representational mistakes that never would have been made by the likes of Henry Hampton.

The film's most egregious error is to narrate a signal event of the Civil Rights era from an overwhelmingly white (male) point of view. Gerolmo's fanciful script focuses on two FBI agents assigned to the murder investigation: Agent Anderson (Gene Hackman), a white working-class southerner not above brutal methods, and Agent Ward (Willem Dafoe), a by-the-book, college-educated white northerner who abhors Anderson's less-than-scrupulous adherence to legal procedures. As bad cop and good cop, Anderson and Ward clash—which makes for good melodrama—but ultimately succeed in solving the case, thanks in large part to Anderson's vigilante methods. With its deployment of the outlaw hero (Hackman) and the official hero (Dafoe) who must understand each other and ultimately join forces to defeat a common enemy, *Mississippi Burning* taps into a classic Hollywood narrative paradigm exemplified by films as diverse as Michael Curtiz's *Casablanca* (1942), John Ford's *The Man Who Shot Liberty Valance* (1962), or Curtis Hanson's *L. A. Confidential* (1997). However, in the case of *Mississippi Burning*, there is no drift of the outlaw hero toward virtuousness commensurate with the official hero's acceptance of moral ambiguity and corruption as facts of life. Instead, by lionizing Hackman's Agent Anderson, *Mississippi Burning* implicitly argues that brutality can only be overcome by a proportionate brutality. Equally dubious is the film's depiction of the FBI as righteous pursuers of justice and guardians of African American civil rights. In point of fact, J. Edgar Hoover was a racist enemy of Dr. Martin Luther King Jr. and the FBI was never particularly sympathetic to the Civil Rights cause. The Bureau did indeed mount a massive and ultimately successful effort to solve the Chaney-Goodman-Schwerner murders but did so not out of any heightened ethical sense but because President Lyndon B. Johnson brought extraordinary pressure to bear. Perhaps worst of all *Mississippi Burning* largely depicts African Americans in the early 1960s Deep South as terrified bystanders and victims—a reprehensible distortion of history.

Malcolm X (1992)

Fortunately, African American filmmaker Shelton Jackson "Spike" Lee (*Do the Right Thing*) adhered to a much higher standard of historical veracity when he made *Malcolm X* (1992). The project actually had its origins in 1969 when television writer turned movie producer Marvin Worth acquired the film rights to *The Autobiography of Malcolm X* (New York: Grove Press, 1965), cowritten by Malcolm X (real name: Malcolm Little, 1925–1965) and Alex Haley (and published eight months after Malcolm's assassination by Nation of Islam hitmen at the Audubon Ballroom, New York City, on February 21, 1965). Worth closed a production deal with Columbia Pictures, and future Nobel Prize–winner James Baldwin (1924–1987) collaborated with playwright Arnold Perl (1914–1971) to write a script based on *The Autobiography*. Despite bizarre rumors that Sidney Poitier might play Malcolm X, a dramatic biopic did not materialize, probably because Malcolm was erroneously remembered as a dangerous black separatist and racial hate-monger, the villain who provided a perfect foil to the recently martyred Dr.

*Malcolm X (1925–1965), waiting at a Martin Luther King Jr. press conference.
(Library of Congress)*

King. Arnold Perl settled on a more modest project: producing and directing *Malcolm X* (1992), a Warner Bros. compilation documentary narrated by James Earl Jones, Ossie Davis, and Steve Benderoth that was not particularly successful. Like an unwanted orphan, the Baldwin-Perl script circulated in Hollywood for eighteen years before Warner Bros. launched an attempt to make a dramatic film about Malcolm X. Canadian director Norman Jewison (*In the Heat of the Night; A Soldier's Story*) and playwright-screenwriter Charles Fuller (*A Soldier's Story*) spent months in 1990 toiling on a new script but could not get it to crystallize. When Spike Lee publicly objected to a white man directing a film on Malcolm X, Jewison withdrew from the picture in January 1991 and Lee replaced him.

Reverting to the original Baldwin-Perl script and casting Denzel Washington (*A Soldier's Story; Glory*) as Malcolm X and Angela Bassett (*Boyz 'n in Hood*) as Malcolm's wife, Betty Shabazz, Spike Lee began shooting the film in mid-September 1991—amid controversy. Unimpressed with Lee's political depth or his grasp of black history, poet-ideologue Amiri Baraka (Everett LeRoi Jones) organized a rally in Harlem decrying Lee's involvement in the project. Lee had bigger headaches, though, with financing. Nervous about the commercial potential of a black-oriented film, Warner Bros. would put up no more than $20 million (plus $8 million from Largo Entertainment for foreign rights). Lee felt he needed at least $33 million for the large-scale film he envisioned, which involved costly location shooting in New York, Boston, Saudi Arabia, Egypt, South Africa, and other places. By the end of the year the project had indeed run $5 million over budget, prompting the Completion Bond Company to assume financial control of the film. When Lee refused to comply with Warner's demand, reiterated by the bond company, that the film come in at 2 hours, 15 minutes, no more funds were forthcoming. Stymied, Spike Lee had to appeal to wealthy black donors (Bill Cosby, Oprah Winfry, Earvin "Magic" Johnson, Janet Jackson, and others) to pony up large sums of money. They obliged, principal photography was completed in late January 1992, a rough cut was viewed and approved by Warner Bros. executives in late August, and the completed film was released just before Thanksgiving, 1992.

Though ponderously overlong at 3 hours and 21 minutes, *Malcolm X* calmed fears in the black community that Spike Lee would sensationalize Malcolm X's early life as a petty criminal and/or soften his later radicalism. The film turned out to be a sweeping but staid and reverential biopic in the David Lean mode that was faithful to *The Autobiography* (which was probably not entirely faithful to the facts) in tracing Malcolm Little's complex evolution from naïve midwesterner to Boston street hustler to convicted felon to "Malcolm X," Black Muslim firebrand, to his final—and most politically dangerous—metamorphosis into a racial conciliator and peace advocate. Denzel Washington's masterful and entirely convincing rendition of Malcolm X raised the film from respectable mediocrity to near greatness.

Current events also magnified the film's relevance and visceral impact. On March 3, 1991, a group of white Los Angeles police officers were videotaped viciously beating a prone, drug-intoxicated black motorist named (Glen) Rodney King. After the disturbing tape was played and replayed on national news, the black community clamored for the prosecution and conviction of the policemen. Four were brought to trial but the venue was moved from urban Los Angeles to Simi Valley, a white town in outlying Ventura County. On April 29, 1992, while *Malcolm X* was in postproduction, a mostly white jury acquitted the police officers of any wrongdoing—a patently absurd verdict that stunned the nation and caused Los Angeles to erupt in massive rioting that resulted in the destruction of hundreds of buildings, 40 dead, and 1,200 injured. To show that racial oppression in America was by no means a passé phenomenon, Spike Lee incorporated the Rodney King tape into the early moments of *Malcolm X*—a ploy decried as unnecessarily inflammatory by some critics but certainly defensible given the film's subject matter. Not long after the film debuted, Spike Lee brought out a companion book: *By Any Means Necessary: The Trials and Tribulations of Making Malcolm X* (New York: Hyperion, 1992).

Ghosts of Mississippi (1996)

After midnight on June 12, 1963, as he stood in the driveway of his home in Jackson, Mississippi, black civil rights activist Medgar Evers was shot and killed by a sniper. Police soon arrested the guilty party—a white supremacist named Byron De La Beckwith—but De La Beckwith escaped punishment after two murder trials in 1964 ended in hung juries. Thirty years later, at the insistence of Evers' widow, Myrlie Evers, Bobby DeLaughter, assistant district attorney of Hinds County, Mississippi, indicted Byron De La Beckwith a third time. Tried in January 1994, De La Beckwith was finally convicted of murdering Medgar Evers. He was sentenced to life imprisonment.

Among those who closely followed De La Beckwith's third trial was Willie Morris, a white Mississippian famous for writing folksy memoirs about the culture of the South. Morris convinced a movie producer friend, Fred Zollo (*Quiz Show*), to make the Evers case into a film. Coproduced and directed by Rob Reiner (*Stand by Me; Misery*), *Ghosts of Mississippi* (1996) was based on Maryanne Voller's *Ghosts of Mississippi: The Murder of Medgar Evers, the Trials of Byron de la Beckwith and the Haunting of the New South* (Boston: Little,

Brown, 1995) and starred Alec Baldwin as the intrepid Bobby DeLaughter and James Woods as the arrogant and deeply loathsome Byron De La Beckwith, a juicy role for which he was nominated for a Best Supporting Actor Oscar. Though it cost some $33 million to make—a budget comparable to that of *Malcolm X*—*Ghosts of Mississippi* exuded the tame, perfunctory feel of a television movie; it was dismissed by critics and flopped at the box office. The failure of *Ghosts* probably was owed to ideological clumsiness and unfortunate timing. To maximize dramatic interest, screenwriter Lewis Colick (*Bulletproof*) chose to place the narrative focus on the battle of wits between Bobby DeLaughter, an honorable white liberal, and Byron De La Beckwith, a stereotypical racist yahoo. In so doing the film echoed the more egregiously wrongheaded *Mississippi Burning* in its tendency to de-emphasize the *black* struggle for self-determination that was at the core of Civil Rights: a move sure to alienate African American audiences tired of seeing noble whites fight their battles for them on-screen. At the same time *Ghosts* seems to blame southern rednecks for the nation's race problems: a stance repugnant to white working-class audiences tired of being preached to by wealthy Hollywood liberals. Furthermore, the film dealt with the attenuated consequences of an event that happened thirty years earlier: a topic that lacked immediacy and emotional resonance in the times of the L.A. riots (1992) and the O. J. Simpson trial (1993–1995).

Amistad (1997)

In the early morning hours of July 2, 1839, a recently enslaved African named Sengbe Pieh ("Cinqué") managed to free himself from his manacles. Cinqué then freed the other fifty-two captives in the hold of a 65-foot schooner ironically named *La Amistad* (*Friendship*) that was transporting them from Havana to slavery in Puerto Principe, Cuba. The Africans took over the ship and killed its captain and another crew member but spared their "owners," Spanish planters Jose Ruiz and Pedro Montes. Ruiz and Montes promised to sail their former captives back to Africa but actually tacked north along the eastern coast of the United States. After almost two months at sea the *Amistad* was finally captured by a U.S. Navy vessel off Montauk, Long Island, and escorted to New London, Connecticut, on August 27, 1839. The forty-four surviving Africans were put in jail and charged with murder and mutiny. Ruiz and Montes, backed by the Spanish government, demanded that the Africans be extradited back to Cuba but American abolitionists initiated lengthy and complex court proceedings to determine if the Africans were *ladinos* (Cuban-born, therefore legal slaves) or *bozales*

(Africans kidnapped and illegally sold into slavery in the Americas). Amid intense publicity the legal wrangling began on September 19, 1839. Over the next seventeen months the *Amistad* case wended its way through the federal court system all the way to the Supreme Court. President Martin Van Buren (1782–1862), anxious to placate southern Democrats, was in favor of turning the escaped slaves over to the Spaniards and probable execution. Representing the Africans, former President John Quincy Adams (1767–1848) eloquently argued that they had been enslaved illegally and should be returned to Africa as free people. Won over by Adams' plea, the Supreme Court ruled in the Africans' favor on March 9, 1841, and they were returned to their homeland.

A long forgotten incident in the history of the transatlantic slave trade, the *Amistad* affair would have remained obscure were it not for the efforts of actor-producer-director Debbie Allen (*Fame*). In 1978 Allen learned about the *Amistad* case in the bookstore of her alma mater, Howard University (Washington, D.C.), when she came across William A. Owens' *Black Mutiny: The Revolt on the Schooner Amistad* (1st ed., entitled *Slave Mutiny: The Revolt on the Schooner Amistad*, New York: J. Day Co., 1953; 2nd ed.: Philadelphia: Pilgrim Press, 1968). Allen optioned the book but could not get a film made until Steven Spielberg (who had just made *Schindler's List*) took on the project in 1994. In Spielberg's hands *Amistad* (1997) does its best to present the complicated legal issues as clearly as possible but the film's form and tone are skewed by the politico-cultural climate prevailing in the late 1990s. Well aware that black history films were subject to intense scrutiny, Spielberg, a well-meaning albeit commercially shrewd white liberal, was avid to achieve perfect and unassailable political correctness by portraying Cinqué (Djimon Housou) in unambiguously heroic terms. The same goes for John Quincy Adams (Anthony Hopkins) as the very embodiment of American idealism. Interestingly, *Amistad* portrays abolitionists such as Lewis Tappan (1788–1863) (Stellan Skarsgård) as meddlesome political opportunists who would be just as happy to see the Africans martyred for the abolitionist cause. In point of fact, Tappan, a leading antebellum abolitionist acting out of deep religious convictions, did more than anyone to save the Africans on board the *Amistad*. The film's affirmations of law and the American republic as bulwarks of freedom reflect Spielberg's centrist politics and corporatist sensibilities. Likewise, the film's defamation of the religious abolitionists bespeaks a deep suspicion of emotionalism, ideological zeal, and grassroots movements of any kind as destabilizing influences on a fundamentally sound system. Furthermore, as historian Eric Foner points out, the film tends to overplay the political significance of the *Amistad* decision; virtually the same Supreme Court ruled in favor of slavery with the Dred Scott decision of 1857.

Rosewood (1997)

On January 1, 1923, Fannie Taylor, a white woman from the hamlet of Sumner in northwest Florida on the Gulf of Mexico, falsely claimed that a black man named Jesse Hunter accosted her (in fact, she was beaten by her white lover). Levy County Sheriff Elias Walker borrowed bloodhounds and gathered a posse from surrounding towns. The dogs tracked Hunter to the home of Aaron Carrier just outside Rosewood, a mostly black town 3 miles away. The white mob wanted to lynch Carrier for helping Hunter escape but Sheriff Walker took him under protective custody. Frustrated, the white vigilantes tortured and lynched Sam Carter, another black man passing through the area in a wagon. On the evening of Thursday, January 4, twenty or thirty drunken vigilantes attacked the home of Aaron Carrier's cousin, Sylvester. In self-defense Sylvester Carrier shot and killed two of his attackers and wounded three others. The vigilantes retreated after running out of buckshot—but not before killing Sylvester's mother, Sarah, and burning down several nearby buildings. Incensed that blacks had offered armed resistance, racist whites from all over Levy County, many of them Ku Klux Klan members, gathered for another attack on Rosewood. On Friday morning, January 5, a rampaging mob of 200–300 set fire to most of the buildings in town and then returned on Sunday to burn down the ones that remained. Most of Rosewood's residents fled to nearby swamps or were taken in and hidden by a white storekeeper named John Wright. Many refugees, all women and children, were transported north to Gainesville aboard a train driven by John and William Bryce, two white railroad workers sympathetic to their plight. Completely razed—except for two white-owned houses—Rosewood, founded in 1848, ceased to exist on January 7, 1923. There were at least six black people confirmed killed but as many as twenty-seven may have died. Three whites were killed and three wounded. No one was ever brought to trial.

The Rosewood "riots" were reported in major newspapers all over the country at the time but the incident was soon forgotten by the perpetrators and repressed by the survivors as a thing too terrible to talk about. In 1982 Gary Moore, a reporter for the *St. Petersburg Times*, was writing a feature story on Levy County and came to wonder why there seemed to be no blacks living there. After doing some research and talking to locals, Moore uncovered the story of Rosewood, eventually located and interviewed twenty elderly survivors, and wrote up his findings in the *St. Petersburg Times*. In 1983 the CBS-TV news magazine show, *60 Minutes*, did a segment on Rosewood and did a follow-up piece in April 1994 after a bill was passed in the Florida legislature granting reparations to Rosewood survivors. Movie producer Jon Peters (*The Color Purple; Rain*

Man) saw the *60 Minutes* piece, immediately grasped its dramatic potential, and started to develop a film. Peters hired John Singleton (*Boyz 'n the Hood*) to direct and Gregory Poirier to write the screenplay. Singleton, Poirier, and executive producer Tracy Barone researched historical records, visited the site where Rosewood had stood, and interviewed survivors and descendants to create an accurate approximation of the events of that first week in January 1923.

Starring Jon Voight as John Wright, Don Cheadle as Sylvester Carrier, and Michael Rooker as Sheriff Walker, *Rosewood* (1997) also invents a Shane-like character named Mann (Ving Rhames), a tough World War I veteran turned drifter who happens into Rosewood and gets caught up in its troubles. While largely faithful to the historical facts to the extent that they are known, John Singleton's *Rosewood* may have erred slightly on the side of excess in its extremely graphic depictions of violence and of the number of people killed. What could have been simply a ham-fisted antiracist polemic is leavened by an attempt to explain the underlying psychological motivations of the white mob (e.g., jealousy over the relative prosperity of Rosewood). The film also shows that some whites (e.g., John Wright) refused to succumb to the mob's depravity and that blacks (e.g., Sylvester Carrier) bravely defended themselves when attacked. Though a powerful, even draining, viewing experience, *Rosewood* did not do well at the box office. Evidently white audiences wished not to be reminded of a vile moment in the nation's history and black audiences could not savor a hellish vision of racist insanity run amok.

4 Little Girls (1997)

On Sunday, September 15, 1963, a bomb tore through the 16th Street Baptist Church in Birmingham, Alabama. The blast injured fourteen people and killed four black girls attending Sunday school in the church basement: eleven-year-old Carol Denise McNair and fourteen-year-olds Cynthia Wesley, Addie Mae Collins, and Carole Robertson. Like no other racist atrocity in the history of the South, the hideously brutal murder of four innocent schoolgirls galvanized the nation behind the Civil Rights movement and sealed the doom of Jim Crow. A Ku Klux Klan member named Robert Chambliss was arrested, tried for the killings, convicted, and sentenced to life in prison where he died in 1985, never having disclosed the names of the other men involved in the bombing. Some weeks before the twentieth anniversary of the bombing, Howell Raines published "The Birmingham Bombing," *New York Times Magazine* (July 24, 1983), a long article not only about the crime but also the botched investigation that followed. Spike Lee, then a recent alumnus of NYU's Tisch School of Arts film program, read Raines's article and—though he had not yet made a feature film—decided that he would one day make a film about the bombing. Fourteen years and ten acclaimed feature films later, Lee followed through on his original intention with *4 Little Girls* (1997), a heart-wrenching, Oscar-nominated documentary for HBO that uses archival footage and interviews with the victims' surviving family and friends to flesh out the victims and explore the larger implications of the bombing. After airing on television in February 1997 (Black History Month), *4 Little Girls* had a limited theatrical release. Widely praised by critics, the film is considered one of Lee's best efforts, even though it only cost $1 million to make. Another salutary outcome: a few weeks after the film was released the FBI reopened its investigation into the bombing. In May 2000 former Ku Klux Klan members Thomas E. Blanton Jr. and Bobby Frank Cherry were each indicted on four counts of murder. Cherry proved mentally incompetent to stand trial but in May 2001 Blanton was convicted of participating in the bombing and sentenced to life in prison.

Africans in America: America's Journey through Slavery (1998)

Less inflammatory and infinitely more enlightening is Orlando Bagwell's superb *Africans in America: America's Journey through Slavery* (1998), an enormously ambitious miniseries consisting of four 90-minute episodes produced over a ten-year period by WGBH Boston and aired nationally on PBS, Monday through Thursday, October 19–22, 1998. Dubbed the "documentary equivalent of *Roots*," *Africans in America* traces the entire history of the American slave trade from its origins in the fifteenth century to the Emancipation Proclamation. Episode I— *The Terrible Transformation* (1450–1750) examines the long and gradual transformation of indentured servitude into a racialized and industrialized slave trade that would form a vital part of the economic base of the British colonies in America. Episode II—*Revolution* (1750–1805) recounts African American participation in the War of Independence, betrayed by the subsequent codification of slavery in the fledgling nation's Constitution. Episode III—*Brotherly Love* (1781– 1834) deals with the expansion of slavery after Eli Whitney's invention of the cotton gin in 1793 makes southern cotton a profitable crop for the first time. The episode also traces the early slave rebellions and the beginnings of the abolitionist movement in the early nineteenth century. Episode IV—*Judgment Day* (1831– 1861) delineates the country's westward expansion, which fuels rising tensions between the abolitionist movement and the entrenched institution of slavery in the South, tensions that finally explode into the Civil War. Shot on location in twelve states, England, and Ghana, *Africans in America* (narrated by Angela

Bassett) uses period photographs, recitations, reenactments, and interviews with Chinua Achebe, Eric Foner, Colin Powell, John Edgar Wideman, and many other notables, historians, and experts to convey both the massive scope and human dimensions of the tragedy of slavery. Both highly informative and deeply evocative, *Africans in America* won a Peabody Award in 1999. An illustrated companion book, Charles Johnson's *Africans in America: America's Journey through Slavery* (Harcourt Brace), was published in April 2000.

Antwone Fisher (2002)

The African American counterpart to Ken Burns, Orlando Bagwell makes carefully researched, intelligent documentaries on racial topics that will have lasting significance as historical testaments. Bagwell's distance from mainstream, commercial filmmaking on the handling of race issues is well illustrated by a film like Denzel Washington's *Antwone Fisher* (2002). Born in prison in 1959 to seventeen-year-old Eva Mae Fisher, Antwone Quenton "Fish" Fisher was immediately put in the Ohio state foster care system. When Fisher was two years old he was placed in the Cleveland home of a Reverend and Mrs. Pickett. During his fourteen-year stay with the Picketts, Antwone Fisher was verbally and physically abused by the cruel and possibly psychotic Mrs. Pickett and sexually abused by a female neighbor. Unceremoniously returned to child welfare as a teenager, Fisher lived in a YMCA and on the streets until he decided to join the U.S. Navy in 1977. An introverted but rage-filled and volatile young man, Fisher was nearly ejected from the navy for fighting. In 1981 a perceptive and sympathetic navy psychiatrist helped Fisher confront his demons and begin to make peace with his troubled past. Fisher spent eleven years in the navy, worked as a corrections officer, and then took a job as a security guard at Sony Pictures Studio, Culver City, in 1989. In 1993 Fisher enrolled in a Hollywood screenwriting class where he met producer Todd Black (*A Knight's Tale*). His interest piqued by Fisher's story, Black hired Fisher to turn his survivor's saga into a screenplay. Denzel Washington signed on to direct "The Antwone Fisher Story" in 1997 but prior commitments prevented him from starting until 2001, by which time Fisher had expanded his script into a best-selling autobiography (cowritten with Mim Eichler Rivas), *Finding Fish: A Memoir* (New York: William Morrow, 2001).

    Antwone Fisher, Denzel Washington's directorial debut, stars Derek Luke (*Friday Night Lights*) as Antwone Fisher and Washington as Dr. Jerome Davenport, Fisher's analyst, mentor, and father figure. Though solidly directed, well acted, and at times deeply affecting, *Antwone Fisher* is, in many ways, a predictable feel-good movie that owes its tone and overall ideology to contempo-

Antwone Fisher poses at a screening of the movie, Antwone Fisher, *based on his auto-biography,* Finding Fish. *(Adrees Latif/Reuters/Corbis)*

rary therapeutic discourse. Indeed, the film has a derivative quality; whether true to life or not, the blossoming therapist-client relationship at its center recalls earlier renditions of the same scenario in *Ordinary People* (1980), *Prince of Tides* (1991), and *Good Will Hunting* (1997). In real life Antwone Fisher definitely benefited from therapy but the film's emphasis on psychological and emotional healing tends to obscure the fact that Fisher's horrible childhood and youth—his father was murdered, his mother incarcerated before Fisher was born—can be traced to *systemic* conditions, that is, the degraded world of Cleveland's black ghetto, an inner-city nightmare of poverty and desperation built by race and class discrimination. All the individualized psychotherapy in the world will not create a standard of education, employment, culture, and public safety conducive to the healthy socialization that produces well-adjusted, responsible adults. In other words, Antwone Fisher's self-redemption is an exceptional occurrence not to be generalized to the black urban underclass as a whole. Mass social problems need individual *and* collective solutions. In "Leaving the Others Behind," an online review for the World Socialist website (January 29, 2003), David Walsh perceptively notes that *Antwone Fisher* reduces "life and human relationships to quite manageable bite-size pieces, arranged to illustrate a series of platitudes about 'coming to terms with your past,' 'having the courage to reach out for help,' 'overcoming all obstacles' and 'demonstrating the resilience of the human spirit' . . . Instead of anger over the conditions ultimately responsible for Fisher's misfortunes, it offers racial pride, self-help advice and facile psychology."

With All Deliberate Speed (2004)

May 17, 2004, marked the fiftieth anniversary of the Supreme Court's decision in the landmark *Brown v. Board of Education* case. In 1951 a group of thirteen African American parents, aided by the NAACP, filed a class action suit against the Board of Education of Topeka [Kansas] schools calling for an injunction that would end racial segregation in Topeka's public schools. After losing their case in U.S. District Court in Kansas in June 1951, the parents appealed to the Supreme Court, which first heard the case in December 1952 but could not reach a decision. *Brown v. Board of Education* was reargued a year later. The Supreme Court rendered a unanimous decision on May 17, 1954, that invalidated *Plessy v. Ferguson*, the 1892 ruling that legalized the "separate but equal" doctrine that allowed for mandated or permitted segregation in many areas of public life (e.g., schools, theaters, restaurants, and transportation) in twenty-one states. Though it only desegregated public schools, *Brown v. Board of Education* was the first major nail in the coffin of Jim Crow and marked a key moment in the genesis of the Civil Rights movement.

To commemorate the fiftieth anniversary of *Brown v. Board of Education*, producer-director Peter Gilbert (*Hoop Dreams*) made *With All Deliberate Speed* (2004), a documentary narrated by Jeffrey Wright (*Angels in America*) that recounts the court battles that led to the historic ruling. The film then goes on to survey the decades hence in terms of progress in improving American public education for African Americans. Unfortunately, its conclusions are grim. The Supreme Court was in earnest when it demanded desegregation "with all deliberate speed." The film uses the phrase ironically. In actuality desegregation has often been implemented at an exceedingly slow pace and in such a halfhearted way that vast inequalities still prevail between white and black public schools. An important documentary on an important topic, *With All Deliberate Speed* nonetheless suffers from excessive length, complexity, and a diffuse narrative focus that bespeaks an overly ambitious agenda on Peter Gilbert's part—flaws also evident in *Hoop Dreams*.

10

History of Crime on Film and Television

A popular nonfiction literary genre since the 1920s, "true crime" has since become a staple feature of film and television, especially after the 1960s. At first, the genre owed its popularity to the public's lurid fascination with the transgressive, tragic, and even vicariously liberating aspects of criminality. No one wanted to share the gruesome fate of Bonnie and Clyde or John Dillinger but one could read about or watch reenactments of their exploits and experience the simulated exhilaration of breaking the law and getting away with it—for a time. In the 1960s the American social fabric began to unravel in ways not even dreamt of in the 1930s. Suddenly, with the emergence of Lee Harvey Oswald, Albert De Salvo, Richard Speck, Charles Whitman, Sirhan Sirhan, Charles Manson, and others, random, grotesque acts of homicidal violence seemed to become ordinary occurrences symptomatic of a society in extreme crisis. In the decades that followed, true crime stories have proliferated in all media, not as innocent entertainment but as a kind of morbidly fascinated stare into the attenuated demise of a civilization.

The Thirties

I Am a Fugitive from a Chain Gang (1932)

In the first six months of 1931 Benarr Macfadden's *True Detective Mysteries* magazine published serialized installments of *I Am a Fugitive from a Georgia Chain Gang,* a chilling exposé of Georgia's medieval penal system by Robert Elliott Burns (1891–1955). Published in book form by Vanguard Press in January 1932, Burns's story garnered national attention and prompted impassioned calls for reform that ultimately resulted in the abolition of the chain gang in Georgia in 1937. Warner Bros. producer Hal B. Wallis (*Little Caesar*) purchased the film rights and assigned Howard J. Green (*The Kid Brother*), Brown Holmes (*20,000*

Years in Sing Sing), and Sheridan Gibney (*The Story of Louis Pasteur*) to adapt Burns's story to the screen. Directed by Mervyn Leroy (*Little Caesar*) and starring Paul Muni as James Allen (aka Allen James), the Robert E. Burns figure, *I Am a Fugitive from a Chain Gang* (1932) bears the distinction of being the first social problem talkie and an early forerunner of the film noir genre. Released on November 19, 1932, the film proved to be a great success for Warner Bros.

For the most part, *I Am a Fugitive* stays fairly close to the facts of Burns's case. One notable exception is the removal of the word "Georgia" from the title of the film for fear it would cause too much controversy. Other changes are designed to engender sympathy for Burns by painting him as more of a hapless victim of circumstance than he actually was. For example, the film suggests that Burns's service in the First World War made him too restless to stay at his old job when he returned home after the war. In point of fact, Burns's $50-a-week factory job had been filled in his absence; his employers offered him a job paying only $17.60. Rather than accept such a pay cut, Burns took to the road. Falling in with two other drifters in Atlanta, Burns participated in a 1922 grocery store holdup that netted $5.80. (The film erases Burns's culpability by having him unwittingly implicated in the robbery of a diner by a traveling companion.) Arrested immediately, all three were tried, convicted, and sentenced to long terms at hard labor.

The movie accurately depicts Burns's first escape. On June 21, 1922, some six months into his six- to ten-year sentence, Burns escaped from a Campbell County chain gang with the help of a black prisoner, who agreed to bend his shackles with a sledgehammer. As also depicted in the film, Burns made his way to Chicago, changed his name, married his landlady, Emily del Phino Pacheo, and went on to become a successful businessman by founding *The Greater Chicago Magazine* in 1926. As the magazine's editor in chief, Burns made a good living and was a respected civic leader. Sadly his world came crashing down in the summer of 1929 when he sought a divorce from his wife, Emily, after falling in love with a woman named Lillian Salo. Seeking revenge, his jealous wife alerted Georgia authorities as to his real identity and whereabouts. Waiving a legal fight over his extradition, Burns agreed to return to Georgia on the understanding that he would only have to serve forty-five to ninety days. Once they had Burns back in custody, Georgia authorities transformed his light sentence into a minimum of twelve months hard labor (probably because he did not have the requisite $500 needed to bribe members of the Georgia Prison Commission). Denied parole on July 9, 1930, after having served a hellish year on a Troup County chain gang, Burns vowed to escape again—which he did on September 4, 1930. The movie dramatically depicts Burns commandeering a dump truck and hurling dynamite to elude his pursuers. The reality was much more prosaic: Burns simply slipped away from his guards on a road project near Mountville, Georgia, and paid two farmers to give him a ride to Atlanta. He then made his way to New Jersey and some months later published his story in *True Detective Mysteries.* In the film, Burns is depicted, hauntingly, as a fugitive forever doomed to a life of hiding in the shadows and stealing to survive.

Once again, the extracinematic reality was a good deal more prosaic. Under an alias Burns ran a small toy store in New Jersey after his second escape from Georgia. On December 15, 1932, less than a month after the premier of the film version of his saga, Newark police detectives arrested Burns. With the magazine series, book, and film having made Burns a much-pitied national celebrity, he garnered strong support when he appealed to New Jersey Governor A. Harry Moore to refuse Georgia's request for extradition. To Burns's immense relief— and Georgia's outrage—Governor Moore did indeed refuse to sign the extradition papers, as did Moore's successors. On November 1, 1945, Burns voluntarily appeared before Georgia's State Pardon and Parole Board, which finally exonerated him twenty-three years after the Atlanta robbery. He spent the last ten years of his life an entirely free man.

The Forties

Rope (1948)

At 5:25 on Wednesday afternoon, May 21, 1924, Richard "Dickie" Loeb, eighteen, and Nathan "Babe" Leopold Jr., nineteen years old, picked up a Loeb family friend named Bobby Franks, fourteen, as he was walking home from a Chicago park. Moments after Franks got in the front seat next to Loeb, Nathan Leopold clasped a hand around Franks' mouth from behind and then proceeded to bash his skull with a steel coal chisel and strangle him for good measure. Loeb and Leopold then drove Franks' lifeless body to a swampy area near Wolf Lake on the South Side of Chicago. There they undressed Franks, poured acid on his face, and then stuffed his corpse into a culvert by some railroad tracks. Loeb and Leopold were in the midst of trying to collect a kidnap ransom from Bobby Franks' parents when the body was discovered, as were a pair of distinctive eyeglasses that accidentally fell out of Leopold's pocket. Soon linked to the murder, Loeb and Leopold confessed to the crime on May 29, 1924. Both being from wealthy families, Loeb and Leopold did not need the ransom money, nor did they have any personal animus against Bobby Franks. Followers of Nietzsche, they simply wanted to commit the proverbial "perfect crime" as a means to prove their intellectual superiority and cement their bond as homosexual lovers. Amid sensational publicity, their defense attorney, the legendary Clarence Darrow

(1857–1938), persuaded Loeb and Leopold to plead guilty and thus avoid a jury trial that was certain to lead to the death penalty. In a summation that lasted two days, Darrow argued against capital punishment, citing among other reasons that their "inverted" sexuality had made the two young men insane. Judge John Caverty agreed and sentenced Loeb and Leopold to "life plus 99 years" for kidnapping and murder. Richard Loeb was slain by another inmate at Joliet Prison in 1936. Paroled in 1958 after serving more than thirty years, Nathan Leopold died in Puerto Rico in 1971.

In 1929 British playwright Patrick Hamilton (1904–1962) had his first success in the London theater with *Rope*, a three-act thriller about Wyndham Brandon and Charles Granillo, two Oxford University undergraduates steeped in Nietzsche's philosophy of the Superman, who attempt to commit the "perfect murder." After murdering a fellow student, they put his body in a steamer trunk and then hold a dinner party using the trunk as a table. Among those invited: Rupert Cadell, the boys' philosophy professor and mentor who introduced them to the writings of Nietzsche. In a tense verbal cat-and-mouse game, Cadell, who suspects the truth, causes Brandon and Granillo to eventually reveal their terrible secret. While clearly based on the Loeb-Leopold case (despite the coy disclaimers of Patrick Hamilton), *Rope* drained the case of most of its historical specificity. That the actual killers were affluent Jewish homosexuals from the American heartland was lost in shifting the action to Oxford: a diminution of context that resulted in a misrepresentation of the crime as some sort of perverse philosophical exercise.

Interested in filming the play since the mid-1930s, Alfred Hitchcock finally brought *Rope* (his first color film) to the screen in 1949. Adapted from Hamilton's play by Arthur Laurents and Hume Cronyn, *Rope* stars James Stewart as Rupert Cadell, John Dall as Brandon Shaw, and Farley Granger as Philip Morgan. In 1939 Dallas Bower, Hitchcock's soundman on *Blackmail* (1929), did a BBC-TV production of *Rope* that used long takes to keep the camera on the murder chest. Hitchcock decided to experiment with a similar strategy when he filmed *Rope*. The 80-minute film was shot in ten 8-minute-long takes—defined by the amount of film the camera could hold before it needed to be reloaded—with most cuts between takes concealed by having the camera zoom in on a dark object (for example, a vase or a man's back) then pull out again to start the next take. The goal was to create the illusion of one seamless and virtually continuous shot. The actual result was a static, gimmicky film that lacked the taut suspense usually associated with Hitchcock. Though the scenario bore only the most general resemblance to the Loeb-Leopold case, the conspiratorial closeness of the two effete young men hinted at a homosexual liaison—which caused the film to be banned in Chicago, Seattle, Memphis, and other cities and towns.

The Fifties

A Place in the Sun (1951)

Predating the infamous Loeb-Leopold case by some sixteen years, the murder conviction and execution of Chester Gillette of Cortland, New York, would have fallen into obscurity were it not for the efforts of the great American naturalist writer Theodore Dreiser (1871–1945). During his days as a newspaperman, Dreiser noticed the continual reoccurrence of a certain type of homicide: that of a lower-middle-class young man doing away with a pregnant girlfriend who threatened to tie him down with an unwanted marriage and family and ruin his prospects for social advancement. Dreiser thought that such crimes spoke volumes about the essentially intractable nature of the American class structure, a system that nonetheless fosters in many of its minions a ruthless desire to "rise in the world" regardless of the costs or the consequences. A foreman in his rich uncle's skirt factory in central New York, Chester Gillette became romantically involved with Grace "Billy" Brown, one of the girls in his department. After a few months Gillette dumped Miss Brown to pursue a local society girl but it soon came to light that Brown was pregnant with Gillette's baby. Desperate for a way out of his dilemma, Chester Gillette lured Grace Brown to Big Moose Lake in the Adironacks on July 11, 1906, where he murdered her and tried to make it look like an accidental drowning. Convicted of first-degree murder in a highly publicized trial, Gillette died in the electric chair at Auburn State Prison on March 30, 1908.

An epic fictionalization of the Chester Gillette story, Theodore Dreiser's masterpiece, *An American Tragedy* (1925), painstakingly traces the life of Clyde Griffiths (the Gillette figure) to show how he was particularly susceptible to the blandishments of American dream ideology. Hailing from a family of impoverished, itinerant evangelists, Griffiths almost instinctively seeks escape from his materially and culturally barren social class origins: a fierce and quite understandable impulse that leads to the deaths of two people. Dreiser does not romanticize Griffiths or condone his crime; he merely tries to suggest that the sad fate of young men like Chester Gillette and young women like Grace Brown (called Roberta Alden in the novel) show that the yawning chasm between desire and actuality in twentieth-century American society presents unbearable contradictions that can cause all manner of desperation and depravity.

Despite Dreiser's prolix and sometimes turgid writing style, *An American Tragedy* became a highly acclaimed bestseller that soon spawned dramatic and film adaptations. The first movie version, Joseph von Sternberg's *An American Tragedy* (1931), vexed Dreiser by turning his allegorical critique of American civilization into a simplistic crime yarn. Twenty years later Hollywood took another crack at Dreiser's novel with George Stevens' *A Place in the Sun* (1951). Made when anticommunist hysteria was at an all-time high, Stevens' version could hardly be expected to endorse Dreiser's scathing indictment of class society. Indeed, *A Place in the Sun* effectively subverts Dreiser's message by glamorizing the wealthy Eastman family and their social set while depicting the Chester Gillette figure, George Eastman (Montgomery Clift), as quite right to aspire for acceptance from them. In Dreiser's novel, Sondra Finchley, the society ingenue with whom Clyde Griffiths is infatuated, is portrayed as a spoiled, emotionally manipulative brat who is using Clyde to make another suitor—Clyde's cousin, Gilbert—jealous. In *A Place in the Sun*, the narcissistic Sondra Finchley is transformed into Angela Vickers (Elizabeth Taylor), a very beautiful, glamorous, and kindhearted young woman who has it all over the Grace Brown figure, Alice Tripp (Shelley Winters), a dowdy and excessively whiny factory girl with a grating voice and manner. Further skewing the glaring disparity in attractiveness between the two women is the fact that Taylor was only eighteen years old at the time, while Shelley Winters was thirty. Given these casting choices and characterizations, the audience is quite happy to see George Eastman dispatch Alice Tripp—not at all what Theodore Dreiser had in mind. The film also has Angela Vickers visiting George Eastman in prison just before his execution to profess her undying love—cloying, romantic nonsense that has no basis in Dreiser or the Chester Gillette case.

I Want to Live! (1958)

On June 4, 1955, the state of California sent three death row inmates to the gas chamber at San Quentin: Jack Santo, fifty-four; Emmett Perkins, forty-seven; and Barbara Graham, thirty-two. All three had been convicted of the strangulation and bludgeoning murder of Mrs. Mabel Monohan, sixty-two, a wealthy widow, whose Burbank, California, home the trio entered and ransacked on the night of March 10, 1953. Caught after a highly publicized three-week manhunt, Santo, Perkins, and Graham were tried, convicted, and sentenced to death in a Los Angeles court in the late summer of 1953. Santo and Perkins were run-of-the-mill career criminals. What made the case a media sensation was the involvement of Barbara Graham, a young, attractive mother of three who, though sometimes a prostitute and heroin addict, did not conform to the popular stereotype of a cold-blooded killer. Her death sentence was also unusual. Of 154 convicts executed at San Quentin's gas chamber since it started operating in 1937, only 2 had been women prior to Graham. The other factor that made Graham stand out was her high-strung, volatile personality; she wept openly at the verdict and repeatedly and loudly cursed her fate, her partners in crime, and her jailers during her twenty-month stint on death row. After two brief but agonizing stays on the morning of execution, Graham finally died in the gas chamber at 11:42 A.M.

In 1957, while the public's memory of Barbara Graham was still fresh, film producer Walter Wanger of Figaro commissioned "The Barbara Graham Story," later retitled *I Want to Live!* (1958). Don Mankiewicz (nephew of Figaro's CEO, Joseph Mankiewicz) and Nelson Gidding (*The Helen Morgan Story*) collaborated on a screenplay based on newspaper stories by journalist Ed Montgomery and Barbara Graham's letters from prison. Directed by Robert Wise (*Somebody Up There Likes Me*) and starring Susan Hayward as Barbara Graham, the first half of *I Want to Live!* traces Graham's delinquent life up to the murder while the film's second half, actually shot at San Quentin, deals entirely with her nerve-wracking wait to be executed. Taut direction by Wise and a brilliantly agonized, Oscar-winning performance by Haywood make *I Want to Live!* a tour de force and a revealing barometer of cultural anxieties generated by rapidly changing ways of life in late 1950s America, when wanton murder suddenly seemed more commonplace and women were no longer reliably docile.

Compulsion (1959)

Already dealt with on stage and screen in the previous decade, the infamous Loeb-Leopold case received another airing with Richard D. Zanuck's *Compulsion* (1959). The film had its first incarnation as a best-selling novel by Meyer Levin (New York: Simon & Schuster, 1956), which Levin immediately adapted into a stage play. Starring Roddy McDowall as Artie Straus (Richard Loeb) and Dean Stockwell as Judd Steiner (Nathan Leopold), *Compulsion* premiered at the Ambassador Theatre, West 49th Street, New York City, on October 24, 1957, and ran until February 24, 1958 (140 performances). Unlike the stage and film versions of *Rope*, the stage version of *Compulsion* was, to the chagrin of some critics and audience members, a little more explicit about the homosexual relationship between the killers but nonetheless took pains to mitigate the shock of a taboo being broken by depicting Steiner as pathetically desperate to function as heterosexual. Ironically, just a few days before the play closed, the real Nathan Leopold was paroled from prison, after serving thirty-three and a half years. A month after his release, Leopold published his autobiography, *Life Plus 99 Years* (New York: Doubleday, 1958).

Richard Zanuck, the then twenty-four-year-old son of 20th Century Fox Studios founder Darryl F. Zanuck, selected *Compulsion* as the first property he would produce. Directed by Richard Fleischer (*The Vikings*), *Compulsion*

(1959) stars Orson Welles as Jonathan Wilk (the Clarence Darrow figure), Dean Stockwell reprising his stage role as Judd Steiner, Bradford Dillman replacing Roddy McDowall as Artie Straus, and Diane Varsi as Ruth Evans (Ruth Goldenberg in the play), Steiner's other love interest. Tellingly, the film completely represses the homosexual aspects of the case and concentrates on repudiating the killers' deluded Nietzcheanism, as contrasted to Wilk's eloquent, compassionate humanism that reputedly saves their lives. To a greater extent than the stage version, the film was avid to contain Loeb and Leopold's transgressions against social, sexual, and legal norms at a time when status quo verities were being challenged.

The Sixties

Birdman of Alcatraz (1962)

In the early 1950s Thomas E. Gaddis, a former corrections officer who became a prison reform advocate, began corresponding with Robert Stroud (1890–1963), an inmate at Alcatraz serving a life sentence for murder. Stroud's story was both grim and fascinating. In 1909 Stroud was sentenced to twelve years at McNeil Island (WA) Penitentiary for killing a bartender named Charles F. Damer (variously "Dahmer") in Juneau, Alaska, after Damer assaulted Kitty O'Brien, a prostitute for whom Stroud was pimping. Transferred to Leavenworth Federal Penitentiary in 1912, Stroud fatally stabbed a brutal guard named Andrew F. Turner in the prison mess hall in full view of 1,100 witnesses on March 26, 1916. After three separate trials, Stroud was found guilty of first-degree murder and sentenced to death by hanging in 1918 but had his death sentence commuted to life by President Woodrow Wilson. A. Mitchell Palmer, Wilson's vindictive attorney general, directed that Stroud's life sentence be spent in solitary confinement.

In 1920 Stroud's blighted life took a turn for the better. While walking alone in the prison exercise yard, Stroud found three live baby sparrows fallen from a nest, took them back to his cell, and began to care for them—and to develop an intense interest in ornithology. Over the next twenty-two years Stroud raised dozens of canaries, studied their diseases, and developed cures. In the early 1930s Stroud wrote a 60,000-word treatise on canary diseases that was smuggled out of Leavenworth and published in 1933 (Stroud published a second book, *Stroud's Digest of the Diseases of Birds*, in 1943). For Leavenworth officials, Stroud's increasing fame as a bird expert brought unwanted publicity; they arranged to have him transferred to Alcatraz in San Francisco Bay on December 19, 1942. Ironically, by the time Thomas Gaddis's biography, *Birdman of Alca-*

traz: The Story of Robert Stroud (Random House), was published in September 1955, Stroud had not worked with birds—which were not allowed at Alcatraz— for almost thirteen years (doubly ironic given the name of the prison, which is Spanish for pelican). Transferred from Alcatraz to a Missouri minimum-security prison hospital in 1959, Robert Stroud died behind bars on November 21, 1963. He had spent fifty-four of his seventy-one years in prison, forty-one in some form of solitary confinement.

Based almost entirely on Robert Stroud's own account of his life, as interpreted by Tom Gaddis, a zealous advocate for rehabilitation, *Birdman of Alcatraz* presents only one side of the story. While it is true that Stroud, who had a superior intellect, educated himself in a number of fields, became a first-rate ornithologist and author, even learned French in his sixties, he was at base an extremely dangerous and menacing psychopath disliked and distrusted by his jailers and fellow inmates. Adapted to the screen and produced by Guy Trosper (*The Stratton Story; The Pride of St. Louis*) and directed by John Frankenheimer (*The Manchurian Candidate; Seven Days in May*), *Birdman of Alcatraz* (1962) merely reiterates Thomas Gaddis's fanciful portrait of Robert Stroud (Burt Lancaster in the film) as a mild-mannered model prisoner incarcerated long after he should have been paroled. Indeed, after the film premiered in July 1962, hundreds of sympathetic filmgoers wrote the U.S. Bureau of Prisons pleading for Stroud's release that Attorney General Robert F. Kennedy wisely refused to grant.

Bonnie & Clyde (1967)

The five years that elapsed between *Birdman of Alcatraz* (1962) and the next major true crime film—Arthur Penn's *Bonnie & Clyde* (1967)—saw a sea change in the American zeitgeist. In those five years John F. Kennedy had been assassinated, the nation's black ghettos had exploded in rioting, the Vietnam War had begun in earnest, and a youth counterculture fueled by psychotropic drugs, rock music, growing antiwar fervor, and disillusionment with business civilization was on the rise. While *Birdman* epitomized New Frontier liberalism, *Bonnie & Clyde* spoke to a different ethos altogether, one that slyly glorified violent criminality as the ultimate expression of youth rebellion. When *Bonnie & Clyde* premiered at the 8th Annual Montreal International Film Festival on August 5, 1967, the largely Canadian and European audience loved it but a week later senior *New York Times* film critic Bosley Crowther pounced on the film, calling it "a cheap piece of bald-faced slapstick comedy that treats the hideous depredations of that sleazy, moronic pair as though they were as full of fun and frolic as the jazz-age cut-ups in 'Thoroughly Modern Millie'" (Crowther 1967).

The infamous Bonnie and Clyde, as seen in May 1934. Bonnie and Clyde were later killed in a clash with the Texas Rangers. (Associated Press)

Though a sixty-two-year-old curmudgeon on the verge of retirement and far removed from the youth pulses of the 1960s, Crowther was in fact quite right: *Bonnie & Clyde* romanticized people who should never be romanticized. The real Clyde Barrow and Bonnie Parker were crude, vicious, psychopathic killers—hardly the lovable, crazy, mixed-up kids portrayed by Warren Beatty and Faye

Dunaway. The mythic distortion of Bonnie and Clyde began with David Newman and Robert Benton, editors at *Esquire* magazine who wrote a French New Wave cinema-influenced seventy-five-page treatment in 1963–1964 that turned the criminals into chic youth rebels. Indeed, Newman and Benton hoped that François Truffaut (*The 400 Blows; Jules and Jim*) would direct their Bonnie and Clyde movie but Truffaut was too busy to do it. Told about the film script by Truffaut, Warren Beatty read it, loved it, and decided that he would produce and star in the picture. Graced by the inspired direction of Arthur Penn (*The Miracle Worker; Mickey One*), *Bonnie & Clyde* featured strong performances by Beatty, Dunaway, Michael J. Pollard as gang member C. W. Moss (actually an amalgam of gang members W. D. Jones and Henry Methvin), Gene Hackman as Clyde's brother Marvin ("Buck"), Estelle Parson as Buck's wife Blanche, and Denver Pyle as Frank Hamer, the dogged lawman who pursued the Barrow gang. As for tone, *Bonnie & Clyde* blended extreme violence, comedy, romance, and car chases (accompanied musically by Flatt and Scruggs' exhilarating "Foggy Mountain Breakdown") in a way that confounded genre formulas and made the film hard to read. As a result *Bonnie & Clyde* generated a strange and unprecedented critical reaction. Following Bosley Crowther's lead, other top film critics initially panned the film but a laudatory review by Pauline Kael, the film critic at *The New Yorker* magazine, instigated a critical reassessment and great box office returns. The film went on to huge box office success and ten Oscar nominations, winning two Oscars: one to Burnett Guffey for Cinematography and another to the screechy Estelle Parsons for Best Actress in a Supporting Role.

Though putatively about 1930s gangsters, *Bonnie & Clyde* was quite obviously a self-congratulatory celebration of the antiauthoritarian, youth-oriented mood of the 1960s. This orientation is especially evident in the relationship between the fictional C. W. Moss and his equally fictional father, Ivan (Dub Taylor). Young C. W. is enchanted with Bonnie and Clyde as the epitome of bold, brave spontaneity in a dull, run-down world ruled by money worries, want, and meek conformity. In marked contrast to his son, Ivan Moss despises Bonnie and Clyde as criminal lowlifes and is particularly upset when C. W. acquires a tattoo: an outlaw example of gratuitous self-adornment that goes against Mr. Moss's puritanical working-class creed. The embodiment of the older generation, the duplicitous Ivan Moss is instrumental in the betrayal and assassination of Bonnie and Clyde that brings the movie to an abrupt, stunning, and apocalyptic end. Equally villainous is Bonnie and Clyde's adult authority figure, Frank Hamer, a humorless, cowardly lawman bent on personal revenge. In its explicit and graphic depiction of violence and its effects, *Bonnie & Clyde* put the final nails in the coffin of the Hays Code and helped to usher in the New American Cinema, an auteur-oriented counterculture cinema that produced a string of great films in the 1960s and 1970s. At the same time, *Bonnie & Clyde* did inestimable damage to American popular culture by glorifying psychopaths and making bloodshed and violent death (in slow motion) beautiful to watch: morbid and perverse tendencies that would be taken to absurd heights in the decades that followed.

In Cold Blood (1967)

On November 16, 1959, writer Truman Capote (1924–1984) was perusing the *New York Times* in his Manhattan apartment when he happened upon a brief account of a mass murder in Holcomb, Kansas. The previous night Herbert W. Clutter, forty-eight, a wealthy wheat farmer; his wife, Bonnie, forty-five; and two children still living at home—Nancy, sixteen, and Kenyon, fifteen—were bound and gagged and had their throats slashed and/or heads disfigured by close-range shotgun blasts. Searching for a topic for an experimental hybrid of pure fiction and accurate reportage he termed the "nonfiction novel," Capote quickly decided that the Clutter family murders would suit his purposes, perhaps because the Clutters' grisly fate so shattered and defiled the heartland American normalcy they seemed to epitomize. Capote, initially accompanied by Nelle Harper Lee (*To Kill a Mockingbird*), made numerous long sojourns from New York City to Kansas and other relevant places to investigate the crime and its aftermath. When two paroled convicts named Perry Edward Smith, thirty-one, and Richard Eugene "Dick" Hickock, twenty-eight, were apprehended in Las Vegas a month after the slayings and charged with the murders, Capote attended their extradition and trial and later visited and corresponded with them on death row after they were convicted in late March 1960. Five years later Capote was on hand to witness Dick Hickock's hanging at Kansas State Penitentiary in Lansing (April 14, 1965) but could not bring himself to watch Perry Smith's execution a few moments later. With Hickcock and Smith dead, Capote was finally able to write an ending to *In Cold Blood*, his 135,000-word book on the Clutter case. *The New Yorker* magazine published it in four installments that fall and Random House published it in book form on January 17, 1966, to much hoopla, almost universal critical acclaim, and brisk sales. Along with magazine and hardcover rights, Capote also sold paperback rights to New American Library and film rights to Columbia Pictures for a grand total of $2 million (more than US$12 million in 2005). *In Cold Blood* made Capote a rich man and a household name and proved to be a seminal work of the true crime genre that would explode in popularity in the decades that followed.

Columbia wanted to exploit the success of the book by shooting a blockbuster film version of *In Cold Blood* starring Steve McQueen as Perry Smith and

A 1959 portrait of author Truman Capote, famous for his 1966 novel In Cold Blood. *(Library of Congress)*

Paul Newman as Dick Hickock. Pressure from studio executives notwithstanding, veteran noir producer-director Richard Brooks (*Brute Force; Crossfire*) insisted on casting unknowns Robert Blake and Scott Wilson as the killers and opted to have his cinematographer, Conrad Hall (*Cool Hand Luke*), shoot the movie in black and white: wise choices that made for a more muted, credible, and eerily atmospheric film. Brooks also shot the movie at most of the actual locations, including the Clutter home, and faithfully followed Capote's four-part narrative structure, terse documentary style, and—most crucially—Capote's interpretive slant, which tended to portray Hickock as the villain and Smith as his unwitting accomplice even though it was Perry Smith who actually committed all four murders. In book and film, the theory advanced for Smith's homicidal rampage is that he had some sort of mental fugue brought on by a life of poverty, violent parental abuse, failure, and frustration. Released for the Christmas holidays, 1967, *In Cold Blood* did not match the smashing success of the book but nonetheless did quite well at the box office and was nominated for four 1968 Oscars.

Some thirty years later, J. J. Maloney (1940–1999), a paroled murderer who became a five-time Pulitzer Prize–nominated journalist, published a fascinating revisionist piece on Capote's novel: "*In Cold Blood:* A Dishonest Book" (*Crime Magazine: An Encyclopedia of Crime*, a website devoted to true crime [http://crimemagazine.com/CrimeBooks/incold.htm]). In his savvy but nonetheless speculative article, Maloney concedes the accuracy of the basic facts related by Capote but goes on to argue that Capote's theory regarding the motive behind the killings is deeply disingenuous. Both book and film depict Perry Smith and Dick Hickock as heterosexual. Maloney asserts that Smith was decidedly gay and that Hickock, though straight, did resort to a homosexual liaison with Smith while both were in prison together—a common occurrence. When Perry Smith caught Dick Hickock trying to rape sixteen-year-old Nancy Clutter during what was supposed to be strictly a robbery, he flew into a jealous rage and massacred the Clutter family to get back at Hickock, his errant lover. Maloney also asserts that Capote, a flamboyantly effeminate gay man, fell in love with Perry Smith during his stint on death row: ample reasons, both ideological and personal, for Capote to suppress the homosexual aspect of the story and advance a then-fashionable environmentalist theory of the crime.

The Boston Strangler (1968)

Over an eighteen-month period (June 14, 1962–January 4, 1964), a person or persons unknown sexually assaulted and strangled thirteen Boston area women ranging in age from nineteen to eighty-five. In late October 1964 police arrested a married factory worker named Albert De Salvo on rape charges. On March 6, 1965, De Salvo met with defense attorney F. Lee Bailey and claimed, in a tape-recorded confession, that he was the infamous "Boston Strangler." De Salvo was, however, a habitual braggart and the police were not able to produce a shred of physical evidence linking him to any of the crimes. Tried in 1966 on unrelated robbery and sex charges, Albert De Salvo was sentenced to life in prison in January 1967. He died at the hands of another inmate in 1973. Because De Salvo's confession could not be corroborated, lingering doubts remain as to the true identity of the Boston Strangler.

From the first murders in the summer of 1962 to De Salvo's conviction in 1967, the Boston Strangler case garnered national attention. Celebrity ghost-writer Gerold Frank exploited the notoriety of the case with *The Boston Strangler* (New American Library), a book that hit the *New York Times* bestseller list shortly after its 1966 Christmas season publication—and just as De Salvo's trial was coming to an end. The book's considerable popularity caught the attention of Hollywood. Producer Robert Fryer bought the film rights and persuaded 20th Century Fox to make a movie version. The original screenwriter, British playwright Terrence Rattigan, wrote a farcical script that had a computer identify 20th Century Fox mogul Darryl F. Zanuck as the Boston Strangler! Not at all amused, the studio dropped Rattigan and hired Edward Anhalt (*The Young Lions*) to write a serious treatment. Directed by Richard Fleischer (*The Vikings; Compulsion*), *The Boston Strangler* (1968) bifurcates the story. Its first half is a terse police procedural shot in semidocumentary style—with liberal use of split screen (a 1960s cinematic fashion that has not exactly stood the test of time). As the murder count rises and Boston area police are unable to find the killer, Massachusetts Attorney General Edward W. Brooke (William Marshall) takes over the case, appointing his Assistant A.G., John S. Bottomly (Henry Fonda), to head a "Strangler Bureau" consisting of several Boston PD and State Police detectives and other forensic experts. The second half of the film focuses on Bottomly's probing interrogation of Albert De Salvo (Tony Curtis) after the bureau concludes that he is probably the strangler. It turns out that De Salvo is a schizoid personality who has managed to repress the memory of his crimes. In the end, Bottomly is able to make De Salvo face and acknowledge his dark side. In point of fact, the real John Bottomly was a buffoon widely reviled by his law enforcement colleagues—far from the calm, intelligent figure depicted by Henry Fonda.

The Seventies

Bloody Mama (1970)

Arizona Donnie Kate "Ma" Barker (1872–1935) and her four sons—Herman (1894–1927), Lloyd (1896–1949), Arthur, aka "Doc" (1899–1939), and Fred (1902–1935)—later joined by Alvin "Creepy" Karpis (1908–1979) and other criminals, made headlines in the 1920s and early 1930s by perpetrating a long string of bank robberies, hijackings, kidnappings, and murders, mostly in the Midwest. Herman committed suicide in 1927 in the wake of a deadly shoot-out with police; Ma and Fred were killed in a marathon shoot-out with FBI agents in 1935; Doc died trying to escape from Alcatraz in 1939; Lloyd was murdered by his wife in 1949; Alvin Karpis, paroled after serving thirty-three years in prison (1936–1969), committed suicide in 1979. Though it is still not clear whether Ma Barker was the Barker-Karpis gang's mastermind or merely went along for the ride, J. Edgar Hoover's FBI termed her "Bloody Mama" and characterized her as the gang's diabolical leader, perhaps to justify her shooting by government agents.

Having already broached the true crime genre with *The St. Valentine's Day Massacre*, Roger Corman attempted to further exploit the 1930s crime film revival opened up by *Bonnie & Clyde* by making a drive-in movie about Ma Barker and her notorious gang. Cowritten by Robert Thom (*All the Fine Young Cannibals; Wild in the Streets*) and artist-writer Don Peters (*The Naked Prey*), *Bloody Mama* (1970) stars Shelley Winters as Ma Barker, Don Stroud as Herman, Robert De Niro as Lloyd, Clint Kimbrough as Arthur, and Robert Walden as Fred. A chaotic exploitation movie full of gratuitous nudity and tasteless examples of incest, rape, drug taking, gory murder, and bad acting, *Bloody Mama* is worthless as crime history but does say something about the increasing cultural degradation of lower-middle-class America circa 1970.

The Honeymoon Killers (1970)

Annoyed by *Bonnie & Clyde*'s mendacious portrayal of the vicious duo as glamorous counterculture rebels, music composer Leonard Kastle decided to write a film script based on the exploits of another, less notorious couple: Raymond M. Fernandez and Martha (Seabrook) Beck, aka the "Lonely Hearts Slayers." Fernandez (1914–1951), a Latino born in Hawaii, returned to the United States in December 1945 after spending thirteen years in Spain, where he had married and had several children. Reputedly a law-abiding citizen until a severe head injury caused major personality changes, Fernandez spent 1946 in a Florida prison for the theft of some clothing. After his parole in March 1947, Fernandez hit on a tried-and-true way to make a living without working. He met older single women through lonely hearts clubs, courted them, proposed marriage, then bilked them of whatever assets they had before moving on to his next victim. One of his intended victims was Mrs. Martha Beck (1920–1951), an obese twenty-seven-year-old nurse from Pensacola, Florida. After being jilted by Fernandez in Florida, the love-struck Beck showed up at Fernandez's apartment in New York City on January 18, 1948, with her two young children in tow. After abandoning her children at a Salvation Army mission at Fernandez's insistence, Beck became

Raymond Fernandez and Martha Beck, self-confessed "Lonely Heart Slayers," en route to New York to face murder charges, March 15, 1949. (Bettmann/Corbis)

his lover and accomplice as he continued to work his scheme all over the eastern United States. During the next year Fernandez and Beck (posing as his sister) tricked scores of lonely women out of their life savings—and murdered the ones who became suspicious. Arrested in Michigan on February 28, 1949, Fernandez and Beck stood trial, amid sensational media coverage, during the sweltering summer of 1949 for the murder of Mrs. Janet Fay of Albany, New York. Convicted in mid-August, the infamous pair spent the next six months in separate cells on death row at Sing Sing before going to the electric chair on March 3, 1951.

Leonard Kastle's producer, Warren Steibel (*Firing Line*) accorded him a shoestring production budget, necessitating that *The Honeymoon Killers* (1970) be shot as quickly and inexpensively as possible. Much in the manner of *Poverty Row* director Edgar G. Ulmer, Kastle made the most of scant resources by shooting on location, in black and white, with minimal takes and makeshift lighting. Curly-haired Tony Lo Bianco (*The French Connection; Serpico*) did not much resemble the bald, thin Ray Fernandez physically but played him with great brio. In her debut film role Shirley Stoller (*Klute; The Deer Hunter*) looked like

Martha Beck and delivered a stunning performance of a woman so deeply in love that she is willing to kill and die for her man. *The Honeymoon Killers* takes some liberties with the facts of the case but the film is so tawdry, brutal, and eerily realistic in its crude effects that it achieves a terrifying authenticity. The great French director François Truffaut declared it his favorite American movie.

Manson (1973)

The depredations of Fernandez and Beck seem almost quaint compared to the horrific Tate-LaBianca murders committed by Charlie Manson's crime "family" in August 1969. Caught and tried, Manson and many of his followers—Patricia "Katie" Krenwinkel, Susan Atkins, Leslie Van Houten, Charles "Tex" Watson, Bobby Beausoleil, Charles Watson, Bruce Davis, and Steve "Clem" Grogan— were all eventually convicted of murder and many were sentenced to death but had their sentences commuted to life imprisonment after California abolished the death penalty in 1972. Along with the Rolling Stones debacle at Altamont in December 1969, the Manson murders marked the end of the short-lived hippie ethos—a naïve form of Dionysian abandon that proved highly susceptible to the manipulations of lumpen psychopaths like Manson who intuited that antiestablishment ideology, sexual license, and psychoactive drugs could be used to control the suggestible minds of American middle-class youth.

Not long after the Manson trials ended, independent filmmakers Robert Hendrickson and Laurence Merrick made *Manson* (1973), a 93-minute low-budget documentary that features interviews with members of the Manson "family" and Vincent Bugliosi, the deputy district attorney who prosecuted the Manson case. The vapid, sometimes idiotic, conversational meanderings of Manson's starry-eyed followers—Lynette "Squeaky" Fromme (who later tried to assassinate President Gerald Ford), Sandra Good, Mary Brunner, Catherine Share— manifest the intellectual bankruptcy of the hippie movement but also suggest a less-than-flattering truth about the larger bourgeois civilization from which it emerged. Despite its rough production values and repugnant content, *Manson* was nominated for the Academy Award for Best Documentary in 1973. *Helter Skelter*, a clumsy, exploitative made-for-television movie, appeared in 1976.

Badlands (1973)

On December 1, 1957, Charles Starkweather, a nineteen-year-old ex–garbage collector from Lincoln, Nebraska, shot and killed a gas station attendant who refused him credit. The murder, unsolved at the time, was a dress rehearsal for many more to come. On January 21, 1958, Starkweather and his fourteen-year-old girlfriend, Caril Ann Fugate, began a nine-day murder spree by shooting and stabbing Fugate's mother, stepfather, and two-year-old sister. After disposing of the bodies, Starkweather and Fugate casually remained on the property for several days before deciding to make a run for it. By the time the police captured them in Douglas, Wyoming, on January 29, Starkweather and Fugate had robbed and killed seven other persons. Tried and convicted on murder charges, Charles Starkweather was sent to the electric chair on June 25, 1959. Caril Fugate was also convicted but because she was only fourteen she received a life sentence. After serving nearly eighteen years, Fugate was paroled in June 1976. Needless to say, the public was shocked by the bizarre spectacle of a couple of teenaged mass murderers from the American heartland. The killings were brutal and senseless—perhaps the tragic expression of inchoate alienation and rage at an indifferent society, perhaps nothing more than the mindless depravity of half-civilized dimwits.

Fourteen years after the state of Nebraska executed Charles Starkweather, first-time film director Terrence Malick made *Badlands* (1973), a very loose adaptation of the Starkweather-Fugate murders starring Martin Sheen as Kit Carruthers (Starkweather) and Sissy Spacek as Holly Sargis (Fugate). Inasmuch as Caril Fugate was still in prison when *Badlands* was made, Malick had to change the names of his protagonists to avoid a possible lawsuit. But Malick also changed elements of the setting in ways that suggest a bid to mythologize his subject matter. Most of the Starkweather killings took place in the Midwest (i.e., the Lincoln, Nebraska, area) in the winter of 1957–1958. Though actually filmed in Colorado, Malick's *Badlands* is set in South Dakota and Montana in the summer of 1959—a warm, vast, empty, and arid milieu clearly meant to evoke John Ford's mythic West at the end of the Eisenhower era. The real Charles Starkweather was stocky, nearsighted, and bowlegged: an unemployed lumpen teenager estranged from his family, evicted from his rented room, and seething with nihilistic rage at his life's poor prospects. Martin Sheen's Kit Carruthers is older (twenty-five), distinctly more fit and handsome, and though also at loose ends, exhibits none of Starkweather's bitter class resentment, just a careless indifference to the world around him. The real Caril Fugate was a blank-faced, lonely, and woefully ignorant schoolgirl who came out of rural squalor. Sissy Spacek's Holly Sargis is an attractive, naïve waif who resides in the stable lower-middle-class household of her stern widower father (Warren Oates), a professional sign painter. In the film, Carruthers merely shoots his victims (some of whom are anonymous bounty hunters); Starkweather shot, repeatedly stabbed, and bludgeoned his. All of these differences add up to a perverse glamorization of the Starkweather-Fugate figures that closely parallels the same sort of gross image distortion that was visited on Bonnie Parker and Clyde Barrow in *Bonnie & Clyde.* In sum, *Badlands* says more about the cultural alienation of politically progressive intellectuals like Terrence Malick in the early 1970s than it does about the zeitgeist of Nebraska in the late 1950s. Malick's antiheroes are sociopaths only by virtue of the general vapidity of American culture. In point of fact, the nihilism of Charles Starkweather and Caril Fugate had much more to do with their lowly social class origins than Terrence Malick is able to imagine.

Dillinger (1945) and *Dillinger* (1973)

John Herbert Dillinger Jr. (1903–1934) was a juvenile delinquent and petty thief from Indianapolis, Indiana, who graduated to bank robberies after serving a nine-year prison sentence for the attempted holdup of a grocery store in 1924. Between July 17, 1933, and June 30, 1934, Dillinger and various associates robbed eleven banks spread over six states in the Midwest and took more than $300,000 (US$ 5 million in 2005). John Dillinger's memorable name, cocky mien, daring jail escapes, and uncanny ability to shoot his way out of FBI ambushes made him hot newspaper copy and something of a Depression-era folk hero among the downtrodden. Dillinger's notoriety prompted FBI Director J. Edgar Hoover to designate him "Public Enemy No. 1" and put a $15,000 bounty on his head. Betrayed by the infamous "Lady in Red," Dillinger, unarmed, was gunned down by FBI agents outside the Biograph Theatre in Chicago on July 22, 1934.

Ironically, it was the FBI itself that commissioned the first Dillinger film. The fact that Dillinger was shot six times in the back while fleeing G-men did not sit well with the public. Always vigilant about his fledgling Bureau's public image, J. Edgar Hoover commissioned the Midland Film Company to make *Dillinger: Public Enemy No. 1*, a short newsreel that depicted Dillinger as an extremely dangerous archcriminal to justify his less-than-glorious assassination. A decade after his death, Monogram Pictures brought out *Dillinger* (1945), a short (70 minutes), fast-paced B movie written by Philip Yordan (*Johnny Guitar*; *The Big Combo*) and William Castle and starring Hollywood bad boy Lawrence Tierney as Dillinger and Edmund Lowe as "Specs Green," probably the fictional counterpart to Harry "Pete" Pierpont (1902–1934), Dillinger's right-hand man. Though, in reality, Pierpont was the gang's most reckless member and Dillinger more levelheaded, the film reverses this characterization in keeping with the FBI and media-generated myth of Dillinger as a homicidal mad dog.

Nearly thirty years later right-wing screenwriter John Milius (*Jeremiah Johnson*) made his directorial debut with *Dillinger* (1973), which he also wrote.

Though clearly meant to take advantage of the Depression-era gangster revival instigated by *Bonnie & Clyde*, Milius's *Dillinger* owes more, stylistically and ideologically, to Clint Eastwood's *Dirty Harry* (1971) and Sam Peckinpah's ultra-violent films, especially *The Wild Bunch* (1969), a Western that featured a level of bloodshed previously unseen outside the war film genre. Milius's almost exclusive focus on the cinematographic glories of the firefight is evident by the trajectory of his script. *Dillinger* begins with John Dillinger (Warren Oates) taking up bank robbery with his gang in the summer of 1933. Noisy, kinetic, blood-spattered shootouts abound but almost no attempt is made to explain Dillinger's motivations or provide background as to how he and his cohorts became career criminals.

Serpico (1973)

Countering the dashing right-wing machismo of *Dillinger* is Sidney Lumet's *Serpico* (1973), a Martin Bregman–Dino De Laurentiis production closely based on Peter Maas's bestseller, *Serpico, The Cop Who Defied the System* (New York: Viking, 1973). The Serpico of book and film is Francisco "Frank" Vincent Serpico, the son of an Italian immigrant cobbler from Bedford-Stuyvesant, Brooklyn, who became a New York City policeman in 1959 at the age of twenty-three. On June 18, 1970, patrolman Frank Serpico testified as a prosecution witness in the trial of Robert Stanard, a fellow patrolman indicted for taking bribes from gamblers in the Bronx. Serpico's testimony made front-page news in the *New York Times* and touched off a protracted and highly publicized corruption scandal that would rock the NYPD and eventually result in the indictment of some twenty police officers by Mayor John V. Lindsay's Knapp Commission. Serpico's comrades on the force resented the fact that he adamantly refused to take bribes; they were all the more incensed when Serpico became a whistle-blower. On February 4, 1971, less than eight months after his testimony against Stannard, Serpico was trying to arrest a Brooklyn heroin dealer when the man shot him in the face through a partially open door. It was widely suspected that Serpico had been set up for assassination or at the very least that his two partners in on the botched arrest deliberately failed to back him up. Though nearly killed, Serpico (mostly) recovered from the shooting, was promoted to detective, and continued to testify before the Knapp Commission. He was, however, a marked man who, ironically, required round-the-clock police protection from other cops. Eventually the stress and danger proved too much: Serpico retired from the NYPD in 1972 and spent many years wandering Europe. He returned to America in the mid-1980s and settled in upstate New York, keeping his location and real identity a closely guarded secret.

In the summer of 1971, at the height of the NYPD corruption scandal, Viking Press commissioned Peter Maas to write a book about Frank Serpico. By August 1972 Maas (*The Vallachi Papers*) had completed his book for Viking and sold the paperback rights to Bantam and the film rights to Dino De Laurentiis Productions for more than $400,000 (US$2 million in 2005). De Laurentiis's casting director, Shirley Rich, cast Al Pacino, fresh from his breakthrough role as Michael Corleone in *The Godfather* (1972), as Frank Serpico; John Randolph (*Seconds*) as New York's police chief; and Tony Roberts as Bob Blair, a fictionalized and unfairly diminished version of Detective Sergeant David Durk, Serpico's friend and only ally on the NYPD in the early days of his anticorruption crusade. John Avildsen, who directed *Joe* (1970) and would go on to direct *Rocky* (1976) and the *Karate Kid* movies, was slated to direct but dropped out over creative differences with his producers. Luckily Sidney Lumet (*Twelve Angry Men*) replaced Avildsen. Lumet had a passion for social justice topics and, as a long-time New York City resident, had a deep understanding of the city's sociopolitical ambience. He was, in short, the perfect director for *Serpico*. As adapted to the screen by Waldo Salt (*Midnight Cowboy*) and Norman Wexler (*Joe; Saturday Night Fever*), *Serpico* was factually accurate, fast-paced, suspenseful, and graced with a bravura performance by Pacino. Critically acclaimed and a major box office success, *Serpico* confirmed Pacino's stardom but more importantly affirmed 1960s-style nonconformism and individual conscience over the blandishments of a corrupt social order and also suggested that the vaunted forces of law and order were deeply flawed.

Dog Day Afternoon (1975), *The Third Memory* (2000), and *Based on a True Story* (2005)

Two years after *Serpico* Sidney Lumet and Al Pacino joined forces once again to make *Dog Day Afternoon* (1975), a rather bizarre true crime story based on an article by P. F. Kluge and Thomas Moore, "The Boys in the Bank," *Life* (September 22, 1972). John Wojtowicz, a gay man, needed a large sum of money to finance a sex-change operation for Ernest Aaron, his gay "wife" (Wojtowicz was separated from his actual wife, Carmen). On the afternoon of August 22, 1972 Wojtowicz, twenty-seven, and two accomplices—Arthur Westenberg, twenty-one, and Salvatore Naturile, eighteen—undertook to rob the Bensonhurst branch of the Chase Manhattan Bank located at Avenue P and East Third Street, Brooklyn. Unnerved by the appearance of a police car on the street, Westenberg fled the scene before the robbery actually got under way. Wojtowicz and Naturile proceeded with the holdup but were unable to make their escape before police were alerted and the bank surrounded. What ensued was a tense fourteen-hour stand-off between the hapless robbers, who held bank employees hostage, and the cops and FBI. Further complicating the situation was the presence of radio reporters and TV news cameras and a crowd of some 3,000 boisterous Brooklynites watching the drama unfold behind police barricades. Indeed, the scene resembled the carnival-like atmosphere that accompanied the 1925 cave entrapment of Floyd Collins as dramatized by Billy Wilder's *Ace in the Hole* (1951). More than just a botched robbery, the Bensonhurst caper became a gripping media spectacle, with underdog folk heroes (the bank robbers), villains (law enforcement), endangered hostages, and the suspense of an uncertain outcome. In times past, publicity-hungry criminals had to wait a day to see their exploits reported in newspapers. By the 1970s on-the-spot news teams allowed for instantaneous coverage, a fact not lost on John Wojtowicz, who repeatedly ventured outside the bank to negotiate with authorities—and grandstand for the crowd and news cameras. At one point in the film the Wojtowicz figure, Sonny Wortzik (Pacino), whips up the crowd by chanting "Attica!" in reference to the Attica Correctional Facility riot of September 1971. In the process of putting down an inmate insurrection, New York State Police and National Guardsmen killed forty-two (including ten hostages), perpetrating the worst massacre in U.S. prison history.

Scene still from Dog Day Afternoon, *starring Al Pacino (right) and John Cazale.* *(Warner Bros./The Kobal Collection)*

The antiestablishment temper of the times, the absurd amateurishness of the attempted robbery, the robbers' strange motives and benign treatment of their hostages, and the cool efficiency of the FBI all conspire to slant viewer sympathy toward Sonny and his dim-witted sidekick, Sal, played by John Cazale (*The Godfather I* and *II*), a dark-haired, thirty-nine-year-old actor in place of the real Sal Naturile, a blond teenager. Toward the end of the ordeal Sonny and Sal arrange for a shuttle limousine to take them and their remaining hostages to Kennedy Airport and a waiting jet that will supposedly fly them out of the country. True to life, the FBI foils the escape, shooting Sal in the forehead and capturing Sonny (in fact, Sal Naturile was shot, less dramatically, in the chest). Contemporary audiences, not yet fully converted to the rightist law-and-order ideology that would dominate public opinion in the decades that followed, were somewhat taken aback by the film's brutal outcome.

In "Real *Dog Day* Hero Tells His Story," an article for *Jump Cut* (no. 15, 1977, pp. 31–32), John Wojtowicz, then incarcerated in Lewisburg Federal Penitentiary, praised Sidney Lumet's direction and the acting of Al Pacino and Chris Sarandon (who played his gay lover) but declared the film only about "30 percent accurate" and he was particularly upset by the characterization of his female wife (called Angela in the film and played by Susan Peretz) as homely, obese, and dim-witted. Wojtowicz served seven years of a twenty-year sentence and was paroled in 1984. He has since appeared in two documentaries that further explore his story: Pierre Huyghe's *The Third Memory* (2000) and Walter Stokman's *Based on a True Story* (2005).

Looking for Mr. Goodbar (1977)

Even more shocking was the ending of *Looking for Mr. Goodbar* (1977), Richard Brooks' harrowing adaptation of the eponymous 1975 bestseller by Judith Rossner (Simon & Schuster), which was in turn loosely based on an actual murder case. On the evening of New Year's Day, 1973, Roseann Quinn, a twenty-eight-year-old New York City schoolteacher, met John Wayne Wilson, a twenty-three-year-old Indiana drifter, at W. M. Tweed's (now the All State Café), a cellar bar she frequented across the street from her studio apartment at 253 W. 72nd Street. The two later repaired to Quinn's place, where they had sex, after which Wilson, enraged by something Roseann Quinn said to him about his sexual prowess, proceeded to stab her fourteen times, stick a candle in her vagina, and place a cement statuette on her face. Arrested in Indianapolis eight days after the murder, John Wilson was returned to New York City to stand trial. He committed suicide in his jail cell at The Tombs on May 5, 1973.

Though Judith Rossner always insisted that *Looking for Mr. Goodbar* was largely imagined, the novel (and film) follow the life of Roseann Quinn quite closely. In novel and movie versions Teresa Dunn (the Roseann Quinn figure) is a complex, troubled young woman from a repressed Irish Catholic background who leads two lives. By day she is a skilled and devoted teacher of deaf children (as was Quinn). By night she roves the singles bars on West 72nd and picks up men for sex at her nearby apartment (as did Quinn). The schism in Teresa's personality stems from childhood trauma. When Dunn was twelve years old she had surgery to remove a large lump from her spine (as did Quinn). In a full body cast for a year, Dunn/Quinn recovered but was left with a limp and some scar tissue: physical imperfections that fostered social awkwardness and self-loathing. After a long, degrading affair with a college professor, Rossner's Teresa Dunn is convinced that she is unworthy of a long-term, loving relationship. Her risky immersion in the city singles scene is a masochistic way to get her sexual needs met and to feel some (illusory) sense of control. Tragically, her walks on the wild side lead to her death.

Richard Brooks' film version of *Looking for Mr. Goodbar* follows the contours of Rossner's novel but alters the characterization of Teresa Dunn/Roseann Quinn (Diane Keaton in the film). The real Roseann Quinn was a wispy woman of average looks; Keaton's Teresa Dunn is far more beautiful and probably more mercurial and vibrant—qualities that make it difficult to believe that Teresa Dunn suffers from chronic low self-esteem. At a time when feminism was resurgent and American women were enjoying unparalleled sexual freedom, *Looking for Mr. Goodbar* can be read as a poignant exploration of the dark side of the urban singles scene or, more likely, as a misogynist swipe at women's newfound social, sexual, and political power.

The Onion Field (1979)

Four years after Sidney Lumet's *Dog Day Afternoon*, producer Walter Coblenz (*All the President's Men*) and director Harold Becker (*Sea of Love*) offered a very different take on real-life cops and robbers with their film version of Joseph Wambaugh's bestseller, *The Onion Field* (New York: Delacorte, 1973). Adapted for the screen by Wambaugh (an ex-LAPD detective) and script doctor Eric Roth, *The Onion Field* (1979) tells the grim story of Karl Francis Hettinger, a Los Angeles police officer whose life is marred by intense trauma and disgrace. On the night of March 9, 1963, Hettinger and his partner, Ian Campbell, were disarmed and kidnapped by a pair of petty criminals named Gregory Ulas Powell and Jimmy Lee Smith after a traffic stop in Hollywood. Powell and Smith drove

Hettinger and Campbell to an onion field in Kern County, 75 miles north of Los Angeles. There they shot and killed Campbell but Hettinger managed to run away and seek help at a nearby farmhouse. Powell and Smith were caught, tried, convicted, and sentenced to death for the murder of Officer Campbell but a seemingly endless series of appeals; legal maneuverings by Powell, a brilliant psychopath; and retrials forestalled their executions. All the while Karl Hettinger—shunned by his fellow cops and plagued by overwhelming feelings of shame, guilt, and frustration—underwent a slow but steady psychological disintegration marked by the loss of his job, alcoholism, the abuse of his children, and suicidal tendencies. He died a broken man in 1994 at the age of fifty-nine. As America prepared to swing drastically to the Right by electing Ronald Reagan, films like *The Onion Field* countered the romantic rebel imagery promulgated by the New American Cinema with a representation of cops as vulnerable, suffering human beings.

The Eighties

Brubaker (1980)

In late February 1967, Winthrop Rockefeller (1912–1973), the newly elected governor of Arkansas, appointed Thomas O. Murton warden of Tucker Prison Farm, a 4,500-acre facility holding 300 inmates. Murton, a criminology professor at Southern Illinois University and an outspoken prison reform advocate, found terrible conditions at Tucker: poor food, overcrowding, rampant corruption, and vicious mistreatment of inmates by guards. During his ten months at Tucker Farm, Murton instituted major reforms. Impressed with Murton's abilities, Governor Rockefeller appointed him superintendent of the 16,277-acre Cummins Prison Farm on January 4, 1968. Before the month was over Murton began investigating allegations by inmates that, over the years, many prisoners had been beaten to death by guards and surreptitiously buried on the facility's vast grounds. Three skeletons were exhumed on January 29 and Murton planned more exploratory digging when Governor Rockefeller shut down the investigation to forestall damning publicity. Murton was fired from his job on March 7, 1968, and his reforms were soon rolled back. The following year Thomas Murton and Joe Hyams published *Accomplices to the Crime: The Arkansas Prison Scandal* (New York: Grove Press, 1969), an account of Murton's frustrated attempts to reform the Arkansas penal system.

A decade after the appearance of Murton's book Hollywood set out to make a fictionalized film version initially helmed by Bob Rafelson (*Five Easy Pieces*) but soon replaced by Stuart Rosenberg (*Cool Hand Luke*). Written by W. D. Richter and Arthur A. Ross, *Brubaker* (1980) starred Robert Redford (*All the President's Men*) as Warden Henry Brubaker, the Thomas Murton figure. To heighten drama and suspense, the screenwriters have Brubaker enter Wakefield Prison Farm (an amalgam of Tucker and Cummins) posing as a convict so that he can get an uncensored view of conditions therein. Needless to say, conditions are horrible. Once Brubaker reveals his true identity as the new, reform-minded warden, he comes to earn the respect of the inmates but the enmity of government officials. As in the real case, inmate corpses are unearthed, the investigation preempted, the prison reformer dismissed for his efforts, and then conditions revert to what they had been.

In "Mr. Carter Goes to Washington—An Analysis of Three Films in Relation to Jimmy Carter's Presidency," *Journal of Popular Film and Television* (Summer 1997), lawyer Allen Rostron reads *Brubaker* as an allegory about the failure of Jimmy Carter's presidency (1977–1981). Like Carter, Brubaker is an idealistic, politically liberal outsider seeking to reform a corrupt power structure but failing because he is unwilling or unable to engage in the necessary political compromises. *Brubaker* came out in late June 1980, five months before Jimmy Carter was handily defeated by Ronald Reagan: an electoral defeat that signaled the end of postwar liberalism as a viable political philosophy.

Prince of the City (1981)

Not long after the release of *Brubaker* a different kind of story about a lawman caught in an implacably corrupt system was dramatized in Sidney Lumet's sadly underrated masterpiece, *Prince of the City* (1981). Based on Robert Daley's *Prince of the City: The True Story of a Cop Who Knew Too Much* (Boston: Houghton Mifflin, 1978), the film recounts the travails of NYPD Detective Daniel Ciello (Treat Williams), the filmic counterpart to a real cop named Robert Leuci. The leader of an elite narcotics squad, Leuci was willing to cooperate with an early 1970s federal anticorruption probe but unwilling to inform on any of his partners, which would be an unforgivable breach of the cop's code of fraternal solidarity. Eventually, Detective Leuci became so deeply implicated in corruption himself that he was forced to betray his colleagues—and his honor—to avoid prison time. Long at nearly 3 hours but riveting, *Prince of the City* was mistakenly written off as a rehash of Lumet's *Serpico* (1973). Though both stories involve corruption in the New York City Police Department, they are very different in character. The other factor that made *Prince of the City* a commercial failure was a marked change in the American temperament with the ascendancy of

Ronald Reagan. By 1981 the public had grown weary of decidedly pessimistic assessments of American institutions from a left-wing point of view.

The Executioner's Song (1982)

On Monday morning, January 17, 1977, Gary Mark Gilmore, thirty-six, made history by being the first man legally executed in the United States after reinstatement of the death penalty in 1976 after a ten-year moratorium. Though intelligent and gifted with artistic talent, Gilmore was a criminal psychopath. In July 1976 Gilmore senselessly murdered a gas station employee in Orem, Utah, and a motel manager in Provo, Utah. Convicted of the second murder, Gilmore waived all appeals and opted to be executed as soon as legally possible. The state of Utah obliged and Gilmore's execution by firing squad opened the floodgates for a new era of executions that continues unabated to the present. Had he not been so vociferous in his insistence to die, Gilmore would have remained an obscure misfit.

Working with letters, interviews, trial transcripts, and other materials gathered by journalist-producer Lawrence Schiller who interviewed Gary Gilmore for *Playboy* (April 1977), Norman Mailer immortalized Gilmore in *The Executioner's Song* (Boston: Little, Brown, 1979), a best-selling nonfiction novel of 1,056 pages that traces Gilmore's life and death. The Gilmore case and Mailer's book on it were so notorious in their depictions of a peculiarly American form of nihilistic rebellion that a filmic treatment was almost inevitable. Starring Tommy Lee Jones as Gary Gilmore and Rosanna Arquette as Gilmore's girlfriend, Nicole Baker, Lawrence Schiller's made-for-television movie, *The Executioner's Song* (1982), is a factually accurate, well-acted, and compelling rendition of the last part of Gilmore's ruined life. On the downside, Tommy Lee Jones's portrayal of Gilmore as loquacious, emotionally volatile, and self-pitying does not reflect the real Gilmore, who had the personality befitting a man who had spent half his life behind bars: hard as nails, taciturn, and menacing. *The Executioner's Song* is also deficient in providing enough family history to adequately account for Gilmore's severely maladaptive ways. Finally, in making the pathetic, despicable Gary Gilmore into a sympathetic antihero, both book and film versions of *The Executioner's Song* promulgate the facile and deluded counterculture romanticism that equates rebellion with virtue (cf. *Bonnie & Clyde*).

Shot in the Heart (2001)

Gilmore's full story came out twelve years later when Gary's younger brother Mikal Gilmore published *Shot in the Heart* (New York: Doubleday, 1994), a brilliantly written and chilling memoir of a hideously dysfunctional family headed by a cruel, authoritarian alcoholic that explains Gary Gilmore's intense alienation and rage. Mikal Gilmore's book also became a made-for-television HBO movie, *Shot in the Heart* (2001). Adapted for the screen by Frank Pugliese, directed by Agnieszka Holland (*Europa, Europa*), and starring Giovanni Ribisi as Mikal Gilmore and Elias Koteas as Gary Gilmore, *Shot in the Heart* oscillates between scenes of Mikal visiting Gary in prison shortly before his execution and nightmarish flashbacks of life inside the Frank and Bessie Gilmore home: a narrative structure suited to film but one that dilutes the cumulative power of Mikal Gilmore's book.

The Killing of America (1982)

Screenwriter Paul Schrader deftly captured America's precipitous slide into alienation and violence in the 1960s and 1970s with Martin Scorsese's *Taxi Driver* (1976). Six years later, Schrader's brother, Leonard, joined Sheldon Renan and Japanese producer Mata Yamamoto to make *The Killing of America* (Japanese title: *Violence U.S.A.*) (1982). A narrated compilation documentary that surveys violence in the United States from the assassination of JFK in 1963 to the killing of John Lennon in 1980, *The Killing of America* presents a plethora of disturbing images of crime, violent death, and mayhem. Archival footage of notorious killers (e.g., Charles Whitman, Charles Manson, Ted Bundy, John Wayne Gacy) is supplemented by interviews with Robert F. Kennedy's assassin, Sirhan Sirhan, and convicted serial killers Lawrence Bittaker and Ed Kemper. Pressured by his Japanese financial backers to end an otherwise deeply depressing film on a more positive note, Leonard Schrader added footage covering peace vigils in honor of John Lennon after he was murdered outside his home in New York City by Mark David Chapman on December 8, 1980. Though widely shown in Japan, *The Killing of America* has never been released commercially in the United States. A British media company released uncut VHS and DVD versions of the film in 2001.

Star 80 (1983)

While working at a Dairy Queen in Vancouver, British Columbia, in 1977, a beautiful teenaged girl named Dorothy Ruth Hoogstraten was discovered by Paul Leslie Snider, twenty-six, a smooth-talking pimp and hustler. Convinced that she had star potential, Snider relentlessly courted the shy, naïve Hoogstraten, soon became her lover and self-styled manager, and eventually persuaded her to pose nude for photographs he then submitted to *Playboy*. Impressed with her fresh face and natural beauty, Hugh Hefner flew Dorothy Stratten (shortened from Hoogstraten) to Los Angeles and made her Playmate of the Month for the August 1979 issue of the magazine and began to groom her for a career in film. Named Playmate of the Year for 1979, Stratten was cast in *They All Laughed* (1980), a comedy by Peter Bogdanovich (*The Last Picture Show*). Though she had married Paul Snider in June 1979 out of a sense of obligation to him, Dorothy Stratten separated from him in the spring of 1980 and began living with Bogdanovich. Crazed over losing control of his priceless meal ticket, Snider lured Stratten to his apartment in West Los Angeles on August 14, 1980. There he bound and raped her, murdered her with a 12-gauge shotgun blast to the face, and then sodomized her corpse before turning the gun on himself.

Haunted by Stratten's surreal and tragic story, dancer-choreographer-writer-producer-director Bob Fosse (*Cabaret; All That Jazz*) brought it to the screen with *Star 80* (1983). Starring Mariel Hemingway as Dorothy Stratten, Eric Roberts as Paul Snider, Cliff Roberston as Hugh Hefner, Carol Baker as Dorothy's mother, Nelly, and Roger Rees as Aram Nicholas (the Peter Bogdanovich figure), *Star 80* opens with Stratten's grisly murder and then covers the previous three years leading up to it through flashback—a classic noir structure that lends the story a somber, fatalistic quality. Brilliantly written and directed by Fosse and graced with a mesmerizing performance by Eric Roberts—the best of his career—as a loathsome yet somehow pitiable Paul Snider, *Star 80* (title derived from Snider's vanity license plate) explores the cultic status of beauty, celebrity, and money in contemporary society and shows how its desperate pursuit can destroy innocence and even life itself. In its deeply troubling look into the darkest recesses of the American dream, *Star 80* was at least twenty years ahead of its time in delineating the brooding, selfish nihilism that lies beneath the commercial culture of narcissism that created and destroyed Dorothy Stratten and Paul Snider. (A stickler for authenticity, Fosse filmed at the actual locations, for example, the Dairy Queen at 2901 East Hastings Street in Vancouver where Snider and Stratten met and the actual apartment at 10881 West Clarkson Road in Los Angeles where the murder-suicide took place.)

Fatal Vision (1984)

On August 30, 1979, after a six-week trial and six and a half hours of deliberation, a jury in Raleigh, North Carolina, convicted Dr. Jeffrey R. MacDonald of murdering his pregnant wife, Colette, and their two young daughters, Kimberly and Kristen, in their Fort Bragg duplex during the early morning hours of February 17, 1970. MacDonald, an Ivy League graduate and former Green Beret physician, received three consecutive life sentences. Almost a year later, a Federal Appeals Court overturned MacDonald's conviction on the grounds that he had been denied the right to a speedy trial. MacDonald enjoyed nine months of freedom until the Supreme Court reinstated his murder conviction on April 1, 1982. Jeffrey MacDonald has been in prison since that day and still insists he is innocent.

Before his trial in 1979 MacDonald struck a deal with journalist Joe McGinniss to write a book about the case that would hopefully help to exonerate him. (The contract stipulated that MacDonald would receive 25.6 percent of the publisher's advance and 33 percent of the royalties but would not be able to sue McGinniss if the book did not prove to his liking.) McGinniss believed or, more likely, pretended to believe MacDonald's story that his home had been invaded by four drug-crazed hippies who knocked him out and then killed his family. Yet to MacDonald's shock and dismay, when McGinniss's book *Fatal Vision* (New York: Putnam, 1983) came out, it presented compelling circumstantial evidence that Jeffrey MacDonald had, in fact, slaughtered his family on that fateful night in 1971. McGinniss went on to advance the theory that MacDonald was a pathological narcissist who killed his wife in the midst of an amphetamine-fueled rage and then decided to kill his children in order to fabricate a home invasion story. MacDonald had considered McGinniss a friend and supporter; the book proved that McGinniss had brazenly manipulated him. Despite the no-suit clause in their contract, MacDonald sued McGinniss for breach of contract and eventually settled out of court, with McGinniss paying him $325,000.

A year after the appearance of the hardcover version of McGinniss's book and a few months after the paperback edition appeared, NBC-TV aired *Fatal Vision* (1984), a two-night, 4-hour miniseries adapted by John Gay and starring then-unknown Gary Cole as MacDonald and Eve Marie Saint and Karl Malden (who had both appeared in Elia Kazan's *On the Waterfront*) as Mildred and Freddy Kassab, the mother and stepfather of MacDonald's wife, Colette. Initially Freddy Kassab had been a firm believer in his son-in-law's innocence but as time went on, MacDonald's arrogance and discrepancies in his story caused Kassab to exhaustively research the case. He eventually came to believe that MacDonald was guilty and lobbied to have him tried. Well written and powerfully acted,

Fatal Vision solidified public opinion that Jeffrey MacDonald was indeed guilty. Developments since then have raised many doubts. Joe McGinniss's credibility as a nonfiction writer was severely damaged when he published a heavily embroidered biography of Ted Kennedy, *The Last Brother* (New York: Simon & Schuster, 1993). Denied all access by the Kennedy family, McGinniss resorted to inventing quotes, internalized monologues, and situations on a wholesale basis— and was widely excoriated for doing so. With McGinniss's credibility at an all-time low, Jerry Allen Potter and Fred Bost's *Fatal Justice: Reinvestigating the MacDonald Murders* (New York: W. W. Norton, 1995) presented an exhaustively researched and well-reasoned rebuttal to *Fatal Vision*, alleging that the prosecution suppressed evidence pointing to MacDonald's innocence. It should be noted, though, that as a Texas-born former minister and a former Green Beret Vietnam veteran, respectively, Potter and Bost had an ideological interest in defending MacDonald; his triple-murder conviction brought dishonor on the military. Potter and Bost would much prefer to place the blame for the killings on hippie degenerates. In the final analysis Joe McGinniss is a writer of very dubious integrity and *Fatal Vision*, book and miniseries, though they pretend to be objective, are carefully slanted to prove MacDonald's guilt. On the other hand, flaws in the case against MacDonald do not prove that he is innocent. The MacDonald case remains vexing and the debate rages on.

The Deliberate Stranger (1986)

While there are lingering doubts as to whether or not Dr. Jeffrey MacDonald is a psychopath or a wronged man, no such doubts apply to Theodore Robert Bundy (1946–1989). Tried and convicted by the state of Florida on two counts of murder in July 1979, Ted Bundy went to the electric chair on January 24, 1989, after exhausting all his appeals. Though handsome, intelligent, and outwardly charming, Bundy was in reality a rapist, sexual sadist, murderer, and necrophiliac. He is known to have kidnapped, bludgeoned, and strangled at least thirty-six women in four states between 1974 and 1978 but may have started killing as early as 1961 (at the age of fifteen) and might have murdered as many as fifty women and girls; the exact number will never be known. Despite numerous competitors for the dubious honor, Bundy remains America's most notorious serial killer.

After Ted Bundy's sensational trial and conviction in 1979, books about him began to proliferate. One such tome was Richard W. Larsen's *Bundy: The Deliberate Stranger* (Englewood Cliffs, NJ: Prentice-Hall, 1980). Six years later, as Bundy began to reach the end of his death row appeals process, veteran television producer Marvin J. Chomsky (*Roots*) produced and directed *The Deliberate*

Stranger (1986). A made-for-television miniseries adapted to the screen from Larsen's book by Hesper Anderson (*Children of a Lesser God*) and starring Mark Harmon as Bundy, *The Deliberate Stranger* more or less accurately surveys Bundy's four-year killing spree. Harmon looks like Ted Bundy and credibly suggests the yawning chasm between Bundy's evil compulsions and the sunny disposition he showed to the outer world. Unfortunately, as a made-for-TV movie, *The Deliberate Stranger* could not even begin to reveal the depths of Bundy's depravity. Viewers were subject to a sanitized depiction of Ted Bundy that bears only a glancing resemblance to the real monster.

The Thin Blue Line (1988)

In the mid-1980s, offbeat documentary filmmaker Errol Morris (*Gates of Heaven; Vernon, Florida*) set out to make a film about Dr. James Grigson (1932–2004). Grigson, a Dallas forensic psychiatrist, was known as "Dr. Death" because he testified as an expert witness for the prosecution in scores of capital murder cases and almost always found the defendant to be a dangerous psychopath who would kill again in the future—testimony that usually prompted juries to opt for the death penalty. While interviewing inmates against whom Grigson had testified, Morris stumbled on a case that piqued his interest. A man by the name of Randall Dale Adams was serving a life sentence (commuted from death) for the murder of Dallas police officer Robert Wood during a routine traffic stop on the night of November 26, 1976. Adams claimed that he was innocent and that the real killer was most likely David Ray Harris, a young acquaintance he had met on the day of the killing. Over the next two years, Morris, a former private detective, conducted an exhaustive investigation into the case and tracked down and interviewed almost all relevant witnesses. The result of his labors was *The Thin Blue Line* (1988), a brilliantly executed, stylistically innovative, and utterly persuasive film that managed to expand the formal and conceptual boundaries of documentary filmmaking.

Morris breaks with documentary conventions in a number of ways. He shoots his interviewees from a uniform distance and always frames and lights them the same way: a subtle device that implicitly gives equal credence to every point of view. Morris also deliberately neglects to identify his interviewees with on-screen captions; it is left to the viewer to figure out who the person is and how he or she figures in the film's overall narrative—a trope that encourages greater viewer attention and involvement. In terms of structure, Morris eschews the standard, plodding chronological presentation that constructs an argument through steady accretion of objective facts. Instead he opts to lay out the elements of the case in an ever-widening spiral of often conflicting testimony that keeps on return-ing to the primal event of the murder, reenacted in various ways, according to the subjective recollections of key witnesses. The film also uses graphics in a unique way. An aerial photograph of Greater Dallas transmogrifies into a road map of the same area. The mention of a gun is accompanied by a drawing of a pistol that whirls slowly into space. Extreme close-ups of objects—the revolving light on a police cruiser, blurry newsprint photos, a spilled chocolate shake, a butt-filled ash-tray, a hypnotist's pocket watch, a bit of popcorn—all focus and arrest attention in oddly evocative ways. Finally, the hauntingly evocative music of postmodern composer Philip Glass gives the film a surreal aura of wonder and doom.

As for content, *The Thin Blue Line* contrasts Randall Adams' rendition of the day of the murder with that of David Harris. To amplify and articulate the dif-ferences between the two versions, the film presents interviews with a number of Dallas detectives; presiding trial judge Don Metcalf; two of Harris's friends from his hometown of Vidor, Texas; Adams' defense attorneys Dennis White and Edith James; Sam Kitrell, a Vidor detective; and a number of supposed witnesses to the shooting. The story that emerges is that Harris picked up Adams on a Dal-las highway after Adams' car ran out of gas. The pair ended up spending the day together and went to a drive-in movie in the evening. Then Randall Adams had David Harris return him to the motel where he was staying with his brother but did not invite Harris to spend the night. Left to his own devices David Harris sped off into the night and shot Officer Wood shortly thereafter. Having bragged about killing a Dallas cop back in Vidor, Harris was soon arrested. To save him-self Harris implicated Adams—who, at twenty-seven, was a more attractive sus-pect than Harris, sixteen, because he (Adams) was eligible for the death penalty. However, the case against Adams was weak so Dallas law enforcement officials likely bribed a witness named Emily Miller to make a positive identification of Randall Adams as the man driving the car stopped by Officer Wood, even though she only caught a shadowy and distant glimpse of that man. The film ends with a chilling tape-recorded excerpt of Morris's final interview with David Harris (in prison for an unrelated murder). Though cagey, Harris declares Adams innocent and strongly hints that he, David Harris, is the guilty party. Utterly convincing in its exoneration of Randall Adams, *The Thin Blue Line* nonetheless suffers from certain key omissions. There are no interviews with the prime witness to the shooting, Robert Wood's patrol partner, Officer Teresa Turko, or Randall Adams' brother, or, ironically, Dr. James Grigson, the original subject of the film. Fur-thermore, the film does not question or attempt to explain why a twenty-seven-year-old man would spend the day with a sixteen-year-old boy he had just met.

Released in the late summer of 1988, *The Thin Blue Line* gave the Adams case national exposure and soon achieved a remarkable result for a film: it prompted a new hearing at which Dallas judge Larry Baraka overturned Adams' conviction, a finding upheld by the Texas Court of Criminal Appeals. After serving twelve and a half years in prison, part of that time on death row, for a crime he did not commit, Randall Adams was freed on March 12, 1989. Shortly thereafter Winfield Scott, one of the corrupt Dallas prosecutors who railroaded Adams, was forced to resign from office. Ironically, Randall Dale Adams went on to successfully sue Errol Morris over the rights to his life story: strange repayment for the man who got him out of prison. Adams has since become an anti–death penalty advocate. A final footnote: on June 30, 2004, David Harris was executed by the state of Texas for the 1985 murder of Mark Mays of Beaumont, Texas.

The Accused (1988)

Around 9:00 P.M. on Sunday evening March 6, 1983, Cheryl Ann Araujo, a twenty-one-year-old mother of two, walked into Big Dan's Tavern in New Bedford, Massachusetts, to buy cigarettes. She stayed to have a drink or two at the bar and to play the jukebox. Around 10:00 P.M., as she was leaving, a man grabbed her from behind and threw her down on a pool table. Cheryl Araujo was then stripped from the waist down and over the next two hours, gang-raped by three men, while another five or six bar patrons laughed, taunted the victim, and cheered on her attackers.

Initially the city of New Bedford was outraged by the incident. But after newspapers widely reported that the rape suspects were all Portuguese-speaking immigrants from the Azores, a backlash of anti-Portuguese sentiment in the area caused New Bedford residents (50 percent Portuguese) to close ranks in support of the accused men. A year later in what became infamous as the Big Dan's rape case, six defendants went to trial at Superior Court in Fall River. Defense lawyers portrayed Cheryl Araujo as a willing participant in group sex rather than a rape victim—a characterization that incensed women's groups all over the nation. Equally egregious: court officials allowed the trial to be covered by a local cable station and Cheryl Ann Araujo's identity became well known in Bristol County, information that prompted other media outlets to make an exception to the long-standing practice of protecting a rape victim's anonymity. As a result Araujo was harassed and threatened, especially after guilty verdicts were handed down on March 26, 1984, and four of the six defendants were sentenced to lengthy prison terms (the other two were acquitted). Hounded out of New Bedford, Araujo and her family moved to Miami, Florida. Sadly Cheryl Ann Araujo was killed in a car accident in Florida on December 14, 1986, well before her rapists were paroled.

Loosely based on the Big Dan's incident, Jonathan Kaplan's *The Accused* (1988) departs from the specific facts of the case in many ways. Written by former journalist Tom Topor (*Nuts*), shot in Vancouver, and set in the spring of 1987 in some indeterminate North American city, *The Accused* features Jodie Foster as Sarah "Sadie" Tobias, a single young woman of working-class pedigree, loose morals, and a fondness for alcohol who is accosted in a bar called The Mill and gang-raped on a pinball machine in front of an ebullient crowd of fraternity boys and locals. Angry that her rapists are given light sentences, Sadie Tobias enlists the help of Kathryn Murphy (Kelly McGillis), the local A.D.A. and a bourgeois career woman, who knows that the young and sexy Tobias will be pilloried because she was quite drunk, provocatively dressed, and in a rough bar alone at night. In an uphill battle against entrenched male chauvinism, Tobias and Murphy ultimately join forces across social class lines and at least win their case against the spectators of the rape who did nothing to prevent it. While an admirably progressive feminist critique of the misogynist mind-set that condones rape and even blames the rape victim, *The Accused* loses much of its historical specificity by choosing not to engage the unique ethnic, cultural, and class tensions that plagued the economically depressed city of New Bedford in the early 1980s. These factors do not excuse or mitigate a gang rape but they need to be addressed to understand the debased moral and psychological atmosphere of a place like Big Dan's Tavern.

The Nineties

Goodfellas (1990)

Crime journalist Nicholas Pileggi's bestseller, *Wiseguy: Life in a Mafia Family* (New York: Simon & Schuster, 1986), told the true story of Henry Hill, the Brooklyn-born son of an Irish American electrician and a Sicilian American housewife, who in 1955 at the age of ten became an errand boy for "Paulie" Vario, a Lucchese crime family capo. Because he was only half Italian, Henry Hill could never be a "made man" (official Mafia member) but he did go on to become a "wiseguy" (mob-connected career criminal) operating closely with organized crime cohorts in a wide range of illegal activities, from point-shaving college basketball games to truck hijacking. The high point of Hill's career was his participation in the famous Lufthansa air cargo terminal heist at Kennedy Airport, December 12, 1978, which netted $5.8 million in cash and jewels. While serving time in prison for assault, Henry Hill made contacts with drug dealers. Once paroled, Hill ran a freelance cocaine smuggling operation between Brooklyn and Pittsburgh

Movie poster for Goodfellas, *starring Ray Liotta, Robert De Niro, and Joe Pesci and directed by Martin Scorcese. (Warner Bros./The Kobal Collection)*

behind the back of his boss, Paul Vario, who abhorred the drug trade. Arrested by the FBI on narcotics charges in 1980, Henry Hill entered the Witness Protection Program rather than face Vario's wrath. His testimony against Vario and James "Jimmy the Gent" Burke put them both in prison for the rest of their lives.

Pouncing on a sensational true story about New York City mobsters, Martin Scorsese hired Nicholas Pileggi to turn *Wiseguy* into a screenplay. The resulting film, *Goodfellas* (1990), streamlined the book and changed the names of Henry Hill's partners-in-crime but generally stayed very close to the facts of Hill's life, even using numerous verbatim quotes from the book for voice-over narration by Hill (Ray Liotta) and his wife, Karen (Lorraine Bracco). Pileggi and Scorsese exercised the most artistic license in terms of characterization. Paul Sorvino's handsome, dapper Paul Cicero is a much more attractive figure than his real-life counterpart, Paul Vario, who was a jowly, boorish glutton of a man and also extremely violent, which Cicero is never shown to be. As played by Ray Liotta, the movie's Henry Hill is smarter and considerably more attractive than the real man. Robert De Niro's Jimmy Conway is a sanitized version of "Jimmy the Gent" Burke. The real Jimmy, a brawny thug, is reputed to have personally murdered dozens of men; De Niro's Jimmy is never shown being violent. Joe Pesci's impersonation comes closest to authenticity. His psychotic Tommy DeVito nicely approximates the exceedingly volatile and dangerous Thomas "Two-gun Tommy" DeSimone—except that the real Tommy was a tall Errol Flynn type whereas Pesci is a diminutive, balding man. Most of these changes in characterization tend to glamorize Hill and his mobster friends. Francis Ford Coppola's quasi-allegorical *Godfather* series romanticizes the Corleones in solemn, tragic tones. *Goodfellas* portrays life in organized crime as more proletarian, haphazard, down-to-earth, and funny: a vision probably closer to the truth but one that also smacks of whitewashing.

The Krays (1990)

England's oblique answer to *Goodfellas* was *The Krays* (1990), a biopic written by Philip Ridley and directed by Peter Medak (*The Ruling Class*) about Ronald Kray (1933–1995) and Reginald Kray (1933–2000), identical twins from London's East End who owned a string of nightclubs and ran a large-scale extortion racket in the 1960s through sheer force and violence. Convicted of murder in 1969, the Krays were both sentenced to thirty-year prison terms. Ronnie Kray died of a heart attack in prison four years short of his parole date, and his brother, Reggie, died shortly after his release. In their time they were the most notorious and feared gangsters in Britain.

Instead of making a standard gangster film, Ridley and Medak chose to focus on the Kray brothers from a psychological point of view. With the paterfamilias, Charlie Kray (Alfred Lynch), either absent or uninterested, his wife, Violet (Billie Whitelaw), raises their three sons: Charlie Jr. (Roger Monk) and the twins Ronnie and Reggie (played as adults by Gary and Martin Kemp of the pop group, Spandau Ballet). Doted on by their domineering, love-smothering mother, the Kray twins form a strange and primal bond with her and with each other. Ronnie, the more dominant and violent one, is homosexual and a paranoid schizophrenic. Though less disturbed than his brother, Reggie is just as caught up in the pathological family dynamic. Both men are physically tough and strong, and they get what they want through intimidation, torture, and gory violence. Yet, for all their menacing machismo, the Krays continue to be devoted momma's boys stuck in an odd, pre-Oedipal twilight existence. Haunting in tone and unconventional in approach, *The Krays* commendably raises more questions than it answers.

Reversal of Fortune (1990)

On Sunday morning, December 21, 1980, socialite Martha "Sunny" von Bülow was found lying unconscious on the marble floor of her bathroom at Clarendon Court, her multimillion-dollar mansion in Newport, Rhode Island. At the time she was discovered, Mrs. von Bülow was already in a deep coma from which she never awakened (she remains in a persistent vegetative state in a New York City hospital). Alexander and Annie Laurie ("Ala") von Auersperg, Sunny von Bülow's adult children from her first marriage, accused Sunny's husband, Claus von Bülow, of trying to kill her by injecting her with an overdose of insulin (she had suffered a coma, from which she recovered, a year earlier). During the ensuing six-week trial, the von Auerspergs; Sunny's loyal maid, Maria; and Claus von Bülow's mistress, soap-opera actress Alexandra Isles, all testified against him and a plausible motive was established to wit: if Sunny died, Claus would inherit $14 million and would be free to marry his mistress. The jury returned a guilty verdict on March 17, 1982. On May 8 Claus von Bülow was sentenced to thirty years in prison on two counts of attempted murder.

Out on bail, von Bülow hired famed Harvard University law professor Alan Dershowitz to argue an appeal. On April 27, 1984, Dershowitz succeeded in persuading the Rhode Island Supreme Court to overturn von Bülow's convictions and grant a new trial. Retried the following summer, with Dershowitz acting as defense consultant, Claus von Bülow was acquitted of all charges on June 10, 1985. A four-and-a-half-year saga that featured possible drugging, attempted murder, family squabbling, marital infidelity, and a glimpse into the lives of the very wealthy, the von Bülow affair was accorded massive media exposure. Alan Dershowitz jumped on the bandwagon with his own book, *Reversal of Fortune: Inside the von Bülow Case* (New York: Random House, 1986). Just as his book was coming out, Dershowitz signed a movie deal with producer Edward R. Pressman (*Wall Street; Talk Radio*) for whom Dershowitz's son, Elon, worked.

Adapted for the screen by Elia Kazan's son, Nicholas Kazan (*Frances*), and directed by Barbet Schroeder (*Barfly*), *Reversal of Fortune* (1990) stars Jeremy Irons as the enigmatic Claus von Bülow, Glenn Close as Sunny, and Ron Silver as the energetic Alan Dershowitz. In his book Dershowitz quite understandably portrayed himself as a principled crusader for justice and the constitutional rights of the accused. With Elon Dershowitz as one of its executive producers, the film does likewise; Ron Silver's Professor Dershowitz comes off as a brilliant legal tactician, a wonderfully nurturing teacher, and an all-around good guy. (The real Alan Dershowitz may indeed be all of these things but writing a book and helping to make a movie extolling one's virtues could be considered a tad unseemly.) On a more positive note, book and film avoid gossipy speculation and restrict their focus to the legal complexities of the case. The film is especially scrupulous in its refusal to judge Claus von Bülow. In the end, though the law has exonerated him, it is left to the viewer to decide if von Bülow is *morally* guilty or innocent. Jeremy Irons' brilliantly nuanced depiction of Claus von Bülow as a jaded Danish aristocrat won him the 1991 Oscar for Best Actor in a Leading Role. As it appeared shortly after the Reagan era and focused on a high-society scandal that consumed public attention through much of that period, one could consider *Reversal of Fortune* an allegory of the "Age of Reagan," with its corruption, excess, and an unfathomable gap between reality and perception. Uncertainty as to whether Claus von Bülow was a malevolent figure equates to unspoken ambivalence over Ronald Reagan's legacy. America was reinvigorated by Reagan's entrepreneurial creed but at what price to its soul?

Brother's Keeper (1992)

An alleged murder that may not have been a murder at all is also the subject of *Brother's Keeper* (1992), a *Thin Blue Line*–type advocacy documentary made by Joe Berlinger and Bruce Sinofsky, cinema verité filmmakers formerly associated with Maysles Films. In marked contrast to the glamorous and sophisticated world presented in *Reversal of Fortune, Brother's Keeper* offers a glimpse into astonishing squalor, poverty, and backwardness. On June 6, 1990, William Ward, a sixty-four-year-old bachelor dairy farmer from upstate New York, was found dead in the bed he shared with his brother Aldelbert (called Delbert), fifty-nine, in a filthy, ramshackle farmhouse also shared by brothers Roscoe, seventy-one, and Lyman, sixty-two. Having been in poor heath, Bill Ward may have died from natural causes but Delbert, barely literate and of subnormal intelligence, confesses to the alleged crime after hours of coercive state police interrogation. Furthermore, an autopsy suggests Delbert may have euthanized his sick brother by smothering him with a pillow (the coroner finds petechiae in the eyes—minute hemorrhages sometimes, but not always, indicative of death by asphyxia). After Delbert is arrested and indicted for murder, the nearby town of Munnsville, New York (pop. 400), rallies to his defense, raising $10,000 in one day to provide bail. The film follows the course of the trial, amid sensational publicity (including a visit by pseudojournalist Connie Chung), over the next ten months as obtuse police officers and a martinet district attorney with political ambitions seek to convict the defenseless Delbert Ward of a dubious crime. In the end, thanks to the hard work of resourceful defense attorney Ralph A. Cognetti, Delbert is acquitted. A movie that pits a crusading lawyer and smart, decent country folk defending the lowliest among them against clueless, perhaps venal city bureaucrats, *Brother's Keeper* delivers a satisfying emotional experience that nonetheless obscures the film's voyeuristic tendencies. When all is said and done, a central feature of *Brother's Keeper* is its lurid fascination with the incredibly primitive, otherworldly conditions in which the Ward brothers live: one wallowing in country bumpkin stereotypes incarnate that calls the film's putative good intentions into question.

Swoon (1992)

Having been dramatized by Hitchcock's *Rope* (1948) and Richard Zanuck's *Compulsion* (1959), the Loeb-Leopold case received a third cinematic treatment with Tom Kalin's *Swoon* (1992). While the first two films downplayed the issue of the killers' homosexuality, Kalin, a gay filmmaker with an ideological ax to grind, puts it at the center of his movie, as it should be. The homosexuality of Loeb and Leopold was, indeed, a salient factor in their lives, their crime, the way their trial was conducted, and in the way they were viewed by the public—although anti-Semitism, anti-intellectualism, and social class resentment also helped to shape popular perception of the young men and the senseless atrocity they committed. Highly stylized and oblique in the postmodern mode, *Swoon* is ultimately vague about what it is trying to assert, perhaps because the cold-blooded murder of

Bobby Franks cannot be justified by the homophobia rampant in the 1920s, the sadomasochistic, master-slave relationship that prevailed between Loeb and Leopold, or any other reason. Though *Swoon* is avid to contradict the old knee-jerk prejudice that Loeb (Daniel Schlachet) and Leopold (Craig Chester) killed because they were gay, it cannot offer an alternative explanation except to hint at the notion that killing Franks was the only way that Loeb and Leopold could sanctify and immortalize their intense love for each other in a society that considered such love an abomination. Unfortunately, Kalin's depiction of Loeb and Leopold as utterly self-involved, languorous, misanthropic scions of privilege does not help his cause.

To Die For (1995)

On the evening of May 1, 1990, a twenty-four-year-old insurance salesman named Gregg Smart was shot and killed as he entered the front door of the condo he shared with his wife, Pamela Ann (Wojas) Smart, in Derry, New Hampshire. Staged to look like a burglary interrupted, the killing of Gregg Smart turned out to be a premeditated homicide engineered by Smart's wife and carried out by her teenage lover, William Flynn, fifteen, and three of his friends from Winnacunnet High School in Hampton, New Hampshire, where Pam Smart worked as media services coordinator. The truth began to emerge when a friend of one of Flynn's accomplices told police he overheard them discussing the murder. On June 10, 1990, Derry police arrested Bill Flynn and two of his coconspirators. They implicated Pam Smart, whereupon police recruited high school student Cecelia Pierce, a friend of Smart and Flynn, to secretly tape-record Smart incriminating herself. Flynn and his young partners-in-crime soon struck a plea bargain for lighter sentences in exchange for testifying against Pamela Smart. With her coconspirators turned witnesses for the prosecution and damning statements on tape, Smart was convicted of murder on March 22, 1991, and sentenced to life without the possibility of parole. Though soon overshadowed by the O. J. Simpson case, the Pamela Smart saga stirred the proverbial media feeding frenzy. With a love story, infidelity, deception, betrayal, murder, and the classic wily and sexually manipulative femme fatale, the Smart case had all the juicy noir ingredients for maximum public titillation.

Among the envied few that got to attend the trial in person was New Hampshire native Joyce Maynard, author of *Looking Back* (New York: Doubleday, 1973) and *Baby Love* (New York: Knopf, 1981) who undertook a novel on the Pam Smart story entitled *To Die For* (New York: E. P. Dutton, 1992). In Maynard's fictionalized version of the story, Pam Smart becomes Suzanne Maretto, a narcissistic and maniacally ambitious but not very bright young woman who aspires to be a television journalist (tellingly, Barbara Walters is her role model). Feeling held back in her career ambitions by her loving but dim-witted husband, Larry, Suzanne seduces a smitten teenager named Jimmy Emmett and then enlists Jimmy and two of his friends to do away with Larry. Indictments and a trial ensue but Suzanne dodges conviction, only to be murdered by Larry's vengeful, Mafia-connected family. Though it uses the Smart case as a point of departure, Maynard's *To Die For* really constitutes a very broad satire of American popular culture, as constructed and promulgated by television and its puerile obsessions with fame, beauty, conventional notions of success, and everything commercial.

Maynard's novel began its journey to the screen when Leslie Morgan, an associate of Hollywood producer Laura Ziskin (*D.O.A.*; *What about Bob?*), read a review of the book and felt that it would make a great movie. The rights were purchased, Buck Henry (*The Graduate*) was hired to write a screen adaptation, and Gus Van Sant (*Drugstore Cowboy*) was hired to direct. Meg Ryan was originally slated to play Suzanne Maretto but dropped out and the part went to Nicole Kidman (and proved to be her breakthrough role). Matt Dillon, a frequent Van Sant collaborator, plays Larry Maretto and Joaquin Phoenix, Jimmy Emmett. In book and film, Suzanne Maretto is considerably more ambitious and media-obsessed than her real counterpart, Pamela Smart, but her other attributes—an almost autistic self-absorption, callousness, and a rigid adherence to cheap values—are consistent with the actual person. A hit at Cannes, the movie was well received by critics and moderately successful at the box office. Ironically, *To Die For* (1995) almost did not get made because studio executives were worried that it was too depressing and pointed in its satire of the very media culture it depended on for commercial success. A final irony: *To Die For* went into national release on September 27, 1995: the day after the O. J. Simpson not-guilty verdict was handed down—art imitating life imitating art.

Paradise Lost: The Child Murders at Robin Hood Hills (1996)

When Joe Berlinger and Bruce Sinofsky (*Brother's Keeper*) released their second major documentary, *Paradise Lost: The Child Murders at Robin Hood Hills* (1996), it became clear that, whatever their professed motives, Berlinger and Sinofsky trade in lurid versions of country gothic. Miltonic echoes notwithstanding, *Paradise Lost* deals with a sensationally ugly crime. On May 5, 1993, three second-grade boys from the Mississippi River town of West Memphis, Arkansas (pop. 28,000), were found murdered (one of them sexually mutilated) in a remote area. Because the killings seemed to have a ritualistic aspect, the Christian citizenry of West Memphis suspected that some sort of satanic cult was responsible. Soon three goth teenagers—Damien Wayne Echols, eighteen; Jessie Misskelley, seventeen; and Charles Jason Baldwin, sixteen—were arrested and charged with the crimes. All three were convicted and sentenced to long prison terms despite the fact that no physical evidence tied them to the murders. Overlong, shapeless, sensationalistic, and manipulative—key bits of information are deferred or missing—*Paradise Lost* aspires to be another *Brother's Keeper* but inadvertently reveals a sinister P. T. Barnum sensibility. Seeking to arouse righteous anger at justice miscarried but, at the same time, to stimulate grim amusement at the superstitious ignorance and sheer stupidity displayed by most of the film's subjects, *Paradise Lost* is ultimately distasteful.

Killer: A Journal of Murder (1996)

Though not a household name in the annals of crime, Carl Panzram (1891–1930) was one of the most vicious, rage-filled, misanthropic criminals who ever lived. Either the pure product of an incredibly brutal early twentieth-century American penal system or inherently evil, Panzram, by his own admission, murdered "21 human beings . . . committed thousands of burglaries, robberies, larcenies, arsons and last but not least . . . committed sodomy on more than 1,000 male human beings" (Gado n.d.). Panzram added with nihilistic pride, "For all these things I am not in the least bit sorry." In June 1929, while serving a twenty-five-year sentence for burglary, Panzram bludgeoned a fellow inmate with an iron bar and was sentenced to death. On death row at Leavenworth Prison awaiting his sentence (which was carried out on September 5, 1930), Panzram wrote a series of letters to Henry Lesser, a guard he had befriended while imprisoned in Washington, D.C. Constituting a de facto autobiography, Panzram's letters were edited by Thomas E. Gaddis (*The Birdman of Alcatraz*) and James O. Long and finally published as *Killer: A Journal of Murder* (New York: Macmillan, 1970). A quarter century after the publication of *Killer*, screenwriter Tim Metcalfe (*Kalifornia*) adapted the book and used it to make his debut as a director. Starring James Woods as Carl Panzram, *Killer: A Journal of Murder* (1996) takes poetic license by situating Panzram on Leavenworth's death row in 1929–1930 and telling his story directly to Henry Lesser (Robert Sean Leonard) rather than through correspondence. Woods, an excellent actor, is as menacing as he can be but the real

Carl Panzram was a truly frightening individual and his crimes far surpass anything that could be suggested in a 90-minute film. Taking on evil beyond its scope to adequately represent or conceptualize, *Killer* comes off as an anemic exercise in dark sensationalism.

Donnie Brasco (1997)

In 1976 FBI undercover agent Joseph D. Pistone infiltrated organized crime in New York City by posing as a jewel thief under the assumed name "Donnie Brasco." The undercover operation, intended to identify major fences of stolen goods in the city, was only supposed to last six months but Pistone managed to form friendships with Benjamin "Lefty" Ruggerio and Dominick "Sonny Black" Napolitano: two "made" members of the Bonanno crime family. Over the next five years, Pistone sacrificed his family life and risked life and limb to observe and sometimes secretly tape-record enough criminal activity to convict more than 100 mobsters by his testimony at a series of trials in the early 1980s. In 1986 Pistone retired from the FBI and wrote *Donnie Brasco: My Undercover Life in the Mafia* (with Richard Woodley, New York: New American Library, 1987).

A decade later producer-director Barry Levinson (*Diner; Sleepers*) brought Joseph Pistone's story to the screen in a version adapted by Paul Attansio (*Quiz Show; Disclosure*), directed by Mike Newell (*The Good Father*), and starring Johnny Depp as Donnie Brasco, Al Pacino as Lefty Ruggerio, and Michael Madsen as Sonny Black. Continuing and deepening the revisionist view of the Mafia introduced by *Goodfellas*, *Donnie Brasco* (1997) shows that life in the mob is not glamorous or exciting for those stuck at the bottom rungs of the organization. Having played the elegant Mafia prince, Sonny Corleone, in the *Godfather* series, Al Pacino made amends for romanticizing wise guys with his unusually restrained and poignant portrayal of Lefty Ruggerio as an aging, lonely, disillusioned subaltern passed over for promotion numerous times even though he has performed more than two dozen hits for his bosses. Actually Donnie Brasco was closer to Sonny Black but Paul Attansio's script exaggerates the Brasco-Ruggerio relationship to heighten the emotional and moral impact of Brasco's inevitable betrayal of Ruggerio. The film strongly implies that Lefty Ruggerio was murdered for having let Brasco into the organization. In reality it was Sonny Black who was assassinated by his mob colleagues. Arrested by the FBI in August 1982, Ruggerio was sentenced to twenty years in prison and died at home of cancer in 1995 after serving thirteen years. Johnny Depp's Donnie Brasco closely identifies with his mobster friends and comes to disdain the FBI. In reality, Joseph Pistone felt no compunctions about betraying the likes of Lefty Ruggerio and Sonny Black; he knew that, friendship notwithstanding, they would not hesitate to kill him if they found out he was a federal agent.

The Brandon Teena Story (1998) and *Boys Don't Cry* (1999)

Around 1:00 A.M. on New Year's Eve, 1993, ex-convicts John Lotter and Marvin Thomas "Tom" Nissen burst into a rented farmhouse in Humboldt, Nebraska. In a matter of a minute or two Lotter shot and killed three of the four occupants: a handicapped man named Philip DeVine, nineteen; a young mother named Lisa Lambert, twenty-four; and Brandon Teena, twenty-one (Lisa Lambert's eight-month-old son, Tanner, was spared). The prime motive for the triple homicide was to silence Brandon Teena; the other two were dispatched because they were potential witnesses. The chain of events that led to the slaughter at the farmhouse began two weeks earlier when Teena was arrested for check forgery. Discrepancies in identity documents quickly led police to discover that Brandon Teena was actually Teena Brandon—a biological female posing as a male. When the arrest was posted in the local paper, the name Teena Brandon was used, prompting Lotter and Nissen to become suspicious of their friend's true gender. On Christmas Eve they caught up with her at the house of her girlfriend, Lana Tisdel, and forcibly stripped her. Outraged at the deception, Lotter and Nissen took Teena out to a remote spot and raped her with utmost violence. She reported the crime to Richardson County Sheriff Charles B. Laux, who showed no sympathy whatsoever. Indeed, Laux interrogated the victim as if she were somehow responsible for the assault and to make matters infinitely worse, telephoned Lotter and Nissen to tell them rape charges were being filed against them but inexplicably neglected to actually arrest them. A week later, Teena Brandon and two bystanders were dead. Tried and convicted for the murders, John Lotter was sentenced to death and Tom Nissen to life imprisonment on February 21, 1996.

Five years after the murders, a New York City lesbian couple—Susan Muska, an independent video producer, and Gréta Olafsdóttir, a professional photographer—decided to make a documentary about Teena Brandon/Brandon Teena. Among those they interviewed on numerous visits to Nebraska: JoAnn Brandon, Teena's mother; Lana Tisdel, Brandon Teena's girlfriend; John Lotter and Tom Nissen (in prison); and a transgendered writer-activist named Kate Bornstein. The resulting film, *The Brandon Teena Story* (1998), conveyed the backwardness and bigotry of the rural Midwest around gender issues but also suffered from sketchy cinematography, choppy editing, and a generally amateurish quality that could be attributed to the filmmakers' lack of experience and funding.

Money and expertise were in much better supply when independent producer Christine Vachon (*Swoon; I Shot Andy Warhol*) and director Kimberly Peirce set out to make a docudrama on the Brandon Teena story. Starring Hilary Swank as Teena Brandon/Brandon Teena, Chloë Sevigny as Lana Tisdel, Peter Sarsgaard as John Lotter, and Brendan Sexton III as Tom Nissen, *Boys Don't Cry* (1999) was realistic, overwhelmingly grim, and stayed close to the facts—except for its rendition of the murders. *Boys Don't Cry* completely elides Philip DeVine, one of the murder victims, and changes the specific details of the killings, for example, Lambert and Teena were actually shot in bed. But these are relatively minor quibbles compared to what the film gets right. Hilary Swank (born in Lincoln, Nebraska, in 1974, two years after Teena Brandon was born in the same city) delivered an incredibly convincing performance as Teena for which she won twenty-one film festival and industry awards including the 2000 Oscar for Best Actress in a Leading Role. Numerous awards and nominations also went to Chloë Sevigny and Kimberly Peirce. Highly praised by critics, *Boys Don't Cry* was also a box office success, earning three times what it cost to make. The fact that the film was made at all and that it was a resounding critical and commercial success owe to the skill and tenacity of the filmmakers but also bespeak a major liberalization of public attitudes toward questions of gender that would have been unthinkable just a few years earlier.

The Hurricane (1999)

Just before closing time at 2:30 A.M. on Saturday morning June 17, 1966, two black men walked into Bob's Lafayette Grill at 428 East 18th Street in Paterson, New Jersey. One man was armed with a double-barreled shotgun and the other carried a .32-caliber revolver. Without uttering a word both immediately opened fire on the four people inside. Two of those shot—Fred Nauyoks, a patron, and Jim Oliver, the bartender and part owner—died instantly. A second patron, Hazel Tanis, died from her wounds almost a month later. A third patron, William Marins, took a bullet in the head but survived. Half an hour after the shootings (and about a mile from the murder scene), police stopped a 1966 white Dodge Polara with out-of-state plates that fit witnesses' descriptions of the car the assailants used to flee the scene. The car's two occupants—John Artis and Rubin "Hurricane" Carter, a former middleweight contender—were arrested, tried, and convicted of the triple homicide and sentenced to life terms in prison. On appeal, the New Jersey Supreme Court upheld their convictions in 1969.

The story might have ended there were it not for Rubin Carter's dogged insistence that he was innocent and had been framed by racist whites because of his black militancy and high visibility in Paterson. Fred W. Hogan, an investigator with the New Jersey Public Defender's Office, took up Carter's case in 1970. Four years later Hogan was able to secure recantations by Alfred Patrick Bello and Arthur Dexter Bradley, the state's chief prosecution witnesses against Carter and Artis (both Bello and Bradley testified that they saw the defendants leaving the Lafayette Grill seconds after the shootings). Concurrent with the announcement (in late September 1974) that Bello and Bradley—both convicted criminals—had recanted, Rubin Carter published *The Sixteenth Round: From Number 1 Contender to #45472* (New York: Viking, 1974), a passionate memoir declaring his innocence. Swayed by the recantations and Carter's book, powerful celebrities took up Carter's cause. Among them were Ellen Burstyn and Mohammed Ali, who provided financial assistance, and Bob Dylan, who joined lyricist Jacques Levy in writing "Hurricane," a long but rousing protest song that argued Carter's side of the story (released on Dylan's best-selling *Desire* album on January 5, 1976). Dylan also played a benefit concert for Carter at Clinton State Prison (December 6, 1975). Author Nelson Algren put in his oar with a novel based on the Carter case entitled *The Devil's Stocking: A Last Interview with W.J. Weatherby* (New York: Arbor House, 1983). The groundswell of sympathetic media attention led to a new trial but, once again, a jury found Carter and Artis guilty on December 22, 1976.

The last phase of the Hurricane Carter saga began in 1980, when a fifteen-year-old black boy named Lesra (Lazarus) Martin read Carter's autobiography and was prompted to write to Carter in prison. Martin's correspondence with Carter attracted the attention of his adoptive parents who were members of an activist commune in Toronto. Three members of the commune—Lisa Peters, Sam Chaiton, and Terry Swinton—took up Carter's case and joined Martin in moving to New Jersey to visit Carter in prison and help conduct an exhaustive investigation into the case that eventually uncovered enough racial bias and prosecutorial misconduct to warrant a new review. In November 1985 federal judge H. Lee Sarokin overturned the second set of convictions but Rubin "Hurricane" Carter would have to wait until late February 1988 for the state of New Jersey to formally dismiss all charges—after the U.S. Supreme Court refused to hear its appeal to reinstate the convictions. (John Artis was released in 1981 after serving fourteen years but was subsequently sentenced to a six-year term for cocaine dealing.) Though relations between the commune and Carter soon soured, Sam Chaiton and Terry Swinton brought out *Lazarus and the Hurricane: The Freeing of Rubin "Hurricane" Carter* (New York: Viking, 1991), a rosy

Hurricane Carter speaking to reporters with John Artis at his left. (Bettmann/Corbis)

narrative of uplift and liberation that overlooked troubling inconsistencies in Carter's version of events.

Not long after the publication of *Lazarus and the Hurricane*, producer Armyan Bernstein (*One from the Heart; The Road to Wellville*) won a fierce bidding war to bring Rubin Carter's story to the screen. Bernstein and screenwriter Dan Gordon (*Passenger 57*) spent years developing a screenplay until they settled on a script that focused on the mutually redemptive relationship between young Lesra Martin and Rubin Carter—at the expense of the investigators and lawyers who played a more crucial role. Directed by Norman Jewison (*In the Heat of the Night; A Soldier's Story*) and starring Denzel Washington as Carter and Vicellous Reon Shannon as Lesra Martin, *The Hurricane* was taut, intensely dramatic, well acted, and offered a triumphant conclusion. The film proved a box office success and earned Denzel Washington an Oscar nomination (since 1988 Washington has garnered five nominations and two Oscars).

But was it good history? Joseph "Cal" Deal emphatically does not think so. A former reporter-photographer for *The Passaic [NJ] Herald-News*, Deal wrote about the Lafayette Grill murders and interviewed Carter in prison in 1975. Though he initially thought Rubin Carter was innocent, Deal was troubled by Carter's refusal to submit to a lie detector test. In 1999 Deal (now the proprietor of a trial graphics business in Fort Lauderdale, Florida) posted *Hurricane Carter: The Other Side of the Story* (http://graphicwitness.com/carter), an elaborate and heavily documented website that presents a revisionist view of the Carter case that is too detailed and persuasive to dismiss. Part of the site is dedicated to a systematic debunking of *The Hurricane*. The film posits the figure of Detective Vincent Della Pesca (played by stock villain Dan Hedaya): a vile, racist cop who has had it in for Rubin Carter for decades. Della Pesca is supposedly based on Detective Lt. Vincent DeSimone, but Deal points out that DeSimone was mild-mannered and never met Carter before the murders occurred. The film also falsely depicts Carter as pummeling middleweight champion Joey Giardello in a title fight (December 14, 1964) but losing the bout on a biased decision rendered by racist boxing judges (in reality, Giardello decisively defeated Carter). Indeed, Joey Giardello (real name: Carmine Orlando Tilelli) saw *The Hurricane*, was incensed by its fictitious depiction of the fight, and successfully sued the filmmakers for defaming his legacy. In the same vein, the film supports Carter's own assertion that he was still a serious contender for the middleweight crown in 1966. In reality, Hurricane Carter's career as a professional boxer was in sharp decline—he won only four of his last ten bouts—in the year preceding the murders. The film also portrays Rubin Carter's military service as exemplary when, in fact, Carter was court-martialed four times during his twenty-one months in the army and finally dismissed as unfit. Likewise, the film also glides lightly over Carter's extensive juvenile criminal record and long history of violence outside the ring. More egregiously the film depicts Alfred Bello falsely naming Carter as one of the shooters so that he (Bello) could keep himself out of jail for attempted burglary. In point of fact, Bello was reluctant to identify Carter for fear of reprisal but nonetheless did so on three separate occasions. The only quid pro quo offered by police was that they would protect him from a vengeful Carter. In sum, the portrait of Rubin Carter that emerges from Cal Deal's extensive archives (complete with numerous transcripts of psychiatric evaluations) is not of a noble and beleaguered martyr to American racism but rather of a very dangerous and frightening sociopath.

The New Millenium

Blow (2001)

The story of George Jung is, in many ways, a story about the enormous cultural changes America underwent in the 1960s, 1970s, and 1980s—many of them not for the good. Born into a working-class family in Weymouth, Massachusetts, in 1946, George Jung was a high school football hero who got swept up in the hippie counterculture of the mid-1960s. A natural born entrepreneur and not a little greedy, Jung soon realized that he could make a lot of money smuggling cheap West Coast marijuana to East Coast universities where scarcity made prices steep. Operating out of Southern California and Mexico, Jung made a fortune before he was arrested in 1974. While an inmate at the Federal Corrections Institution (FCI) in Danbury, Connecticut, George Jung met Carlos Lehder, head of the Medellin (Colombia) cocaine cartel whose stated goal was to destroy the social fabric of the United States by flooding the country with cocaine (he succeeded to an alarming degree). As Lehder's American middleman, George Jung made money hand over fist; in the 1970s the Medellin cartel was making an astonishing $35 *billion* a year. Indeed, Jung had so much illegal cash on hand that he took to lining the floors and walls of a house he called his bank with hundred-dollar bills. After a falling out with Carlos Lehder, Jung allied himself with coke kingpin Pablo Escobar (1949–1993). Cocaine-addicted from too much product sampling, Jung eventually got sloppy and let federal undercover narcotics agents infiltrate his operation. Arrested again in 1988, Jung became the U.S. government's primary witness against Carlos Lehder and was granted immunity from prosecution. Stupidly, Jung began trafficking again, was arrested, and sentenced to sixty years in prison. His earliest possible parole date is 2014.

Bruce Porter's *Blow: How a Small-Town Boy Made 100 Million with the*

Medellin Cocaine Cartel & Lost It All (New York: HarperCollins, 1993) brought George Jung's incredible story to light and prompted the making of *Blow* (2001), a film version directed by Ted Demme and starring Johnny Depp as George Jung; Penélope Cruz as his Cuban wife, Mirtha; Jordi Mollà as Diego Delgado (the Carlos Lehder figure); and Cliff Curtis as the late and unlamented Pablo Escobar. Though the lithe, handsome Johnny Depp looked nothing at all like the real George Jung (who is shown, in prison, at the end of the film), he delivered a convincing rendition of an ordinary man caught up in a mesmerizing caricature of the American dream: a lifestyle too lucrative and seductively decadent to walk away from. Though it is guilty of glamorizing Jung—and overplaying the tragic nature of his relationship with his long-lost daughter, Kristina—*Blow* does present the salient facts of Jung's strange odyssey while, at the same time, showing how the cocaine epidemic of the 1970s and 1980s permanently altered the American cultural landscape. Ironically, director Ted Demme died of a cocaine-related heart attack ten months after *Blow* was released.

Bully (2001)

At the dawn of the twenty-first century, the law of diminishing returns began to overtake the American true crime genre. An increasingly coarsened and impoverished cultural sensibility called for ever more drastic forays into macabre sensationalism. Always much in evidence on television, crime shows proliferated at a dizzying pace, and both fiction and nonfiction approaches became more pornographic in their fixation on the grisly forensic details of bloody murder, dismemberment, death, and decay—very often tinged with twisted sexuality. Though the media focus on inexplicable acts of nihilistic violence as titillating cultural spectacle probably dates from the Loeb-Leopold case, what was once considered a fascinating aberration now passes for ordinary entertainment.

Amply manifest on television, the trend toward morbid voyeurism is somewhat less pronounced in recent crime history films made for theatrical release. Larry Clark's *Bully* (2001) probably falls between sensationalism and serious social critique. *Bully* focuses on a group of morally, culturally, and intellectual vapid Fort Lauderdale, Florida, teenagers who join forces to murder one of their own: a menacing bully named Bobby Kent. Based on Jim Schultze's *Bully: Does Anyone Deserve to Die?—A True Story of High School Revenge* (New York: William Morrow, 1997), *Bully* describes a depraved, amoral, contemporary suburban youth culture addicted to sex, drugs, and video games—a dim-witted, swinish generation that bodes ill for the future of American society.

Auto Focus (2002)

Paul Schrader's *Auto Focus* (2002), based on Robert Graysmith's *The Murder of Bob Crane* (New York: Crown, 1993), explores the last fourteen years in the life of radio-television star Bob Crane (1928–1978), best known for his starring role in the bizarre television sitcom, *Hogan's Heroes* (1965–1971), which was set in a WWII German POW camp. Once Crane (Greg Kinnear in the film) became truly famous he left behind a conventional suburban family life and began to indulge his passions for womanizing, pornography, and self-videotaped sex: passions that took over his life and probably resulted in his murder in Scottsdale, Arizona, on June 28, 1978. Though never convicted, Bob Crane's killer was likely John "Carpy" Carpenter (Willem Dafoe in the film), a Los Angeles video technician who had been Crane's sidekick in his sexual adventures for many years. The film suggests that Carpenter's relationship with Crane was charged with (unreciprocated) homoeroticism. When Crane attempted to break off the relationship, Carpenter murdered him. A variation on themes broached in Bob Fosse's *Star 80*, *Auto Focus* shows how large doses of fame, sex, and narcissistic self-indulgence—modern America's favorite obsessions—can lead inexorably to moral disintegration and death.

Aileen Wuornos on Film

Aileen "Lee" Carol Wuornos (1956–2002) was a Daytona Beach highway prostitute who shot and killed seven men, mostly truck drivers, in 1989 and 1990. As America's first *known* female serial killer, Wuornos garnered extraordinary news coverage and publicity during and after her arrest, murder trial, and conviction in 1991–1992. There were several television biographies: *Overkill: The Aileen Wuornos Story* (1992), a made-for-TV movie by Peter Levin, and two documentaries by British filmmaker Nick Broomfield—*Aileen Wuornos: The Selling of a Serial Killer* (1992) and *Aileen: Life and Death of a Serial Killer* (2003). While other depictions of Aileen Wuornos painted her as a cold-blooded, psychotic killer, Broomfield's films pointed out that her legal defense was pathetically incompetent and at least took seriously Wuornos' claim that she killed in self-defense (though killing *repeatedly* in self-defense is a little hard to credit). After more than ten years on death row at Lowell (FL) Correctional Institution, Aileen Wuornos was executed by lethal injection on October 9, 2002.

Filmmaker Patty Jenkins first became interested in the Wuornos case while she was in college in the early 1990s. At the time, Jenkins instinctively felt that

Film still from the movie Monster *(2004), starring Charlize Theron (right) and Christina Ricci, based on the life of convicted serial killer Aileen Wuornos. (Zodiac Productions/ZUMA/Corbis)*

popular media depictions of Wuornos as a raging, homicidal, lesbian prostitute had to be reductive. By the time she graduated from the director's program of the American Film Institute (AFI) Conservatory in 2000, Jenkins learned that funding was available to do straight-to-video exploitation pictures on serial killers, but after corresponding with Wuornos on death row, Jenkins decided to make a film that was neither exploitative nor sentimentalizing. Just before Wuornos was executed she decided to give Jenkins all her death row letters to childhood friend Dawn Botkins: an invaluable source of insight into Wuornos' tortured psyche. Accorded a $5 million budget by a group of producers, Jenkins managed to recruit South African model-actress Charlize Theron (*The Italian Job*) to play Wuornos and Christina Ricci (*Sleepy Hollow*) to play Aileen's young lesbian lover, Selby Walls (loosely based on Tyria Jolene Moore, Wuornos' lover from 1986 to 1990). Shot on location in Florida in April 2003, *Monster* premiered at the AFI Film Institute on November 15 and went into national release in January 2004.

The Aileen Wuornos depicted by Charlize Theron (thirty pounds heavier for the role and made ugly by prosthetics) is not a sympathetic figure in any ordinary sense. It is quite clear that her first killing is in self-defense but that the subsequent shootings are murder, pure and simple. The film does, however, introduce a major mitigating factor: Wuornos' love for her lesbian lover, Selby, a unique experience for a tough runaway woman of the streets who has known horrific childhood abuse, degradation, and scorn. Wanting to provide some sort of home for Selby, who has been ejected from her parents' house but no longer wanting to work as a prostitute—and otherwise unemployable—Wuornos starts killing in order to steal money (and cars) from her victims. In the end, Selby turns in Wuornos, partly out of moral revulsion for the murders but mostly out of a sense of self-preservation. *Monster* does not condone Wuornos' crimes but does argue—with considerable justification—that her absolutely hellish life at the bottom of the American abyss helps to explain her heinous actions. Previously thought of as a thespian lightweight, Charlize Theron amazed audiences and critics with a bravura performance that won eighteen awards including the 2004 Oscar for Best Actress in a Leading Role.

Capote (2005)

More than twenty years after the magazine, book, and film versions of Truman Capote's *In Cold Blood* appeared, former *Time* writer turned celebrity biographer Gerald Clarke brought out *Capote: A Biography* (New York: Simon & Schuster, 1988). Clarke devotes five of fifty-nine chapters (about 50 of the book's more than 600 pages) to the grueling six-year period Capote spent researching and writing *In Cold Blood* (1959–1965)—and waiting for Perry Smith and Dick Hickock to exhaust their appeals and be executed so that he could finally write the ending to his book. Having become a trusted friend and confidant to the two convicted killers—especially Perry Smith—Capote dreaded their impending executions but also deeply longed for their deaths so that he could publish his masterwork: a protracted, excruciating exercise in moral ambiguity and deception that nearly drove Capote mad and may have precipitated his decline as a writer.

　　Some time around the year 2001, actor Dan Futterman (*The Birdcage*) read Gerald Clarke's biography of Capote and grasped the rich dramatic possibilities inherent in the backstory of *In Cold Blood*. Futterman wrote a screenplay—his first—and presented the project to his friends, director Bennett Miller (*The Cruise*) and actor Philip Seymour Hoffman (*Boogie Nights; Magnolia*); Miller and Hoffman agreed that the story would make a powerful movie. The trio eventually secured $7 million in funding, Hoffman spent months studying footage of Capote, and the film was shot in Winnipeg, Manitoba, and Austin, Texas, in the autumn of 2004. Released a year later, *Capote* proved to be superbly crafted and largely accurate—although some exchanges that took place by letter or telephone are dramatized as person-to-person encounters. *Capote* also featured astonishing performances all around, especially Hoffman's mesmerizing rendition of Capote (whom he closely resembles) and Clifton Collins Jr.'s wholly convincing and deeply poignant portrayal of Perry Smith. More problematic—though probably unavoidable, given the film's slant—is its scant attention to the Clutter family. *In Cold Blood* supplies complete characterizations of the four murder victims. Also dubious is the film's implicit thesis that Truman Capote's obsession with the Clutter case destroyed him. In point of fact, Capote's subsequent decline had much more to do with celebrity mongering, hedonistic excess, and a propensity for alcohol and drugs—lifestyle choices that probably owe more to Capote's narcissistic tendencies than to the spiritual damage sustained during his *In Cold Blood* years.

Bibliography

Algren, Nelson. *The Devil's Stocking: A Last Interview with W. J. Weatherby*. New York: Arbor House, 1983.

Ali, Mohammed, and Durham, Richard. *The Greatest: My Own Story*. New York: Random House, 1975.

Ambrose, Stephen. *Band of Brothers: E Company, 506th Regiment, 101st Airborne from Normandy to Hitler's Eagle's Nest*. New York: Simon & Schuster, 1992.

———. *D-Day (June 6, 1944): The Climactic Battle of World War II*. New York: Simon & Schuster, 1994.

Ardrey, Robert. *African Genesis: A Personal Investigation into the Animal Origins and Nature of Man*. New York: Simon & Schuster, 1961.

———. *The Territorial Imperative: A Personal Inquiry into the Animal Origins of Property and Nations*. New York: Atheneum, 1966.

———. *The Social Contract: A Personal Inquiry into the Evolutionary Sources of Order and Disorder*. New York: Atheneum, 1970.

Asinof, Eliot. *Eight Men Out: The Black Sox and the 1919 World Series*. New York: Holt, 1963.

Ballard, J. G. *Empire of the Sun*. London: Victor Gollancz, 1984.

Barra, Allen. "Alamo Redux: A Mission Impossible," *New York Times*, March 10, 2002, D5.

Barta, Tony, ed. *Screening the Past: Film and the Representation of History*. Westport, CT: Praeger, 1997.

Beato, G. "The Lords of Dogtown," *Spin*, March 1999.

Berardinelli, James. *Reelviews—Berardinelli Sees Film:* Review of *Without Limits*, September 25, 1998. http//movie-reviews.colossus.net/movies/w/without.htm.

Bernstein, Carl, and Bob Woodward. *The Stepford Wives*. New York: Simon & Schuster, 1974.

Bimba, Anthony. *The Molly Maguires*. New York: International Publishers, 1932.

Bissinger, H. G. *Friday Night Lights: A Town, a Team, and a Dream.* Reading, MA: Addison-Wesley, 1990.

Bleszynski, Nick. *Shoot Straight, You Bastards! The Truth behind the Killing of "Breaker" Morant.* New York: Random House, 2002.

Bohn, Thomas W. *An Historical and Descriptive Analysis of the "Why We Fight" Series.* New York: Arno Press, 1977.

Bolt, Robert. "Apologia," *T. E. Lawrence Studies Journal*, Vol. 5, No. 1, pp. 76–81, Autumn 1995.

Boulle, Pierre. *Le Pont de la rivière Kwai.* Paris: Rene Julliard, 1952. English translation, London: Secker & Warburg, 1954.

Bowden, Mark. *Black Hawk Down: A Story of Modern War.* New York: Atlantic Monthly Press, 1999.

Bradford, J. Selby, and Ewan Butler. *Keep the Memory Green.* London: Hutchinson & Co., 1950.

Bradley, Omar N. *A Soldier's Story.* New York: Henry Holt, 1951.

Brickhill, Paul. *The Great Escape.* New York: W. W. Norton, 1950.

———. *The Dam Busters.* London: Evans Bros., 1951.

Briley, Ron. "Film & History," *H-Net Reviews*, June 1998.

Broehl, Wayne. *The Molly Maguires.* Cambridge, MA: Harvard University Press, 1964.

Brokaw, Tom. *The Greatest Generation.* New York: Random House, 1998.

Buchheim, Lothar-Günther. *Das Boot.* Munich: Piper, 1973.

———. *U-Boat-Krieg.* Munich: Piper, 1976.

Burchard, Peter. *One Gallant Rush.* New York: St. Martin's, 1965.

Burgoyne, Robert. *Film Nation: Hollywood Looks at U.S. History.* Minneapolis: University of Minnesota Press, 1997.

Burns, Ken. *Baseball*, A Film by Ken Burns. PBS website, 2002, http://www.pbs.org.

Bush, John. "Holiday for the Blues . . . Billie of Course!" AMG [All Music Guide], http://www.allmusic.com.

Cameron, Kenneth M. *America on Film: Hollywood and American History.* New York: Continuum, 1997.

Carnes, Mark C., ed. *Past Imperfect: History according to the Movies.* New York: Henry Holt, 1995.

Carter, Rubin. *The Sixteenth Round: From Number 1 Contender to #45472.* New York: Viking, 1974.

Cartmell, Deborah, I. Q. Hunter, and Imelda Whelehan, eds. *Retrovisions: Reinventing the Past in Film and Fiction.* London: Pluto Press, 2001.

Chaiton, Sam, and Terry Swinton. *Lazarus and the Hurricane: The Freeing of Rubin "Hurricane" Carter.* New York: Viking, 1991.

Charles, Ray, and David Ritz. *Brother Ray: Ray Charles' Own Story*. New York: Dial Press, 1978.

Clark, Alan. *Barbarossa*. New York: Signet, 1966.

Clarke, Gerald. *Capote: A Biography*. New York: Simon & Schuster, 1988.

Clifton-James, Myrick E. *I Was Monty's Double*. London: Rider & Co., 1954.

Cobb, Humphrey. *Paths of Glory*. New York: Viking, 1935.

Coleman, James W. *The Molly Maguire Riots: Industrial Conflict in the Pennsylvania Coal Region*. Richmond, VA: Garrett and Massie, 1936.

Colijn, Helen. *Song of Survival: Women Interned*. Ashland, OR: White Cloud Press, 1995.

Connell, Evan S. *Son of the Morning Star*. San Francisco: North Point Press, 1984.

Corbett, James J. *The Roar of the Crowd*. New York: Grosset & Dunlap, 1925.

Craig, William. *Enemy at the Gate: The Battle for Stalingrad*. New York: Reader's Digest/E. P. Dutton, 1973.

Crime Magazine: An Encyclopedia of Crime, http://crimemagazine.com/Crime Books/incold.htm.

Crowther, Bosley. "Screen: 'Bonnie & Clyde' Arrives," *New York Times*, August 14, 1967, 36.

Crowther, Bruce. *Hollywood Faction: Reality and Myth in the Movies*. London: Columbus Books, 1984.

Custen, George F. *Bio/Pics: How Hollywood Constructed Public History*. New Brunswick, NJ: Rutgers University Press, 1992.

Daley, Robert. *Prince of the City: The True Story of a Cop Who Knew Too Much*. Boston: Houghton Mifflin, 1978.

Davis, Natalie Zemon. *Slaves on Screen: Film and Historical Vision*. Cambridge, MA: Harvard University Press, 2000.

Denton, Kit. *The Breaker*. London: Angus and Robertson, 1973.

Dershowitz, Alan. *Reversal of Fortune: Inside the von Bülow Case*. New York: Random House, 1986.

Dibbets, Karel, and Bert Hogenkamp, eds. *Film and the First World War*. Amsterdam: Amsterdam University Press, 1994. (Out of print).

Dietrich, Noah. *The Amazing Mr. Hughes*. New York: Fawcett, 1972.

Donato, Pietro di. *Christ in Concrete*. Indianapolis, IN: Bobbs-Merrill, 1939.

Donovan, Robert J. *P.T. 109: John F. Kennedy in WWII*. New York: McGraw-Hill, 1961.

Ebert, Roger. [Review]. "The Buena Vista Social Club," *Chicago Sun-Times*, June 25, 1999.

———. "The Alamo," *Chicago Sun Times*, April 9, 2004.

Edelman, Bernard. *Dear America: Letters Home from Vietnam.* New York: W. W. Norton, 1985.

Elliot, Craig. [Review]. "The Genius of Lenny Breau," *See Magazine*, March 23, 1999.

Endore, Guy. *Babouk.* New York: Vanguard Press, 1934.

Farago, Ladislas. *The Broken Seal: The Story of "Operation Magic" and the Pearl Harbor Disaster.* New York: Random House, 1967.

———. *Patton: Ordeal and Triumph.* New York: Ivan Obelensky, 1963.

Farson, Daniel. *The Gilded Gutter Life of Francis Bacon.* New York: Pantheon, 1993.

Femina, Jerry Della. *From Those Wonderful Folks Who Gave You Pearl Harbor.* New York: Simon & Schuster, 1970.

Fénelon, Fania. *Playing for Time.* New York: Atheneum, 1977.

Fensch, Thomas, ed. *Oskar Schindler and His List: The Man, the Book, the Film, the Holocaust and Its Survivors.* Forest Dale, VT: Paul S. Eriksson, 1995.

Ferro, Marc. *Cinema and History.* Translated by Naomi Greene. Detroit, MI: Wayne State University Press, 1988.

Fisher, Antwone, and Mim Eichler Rivas. *Finding Fish: A Memoir.* New York: William Morrow, 2001.

Forester, C. S. *The Last Nine Days of the Bismarck.* Boston: Little, Brown, 1959.

Frank, Annalise. *The Diary of a Young Girl.* New York: Doubleday, 1952.

Fraser, George MacDonald. *The Hollywood History of the World: From One Million Years B.C. to Apocalypse Now.* New York: Fawcett Columbine, 1989.

Gaddis, Thomas E., and James O. Long, eds. *Killer: A Journal of Murder.* New York: Macmillan, 1970.

Gado, Mark. "Carl Panzram: Too Evil to Live," *Court TV's Crime Library*, http://www.crimelibrary.com/serial_killers/history/panzram1/1.html.

Garrison, Jim. Garrison's *On the Trail of the Assassins.* New York: Sheridan Square Press, 1988.

Geertz, Clifford. "Thick Description: Toward an Interpretative Theory of Culture." In *The Interpretation of Cultures.* New York: Basic Books, 1973.

Gibson, Guy. *Enemy Coast Ahead.* London: M. Joseph, 1946.

Gilmore, Mikal. *Shot in the Heart.* New York: Doubleday, 1994.

Girgus, Sam B. *America on Film: Modernism, Documentary, and a Changing America.* New York: Cambridge University Press, 2002.

Gordon, Ernest. *Through the Valley of the Kwai.* New York: Harper, 1962.

———. *The Miracle on the River Kwai.* London: Collins, 1963.

Graysmith, Robert. *The Murder of Bob Crane*. New York: Crown, 1993.

Graziano, Rocky. *Somebody Up There Likes Me: My Life So Far*. New York: Simon & Schuster, 1955.

Griffin, John Howard. *Black Like Me*. Boston: Houghton Mifflin, 1961.

Grinden, Leger. *Shadows on the Past: Studies in the Historical Fiction Film*. Philadelphia: Temple University Press, 1994.

Hansen, Miriam. *Babel and Babylon: Spectatorship in American Silent Film*. Cambridge, MA: Harvard University Press, 1991.

Harlan, Veit. *Im Schatten meiner Filme. Selbstbiographie* [*In the Shade of My Films: An Autobigraphy*]. Gütersloh, Germany: Mohn, 1966.

Hauser, Thomas. *The Execution of Charles Horman: An American Sacrifice*. New York: Harcourt Brace Jovanovich, 1978.

Hayslips, Le Ly, and Jay Wurts. *When Heaven and Earth Changed Places*. New York: Doubleday, 1989.

———. *Child of War, Woman of Peace*. New York: Doubleday, 1993.

Helfgott, Gillian. *Love You to Bits and Pieces*. New York: Penguin Books, 1997.

Helfgott, Margaret, and Tom Gross. *Out of Tune: David Helfgott and the Myth of "Shine."* New York: Warner Books, 1998.

Helm, Thomas. *Ordeal by Sea*. New York: Dodd, Mead, 1963.

Herrera, Hayden. *Frida: A Biography of Frida Kahlo*. New York: Harper & Row, 1983.

Hoberman, J. "Existential Heroism and Mild Revisionism in a 9-11 *Alamo*," *The Village Voice*, April 9, 2004.

Huffington, Arianna Stassinopoulos. *Picasso: Creator and Destroyer*. New York: Simon & Schuster, 1988.

Huie, William Bradford. *The Execution of Private Slovik: The Hitherto Secret Story of the Only American Soldier since 1864 to Be Shot for Desertion*. New York: Duell, Sloan & Pearce, 1954.

Huston, John. *An Open Book*. New York: Macmillan, 1981.

Internet Movie Database, http://www.imdb.com.

Isenberg, Michael T. *War on Film: the American Cinema and World War I, 1914–1941*. Rutherford, NJ: Fairleigh Dickinson University Press, 1981.

James, Steve. "The American Right and Scottish Nationalism," World Socialist website, February 3, 1999, http://www.wsws.org.

Jeffrey, Betty. *White Coolies*. Sydney, Australia: Angus and Robertson, 1954.

Johnson, Malcolm. *Crime on the Labor Front: The Inside Story of Murder, Violence, and Organized Gangsterism in Labor Unions*. New York: McGraw-Hill, 1950.

Kaes, Anton. *From Hitler to Heimat: The Return of History as Film*. Cambridge, MA: Harvard University Press, 1989.

Kempner, Aviva. The Ciesla Foundation Presents *The Life and Times of Hank Greenberg*, an Aviva Kempner film, www.hankgreenbergfilm.org.

Keneally, Thomas. *Schindler's Ark.* London: Hodder & Stoughton, 1982.

Kennedy, Ted. *The Last Brother.* New York: Simon & Schuster, 1993.

Kirstein, Lincoln. *Lay This Laurel: An Album on the Saint-Gaudens Memorial on Boston Common Honoring Black and White Men Together Who Served the Union Cause with Robert Gould Shaw and Died with Him July 18, 1863.* New York: Eakins Press, 1973.

Kohn, Howard. *Who Killed Karen Silkwood?* New York: Summit Books, 1981.

Krakauer, Jon. *Into Thin Air: A Personal Account of the Mt. Everest Disaster.* New York: Villard, 1997.

Kurzman, Dan. *Fatal Voyage.* New York: Atheneum, 1990.

Landy, Marcia. *Cinematic Uses of the Past.* Minneapolis: University of Minnesota Press, 1996.

———, ed. *The Historical Film: History and Memory in Media.* New Brunswick, NJ: Rutgers University Press, 2001.

Larsen, Richard W. *Bundy: The Deliberate Stranger.* Englewood Cliffs, NJ: Prentice-Hall, 1980.

Lask, Thomas. "Author Decries Casting of Miss Redgrave by CBS," *New York Times*, October 23, 1979, C7.

Lawrence, Thomas Edward. *Seven Pillars of Wisdom.* London: Self-published, 1926.

Lawson, Ted W. *Thirty Seconds over Tokyo*, ed. by Robert Considine. New York: Random House, 1943.

Lech, Raymond. *All the Drowned Sailors.* New York: Military Heritage Press, 1982.

Lee, Spike. *By Any Means Necessary: The Trials and Tribulations of Making Malcolm X.* New York: Hyperion, 1992.

LeFlore, Ron. *Breakout: From Prison to the Big Leagues.* New York: Harper & Row, 1978.

Lehrer, Jim. *Viva Max!* New York: Duell, Sloan, and Pearce, 1966.

Leifermann, Henry P. *Crystal Lee: A Woman of Inheritance.* New York: Macmillan, 1975.

Leopold, Nathan. *Life Plus 99 Years.* New York: Doubleday, 1958.

Levin, Meyer. *Compulsion.* New York: Simon & Schuster, 1956.

Lewis, Arthur H. *Lament for the Molly Maguires.* New York: Harcourt, Brace & World, 1964.

Linville, Susan E. *History Films, Women, and Freud's Uncanny.* Austin: University of Texas Press, 2004.

Lipkin, Steven N. *Real Emotional Logic: Film and Television Docudrama as Persuasive Practice.* Carbondale: Southern Illinois University Press, 2002.

Lorence, James J. *Screening America: United States History through Film since 1900.* New York: Pearson Longman, 2006.

Lowenstein, Adam. *Shocking Representation: Historical Trauma, National Cinema, and the Modern Horror Film.* New York: Columbia University Press, 2005.

Lynd, Staughton, and Alice Lynd. *Rank and File: Personal Histories of Working-Class Organizers.* Boston: Beacon Press, 1973.

Mackay, James A. *William Wallace: Brave Heart.* Edinburgh, Scotland: Mainstream, 1995.

Mailer, Norman. *The Executioner's Song.* Boston: Little, Brown, 1979.

Malcolm X, and Alex Haley. *The Autobiography of Malcolm X.* New York: Grove Press, 1965.

Manchester, William. *American Caesar: Douglas MacArthur 1880–1964.* Boston: Little, Brown, 1978.

Marshall, Samuel Lyman Atwood. *Pork Chop Hill: The American Fighting Man in Action—Korea, Spring 1953.* New York: William Morrow, 1956.

Marr, Jim. *Crossfire: The Plot That Killed Kennedy.* New York: Carroll & Graf, 1989.

Mass, Peter. *Serpico, The Cop Who Defied the System.* New York: Viking, 1973.

Matelski, Marilyn J., and Nancy Lynch Street, eds. *War and Film in America: Historical and Critical Essays.* Jefferson, NC: McFarland, 2003.

Maynard, Joyce. *Looking Back.* New York: Doubleday, 1973.

———. *Baby Love.* New York: Knopf, 1981.

———. *To Die For.* New York: E. P. Dutton, 1992.

McCain, Gillian, and Roderick McNeil, eds. *Please Kill Me: The Uncensored Oral History of Punk.* New York: Grove Press, 1996.

McCrisken, Trevor B., and Andrew Pepper. *American History and Contemporary Hollywood Film.* New Brunswick, NJ: Rutgers University Press, 2005.

McGinniss, Joe. *Fatal Vision.* New York: Putnam, 1983.

Miller, Merle. *Plain Speaking, An Oral Biography of Harry S. Truman.* New York: Berkeley Publishing/G.P. Putnam, 1974.

Mills, Michael. Moderntimes Classic Film Pages, http://www.moderntimes.com.

Mitchell, William. "Mitchell Charges 'Gross Negligence' in Shenandoah Loss," *New York Times*, September 6, 1925, 1.

Montagu, Ewen. *The Man Who Never Was.* Philadelphia: J. B. Lippincott, 1954.

Moore, Art. "Civil War Epic Shut Down by 'PC Crowd'?: 'Gods and Generals' a Painful Disappointment at Box Office," *WorldNetDaily*, March 22, 2003, http://www.worldnetdaily.com/news/article.

Moore, Hal, and Joseph L. Galloway. *We Were Soldiers Once . . . And Young: Ia Drang—The Battle That Changed the War in Vietnam.* New York: Random House, 1992.

Murphy, Audie Leon. *To Hell and Back.* New York: Henry Holt, 1949.

Murton, Thomas, and Joe Hyams. *Accomplices to the Crime: The Arkansas Prison Scandal.* New York: Grove Press, 1969.

Naifeh, Steven, and Gregory White Smith. *Jackson Pollock: An American Saga.* New York: Clarkson N. Potter, 1989.

Nelson, Peter. *Left for Dead.* New York: Delacorte, 2001.

Nesbit, John. "Dizzy Deserves Better" [Review of *The Pride of St. Louis*] *CultureDose.net*, 2002.

Newcomb, Richard F. *Abandon Ship!* New York: Henry Holt, 1958.

Newfield, Jack. *Only in America: The Life and Crimes of Don King.* New York: William Morrow, 1995.

O'Connor, John E., and Martin A. Jackson, eds. *American History/American Film: Interpreting the Hollywood Image.* Exp. ed. New York: Continuum, 1988.

Osterberg, Bertil O. *Colonial America on Film and Television: A Filmography.* Jefferson, NC: McFarland, 2000.

Owens, William A. *Slave Mutiny: The Revolt on the Schooner Amistad.* New York: J. Day Co., 1953.

———. *Black Mutiny: The Revolt on the Schooner Amistad.* 2nd ed. Philadelphia: Pilgrim Press, 1968.

Patterson, Alex. "Review of 'The Filth and the Fury,'" *Eye* magazine, May 4, 2000.

Piersall, Jim, and Al Hirschberg. *Fear Strikes Out: The Jim Piersall Story.* Boston: Little, Brown, 1955.

Pileggi, Nicholas. *Wiseguy: Life in a Mafia Family.* New York: Simon & Schuster, 1986.

Pinkerton, Alan. *The Molly Maguires and the Detectives.* New York: G. W. Carleton, 1877.

Pistone, Joseph D., and Richard Woodley. *Donnie Brasco: My Undercover Life in the Mafia.* New York: New American Library, 1987.

Porter, Bruce. *Blow: How a Small-Town Boy Made 100 Million with the Medellin Cocaine Cartel & Lost It All.* New York: HarperCollins, 1993.

Potter, Allen, and Fred Bost. *Fatal Justice: Reinvestigating the MacDonald Murders.* New York: W. W. Norton, 1995.

Potter, Jeffrey. *To a Violent Grave: An Oral Biography of Jackson Pollock.* New York: Putnam, 1985.

Powell, Colin. *Nuremberg: Infamy on Trial.* New York: Viking, 1994.

————. *My American Journey.* New York: Random House, 1995.

Prebble, John. *Culloden.* London: Secker & Warburg, 1961.

Pyle, Ernie. *Here Is Your War.* New York: Henry Holt, 1943.

————. *Brave Men.* New York: Henry Holt, 1944.

Rashke, Richard. *The Killing of Karen Silkwood: The Story behind the Kerr-McGee Plutonium Case.* Boston: Houghton Mifflin, 1981.

Raymond, Ernest. *Tell England: A Study in a Generation.* London: Cassel, 1922.

Rebhorn, Marlette. *Screening America: Using Hollywood Films to Teach History.* New York: P. Lang, 1988.

Redhot.org, http://www.redhot.org.

Reed, John Silas. *Ten Days That Shook the World.* New York: Boni & Liveright, 1919.

Reid, Patrick. *The Colditz Story.* London: Hodder and Stoughton, 1952.

Remarque, Erich Maria. *All Quiet on the Western Front.* Boston: Little, Brown, 1929.

————. *Im Westen Nichts Neue.* Berlin, Propyläen-Verlag, 1929.

Ribowsky, Mark. *Don't Look Back: Satchel Paige in the Shadows of Baseball.* New York: De Capo, 2000.

Richards, Jeffrey, and Anthony Aldgate. *British Cinema and Society, 1930–1970.* Totowa, NJ: Barnes & Noble Books, 1983.

Robbin, David L. *War of the Rats.* New York: Bantam, 1999.

Rollins, Peter C., ed. *Hollywood as Historian: American Film in a Cultural Context.* Rev. ed. Lexington: University Press of Kentucky, 1997.

————. *The Columbia Companion to American History on Film: How the Movies Have Portrayed the American Past.* New York: Columbia University Press, 2003.

————, and Gary R. Edgerton, eds. *Television Histories: Shaping Collective Memory in the Media Age*, 2nd ed. Lexington: University Press of Kentucky, 2003.

————, and John E. O'Connor, eds. *Hollywood's White House: The American Presidency in Film and History.* Lexington: University Press of Kentucky, 2003.

Roquemore, Joseph. *History Goes to the Movies: A Viewer's Guide to the Best (and Some of the Worst) Historical Films Ever Made.* New York: Broadway Books, 1999.

Rosen, Philip. *Change Mummified: Cinema, Historicity, Theory.* Minneapolis: University of Minnesota Press, 2001.

Rosenstone, Robert A. *Visions of the Past: The Challenge of Film to Our Idea of History.* Cambridge, MA: Harvard University Press, 1995.

————, ed. *Revisioning History: Film and the Construction of a New Past.* Princeton, NJ: Princeton University Press, 1995.

Rosenthal, Alan, ed. *Why Docudrama? Fact-Fiction on Film and TV.* Carbondale: Southern Illinois University Press, 1999.

Ryan, Cornelius. *The Longest Day: June 6, 1944.* New York: Simon & Schuster, 1959.

————. *The Last Battle.* New York: Simon & Schuster, 1966.

————. *A Bridge Too Far.* New York: Simon & Schuster, 1974.

Sanello, Frank. *Reel v. Real: How Hollywood Turns Fact into Fiction.* Lanham, MD: Taylor Trade Pub., 2003.

Satterfield, Jack A. *We Band of Brothers: The Sullivans & World War II.* Parkersburg, IA: Mid-Prairie Books, 1995.

Sayles, John. *Union Dues.* Boston: Little, Brown, 1977.

————. *Thinking in Pictures: The Making of the Movie.* Matewan. Boston: Houghton Mifflin, 1987.

Schultze, Jim. *Bully: Does Anyone Deserve to Die?—A True Story of High School Revenge.* New York: William Morrow, 1997.

Scoresesfilms.com, www.scorsesefilms.com/blues.htm.

Shaara, Jeff. *Gods and Generals.* New York: Ballantine, 1996.

Shaara, Michael. *The Killer Angels.* New York: McKay, 1974.

Shaw, Artie. *The Trouble with Cinderella: An Outline of Identity.* New York: Farrar, Straus & Giroux, 1952.

————. *I Love You, I Hate You, Drop Dead! Variations on a Theme.* New York: Fleet Publishing, 1965.

————. *The Best of Intentions and Other Stories.* Santa Barbara, CA: John Daniel & Co., 1989.

Shawcross, William T. *Sideshow: Kissinger, Nixon, and the Destruction of Cambodia.* New York: Simon & Schuster, 1979.

Sheehan, Neil. *A Bright Shining Lie: John Paul Vann and America in Vietnam.* New York: Random House, 1988.

Shindler, Colin. *Hollywood in Crisis: Cinema and American Society, 1929–1939.* New York: Routledge, 1996.

Sklar, Robert, and Charles Musser, eds. *Resisting Images: Essays on Cinema and History.* Philadelphia: Temple University Press, 1990.

Slutsky, Alan. *Standing in the Shadows of Motown: The Life and Music of Legendary Bassist James Jamerson.* Milwaukee, WI: Hal Leonard Publishing, 1989.

Smith, Charles Saumarez. "More about Bruce Weber," http://www.deppography.com/weber.htm.

Smith, Gary Allen. *Epic Films: Casts, Credits and Commentary on Over 350 Historical Spectacle Movies*. 2nd ed. Jefferson, NC: McFarland, 2004.

Sobchack, Vivian, ed. *The Persistence of History: Cinema, Television, and the Modern Event*. New York: Routledge, 1996.

Solanas, Valerie. *SCUM Manifesto*. London: Verso, 2004.

Solomon, Deborah. *Jackson Pollock: A Biography*. New York: Simon & Schuster, 1987.

Solomon, Jon. *The Ancient World in the Cinema*. Rev. and exp. ed. New Haven, CT: Yale University Press, 2001.

Sorlin, Pierre. *The Film in History: Restaging the Past*. Totowa, NJ: Barnes & Noble Books, 1980.

Stanton, Doug. *In Harm's Way*. New York: Henry Holt, 2001.

Stegner, Wallace. *The Preacher and the Slave*. Boston: Houghton Mifflin, 1950. Reprint, *Joe Hill*. New York: Doubleday, 1969.

Stevens, Michael G. *Reel Portrayals: The Lives of 640 Historical Persons on Film, 1929 through 2001*. Jefferson, NC: McFarland, 2003.

Stone, Irving. *Lust for Life*. London: Longman's, Green & Co., 1934.

———. *The Agony and the Ecstasy*. New York: Doubleday, 1961.

Sturken, Marita. *Tangled Memories: The Vietnam War, the AIDS Epidemic, and the Politics of Remembering*. Berkeley: University of California Press, 1997.

Summersby, Kay. *Eisenhower Was My Boss*. New York: Prentice-Hall, 1948.

———. *Past Forgetting: My Affair with Dwight Eisenhower*. New York: Simon & Schuster, 1976.

T. E. Lawrence Studies website. www.telstudies.org.

Talmer, Jerry. "Screenwriter Budd Schulberg, 90, Reminisces on Making 'Waterfront,'" *The Villager* 74, no. 27, November 3–9, 2004.

Terkel, Studs. *The Good War: An Oral History of World War II*. New York: Pantheon, 1984.

Thomas, Lowell. *With Lawrence in Arabia*. New York: Century, 1924.

Tinkle, Lon. *13 Days to Glory*. New York: McGraw-Hill, 1958.

Toplin, Robert Brent. *History by Hollywood: The Use and Abuse of the American Past*. Urbana: University of Illinois Press, 1996.

———. *Reel History: In Defense of Hollywood*. Lawrence: University Press of Kansas, 2002.

———. *Oliver Stone's USA: Film, History, and Controversy*. Lawrence: University Press of Kansas, 2003.

Tracey, Grant Annis George. *Filmography of American History*. Westport, CT: Greenwood Press, 2002.

Tregaski, Richard. *Guadalcanal Diary.* New York: Random House, 1943.

Trevor, Elleston. *The Big Pick-Up.* London: Heinemann, 1955.

Trumbo, Dalton. *Johnny Got His Gun.* Philadelphia: J. B. Lippincott, 1939.

Turner, Tina, and Kurt Loder. *I, Tina.* New York: William Morrow, 1986.

Vaughan-Thomas, Wynford. *Anzio: The Massacre at the Beachhead.* New York: Holt, Rinehart & Winston, 1961.

Vidal, Gore. *Screening History.* Cambridge, MA: Harvard University Press, 1992.

Voller, Maryanne. *Ghosts of Mississippi: The Murder of Medgar Evers, the Trials of Byron de la Beckwith and the Haunting of the New South.* Boston: Little, Brown, 1995.

Vonderau, Patrick, ed. *Film as History, History as Film.* Berlin: Humboldt-Universität zu Berlin, 1999.

Walsh, David. "'Hoop Dreams': Something Approaching Reality for a Change," World Socialist website, October 10, 1994.

Wambaugh, Joseph. *The Onion Field.* New York: Delacorte, 1973.

Wenders, Wim. Wim Wenders—The Official Site, www.wim-wenders.com.

Whalen, John, and Jonathin Vankin. *Based on a True Story: Fact and Fantasy in 100 Favorite Movies.* Chicago: Chicago Review Press, 2005.

White, W. L. *They Were Expendable.* New York: Harcourt Brace, 1942.

Williams, Eric E. *The Tunnel.* New York: Coward-McCann, 1952.

Winkler, Martin M., ed. *Gladiator: Film and History.* London: Blackwell, 2004.

Witton, George. *Scapegoats of the Empire: The True Story of Breaker Morant's Bushveldt Carbineers.* Melbourne, Australia: D. W. Patterson, 1907.

Wojtowicz, John. "Real *Dog Day* Hero Tells His Story." *Jump Cut,* no. 15 (1977): 31–32.

Woodham-Smith, Cecil. *The Reason Why: The Fatal Charge of the Light Brigade.* New York: McGraw-Hill, 1954.

Wyke, Maria. *Projecting the Past: Ancient Rome, Cinema, and History.* London: Routledge, 1997.

Young, Desmond. *Rommel.* New York: Collins, 1950.

Young, James E. "Göring Yawns: This Account of the Nuremberg Trials Takes Imaginative License," *New York Times Book Review,* May 29, 1994, 13.

Zaniello, Tom. *Working Stiffs, Union Maids, Reds, and Riffraff: An Organized Guide to Films about Labor.* Ithaca, NY: Cornell University Press, 1996.

Index

Main entries have page numbers in **bold type**.

About the Author

Dr. Robert Niemi is Associate Professor of English and current coordinator of the American Studies Program at St. Michael's College in Colchester, Vermont. He teaches courses on modern American literature, film, and cultural studies and is the author of numerous essays and two previous books: *Russell Banks* (Simon & Schuster/Macmillan, 1997) and (with Daniel C. Gillane) *The Bibliography of Weldon Kees* (Parrish House, 1997). He and his family live in Barre, Vermont.